ELEVATE YOURSELF
TO MANHOOD

WHAT EVERY YOUNG MAN
NEEDS TO KNOW ON HIS QUEST

Presented To

BEN

By

Praise for Elevate Yourself to Manhood

Shelley Ashworth's Review

Growing up in today's media rich environment brings new challenges for young men. Parenting young men to adulthood becomes increasingly complex with the many enticements competing for their time. The teenage years are pivotal for young men as they make choices that have a lasting impact on their lives. *Elevate Yourself to Manhood: What Every Young Man Needs to Know on His Quest* aids young men as they navigate through life by helping them understand how their decisions affect their future. It provides perspective and helps them understand the importance of overcoming obstacles that must be navigated to become responsible men. This book resonated with many of the issues that we have wrestled with in raising our boys. Every young man should read *Elevate Yourself to Manhood*. I recommend that parents read this book with their sons, discuss the topics, work together to set goals, and track progress.

Shelley Ashworth

Carlsbad, California

Shelley is the mother of an Eagle Scout, a Boy Scout, a Cub Scout, and a teenage daughter who is attending university. She has worked in several capacities as a Boy Scouts of America volunteer: Boy Scout Committee Chair, Merit Badge Counselor, Cub Scout Leader, and Cub Committee Chair. Shelley has also worked with youth as PTO Vice President, Young Women's President, and soccer coach. She has supported her husband as he volunteered as Unit Commissioner, Scout Master, Assistant Scout Master, Varsity Coach, Venture Advisor, and Scout Committee Chair. Shelley is currently a Cub Scout Leader.

Dr. Shane C. Leavitt's Review

It has never been harder for young men to transition into manhood than it is today. There seems to be a famine of genuine, strong, alpha males who lead their families, churches, work, and communities in the right direction. We have lost our purpose, strength, courage, and intelligence at the altar of electronics, addictions, and the uncommitted life. We no longer protect families, nations, or ourselves because we do not have the physical or mental capabilities needed to show the way. We avoid marriage, children, and the religion of our fathers. Donell and Elaine Cox's book, *Elevate Yourself to Manhood: What Every Young Man Needs to Know on His Quest*, is a tool that will help every young man move forward into manhood and identify the characteristics and traits of true men told from their perspective. This in-depth and personal guide will serve as a worthy guide to any boy or man who desires to overcome obstacles the world puts in front of men today.

Shane C. Leavitt, M.D.

Mukilteo, Washington

Dr. Leavitt is an Orthopaedic Surgeon and an Eagle Scout. He has also been a Varsity Scout Advisor and Scout Commissioner. He lives with his wife and six children.

ELEVATE YOURSELF TO MANHOOD

WHAT EVERY YOUNG MAN NEEDS TO KNOW ON HIS QUEST

Donell Cox & Elaine J. Barbeau Cox

La Fleur
Publishing

Mukilteo, Washington

Published by La Fleur Publishing

ISBN: 0692621911
ISBN 13: 9780692621912
Library of Congress Control Number: 2016901237
La Fleur Publishing, Bothell, WA

TABLE OF CONTENTS

FOREWORD BY
DR. GORDON S. NISHIMOTO

SEVERAL YEARS AGO, I WAS traveling with my five-year-old daughter to a house I had never before visited. I had a street address but was struggling to find the location. The address just didn't seem to exist! My daughter turned to me and said, "Dad, you're not smart! Mom is smart. She brings a map!" Well, this comment made me think. In life, is there a map to navigate the challenging terrain that the youth of today face? Specifically, how does a young man know what is appropriate or what will bring him the greatest satisfaction in life, without a guide or compass to direct him? With so many voices out there, where can young men turn to for direction?

In the many years that I have had to work with young men, I have learned that choices, made at crucial times in life, are of the greatest importance. A single decision can have a life-changing impact. If a young man could see the future, would it affect the decisions he would make? If he knew what dangers were on the road ahead, could he be warned in some way? If other people had traveled that same road previously, would their experience help this young man?

Donell and Elaine Cox, have written just such an inspired book with a map to help young men through the transition into manhood. *Elevate Yourself to Manhood* is written in a manner as to answer most of the questions a young man may ask. Sections on self-confidence, how to succeed in school, and emotional intelligence are right resources for a young man. Not only that, but the book also shares the authors' life experiences to guide young men and how to avoid the pitfalls and dangers of laziness, drugs, and poor nutrition. The book is written with optimism and encouragement and incorporates concrete guides to help a young man develop physically, mentally, emotionally, and spiritually.

Much like a small snowball rolling down the top of a snow-capped mountain, the decisions a young man will make may turn into an avalanche of success or, in other cases, outright failure. Realizing that young men are required to make important decisions every day, what is going to help them the most? Can we rely on society helping them, when role models in music and sports often have lives that are in a certain destructive mode? A popular previous NBA basketball player and sports broadcaster, Charles Barkley, states, "I'm not a role model. Just because I dunk a basketball doesn't mean I should raise your kids." Yet, through the years, it has always been that young men look up to others and model themselves after those they admire. For these young men, can they trust the example of a young movie star, whose life is crumbling around him from the problems associated with fame and fortune? Some will say, "It has always been that way." But, even these people, must realize that the world today is not the same as it was twenty years ago. In today's world, a single "private" line of text or a picture sent from a cell phone, (which almost every young man has), could haunt this young man for the rest of his life as it is published to his entire school, community, and the world. This personal media may not be able ever to be erased. Certainly, then, young men today are faced with incredible challenges. Where can they turn? They will have mentors. But, who will that be? Who will help them with the important decisions they make in their lives? Parents, teachers, grandparents, community and church leaders, will find the ideas and concepts presented in this book to be most helpful and persuasive, but the book is primarily written for the young man himself. The content provides a powerful map that will help young men in their life journey. There are "certificates of achievement" that are "quest guides" that a young man may complete as he integrates the book's concepts into his life. By doing so, a young man can guide his own destiny as the snowball becomes an avalanche of fulfillment and joy.

The authors have done a wonderful job ferreting out many of the challenges of the youth of today -- challenges that parents and grandparents have had little experience in dealing with "in their day." With radical changes in society and an exponential explosion of information and technology, older members of society are struggling to keep up themselves. Interestingly, this new "millennial" generation is most adept at absorbing these changes. At a recent school function, where Internet and social media safety were being discussed with parents, one concerned grandmother said, "How am I supposed to protect my grandchild? I have to ask them how to use my cell phone and computer!" The section dealing with technology are helpful in this regard. Also, the book will help young men see that there is so much more to life than what is seen on a computer screen.

Lastly, the authors have provided an amazing collection of moral maps and guidelines. Spiritual health is not often examined in books today but is essential to a young man finding his way. Chapters on spiritual happiness, the importance of families, and moral purity are particularly insightful. Towards the end of the book, the authors take a brief look into social aspects and the legacy that one may leave behind.

Moreover, I think you will find a great treasure in this book. For you, young man, having a map will be a fabulous tool that will help you while traversing your life experience in becoming a man. This is your quest -- to become the person that you want to be. Thanks so much to the authors for sharing their ideas.

All the best,

Dr. Gordon S. Nishimoto, DPM

Dr. Nishimoto is a Podiatric Surgeon, a Bishop, and an Eagle Scout. He has worked with youth for more than twenty years. He currently lives in Mukilteo, Washington with his wife and three of his five children. Two of his children are attending university. His eldest son is also an Eagle Scout.

ACKNOWLEDGEMENTS

WE FIRST OFFER THANKS TO our Heavenly Father for guidance and inspiration while writing this book and for sustaining us throughout the process. We thank Jesus for His Atoning Sacrifice and the Holy Spirit who placed critical resources and people in our path that enabled us to complete this work.

We acknowledge all the wonderful people who offered materials, insights, personal stories, and encouragement, especially the Honorable Leone Panetta, former Secretary of Defense and former Director of The Central Intelligence Agency.

We thank Secretary Panetta for responding to the six-page letter my wife, Elaine, wrote to President Obama on January 20, 2014 voicing her concern for young men in our country and the solutions that she thought would strengthen young men. In that letter, she also mentioned a disturbing statistic expressed by Secretary Panetta whom she heard speak on CNN the day before we married, on July 13, 2012. During the CNN interview, Secretary Panetta expressed his concern for young men in our society saying, "Our veterans are committing suicide at a rate of 17 per day, and we don't know why." Elaine felt his genuine concern. She sent copies of the Letter to the President to First Lady Michelle Obama, former presidents, former first ladies, governors, politicians, and media personalities, including Secretary Panetta, who was the only person who responded back to her. The letter that Mr. Panetta wrote to Elaine dated February 13, 2014 encouraged her to start a grassroots effort to strengthen young men. Elaine took this as a call to action from an "earthly" commander. Secretary Panetta's letter became an impetus to write this book and confirmed an earlier calling Elaine had received in her Patriarchal Blessing.

Elaine began her efforts by alerting mayors in ten major cities in every state. One night in April 2014 we watched an episode of *Chicagoland*, a special television series produced by Robert Redford and aired on CNN. We were touched deeply by the sad plight of young men portrayed in the story and the uphill battle they faced each day just to survive, go to school, and live normal lives. Elaine was very moved by an Emergency Room trauma surgeon, Dr. Andrew Dennis, who fought furiously to save the lives of a continuous stream of young men brought to the ER with gunshot and knife wounds. Even though this surgeon had a wife and two daughters, he felt compelled to do more to save the lives of young men. In his spare time, Dr. Dennis became a police officer and was assigned to accompany the Special Weapons and Tactics (SWAT) teams so he could be available to help the wounded young men and officers. After seeing this episode, my wife turned to me and asked, "Will you please write a book to help young men?" I figured that if a surgeon would risk his life to save young men, at least, I could write a book to help them. We created a plan and began to write *Elevate Yourself to Manhood* to empower young men of all races who are 12 years of age and up.

Though Elaine is a Canadian, she wears a badge of compassion for the children of the United States on her sleeves, as she does for all children. It was from her concern for the salvation of America that this book was born. Elaine's undying passion for saving the lives of our children, for protecting them from the ravages of bullying, for strengthening them, for saving parents the heartache of losing a child to violence and suicide, and for creating a healthier society inspires us into action. Prior books she has written, *Bullies and Denial Kill* and *Kids Care for Kids*, available in Google Library, were her seminal works in this arena and have inspired a generation of other books and programs to continue the fight. Today, anti-bullying programs and campaigns abound in part due to her unceasing pioneering efforts.

While we were writing *Elevate Yourself to Manhood*, I was diagnosed with cancer, underwent surgery, and we moved, which delayed the completion of the book. The members of our church were very supportive, and now through the grace of God, we have been able to complete this book to strengthen young men.

Special thanks go to Dr. Gordon Nishimoto, Mrs. Shelley Ashworth and Dr. Shane Leavitt who offered editorial services, suggested improvements to the book, and inspired us in so many ways. We give thanks to all the other people who shared their knowledge, expertise, and experience, including Scott Ashworth, Jim Farmer, Lara Buchmiller, David Porter, Steve Fitch, Spencer Davis, Jacob Batchelor, Daniel Harris, and Isaiah Lopossa. Thanks go to Bishop Eric Jacobsen for his warm support and for sharing his famous Root Beer recipe.

We thank, most graciously, Fernando DiLabio, who contributed stories and pictures of Elaine's father when they were young and growing up in Ottawa, Canada.

I am eternally grateful to Mrs. Allen, my former High School English and Literature teacher for a lifetime of encouragement, support, and inspiration. She also inspired other members of my family and our East Texas communities by her ceaseless service, leadership and grace.

Last but not least, I give special thanks to my beautiful and talented wife, Elaine, for her tireless support, encouragement, sage advice, warm guidance, thoughtfulness, prayers, expert assistance and massive contributions to this book. She reviewed books, articles, and websites, condensing and filtering the information, and provided powerful input on all sections of this book. She authored and co-authored much of this book. She also edited this work. Without her love, kind attendance, attention to detail and unceasing effort, this book would probably not have been completed.

PREFACE

It is easier to build strong children
than to repair broken men.

- FREDERICK DOUGLASS

ELEVATE YOURSELF TO MANHOOD WAS written to enable young men to transition successfully from adolescence to manhood. The book will guide young men on their quest for manhood through an awakening, development of the mind, body, spirit, character, family relationships, social aspects, and legacy. *Elevate Yourself to Manhood* was written as a catalyst to strengthen young men to enable them to become healthy, wise, and empowered men.

One of the intentions of this book is to level the playing field for many young men who have not had ideal lives and to improve the lives of those who have been more fortunate. This will be accomplished for young men by filling in the gaps of their "common sense" knowledge, adding to their knowledge the latest findings of cutting-edge research, and by encouraging experiences that they may otherwise miss due to circumstances in their life. The information in this book will enable young men to have a "more equal" mentorship experience as they prepare for their journey to manhood and launch into manhood.

Elevate Yourself to Manhood is a labor of love. The idea grew out of a deep concern for young men, who have so much potential to have a glorious and happy life. It is our sincere hope that young men who read *Elevate Yourself to Manhood* will grow to love themselves, love their parents, love their wives, love their children, love their communities, love their country, and love God - for we have all been sent to the earth to learn how to love and to develop to our full potential.

The book cover, designed by Justin Randolph Cox, is very symbolic. Each element and color has a significant meaning, which we hope will inspire our future brotherhood of men.

The black background symbolizes our universe and "constancy,"[1] as endurance is needed to achieve anything in life.

On the front cover, the shield symbolizes protection, and its color azure blue signifies "truth and loyalty."[2]

A white fleur-de-lys is superimposed on the blue shield. White symbolizes "peace and sincerity."[3] "Traditionally, the fleur-de-lys has been used to represent French royalty, and in that sense, it is said to signify perfection, light, and life. Military units, including divisions of the United States Army, have used the symbol's resemblance to a spearhead to identify military power and strength,"[4] according to the website Fleur-de-lys Designs. The Boy Scouts of America incorporates the fleur-de-lys as part of its "World Crest" design due to its rich symbology. The three tips of the fleur-de-lys on the World Crest represent the three points of the Scout Promise. The three tips of the fleur-de-lys on the *Elevate Yourself to Manhood* book cover symbolize the book's mission to strengthen young men, their families, and our communities.

Superimposed on the fleur-de-lys is a green-faceted mountain, which symbolizes each young man's quest for manhood. The seven white lines running to its summit make eight facets, which represent the eight chapters in *Elevate Yourself to Manhood*, and the growth needed to become a healthy man. Green symbolizes "hope, joy, and loyalty in love."[5] It also symbolizes time spent in nature, which is pivotal.

Superimposed on the mountain is a gold man in a victory stance. Gold signifies electrical conductivity of the elevation of the mind, body and spirit, enabling a current that will charge your life, your family's life, your society, your world, and your eternity.

Our hope is that *Elevate Yourself to Manhood* will be a beacon, which will light the way for new generations of manly men - generations, which will honor themselves, honor their family, honor their community, honor their country, and honor God.

Ray Edward Cox, Sr., Circa 1948

DEDICATION TO RAY EDWARD COX

This book is dedicated to my dad, Ray Edward Cox. By any measure, he was a manly man. His life exemplified the traits and behaviors expected of adult males then and now. My dad's legacy is one of a loving husband to my mother, Maria Massenburg, for fifty-two years, a great father to nine surviving children (five girls and four boys), a wonderful provider for his family, an innovative thinker, and a hard worker. He was a sterling role model for boys including myself, my three male siblings and all other boys who were privileged enough to know him.

Ray Cox was a Renaissance man. Though his accomplishments may not be nationally renowned, he was monumental to those who counted most - his family, friends, co-workers, members of the community and acquaintances.

Living in the Deep South in a deeply segregated society, my dad found ways to co-exist peacefully, find his path, raise a family and establish himself as a well-respected member of our community. Because of his character, all who knew him - men and women, black and white alike, revered him. He was sought out for life skills, his talents, his wisdom, or simply for friendship.

I never knew him ever to raise his voice, but he was a man of little fear and great physical strength. Though not a violent man, he knew how to protect himself and his family. He maintained a small arsenal as part of our existence on the family farm due to a history of our property being attacked by violent racists, and as protection from wild animals. He taught me how to handle guns, hunt, fish, manage animals, farm and drive a tractor by the age of ten.

He learned to do hard things at an early age. He built our family home with his bare hands. On weekdays, he worked full-time at a factory.

Evenings and weekends, he ran a large farm, where he raised prize-winning produce for his immediate and extended family. In addition to those responsibilities, he also worked a grueling part-time job, for a while, at an iron refinery at night. One night, when he picked me up from my part-time employment, he looked particularly exhausted. On his tired, haggard face I could see a coating of fine black soot from the hot furnaces. Although that job tested his human physical limits, his determination and sense of self-reliance to serve his family never diminished.

He did everything with skill, care and attention to detail. He demonstrated love and patience when mentoring me. For this, I am most grateful and indebted.

At home, he was a carpenter, a hunter, a fisherman, an electrician, a plumber, a horticulturist, and a mechanical genius.

Professionally, he was a master mixologist for high-temperature commercial ceramics. He had an uncanny knack for creating optimal formulas for clays and glazes from raw materials. Decades later, man developed technology to automatically create specific colors for ceramics, a task that my dad pioneered through natural talent.

He feared God and his moral values were beyond reproach. I understand that he was a Master Freemason. He regularly attended church services at our church, New Mountain, C.M.E. (Christian, Methodist, Episcopal), and served as Deacon. He was a leader of men.

One of his more mysterious gifts was the ability to "divine" water. I remember people would consult him to help locate areas for drilling water wells – a valuable skill in Texas in the days of "wildcat" oil and gas wells. Before investing tons of time, labor and money into digging a well, people wanted to have the best possible chance of finding water, gas, or oil. My dad was locally renowned for this ability.

As his photo attests, he was a dapper dresser. When he purchased clothing, shoes, or accessories, they were always of the highest quality without going overboard on price.

My dad had to drop out of school in the eighth grade to help support his mom, dad, and younger siblings on the family farm. He bore that duty as a badge of honor.

He elevated his family out of post-slavery and post-Great Depression circumstance. He had a modicum of education and precious little monetary inheritance. With hard work and determination he successfully worked his way up from the bottom to become foreman, supervisor, and eventually, Vice President of his company where he retired after 45 years.

He was our hero – showing us and teaching us how to elevate ourselves and how to follow our dreams. He was able to shepherd my male siblings and me into manhood by his example and guiding words. Though he has passed away, his legacy inspires me as I strive to show myself as a man as he did.

Major Arthur Eugene Joseph Barbeau, C.D., Physical Education and Recreation in the Royal Canadian Air Force and the Canadian Armed Forces, Circa 1970

DEDICATION TO MAJOR ARTHUR EUGENE JOSEPH BARBEAU

This book is also dedicated to Major Arthur Eugene Joseph Barbeau, my wife's father. He, too, was a manly man, and a Renaissance man, whose military career and civilian career led him to live in Europe and throughout Canada. He is the father of seven children, including six daughters and a son.

Arthur was born in Ottawa, Canada, two months premature during a time when incubators did not exist. He was born prematurely because his seventeen-year-old mother, Jeannette Janveau Barbeau, fell down icy stairs. His nineteen-year-old father, Arthur Alexandre Barbeau, cried when he saw his tiny premature baby because he did not look healthy – he was not yet fully formed. The poor baby's head was rather lopsided. Also, his father knew that very few premature babies survived in those days.

His mother placed her tiny baby in a shoebox, on the open door of her wood-burning stove, to keep him warm. The oven was not too hot – just warm enough to keep his body at about the temperature he would have been in her womb. Miraculously, due to his mother's meticulous care and much prayer, he not only survived, but he thrived steadily in strength and stature.

When Arthur was around five years old, he began to play outdoors for hours each day, in a modest multi-cultural neighborhood, slightly north of "Little Italy" in Ottawa, Canada. He made many friends. As they grew, they started to call themselves the "Balsam

Street Pals," (see photograph in the Legacy chapter). There was a large field owned by J.R. Booth Lumber Mill, in their neighborhood, which "saved them" from getting into trouble, according to Fernando DiLabio one of Arthur's boyhood friends who became an aeronautical engineer. The field was adjacent to a lumberyard with a railroad on one side and the Ottawa River on the other side. In this field, the boys built forts out of logs from the lumberyard in the summer and fall, and played baseball, football and soccer. In the winter they built snow forts. In the spring, they sailed their homemade boats down the spring run-off. The field also hosted the Ringling Bros. and Barnum & Bailey three-ring circus whenever it came to town.

Arthur was raised in the Catholic faith. When he was a boy he would sing at an early mass in his church. Afterward, he would run over to a Methodist church to sing in their choir. In those days, it really was not acceptable for a Catholic to go into a Protestant church and vice-versa but he loved to sing.

The fresh air, exercise and creative skills Arthur developed playing with his boyhood friends and singing in choirs paid off. The following is an excerpt from Arthur's memoirs:

"He attended St. Jean Baptiste primary school and Ottawa Technical High School. A member of the special HS music class through four years as a trombonist and became assistant conductor leading the first half-time shows for the Ottawa Rough Rider football games at many Saturday games with a single majorette (1946-1947). Won the 16-year old trombone soloist at the Ottawa Music Festival in 1946 (see photograph in the Legacy chapter). A member of the Ottawa Technical High School Gymnastic teams that dominated the Ottawa and District and Provincial high school gymnastics in the mid-40s, he led the team to the Senior Provincial Title in 1948 and, with Ray Gauthier and Gerry Cotter, won the Junior Canadian Gymnastics Championship in 1947 (see photograph in the Legacy chapter). They were considered for the Olympics but due to financial restrictions, Dr. Orban from McGill [University] was sent as an observer instead. At this meet, Barbeau won the Dominion Championship individual silver medal on the High Bar (see photograph in the Legacy chapter). The gymnastics and music established the foundations for his lifetime career. He joined the Royal Canadian Air Force (RCAF) on October 26, 1948."

From a young age Arthur challenged himself to do hard things. He excelled in sports competitions and music competitions. As a twenty-one-year-old he was transferred to the Manning Depot to train French-speaking recruits at the R.C.A.F. St. Jean, Quebec, School of English. While he was at the school, "he challenged the 300 English-speaking recruits to a drill competition and successfully took on the best of the whole Manning Depot with his 30 French recruits. With a single departure command, his squad performed for 12 minutes without a single mistake and won." Shortly after, he became the School of English Disciplinarian responsible for 300 students who were learning to speak French.

In 1952, he married Cécile Fernande Blais whom he had met when he was at the R.C.A.F. School of English. They were married for 54 years.

After he married, he climbed the ranks of the Royal Canadian Air Force (RCAF), and the Canadian Armed Forces. As a young Corporal he was the honor student for the first Recreation Athletic Specialist course. He was given a choice of postings in recognition of this. He received numerous awards throughout his career.

During the early years, he often played trombone in dance bands to earn extra money to help support his family. He also went hunting for moose, deer, and elk and fished in the wild Canadian North to stock their deep freezer for winter months. He took a few of his children on some of these hunting and fishing trips. Summer vacations usually included a camping trip with his family.

On Sundays, he went to church with his family, directed many church choirs and frequently sang solos. His bilingual rendition of O Holy Night every Christmas was breathtaking and memorable. He had a naturally operatic tenor voice though he never received voice training. Sunday afternoons were reserved for family outings – a swim in a pool that was closed to everyone else but his children, (for as the military base's Recreation Director he had the keys to the pool); picnics; car rides to explore the countryside; horseback riding; and skiing.

He was an excellent snow skier and a talented water-skier who performed tricks to amuse crowds of onlookers during summer carnival festivities. He also performed in plays and musicals, such as "H.M.S. Pinafore."

He became a Major in the Canadian Armed Forces – a Recreation and Sports Specialist, and a Protocol Officer. His Turf Management program was widely accepted throughout the R.C.A.F. for early putting golf greens in the North. He was also a respected member of the Knights of Columbus, and the Royal Canadian Legion.

The Mynarski Trophy at this time was awarded to the most outstanding community recreation program in the RCAF with the onus on children's programs. Arthur's team of recreation specialists won this prestigious award twice – on one of the smallest RCAF stations Parent, Quebec and on one of the largest units Cold Lake, Alberta.

He retired from the Air Force after 27 years to pursue a career establishing recreation facilities for the James Bay Hydro Project, to occupy 5,000 men and women with healthful activities in the wild, isolated Canadian North, where temperatures drop to 60 degrees below zero (Fahrenheit). The facilities and programs that Arthur established were crucial for maintaining the physical health and mental health of the members of the community.

Upon returning to civilization from the north, he became the manager of a real estate branch. He taught real estate in French and in English at a college and became the president of the province of Quebec's real estate board.

Whatever he did in life he did to the best of his abilities. His motto was, "If something is worth doing, it is worth doing well." He also had a "joie de vivre." He enjoyed fine dining, and traveling but mostly he enjoyed spending time with his family. He came across as a serious man, who demanded perfection of himself and his family, but he was also young at heart. His objective in life was to set a good example for his family so that subsequent generations would be strong in mind, body and spirit. His intention was always to elevate himself and his family.

Arthur was an avid reader all through his life. He read newspapers daily, always staying abreast of current events, and he liked science fiction - Isaac Asimov in particular - and books such as "Time Line." He read "The Lord of the Rings" in his youth and enjoyed the "Harry Potter" series when he was convalescing in the hospital as an older man.

In retirement, he was a regional coordinator for the Canadian Veterans' poppy campaign through the Royal Canadian Legion, went to the library daily, and he sang with the Stuart Hall Chorus, in Beaconsfield, Quebec, (a professional level choir) and a church choir. It was painful for him to stand for hours while singing in the choir due to injuries he sustained to his knees in his youth from gymnastic activities. He had also had a hip replacement operation. It was even difficult for him to walk and to go up and down stairs. He certainly loved music, loved life, and never gave up throughout all of his life's challenges.

When he was 75 years old, he died of a massive heart attack standing up at his front door and fell straight back to the floor. His many friends and large family attended his funeral that commemorated a life well lived. He is missed and loved by his wife, all of his children, his grandchildren, and his many friends.

In my opinion, Arthur's crowning glory was becoming the father of Elaine, his eldest daughter, who would become my wife, and co-author of this book. For this, I am most thankful.

INTRODUCTION

BY VARYING DEGREES, YOUNG MEN of today struggle to grow up, find independence and become productive men of society. They struggle to stake their rightful claim to manhood. You may have heard about or read about this phenomenon. Through research, we have discovered many reasons why this is occurring. Almost every adult we spoke to about this book knows of a young man struggling to find his footing in society. When we were doing research for this book, we discovered that a handbook to guide young men in their teen years through all facets of life did not exist. We have written *Elevate Yourself to Manhood* to enlighten and to strengthen all young men. It is intended to be a holistic survival guide that offers crucial information to help get you on track for your quest to becoming a manly man. By the word "manly" we mean a caliber of men like modern day versions of my father and father-in-law. We mean to say, men who love to learn, men who have a predisposition for action, men who are responsible, men who earn love and respect, men who can support themselves, their family and give back to their community. We are talking about men who become the best they can be, inspire other people to do the same, and because they live, the world is a better place.

It is important for you, young man, to realize that each person has three core areas of existence:

* Mind
* Body
* Spirit

All other facets of a person build upon these three key areas. In this book, I plan to guide you through an awakening, the development of your mind, body, and spirit - as well as your character, family relationships, social aspects, and how to leave a respectable legacy for yourself, your children and your grandchildren. Essentially, this book will coach you through adolescence on your quest to manhood to enable you to become healthy and wise. What is the sense in waking up at the age of fifty, only to say, "I wish I knew this when I was eighteen years old?" After reading this book, the odds are very favorable that you will have a much easier time making the leap from adolescence to manhood, to become a great man.

We will offer solutions to the problems that plague you as a modern young man. These solutions are based on the latest research as well as information that has been passed on from some of the wisest and most caring men and women of our time. We have no doubt that this book will answer many of the questions on your mind, as well as answering questions that you have not yet been able to formulate in your mind but which may exist in your heart. It is our hope that it will help guide you through the maze of challenges associated with being a young man growing up in today's society to the road that leads up to the summit of manhood.

We believe that this book will continue to benefit young men aged twelve and up from any generation for years to come - regardless of the "Generation" designation – such as Generations X, Y, Z, Millennials, or whatever. The generation designations are very subjective and controversial - government documents, the media, and social science do not agree upon when each generation name begins and ends.

Young man, you may feel that this awkward period in your life – this indescribable stage of life when you are no longer a child but not yet a man - is hard to navigate. This book will steer you like a compass. Also, this book will soothe some of your fears about dealing with your present life and your future. Mastering the topics in this book will help you make that giant leap to manhood with strength and confidence.

We chose the title *Elevate Yourself to Manhood* because we want to empower you. We want you to learn to uplift yourself by taking in your knapsack on your quest for manhood, interesting and useful knowledge and skills – some of which you may not have heard about or read about before. We have provided cutting-edge research distilled down into easily-understood language, some practical information, and ideas to stretch your imagination. We hope you will take it all to heart, but that will be up to you. We also hope you find it entertaining.

The goals of this book are to:

* Help you to awaken to life
* Help you to achieve happiness and gain hope
* Strengthen your mind by providing solutions for the ills that plague the minds of modern young men
* Enhance your body through proper health, nutrition, and fitness
* Enable you to recognize your spiritual nature and enable you to grow and refine your spirit as you mature into manhood
* Strengthen your character by teaching you how to avoid those things that thwart proper character-building in our modern society
* Enable you to strengthen family relationships
* Enable you to develop critical social skills
* Help you to develop confidence
* Enable you to become wise

Our hope is that you will flourish as you mature into a fine, well-adjusted adult who will be able to establish, protect, and sustain yourself and your family.

If your parents gave this book to you, be grateful that they love you and that they are also trying to enable you to become all you want to be. If you are studying this book with a friend, you are lucky to have an inspired buddy. Many quests have been undertaken successfully with partners. Explorers such as Columbus, the Vikings, Jacques Cartier, and Lewis and Clark embarked upon their quest with a whole contingent of men. If you are studying this book with the scouts or with a class in your school for boys, be glad that you have companionship on your journey and that you are part of a team. You may want to team up with a parent or grandparent if that would be more fun for you. At a later date, however, you will want to continue the quest on your own.

How My Father Helped Me to Prepare for My Quest; the Role Played by My Extended Family, and Other Members of My Community

My father started mentoring me early in life. Some of my earliest and fondest memories are from when I was around four or five years old. My dad would jack up the family Oldsmobile on wooden blocks, and we would crawl underneath to do repairs together. I do not know if I actually provided any useful help, but he allowed me to pretend anyway.

Our cars always seemed to need work, and we were forever tinkering around with them. Repairing our automobiles was a lesson in self-reliance – that is – we relied on our own abilities (out of necessity), because we could not afford to pay for professional automobile servicing. Also because of pride, we would never think of having our cars repaired by outsiders except in circumstances beyond our capability. For example, we might need professional help with crankshaft resurfacing or auto body repair work.

Just spending time with my dad, even if only doing chores, was special to me. As his oldest son, I got enormous amounts of on-the-job training in "manly" skills. Dad was a rock-solid man of few words, but the words he did impart to me, I still treasure decades later. Mostly, he guided me by example. He taught me how to be a man by showing me how to be responsible, how not to whine when things did not go my way, and how to accomplish large tasks in small steps on a compressed schedule. He was definitely a "show-me" not a "tell-me" kind of guy. My dad's words of wisdom and my experiences growing up on the family farm, out in raw nature helped give me bearing as I navigated through times of plenty and times of trouble throughout my life. Without the distractions of cell phones and Internet connections when I was growing up, adults had more opportunity to pass down stories from my forbears, share personal philosophies, and to help model my future life. I never had the occasion to tell my father before he died, how much his mentoring meant to me.

My grandmother, Effie Webb Cox, taught me many things about life in the brief years that I knew her. She was my best friend. Grandmother taught me mostly about things of a spiritual nature. She encouraged me always to "be good." She praised me for the positive deeds I performed and for getting good grades in school. She also cautioned me about evil in the world - to be aware of it and to avoid it. There were certain circumstances in my life where her counsel may have saved my life.

My grandfather died when I was just a little tyke of two years old, so my memories of him are very faint, if any. I am sure that he attempted to impart words of wisdom to me during our times together. Being the first and only grandchild when he passed away, I can only imagine how he wanted to teach me things that he had learned during his lifetime, but at that age, I am sure my poor little brain just would not have been able to take it all in.

I had four uncles that lived close by who also shared valuable knowledge with me and served as male role models as well. Uncle Arzo was a former Army Paratrooper. After he had left the Army, he joined my teenage gospel band, "The Heavenly Wonders." He enthusiastically sang, played guitar, provided musical direction, and provided adult leadership. He made sure we practiced, perfected our art, and got to performances on time as we played at various churches throughout our county. He was also a mentor to the other teenage band members.

Uncle Dainty and Uncle Herman, as well, were wise, hard-working manly men who spent copious amounts of time shepherding me to manhood. At times, my dad and all my uncles would invite me to go hunting and fishing with them. At other occasions, we all worked around the general homestead in which we lived. I learned so much by osmosis just being around them, feeding off their energy, stories, and games.

Aunt Cora, Aunt Velma, and Aunt Bertha were very generous and loving towards me as I grew up. They always seemed to have time for me and taught me about life from a female perspective. Aunt Cora even had the courage to teach me to drive a car on our rural property when I was nine years old. When I was twelve, Aunt Velma and Aunt Cora took me to a James Bond double-header at the Starlight Drive-In Theater, which was my first official outing into the "night life" and one experience that I will never forget.

My high school teachers went absolutely beyond the call of duty by setting aside extra tutoring time for me. During my senior year, they ensured that I had the knowledge and skills to enter into college and pursue my college and professional dreams. My high school was small and did not offer a full cadre of courses that a college fresh-man engineering student would need. Mrs. Bell personally tutored me in Trigonometry. She was also my French teacher. Mrs. Muldrew tutored me in language, and Mrs. Hill tutored me in English and lit-erature. Without their personal sacrifices, effort and support, I would not have been able to enter college that year to study engineering.

Also during high school, my dad's boss gave me an unprec-edented opportunity to work in the company laboratory to learn testing procedures and quality control measures. Working in the laboratory was a promotion from my part-time custodian role, which I had held for a couple of years. Prior to this, I had worked in the hot sun for hours with a wire brush scraping residue off kiln-fired clay products. That was most definitely a character-building job, if there ever was one.

I took this lab opportunity, not only to make money but also to continue learning the value of hard work. My dad's co-workers and friends always included me in their conversations and shared small talk as well as advice on various life topics. I always listened intently to learn as much about life from them as I could. I loved hanging out with the "old folks." In those days, children were taught to respect their elders and learn from them. Everything I learned from them as a young child and teenager, I remembered and employed in my everyday life.

Members of my church, New Mountain, C.M.E., elevated me by giving me various jobs to do for the church. As a fourteen-year-old,

I was paid to clean the church on Sundays before services began. At fifteen, I began to teach Sunday School, and at seventeen, I became the Assistant Sunday School Superintendent. In these roles I learned leadership. I also sang lead in the church choir during "call-and-response" style songs – which was a big deal for me because I loved music.

After graduating high school, I was offered membership in the Junior Kiwanis Club, a civic organization founded for men in 1915 to promote community service. We would gather together on Thursday mornings at an old hotel for breakfast. In attendance would be a bunch of older guys and myself. One jolly old fellow would play a couple of rousing songs on the piano, and we would all sing with gusto prior to going to work or in my case, to the local college. With my being a young black teenager and they being much older white men in the Deep South in the "civil rights" days, it was quite an honor to be treated with such dignity and accepted as one of their children. They afforded me a glimpse into a world that I had never known.

At my dad's company, supervisors, foremen, managers, and executives all shared their friendship, knowledge, wisdom and examples of leadership.

I was fortunate to have had these and many more mentors in my life who cared enough for me to share their time, wisdom and love. I would like to think that all their support made me a better man than I would have been otherwise.

FILL YOUR KNAPSACK – SEEK OUT RIGHTEOUS MENTORS AS YOU PREPARE FOR YOUR QUEST FOR MANHOOD

I know you can find mentors in your life to help you on your quest if you seek and accept help and guidance from your parents, church members, scout leaders, teachers, coaches, bosses, and community leaders. Seek out those who will give you righteous advice. Keep a distance from those who would lead you astray if you gave them a chance. Be in control.

With this book, I am part of your extended earthly family - one of the mentors who will help you to fill your knapsack with tools to take on your quest for manhood. My hope is that this book will strengthen you as you read its pages. I hope you will gain an awareness of self; an awareness of life; a joie de vivre (a joy for life); an awareness of how to care for your mind, body, and spirit. I hope you will also gain a profound awareness of your particular purpose in life and share it with your family and community. With them, I hope you will develop a mutual trust, love, gratitude, and joy.

ADULTS HAVE A RESPONSIBILITY TO GUIDE YOUNG MEN

It is our belief that adults need to do more to protect and guide our children – all children – whether we share DNA with them or not. An old African expression was popularized by Hillary Clinton in 1996, in her book, *It Takes a Village*. "It takes a village to raise a child" means that it is the responsibility of all adults to see after all the children in their communities.

Please notice in the *Bible* in Malachi (excerpt below) that it is the heart of the fathers, which turn to (all) the children first.

*Behold, I will send you Elijah the prophet before the coming of the great and dreadful day of the Lord: And he shall turn the heart of the fathers to **the** children, and the heart of the children to **their** fathers, lest I come and smite the earth with a curse.*

– MALACHI 4:5-6 KJV

Malachi did not state, "the fathers to their (own) children." "The fathers to **the** children," implies that fathers everywhere need to protect all children - not just their own children - or Jesus will punish the earth. We obviously do not take this biblical verse lightly. It is one of the main reasons we wrote this book.

I hope someday you will teach your children and other children in your community the lessons of your life. I hope you will tell the children stories and engage them with wise counsel to shape their young lives. With the life experiences you will gain, and with sincere intent, you will bestow upon the children such a precious gift.

We are doing our part by writing this book to help you. As you go through the book, think about what you would like your life to look like when you become an adult.

ELEVATING YOURSELF ON YOUR QUEST FOR MANHOOD

In order for a young man to prepare for the responsibilities of manhood, he must learn to take on challenges and shoulder responsibilities early on. Learning to deal with problems while you are young creates "responsibility muscles" that you will need as a man.

So just how exactly will you go about "elevating yourself" to manhood?

This book uses a pyramid model similar in construction to the famous Maslow's Hierarchy of Needs pyramid to demonstrate the concept. His theory was that people have a hierarchy of needs, and they are motivated to satisfy those needs in five stages, starting at the bottom stage of the pyramid, moving up the pyramid as each need is satisfied.

However, in *Elevate Yourself to Manhood*, a young man's life is symbolized by a mountain with eight facets and a path which meanders through the eight facets as the young man learns and practices new skills on his quest to the summit of manhood. The eight facets on the mountain represent the eight facets of growth which young men attain to become manly men. These eight facets of growth are depicted in the eight chapters in *Elevate Yourself to Manhood*. You will start at the bottom of the *Elevate Yourself to Manhood* Mountain, exploring all eight facets of your life as you read this book. You will then put into practice your new skills and tools to move "up" the mountain - creating a zigzag path through all eight facets as you climb to conquer the mountain's summit to manhood as depicted below. Throughout your quest, you will explore and grow through all of these facets continuously.

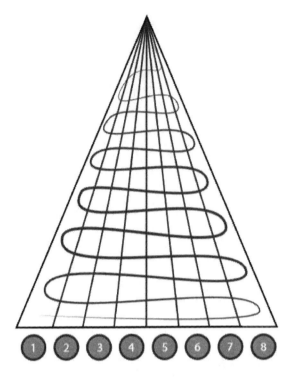

- Facet 1 - *Awaken and Begin Your Quest* – Establish your sense of identity and self-worth while identifying unnecessary baggage to leave behind as you begin your quest.
- Facet 2 – *Elevate Your Mind* – Prepare your mind for the quest by learning the effects of environmental influences on the brain and learning mind development skills. You will first need to assess the state of your mind, get rid of old bad habits, learn new skills, develop talents and take on new habits.
- Facet 3 - *Elevate Your Body*: - Load up on the all-important information regarding health, nutrition, and fitness. Having a fit body is needed to help you succeed and to complete the journey.
- Facet 4 – *Elevate Your Spirit*: - Lighten your load to elevate yourself even higher with God's strength under your wings. Fill your knapsack with spiritual fire, which will help to sustain you and may save your life during stormy weather.
- Facet 5 – *Elevate Your Character*: - Gather tools and skills to build a strong character.

- Facet 6 – *Elevate Your Family:* - Learn to deal with family members and issues gracefully and learn to establish your own family someday.
- Facet 7 – *Elevate Your Place in Society:* - Learn the "savoir-faire" you will need to deal with the people and situations you will encounter on your Quest. Savoir-faire involves having the ability to behave or speak appropriately in social situations.
- Facet 8 – *Create Your Legacy:* - Reflect on what you want to do to build a legacy for yourself and your posterity.

BEFORE YOU BEGIN YOUR QUEST GET RID OF FALSE BAGGAGE

As I have already mentioned, young men in our society are in trouble. There has been an increase in youth violence, youth suicide, depression, and general disrespect for authority. Many boys seem to be in a "fog" whereby they may seem distant, overwhelmed, overstressed, and un-controllably disconnected with their real life. I fear they cannot see the hidden dangers directly before them. We will expose primary reasons why young men may seem distracted, disengaged, or unmotivated in later chapters. What we need to do now is to identify the false baggage and false assumptions you need to leave behind before starting your quest. We need to identify what is NOT causing the fog, confusion or stress disconnection.

People often make excuses for youth violence, youth suicide and other destructive behavior without knowing the real reasons. Misconceptions are false baggage, and you will need to leave them behind.

"MY PARENTS GOT DIVORCED" BAGGAGE

Too often people blame youth unhappiness and youth violence on their parents' divorce. The truth is that young men have experienced the challenge of being in single parent families for centuries. Being a member of a single parent family is not an excuse for violence. When we look at the historical perspective, we see that in the past, hundreds of thousands of children became fatherless in America due to wars. The statistics below will enable you to see the number of American men who perished in wars, many leaving their wives and children, during times when women were not able to find employment that could sustain their large families. Keep in mind also that back then there was no social net or welfare to help them.

During the American Civil War, 625,000 men were lost. During the Second World War (WWII), 407,000 American soldiers were lost. During the Vietnam War 58,220 U.S. military men and women perished.[6] After these wars, there were a lot of single parent families, and orphans.

Due to the sacrifices made by the men and women who fought for our freedom, we are among "the fewer than 5% of all the people who have ever lived on the earth who have lived under conditions that we could consider free."[7] We are so fortunate to live in a country where we enjoy freedom!

We must consistently be realistic in assessing our blessings in regards to living in a country where freedom is a right. We must never forget the horrors of war - the tearing apart of families, the senseless slaughter, for evil ideologies. The powerful movie *Run Boy Run* gives us a glimpse of the reality of what it feels like to live in a country without freedom. In essence, the movie is a reality check that helps us to focus on what really matters in life. The film depicts the amazing true story of Yoran Friedman, an eight-year-old boy, who escaped the Warsaw Ghetto, during World War II. This extraordinary Menemsha Film (2014), Directed by the Academy Award Winning Director, Pepe Danquart. You will need to watch this foreign film with the subtitles turned on. This movie will inspire you to thrive even through life's most difficult challenges. When you think that life is tough you will always remember this movie and you will feel, "If this boy could survive, remain steadfast and go on to have a full life, so can I."

Also, the film reminds us, that we must be vigilant to never let these atrocities happen again. We must raise up our children to be loving, kind, and respectful (someday many of you young men will have children of your own). We must thoughtfully exercise our right to vote for righteous, just and wise leaders, and commit to taking office when we feel called to do so. Thusly, we will each do our part to safeguard our freedom and democracy.

Note: The Warsaw Ghetto was a concentration camp where Jewish people were imprisoned and killed during World War II.

Currently, the divorce rate in the United States is between 40-50%[8]. In the 1940s, the divorce rate was between 20-43%.[9] Though divorces did happen in the 1940s and 1950s, the rate of youth violence and youth suicide was much lower than it is today. So let us not complain about being from a single-parent family. As an example, President Barack Obama's mother was divorced. Barack Obama was raised in a single parent family.

Ben Carson, a retired leading pediatric neurosurgeon, was also raised in a single parent family. His mother was a maid who noticed that the children of the wealthy read many books. She limited her sons' television viewing time to three programs per week and asked them to write two book reports per week. It paid off. Her son, Dr. Ben Carson, attributes his success to her guidance. He has separated conjoined twins, performed surgeries on tiny babies' brains all over the world, and saved many lives.

"There is no such thing as an average human being.
If you have a normal brain, you are superior."

BEN CARSON, PEDIATRIC NEUROSURGEON

The Prime Minister of Canada Justin Pierre Trudeau, who at 43 became the second youngest person ever to hold the office, was elected October 19, 2015. He, like Ben Carson and Barack Obama, came from a single parent family. Susana Mas,[10] a CBC reporter, in her article *Justin Trudeau Memoir: 7 Surprising Revelations from Common Ground* stated that Justin Trudeau shared the difficult periods in his life:

"While his upbringing was one of privilege, it was also one shaped by the breakup of his parents and his mother's struggle with bipolar disorder."

Justin Trudeau stated, "I remember the bad times as a succession of painful emotional snapshots: Me walking into the library at 24 Sussex, seeing my mother in tears and hearing her talk about leaving while my father stood facing her, stern and ashen."

Justin's father, Pierre Elliot Trudeau, was Prime Minister of Canada when his marriage to Justin's mother ended. However, Justin was able to focus on the positive aspects of his life, which strengthened him. At his father's funeral in 2000, Justin gave the eulogy to his father while a whole nation listened in awe of the wisdom Justin had at such an early age.[11]

"Simple tolerance, mere tolerance, is not enough," Trudeau, then 28, told the crowd in French:

"We need genuine and deep respect for each and every human being, notwithstanding their thoughts, their values, their beliefs, their origins. That's what my father demanded of his sons and that's what he demanded of his country. He demanded this out of a sense of love. Love of his sons. Love of his country, and that's why we love him so."

Prior to the election on October 19, 2015 the Liberal Party of Canada was in third place with 36 seats, in the House of Commons. Under Justin Trudeau's leadership the party won 184 seats, and Justin was elected Prime Minister. That was a huge victory!

If you have experienced the turmoil of a parent's death, or your parents' divorce, you can rise above these events. At the moment you may feel emotionally weighted down – just be patient with yourself and with life. The skills learned in this book will strengthen you and with time you will feel renewed. Take one step at a time on your journey.

"LIFE IS TOO STRESSFUL" BAGGAGE
Other than civil war, there are more ways in which our lives are less stressful today than they were one hundred years ago. We have running water in our homes. We can go to a grocery store to buy food - we do not need to hunt for our dinner. When we move to

a different city, we can fly, drive, or take a bus instead of traveling by foot pushing handcarts across thousands of miles for months with little or no food - as did American pioneers with their large families. We are among the luckiest people who have ever lived. Our lives are much easier today because we enjoy modern conveniences. We are some of the most prosperous people on our planet today.

You have only to watch The Roosevelts, a documentary series about the life and times of President Theodore Roosevelt and President Franklin D. Roosevelt (1858-1962) to realize that during those years many, many people suffered and experienced enormous stress in the U.S.A. and around the world. Watching this film helps to put everything into perspective. How President Franklin D. Roosevelt saved the U.S.A. and helped to save the free world while enduring critical personal challenges, is particularly inspiring. I feel that Franklin D. Roosevelt likely inspired my father and father-in-law because they were young men during this time period.

"LIFE IS TOO FAST-PACED" BAGGAGE
When I was young I fed the pigs and milked cows at 6:00 a.m., gobbled down some oatmeal, went to school all day, then worked in a factory (25 miles away) after school until 9:30 p.m. or 10:00 p.m. On some evenings, I had band practice as well. When I got home, I did my homework and continued this routine during the week. On the weekend, I had many farm chores to do as well as working at the factory: caring for animals, milking cows, clearing fields, plowing fields, seeding, weeding crops, harvesting crops, cutting down trees, sawing logs for the fireplace, slaughtering chickens for food, churning butter, running errands, drawing fresh water from the well, cleaning floors, washing clothes, band practice, and gospel group practice. I had to learn auto mechanics, plumbing, construction, and other related skills on the farm. The list goes on and on. My life on weekdays and weekends was fast-paced – no time for slacking off. In other words,

I had to do hard things well. But we always rested on Sundays while observing the Sabbath Day. I have the Lord to thank for a day of rest.

Science has now revealed that learning to do real-life hard things and learning a variety of skills builds and strengthens neurological pathways in the brain. If we do not use these pathways, we lose them. We will discuss these facts in detail with supporting evidence later in this book.

Before beginning a journey or a quest, it is important to see clearly the path ahead. We have discovered why so many youths are unhappy and why so many children are violent in both wealthy and impoverished communities. We intend to give you all the information you will need to maneuver through modern life, to enable you to elevate yourself to be your best self, but for now, just get rid of the false excuses that cloud your perspective.

WHY THIS BOOK AND WHY NOW?

We hope that *Elevate Yourself to Manhood* will become a rite of passage for young men. It is needed because heretofore, there has been no rite of passage for young men in Western society.

To illustrate why *Elevate Yourself to Manhood* is needed, take note of Scott Peck's observations in his seminal work, *The Road Less Traveled.*[12] He brings to light the risks of growing up and how hard it is to find your place in the world. He says,

> *"Of the thousands, maybe even millions, of risks we can take in a lifetime the greatest is the risk of growing up. Growing up is the act of stepping from childhood into adulthood. Actually it is more of a fearful leap than a step, and it is a leap that many people never really take in their lifetimes. Though they may outwardly appear to be adults, even successful adults, perhaps the majority of 'grown-ups' remain until their death psychological children who have never truly separated themselves from their parents and the power that their parents have over them."*

Peck also mentions that the process of growing up does not happen all at once. He observes that maturity occurs slowly over time "very gradually, with multiple little leaps into the unknown."[13]

As you take your bold steps out into the unknown along your quest for maturity, we want you to keep this book as your trusty guide.

THE MALE CHALLENGE

We have acknowledged that growing up through the teen years can be tough work, but we know that you are up for the challenge. Although my childhood experience may have been different from yours, the basics of growing up remain unchanged. It was a challenge for me back then, and it is a challenge for you today.

Sometimes the easiest way to prepare for a journey is to consult a person who has already "been there" and "done that." It is smart to study a map of the road ahead. Parents and schools do what they can to prepare young men for adulthood, but often it is not enough. Parents from dual-earner families have less time to mentor young men than families had in the past when mothers were primarily homemakers. Increasingly today, in schools, teachers are not able to impart as much knowledge as they would like due to disciplinary problems in class. Also, teachers are not mandated to teach young men how to become healthy, wise and empowered men.

One of our objectives is to help young people realize that life is meant to be happy. Many of our youth have seen so much pain and suffering in their lifetime that they have become discouraged, stressed and worried. They are afraid and wonder if they can ever have a happy life. Yes, you can rise above your current circumstances even if you are living in a broken or unhappy home; or residing in a gang-infested neighborhood; or if your girlfriend broke up with you; or if you failed an exam; or if you are just floating along in life. You can learn to elevate yourself successfully to a wholesome, healthy adulthood. Some of you may be from affluent homes and rarely see your parents due to their busy schedules. Some of you may have health challenges, or you may be caring for a family member who has health concerns. Some of you may be members of a gang and want out. Whatever your present situation is, this book is here to help you. Being overwhelmed by the problems in life can obscure the fact that God wants us all to be happy and has the means to make it so. I realize that everybody defines happiness differently, but I hope that after you read this book cover to cover, we can agree on what true happiness really means and how to attain it. More importantly, I hope that you will be strengthened with new insights and skills that will empower you to meet life's challenges in the pursuit of happiness.

What if I told you that despite the fact that we have never met – I think you are a truly awesome person - that you are without a doubt, one of the most awesome people who has ever lived? Further, what if I said that you are a miracle?

Check the *Elevate Yourself to Manhood* website at www. elevateyourselftomanhood.com/videos for the availability of the "Miracle of Life" video.

You are a unique human being. Your existence plays a vital role in the destiny of all humanity because we are all a part of the fabric of society. We hope you will come away from reading this book with a more elevated opinion of yourself – not to the point where you will feel the need to boast or be overly proud, but to the point where you will, hopefully, possess a much stronger feeling of self-appreciation and self-confidence. You should come to know how truly awesome you are and that you have the strength to meet the challenges of life and to make that giant leap into adulthood.

There is so much more to learn than what you are getting in school. Although we present much information in this book, we cannot include all of life's lessons. Consider this book a supplement or an extension of your current learnings. However, be prepared to continue learning throughout your life.

Elevate Yourself to Manhood contains potentially life-changing and even life-saving information, and it will help you cut through the clutter of life and give you a clearer picture of the road ahead.

Ultimately, I want to spark you and other young men into action. My desire is that you will awaken from the slumber of life, sense the reality and urgency of your immediate environment, self-actuate, take charge, and become the motivating force in your life. It is my hope that you will come away with a renewed sense of self and an invigorated spirit.

You may already be familiar with some of the concepts in this book, but it is important for you to know what you do not know. We will explore and tie together concepts you may or may not know or be familiar with, revealing new truths and realities to you.

How to Know If this Book Is Written for You

Perhaps you are a young, red-blooded male maybe not yet old enough to vote. Perhaps you are already old enough to vote. You may be poor, affluent, or middle class. You may have been raised by a single parent, a "nuclear" family, or within some other family genre. You may be or have been a foster child. You may be African-American, Caucasian, Asian, Hispanic, of a blended background, or have whatever heritage you please - your background does not matter.

You may be what people consider a good person, or you may be known as a troublemaker or anything in between. I do not care. This book is for you. I can see you now. You may be decked out in the latest skateboarder tee shirt and sneakers sporting a set of specialty shoestrings to withstand the torque of a world-class boarder, or you may be standing there with your pants hanging halfway off your derriere because you are cool like that. You might also be a conservative, preppy type. Whatever - it does not matter.

You may be a bully or have been bullied in the past. You may lack confidence in yourself. You may think you are ugly or feel worthless sometimes. That sounds like me when I was young. I was full of doom and gloom. I felt like I would not live to be thirty years old. I had no reason to think that. I just did. Maybe, you do not think you are smart enough to be successful in this world. Maybe, you do not feel athletically capable of competing in sports. Perhaps, you think you are fat or too skinny. Maybe, you are chronically ill and feel miserable most of the time, or maybe you just do not have any energy. If so, this book may be especially for you. Even if you think you are God's gift to women and the world and hey, you may be! This book is still for you.

HAVE I WHETTED YOUR APPETITE? WANT TO KNOW MORE?

In this world, you are exposed to physical, emotional, physiological and spiritual dangers constantly - whether you know it or not. Plus, you might have high stress or burnout from your everyday life. You may not be able to see all the dangers around you or just over the horizon. In America, we have been shielded – with a few notable exceptions - from the scourge of foreign terrorism thanks to our natural defenses (Atlantic and Pacific oceans), military, law enforcement agencies, and diplomacy, but the bad guys are always trying to reckon our weak spots. Domestic violence inside America like gang warfare, domestic terrorists, and common criminals are on the rise. There seems to be a mass shooting somewhere in America each week. The cities are teeming with unscrupulous people who, as the old song by Carol King goes, "They'll take your soul if you let them, oh, but don't you let them." It is hard for you to trust anybody or anything. We hope this book will help you to develop street smarts, common sense, or "horse sense" as my father called it. It will enable you to seek the truth to help you avoid danger - whom to choose as friends, whom to choose as mentors, how to choose your educational path, how to choose your spouse, and how to chart your future in an enlightened fashion. It will help you to identify things that will make you strong and help you identify those things that are detrimental to your health and well-being so you can avoid or mitigate them. It will even help enrich your spirit and teach you how to know that God is real. These are the things you need to thrive now and in the future.

DO YOU FEEL THAT YOU ARE SENSITIVE AND INSPIRED?

Ask yourself the following questions and answer them honestly because you would not want to delude yourself, lest you become your own worst enemy:

- Do you feel that you have a broad understanding about things? Do you have an analytical mind? Do you tend to speak your mind, even when it may offend someone?
- Do you often say, "I know that"?
- Do you feel that you have a mission in life?
- Do you see things differently than most people, such as the school curriculum?
- Have you been bullied?
- Are your wounds painful and deep?
- Do you empathize with the pain other people feel?
- Do you have difficulty turning off your emotions when you feel bad?
- Is the fear of being persecuted holding you back from participating in sports, from socializing, from going to family gatherings, from doing volunteer work, from getting a job?
- Do you feel stuck?
- Do you feel pain, confusion, and frustration?
- Do you have suicidal thoughts?
- Do you feel that you are in a black hole?
- Are you reluctant to ask for help?
- Are you reluctant to accept help from your parents, siblings, teachers or friends?
- Do you have a tendency to say, "I'm OK," when the truth is that you feel as if you are in a black hole and do not know how to get out?

If you answered, "Yes," to some or most of these questions you might be a "sensitive" and "inspired" and depressed young man. Breathe deeply. Take one step at a time – the first step is to read this book. There is a way out of the abyss.

You do have a mission in life. It will be revealed to you in due time. This book will help you to develop coping skills.

Life is not like a video game. In life you cannot die, hit the reset button, and get a new life. You only get one chance at life. When people talk about past lives or reincarnation, they are likely remembering the lives of other people they saw from the Pre-Mortal existence (before they were born) when they were spirit children of God. Before you were born, you asked to come to Earth to be tested but have forgotten because you went through the Veil of Forgetting. Fulfilling your mission in life is paramount because otherwise you will be very disappointed with yourself when you die and return to the spiritual realm. Being reckless or suicidal with your life is not a wise choice. Besides, when you get over this difficult period in your life (it is temporary), you will be in a better position to teach other sensitive children to remain on their path so that they can fulfill their mission. You are desperately needed here on this earth to help and inspire others as well as to progress yourself.

Your primary mission is here on Earth. Accept your parents' help. They will help you to move to the next level. Share this book with them. It will assist them to prepare for your new elevated self, and it will help them to guide you to find the best outlets to develop your special skills and gifts because they know you, they love you, and they want you to be happy. Then you will be able to live your life with strength and passion.

Job #1 for parents, grandparents, teachers, and mentors is to teach their children and to help them succeed in life. Be careful, though, how you define success.

How to Read This Book

It is best to read this book cover to cover. I cannot stress that enough because we are so concerned about your welfare. We want you to develop all the skills and learn all the tools you will need to be successful on your Quest for Manhood. Each chapter stands alone.

All the chapters together will give you the complete story. However, the world will not end if you decide to jump around in your reading. We will be happy just to know that you read the whole book.

I have done my best to bring you the most up-to-date scientific research from leading psychologists, medical doctors, spiritual leaders, and others regarding how to safely navigate the waters of adolescence and adulthood. For example, while doing research for this book, we discovered some incredible information that you absolutely need to know to make wise decisions concerning your mental health and physical well-being because your mind, body, and spirit are still developing.

The tone and writing style are in the manner of an older gentleman mentor imparting wisdom to a younger man. Think Karate Kid.

With a female co-author, you will benefit from a woman's perspective as well. This formula is key because a man is not complete without a woman. One of your biggest struggles in life will be learning to accept and embrace this concept, but know that it is vital for your progression.

If you read the contents of this book with an open mind, it will help you create a vision and map for your life to come. Each chapter in this book will allow you to build upon that vision you are creating for your life.

WHY YOU MATTER

You must never underestimate how much you matter to this world. You and every other individual are divine human beings made in the likeness of God. It took me decades to come to this logical reality. I hope you will make a quantum leap to reach that conclusion in a shorter time period than I did. We all deserve the love and respect of every other being on this earth – friends and enemies alike. Ultimately, we are all connected. Your life touches many other lives. These lives touch other lives. Your actions affect hundreds, thousands, or maybe millions of others directly or indirectly. You are the star in your movie titled *(your name)'s Quest for Manhood*, and many people view your role. Other people and their actions also affect you. Along the journey, you may make mistakes (we all do). You may even get beaten down a couple of times but with the guidance from this book and your preparation for your quest you will be resilient, and you will most definitely become the hero of your own movie.

So, let's awaken and begin this divine journey together.

The Awakening

AWAKEN - YOUR QUEST BEGINS

WHY AWAKEN?

MANY HAVE RECOGNIZED A GROWING problem of young men who are struggling to assume the traditional social responsibilities of getting an education, finding a job, and getting married and fulfilling their role in a family of their own.

Some people blame the plight of men who "fail to launch," on the increase in the number of successful women on campuses and the workplace. Some people blame feminism for this phenomenon. In her book "Manning Up", Kay Hymowitz[14] argues that men of today do not feel that they should be subjected to the traditional tests of manhood. However, she says that this attitude comes at a price - what she calls "Permanent Adolescence" - the phenomenon where one grows up physically but not emotionally. This happens to be the same phenomenon that Dr. Peck observed in his psychiatric practice – that for whatever reason, some young men are in danger of not reaching a satisfactory level of maturity at the generally expected timeframe, if at all.

In the book, *Permanent Adolescence: Why Boys Do not Grow Up*, the author Joe Carmichael[15] wondered why boys are falling behind girls in school and have now become a minority on college campuses. He wanted to know what was happening in society to encourage juvenile behavior and discourage adult responsibility. He also sought to find out why boys were drawn to violence, what made them mistrust adults, and what led to their underachievement with respect to girls. We hope to answer those questions in this book.

Yes, there is a dear price to be paid for a young man's permanent adolescence. It is a big problem not only for our society's young men, but it is a significant problem for our society as well.

A percentage of young men get stuck in adolescence due to personal sabotage through laziness and lack of motivation, perhaps copying the behavior of other young men who have failed to launch to manhood. However, research has revealed that young men get stuck in adolescence, largely, because of the unexpected consequences of modern life. We will address factors of modern day life that we discovered are harmful, and are not widely known. This critical information and guidance will ultimately lead to your health, happiness, and success if you keep an open mind and choose to have the courage to make course corrections when needed.

This book attempts to offer actual remedies or solutions to whatever issues currently beset young men. On your quest, you will not be on the journey alone.

For this purpose, we ask you, young man, to awaken, and get yourself together before you get started on your quest for manhood.

But First, Who Exactly Are You?

Take a look at yourself in front of a full-length mirror. Study the image in front of you. What do you see? Do you see yourself? Is that really you?

SHOCKING FACT #1: YOU ARE NOT WHO YOU SEE IN THE MIRROR.

You are totally NOT that person. You are something else. You are somebody else. You are what's on the inside. You are inhabiting a human body. That's right. I did not come to this realization until I was well into adulthood. Learning this shocking fact has had an enormous impact on my life. It has given me a whole new perspective on life and changed the way I have come to know myself. It is one of those things that you may already KNOW deep inside, but it has not yet RESONATED with you.

SHOCKING FACT #2: YOU ARE NOT YOUR THOUGHTS

As you will learn later in this book, you are not your thoughts either, but you can learn to observe and control your thoughts. This turns out to be a critical skill you will need to develop for your quest.

If you are with me so far, then you must now be thinking, "So, if I am not who I see in the mirror, and I am not my thoughts, then who am I?"

Well, I am glad you asked that question, and I must apologize for having to shock you again.

SHOCKING FACT #3: YOU ARE A SPIRITUAL BEING, WHO LIVES INSIDE THE PHYSICAL BODY YOU SEE IN THE MIRROR.

In the book, *The Power of Now: A Guide to Spiritual Enlightenment*, Eckhart Tolle[16] explains that our spirit can control our thoughts. Our spirit can also control our body. Think long and hard about this because it is key to your development.

How many people wonder who they truly are? How many people wonder what they are doing here on Earth? What's your purpose in life? Who even cares that you are here? Have you ever had these thoughts? It is not unusual for people to step outside of themselves and wonder these things.

We human beings DO HAVE a purpose in life. Many people never realize that. They never recognize their importance in life. They never come to realize how many people love them and want them to succeed in life. They never really "get it."

As you go through this book, we hope that you will begin, if you have not already begun, to get a stronger sense of yourself.

AWAKEN TO BEGIN ELEVATING YOUR MIND, BODY AND SPIRIT

SCOUTING: A SHORT-CUT TO ALL ASPECTS OF DEVELOPMENT

As you read this book, keep the information about the Boy Scouts of America, Outward Bound and the National Outdoor Leadership

School (NOLS) in the back of your mind. It is meant to be food for thought.

Of all the organizations that mentor boys, Boy Scouts of America may be the organization, which encompasses the quest for manhood the best. Scout leaders care for the development of the whole person, more precisely the boys' mind, body, spirit, and the development of a multitude of life skills, for all of the facets of life. Scouting is an excellent way to have fun, make friends, and to get out into nature, which we will see - later on in the book - is crucial to the healthy development of your mind and your quest for manhood.

> *"On my honor I will do my best*
> *To do my duty to God and my country*
> *And to obey the Scout Law,*
> *To help other people at all times,*
> *To keep myself physically strong,*
> *Mentally awake, and morally straight."*

- Boy Scout Oath (or Promise) Boy Scouts of America (BSA)

The Boy Scout Oath tells us a lot about the character of what we would call a "fine young man." The oath tells us that a fine young man has honor, recognizes a duty to God and country, and gives service to others. A fine young man also keeps his body physically strong, remains mentally awake, and stays morally straight - addressing the whole person: mind, body, and spirit. By becoming a Boy Scout and progressing to achieve the rank of Eagle Scout, you will be well on your way to becoming a man in the real definition of a man.

You are ultimately accountable to yourself for growing up and becoming a man. Society has not been doing such a great job of mentoring and raising up our young men. We want you to succeed in this quest for manhood. Knowing where to find good mentors and like-minded young men who are also on a quest to elevate themselves to manhood will help you.

The scouting program has a Bullying Awareness Initiative to promote civil and kind behavior between scouts. A Scout should treat others as he wants to be treated. "A Scout is kind" - is woven throughout the programs and literature of the Boy Scouts of America. When a Scout follows the principles of the Scout Oath and Scout Law, bullying, and hazing situations should never occur. Scouting provides a safe and healthful environment in which to become sharp, knowledgeable and skilled, and make friendships that can last a lifetime.

Scout Law

"A Scout is trustworthy, loyal, helpful,
friendly, courteous, kind, obedient, cheerful,
thrifty, brave, clean, and reverent."

BOY SCOUTS OF AMERICA

In the Scouting organization, there are numerous young men who would make great friends. There is a whole new interesting world out there where you can have fun exploring while on your quest to become a man.

Boy Scouts on High Adventure

I asked several boy scouts to share their experience of scouting with you. They had just come back home from a 5-day, 50-mile trek along the Pacific North West coastline in the shadow of the Olympic Mountains. Their passionate testimonials follow:

David Porter wrote,

> "Boy Scouts to me has been my life. I started as a Wolf Cub in Cub Scouts and have been living the dream since. When I was 14, my dad had the idea that I should work at a Boy

Scout camp. The summer camp I went to was for one week out of the summer with my troop. It was called Camp Cuyana in Cross Lake, Minnesota. I wasn't liking the idea of working it as staff but decided to give it a try. I loved it so much I've gone every summer for the last four years working as a Camp Counselor. I taught the Wilderness Survival, Cook, Camping, Pioneering, and Leather Work Merit Badges. The Skills and Leadership Skills Boy Scouts have taught me for life is something I would never be able to get anywhere else. Along with that, I have performed several other high adventure activities including a 50-mile hike, various week-long canoe trips, bike trips, and more. I do not know what I would do without the scouting program. Another big thing Scouts has taught me is Goal Setting. Scouting is all about goal-setting."

Steve Fitch wrote,

"Scouting is one of the greatest things that has ever happened in my life. You learn so many life skills. The Boy Scouts organization teaches you many things you will always use for the rest of your life, such as, money management, social skills, and leadership skills. Getting my Eagle Scout was one of the best choices in my life. Getting your Eagle is not easy. Accomplishing that is a large thing in my family. All of my uncles have their Eagle Scout, so I was going to be like them. I love it! It is so much fun I can't explain it.

"Sometimes it is the worst at the same time, but when you are done, you would totally do it again. That's like every trip you go on :)"

Spencer Davis wrote,

"The Boy Scouts have given me one influence after another. Carrying on the traditions, obtaining ranks and badges - scouting has not just benefitted me physically with badges, but also spiritually and mentally. The Scout Oath states, "Do my best to do my duty to God and my country, to help other people at all times and to keep myself physically strong, mentally awake, and morally straight." Those last lines are the most important and most influential to me.

"Physically strong" - keeping my body clean and healthy

"Mentally awake" - keeping my mind busy and getting smarter

"Morally straight" - keeping my honor and self-worth as high as I can.

"On the spiritual side, the Lord stated, 'Thou shalt not be idle; for he that is idle shall not eat the bread nor wear the garments of the laborer.'[17] To myself scouting has a lot bigger picture for me; it has helped to strengthen my leadership skills, communications with others, and my personal goal-setting skills."

Jacob Batchelor wrote,

"Boy Scouts has taught me the things I need to know to be a man."

Daniel Harris wrote,

"Scouting to me is learning new skills and things that can help us later in life while helping us learn what we need to do to become a responsible adult. I have learned to do your best, and you will be fine."

Isaiah Lopossa wrote,

"That awkward stage between boy and man is completely mended by the Boy Scout program. It helps people take responsibility for their actions and builds positive character."

How proud we are that these young men successfully undertook such an ambitious trek. There were bruises and scrapes abound, but they all had smiles on their faces as they recounted their big adventure.

A Lesson in How Scouting Prepares Boys to Handle Life
On November 6, 2013, my wife, Elaine, attended a seminar on Post Traumatic Stress Disorder (PTSD) at Edmonds Community College/ Continuing Education Department. Dr. Greg Anderson gave the seminar on PTSD with passion and genuine concern. Dr. Anderson has practiced medicine for 40 years, specializing in PTSD. "Greg Anderson is a board certified family physician who works for the Army writing medical histories of soldiers being medically discharged from the Army. He also taught for the Physician Assistance program for many years at the University of Washington," (from the Edmonds Community College course outline). Please read Dr. Anderson's thoughts regarding the scouting program:

During Dr. Anderson's talk, he mentioned that his father had served in World War II, saw combat and became a psychiatrist. Dr. Anderson also served - in the Navy - and became a medical doctor. Later in his talk he mentioned that children of soldiers suffer turmoil, and some suffer from PTSD.

Elaine asked him, "Why were you able to cope? You were the son of a veteran."

He replied, "I was a boy scout. Not a very good boy scout but it helped."

As he concluded the first half of the session my wife commented from her seat, "You mentioned something very interesting - that being a boy scout helped you." He responded, "Give me an Eagle Scout and a regular individual - the Eagle Scout will fare a lot better [after trauma] than an individual who has not been through the scouting program."

Further on in the book we will explain scientifically how your brain can benefit from your participation in the scouting program - strengthening you and enabling you on your quest for manhood.

There is no better way for boys to become men of excellence than through the Boy Scouts. We believe that exposure to scouting is the keystone solution to many problems that young men face in today's world. Why? The Boy Scouts infuse the young men with priceless values they will need to meet the challenges of growing up and becoming a responsible/vital adult male. Since 1910, scouting programs have instilled in our young men the values of honor, trustworthiness, and courage to tackle hard things.

These values are as important today as they were back then - to help young men realize their full potential. The scouting program provides young men with programs and activities that allow them to explore, to develop skills, to grow academically, to provide service to others, to build confidence, to demonstrate leadership, and to build ethical standards.

Scouting provides young men with a sense of belonging, a sense of purpose, and demonstrates their individual worth to themselves, the team, to their families, and to the world. Also, they come to develop a deep appreciation for nature and learn a sense of responsibility for the environment.

US Presidents Involved in Scouting

Since the inception of Boy Scouts of America in 1910, each US president from Theodore Roosevelt to Barack Obama has been personally involved with scouting. This alone shows us how very important the scouting program is to our country.

John F. Kennedy was the first US president to become a Boy Scout when he was a youth as a member of Troop 2 in Bronxville, New York. In a speech as president, he said, "For more than 50 years, Scouting has played an important part in the lives of the Boy Scouts of this nation. It has helped to mold character, to form friendships, to provide a worthwhile outlet for the natural energies of growing boys, and to train these boys to become good citizens of the future." Kennedy stressed that "In a very real sense, the principles learned and practiced as Boy Scouts add to the strength of America and her ideals." [18]

Gerald R. Ford became an Eagle Scout in Troop 15. About his experience in scouting, he said, "One of the proudest moments of my life came in the court of honor when I was awarded the Eagle Scout badge. The three great principles, which Scouting provides--self-discipline, teamwork, and moral and patriotic values--are the basic building blocks of leadership. I am confident that your ability to bring ideals, values, and leadership training for millions of our young people will help to bring about a new era--a time in which not only our republic will progress in peace and freedom, but a time in which the entire world shall be secure, and all its people free."[19]

President Reagan said to the Boy Scouts organization, "I applaud your many efforts and programs encouraging character development and leadership among American youth. By sponsoring many useful physical, mental, and social activities designed to promote self-responsibility, the Scouts strengthen the cornerstone of individual freedom in our nation. These programs develop the youngster's confidence in his ability to deal with nature, society, and a challenging world."[20]

Most recently, President Barack Obama praised Scouting for its first 100 years of service during a video address to attendees at the 2010 National Scout Jamboree. He said, "For a century, Scouts just like you have served your communities and your nation in ways both large and small. Today, Scouts across the country continue the tradition of collecting food for those in need, improving our neighborhoods, and reaching out to those less fortunate. Congratulations on your first hundred years."[21]

Check the *Elevate Yourself to Manhood* website at www.elevateyourselftomanhood.com/videos for the availability of addresses by President Barack Obama and President George W. Bush to the Boy Scouts of America. You can also view a marvelous scouting presentation, *A Century of Honor*, on the site.

The Boy Scouts of America website shows exemplary Boy Scout Alumni below:

* 181 NASA astronauts were involved in Scouting (57.4 percent of astronauts)- 39 are Eagle Scouts
* 36.4 percent of the United States Military Academy (West Point) cadets were involved in Scouting as youth - 16.3 percent of cadets are Eagle Scouts
* 22.5 percent of United States Air Force Academy cadets were involved in Scouting as youth - 11.9 percent of cadets are Eagle Scouts
* 25 percent of United States Naval Academy (Annapolis) midshipmen were involved in Scouting as youth - 11 percent of midshipmen are Eagle Scouts
* 191 members of the 113th Congress participated in Scouting as a youth and/or adult leader - 28 are Eagle Scouts.
* 18 current U.S. governors participated in Scouting as a youth and/or adult volunteer (2015) - 4 are Eagle Scouts

(Source: Membership figures from each organization. Found on the BSA website.)

Scouting Provides Lifelong Learning Opportunities

As the world shrinks and grows more complex, people will need to learn to be adaptive throughout their lives. Learning core values early in life can help build resilience, which will help you to adapt and grow, acquiring new skills and knowledge to keep you abreast of developments. This will boost your self-confidence. The health, safety, and well-being of your future family will depend upon your ability to learn and adapt. You will be able to impart this knowledge to the benefit of younger generations while keeping yourself relevant and productive.

Scouting Helps Build the Spirit

One of the key tenets of scouting is "duty to God." Like adults, young people need faith or spiritual nourishment. The Boy Scouts do not define religious beliefs for its members, but they encourage each young man to begin a spiritual journey through the practice of faith in their chosen tradition or religion. The Church of Jesus Christ of Latter-day Saints (LDS) has been associated with the Boy Scouting movement since 1913! Scouting is one of the major programs that young men of their faith are encouraged to participate in from the time they are seven years old. By observing faith-based activities, it is expected that the young men will develop hope, optimism, compassion and a belief in a better tomorrow.

Scouting Builds Character "Do a Good Turn Daily" (Serving Others)

Beginning with the *Scout Oath* and *Scout Law*, scouting is full of character-building activities and guidance for young men. For example, giving service to others is one of the avenues used to build character. From its inception, scouting has deeply ingrained the notion of service with its members. The concept of doing a good turn daily helps young people to develop empathy as they recognize the needs of others, and it enables them actually to do good deeds in response to those needs. This concept also enables young men to put life into perspective – that they are needed –that their life matters – and that the little kindnesses in life matter. Also, these activities give Scouts a greater perspective of life:

* How do I want to live my life?
* What do I need to do to have that kind of life?
* How will I secure my future for my family and myself?

Sometimes focusing on the needs of other members of our earthly family makes our problems seem more manageable. Service to others enables us to take a break from thinking about our own problems for a while. When we help other people, it feels good to know that our assistance and talents are appreciated. Also, providing service can lead to the development of new talents. Service to others develops social skills and it helps us to develop friendships as we work alongside people who are also being of service. Chances are the people who are working with you to be of service will make good friends who will help you if you are ever in need of help. You need never feel alone.

Scouting Provides Mentoring

Much like this book, Boy Scouts of America provides mentors or Scout Leaders to guide the young men and to set real life examples for them. Young men need mentors, for they provide a tremendous, positive impact on the life of young men. The Scout-Leaders-to-be are screened, selected through a rigorous process, and trained so they can provide the attention and knowledge necessary for young men to grow up to become well-adjusted adults.

Scouting Promotes Healthy Living

Being mentally and physically fit is vital if you want to get the most out of life. The Boy Scouts have programs for physical activity such as hiking, swimming, camping, climbing, conservation and more. These programs naturally promote physical fitness and health.

Scouting Gets You Involved with Nature and Shows You Why You Need Nature

Did you have a favorite stuffed animal toy when you were younger? Was it a teddy bear, a monkey, an alligator, a penguin, a puppy, a cat, a lion, a tiger, a turtle, an armadillo, or an orangutan? Do you still have it? Many stores have shelves of stuffed toys – toy stores, book-stores, pharmacies, department stores. Research has shown why children are so drawn to nature:

1. Being close to nature relieves stress.
2. Nature also offers nurturing solitude.

3. Nature develops our senses.
4. Nature develops the eighth intelligence. Children can develop all eight types of intelligence if they have the opportunity to have experiences that help to develop each type of intelligence. The first seven intelligences identified by Howard Gardner a professor at Harvard University, in 1983 are: linguistic intelligence ("word smart"); logical-mathematical intelligence (number/reasoning smart"); spatial intelligence ("picture smart"); bodily-kinesthetic intelligence ("body smart"); musical intelligence ("music smart"); interpersonal intelligence ("people smart"); and intrapersonal intelligence ("self-smart"); to which he added the eighth intelligence naturalist intelligence ("nature smart"),[22]

Benjamin Franklin is an example of someone who was nature smart. He lived a block from Boston Harbor when he was a boy.

Professor Leslie Owen Wilson teaches courses in educational psychology and theories of learning in the School of Education at the University of Wisconsin. She offers a list that describes children with the eighth intelligence- or nature-smart:

* They have keen sensory skills, including sight, sound, smell, taste, and touch.
* They readily use heightened sensory skills to notice and categorize things from the outside world.
* They like to be outside, or like outside activities like gardening, nature walks, or field trips geared toward observing nature or natural phenomena.
* They quickly notice patterns from their surroundings – likes, differences, similarities, and anomalies.
* They are interested in and care about animals or plants.
* They notice things in the environment others often miss.
* They create, keep, or have collections, scrapbooks, logs, or journals about natural objects – these may include written observations, drawings, pictures, and photographs, or specimens.

- They are very interested, from an early age, in television shows, videos, books, or objects from or about nature, science, or animals.
- They show heightened awareness of and concern for the environment and/or for endangered species.
- They quickly learn characteristics, names, categorizations, and data about objects or species found in the natural world.[23]

5. Being in nature helps to keep children healthy because they move around so much when they are climbing trees, running through meadows, picking up rocks and leaves, and looking for tadpoles.

6. Having unstructured time in nature enables youth to be mentally healthy. In one example, a young person described a hectic schedule - time pressure due to schoolwork, participation in sport, socializing, and civic involvement. The outcome was that being so busy led to suicidal feelings. She said she would rather hurt herself than let her family and friends down. Clearly being too busy caused brain fog – she was no longer capable of thinking clearly, and she was probably exhausted. If she had fewer activities and had unstructured time in nature, she would have felt less stress.[24]

In inner cities, some parks have been taken over by thugs. Some children spend their entire childhood in their apartments. This is too much time spent indoors - scouting can help kids to spend time in nature. Boy Scouts of America offers nature experience and life skills education for every boy and young man in a supervised environment. We highly recommend participation in the Boy Scouts movement in your quest to elevate yourself.

7. Being in nature builds and strengthens character. Most young men in the LDS church are members or have been members of Boy Scouts of America. It is interesting to note that many of these young men grow to be capable of supporting large families. It

is not uncommon for these young men to have the resources to support five, six or seven children, and their wives are not obliged to work outside of their home. They become strong men.

In 2014, as Family History consultants, my wife and I spent an evening helping the Cross family, a mother and father and their seven children, with family history work using the online family history tools, *Family Search* and *Ancestry*. While we were in their house, the young father turned to me and said, "I am living the dream." He was so happy to have a lovely, righteous wife and seven healthy and well-behaved children. His wife is not obliged to work outside of their house. She homeschools their seven children, and sews fancy pillowcases and sells jewelry to earn a little more money to help to pay for her family's outings and vacations. Lonny Cross was not a boy scout in his youth. He converted to the LDS church, which would have offered participation in scouting had he been a member but he had many experiences that were similar to those experienced by scouts, and he had a twin brother with whom he found camaraderie, very much like the camaraderie a young man would experience in scouting. They spent a great deal of time in nature – camping, caring for their family's chickens and horses, and chopping wood. Terra Cross told us that their eldest son is working to attain the highest level of scouting achievement to become an Eagle Scout and that all of their sons are obliged to earn their Eagle before they can get their driver's license. The girls must earn the Young Womanhood Recognition Award and proudly wear the gold medallion before they can obtain their driver's license. This is a marvelous incentive! I am certain that when it comes time for the girls in this family to choose husbands they will seek someone who has the strength of character – more than likely an Eagle Scout.

I am always impressed to see these large families arrive punctually, and well-groomed for church every Sunday. That takes goal-setting skills, planning, and cooperation, which are Scouting and Young Women's attributes. So it is understandable that young men and young women who have received such excellent mentorship through Scouting and Young Women's would be able to be so well organized.

We assert that the young men's strength, organizational skills, and tenacity to get a good education, and to support their families comes largely from the skills they learned in scouting and working and playing in nature. This phenomenon is in sharp contrast to the current trend in the general population of an epidemic of young men, who are not motivated to go to school, nor are they motivated to go to work, nor are they motivated to date, nor are they motivated to marry and have a family. We will discuss what has caused this new trend in detail, in a later chapter. Participation in Boy Scouts of America prepares young men for real life – as long as Brain Dangers are avoided – which we will also discuss in detail in this book.

8. Being in nature awakens the connection between nature and spirit: Many religious groups realize and are promoting the relationship between nature and spirit. "We cannot care for God if we do not care for His creation. The extent that we separate our children from Creation is the extent to which we separate them from The Creator – from God," says Paul Gorman, founder and director of the National Religious Partnership for the Environment, headquartered in Amherst, Massachusetts. Gorman's organization, formed in 1993, is an alliance of major Jewish and Christian faith groups and denominations."[25]

How Nature Connected to Me Spiritually
In 2011, I lived in the beautiful Michigan countryside about fifteen minutes outside Traverse City, a popular resort town. Near my home there was a large, fresh water lake named Long Lake where I was baptized on August 20th. After I arose from the waters of this most sacred event, and after the crowd gathered around me on the shore, a lone white dove made its way to where we had all gathered. I saw the bird approach and thought that it was simply passing by. But the bird began to circle overhead. At first, I thought that only I had noticed it, but the president of the women's association for our church recognized the dove's continuous encirclement and said, "Don, there

is your dove!" She was referring to the biblical account of Jesus' baptism. After John the Baptist baptized Jesus, "he saw the Spirit of God descending like a dove, and lighting upon him" (see Matthew 3:16 KJV). As I recall, the dove circled 5-7 times before it departed. I feel that this creature was drawn to us by the presence of the Holy Spirit and as a sign of God's love for me.

The next morning while I sat near the window of my living room, which faced the woods at the rear of my house, my body still vibrating with awe from my baptism, a white-tailed buck came to graze five feet from my living room window. I was accustomed to seeing deer – female deer with their fawns from afar, but I had never seen a male deer anywhere near my house before. In Northern Michigan, near deer season, male deer usually disappear as if they know they will be the prime target of local hunters. But this deer seemed not to have a care in the world. I took videos of him grazing peacefully right in front of me as if he knew that something very spiritually significant had happened, and he had come to pay his respects.

My spirit soared mightily on the day of my baptism and for many days afterward - almost as if I were floating on air. It seemed to me that Nature, through a dove and a deer, shared its testimony of God's love before me.

My Wife's Experience in the Woods

In 2005, the day after my wife's baptism she went camping with her two daughters and four young grandchildren. The first evening they camped in a provincial park that was very dark, due to the tree cover, and their campsite was covered with gravel. After putting the children to bed in the tent and while clearing the dinner table she felt a presence in the woods. She turned and saw a huge black dog/wolf who bowed his head so as not to look menacing. She felt that he was hungry and gave him table scraps. All night long she felt that the dog/wolf watched over her, her daughters and her grandchildren, ensuring their safety. The next day they decided to move to another campsite. Their new campsite was covered with grass and tiny flowers for the baby to crawl through. Beside the new campsite, there was a farmer's field in which her three grandsons could fly their kites and play in haystacks.

While she minded her grandsons, an eagle flew over them, and then a second eagle joined him, and then a third eagle and a fourth eagle and then a fifth eagle, and a sixth eagle, and a seventh eagle all flew over them. She felt that God sent the eagles to let her know that she had taken the correct path for herself and her family. My wife, her two daughters, and their four children numbered seven. The same number of eagles came to pay their respect as there were people in her party.

The Flower God Sent Us as Encouragement to Write this Book Together

As we were discussing whether or not I should include the raisin exercise in this book, which promotes mindfulness, my wife, suggested, "Encourage the boys to use a golden raisin. They have such a beautiful color. Brown raisins are a bit boring."

"Brown raisins are actually purple. Like grapes," I said.

She immediately turned around and looked at me and said, "Well, you're brown, and you're interesting."

"No, actually I'm purple!" I said.

After which we both burst out laughing. Then we forgot about the matter.

The next day, while working in our garden my wife noticed an unusual purple and white chrysanthemum - half of the flower was purple, and the other half was white. All the other chrysanthemums were purple all over. We felt that the white half of the unusual flower represented my wife because she is white, and the purple half represented me because I jokingly identified myself as being purple. I searched Google to find images of half-white chrysanthemums and found only one picture, but its other half was yellow, not purple. This was truly a unique flower. We felt that God was sending us a message to include the raisin exercise in this book, to continue to write together, to show us that He knows us and that He also has a sense of humor. We felt that

God wanted us to share this story with you because He wants young men to know that He knows each one of us and that He loves all of his children. You cannot know how much this tender experience touched our hearts. A photograph of that flower has now become the mascot/logo for La Fleur Publishing and adorns the spine of this book.

What messages will God send to you when you are in nature? You can only receive these messages when you immerse yourself in nature. You can find fulfillment in Nature with the Boy Scout of America.

EAGLE SCOUTS

The Eagle Scout Award is the pinnacle of scouting. Young men who reach this level are proud to know that they have achieved an impressive amount of experience and growth that will bode them well in life. The Boy Scouts of America detail the obligations that an Eagle Scout takes upon himself below:

Obligation #1 - Honor

The foremost responsibility of an Eagle Scout is to live with honor. To an Eagle Scout, honor is the foundation of all character. He knows that "A Scout is trustworthy" is the very first point of the Scout Law for good reason. An Eagle Scout lives honorably, not only because honor is important to him but because of the vital significance of the example he sets for other scouts. Living an honorable life reflects credit on his home, his place of worship, his troop, and his community. The white of the Eagle badge reminds them always to live with honor.

Obligation #2 - Loyalty

The second obligation of an Eagle Scout is loyalty. A Scout is true to his family, Scout leaders, friends, school, community, and nation. His loyalty to his troop and brother Scouts inspire him to pitch in and carry his share of the load. This load sharing, and caring for other scouts, enables the scout to build his empathic loyalty muscle, creating a bond between scouts. A scout can then use this empathic loyalty muscle when developing relationships with himself, his family, his friends and his community. Loyalty means devotion to family, to the community, to the country, to one's own ideals, and to God. The blue of the Eagle badge inspires their loyalty.

Obligation #3 - Courage
The third obligation of an Eagle Scout is to be courageous. Courage has always been a quality by which people measure themselves and others. To a Scout, bravery means not only the courage to face danger, but also the determination to stand up for what is right. Trusting in God, with faith in his fellow citizens, he looks forward to each day, seeking his share of the world's work to do. The red of the Eagle badge reminds them always to have courage.

Obligation #4 - Cheerfulness
The fourth obligation of an Eagle Scout is to be cheerful. It reminds the Eagle Scout always to wear a smile. The red, white, and blue ribbon is attached to the scroll of the Second Class Scout rank, which has its ends turned up in a smile.

Obligation #5 - Service
Another critical responsibility of an Eagle Scout is service. The Eagle Scout extends a helping hand to those who still toil up Scouting's trail, just as others helped him in his climb. The performance of the "Daily Good Turn" takes on a new meaning when he enters an adult life of continuing service to others. The Eagle stands as a protector of the weak and helpless. He aids and comforts the unfortunate and the oppressed. He upholds the rights of others while defending his own. He will always "Be Prepared" to put forth his best for himself and others. [26]

Eagle Scouts deserve much credit for having achieved Scouting's highest rank. They wear their award with humility, ever mindful that the Eagle Scout is looked up to as an example.

Four Boy Scout Heroes

Hero #1 - Lawrence Sellers
Incident happened in 2013

"(CBS) – This evening – a South Side teenager will get an award from the Boy Scouts of America: an honor only a few other scouts have ever received in this country. It is the Honor Medal. Since 1923, fewer than 2,500 have been given out by the Boy Scouts.

"And now 18-year-old Lawrence Sellers – a senior at King High School – is getting one because he shielded his girl-friend from bullets just over a year ago – and he was shot in the leg.

"It was the same incident where Hadiya Pendleton was killed.

"Sellers says he's not an 'awards person.'

"It's not – well, it's a big deal, but I just feel like you do not deserve an award for doing what's right.

"He says he and his girlfriend Danetria Hutson have been closer since the shooting.

"'Maybe a little, I do not know.'

"'He talks to me about his nightmares and stuff,' says Danetria. 'He never talked to me about nightmares before... so I think that's close.'

"Nightmares where he reenacts the events of that day – when 15-year-old Hadiya Pendleton died."[27]

Hero #2 - Karsten Singh
Incident happened in 2013

"14 -year-old Northfield Boy Scout Karsten Singh saved his dad from drowning after a freak hot tub accident. He received the national organization's prestigious Honor Medal.

"A Northfield teenager who saved his father from drowning after a hot tub accident credits his Boy Scout training for helping him be prepared for the crisis.

"In recognition of his efforts, the Boy Scouts of America awarded Karsten Singh the Honor Medal. He received the national award during ceremonies in St. Paul last week.

"Last April, Karsten, then 14, came to the aid of his father, Raghav Singh, after a cover for the family's hot tub suddenly collapsed. The wood-and-foam folding cover, which had been supported upright like a cooler lid by hydraulics, fell and broke Raghav Singh's neck.

"Karsten discovered that he could not lift the cover, which had absorbed water that increased its weight. Instead, he swam into the large hot tub outside the family's country home, pulled his father's head out of the water and kept him alive until paramedics could arrive.

"He recalled his training with the Boy Scouts to resist moving a person who has broken a back or neck, stabilizing him as well as he could inside the hot tub instead.

"'If I had moved him out of the hot tub, he probably would have been hurt worse,' Karsten said.

"After paramedics arrived, a helicopter airlifted Raghav Singh to Hennepin County Medical Center.

"Raghav Singh remains paralyzed below his waist from the accident but is certain he would not be alive if his son had not known what to do.

"'When the accident happened, I was completely para-lyzed, and if he hadn't have been there, I would have drowned,' Raghav Singh said. 'He kept his cool.'

"Even Karsten admits he is surprised at how methodical he remained in his reactions during the ordeal.

"'I think it's pretty amazing I could do that," he said. "I was calm, but I was still nervous.'

"Karsten's mother, Kristin Moorhead, momentarily found herself at a loss for words after he received the Honor Medal Dec. 11 before hundreds of supporters of the Boy Scouts at the Crowne Plaza St. Paul-Riverfront Hotel.

"'He's very noble about it,' she said before pausing to compose herself. 'He definitely saved his life.'

"Moorhead had been inside, unaware of the situation ini-tially. She called the hot tub incident a freak accident.

"'It's not something you think of as a dangerous activity,' Moorhead said.

"She did not learn of the incident until after Karsten man-aged to tell his sister, Hannah Singh, then 11, to tell their mother to call 911.

"Because Karsten managed to move Raghav Singh's head above the surface so quickly, he did not suffer any brain dam-age, Moorhead noted.

"Moorhead said she had difficulty imagining what life would be like without Raghav Singh.

"'I think this, along with other experiences, will really shape Karsten's life and will have a profound impact on him going forward,' she said. 'He'll be very mindful of the gift of life and appreciate what he has.'

"A nodding Karsten agreed.

"'My dad is an important person," he said. "I'm really hap-py he can still be here.'

"Raghav Singh noted that Karsten's great-grandfather had been a Boy Scout in India, but neither of Karsten's parents ex-pected the organization to influence their son so significantly.

"'It was just an activity to be occupied in and have fun,' Moorhead said.

"Raghav Singh said, 'We knew it would have very positive impacts. I certainly didn't think it would be something that would save my life.'

"Karsten's troop leader, Jay Kuivinen, nominated him for the Honor Medal, which is awarded for unusual heroism and skill in saving or attempting to save a life at considerable risk to self.

"Karsten's actions upheld the goals of the Boy Scouts of America to teach participants to be prepared to take action quickly while remaining calm and reacting to serious challenges, said Ken York, director of marketing and communications for the Northern Star Council regional branch.

"'It sums up in a nutshell what we do as an organization,' York said.

"Staff Sgt. John Kriesel, a former legislator from Cottage Grove who appeared with Karsten Singh at the Northern Star Council's "Million Dollar Day for Scouting" ceremony to discuss how he dealt with the loss of his legs in Iraq, marveled at Karsten's story.

"'I think it's an awesome example of what scouting is all about,' Kriesel said. 'I was tremendously proud of that young man. He's already been through more than people five times his age.'"[28]

Hero #3 - Christopher Alvelo
Incident happened in 2013

* Christopher Alvelo, 17, grabbed the steering wheel and narrowly avoided a jet fuel tanker truck after his step-father passed out while driving
* Alvelo died, but the other three people in the SUV survived
* He was returning home from work on the final service project he needed to achieve rank of Eagle Scout

"A Philadelphia teenager has died in a car crash on his way home from his final project to become an Eagle Scout - but not before he saved four lives.

"When Christopher Alvelo's step-father blacked out while driving Saturday, he unbuckled his seat belt and grabbed the wheel, steering the SUV clear of a tanker truck full of jet fuel it was about to hit.

"The 17-year-old's actions saved the lives of his step-father, the two other Boy Scouts in the back of the SUV and the driver of the fuel truck, his family says.

"Because he was not wearing a seatbelt, he was killed on impact after the SUV smashed into a hangar at the Northeast Philadelphia Airport.

"Alvelo was a beloved student at New Foundations Charter School in Philadelphia with a promising future ahead of him. He planned to join the Air Force after he graduated this spring.

"Alvelo's step-father Joseph Snyder, 51, was taken to the hospital in critical condition, but is expected to survive. The two other Scouts were treated for minor injuries.

"Foremski told the Philadelphia Inquirer that Snyder was driving Alvelo and two other Scouts home from a morning of cleaning up a city park.

"It was the last project Alvelo needed to complete before he could be promoted to Eagle Scout - the highest rank in scouting.

"It was an achievement, which was the result of years of hard work and dedication to the Boy Scouts.

"And it was just another outstanding aspect of Alvelo's short life, his friends and family say.

"'He was a gentleman's gentleman. If you have a son, you wanted him to be your son, and if you had a daughter, you wanted him to date your daughter,' his principal Bill Schilling said."[29]

Hero #4 - Eric Ray
Incident happened in 2013

"WINDSOR, Colo. (CBS4) – A family in Windsor is counting their blessings after a young boy nearly choked to death on a piece of candy.

"The boy was alone with his siblings when the incident happened, and his 11-year-old brother came to the rescue.

"Eric and Gavin Ray do not sweat the details, but the pair definitely have each other's backs.

"'I first yelled for mom for help,' Eric said.

"On a routine visit to a nearby stable earlier this month the boys' mother, Shaundra Ray, gave each boy a peppermint to feed a horse and briefly left the boys alone.

"'Gavin inhaled the mint on accident and started choking,' Eric said.

"Seeing his little brother in trouble, Eric took action.

"'I clutched my hand over my fist, and I pushed down and up underneath his rib cage,' he said.

"He's not sure if he learned it in Boy Scouts or from his mother, but he successfully performed the Heimlich maneuver.

"'I had like three tries and the last try the mint came out with the rest of his Wendy's potato,' Eric said.

"I just heard him scream, 'Gavin is choking, Mom!', Shaundra said.

Mom arrived in seconds to find Gavin shaken but breathing again, and thankful.

"'As I tell him each day, he's the angel that watched over Gavin,' she said.

"Though he doesn't like to talk about what happened, Gavin is clear about one thing -- no more peppermints.

"'I am scared of them,' Gavin said.

"As for Eric, he's eager to add to his collection of Boy Scout merits, although he's not sure if they have a Heimlich badge, he's is sure of something.

"'I feel glad that I didn't lose my brother,' Eric said."[30]

Scott Ashworth's Testimony of Scouting

The following is a testimony of how scouting has influenced the life of a successful man and personal friend, Scott S. Ashworth. He is an Eagle Scout, a manufacturing engineer, a senior operations manager, veteran scout leader and father of three boys and one girl. He has volunteered as Unit Commissioner, Scout Master, Assistant Scout Master, Varsity Coach, Venture Advisor, and Scout Committee Chair:

"The Boy Scouts of America has been a great blessing in my life. It is a principled organization with strong values and standards. What sets it apart from many other principled organizations are the programs and activities that are woven together into an interactive experience. These programs and the method by which they are realized afford great possibilities for a young man to learn, develop, and grow in confidence. From the patrol method and shadow leadership to achievement and rank opportunities, every young person involved in scouting can choose a unique path or experience that will open their eyes to new possibilities. This path starts to unlock life's opportunities and starts to cultivate their personal potential.

"I remember well the scout leaders that I had throughout the years. All of them were good men, examples of integrity, and possessed great character. As a youth participant in the Boy Scouts of America, I mistakenly thought that we were just headed into the woods to camp. From my perspective at the time I was simply learning some basic skills and being introduced to camping and wilderness etiquette. What I was unaware of was the greater blessing of developing effective social interaction and advanced group skills. There were several times that I can recall when I became frustrated but was able to work through my problems with patient and wise coaching from a leader. It was in these settings, away from ordinary distractions that the imprinting of character was very effective.

"As I earned merit badges and rank advancement, I was exposed to many different skills and concepts. I was afforded [shadow] leadership opportunities and was coached to be successful and challenged to enable me to stretch and grow. More importantly, I was developing confidence in my ability to tackle and solve problems and learning new skills. This for me is the beauty of scouting. The programs and coaching and mentorship are organized into manageable pieces that build on each other. The character, faith and self-esteem of each young man are slowly but surely built skill by skill, merit badge by merit badge, rank by rank, success by success."

JIM FARMER'S APPROACH FOR DEVELOPING YOUNG MEN
We are amazed at how scout leaders care for developing a young man's independence and leadership skills while protecting and teaching them. Jim Farmer, another personal friend who is also a Scout Leader, shared his approach with us. Here he summarizes what he feels is one of the most important aspects of scouting and what he notices truly helps the boys feel empowered as they develop leadership skills:

"As a venturing crew advisor, I've found you really need to be careful not to micromanage the boys. You often times will know the problems that they will face on the trail before they do - stuff they learned in training, but might rediscover in the wilderness. I find it's good to let them rediscover the problems on their own rather than pointing everything out to them. That way they want to own the problem, and have the desire to take it on. If the boys are at a loss for what to do, we can ask questions to get them thinking about the problem in other ways. The adults can help point them in the right direction, but also need to get out of the way in order to let them lead.

"I think this is very similar to helping build testimonies. Young men are taught right and wrong at home, in seminary and in their quorum lessons. As leaders we don't want to answer every gospel question for them. We want to help them think for themselves, to learn to turn to the Lord and develop a relationship with Him so that they can use His help to solve problems and gain a testimony. We want them to learn to feel confident in their own ability to find answers."

Jim Farmer, Venturing Crew Advisor, Boy Scouts of America

Men and women like Jim Farmer provide the very best caliber of mentorship that our society can offer young men. Being a father of five small children, Jim volunteers his precious time and talent for the fostering of young men under his stewardship. As a young man yourself, it would be wise to take advantage of such wisdom, kindness, and talent and count yourself lucky to have wonderful scout mentors as Gordon Nishimoto, Scott Ashworth, Shelley Ashworth, Jim Farmer, Shane Leavitt, and others.

Outward Bound and NOLS

There are two other organizations that I would recommend for young men: Outward Bound and National Outdoor Leadership School (NOLS).

Outward Bound is an amazing organization for middle school and high school students offering outdoor experiential courses. Many of the students who attend Outward Bound courses receive scholarships from Outward Bound. Outward Bound's mission is to "change lives through challenge and discovery." Outward Bound seeks to "help individuals and teams discover the strength of character and an aptitude for leadership, needed to serve others in their community and care for the world around them."

"There are courses for motivated middle school and high school students seeking a physically and mentally demanding skill building experience in the wilderness. There are courses specifically designed for young adults transitioning from high school to college or taking a gap year to spend time in a foreign country. There are courses for teenagers struggling with personal challenges at home or at school."[31]

"There are courses for 12-13-year-olds, 14-16-year-olds, and 16-18-year-olds. The courses last from 7 days to 28 days. Some of these awesome courses are:

- St. Croix Riverway Canoeing for Boys
- Maine Coast Sailing
- Colorado Alpine Backpacking
- Lake Superior Sea Kayaking
- Southwest Rafting and Backpacking
- Blue Ridge Mountains Backpacking and Rock-climbing"

The other organization I would recommend is NOLS, the leader in wilderness training. NOLS trains students to be leaders. NOLS' courses are for highly motivated older students who are at least 16 years of age. Students can get university credits for participating in the NOLS program. This is something to keep in mind. Courses range from 10 days to full academic years. Some of the courses offered are:

- Scandinavian Sea Kayaking and Backpacking – 30 days
- Fall Semester in the Rockies with WFA – 89 days
- Southwest Alaska Sea Kayaking – 30 days
- Spring Semester in New Zealand – 77 days

NOLS offers many courses in the U.S.A. and in other countries. They are all marvelous adventures.

There are other ways to spend time in nature and to learn to do hard things. However, some of these tend to cost more than participating in scouting, especially if the activities occur on a weekly basis – such as scuba diving, and sailing in the summer; and skiing in the winter. Frequently participating in a variety of activities is important to stimulate the health and growth of all neurological pathways in the brain. Here are a few ideas:

1. Surfing
2. Mountain biking
3. Living on a sailboat
4. Sailing 100 miles from shore in a 36-foot boat in 25-foot waves for two days (not recommended but this is definitely a hard thing to do – as our grandsons will attest)
5. Sailboat racing
6. Hang gliding
7. Working to maintain your family's farm
8. Golfing
9. Outdoor hockey
10. Soccer

If you are not a scout, give yourself opportunities to have community service experiences doing hard things, because helping other people is the right thing to do and it is an important factor in developing social skills, connections and empathy. Service helps to develop new talents, and it also helps to put life into perspective, which will help you to avoid depression. You can record these experiences on your resume, which could eventually help you to get a good job. Here are a few ideas:

1. Offer your service as a volunteer to build homes with Habitat for Humanity,
2. Plan to help someone in your school or family or community each day,
3. If you play a musical instrument offer to perform for seniors in a residence, or offer to perform for children in a hospital,
4. Get involved supporting your favorite political candidate,
5. Offer your services at a food bank,

6. Become a scout leader,
7. If you are an artist – donate one of your paintings or sculptures to a museum for their fund-raising campaign, and offer to help at the fundraiser, or
8. Join the Kiwanis Club, or Rotary Club, or Masons, or Knights of Columbus, and help in any way you can.

WHY ELEVATE YOURSELF TO MANHOOD?

*"Masculinity is not something given to you,
but something you gain. And you gain it by
winning small battles with honor."*

(NORMAN MAILER)

As we mentioned before, your life on this earth is like a movie - your own personal movie, and you're the star! How is your movie going to play out? Will you, the hero, ride off into the sunset with the girl? Your film began with your early childhood, but now, as a young man, you have the power to take over writing your own script. If you do not write your own script, someone else will.

Just like in the movies, it is the good, self-sufficient men who will conquer the hearts of the best women and have the best lives. Many women today are choosing to become single parents because they have given up trying to find a suitable husband. They are not "waiting for the right man to come along" anymore. They do not want to take care of a baby and also take care of a man who is not capable of "manning up." This is neither the proper order of society, nor is it God's order as described in the *Bible* – nor is it the fault of young women. They are exasperated because they cannot find husbands who are willing and capable of supporting a family. A young lady expects her spouse to be educated, to have the courage to find employment, to demonstrate responsibility, to be healthy in mind, body and spirit, to be gentlemanly, to be kind, and to be supportive of her efforts. A woman has these criteria because it is her responsibility to choose a capable man who will be a good husband, good provider, and a good father to her future children. She knows that she may not be able to return to work after childbirth. She knows that she may have a special needs child. She knows that she may love her babies so much that she may not want to return to work. She knows that she may not have the strength to be a wife, a mother and work outside the home at the same time. So what is your plan for becoming a man? How do you propose to become your best self?

The preparations for the quest for manhood begin by awakening, by opening your eyes, and yes your mind, to the world of yourself.

AWAKEN AND GAIN AWARENESS OF YOUR WORLD

"Awakening" is a deep, personal awareness of yourself and your world that increases as you get older and gain life experience. It is usually a slow process, but sometimes it can sometimes strike you suddenly like a bolt of lightning. Life is full of surprises and sometimes those surprises can be daunting. *Elevate Yourself to Manhood* aims to prepare you for handling these surprises.

Awakening can also be likened to the peeling away of layers of an onion skin – as you peel away more and more layers of the onion, more of its insides are revealed. *Elevate Yourself to Manhood* aims to accelerate this process for you - to enable you to start to gain wisdom at a younger age than you would have without this book.

Hundreds of years before Christ was born, on his deathbed, the old prophet, Lehi, called his sons to his side and said to them,

> O that ye would awake; awake from a deep sleep, yea,
> even from the sleep of hell, and shake off the awful
> chains by which ye are bound, which are the chains which
> bind the children of men, that they are carried away
> captive down to the eternal gulf of misery and woe.

- 2 NEPHI 1:13

The old man, Lehi, took this last-minute, desperate occasion to encourage his sons to awaken, stop being boys and start being men. He wanted them to wake up, get serious, mature, and begin to take responsibility for themselves and for the family he would soon be leaving behind upon his death. More than that, Lehi was hoping that there would be a sudden spark, which would start a fire in his sons' bellies to awaken them and to cause them to mature quickly to grow in mind, body and spirit into the fullness of a man.

How and when will YOU begin to awaken? Most of us walk around all day seemingly awake. If truth be told, due to the stresses of daily living, most of us are probably not fully awake and aware of our lives. We hope to be a catalyst or spark to your awakening. You will awaken, learn to overcome challenges, and elevate yourself to higher levels of consciousness. As layers of your onion peel away, you will reveal your true self, see the real world, and discover your true power in the world. With each new "revelation" your understanding will deepen, accelerating your physical, emotional and spiritual growth. For many young people, adolescence may feel like a fog. We hope this book will help lead you out of that fog.

My First Awakening Lightning Bolt

My first awakening "lightning bolt" came when I was 14. I remember it as if it happened only yesterday. I can still sense that my father was patiently waiting for me to start showing more maturity, even though I felt like I already knew everything there was to know in life (don't we all think that?). He had probably shown maturity early as a young man himself and wanted the same for me. Being part of one of the first few generations out of slavery and having only an eighth-grade education at the time of my birth, I am sure he had to grow up quickly. It seems that he had become somewhat frustrated with my lack of attention to detail and follow-through when I performed my duties on the family farm. I am sure I was always distracted by something similar to how young people today are constantly distracted by electronic screens. Although mostly straightforward, my chores were important because we depended upon our crops and animals to supplement my father's wage. He was to have ten children. As the oldest child, my father depended on me to assist him efficiently and effectively manage the farm. I needed the discipline to complete my chores accurately and in a timely fashion. There was not much room or time for mistakes, nor slothfulness. Often, I would procrastinate, take shortcuts, or otherwise perform shoddy work. These errors required rework, which took even more time.

However, I was always a good student in school. My teachers always praised my academic achievement and my demeanor. I received lots of awards and kudos and yes, sometimes, it went to my head. However, on one particular day, my father felt he had to bring me down to Earth by telling me, "Son, you know, you may be book smart, but you don't have horse sense!" Lightning bolt. That shocked me! What a psychological jolt it was to know suddenly that, first, I had faults, and second, that my father looked upon me as second-rate! Now he did not take full advantage of this "teaching moment" to lecture me on how I was supposed to fill in this enormous hole. He just dug into my psyche. It slowly began to seep into my brain that I was not mentally "present." My mind was always on something other than the thing I should have been doing. I seemed listless at times. Uninterested. I was just going through the motions. I was not having fun, either, and this all reflected in my work. I suppose he just figured that I would recall the instructions he had given me before and that I would be able to self-parent. It was up to me to learn from this incident, to make the necessary course corrections since I was so "smart." Luckily for me, the incident did not send me into depression. Surprisingly, it energized me! I chose not to take it personally, but as a call-to-action. This was quite the epiphany for a 14-year-old. Also, I wanted more than anything to please my father because I loved him and respected him. He was a man full of wisdom, and he had ingrained in me since I was very young the words, "Use your own best judgment." I came to know and understand that I was to use my own free will righteously and judiciously, use my talent of creativity, to have a positive attitude, and to always try to do my best with what I have been given. That lesson has guided me until this day. I still have an insatiable curiosity for life, and I continuously strive to learn more and improve myself.

Getting Through the Test of the Fog

As a young man, there may come a critical time in your life when you feel that you are in a "fog" – better described as a time when you feel like you have no control over your life, or that you have no purpose or direction, and you are simply overwhelmed by the feeling of emptiness. You may feel totally stressed or exhausted. Or you may not have any drive or interest in anything. You may experience feelings of total confusion or helplessness, which I will talk about in a later chapter. You may even have feelings of anger or hate. Be aware that these are the times when you are the most vulnerable. These are the times when darkness can envelop your life and your soul and lead you to temptations such as drugs, alcohol, or even to violence towards yourself or others.

I feel that a lot of young men go through a fog at some point in their lives and sometimes at the most crucial times such as when starting college. This book will help you to get through the fog. Right up front, if you are experiencing this fog, there is no cause for you to panic, or act rashly by judging yourself too harshly, or by lashing out to hurt others or yourself. This is just something that you have to work through. You are being put to the test. Part of your mission here on Earth is to be tested to see if you can overcome and prevail in the face of challenges through those times of apathy, stress, exhaustion and times of vulnerability when the devil will approach you. **YOU WILL FAIL THIS TEST IF YOU ARE NOT VIGILANT AND NOT WILLING TO MEET THE CHALLENGE. Just keep an open mind and keep moving forward one step at a time. Be patient with yourself. Be patient with life. You are not alone.**

What causes this fog? Any number of things can lead a person down into a fog. Loneliness. Stress. Apathy. Bullying. Rejection. Environmental factors. Changing hormones. Video gaming. Poor nutrition leading to hormonal imbalances. Lack of exercise can decrease healthy endorphins. Failing an exam. Lack of motivation can lead to having a mountainous "to do list," and a feeling of failure. Feeling that you do not fit in. Disappointment. Being around people who are unkind to others, who are unrighteous, and who are unwise. Rage.

I know it can happen because I found myself in a deep mental crevasse – a fog that I, to this day, cannot fathom when I look back years later:

While attending junior college, I lived at home with my parents. I had a car, a job, spending money, and freedom. I attended summer Air Force Reserve Officer Training Corps (ROTC) boot camp where I excelled at physical and academic challenges. After my second year of junior college, and after completing summer ROTC boot camp, I transferred to a university 175 miles away to a whole different, dark and onerous environment. I was studying Nuclear Engineering – not the easiest major to be undertaken. Being homesick, lonely, and essentially bullied because of the racially charged environment, I was obviously at a disadvantage and was being critically stressed to the point of having headaches and nose bleeds daily. I fell into a dark, deep fog. I did not share this with my parents. I did not have anyone with whom to share my situation. Missing lots of classes and seeing my grades fall precipitously, I felt even more overwhelmed because I felt I was squandering my last chance at academic success. My parents and teachers had sacrificed so much to bestow the gift of college upon me, and I was blowing it. It was a golden opportunity on which I, as high school valedictorian, needed desperately to capitalize upon.

While we were in process of writing this book, a 14-year-old young man attending a high school in Marysville, Washington, just a few miles from our home, committed a horrendous crime. He killed three 14-year-old girls with a handgun and injured two others who were his cousins and friends since early childhood. He also killed himself. No one deserves to die this way. It was such a cowardly act. He did not have the courage to forgive, and he did not have the courage to live. He must have been in a very dense fog.

In the days leading up to this event, a bullying incident reportedly allegedly led him to have a vicious fight with one of his cousins. A young lady according to reports had also rejected him. Although he had just been elected Homecoming Prince, was attractive, athletic, and had many friends, he was evidently overcome by feelings of rage. He was in a fog-of-the-moment. A newspaper article indicated that, days earlier, when he was at the podium accepting the honor of Homecoming Prince, he seemed distant and disconnected. While the Homecoming Princess was beaming, smiling, and waving, he acted strangely. One of his friends noticed that he was not his usual self and told him, "I'm here for you." He did not accept the friend's offer. Instead, he harbored these inhuman thoughts and carried out such an unthinkable deed. He did not resist evil. He chose the wrong path. He became evil.

When Jesus fasted in the desert for forty days and forty nights, the devil tempted (taunted) him to make bread out of stones, but Jesus rebuked him. When the devil took Jesus to the pinnacle of the temple and dared him to cast himself down and order the angels to save him, Jesus rebuked him again. Finally, when the devil took Jesus to an exceedingly high mountain and offered all the kingdoms and the glory of them to Him, Jesus rebuked him for the third time. Jesus resisted evil. The Scriptures say that "Then the devil leaveth him, and, behold, angels came and ministered unto Him." I imagine that if Jesus needed to be ministered to by angels, he must have been, as a human, exhausted by the ordeal. He probably needed to recover from his fasting and from temptation in his weakened state. If you ever go through life trials that wear you down to the core, then you will also need to be around people who care for you - your parents, your teachers, your counselors, or your friends. Reach out to them. Accept their help.

Jesus was fully aware of the craftiness of the devil. Jesus used wisdom he had learned from God, his Father, to overcome his trials. He passed his tests. In his human state, he felt pain, and he felt stress as we do. We use this biblical story to illustrate an example of trials that every young man must face at some time in his life - to some degree or another. Your test will not be impossible to bear if you share the load with others. Pray and look to God for a way out. He often works through others to make a way for us out of difficulty – out of the fog. These helpers could be your parents, coaches, scout leaders, teachers, counselors, or friends. You can depend on God's light – the Word of God - to guide you out of the fog. Studying scripture helps – it is amazing how reading a daily morning scripture can be the exact message we need to shed light on a particular circumstance during the day. We will discuss more about how God speaks to us in Facet 4: *Elevate Your Spirit.*

My "fog" in college would not compare to the temptations of Jesus. Neither would my personal mental state appear as dire as the young man's who committed terrible acts in Marysville.

To be fair, though, I must tell you how I was protected or saved from the fog. One day while hanging out on the university campus, a young man, whom I had never seen before, approached me. He was unassuming and non-threatening. He asked, "Do you believe in Jesus?" I said, "Yes" and he prayed over me. Someone cared about me - a stranger! I feel that this simple act from this mysterious young man saved and protected me from falling even deeper into the abyss of the fog. To this day, I am ever grateful to God for sending this stranger to me – to bring a beam of light into my dark life. It was shortly after that encounter that I sought out refuge in the Navy and began a new career, which led to the next step in my awakening. Had I stayed in my earlier situation, who knows what would have happened to me? I do not know if I "passed my test" so much as I was rescued from it. I feel that Heavenly Father sent this young man to me to shine a light to lead me out of my fog.

The young shooter mentioned previously, however, did not pass his test. He failed the test miserably. He gave in to temptation and to anger and evil. His behavior was deplorable. We learned later that he had lured his friends to their death by texting them and inviting them to lunch. He arrived a little after the appointed time and shot them. I only wish someone could have intervened before his dastardly deed. I wish that someone could have taught him to forgive, to be patient, to pray, and to hold on to dear, sweet life. (This is one of the reasons why we wrote this book.) The trials and tribulations of life are tough, but they can be overcome. Our mission is to provide you with a guiding light to help you find your way.

This is an account written by Adam C. Olson, titled, *Where is my Iron Rod?* He passed the test:

[Scriptural references given below are from *The Book of Mormon.*]

"I was 14 and struggling. I didn't have many friends. Those I had were beginning to experiment with alcohol, tobacco, pornography, and immoral behavior. The pressure to participate was growing daily. I was struggling to stand up for my beliefs. I was struggling to find friends. I could understand why temptation was called 'mists of darkness' (1 Ne. 12:17). I felt blind to the light of the Spirit.

"I was trying to do what was right, doing my best to follow "the path which led to the tree" (1 Ne. 8:22). But I could relate to those people 'who had commenced in the path' but were lost because of the 'mist of darkness.' I felt like I had 'wandered off and [was] lost' too (1 Ne. 8:23).

"I rarely cried. But that night in my room, as I read those verses, I couldn't keep the tears from spilling out. I really felt lost, and I wasn't sure what to do. I wanted a solid metal handrail right there by my bed that I could grab onto and follow back to heaven.

"My seminary teacher had said the rod of iron symbolized the word of God in the scriptures and given through the prophets today. But I couldn't hold on to a symbol. I shut my scriptures and poured my heart into prayer: 'Father, where is my iron rod?'

"The question stuck in my head for days. Then one night, like Lehi, I 'dreamed a dream' (1 Ne. 8:2).

"In my dream, I was on my stomach on the seminary classroom floor. Something behind me held my legs so tightly that I couldn't get free, and it was slowly pulling me backward. Terror smashed me so I could hardly breathe. I was too scared to look back, but I knew I was being dragged into a darkness that would mean more than death. It meant spiritual destruction.

"I looked around desperately for anything I could grab onto. It was then that I saw in front of me *The Book of Mormon* resting on a chair. Somehow I knew that if I could just make it to the book, I would be safe.

"I woke up halfway between safety and destruction. I knew I had to go one-way or the other.

"Suddenly, I was more interested in *The Book of Mormon*. But while the dream was my wake-up call to read *The Book of Mormon*, it was the actual reading that changed my life. The Lord blessed me for being obedient. I found spiritual strength in the face of temptations. I found the confidence to break ties with my old friends and reassurance that I was better off by myself until my prayers to find better friends were answered.

"Most important, I could feel the Spirit when I read *The Book of Mormon*. I could feel the love of God. It felt so good I never wanted to put the book down. I had found my iron rod.

"Soon after, tears again blurred the words I was reading. But this time they were tears of joy as I read Nephi's promise to his brothers." [32]

> "And they said unto me: What meaneth the rod of
> iron which our father saw, that led to the tree?
> "And I said unto them that it was the word of God;
> and whoso would hearken unto the word of God,
> and would hold fast unto it, they would never
> perish; neither could the temptations and the fiery
> darts of the adversary (Satan) overpower them unto
> blindness, to lead them away to destruction"
>
> - 1 NE. 15:23–34

FOR A SUCCESSFUL QUEST, YOU MUST UNLOAD YOUR PAIN BODY AND LEAVE IT BEHIND

Your pain body is like an iceberg. The vast majority of it is invisible, buried deep within you.

At your age, you may not have experienced many pains and disappointments, but you may have heard about your parents' pains and the pains of your ancestors. Or you may have vicariously experienced all this pain along with them. This experience has created in you a

42

"Pain Body," which can be likened to an iceberg. Since the area of an iceberg below the water is much larger than the tip sticking up out of the water, when something bad happens to us in the present, 90% of the pain we feel can be due to past wounds.

In order to be successful on your quest, you need to leave your pain body behind. Otherwise, it can drag you down and cause you to implode or explode, as the young shooter we mentioned earlier. How do you shed your pain-body? Give yourself the "gift of forgiveness." Forgive those who have hurt you personally, those who have hurt your family, or those who have hurt your race or insulted the people of your culture.

Forgiving does not necessarily mean forgetting. It is helpful to remember how people have hurt you because it will enable you to treat people as you would like to be treated, and also it will enable you to choose friends, and your future spouse wisely. Forgiveness does not necessarily happen overnight. You can elect to forgive but find that angry feelings will well up inside you towards the people you have already forgiven, then you have to forgive them again. When you feel that you are not quite ready to forgive someone who has hurt you seriously, you can ask God to forgive them for you. Put your anger in God's hands. Let God fight your battles. He will teach the culprits a lesson in His time.

One of the young men shot during the ordeal we just mentioned, from his hospital bed, found a way to forgive the shooter. Nina Golgowski of the Daily News wrote, "Nate Hatch, 14, tweeting from a Seattle hospital Sunday where he's recovering from a gunshot wound to his jaw, posted 'I love you, and I forgive you . . . rest in peace.' Hatch's cousin, [the shooter], 15, took his own life after shooting five teens at Marysville-Pilchuck High School Friday."[33] (We chose not to give the murderer publicity here by mentioning his name.)

Try to view some of the negative things that have happened to you and your family in a positive light. Ask yourself what you learned from those experiences. If you learned lessons, how can you help others? How can you save someone the same heartaches? How can you make this world a better place? We all have a role to play in

Donell Cox & Elaine J. Barbeau Cox

making this world a better place – in our families, schools, places of worship, workplaces, communities, and on the national level. Having a positive outlook on life and having purpose will strengthen you on your quest for a happy and successful manhood.

By removing yourself from negative people and negative circumstances, you will help yourself to move forward on your journey. This is sometimes easier said than done, so take one step at a time. Making a new friend is a good start. You only need one good friend to start. If you have more than one true friend, then you are very blessed. We all have faults. Even the best of friends make little mistakes at times, and they need to forgive each other, but remember there is never any excuse to abuse others.

When faced with a negative event, such as failing an exam, someone's unkind words, the ending of a friendship, or the death of a favorite pet, give yourself time to heal from the pain (time heals) and make an effort to see the larger perspective. We understand that these circumstances are difficult, but people have endured hardships for centuries and they have survived. For example, girls and boys have broken off friendships with each other for centuries. When one door closes, another door opens. There are billions of people on this planet. There are other fish in the ocean (pick your own cliché). In other words, there is a special someone for each of you. Just be patient. Sometimes you will strike out, but someday you will hit a home run. Be mindful before you open your heart completely and love someone. Get to know the young lady in many social settings first. It is truly best to wait until you are eighteen or older to get emotionally involved with a young lady. Before then, keep the emphasis on friendship rather than romantic love.

As a further example, David Williams, applied to medical school three times before being accepted, which means that he was rejected twice. He did not give up. He was not consumed with anger or depression. He eventually became an emergency room doctor and a Canadian astronaut.

If you are enduring more than one negative event, you may suffer from adrenal exhaustion, and your hormones may be out of balance. In such a circumstance, it may take longer to heal than if you had only one event. First, see a physician or naturopath. Then you may need to crash and get a lot of sleep. Eventually, you may need to get out in nature – take a hike, lay in a clearing looking up at trees, or lay in a meadow looking up at the clouds. When you start to feel better, plant a tree, as a symbol of your new beginning, and care for it. Imagine the tree growing tall and strong. It may take you a couple of days to heal and it may take you a couple of years to fully heal, depending on the gravity of your circumstances and the duration of the stressful period you endured. Eckhart Tolle, the author of *The Power of Now* who suffered from depression when he was young, was studying for his doctorate at Cambridge University when he dropped out of school and took two years to contemplate and heal. He wrote *The Power of Now*, which gained worldwide acclaim. In a nutshell, *The Power of Now* encourages the reader to focus on the present. For the past no longer can harm you unless you keep thinking about it, and although we ought to plan for the future we ought not to dwell only on our potential future happiness. We can find peace, and joy in each present moment.

Again be patient with yourself. Forgive others, ask for forgiveness, and don't forget to forgive yourself, if needed. We will share with you more about forgiveness in Facet 4: *Elevate Your Spirit*. Also be grateful for what you have. Developing an attitude of gratitude helps to diminish the effects of negative life events. How to develop an attitude of gratitude will be discussed in Facet 2: *Elevate Your Mind*.

MY SECOND AWAKENING LIGHTNING BOLT

My second "lightning bolt" of awakening came as a 22-year-old US Navy sailor within the first few minutes of Navy Boot Camp.

Because my grades had gone downhill and my motivation had hit rock bottom, I left university and joined the Navy, as I mentioned before.

My first set of orders sent me to Camp Duncan at Great Lakes, Michigan in the dead of winter for boot camp. It was a frigid, dark night in the middle of winter as I stepped off the military shuttle bus from O'Hare airport onto the pavement in front of the barracks of Camp Duncan at

Great Lakes Training Center. I found myself standing toe-to-toe with a seemingly irate Third Class Petty Officer barking obscenity-laden orders, informing me that, because I was a new recruit, my life status had just sunk lower than pond scum and assured me that I would never be the same again. He was also kind enough to inform me with equal vigor that I had better listen up, toughen up, or face consequences beyond my tender imagination. Of course this was all psychological babble to either break me down or to toughen me up.

After they sheared off my long bushy afro, stripped me of my stylish street clothes and provided me with Navy-standard work dungarees and brogans (standard high-top work shoes), my dignity was mostly stripped bare. Cold, homesick and afraid, the stark reality of what I had gotten myself into began to sink in. Life suddenly became very clear. I started to feel a strong sense of my own mortality.

During Navy Boot Camp, all the lessons I learned on the family farm about commitment, hard work, and making right decisions had suddenly became useful. Those lessons helped me - mentally and physically - deal with the enigmatic situation into which I had gotten myself.

Something clicked in my brain, and at this poignant moment that shook me and rattled me, I came to the painful awareness of where I was and what was transpiring right before my eyes. I became suddenly much more mindful of myself. The Navy had my full attention! Over the next few weeks, my awareness of self came front and center. I was appointed Master-at-Arms for my boot camp company, which meant that I was a leader and expected to maintain good order and discipline among the troops. Being handed this responsibility boosted my morale and spirits I was proud that others looked up to me.

Even though the Navy provided numerous other "awakening" experiences for me, honestly, I have gone through several other "awakenings" in my civilian life. As those additional layers of onion skins were lifted from me, each revealed more temporal and eternal truths. Later in the book, I will explain to you the most important ones.

Also, later on, we will be using tools to help you peel away some of your own onion skins, but the experience will, hopefully, be a much more pleasant experience for you. However, there is something to be said about experiential learning akin to what I went through in boot camp.

We ask you to awaken, identify that person in the mirror and begin to savor the beauty of life in this world. Through scouting and adventures in nature, you can probably experience less stressful "awakening" moments.

Use the example of Jesus, the only perfect human to have ever walked upon the face of the earth. Although he was a Supreme Being, when he was born, his mind was just like any other human baby born on earth. His mind was like a clean slate. He had to learn all the ways of the world and the ways of his Heavenly Father, step by step, "line upon line, precept upon precept"[34] until he received a fullness of the glory of the Father.[35]

LEARNING PATIENCE AND SELF-DISCIPLINE

PATIENCE

Some problems take time to solve. As you work to awaken and elevate yourself to manhood, it is important to be patient with yourself.

The well-respected psychiatrist Scott Peck once considered himself a "mechanical idiot." In his book *The Road Less Traveled* Dr. Peck tells the following story:

> "Then one day ... while taking a spring Sunday walk, I happened upon a neighbor in the process of repairing a lawn mower. After greeting him, I remarked, 'Boy, I sure admire you. I've never been able to fix those kind of things or do anything like that.' My neighbor, without a moment's hesitation, shot back, 'That's because you do not take the time.' I resumed my walk, somehow disquieted by the guru like simplicity, spontaneity and definitiveness of his response. 'You do not suppose he could be

right, do you?' I asked myself. Somehow, it registered, and the next time the opportunity presented itself to make a minor repair I was able to remind myself to take my time."[36]

LESSONS LEARNED FROM EIGHT-GRADE MATH

SELF-DISCIPLINE

The second skill we want to mention that you will need to prepare for your quest and throughout your life is self-discipline. Without the ability to control your mind and thus, your actions, your life would be doomed to one of utter chaos. You can begin to exercise your self-discipline by finishing this book. That would make the authors very happy.

The skills I learned in Navy Boot Camp were necessary for my survival most directly in preparation for times of war. The self-discipline skills I learned back in the eighth grade were also necessary for my future survival. I just didn't know it at the time.

In my eighth-grade mathematics class, all the students hated math word problems, and we all struggled with them. The problems always started out simple but got harder as we read more and more about the problem. Perhaps you have experienced challenging math problems and felt a sense of despair as the problem became more complicated. One day I just decided that I was no longer going to be defeated by math problems just because they were presented as words instead of formulas. I decided that I was going to master them if it was the last thing I did. I recalled the words my father always drilled into me whenever I had given up on a project at home that I felt was too difficult for me, "There ain't no such word as can't!" My father was right. It's just eighth-grade math, isn't it? Problems of this type had been around for hundreds of years, and boys had learned to solve them in the past. My self-talk continued with, "So why can't I?" The way I saw it, if one person could do it, then anyone could! So I did.

Here's how:

I found a nice quiet, lighted place to study and focused my attention. First, I selected one of the simplest word math problems and proceeded to break it down into its basic, understandable parts. I drew the problem out in pictures and labeled each part with the associated mathematical information. I then went to the problem and mapped each sentence onto the image so that I could see more clearly what information was known and what information was not known. I discovered that if I was able to document and keep track of the bits of information given, it became an easy matter of plugging that information into known mathematical formulas in order to solve problems.

In this example, I used self-discipline and patience to allow my creative mind to show me how to solve problems in a way that I could understand. This may not have worked for anyone else, but it worked for me. Little did I know that this would become a skill I would use over and over in university to solve complex engineering problems.

On your quest for manhood and also after you attain it, you will encounter many obstacles to overcome and problems to solve. Some of them will be critical to you and your family, so you'll need to stay sharp and learn as much as you can about everything. By demonstrating patience and self-discipline, you will be able to achieve things great and small.

LESSONS LEARNED IN ENGINEERING SCHOOL

As an engineering student, I often spent days or weeks attempting to solve ONE PROBLEM. My electrical engineering professor's mantra was "Through struggle there is enlightenment." So, on purpose, he would assign us these horrendous (at least for me) problems as homework.

Now, do not be shocked when I tell you that I went to engineering school at a time in our technological development when electronic calculators were just being introduced to the public. Most of the students had a calculator, but I could not afford one. So what does an engineering student do to solve complex engineering problems when he doesn't have an electronic calculator? He solves them by hand! Well, I had a little help. I had something called a slide rule, which now, if you're lucky, you can find, in a museum or on eBay. That's how I got through engineering school. But now I am so glad I did not get an electronic calculator because it forced me to develop all those extra neurological pathways. However, I must confess that I finally got a calculator during the final semester from Sears Roebuck for about $150. Nowadays you can get calculators for $5 or even free sometimes. It could not do anything fancy or perform advanced engineering calculations like logarithms, exponentials, or transforms. I could only do the basics - add, subtract, multiply and divide. And, oh yes - percentages. Big whoop, right? Anyway, I was thankful for that and it did save me a lot of time.

But this experience taught me about a couple of things (skills): Determination and Patience.

My computer science professors also taught me another skill:

Stepwise Refinement

This was similar to the time when I was in the eighth grade and taught myself to do math word problems. It is the art of:

1. Breaking down big problems into small ones,
2. Perfecting the simplest, lowest-level parts of the problem,
3. Progressing to the next level and perfecting that level, building on the smaller part,
4. Progressing through all remaining parts of the problem, always building on the last piece, and finally
5. Arriving at the completed task done well.

As a young man, I was able to use this skill to develop one of the world's first computer games written for personal computers, *Forbidden Quest*, which was a text adventure game and a predecessor for modern video games.

If you desire, you should learn to apply this skill - which I used successfully for many years building computer programs – also in solving math problems, in addressing everyday problems and for many different types of projects. It requires planning, discipline, and patience while you build up the skill. It is a great skill to have in your toolbox/knapsack both during and after your quest for manhood!

PROBLEM SOLVING IN GENERAL
Scott Peck, the author of *The Road Less Traveled*, cautions us:

> "...there is a defect in the approach to problem-solving more primitive and more destructive than impatiently inadequate attempts to find instant solutions, a defect even more ubiquitous and universal. It is the hope that problems will go away of their own accord.
>
> "Problems do not go away. They must be worked through or else they remain, forever a barrier to the growth and development of the spirit.
>
> "This inclination to ignore problems is once again a mere manifestation of an unwillingness to delay gratification.
>
> "We cannot solve life's problems except by solving them. This is because we must accept responsibility for a problem before we can solve it. We cannot solve a problem by saying 'It's not my problem.' We cannot solve a problem by hoping that someone else will solve it for us. I can solve a problem only when I say "This is my problem, and it's up to me to solve it." However, many seek to avoid the pain of their problems by saying to themselves: 'This problem was caused me by other people, or by social circumstances beyond my control, and, therefore, it is up to other people or society to solve this problem for me. It is not really my problem."[37]

Is this the truth? Is this reality? No. For example, if you have an exam but have lost the textbook from which you are supposed to study, you need to decide earlier rather than later to either find the book or to get a new one – do not expect the book to appear magically.

If you want social change, you could foster change by protest or boycott - such as at rallies to protect the environment. If you feel that something is unjust, speak up. Grow up to become a better teacher, a better police officer, a better politician, or a better judge. If you do not have any friends in school, ask to transfer to a different school, or make friends out of school by participating in Boy Scouts of America or My Brother's Keeper. For something to change, you need to take action. Whether you like it or not, "it is the squeaky wheel that gets the oil."

SEEKING THE TRUTH IS PART OF SELF-DISCIPLINE

Scott Peck, in *The Road Less Travelled*, has an interesting take on self-discipline. He suggests that we should always be truth-seekers (I agree), and by doing this, we are automatically applying self-discipline:

> "Our view of reality is like a map with which to negotiate the terrain of life. If the map is true and accurate, we will generally know where we are, and if we have decided where we want to go, we will generally know how to get there. If the map is false and inaccurate, we generally will be lost.
>
> "Truth or reality is avoided when it is painful. We can revise our maps only when we have the discipline to overcome that pain. To have such discipline, we must be totally dedicated to truth. That is to say that we must always hold truth, as best we can deter- mine it, to be more important, more vital to our self-interest, than our comfort. Conversely, we must always consider our personal discomfort relatively unimportant and, indeed, even welcome it in the service of the search for truth. Mental health is an ongoing process of dedication to reality at all costs. What does a life of total dedication to the truth mean? It means, first of all, a life of continuous and never-ending stringent self-examination. . . . The life of wisdom must be a life of contemplation combined with ac- tion. . . . I have heard parents tell their adolescent children in all seriousness, 'You think too much.' What an absurdity this is, given

the fact that it is our frontal lobes, our capacity to think and to examine ourselves that most makes us human."[38]

Seeking the truth can take time, and taking the time takes self-discipline. The reward is that you will have an accurate map to guide you on your quest to manhood. *Elevate Yourself to Manhood* will enable you to create your map truths. All you need is the self-discipline to read it.

LEARN TO DELAY GRATIFICATION

In this society, there is an epidemic of instant gratification, the desire to experience pleasure or fulfillment immediately - without delay. Think fast food. Think Google where we get instant information at our fingertips around the clock. Basically, you want what you want when you want it, and that means now!

Waiting is hard.

INSTANT GRATIFICATION AND THE PLEASURE PRINCIPLE

In human psychology, the "pleasure principle" is known to be the instinctual seeking of pleasure and avoiding of pain in order to satisfy biological and psychological needs, wants, and urges. It is the driving force behind these desires and it can be as basic as the need to breathe, eat, or drink or it can be as complex as the "need" for an iPad or some other cool new gadget.

When we do not satisfy our need for pleasure, we experience anxiety or tension.

This is obviously stressful, so it would be better for us - during our quest - if we learned how to delay gratification.

DELAYED GRATIFICATION

Scott Peck discussed delaying gratification in his book, *The Road Less Traveled*. To illustrate this point he told a story about one of his clients who came to him because of a problem with procrastinating on the job. Dr. Peck was inspired to ask his client, "Do you like cake?" The client replied in the affirmative. He went on, "Which part of the cake do you like better," and then asked, "The cake or the frosting?" "Oh, the frosting!" the client replied beaming. "And how do you eat a piece of cake?" he asked. "I eat the frosting first, of course," the client replied. Dr. Peck then helped the client to examine work habits. He discovered that the customer began each day with work that was most gratifying or fun or exciting, and spent the next six hours doing the hard work. As a remedy to the problem of procrastination on the job Dr. Peck suggested that the client spend the first hour of each day on the most difficult work, then the rest of the day would be spent on the work that was most interesting. The client agreed to make this change, and no longer procrastinates.

Dr. Peck explains,

> "Delaying gratification is a process of scheduling the pain and pleasure of life in such a way as to enhance the pleasure by meeting and experiencing the pain first and getting it over with. It is the only decent way to live.
>
> "This tool or process of scheduling is learned by most children quite early in life, sometimes as early as age five. Throughout grammar school, this early capacity to delay gratification is exercised daily, particularly through the performance of homework. By the age of twelve some children are already able to sit down on occasion without any parental prompting and complete their homework before they watch television. By the age of fifteen or sixteen such behavior is expected of the adolescent and is considered normal."[39]

Are you on track? Can you delay gratification? You will feel less stressed and be more likely to have a successful quest to manhood if you can learn to delay gratification. Do the hard things first. Do the right thing first.

Check this off your "to become elevated list" if you are able to delay gratification. We will get into delayed gratification a bit more in Facet 2 – *Elevate Your Mind* - when we discuss video gaming.

GETTING ATTUNED TO AGENCY AND ACCOUNTABILITY

Wherefore men are free to choose liberty and
eternal life, through the great Mediator of all
men, or to choose captivity and death.

– 2 NEPHI 2:27

Great news! You are in charge of your own life! We call this "free will" or "free agency" or just "agency." God, the Creator of the Universe, gave it to you. There is only one thing God cannot do – take away your agency. He will not do that because He gave it to you for a particular reason – to demonstrate that you can make correct choices.

Agency is the ability God gives us to choose and act for ourselves. Your ability to use your mind to make decisions for yourself is a cornerstone of your life here on Earth. It is one of God's most precious gifts to humanity. Without agency, we would not be able to learn or progress spiritually or follow the Savior, Jesus Christ.

Although you have been given agency (the ability to "choose the right" until you learn to make wise decisions on your own), you should discuss things with your parents because they are responsible for your welfare and can be a big help in making wise life choices.

You should always ask yourself, "Are my personal choices leading me towards lasting happiness?"

Throughout your life, you will make decisions that will affect your life and the lives of others. Decisions other people make will affect you, too, either directly or indirectly because they also have the agency to think and act for themselves - in ways that may or may not be to your advantage. In this world, we are all connected, so it's hard to avoid being on the receiving end of other people's decisions.

Anyway, from the time you were eight years old you should have been able to distinguish between right and wrong. If you are not already aware of this awesome gift, you should talk to your parents or spiritual leaders and learn to use this gift wisely. You must remember, however, that agency also comes with responsibility and consequences.

You are accountable for the choices you make - right or wrong. Although you get to choose what actions you take in this life, you do not necessarily get to choose the consequences. For example, you can choose to obey or not obey the laws of the country, and you can choose to obey or not to obey God's laws. However, if you elect to disobey any of these laws, you will be held accountable for having committed offenses and will receive negative consequences or punishment. That's why the expression "free will" is misleading. Using your will is not free of consequences. There is a price to pay if you make incorrect choices.

Also, think about this: you will also be held accountable for the choices that you DO NOT make. For example, it is expected that you choose to use your God-given talents. Believe it or not, you have a unique set of talents - different from anyone else in this world. There are consequences for NOT using your talents to your benefit and for the interest of others.

Hopefully, you will choose to do the right things always.

GET OUT OF YOUR WORLD AND INTO YOUR MIND – MINDFULNESS TRAINING

Life is divided into three terms – that which was, which is, and which will be. Let us learn from the past to profit by the present, to live better in the future.

- WILLIAM WORDSWORTH

We sometimes go through life on autopilot, not fully aware of minute-by-minute or hour-by-hour existence. Young people are particularly vulnerable to this "blanking out" or "drifting" as we Navy folks used to call it when sailors would seemingly "zone out" and not be mentally present for whatever reason. In today's world, there are even more opportunities to be distracted by gadgets, electronic devices, and what not. Without a doubt, some of us do not have an awareness of our most precious assets - our mind and body.

On the quest for manhood, you will need to discover how to become more fully aware of your body and learn to settle your mind. In order to be mindful of the all-important content, we have in this book and to be aware of your surroundings on your quest. There are dangers to avoid. There are tools to gather. There are people who will help you to attain your dreams and goals. In general, being "mindful" means being consciously (mentally) aware of something. We use mindfulness to become more aware of ourselves - being present in the moment and acknowledging feelings, thoughts, and body sensations so that we can learn about ourselves. As teenagers, it could be difficult sometimes to slow down mentally and still the mind in order to achieve mindfulness. This is something that you may not be to learn to do overnight. Depending on the individual, it could take weeks to incorporate mindfulness skills into a daily routine.

Developmental Psychologist Marilyn Price-Mitchell, Ph.D.[40] asks the question "Can meditation positively affect teenagers' lives?" in her article, *Mindful Warriors: Meditation for Teenagers.* She answers the question, "Absolutely it can!"

Price-Mitchell explains that neuroscience research provides evidence that meditation strengthens the neural systems of the brain that are responsible for mental focus and empathy. She says that becoming more mindful helps children and adolescents to regulate better how life circumstances impact their mental health.

"In schools, we teach how to read, write and do arithmetic. However, most schools miss one of the most important aspects of learning – caring and nurturing the mind,"[41] says Price-Mitchell. This was the problem that my dad noticed about me. I was not mindful, and he wanted to shake up my world by bringing it to my attention – to awaken me. This is also what the Prophet Lehi wanted for his sons.

How to Become a Mindful Warrior

Psychology professionals Joseph Ciarrochi Ph.D., Louise Hayes Ph.D., and Ann Bailey wrote *Get Out of Your Mind and Into Your Life for Teens: A Guide to Living an Extraordinary Life*, a book that aims to teach young people how to deal with their emotions. The authors attempt to show young people how to become "mindful warriors" by describing the skills required to become B.O.L.D., an acronym which means:

B - Breathing deeply and slowing down
O - Observing
L - Listening to your values
D - Deciding on actions and doing them[42]

Let's put this process into practical use right now.

Mind Control Exercise

The following exercise will help you develop the skill of controlling your mind. Essentially, this exercise helps you to identify that <u>it is your spirit that can control your mind</u>. The training takes 20-30 minutes to complete. It'll be fun to see if you can pull this off successfully. During the exercise, there are questions you will need to ask yourself to measure the effects and experience the results.

This exercise is from Mark Williams and Danny Penman's book *Mindfulness: an Eight-Week Plan for Finding Peace in a Frantic World*:

1. Start by finding a comfortable position. Either lie on a mat or a thick rug or sit on a firm, straight-backed chair or a meditation stool. If you are sitting on a chair, allow your feet to

be flat on the floor with your legs uncrossed. Your spine should be straight. This posture supports your intention to be awake and aware. In this way, the posture is dignified but comfortable - not stiff or tensed up. If you choose to lie on your back, allow your legs to be uncrossed, while allowing your feet to fall away from each other, with your arms resting alongside, slightly away from your body.

2. Now close your eyes, if that feels comfortable, or lower your gaze. Bring your awareness to the sensations where the body is in contact with whatever you are sitting or lying on. Spend a few moments exploring these feelings.

3. At a certain point, gather your attention and move it to focus on your feet, so that the "spotlight of attention" takes in the toes, the soles of the feet, the heels, the top of the feet and the ankles. Attend to any and all of the physical sensations you can be aware of in your feet and ankles, moment by moment.

4. Notice how sensations arise and dissolve in awareness. If there are no sensations, just register a blank. This is perfectly fine - we are not trying to make feelings happen - we are only recording what is already here when we attend.

5. Now expand your attention to take in the lower legs, the knees, and then the rest of your legs. Hold both legs "center--stage" in awareness - notice whatever physical sensations there may be in the legs.

6. Expand your attention up the body to the pelvis and hips, the lower back and the lower abdomen. Move up the torso to include the chest and the back - right up to the shoulders - noticing all the physical sensations in the torso.

7. Expand your attention again to include the left arm, then the right arm, then the neck and the face and head, until you are holding the whole body in awareness.

8. See if it is possible to allow the whole body and its sensations to be just as they are. Do not try to control anything. At best you can allow sensations to be just as you find them.

9. At a certain point, bring your awareness to the center of the body - to the sensations in the abdomen as the breath moves in and out of the body. Become fully aware of the changing patterns of physical sensations in this region of the body. If you like, you can place your hand here for a few breaths and feel the abdomen rising and falling. There may be mild sensations of stretching as the abdomen gently rises with each in-breath, and there may be different feelings as the abdomen falls with each out-breath. For the full duration of each in-breath and the entire length of each out-breath, be fully alive to the sensations of breathing. [43]

It is important that you not try to control the breath in any way at all - simply let the breath breathe itself. Focus on the physical sensations, breath-by-breath and moment-by-moment.

Sooner or later, you will probably find that the mind wanders away from the breath to thinking, planning, remembering or daydreaming. When this happens, and you notice that your attention is no longer on the breath, there is no need to judge yourself or criticize yourself in any way, and no need to "rush back" to the breath. Instead, taking your time, allow yourself to register where your mind has wandered. Then, when you're ready, very gently but firmly bring your attention to the breath.

Such mind wandering will happen over and over again. Each time your mind wanders, remember that your goal is only to notice where the mind has been, then to escort your attention gently back to the breath. Consider your mind-wandering as a chance to cultivate patience and compassion as you bring your mental attention back. Remind yourself that noticing that the mind has drifted away from focusing on the breath. Bring it back again and again. This is the meditation and the practice.

And now continue to practice this by yourself, coming back to the breath whenever the mind wanders; allowing the breath to be like an anchor, grounding you in the present moment.[44]

How does that feel? Were you able to exhibit mind control when your mind wandered? Were you able to bring it back to center stage?

Did it calm you and give you a sense of centeredness? Do you see how it is YOU (your spirit) that controls your mind?

You have now taken the first steps towards obtaining a better awareness of who you are! Give yourself a pat on the back. You are developing a new talent! Your spirit is learning to control your mind!

WHAT IS YOUR ATTITUDE TOWARDS LIFE?

In the movie *Forrest Gump*, Forrest famously quoted his mom to say, "Life is like a box of chocolates. You never know what you're gonna get."

That's true. Life comes at you fast and hard sometimes. As a teenager, this can be very disconcerting since you are already caught up in the task of just physically and emotionally growing up. When life starts throwing curveballs at you, it can make life even more confusing. I would say that it makes life more "interesting."

If you know anything about baseball pitching and hitting, then you know that there are a lot more tricky pitches than just curve balls. There are also sliders, sinkers, knuckleballs, fastballs, and the list goes on. When the pitcher throws the ball towards the batter, sometimes the batter's brain does not have enough time to figure out what the ball is doing and to adjust the body into position to hit it, or to figure out if the body should NOT swing at the ball. Talented baseball players have developed the talent of mentally "slowing down" the ball in their eye/mind giving them more "time" to make visual judgments and to physically get into position to crush it.

Everybody experiences life differently. If ten people witnessed the same event happening at the same time, and you asked them to describe what they just saw, you could get ten different answers. That is because each of us lives in our own little universe even though we live in the same space. In this instance, there were ten sets of eyeballs and ten different brains analyzing ten different visual images, from different angles, with ten different audio tracks. Those ten brains have ten different life experiences, which affect the way they interpret information. So, yes, you could potentially have ten different answers to the question, "What just happened?" Once you begin to realize this, you will be a lot happier because it will explain a lot about other people's behavior.

Having said this, I know that some people tell lies about other persons. That is why it is important to choose your friends well. It also helps to have friends because they can be your witness. You can have their back, and they can have your back. Always tell the truth and do not let anyone get away with telling a lie against you, nor a lie against someone else. If someone purposely lies about you, they are not worth having as a friend because they are not trustworthy.

Sometimes, people will treat other people unjustly in other ways as well. For example, they might have a habit of being late but they angrily accuse you of being late even when you have arrived at the agreed upon time. This kind of irrational behavior can be baffling, and it is called having a "double standard" at best – at worst, neurotic. Be respectful of everyone, but keep a comfortable distance from such people with double standards.

However, even among the best of friends, disputes will arise because of different points of view. When the issue is of little significance such as which donut shop has the best donuts - you can just agree to disagree - "It isn't a big deal."

What is your view of your life? Is it like a movie? Like a video game? Like a fast-moving train? Are you an active participant, for example, playing a leading role or do you play a bit part? Are you an outside observer of life just going along for the ride? Are you even present in your life? The answers to these and other questions say a lot about what type of life experience you are having.

Your attitude plays a big role in how you experience life.

Despite how you view life or what your life is like right now, it may surprise you or maybe even shock you to learn that life is meant to be experienced, enjoyed, and savored. You are supposed to learn from your life experiences, too. As a teenager or young adult, that may be hard to realize right now dealing with school, parents, friends, teachers, bullies. Please know that you are not sailing on that ship alone even though sometimes it may feel that way. You must realize that other people could be going through similar things that you're going through. Also, realize that there are people who care about you – parents, siblings, peers, teachers, ministers, scout leaders, youth help lines, community youth services, and others.

Meanwhile, no matter what life throws at us, we must be prepared to manage it gracefully. Having a healthy attitude towards life by feeling grateful for your blessings - regardless of circumstances - will definitely help. You will need to learn how to endure life and still remain happy regardless of circumstances. However, when you feel that you are "at the end of your rope" – such as you cannot bear the burden of an unhealthy school environment – ask for help in changing that environment or leaving that environment. Report the behavior of a bully. Attend a different school. Ask to be homeschooled. Go to school by correspondence. Or go to night school. Spend time with a friend. Ask to move to a different area or a different city. In tough times, we learn valuable lessons for which we can be grateful even if it is only out of concern for keeping someone else from experiencing the same tragedy or dilemma.

"When the going gets tough, the tough get going," as the old saying goes. The "tough" - that would be you. You are a machine. You are on a quest. You are unstoppable. You can do this!

REALITY CHECK: LIFE IS NOT A VIDEO GAME

Some people have become so hooked on video games that they have become delusional: they think that their life is a game - like a very sophisticated video game. Well, we are here to tell you that real life is not a video game. On Earth, you only have one real life and it does not come with RESETS. You can't press a button or reboot to get a SECOND LIFE. That only happens in video games. Sadly, there are people selling the idea that video games are good for you - question their motives. Selling video games is a multi-billion dollar industry. The tobacco company had people convinced that smoking cigarettes was good for their health for decades. When scientists proved that smoking caused lung cancer the tobacco companies still persisted telling people that smoking was not a health hazard. Fortunately, today, tobacco companies are forced to have health warnings on cigarette packages. Someday, we may see health warnings on video games.

Navigating through life is much more complicated, challenging, and rewarding than Minecraft or World of Warcraft. However, that should not be an excuse to run away from life and hide inside a video game to avoid life's challenges. Even though life is challenging, you can still find happiness and enjoy success. Think about this. Your ancestors were successful - they survived long enough to become your progenitors, didn't they? So, in this vein, you are quite lucky to be here to participate in this "real life game." Now that your mom has given birth to you and you have attained a certain number of years' growth - enough to be able to read this book - you can start concentrating on getting your life on a healthy track and on tackling some of the vagaries of real life. Your job now needs to become taking over personal management of your life.

This book was written to give you the tools, which are the skills and knowledge that will make you wise to enable you to successfully navigate through your real life on your quest for manhood.

YOUR MIND IS LIKE A RADIO - ARE YOU ON THE RIGHT FREQUENCY?

In May 1998, a gentlemanly waiter at the prestigious Royal York Hotel in Toronto, Canada, told my wife Elaine that "Children's minds are like radios." Mysteriously, he continued to lecture her about children throughout her dinner. Impressed by his knowledge and passion for children, she asked him if he had ever been a university professor. He said, "No. I just love life." He went on to tell her, "You will help children." In retrospect, Elaine feels that this man may have been sent by God to guide her.

Think of your mind as being like a radio - I mean one of those old-fashioned radios with manual tuning dials. In order to hear the voice or music on the old fashioned radios, you have to turn the knob a little to the left or a little to the right to get the correct frequency. Sometimes, the signal will fade away in the middle of a program, and you have to make fine tuning adjustments. Try this out on the AM tuner of a radio.

Kids are good at tuning out parents and teachers. That's not really a smart thing, and we do not condone such action because mentors, parents and teachers have valuable life experiences that can supercharge your efforts along your quest. Essentially, this gives you better footing as you climb up to your summit of manhood and your dreams and goals. You just need to tap into their stream of consciousness.

If you were to pilot a plane, you would be required to dial into the correct frequency to be able to hear voice instructions from the control towers that could help you navigate accurately to your destination.

Like a control tower to airplane pilots, parents and teachers are responsible for transmitting the correct information to children. Sometimes, kids do not appear to be tuned in and listening, but as experienced parents, we know that most of the time kids are actually listening to us. Or, they may have the radio on, but they are not really listening because they are distracted. So let's imagine that you are like a little airplane in flight, trying to tune into your parents' frequencies to hear instructions. Your teenage years are not the time to go "radio-silent." You should only do that if you were a military pilot and your operations required you not to use your radio for fear of the enemy picking up your position. Most times, you are relying on your parents to steer you in through the fog of life to your destination. Parents must loudly and proudly broadcast those loving messages necessary for their children to be able to pilot their little planes safely home. This is a parent's responsibility from which they cannot be relieved except in cases of mental incompetence or death.

So it is important that parents, teachers, and mentors provide proper guidance to children. It is important that you know this. You have the responsibility to yourself to listen on the correct frequency and to hold adults accountable for this guidance. Remember that it "takes a village" to raise a child.

It is the responsibility of ALL adults to guide and mentor ALL the children in our society. Our present and future worlds depend on it. However, it is your responsibility to choose your mentors wisely, to stay attuned to the correct frequencies, to actually hear messages and take them to heart.

SELF-COMPASSION

Earlier, we spoke about the necessity of being patient with yourself. Not only do you need to be patient with yourself, but you also need to learn to be kind to yourself. Sometimes, you might beat yourself up more than life does. You have the responsibility to do the right thing in this world, and you should always try hard to do that. However, you need to stop the cycle of being your own worst enemy. You need to be kind to yourself in order to reduce your stress level and build self-confidence. This is an exquisite skill to perfect.

According to Dr. Kristin Neff, an Associate Professor in Human Development and Culture, Educational Psychology Department, The University of Texas at Austin, the first step in self-compassion is to notice that you are suffering.[45]

To do that, we will ask you to complete a Mindfulness Test shortly. It is important to notice your own suffering especially if it comes from self-judgment and self-criticism. The next step is to be kind to yourself while you are suffering. Be kind, caring and supportive of yourself. That's part of the experience of life. Also, remember that suffering and imperfection is part of the human experience. In other words, you are not alone. You need to recognize this fact so that you do not begin to feel isolated. That could lead to conditions like depression. Depression drains a person of their energy. You will need all your energy to complete your quest to manhood.

You can be realistic about your strengths and weaknesses while practicing self-compassion. We all have strengths and weaknesses.

A Healthier Way of Relating to Yourself

Dr. Neff reminds us that the greatest thing about self-compassion is that you are always there 24/7 to give yourself help when you need it most.[46]

You can probably easily recognize feelings of compassion for others. You can probably recognize feelings of sympathy when someone is sad, or you reach out to help people when they need help. But what about you? Do you know how to feel compassion for yourself? Do you know how to help yourself when you feel down? How do you find out if you have self-compassion? Dr. Neff published a Self-Compassion test in 2009 that can help you know whether or not you have compassion:[47]

Self-Compassion Test

Please read each statement carefully before answering. To the left of each item, indicate how often you behave in a stated manner, using the following scale:

1 Almost Never
2 Occasionally
3 About Half of the Time
4 Fairly Often
5 Almost Always

___ I am disapproving and judgmental about my personal flaws and inadequacies.

___ When I feel down I tend to obsess and fixate on everything that's wrong.

___ When things are going badly for me, I see the difficulties as part of life that everyone goes through.

___ When I think about my inadequacies, it tends to make me feel more separate and cut off from the rest of the world.

___ I try to be loving towards myself when I am feeling emotional pain.

___ When I fail at something important to me I become consumed by feelings of inadequacy.

___ When I am down and out, I remind myself that there are lots of other people in the world feeling the way I do.

___ When times are tough, I tend to be tough on myself.

___ When something upsets me I try to keep my emotions in balance.

___ When I feel inadequate in some way, I try to remind myself that most people share feelings of inadequacy.

___ I am intolerant and impatient towards those aspects of my personality I do not like.

___ When I am going through a very hard time, I give myself the caring and tenderness I need.

___ When I am feeling down, I tend to feel like most other people are probably happier than I am.

___ When something painful happens I try to take a balanced view of the situation.

___ I try to see my failings as part of the human condition.

___ When I see aspects of myself that I do not like, I get down on myself.

___ When I fail at something important to me I try to keep things in perspective.

___ When I am really struggling, I tend to feel like other people must be having an easier time of it.

___ I am kind to myself when I am experiencing suffering.

___ When something upsets me I get carried away with my feelings.

___ I can be a bit cold-hearted towards myself when I am experiencing suffering.

___ When I feel down I try to approach my feelings with curiosity and openness.

___ I am tolerant of my own flaws and inadequacies.

___ When something painful happens I tend to blow the incident out of proportion.

___ When I fail at something that's important to me, I tend to feel alone in my failure.

___ I try to be understanding and patient towards those aspects of my personality I do not like.

Total Score: _____

Add your score and divide by 25.

Score interpretations: Average overall self-compassion scores tend to be around 3.0 on the 1-5 scale, so you can interpret your overall score accordingly. As a rough guide, a score of 1-2.5 for your similar life overall self-compassion score indicates you are Low in self-compassion, 2.5-3.5 shows you are Moderate, and 3.5-5.0 means you are High.

If you scored in the low range, try to work on improving your self-compassion by being kinder to yourself. Share the results with your parents and talk about it.

Check the *Elevate Yourself to Manhood* website at www.elevateyourselftomanhood.com/videos for the availability of the following videos from Dr. Neff:

* Self-Compassion
* Self-Kindness
* Common Humanity
* Mindfulness
* Self-Compassion vs. Self-Esteem

A Happy Quest Means a Successful Quest

"The search for happiness is ultimately and simply a search for self. You can go searching for it in distant lands, but you'll only find it in the palm of your hand.

- Dr. Masuru Emoto, from The Secret Life of Water.

Everybody wants to be happy. If you are feeling relatively happy right now, that's great! But sometimes people are just not happy. Sometimes they do not know why they are not satisfied or what to do about it.

Scientists have been working hard in recent years to discover what makes people happy by doing experiments and asking people to do surveys before and after the experiments so they can make sense of the data.

From these studies, Dr. Ian Smith, MD suggested a list of things that generally seem to make people happy:

* Family, friends, and social relationships
* Helping others
* Appreciating what you already have and not constantly thinking about the things that you do not have
* Making a difference in someone else's life
* Pursuing a passion
* Taking pride in one's work
* Forgiving another person for something they did to you and moving on
* Not trying to keep up with the "Joneses." [48]

We refer to this as "earthly" or "temporal" happiness. We will explore temporal happiness in this chapter, but in later chapters we'll talk about deeper, spiritual happiness.

LEARN THE SKILL OF OWNING YOUR HAPPINESS!

Be careful about allowing other people or circumstances to control your happiness. Remember to use your spirit to control your mind. Use your mind to filter inputs to your psyche. Also, remember that others cannot make you happy. This is something you must do for yourself.

Dr. Smith says, "Base your happiness not on an outcome -- especially one in which others have some influence - but on your contribution or performance in achieving that outcome." For example, if you are the quarterback for your high school football team, base your happiness on how well you played more than whether you win or lose.

My wife cried (with happiness) all through her graduation ceremony because as a single, working parent (before we met) she had overcome many obstacles attaining her degree in Education from McGill University in Montreal, Canada. She knew she had given her all in her studies while caring for her family because she wanted a better life for them. She cried with happiness even though two months before graduating professors told the graduating class "for every 2,500 graduates in Education across Canada there are only 25 jobs."

Despite the odds, she eventually went on to teach, and her education became of great value when she was writing her first two books, *Bullies and Denial Kill*, and *Kids Care for Kids,* which she lovingly made available to the public in Google Library. She took charge of her happiness and made it a reality through hard work and determination. As the saying goes, "When life gives you lemons, it is time to make lemonade."

HAPPINESS POP QUIZ
We thought it would be interesting to give you this pop quiz before you continue to see how you feel now. SPOILER ALERT: We are going to give you the same test AFTER you finish reading this book to see if there has been any improvement. Since there is not a standard definition of happiness, it is not an easy task.

Psychologist, Ed Diener and his research team at the University of Illinois, developed this test for measuring what is called "Global Life Satisfaction" which researchers and others all over the world use to measure happiness.[49]

So, take this short little test and let's see how happy YOU are!

Use this scale (1-7) as shown below to score your test. Remember, there are no wrong or right answers - just answers.

7 - Strongly Agree
6 - Agree

5 - Slightly Agree
4 - Neither Agree nor Disagree (neutral)
3 - Slightly Disagree
2 - Disagree
1 - Strongly Disagree

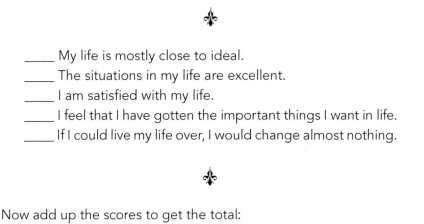

_____ My life is mostly close to ideal.
_____ The situations in my life are excellent.
_____ I am satisfied with my life.
_____ I feel that I have gotten the important things I want in life.
_____ If I could live my life over, I would change almost nothing.

Now add up the scores to get the total:
Happiness Score: _____
Now find out which scoring range your Happiness Score fits in:

35-31 Extremely Satisfied
26-30 Satisfied
21-25 Slightly Satisfied
20 Neutral
15-19 Slight Dissatisfied
10-14 Dissatisfied
5-9 Extremely Dissatisfied

How did you do? I hope you scored 20 points or more. It would be very sad if you didn't. If not, do not despair. We have some exercises from Positive Psychology scientists to help you boost your Happiness Score.

BOOSTING YOUR HAPPINESS QUOTIENT

Do you think you can manufacture happiness? Try giving your personal happiness a booster shot. Ryan M. Niemiec, Psy.D., wrote an article in Psychology Today titled, *7 New Exercises to Boost Happiness.* He used ideas from some of the latest scientific research in happiness to provide us with specific ways to elevate ourselves in the happiness department:[50]

1. <u>Gift of time</u>: Offer the "gift" of your time to someone. This could be time spent helping someone around their house, or sharing a meal with someone who is lonely. Plan these "gifts" in addition to your regular planned activities.
2. <u>Counting kindness</u>: Keep a log of all the kind acts that you do. At the end of each day, write them down in your journal.
3. <u>Three funny things</u>: Did you have any comical experiences today? Record the three funniest things that happened to you - something you created, something spontaneous, or something that you saw.
4. <u>Gratitude letter or visit</u>: Write a letter of gratitude to someone who has had a positive impact on you. If possible, go to deliver the written message in person.
5. <u>Three good things</u>: What are three things that went well for you today? Write them down in your gratitude journal and give an explanation for why you think these things occurred.
6. <u>One door closes, another door opens</u>: Consider a moment in your life/day when a bad thing happened to you, but it led to positive consequences that you were not expecting. For example, our grandsons went sailing with their father in a 36-foot steel sailboat. For fifteen years, they had planned to sail from Victoria, B.C., Canada to Mexico, and were finally able to do so. While sailing about 100 miles off shore a huge storm hit and bounced their relatively small boat up and down 25-foot waves for **two days**. They steered into the waves to help steady the boat. Eventually, the horrific winds died down. Exhausted, they sailed into San Francisco and when

they were about to go under the Golden Gate Bridge, they attempted to start their motor, but it would not start. The U.S. Coast Guard refused to help them to shore. The Coast Guard told them they could drift to shore. They had no control over the boat because there was no wind. Therefore, they had to hire a company to tow them to shore. By this time they were a little disheartened that the problem with the motor would delay their plans to sail to Mexico. A few days later, on October 23, 2015, unexpectedly, Hurricane Patricia hit landfall on Mexico's Pacific coast as a tremendous Category 5 hurricane, with winds of 165 mph (270 kph). Had my grandsons and their father sailed all the way to Mexico when they had planned, their boat would have been destroyed, or worse they may have been caught in the "worst" storm, and lost at sea. In this case, the door that closed was an unexpected delay of their trip to Mexico, and the door that opened was the door to life! The French would call this: "Un mal pour un bien," which means a bad occurrence for a good outcome.

Note: From the time they sailed we prayed to God, asking Him to keep our small band of sailors safe. Our prayers were answered. Thanks be to God! This certainly helped to boost our family's happiness quotient.

Eric Barker[51], an Internet blogger, put together the 4Ps below to help us remember the most important points about attaining earthly happiness. The acronym is based upon work by positive psychology researchers:

REMEMBER THE 4 Ps FOR HAPPINESS

Purpose
Perspective
People
Play

Purpose - The best lives have a purpose. This can be religion, ethics or any set of goals – anything that gives your life structure. Talk with your parents to help brainstorm something that works for you. Ultimately, your goals should be your decision. Though your goals may change over time, you are still young and discovering your talents; you are discovering your options; you are discovering your world and life that surrounds you.

Perspective - Happiness is more about how you look at life than what actually happens. It is <u>not true</u> that happy people have one success after another, repeatedly, and unhappy people have a series of failures. It has been shown that both happy people and unhappy people have very similar life experiences. The only difference is that the average unhappy person thinks about unpleasant events two times more than happy people. Happy people have a tendency to seek and rely upon information that helps them brighten their personal outlook.[52]

If you always compare yourself to those better than you, you'll feel bad. Compare against those who don't do as well as you do and you'll feel better. Or just except that everyone has strengths and weaknesses.

Here is an example. Researchers conducted an experiment where they gave a large group of students a word puzzle to solve. The scientists compared the satisfaction levels of students depending on how quickly or slowly they finished the puzzle. Quick-finishers who compared themselves with other quick-finishers were not usually happy with themselves. Slow-finishers who compared themselves with other slow students felt pretty good about themselves and ignored the speed of the faster students.[53]

Besides, even the people who finish last in an exam ought to feel that they have strengths that the people who finished first may not have. Perhaps they have a talent for playing an instrument, or singing, or painting, or for playing a sport. Perhaps their forte is math and not language or vice versa. Perhaps they have a very sweet spirit and are very close to God. Perhaps they are meticulous, and they get excellent grades.

When negative things happen to happy people, they tend to write them off as one-time events. Unhappy people see bad times as part of who they are. This is a sign of pessimism and low self-esteem.

In a self-esteem study, researchers found that when happy people get defeated, they shake it off as just an isolated incident. They do not let failure go to their heads. They do not let it mean anything about their ability. But when unhappy people fail at something, they make the loss seem bigger than what it was and make it stand for who they really are. They also let it predict the outcome of their future events.[54]

People - 70% of happiness is your relationship with others. Even though people believe that happiness is hard to explain, or that it depends on having great wealth, researchers have identified the core factors in a happy life. They say that the primary components are the number of friends you have, the closeness of those friends, the closeness of family, and relationships with co-workers and neighbors. Together, they claim, these features explain about 70 percent of personal happiness.[55]

According to researchers, Ed Deiner and Frank Fujita, friends and family were nine times more important than money when it comes to being happy. They also found that material resources were nine times less important to one's happiness than personal resources like family and friends.[56]

And it's not just about "getting." Giving has an enormous effect on happiness.

When people gave more of themselves to the service of others, researchers found that life satisfaction improved twenty-four percent.[57]

In an experimental research program, a relationship was found between happiness and helping behavior. By helping (giving service to) others, we create positive bonds with people and enhance our self-image. Individuals who had more opportunities to offer help felt eleven percent better about themselves.[58]

Play

It's not all serious, deep stuff. Sometimes, just having plain old fun will make you feel happy.

Regularly having fun is one of the central factors in leading a satisfied life. Individuals who spend time just having fun are twenty percent more likely to feel happy on a daily basis and thirty-six percent more likely to feel comfortable with their age and stage in life.[59]

MORE RESEARCH ON HAPPINESS – BEYOND THE 4Ps

Other "happiness" researchers suggest a few other simple things you can do to boost happiness. Again, this is all related to "worldly", "temporal" or "secular" happiness. It also touches on "spiritual" happiness, too, but we will be talking more about that in later chapters.

Laughing

In studies of hundreds of adults, happiness was found to be related to humor. The ability to laugh, whether at life itself or a good joke, is a source of life satisfaction. Indeed, those who enjoy silly humor are one-third more likely to feel happy.[60]

Rest

Quality and quantity of sleep matter a lot to health, well-being, and a positive outlook. For those who sleep less than eight hours, every hour of sleep sacrificed results in an eight percent less positive feeling about their day.[61]

Exercising

Research on physical activity finds that regular exercise increases one's self-confidence. This, in turn, strengthens self-evaluations. Regular exercise, including brisk walks, can directly increase happiness twelve percent, and can indirectly make a dramatic contribution to improving one's self-image.[62]

Reading

Reading engages the mind by exercising our memory and imagination. It can contribute to happiness in ways similar to active, positive thinking. Regular readers are about 8 percent more likely to express daily satisfaction.[63]

OTHER TRUTHS ABOUT HAPPINESS AND UNHAPPINESS

There are other fundamental truths about happiness and unhappiness.

Believe, when you are most unhappy, that there is
something for you to do in the world. So long as
you can sweeten another's pain, life is not in vain.

- HELEN KELLER

Emoto Masaru, the author of *The Secret Life of Water*, warns us not to overlook the value of <u>unhappiness</u>. He asserts that unhappiness is the process required for the creation of happiness. Such is life. We all want to be happy every day and never have to experience sadness. How unnatural that would be! Like the waves that rise and fall, if water never falls, then it could never rise or flow ahead. For every happiness in life, there is another side. An appropriate amount of desire is needed to make people strive for something better, and it is what made it possible for human society to rise to its current level. The problem arises when we become slaves to our desires. So what is it that we need to do to escape never-ending desire (which is obsessive) and find happiness? According to Emoto, we must have a thankful heart.[64]

To realize that we are eternal beings helps us to have patience, and to wait for God's time and to wait for His help in enabling us to move the wave back up. For some of you who do not know God, this may be a new concept, which we will revisit in Facet 4: *Elevate Your*

Spirit. Remember to keep an open mind. You will always have your own free will, which God expects you to use wisely.

Some people criticize others for wanting material wealth, and they say that material wealth will not bring you happiness. That is true when people seek material wealth for the purposes of buying things to impress other people - they can find themselves alone in their big house and feel very hollow inside. However, if you work to build wealth to provide a better future for your family or to help others, it is quite a different scenario. Wealth can provide - better health care, better education, safer cars, and decent housing in a crime free neighborhood. If your family members appreciate all the hard work, and the house is filled with love, and joyful times, and caring during times of strife, such as illness, then the feeling is one of gratitude for all of the blessings. Even if wealth is not achieved, there is satisfaction in knowing that we did our best. Family members will appreciate that we did our best. We can be grateful for the opportunities and for all the lessons we learned along the way. Our family members will feel loved because we cared enough to do our best for them, and they will be grateful for the love that was shown to them.

Take, for example, the story of Jon Riquelme, computer application developer from New York, who surprised his parents by paying off their mortgage as Christmas present in 2014.[65] This young man apparently appreciated that his parents had done their best for him and wanted to show his gratitude.

Also, wealth can enable us to help those around us in our community and in this world who are less fortunate. Even if we do not attain great wealth, we can offer what we can to someone who is ill such as a helping hand in their garden; or by mowing their lawn; or shoveling snow from their driveway; or offering a nutritious pot of soup; or a plate of nutritious cookies.

As a final point, remember that success does not drive happiness. Happiness does, however, fuel success. Being happy, therefore, improves your chances of success on your quest for adult manhood!

WHAT WILL YOU DO TO ELEVATE YOURSELF TODAY?

At this Awakening checkpoint we would like for you to reflect on the very important baseline topics in this chapter. Consider this chapter as a "warm up" prior to starting the ascent up the mountain to manhood. However, keep in mind that you will "awaken" during different times in your life. That is why the representation of the mountain shows a zig-zag path through the different facets up the mountain.

By this time, you should be able to:

* Realize that you are an extraordinary person with great personal worth, and
* Recognize that you are not the physical man you see in the mirror. You are the man inside and you are so much more than what you see in the mirror.
* Unload all your unnecessary baggage (excuses) and put in your backpack the tools learned about in this chapter.

QUEST CHECKPOINT: YOUR AWAKENING

In order to satisfy the requirements for the Awakening Certificate, you will need to demonstrate proficiency in the subject areas covered in this chapter by reading and completing the requirements below. After you have completed all the certificate requirements below - using the honor system – fill in the certificate with your name. **You can also download a printed copy from the *Elevate Yourself to Manhood* website at http://www.elevateyourselfto-manhood.com/certificates/.**

CERTIFICATE REQUIREMENTS

☐ **Journaling** - If you do not already have a journal, please obtain one. You will use your journal at all the checkpoint sessions throughout the book.

☐ **Self-Realization** – Make a list of all your good qualities in your journal.

☐ **The Miracle of Life** – Watch the Miracle of Life video on our website.

☐ **Wakefulness** - What did Lehi mean when he asked his sons to "awaken?" This suggests that his sons were "asleep." Do you think about whether or not you are asleep to the realities of life? Do you feel more awake now? What are your thoughts about this? Record your thoughts in your journal.

☐ **Self-Importance** - Rid yourself of electronics for an hour and find a nice private place where you can spend quiet time with yourself. Think about your life and realize how unique and valuable you are to this world and why your life matters.

☐ **Patience** - Realize that you have a lot of life experience ahead of you. You cannot learn everything and do everything all at once. You will need to learn patience for yourself and for others. In your journal write down at least two examples of how you can be patient with yourself and with others.

☐ **Kindness** – Do something kind for yourself today. Record your act of self-kindness in your journal.

☐ **Self-Compassion** - Commit to these Self-Compassion situations:
   ◦ Watch the 5 Self-Compassion videos on our website
   ◦ When you are faced with your own flaws and inadequacies, remind yourself that you are only human and that God loves you regardless of your flaws.
   ◦ When you are feeling down, try to see the bright side of your situation.
   ◦ When things are going badly for you, recognize that life is not perfect and that everybody struggles with life in their own way. You are no different in this regard. Perhaps it will turn out for the better. Hindsight is 20/20.
   ◦ When you are feeling emotional pain, know that the pain will not last always and that you will eventually get over it. Do not feel cut off from the rest of the world. Be loving

towards yourself. Become aware that there are many other people who feel the same way as you do.

* Try to keep your emotions in balance when life happens.
* When you see aspects of yourself that you do not like, do not get down on yourself. Make a plan to change and carry it out.
* When you fail at something important, give yourself credit for trying. Keep things in perspective. Try to recognize why you failed, improve and try again if you want. Be patient with yourself.
* Maintain a sense of optimism, curiosity and openness about life.
* Try to be understanding and patient towards those aspects of your personality you do not like. However, you should work on trying to improve those personality traits.

☐ **Mindfulness** - Repeat the mindfulness exercise to relax and train your mind to focus. Reinforce to yourself that your spirit controls your mind. Practice this exercise daily or weekly or as you see fit.

☐ **Self-Discipline** - Do you carry out your assigned chores without fail? Or do other things distract you before you are finished? Do your chores diligently this week. (**REMINDER**: Although these tasks are given to you for a short period of time for purposes of obtaining this certificate, we expect you to develop these tasks into habits for a lifetime!)

☐ **Delayed Gratification** - When you come home in the evening, do you do chores and homework first or do you play video games first? In your home, demonstrate delayed gratification by forgoing pleasurable pastimes until you finish doing all dull, necessary tasks.

☐ **Agency and Accountability**
* Identify one bad habit you have.
* Decide that you are going to change by stopping your habit of doing this particular thing/behavior.

- Write it down in your journal. State what the bad habit is, how you want to change it, and when you are going to change it.
- Share this with parents, siblings, and friends. Ask them to hold you accountable.
- Promise to hold yourself accountable as well.
- Report the progress regularly to others and write it in your journal.
- Celebrate with your friends and family when you achieve success.

☐ **Happiness –**

- One door closes, and another opens: Write about how a negative event in your life led to something positive happening.
- Gift of Time: Offer the gift of your time to three different people this week.
- Counting Kindness: Write down acts of kindness you perform each day.
- Three Funny Things: Write down the three funniest things you did this week, or things that happened to you, or things that you observed.
- Gratitude Letter or Visit: Write a letter of gratitude to someone who has helped you or someone you appreciate. Deliver this letter in person if you can.
- Things that went well: Write down three things that went well for you this week.

ELEVATE YOURSELF TO MANHOOD

QUEST CERTIFICATE - AWAKENING

THIS CERTIFICATE IS AWARDED TO:

_____

FOR DILIGENCE IN FULFILLING THE *ELEVATE YOURSELF TO MANHOOD*
REQUIREMENTS FOR THE "AWAKENING" ON HIS QUEST

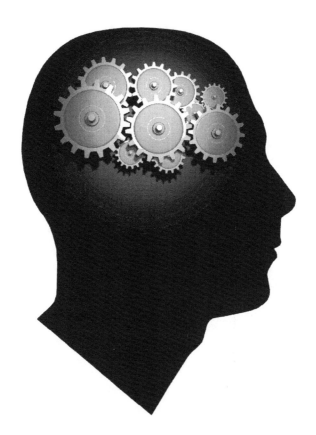

Elevate Your Mind

FACET 2

ELEVATE YOUR MIND

THE WOLF YOU FEED

> *A wise, old Cherokee told his grandson: "My son,*
> *there is a terrible battle between two wolves inside*
> *me. One is evil. He has anger, envy, jealousy,*
> *sorrow, regret, arrogance, self-pity, guilt, greed,*
> *and resentment, inferiority, lies, and ego.*
> *The other is good. He has joy, peace, love, hope,*
> *serenity, benevolence, generosity, humility,*
> *kindness, empathy, truth, gratitude, compassion,*
> *and faith." The same fight is going on inside*
> *you - and inside every other person, too."*
> *The boy thought about it, and asked,*
> *"Grandfather, which wolf wins?"*
> *The old man quietly replied, "The one you feed."*

> *– A TRADITIONAL NATIVE AMERICAN TALE*

TO ELEVATE YOUR MIND, REMEMBER in The Awakening, we talked about Happiness and you took the Happiness Test. Unless you found that you were TOTALLY HAPPY (not many of us fall into that category), you probably have a bit of dissatisfaction with your life. You may not be able to put your finger on it, but we all have unhappiness in our lives. Occasional unhappiness is a part of life. As we explained before, the unhappiness you experience in life will help you appreciate happiness when it comes along, as long as you do not let your unhappiness cloud your vision and worldview.

According to Andrea Wachter, a Licensed Marriage and Family Therapist, we are a culture where chronic dissatisfaction seems to be running at epidemic proportions. In her opinion, we live in a world of "never enough" where we are never rich enough, thin enough, youthful enough, happy enough, accomplished enough or good enough.

Watcher mentions in her article, *Which Wolf Are You Feeding?*, that there are some Eastern and tribal cultures that do not experience dissatisfaction, depression, and addiction. These cultures teach their children to focus on wanting what they already have instead of getting more of what they think they want. The idea is to teach children that they ALREADY HAVE SELF WORTH instead of them having to EARN their worth. This means that we should always have a sense of gratitude for what we already have.[66]

This goes back to what I mentioned before - about how you must recognize your worth to yourself, to society and to the world. You have ENORMOUS intrinsic value, but you must remember to regard that as a starting point. Do not misinterpret this message. You are definitely expected to grow and become more than what you currently are, but you must choose to go about it with humility, compassion, and love as the "good wolf" inside you would do.

Imagine that you are jumping into a shower that has beautiful new decorative tiles all around, but something is not perfect. One tile is missing. What would you do? Would it bother you? Would it ruin your day? Or would you still enjoy the other tiles and feel grateful for the warmth of the cleansing water? I hope you would choose the gratefulness. Of course, if you had paid dearly to have the tile work completed you would call the contractor to install the missing tile. Life tends not to be perfect. Therefore, we must strive for a perfect balance of our emotions. A grateful heart enables us to achieve that balance.

ATTITUDE OF GRATITUDE

It has been said that an ungrateful man is like a
hog under a tree eating apples off the ground but
never looking up to see where they came from.

- TRADITIONAL

Gratitude is an emotion you feel for what you have - big or small, regardless of monetary value. Whenever someone gives us something or does a service for us, we should thank them and be inwardly grateful. We sometimes take food, clothing, shelter, our families and even our own lives for granted. Remember that we came into this world with nothing, so we should be grateful for whatever we have gained.

Focusing on gratitude instead of focusing on the dissatisfaction you feel when you do not have a particular thing (like having the latest smartphone) will make you feel better. If you give thanks for what you already have, and then carefully set RIGHTEOUS goals, you will discover a positive, uplifting attitude emerging.

Psychologists tell us that we can increase our overall well-being and happiness by living in an atmosphere of gratitude. It just makes us feel better!

"And he who receiveth all things with thankfulness shall
be made glorious; and the things of this earth shall be
added unto him, even an hundred fold, yea, more."

DOCTRINE AND COVENANTS *78:19*

"We need to be more grateful. I think there's no
true character without gratitude. It's one of the

*marks of a real strong character, to have a feeling of
thanksgiving and gratitude for blessings that are ours."*

- EZRA TAFT BENSON, "RECEIVE ALL THINGS WITH THANKFULNESS",
ENSIGN NOV. 1976, PRESIDENT OF THE COUNCIL OF THE TWELVE,
THE CHURCH OF JESUS CHRIST OF LATTER-DAY SAINTS

BE GRATEFUL FOR YOURSELF

Whenever you find yourself being too self-critical, try practicing
gratitude: (1) for the talents you have, or the potential to develop
talents, (2) for the fine attributes your body has – such as youthful
health, (3) for the social skills you have developed and the friends
you have gained rather than worrying about the friends you do not
have, and (4) for the knowledge you have gained thus far in your life.

Look at it this way: You're alive! You must be doing something
right. Keep up the good work. Give yourself credit.

BE GRATEFUL FOR THE LITTLE THINGS IN LIFE

Sometimes life can be difficult through no fault of our own - your friends
move away, your parents divorce, or you become very sick or disabled.
During these times, it is important to be grateful for the little things in life
that help to calm us when we are upset. We can be grateful for nature's
bounty – a breath of fresh air, a beautiful sunset and sunrise, a fresh blanket of snow, a starry night, and a pet's affection. In the winter, a warm
cup of cocoa can help calm us. In the summer, a tall glass of lemonade
can be refreshing. In other words, attempt to focus your mind on the
simple things instead of dwelling on how bad things are going.
Consider the lyrics to the song *Smile*:

Smile though your heart is aching
Smile even though it's breaking
When there are clouds in the sky, you'll get by

If you smile through your fear and sorrow
Smile and maybe tomorrow
You'll see the sun come shining through for you
Light up your face with gladness
Hide every trace of sadness
Although a tear may be ever so near
That's the time you must keep on trying
Smile, what's the use of crying?
You'll find that life is still worthwhile
If you just smile
(Written by John Turner and Geoffrey. Composer: Charlie Chaplin)

BEING GRATEFUL IN YOUR CIRCUMSTANCES

You can choose to be grateful in whatever circumstances you find yourself. Instead of only being grateful when things are going your way, you should learn to develop an attitude of gratitude for life in general. That way, you will not focus on just "counting your blessings" and only being grateful in proportion to the number blessings you have received. In other words, gratitude should be part of your disposition - a way of life that stands independent of your circumstances.

OPPORTUNITIES TO SHOW GRATITUDE:

* Say a prayer before you even open your eyes in the morning or after you wake up (suggested daily).
* Say grace before meals (suggested daily).
* Take an inventory of what you have.
* Realize that things could always be worse than what they are.
* Make an entry in a Gratitude Journal of your choice.
* Write a gratitude Letter to someone. Deliver it in person.
* Visit an old teacher and thank him or her.

* Send a gratitude email to someone.
* Make a nice comment on someone's Facebook page.
* Bring your mom fresh cut flowers.
* Take your dad out for breakfast and pay for it.
* Say a prayer before going to bed (suggested nightly)

THE CHOCOLATE EATING MINDFULNESS EXERCISE

To get started elevating our mind, let us do another mindfulness exercise.

Mindfulness training is a relatively recent phenomenon, which we feel would benefit you. This exercise by Danny Penman, Ph.D. and Mark Williams, Ph.D. will help you develop the ability to relax, focus, and control emotions and stress levels - something that we all need to learn to do from time to time.

1. You will need a piece of chocolate for this experiment. Choose something different than you usually eat. Now try this:
2. Open the packet. Inhale the pleasant aroma of the chocolate. Take your time and let it sweep over you.
3. Break off a piece of the chocolate and look at it carefully. Really let your eyes take it in. Analyze it and really see what it looks like. Examine every bit.
4. Now place some of the chocolate in your mouth. While holding the chocolate on your tongue, allow it to melt if you can. Do you notice any desire to suck at it? Did you know that chocolate has over three hundred different flavors? See if you can sense some of them.
5. Notice to see if your mind is wandering while you eat the chocolate. If your mind wandered, casually notice where it went, then gently escort it back to the present moment.
6. Wait until the chocolate has completely melted, then swallow it very slowly. Let the chocolate slide down your throat very slowly.
7. Repeat these steps with the next piece of chocolate until it is all gone. [67]

How did that feel? How did it taste? Did it taste any different from before? Did the chocolate taste better than if you had just eaten it really fast as you may have done so in the past? Do you feel fuller than normal? Do you feel more satisfied than usual? Was that not fun?

Gold, Orange, Blue, Green: Which Color Are You?

Now let's think "outside the box" a bit. The purpose of this experiment is to get you to think about yourself and how you relate to others. Normally, this exercise would be performed by groups of people who work together. By completing the exercise, participants would get to know themselves better and they would come to understand their colleagues and other participants more thoroughly. Psychologists have grouped the individual traits into colors just for discussion purposes.

You may find this exercise beneficial just doing it by yourself, but you can get friends together to do it as a group if you like.

Just for fun, let us say that your personality is a blend of four colors - or we can call them personality styles. Pretend that these four colors or personality styles create a unique plaid pattern of colors for you, with varying degrees of the predominance of color. Everybody's spectrum would look different. There are no bad or good colors. Each plaid pattern is different. Everyone has a predominant color with three other colors in their plaid – gold, orange, blue, or green.

We know that each person has a different and unique personality, too. Even so, we all have some commonalities we share. This little test called, "True Colors" attempts to identify various personality styles and label them with colors. Researchers and psychologists in their work of categorizing personality styles mainly use this. The True Colors Personality Test is based on many years of work.

Many companies administer to potential employees a test called "Briggs-Meyers," a personality test created by Isabel Briggs-Myers, Katherine Briggs, and David Keirsey. Don Lowry, was a student of Keirsey, and he developed the True Colors system below from the Briggs-Meyers test. The True Colors "game" is also used in the corporate world quite a bit to help managers understand their staff better and to be able to build better teams. We are just using it here as a fun way to elevate your understanding of yourself and to elevate your understanding of other people.

So let us take the quiz to identify your individual color spectrum. Follow the directions carefully and then transfer your scores to the score sheet. If you have two colors with the same score, pick the one you think most accurately describes you.

Do this exercise with your friends or members of your family just for fun. Keep in mind, this is just for fun.

DESCRIBE YOURSELF USING THE TRUE COLORS PERSONALITY PROCESS

Instructions: Compare all four boxes in each row. DO NOT ANALYZE EACH WORD; just get a sense of the words inside each box. How much do the words in each box describe your personality? Score each of the four boxes in every row from 1 to 4, with 1 being the lowest score and 4 being the highest score using this scale:

4 = Most, 3 = A Lot, 2 = Somewhat, 1 = Least

Record your answers in the Scoring area below each box.

Box A	Box B	Box C	Box D
Active	Organized	Warm	Learning
Variety	Planned	Helpful	Science
Sports	Neat	Friends	Quiet
Opportunities	Parental	Authentic	Versatile
Spontaneous	Traditional	Harmonious	Inventive
Flexible	Responsible	Compassionate	Competent
Score:	Score:	Score:	Score:

Box E	Box F	Box G	Box H
Curious	Caring	Orderly	Action
Ideas	People	On Time	Challenges
Questions	Oriented	Honest	Competitive
Conceptual	Feelings	Stable	Impetuous
Knowledge	Unique	Sensible	Impactful
Problem Solver	Empathetic	Dependable	
	Communicative		
Score:	Score:	Score:	Score:

Box I	Box J	Box K	Box L
Helpful	Kind	Playful	Independent
Trustworthy	Understanding	Quick	Exploring
Dependable	Giving	Adventurous	Competent
Loyal	Devoted	Confrontive	Theoretical
Conservative	Warm	Open Minded	Why Questions
Organized	Poetic	Independent	Ingenious
Score:	Score:	Score:	Score:

Box M	Box N	Box O	Box P
Follow	Active	Sharing	Thinking
Rules	Free	Getting Along	Solving
Useful	Winning	Feelings	Problems
Save Money	Daring	Tender	Perfectionistic
Concerned	Impulsive	Inspirational	Determined
Procedural	Risk Taker	Dramatic	Complex
Cooperative			Composed
Score:	Score:	Score:	Score:

Box Q	Box R	Box S	Box T
Puzzles	Social Causes	Exciting	Pride
Seeking Info	Easy Going	Lively	Tradition
Making Sense	Happy Endings	Hands On	Do Things Right
Philosophical	Approachable	Courageous	Orderly
Principled	Affectionate	Skillful	Conventional
Rational	Sympathetic	On Stage	Careful
Score:	Score:	Score:	Score:

SCORING THE TRUE COLORS PERSONALITY TEST

Now that you have scored all the boxes, let's add up the scores for each color:

ORANGE SCORE: Add the scores for boxes A, H, K, N, S
GREEN SCORE: Add the scores for boxes D, E, L, P, Q
BLUE SCORE: Add the scores for boxes C, F, J, O, R
GOLD SCORE: Add the scores for boxes B, G, I, M, T

If any of these scores are less than five or more than 20 you have made an error. Go back, read, the instructions, and adjust the scores.

TRUE COLORS ANALYSIS

How did you score yourself? Which color had the highest score when you added up all the scores from the boxes indicated? This would be the color into which your personality mostly falls. If you had two colors with the same score, then pick the one that you feel most closely fits your personality.

Here are some of the typical ways the different Golds, Oranges, Blues, and Greens see themselves according to a True Colors testing website[68]:

Gold:

- I am conventional.
- I am a pillar of strength and have high respect for authority.
- I like to establish and maintain policies, procedures, and schedules.
- I have a strong sense of right and wrong.
- I am naturally parental and dutiful.
- I do things that require organization, dependability, management, and detail.
- I need to be useful and to belong.

- I am the sensible, stable backbone of any group.
- I believe that work comes before play.
- I value home, family, status, security, and tradition.
- I seek relationships that help me ensure a predictable life.
- I am caring, concerned, and loyal.
- I show concern through the practical things I do.

Orange:

- I am courageous.
- I act on a moment's notice.
- I see life as a roll of the dice, a game of chance.
- I am a natural leader, troubleshooter, and performer.
- I like to do things that require variety, results, and participation.
- I often enjoy using tools.
- I am competitive and bounce back quickly from defeat.
- I value action, resourcefulness, and courage.
- I am generous, charming, and impulsive.
- I show affection through physical contact.

Blue:

- I am compassionate.
- I am always encouraging and supporting.
- I am a peacemaker, sensitive to the needs of others.
- I am a natural romantic.
- I like to do things that require caring, counseling, nurturing, and harmonizing.
- I have a strong desire to contribute and to help others lead more significant lives.
- I am poetic and often enjoy the arts.
- I value integrity and unity in relationships.
- I am enthusiastic, idealistic, communicative, and sympathetic.
- I express my feelings easily.

Green:

* I am conceptual.
* I have an investigative mind, intrigued by questions like, "Which came first, the chicken or the egg?"
* I am an independent thinker, a natural nonconformist, and live life by my own standards.
* I like to do things that require vision, problem-solving, strategy, ingenuity, design, and change.
* Once I have perfected an idea, I prefer to move on to a new challenge.
* I value knowledge, intelligence, insight, and justice.
* I enjoy relationships with shared interests.
* I prefer to let my head rule my heart.
* I am cool, calm, and collected.
* I do not express my emotions easily.

How true do you think your "color" reflects your true self? Hopefully, you might understand yourself and others a little better as a result of having taken this little test. Keep this in mind as you interact with other people. Perhaps you can begin to see how people can be so different and why diversity is so important. We all have strengths and as you can see from the table above we all have weaknesses which we can overcome. We hope that your having this knowledge will boost your confidence and help you to improve yourself as you learn from others. Just remember to be your awesome self and it's all good!

IDENTIFY STRENGTHS, WEAKNESSES, PASSIONS, AND TALENTS

IDENTIFYING YOUR STRENGTHS

As you can see from the True Colors Personality Test, we all have strengths and weaknesses. People who have a lot of talent also have weaknesses that they either fixed or just ignored and leveraged into strengths. Take Einstein, one of the world's greatest minds, for example. He once failed a French exam. If he had let that eat away at him and destroy his confidence, he might not have gotten around to developing the Theory of Relativity, and this would be a different world.

Before you can leverage your strengths, you must first identify them. If you want help in identifying your strengths, you could take the Gallup Strength Finder test, or you could look on-line for a Strength Finder test that suits you.

Once you identify your strengths, then work hard to perfect them. Once you have perfected them you must -- practice, practice, and practice until you can perform them in your sleep! Then use your strength to maintain your edge.

"Reflected Best" Self-Exercise

Want a simpler way to discover your strengths? Adam Grant, a professor, and author, finds that the strength finder tests may not be the best way to find strengths. He recommends that if you want to recognize your strengths, you need other people to "hold up a mirror" or in other words, observe you and relay to you their opinions about your strengths.

According to Grant, when you see your own reflection through the eyes of people who know you well, then you can begin to identify your most unique talents. He suggests that you may want to try the Reflected Best Self Exercise. This process is based on research by Robert Quinn, Jane Dutton, Gretchen Spreitzer, and Laura Morgan Roberts.

Here is what you do:

Email or text people you know well and ask them to write a story about a time when you were at your best. Then take these stories and put together a portrait of your strengths. People describe this process as eye-opening. Some even call it life changing. Maybe you will too. Here are the steps:

* Identify 10-20 people who know you well from different walks of life, and ask them to write a story about a time when you were at your best.
* When the feedback arrives, look for the common themes that appear in multiple stories. Make a list of these topics. Identify the key examples that support each area, and what they suggest about your strengths.
* Using the information above, write out a brief profile about yourself when you are at your best.
* Now create an action plan for using the strengths you identified. [69]

IDENTIFYING YOUR WEAKNESSES

Remember, no one is perfect. At your age everyone knows that you are still developing. Your developmental goal ought to be to grow strong and straight like a tree. The earlier you identify your weakness(es) the better so that you can give yourself the best possible chance of growing into a strong individual. Here are a few clues to help you identify and strengthen your weaknesses:

Clue #1: If people tell jokes about you regarding your tardiness, your sloppiness, and your lack of organization - your job is "getting the punch line." Often people will use humor in an effort to tell someone that they need to work on improving certain behaviors. Focus on improving by asking yourself, "What can I do to improve, today?" Then follow through to the next level. You will likely get more attention and compliments when people realize that you are growing to be a strong man.

Clue #2: Be honest with yourself. Ask yourself, "What do I want to achieve?" Then analyze whether or not you are doing the things that will help you to get what you want to achieve. Observe other people who have achieved what you want to achieve. You may want to start by emulating strong, righteous people you admire. Give yourself a gift – the right to change.

You can let others know that you are deliberately changing. A handsome, jovial young man of 19 years who was sitting alone on a pew in front of us in church turned around, introduced himself, and while we were waiting for the service to begin he mentioned his plan. "I am no longer interested in partying. I want to study and I want to go on a mission." The following Sunday he told us that he had started a new part-time job in a grocery store. We were impressed by his determination, his independence, and his enthusiasm.

Clue #3: Ask someone who loves you and whom you respect to help you to identify your weaknesses. This type of heart to heart conversation needs a quiet and calm space. For example, if you decide that a parent would be a good person to give you feedback about your weaknesses, ask them to set up a time at the end of the day, or on the weekend, or during a family vacation, to talk. If you want to ask a kind friend, go for a walk together.

Turning Weakness into Strength

The following stories in this section should be inspirational for all young men. We all have weaknesses of one type or another to overcome. Some issues are quickly resolved, such as lack of punctuality (always being late). Others take more time to resolve, such as experiential challenges (lack of practice); learning challenges; voice challenges; physical challenges, or addiction challenges. People who have overcome major challenges inspire us. If they can overcome a major challenge, so can we.

Overcoming Experiential Challenges

Experiential challenge is probably one of the most common challenges to overcome because of a person's tendency to be lazy, which leads to a lack of practical experience doing something. However, this can be overcome. Some people learn to turn their weakness into strength through practice and gaining a lot of experience in a particular field, sport, or art. One great example is Michael Jordan. When he first tried out for basketball, he was a dismal failure, but through determination and hard work (practice,

practice, practice) Michael became one of the greatest basketball players that ever lived.

Experiential challenges may be overcome by:

* Having the equipment you need to develop a talent or skill, for example, a basketball, soccer ball; football, baseball bat, baseball mitt, piano, flute, violin, harp; or, art supplies
* Transportation to lessons, if you need it
* Instructions or formal lessons
* Support from family, friends and community
* Practice, practice, practice
* Time management
* Patience
* Recognizing and embracing God's unconditional love for you. He will be the wind beneath your wings.

Overcoming Learning Challenges

Years ago I read the remarkable story of Benjamin Carson in his book, *Gifted Hands*. When Ben was 8 years old, his parents divorced. His mother, who was a maid, raised him and his brother Curtis. Ben was an angry young boy from an inner-city school. The kids at school called him the "class dummy." However, Ben grew up to become one of the world's leading pediatric brain surgeons.

When Ben was in university, he was experiencing difficulty with a course he needed to continue his education. He knew that if he did not do well on the final exam, he would fail the course and then he would not likely be able to fulfill his dreams and goals. There was so much to study. The night prior to the exam, he prayed to God. That night, in a dream, he reported that saw the questions on the exam and all of the answers. The next day when he saw the exam all the questions that he saw in his dream were on the exam, and he knew all of the answers because they had already been revealed to him in his dream.

Dr. Carson is credited with being the first surgeon to separate, successfully, conjoined twins who were joined at the head. In 1987, before performing surgery on the Binder twins, Dr. Carson, lead his 50-member surgical team in prayer. The twins were successfully separated and survived independently.

Later, we will share with you scientific proof that the power of prayer is very real.

Most people who have learning difficulties have average to above average intelligence – they just learn differently. Many colleges and universities know this largely because of very successful businessmen who had learning challenges. In the May 13, 2002 issue of Fortune magazine Betsy Morris wrote in her article Overcoming Dyslexia, that four "losers" were Richard Branson, Charles Schwab, John Chambers, and David Boies. Billionaire Branson developed one of Britain's top brands Virgin Records and Virgin Atlantic Airways. Schwab virtually created the discount brokerage business. Chambers is CEO of Cisco. Boies is a celebrated trial attorney, best known as the guy who beat Microsoft. In one of the stranger bits of business trivia, they have something in common: They are all dyslexic. So is billionaire Craig McCaw, who pioneered the cellular industry; John Reed, who led Citibank to the top of banking; Donald Winkler, who until recently headed Ford Financial; Gaston Caperton, former governor of West Virginia and now head of the College Board; Paul Orfalea, founder of Kinko's; Diane Swonk, chief economist of Bank One. [70] The list goes on.

One of Elaine's nephews had learning difficulties throughout elementary school and high school but began to excel in university academically and socially. He attended a preparatory year at Carleton University, in Ottawa, which helped him to gain confidence while improving study habits. He was able to achieve higher levels of time management and organizational skills. During this year, he also took three courses towards his bachelor's degree where he was required to maintain at least a B average. He became Special Events Coordinator for Foreign Students at Carleton University and at Algonquin College on a part-time basis; met a lovely Japanese young lady; studied Anthropology and Japanese; spent a year in Japan as an exchange student at Kansai Gaidai University; graduated from Carleton University; returned to Japan to teach English as a second language in the JET Programme; had his own radio show on a Japanese station; attained the second highest level of proficiency in the Japanese language for foreigners; became a Human Resources Manager at a major English Language Organization that services many schools in Japan (his job involves hiring, training, supervision, evaluation, scheduling, payroll and other); and after an eight-year courtship married his Japanese sweetheart.

In 1994, my wife tutored an 11-year-old boy who did not know how to read. She asked him, "How does your brain work when you are trying to read?"

He answered, "Teachers have told me to skip the words that I don't know in a sentence and to get the meaning of the sentence from the other words."

She was shocked and told the boy, "Never, never skip words. If there is a word that you do not know, look it up in a dictionary." Then she taught him how to use a dictionary. She helped him to find a magazine that he was interested in reading in the school library and with a little more tutoring within one month he was reading on his own. Years later, the young man's older sister thanked Elaine for helping her brother because he was doing well in school.

Some public libraries such as The Seattle Public Library, may offer In Person Homework Help and On-line Homework Help for teens, for free. These libraries may also offer free adult education tutoring for those who do not read. The Seattle Public Library offers the course Adult Education Tutoring "with English language skills; job readiness; GED preparation and high school equivalency; citizenship interview preparation; college placement test preparation; and life skills."[71] We inquired about the age for admittance, for the Adult Education Tutoring program, and we were told that if a person "identifies as an adult," they would be admitted.

Libraries may also offer Adult Literacy classes. If your local library does not offer this service, call your City Hall or Town Hall and ask if there is a civic organization or a church that offers this service for free. You are not alone. Seek and you shall find help. It will be to your advantage to ask for help sooner rather than later. As the old saying goes "a stitch in time saves nine."

For more information about overcoming learning difficulties read the section in this book: *Persons Who Have Learning Difficulties Can also Attain a College or University Education.*

Learning challenges may be overcome by:

- Learning how to read
- Finding an approach to studying that works for you
- Time management
- Perseverance
- Finding your passion
- Engaging with supportive family, friends, and community

Overcoming Voice Challenges

Worried about your voice? If you feel that your voice does not reflect who you are, know that, through practice, you can train your voice to be more pleasing to you and to others. As a young man who stuttered profusely up until the age of 12 or 13, I know how important a pleasing voice can be to you. Of course, your voice may still be undergoing changes as you begin maturing into a man, but nevertheless, you can still train it to sound the way you desire it to sound with practice. Children who stutter have the same level of intelligence as ones who do not stutter, so don't let people run you down because you have any speech impediment. James Earl Jones and King George VI are examples of persons who overcame voice challenges.

James Earl Jones

James Earl Jones, a most distinguished and famous American actor, was brought to live with his grandparents who were poor farmers when he was five years old. Shortly afterward, he began to stutter and was essentially mute for eight years while he attended school. In 2014, Jones told an ABC News reporter on *Person of the Week* that in high school he wrote a poem, which a teacher asked him to read to prove that he had written the poem. Jones was able to read it without stuttering. Thus began his performing arts career. Jones' voice has the deep resonance of a leader's voice. He has won Tony's, Emmy's and an Oscar for his work as an actor. He has performed leading roles in many Shakespearean plays, many Broadway plays, was the voice of Mustafa in *The Lion King* and the voice of Darth Vader in the original *Star Wars* film.[72]

King George VI

In 1936, Prince Albert's father, King George V, died. His brother, King Edward VIII, abdicated the British throne to marry a divorcee the same year, and Prince Albert reluctantly became King George VI of England. At the time, planning to marry a divorcee disqualified Edward from the throne. It must have been quite a shock for George VI, because he was never prepared to be king. One major issue was that he stammered, although he had sought counseling from the voice tutor Lionel Logue for years. Kings are required to give speeches – lots of them – and King George VI was ill-prepared for that. To make matters worse World War II erupted after he became king, and Britain declared war on Germany in 1939. The people of England needed to hear messages of reassurance and encouragement from their king, so he knew he needed to take action.

In order to overcome his voice challenges, George VI continued to work with his voice coach. The tutor and George spent many years improving George's ability to speak eloquently.[73]

George overcame this serious obstacle. He became well-loved by the people in his country, because he had become a great leader, and they knew he had made such an effort to communicate with them. His journey is portrayed in the movie *The King's Speech*.

Voice obstacles may be overcome by:

* Working with a speech therapist
* Breathing exercises
* Reading out loud frequently
* Figuring out in advance what you want to say
* Forcing the first words out of your mouth
* Speaking slowly at first

- Practicing enunciation (pronouncing each word clearly)
- Practicing articulation (speaking fluently and coherently, and expressing emotions)
- Obtaining support of family and friends
- Participating in vocal events, for example, singing in a choir, Toastmasters

If you are concerned about your voice and how others may perceive you, then you should seek help. When I was a young man, I took speech lessons to correct enunciation and articulation problems. With work, you can change your voice to your pleasure. But please remember that you are still growing up and your voice may not yet be mature. Ask others for their opinion about your voice before you begin to worry too much. Often your voice sounds differently to others than it does to yourself. Try taping your voice and listening to it. You may be pleasantly surprised to hear how good it sounds!

Overcoming Physical Challenges
The following stories about President Theodore Roosevelt and Roy Wilson illustrate how physical challenges may be overcome even when doctors have little faith. Notice that these two gentlemen exercised faithfully and spent time in nature.

President Theodore Roosevelt
According to the Ken Burn's documentary, *The Roosevelts: An Intimate History*, Theodore Roosevelt was a sickly, asthmatic child who was unable to participate in regular childhood activities such as playing outside and going to school. He was tutored at home until college, and kept himself busy by writing in his journal and reading voraciously, sometimes three books per day. When he was a young man, his father lectured him on the importance of developing the body to completely develop the mind, and his father built him a gym inside their house. Theodore enthusiastically lifted weights,

practiced gymnastics, swam, rode horseback, hiked, wrestled, boxed and learned judo. Eventually, as his body became strong, his asthma disappeared. Teddy studied at Harvard University and led a very adventurous life, traveling and attaining the highest level of political achievement in the United States – he became President of the United States for two terms, and established many of the National Parks Americans enjoy today in addition to introducing other ground-breaking legislation. His first wife, whom he loved dearly, died tragically two days after giving birth to their only child. His second marriage was to a childhood friend with whom he lived happily until his death. He had five children with his second wife, who also cared for the child from his first marriage.[74]

Roy Wilson

When Roy Wilson was young, doctors told his parents that he had a heart condition, and he would not likely live beyond the age of 15. They warned that Roy ought not to participate in contact sports. Roy graduated high school and enrolled in McGill University where he studied architecture. Once, when he failed a test, he contemplated throwing himself in front of a bus, but decided that that would be too painful for his parents, so he pressed on. He would eventually become a telemark skier, a cross-country skier, a full professor of architecture at McGill University, a husband and a father. He published a book of poetry, painted over 1,500 watercolors, built a sailboat, and sang bass in his church choir. Roy Wilson lived to be 101 years old.

Like Theodore Roosevelt and Roy Wilson, you can enrich your life and overcome physical challenges by:

* Spending time in nature
* Exercising
* Perseverance
* Support of family and friends
* God's help

Overcoming Addiction Challenges

The main reason for overcoming addiction challenges is wanting a better life. Being a slave to addiction must be horrible. The relative short-term pain of withdrawal is worthwhile because a lifetime of being free again is wonderful.

If you have not started smoking, drinking alcohol or taking drugs do everything in your power not to start. During times of stress, don't be tempted to self-medicate with this junk. The following men are glad they overcame their addiction challenges:

Samuel Jackson

Elaine Lipworth reported in *The Telegraph*, that two weeks after Samuel L. Jackson was released from rehab in 1991, he started shooting the movie *Jungle Fever* where he ironically portrayed a crack addict. Jackson said, "It was the first thing I did without a substance in my body." According to the article, offers flooded in and career-defining performances followed. Sobriety, Jackson said, enabled him 'to get inside a character" in a deeper way." Over his career, Samuel L. Jackson's 140+ movies have grossed more than 8 billion dollars, Lipworth reports.[75]

Sobriety pays off!

The inspirational website, BeliefNet reported on how the following three celebrities, Matt Damon, Brian Welch, and Eric Clapton, overcame their addiction challenges:

Matt Damon

Matt Damon was addicted to nicotine and wanted to self-correct. According to BeliefNet, "Matt Damon never had a second thought about his addiction, until he saw a picture of himself smoking and realized how awful it made him look. Disgusted, Damon underwent hypnotic therapy to undo what had been a habit of 20 years. Completely satisfied with his treatment, the actor even convinced good friend Ben Affleck to try hypnosis – and it worked for him too!"[76]

Brian Welch

Brian Welch is one of the co-founders of platinum-selling metal band *Korn*. BeliefNet reported that, "At the height of their success he found himself embroiled in a world of money and drugs. He was addicted to alcohol, sleeping pills, and Xanax. But in 2005 Brian's life changed when he experienced a dramatic conversion to Christianity. He was baptized in the Jordan River and then sought solitude in order to cleanse himself of addiction. He credits God with his rehabilitation, and has been clean ever since his spiritual retreat in a hotel room. Since then he has been making Christian music and dedicating his life to helping others."[77]

Eric Clapton

Eric Clapton once spent $16,000 a week on heroin, according to BeliefNet. They reported that during one of his performances, Clapton actually passed out and had to be revived on stage. "It took *The Who* guitarist Pete Townsend, another former addict, to convince him that there was a better way to live. Clapton has taken his experience and used it for good by establishing the *Crossroads* center for drug and alcohol treatment," says BeliefNet.[78]

Daniel Radcliffe

It has been reported broadly that Daniel Radcliffe, who starred as Harry Potter, struggled with alcohol abuse. He has been sober since 2013, according to reports. Alcoholism is a disease, which can kill a person in the midst of the addiction and during withdrawal. It is critical to follow a doctor's advice.

Addictions may be overcome by:

* Participating in the "twelve step" recovery program
* Removing the addictive substance from your home
* Learning healthy ways to cope with stress
* Going into seclusion, in a peaceful setting, to go through withdrawal
* Avoiding other addicts who are using
* Asking family and friends for support

- Being honest with your doctor and dentist about your past history with addiction. When in need of a painkiller they will administer a drug that is not addictive.
- Praying for God's help
- Spending time in nature
- Exercising
- Examine whether hypnosis will work for you

IDENTIFYING YOUR PASSIONS

Man is only great when he acts from passion."

– BENJAMIN DISRAELI, 19TH CENTURY BRITISH PRIME MINISTER

You will only become truly great if you develop your strengths with passion.

After making a list of your strengths, choose from the list things that are most interesting to you, and things for which you believe you might have a passion. Study them, think about them, and pray about them before embarking on developing the skill or talent. If you develop a passion for a particular activity or field of study: study, study, study, then practice, practice, practice your new skill or talent or interest. Greatness will ensue! But be patient. Remember, you may need to invest a lot of time and focus before claiming absolute success. Read Malcolm Gladwell's book *Outliers* to get a sense that it takes lots of "practice" before one becomes an expert at something. Mr. Gladwell mentions the 10,000-Hour Rule – saying that it takes about 10,000 hours of correct, challenging practice before one can develop world-class expertise. Gladwell explains that the individual must also have a proper environment, opportunity and support in order to cultivate this would-be talent. He cites Bill Gates and the Beatles as two examples. Both had unique opportunities and time to develop their talents, thereby getting the jump on any competitors.

As the classic joke goes: *A visitor to New York City stopped a taxi cab and asked the driver, "How do you get to Carnegie Hall?"* Not missing a beat, the cabbie looked at him squarely in the eye and said, *"Practice, practice, practice!"* If you have talent and passion for your talent, apply practice, give it time, and watch it grow through the roof.

IDENTIFYING HIDDEN TALENTS
Look within yourself to see if you have hidden talents ready to spring forth. You could be multi-talented and not know it. Russell Wilson, quarterback for the Seattle Seahawks, was a baseball player before he became a professional football player. During the 2013 football season, he led the Seahawks as their rookie quarterback, and on February 2, 2014, they tasted victory winning the Seahawks' first Super Bowl Championship, defeating Denver 43–8!

Bo Jackson, an iconic American athlete, excelled in both baseball and football. He is the only player ever selected for both the Major League Baseball All-Star Game and National Football League Pro Bowl.

Leonardo Da Vinci and Benjamin Franklin were also men of many talents.

Try a little experiment. Pick a few persons at random. Ask them what talent(s) they have. Some persons may know their talents and others may be discovering their multiple talents. How many of your own talents have you identified?

WHY IS IT SO IMPORTANT TO DEVELOP TALENTS? IT IS ONE OF GOD'S COMMANDMENTS

One of the best ways to elevate yourself is by developing your skills and talents. Some of those talents you may have been born with and ought to develop. What talents do you already have? Are you a math whiz? Do you play the piano? Violin? Trumpet? Drums? Saxophone? Flute? Sousaphone? Bassoon? French horn? Trombone? Do you play hockey? Basketball? Football? Baseball? Are you a good swimmer? Are you a terrific skateboarder? Do you have a photographic memory? Do you sing? Do you paint? Are you a good photographer? Are you good at chemistry? Biology? Physics? Do you like to visit seniors? Are you entrepreneurial? Are you a good cook? Everyone has talents. Maybe you have not yet discovered your talents. Likely, you have more than one!

You possess a unique set of talents. This may surprise you. God expects you to use your talents and even to develop new ones! In fact, it is a commandment from God. Did you know that you will be held accountable if you do not develop and use your talents?

The Biblical story the *Parable of the Talents* (below) illustrates this commandment, which God has given to us. In the story, the man who is going on a journey symbolizes God and the servants symbolize us, who are the children of God. Jesus used parables to teach lessons and principles based on the Word of God - much in the same way that we use stories to teach lessons and principles in today's society. Jesus also used parables to avoid Roman persecution.

In the parable below, talents are an ancient currency or money. The money symbolizes special gifts or talents each one of us has been given by God. When you think about it, these gifts or talents are like money in that they can enrich our lives and the lives of other people, in many ways, and also they can provide us with income. The story tells us what God expects each one of us to do with the talents we have been given. It also shows what happens when we do not use our talents effectively. **Spoiler Alert**: the final result is not pretty.

THE PARABLE OF THE TALENTS

(The following story is taken from the King James Bible, Matthew Chapter 25, verses 14-30)

> 14 *"For it will be like a man going on a journey, who called his servants[a] and entrusted to them his property.*
> 15 *To one he gave five talents, to another two, to another one, to each according to his ability. Then he went away.*

16 He who had received the five talents went at once and traded with them, and he made five talents more.

17 So also he who had the two talents made two talents more.

18 But he who had received the one talent went and dug in the ground and hid his master's money.

19 Now after a long time the master of those servants came and settled accounts with them.

20 And he who had received the five talents came forward, bringing five talents more, saying, 'Master, you delivered to me five talents; here I have made five talents more.'

21 His master said to him, 'Well done, good and faithful servant. You have been faithful over a little; I will set you over much. Enter into the joy of your master.'

22 And he also who had the two talents came forward, saying, 'Master, you delivered to me two talents; here I have made two talents more.'

23 His master said to him, 'Well done, good and faithful servant. You have been faithful over a little; I will set you over much. Enter into the joy of your master.'

24 He also who had received the one talent came forward, saying, 'Master, I knew you to be a hard man, reaping where you did not sow, and gathering where you scattered no seed,

25 so I was afraid, and I went and hid your talent in the ground. Here you have what is yours.'

26 But his master answered him, 'You wicked and slothful servant! You knew that I reap where I have not sown and gather where I scattered no seed?

27 Then you ought to have invested my money with the bankers, and at my coming I should have received what was my own with interest.

28 So take the talent from him and give it to him who has the ten talents.

29 For to everyone who has will more be given,
and he will have an abundance. But from the one
who has not, even what he has will be taken away.
30 And cast the worthless servant into
the outer darkness. In that place, there will
be weeping and gnashing of teeth.'

Yikes! Slothfulness and laziness are apparently awful character traits! Dr. Peck, whom we have already referenced in the book, while assessing his patients and their problems, determined the bottom line: laziness is "evil" and laziness was the source of his patients' problems.[79]

OVERCOMING LAZINESS AND DEVELOPING TALENTS
Some of us are simply too lazy to develop our talents. Scott Peck, in his book, *The Road Less Traveled,* says shockingly, "If we overcome laziness, all the other impediments will be overcome. If we do not overcome laziness, none of the others will be hurdled."[80] Think about that. It is important that you muster up your self-discipline and shed laziness because laziness will just allow you to waste opportunities for future happiness.

As we have stated before, there are consequences for everything we do - right or wrong. Hopefully, you will choose to do the right things always.

There are three lessons to be learned from *The Parable of the Talents* above:

1. Earnestly seek to discover your God-given talents.
2. Use your talents to help others. Start with your family. Share your talents and skills with them to develop your talents, to be of service, to teach, and to bring joy to your family. Help them add to their talents. Gordon B. Hinckley said, "My talents may not be great, but I can use them to bless the lives of others. I can be one who does his work with pride in that which comes from his hand and mind."[81]

3. Acknowledge God's hand in your success. Athletes and performers often give thanks to God because they know that without God's help, they would not have succeeded.

Developing your strengths and overcoming your weaknesses is like operating a hot air balloon. In order to go higher, you have to increase the amount of heat you pump into the balloon (adding energy or strength). You might also consider getting rid of some of the weight attached to the balloon as well (fixing weakness). Carrying out these actions will allow your balloon to soar ever higher!

You might not be able to do this overnight, so do not feel like you are a loser if it does not happen that way. Through patience and diligence, it will eventually occur. We repeat: Everybody has strengths and weaknesses. We are all human, and nobody is perfect. We just want you to be able to identify your own strengths and weaknesses so you can work on them. Believe in yourself.

A Huge Caution about Self-Doubt
During a conference speech, Jeffrey R. Holland said,

"I wish to speak today of a problem that is universal and that can, at any given hour, strike anywhere on campus — faculty, staff, administration, and especially students. I believe it is a form of evil. At least, I know it can have damaging effects that block our growth, dampen our spirit, diminish our hope, and leave us vulnerable to other more conspicuous evils. I address it here this morning because I know of nothing Satan uses quite so cunningly or cleverly in his work on a young man or woman in your present circumstances. I speak of doubt—especially self-doubt—of discouragement, and of despair."[82]

The message Elder Holland wanted to get across was that self-doubt is something that we should seek to avoid at all cost. Remember the mindfulness exercises? Those are excellent ways to take control of your mind in order to avoid negative thoughts – thoughts which are the source of self-doubt. By taking control of your mind, you can replace those negative thoughts with positive thoughts. You can do it. Be on guard.

Remember, as many have said, you cannot afford the luxury of a negative thought. Have faith in your ability to grow and overcome challenges.

TAKE A CAREER TEST TO HELP YOU DISCOVER HIDDEN TALENTS

A career test can help you gain new insights as to which types of careers would motivate you. Ask your school counselors to give you a Career Test, or try to locate one online. The results of a career test that I took in high school revealed that my highest two interests were Sociology and Psychology; however, my conscious interest was engineering and that is what I majored in during college. Although I became an engineer and computer scientist and have had a long career, my interests now appear to have gravitating back to my innate interests in sociology and psychology. That is manifested in my having developed a passion for writing this book to empower young men. I find this intriguing. So we suggest that you take an interest test to get a reading on where your interests may lie. Talk over the results with your parents and counselors. If there is a disparity between the results and what you consciously seem to be interested in, you may be looking at hidden talents you have not yet considered.

HOW SCOUTING CAN HELP YOU DISCOVER AND BUILD YOUR TALENTS

There are more than one hundred merit badges to earn in Boy Scouts. "You can learn about sports, crafts, science, trades, business, and future careers as you earn merit badges," says the BSA website. These badges cover a broad range of activities and interests which boys have been driven to earn for over 100 years due to the fantastic experience afforded by each badge achievement. From all these activities, you will be able to build skills, develop talents and perhaps discover new ones.

Building Self-Confidence

One important key to success is self-confidence.
A key to self-confidence is preparation.

– Arthur Ashe

Having confidence in yourself is an extremely important trait. If you do not have it, then you might find it difficult to be successful. It is also important to have the right balance: self-confidence but not arrogance. Fortunately, psychologists can show you how to build self-confidence based on a firm sense of reality.

What is Self-Confidence?
Self-confidence is the feeling that you have trust in yourself, you have desirable knowledge or skill, and you have the ability to deal effectively with situations and people.

How Confident Do You Seem to Others?
In the article *Building Self-Confidence: Preparing Yourself for Success*, the Mind Tools team, a group of professionals dedicated to helping others, compared traits and behaviors of confident people against persons with little self-confidence. How do you stack up? Do you portray high confidence or low confidence?

If you have self-confidence, you might project the following traits to other people:

* Doing what you believe to be right, even if others mock or criticize you for it
* Being willing to take risks and go the extra mile to achieve better things
* Admitting your mistakes, and learning from them

* Waiting for others to congratulate you on your accomplishments
* Accepting compliments graciously. "Thanks, I really worked hard on that project. I'm pleased you recognize my efforts." [83]

If you have LOW self-confidence, you might project the following traits to other people:

* Governing your behavior based on what other people think
* Staying in your comfort zone, fearing failure, and so avoid taking risks
* Working hard to cover up mistakes and hoping that you can fix the problem before anyone notices
* Extolling your own virtues as often as possible to as many people as possible
* Dismissing compliments offhandedly like "Oh, that project was nothing really; anyone could have done it." [84]

How to Look Confident

I would add a few factors that would influence how others perceive you:

1) <u>Employ good posture</u>. This will enable you to look confident even if you are not. You can always fake being confident until you become confident in reality. Standing as tall as you can, with shoulders back, stomach in, and chin up will help. You might want to walk around your bedroom balancing a book on your head, but learn to walk naturally - not stiffly.
2) <u>Smile often</u>. Flash those pearly whites. It takes 44 fewer muscles to smile than it does to frown.
3) <u>Give eye contact</u>. Look people in the eyes when speaking to them. Do not stare, though.
4) <u>Give a firm handshake</u> – Do not give a wet noodle handshake. A firm handshake always portrays confidence. Yes, people notice such things.

How to Build More Self-Confidence

The Mind Tools team also points out that <u>goal setting</u> is the most important skill you can learn to improve your self-confidence. They tell us that if you feel the need to boost your self-confidence, you should try these three steps as a start:

Step 1. Prepare for your journey to confidence. Think about who you are, where you are, and where you want to go:

- Take inventory of talents, skills, and accomplishments you already have
- Re-identify all your strengths
- Think about your passions, which ones are most important to you, and what you want to do with them
- Start managing your mind to keep yourself in focus
- Commit yourself to success!

    Preparation involves lots of study and practice. After it "gets into your bones," you will feel confident that you can pass that exam, speak confidently in a foreign language, hit those high notes in the national anthem, or dunk that basketball with power!

Step 2. Setting Out

- Set small goals, then achieve them. For example, set a time limit to learn a new skill; set a time limit to get through a chapter in one of your subjects; or aim for a certain speed or height in sports or dance.
- Build the knowledge you need to succeed. For instance, learn a new sports "move" and practice; learn to play a different tune and practice. Learn how to solve a difficult math problem and practice.
- Focus on the basics, for instance, in typing learn the proper positioning of your arms, wrists, fingers, and elbows.
- Keep managing your mind

Step 3. Accelerating Towards Success

* Make your challenges tougher. Learn how to solve a more difficult math problem, learn how to play a more challenging piece of music or compose a piece of music, or learn how to solve a strategic problem in sport. Learn new skills and develop new talents and deploy them. Measure your success and review your progress regularly.[85]

IDENTIFYING TALENTS AND SKILLS

This is a fine point, but we feel it worth mentioning here.

Talents are special, natural abilities or aptitudes that you may have inherited, such as "perfect pitch when singing," which you can develop further with practice. Michael Jackson, Mozart and Beethoven are reported to have had perfect pitch.[86]

Skills do not necessarily come naturally to us. With practice, however, skills can be developed to look like a natural talent. For example, a young woman we know learned the skill of driving. At first, her skill level was very low – she had three "fender benders" within a short while. We were quite surprised when she started driving a three-ton flower delivery truck, a job at which she excelled and held for years.

I have a natural talent and love for singing. However, after auditioning for and being selected to be in a live musical, I needed to expand my singing talent to meet stringent musical requirements for my role by taking voice lessons and much practice.

There are hard skills and soft skills. Examples of hard skills include auto mechanics, woodworking, and computer programming. Examples of soft skills are communications and diplomacy.

You, too, can identify your God-given talents and set goals to practice in order to develop them. You may also identify skills, that you are not naturally endowed with, for which you can set goals to learn and perfect through practice.

Visit the *Elevate Yourself to Manhood* website at http://www. elevateyourselftomanhood.com/videos to check the availability of the video on *the skill of Self-Confidence* by: Dr. Ivan Joseph.

Discovering the True Condition of Your Brain

So now that we have shown you ways to stimulate your mind positively and build confidence, we need to talk about brain conditioning. You will want to optimize the use of your brain by removing harmful forces and influences, while at the same time, learning how to build a powerful brain. So let us discover how to elevate your mind by optimizing the brain in the next section.

Dorothy: "How can you talk if you do not have a brain?"
Scarecrow: "I do not know…But some people without brains do an awful lot of talking, don't they?"

The Wizard of Oz

Understanding the Importance of Your Brain

Humans have the power to speak, think, imagine, and solve problems. They can do an incredible number of tasks simultaneously. Now, that doesn't necessarily mean you can truly "multitask" as you may think. It simply means that your brain has many things going on at one time, like breathing, controlling body temperature, controlling blood pressure, hearing, seeing, enabling a person to walk, talk, and so forth. You do not have to think to make these things happen yourself; the brain automatically coordinates all these tasks often without your conscious control. However, in order for the brain to do these as well as the cognitive functions such as learning, remembering, storing and problem-solving, the brain needs to be healthy.

The Need for You to Protect Your Brain

Protecting your brain is of utmost importance. The proper functioning of your brain is absolutely essential to your health and well-being, so it is imperative that you take excellent care of your brain. Unfortunately, modern day habits are not always good for brain health, but there are some basic things you can do to protect your brain:

- Get enough sleep,
- Manage stress,
- Eat a healthy diet,
- Get sufficient exercise,
- Provide adequate mental stimulation,
- Wear a helmet when skateboarding, biking, etc.
- Wear a safety belt when riding in a car, and
- Avoid the Seven Brain Dangers below

The Seven Brain Dangers

In recent years, research has shown that lots of young brains have been affected by negative phenomena such as bullying, video gaming, and other harmful phenomena. In this section, we will explore what we call "The Seven Brain Dangers" and see just how much they can wreak havoc on the most precious part of your anatomy.

Brain Danger #1 - Bullying

Have you ever been bullied? Have you ever bullied anyone? Have you been a bystander while someone was being bullied?

What is Bullying?

The Mayo Clinic describes bullying as "a form of aggression, in which one or more persons repeatedly and intentionally intimidate, harass or harm a victim who is perceived as unable to defend him- or herself. Bullying can take many forms."[87]

What are the different types of bullying?

The Mayo Clinic[88] describes four different types of bullying:

Physical: Hitting, kicking, tripping, or destruction of personal property, etc.

Verbal: Teasing, name-calling, taunting and making inappropriate sexual comments. Making derogatory comments about their weight, how they dress, their hair, their race, their culture, or other sensitive personal subjects.

Psychological or Social: Spreading rumors, public embarrassment, or exclusion from a group.

Electronic. Also known as cyberbullying, this involves using electronic media, such as social media, email, video, or text messaging to embarrass, threaten or harm others.

Dr. Phil says that bullying can be physical, emotional, verbal, sexual, or racial in nature.[89]

Neuroscientists have now proven that bullying can affect your brain in ways that can cause damage.

Emily Anthes, in her article *Inside the Bullied Brain – The Alarming Neuroscience of Taunting* says, "...it is becoming clear that harassment by one's peers is something more than just a rite of passage. It is thought that bullied kids are more likely to be depressed, anxious, and suicidal. They are more liable to carry weapons, get in fights, and use drugs.

Many of us who may have experienced bullying may want to write it off as a "soft" form of abuse, Antes says, one that leaves no visible injuries and that most victims simply get over. But a new wave of research into the effects of bullying suggests that bullying can leave an indelible imprint on your brain at a time when your brain is still growing and developing. **Scientists believe that bullying can lead to reduced connectivity in your brain, and even sabotage the growth of new neurons in your brain!**[90]

These neurological scars closely resemble scars borne by children who are physically and sexually abused in early childhood. Neuroscientists are saying that this is not merely an unfortunate rite of passage but a serious form of childhood trauma, including symptoms of depression and anxiety.[91]

Why people bully
Whether in schools or in the workplace, targets (the bullied) are usually children or adults who are perceived as being more capable and might outshine the bully. Or they are seen as being in a weaker position (new to the school or new to the job, or smaller in stature) not a threat at all but they are targeted by the bully as scapegoats to warn others of how they will be treated if they question what the bully is doing. Bullies also bully because it gives them a sense of power. A ten-year-old bully declared to my wife, his teacher at the time, "Bullying is addictive." From the mouth of babes comes the truth.

How Bullying Can Lead to Medical Conditions Such As Chronic Fatigue Syndrome (CFS)
Bullying frequently causes the bullied person to develop chronic fatigue, which is often misdiagnosed as depression. Although the targeted are certainly not happy about being chronically fatigued because it is debilitating, they are not necessarily depressed.

According to Teya Skae, author of the article, *How a Stressful State Leads to Chronic Fatigue*, "When a person is bullied they are stressed. Stress impacts our survival. Our body goes into a 'fight or flight' response, which changes the balance of our body's hormones. If stress (bullying) persists, the constant change in hormone levels, which are not "normal" hormone levels break down the body and leave scars within the body."

Healthy hormone levels are more likely to occur when a person is not being bullied – when a person is in a psychologically-healthy and physically-healthy, safe environment at home, school or in the workplace.

Dr. Hans Selye, the author of 1,700 scholarly papers and books on how stress affects our entire body, pioneered research into the effects of stress on the body and sounded an alarm to make people aware of "General Adaptation Syndrome" (GAS) response, which essentially details how prolonged exposure to stressful situations and environments will lead to chronic fatigue (and many other diseases). If the person who is suffering from chronic fatigue is not given a chance to recuperate, the adrenal glands can stop functioning altogether. In such severe cases, a person's heart can stop beating.[92]

Taking anti-depressant pills will not alleviate chronic fatigue. **The FDA warns that anti-depressant drugs can lead to deep depression and suicide in teens.** Taking anti-depressant drugs and being sent back to the same unhealthy school environment or unhealthy work environment will not alleviate chronic fatigue. The body needs time to recuperate from the trauma of bullying. The unhealthy environment needs to be changed or the person ought to not return to it.

Bullies are a health hazard. School bullies must be taught to make **life-saving** changes to their behaviors using creative discipline, for example, using the Good Deeds Program that is outlined in *Bullies and Denial Kill* (available in Google Library). Teachers need resources and training on how to conduct such a program in their classrooms, which would cost approximately $4 per child per term (the cost of a cup of coffee). If teachers have no such resources at their disposal, removing bullies permanently from schools is the only other option. If this is the case, school districts ought to provide a rehabilitation center for bullies within their immediate community. Children who are in school to learn must be protected from the distraction and health hazard associated with bullying.

Removing bullies from schools and workplaces will give bullies a real reason to change their behavior and seek counseling. They can receive counseling either in school in conjunction with the *Good Deeds Program*[93] or another form of effective discipline, or at rehabilitation centers. Eradicating acts of bullying from schools and workplaces will cut down on the cost of health care. It will also prevent the spread of bullying, which is really a disease. It will prevent the escalation of violence – much like removing the bad apples from a barrel. Until such a time when either of the options stated above are enforced, the following will give young men some coping skills.

Be More than a Bystander or Witness to Bullying

If you are a bystander, your brain is being affected by the bullying, too, because you live in fear of being the next target. Here are a few tips on how to circumvent bullying from the US Department of Health and Human Services website *StopBullying.Gov*:[94]

1. Do not give bullying an audience
    * Do not encourage a bully. Let the bully know that such behavior is intolerable instead of laughing and supporting the bully.
    * When you see bullying, you can act disinterested or blatantly state that you do not think bullying is entertaining or funny.
    Kids who witness bullying are more likely to:
    * Use tobacco, alcohol, or other drugs
    * Experience an increased number of mental health problems, including depression and anxiety
    * Miss or skip school - usually due to the fear of being the next target. It is best to nip bullying in the bud when it happens the first time. Otherwise, it can snowball and get out of control.
2. Help the child who is bullied to get away
    There are a few simple, safe ways you can assist the person being bullied to get away from the situation. However you do it, make sure you keep yourself safe.
    * Create a distraction. Do not reward the bully by paying attention – then the behavior might stop. Bystanders should focus their attention elsewhere.
    * Bystanders can create an avenue of escape for the target, for example, "The teacher needs to see you now."

* You should intervene only if it feels safe to do so, and never use violence in order to help the person get away.

3. Tell a trusted adult
    * An adult can help stop bullying by intervening while it is in progress, preventing it from occurring or giving the person being bullied a shoulder to lean on.
    * You can tell a trusted adult in person or leave them a note.
    * Do not get discouraged when you witness bullying if you have already talked to an adult, and nothing has happened (to stop the bullying). You can ask a family member if they will help. Inform the adult that this is repeated behavior – that you reported the behavior and that nothing was done to stop it.
    * Inform as many teachers, counselors, custodians, nurses, and parents as possible. The more adults get involved, the better. Then you are more likely to speak to someone who will actually take action against the bullying, and the adults may decide to collaborate to end the bullying.
    * Tell the parents of the child who is being bullied that their child is a target of bullying. Keep a record of incidences – including how, what, when, why, and where.

4. Set a good example
    * If you know not to bully others, then other students will follow your example.
    * Make sure children do not bully others and do not encourage bullying behavior.
    * Promote the anti-bullying culture at your school through school clubs and organizations.
    * You can create anti-bullying posters, share stories or show presentations promoting respect for all.

5. Be their friend
    * Be nice to the target. Let them know that they are not alone and that you are their friend. (God loves all of his

children. Emulate Jesus Christ by being kind to those who are bullied. If the bully tries to make you feel sorry for him or her, remember that bullies are frequently con artists and remember that it is their behavior that is abominable. Be civil to the bully but avoid their toxic company because they may get you into trouble. By not paying attention to them, their behavior might change.)

* Listen to the person being bullied, let them talk about the event.
* You can call the person being bullied at home to provide support, encourage them and give advice.
* Send the target a text message. Let them know that what happened was not cool and that you are there for them.
* You can help by telling the person being bullied that you do not like the bullying and asking them if you can do anything to help.
* You can also assist the person being bullied by talking to a trusted adult, and acting as a witness to the bullying.[95]

6. If You Are a Victim of Bullying

As the target, do not feel embarrassed because it is not your fault. Instead, please speak to your parents, a counselor, or someone you trust. Report the bullying incident. Name the bully, where and when the bullying occurred and whether or not this person or anyone else has bullied you before. Also, record this information on your computer or in a notebook for future reference.

Jay McGraw's[96] *Life Strategies for Dealing with Bullies* suggests:

* Do not get into a fight with a bully or try to retaliate in other ways.
* When a bully insults you, do not believe it.
* Do not overestimate a bully's power.
* Bullying won't stop just because you ignore it.

- Do not hang out online in a place where bullies can target you.
- Do not be afraid to think of new ways to solve the conflict.
- Do not believe that you invited or deserved bullying.
- Control your own temper.
- Write journal entries about how you feel.
- Use positive self-talk to keep up your self-esteem and self-image.
- Be confident when you tell the bully not to touch you.
- Expand your circle of friends.
- Try to avoid a bully if you can.

In addition, join the school's anti-bullying campaign. If you are bullied, tell your teacher, counselor, principal, parents, and doctor. RAT is actually an acronym for the "Right Action Taken." So RAT out the bully. You have a right to preserve your God-given life, and your health. People whose behavior harms others should be expelled from school and the workplace. If bullying is still occurring at school after you have done everything that you can do to alert authorities, consider changing schools, or being homeschooled. If the problem is occurring at work, and your company is not doing anything about it, get a lawyer and start looking for another job. Your health is your most important asset.

Note: Even if you do not have any friends at this time in your life be optimistic, you may have a lot of friends later on. Use this quiet period to study or to develop a skill. Join the Boy Scouts and join a church. Become the best you can be – that would be a sweet turn of events. The best retribution will be a life well lived. Remember that many bullies fail miserably in the long run. Many end up in jail.

Check the *Elevate Yourself to Manhood* website at http://www.elevateyourselftomanhood.com/links for web links to homeschooling associations.

If You Are a Bully

If you bully others - stop it. You are hurting yourself because you are likely to be continuously stressed out, in a constant "fight mode" that leads your body to think it is at war, which unbalances your hormones. You are your own worst enemy. You are on the wrong path.

Studies have shown that kids who bully others may also take part in acts of violence or perform risky behaviors even into adulthood. Children who bully are more likely to:

- Abuse alcohol and other drugs in adolescence and as adults
- Get into fights, vandalize property, and drop out of school
- Engage in early sexual activity [and contract sexually transmitted diseases]
- Have criminal convictions and traffic citations as adults
- Be abusive toward their romantic partners, spouses, or children as adults."[97]

Alternative: Take some time off from social pressures. Spend some time in nature. Envision what kind of a man you would like to be. Change your brain and change your behaviors. Change your friends. Change your school. Change your workplace. Develop a new skill. Develop a new persona (a new person). Pray to God. Become the best you can be.

Brain Danger #2 - Internet Addiction and Gaming Addiction

In 2008 China declared Internet addiction to be a clinical disorder, saying it's a top health threat to its teenagers.

THE NEW YORK TIMES, 1/20/2014

Shosh Shlam and Hilla Medalia, Israeli filmmakers, created *Web Junkie* - a gripping documentary on China's Internet addiction rehabilitation clinics. China has over 400 prison-like rehab centers around the country where clinicians are trying to deprogram teens that live mostly in virtual reality.

Shlam and Medalia bring us a shocking view into a typical day at this tough-love camp:

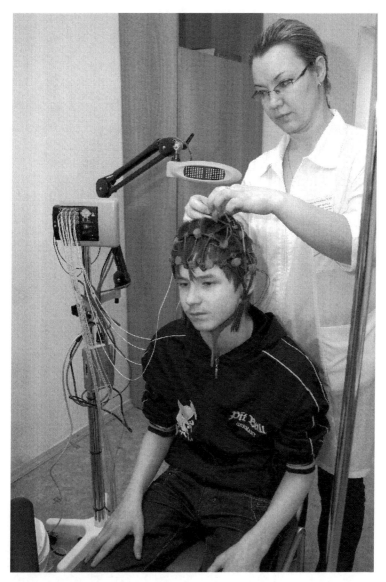

Example for EEG Brain Scanning for Video Game Addiction

"WAKE UP!

"It's still dark outside. A Chinese man in military fatigues bursts into the room after room along a narrow corridor. The drab setting looks like a military barracks, and the rooms are Spartan, consisting of two bunk beds, a window, and nothing more. Young children, who can't be older than sixteen, struggle to rise and shine. For these boys, the man leans in and shines a flickering red light in their faces.

"FALL IN AFTER ONE MINUTE!

"The boys are now assembled outside. They march in line in the freezing winter like miniature soldiers. The camera homes in on a young boy peering out the window, his face faintly visible through its steel security bars. He's weeping uncontrollably. Inside his room, three women in white lab coats try to console him. "Do not cry," they say. He's inconsolable.

"'I'm in a lot of pain,' he says, tears streaming down his face. 'Bring him the medicine,' orders one of the lab-coated women.

"'What did you do?' a man asks the boy. 'I used the Internet,' the boy replies. He's barely able to summon the words. 'My Dad brought me here to see the doctor. But he locked me in here instead.' Tears stream down his face. 'They tied my hands.'

"Welcome to the Internet Addiction Treatment Center in Daxing, a suburb of Beijing, China. Established in 2004, its aim is to deprogram Chinese teenagers--mostly boys--who suffer from an "Internet addiction." China was one of the first countries to brand "Internet addiction" as a clinical disorder, and to claim it's the number one threat to its teenagers today. The Chinese government has erected 400 rehabilitation boot camps like this one to treat Internet addiction disorder.

"It cuts back to the boys, who are now running in line. They stop and, in straight lines, practice punch and kick moves in unison. Afterward, they're served dumplings, rice, and vegetables on metal trays. Every room in the facility is monitored by cameras, like the prison in Oldboy. Teens spend a minimum of three months at Daxing. While they're there, they'll be subjected to a variety of tasks. Wires and nodes will be hooked to their head to measure brain activity (it's a 20-minute process), they're administered daily medication (without being told what it is), they have to keep their rooms spotless, partake in individual and group therapy sessions with their parents and do boot camp-style exercise, with jumping jacks and push-ups. Sometimes, they're forced to line up and sit in a straight-backed crouching position for half an hour.

"Most of the kids do not even know how they got here.

"'Some kids were drugged, others were tricked into coming here,' says one of the kids. 'Usually, it's the parents [who drugged them]. Sometimes, the Center will send staff to do it. One kid was sleeping. Seven or eight drillmasters carried him here. When he woke up, he was at the Camp. Many students got here like that.'

"'My parents tricked me,' adds Nicky, a 16-year-old. 'They told me we were going skiing in Russia.'

"The majority of the kids at Daxing do spend way too much time on the Internet. Nicky played the online computer game *World of Warcraft* for ten hours a day. One kid in the film claims to have played *World of Warcraft* for 300 hours straight, taking only tiny naps in between. "During summer vacation, I played for two whole months," said another. Another boy admits to spending over $8,500 playing a game called *Dream to the West*. Most of the kids at Daxing have been suspended from school at one point due to their constant gaming while some have dropped out entirely.

"'We noticed from these children that they have a bias towards virtual reality," says Prof. Tao Ran, an addiction specialist and director of Daxing Camp. "They think that the real world is not as good as the virtual world.'

"He adds, 'Some kids are so hooked on these games they think going to the bathroom will affect their performance. So they wear a diaper. These are the same as heroin addicts. Heroin addicts crave and look for heroin every day. The teenagers we have here crave and look forward to playing games online every day. That's why we call it electronic heroin.'

"The kids of Daxing do not believe they have a problem and eventually start to break down. When Hope, a 16-year-old in the camp, flips out one day, he's ordered to 10-day isolation where he's locked in a room by himself and, at times, tied to his bed. He's not allowed to speak to anyone. There's another poignant scene midway through the film when the aforementioned Nicky is seen desperately phoning his parents, trying to convince them to remove him from the camp. " [98]

I know this story is a bit harsh, and maybe this solution is only feasible in Communist China. The obvious question now becomes "Are we in the United States that far off from having this same disaster at home?"

Explore the next section and see if it describes you.

Video Game Addiction
WARNING! There Is Evidence That Your Brain May Be Digitally De-Wired.

Do you play video games for hours on end? How many hours are too many? What kinds of games are harmful to you?

There is a world of new evidence that too much video gaming can lead to damage to your brain. People have been talking about the addictive nature of video games and the Internet for years, but now (finally) scientists agree on the negative effects video gaming has on your brain. You might not be aware this is happening to you, but the dangers are real, and the consequences are real. <u>This is definitely meant to scare you.</u> <u>Multiple hours of video game playing is harmful to your brain.</u>

As a young person, it is very important for you to know the signs of video game addiction so that you can get help in order to save your brain. Psychologists agree that many of our teens are already addicted, and we can see the unhappy results in the lives of hundreds of thousands of men in our society who are not behaving like men. They refuse to study at a post-secondary college or university, or they drop out. They refuse to work. They are not interested in dating young women. Nor are they interested in getting married. All they want to do is play hours of video games each day. They are addicts. Period.

What is an addiction? Addiction is a disruptive behavior that makes it obvious that the person has little or no control. Video gaming is addictive because it affects the brain in similar ways that drugs or gambling affect the brain. When scientists observe teenage subject's brain with a functional magnetic resonance imaging (fMRI) device, they can see in real-time the areas of the brain that become active when gaming, specifically the reward or pleasure centers of the brain. These are the same areas of the brain that light up when a subject is exposed to gambling or drug use. Researchers then collect data, measure, and analyze results to compare with other data to come to conclusions. This recent development has made it much easier for scientists to speak with more confidence about their findings.

Many men today live with their parents past what is considered "normal" and neither work, nor go to school, nor make positive contributions to the household. Even birds force their young out of the nest to take their solo flight. It is the natural order of things. Exasperated human parents - in an effort to encourage their son to "grow up" and care for himself – may sometimes move into a smaller abode in which there is no room for their son and his belongings. You do not want to put your parents through this. They expect that all the hard work they put into raising their son will lead to evenings of listening to their son tell them all about his adult adventures in the world. They are hoping that someday they will meet their daughter-in-law and have the joy of holding their grandchildren. They were not expecting their son to become lazy or derelict or addicted and remain stuck in permanent adolescence and dependency. Having to provide for adult children actually inhibits most parents' ability to save for their retirement years, on which their own survival depends. Many parents will start experiencing age discrimination in the workplace around 50 – 60 years of age. Even those with six-figure salaries may all of a sudden find that they can only get a minimum wage job. They need to save in their peak earning years because they will have to support themselves with their savings perhaps until they are 90-100 years old. By age 60, they may find themselves unemployed and unable to get a job due to poor health. Their savings would have to support them for 30 or 40 years. Do you get the picture? In other words, parents usually expect their sons to become independent - supporting themselves and their families. In many cultures, such as in Taiwan, sons are not only expected to become independent - they are expected to care for their parents. Parents give their children the gift of life, and they care for their children's needs for about twenty years. It is up to children to honor that gift by becoming the best they can be, and by being kind and considerate to their parents. The fifth commandment that Moses received from God commands us to honor our parents. This commandment is frequently mentioned in the *Bible* and *The Book of Mormon* too, so it must be significant:

> *For Moses said, Honor thy father and thy mother; and,*
> *Whoso curseth father or mother, let him die the death.*

> – MARK 7:10 KJV

> *For God commanded, saying, Honor thy*
> *father and mother: and, He that curseth*
> *father or mother, let him die the death.*

> – MATTHEW 15:4 KJV

> *Honor thy father and thy mother, that thy days may be*
> *long upon the land which the Lord thy God giveth thee.*

> – MOSIAH 13:20 KJV

Until recently, parents did not know that video gaming was addictive. Very few people knew about this phenomenon. It is interesting to note that Bill Gates and Steve Jobs limited their children's use of electronics and online services. According to the article, *Bill Gates Keeps Close Eye on Kids' Computer Time*, Bill Gates[99] set a limit of

45 minutes a day of total screen time and an hour on weekends plus the time his daughter needed to do homework. In a New York Times article, *Steve Jobs Was a Low-Tech Parent*, Steve Jobs[100] said, "We limit how much technology our kids use at home." He did not specify in the article how long his kids were allowed to play games or surf the web, but apparently it was nowhere near what you would expect from such a high-tech parent. From that same article, it seems other high-tech CEOs and managers have the same attitude towards limiting their kids' access to electronic screens. Perhaps they knew all along that video gaming and continuous screen time was harmful for children? However, now we ALL know that video gaming is harmful to one's mental health and that it is addictive. So, it is up to you, young man, to overcome video gaming addiction. However, that is much easier said than done. Overcoming video gaming addiction requires work and resolve.

You have now been warned. If you are not yet addicted to playing video games, do not start! The more a person plays video games, the harder it becomes to overcome video gaming addiction. Dr. Andrew Doan, MD, Ph.D., a physician with a research background in neuroscience, in his own words, became a "monster" and almost lost his family. You do not want to put your wife and children through this hardship. It is not fair. Dr. Doan, in his book, *Hooked of Games*, mentions that he would not have been able to conquer his video gaming addiction, stopping to play video games entirely, without the strength that he received from God and Jesus. In his book, Dr. Doan, tells his personal story about how he was an addicted gamer and how he struggled with this addiction going through medical school. Dr. Doan determined that he could not play video games in moderation because he was an addict, which means that he could easily return to his old habits of playing video games for hours each day, to the exclusion of more important matters such as his family – so he had to quit altogether. As well, Dr. Doan includes a lot of very valuable information and many other tips on how to overcome video gaming addiction in his book, for all young men including young men who are not ready to accept God and Jesus into their lives.

Dr. Doan was so disturbed and enlightened by this experience that he wrote his book to sound the alarm to parents and children. He now devotes lots of his time to educating others about the hazards of video games, not only in the United States, but in other countries as well where young men spend lots of time playing video games.[101]

Study Identifies Risks for Video Game Addiction

Do you play your favorite video games repeatedly and ignore other activities? Are you impulsive? Do you feel uncomfortable in social situations? Do you feel unhappy when you are not playing video games? Do you lie about how much time you play video games? Do you try to stop playing video games, but you cannot? If you answer "Yes" to any of these questions, then you might be addicted to playing video games. That was the message given in an article by Denise Mann titled, *Researchers Say Depression and Anxiety May Be Among the Consequences of Pathological Gaming.*[102]

In this study, Douglas A. Gentile, Ph.D., an associate professor of psychology at Iowa State University, Ames, spent two years tracking video game usage of 3,000 school-aged children in Singapore to see if they showed signs of video game addiction. His report highlighted risk factors for video game addiction and also some possible consequences of too much gaming, for example, depression, anxiety, social phobia and trouble in school.

"It is not just about how much time is spent playing video games," says Gentile.[103] "It is doing it in such a way that it damages your ability in many other areas, including social function, occupational function, relationships, and school performance."

Mann reports that, "Pathological gamers logged in more time playing video games, exhibited impulsive behavior, and were more likely to be socially awkward compared with those who were not hooked on video games, the study showed. And pathological gaming may not be something that kids just grow out of, the new study suggests." [104]

Mann also pointed out in her article that two years after the study began, 84% of students in the study were still addicted. "It is not a short-term problem," Gentile says. "Once they get into a problematic pattern, it seems to stick with them."

Drop Your Game Controllers - Your Brain May Be Toast
Now we have proof that too much screen time can affect your brain development and operation. In her article, *Gray Matters: Too Much Screen Time Damages the Brain*, Dr. Victoria L. Dunckley, M.D.[105] reports various findings about how Internet and video gaming addiction physically affects the human brain. According to Dunckley, here is your brain on video games:

* Your brain gray matter shrinks and you get loss of brain volume
* Your brain experiences loss of integrity of the white matter
* Your brain's cortical thickness gets reduced
* You have impaired cognitive functioning
* You get cravings and impaired dopamine function

There is now hard evidence that too much gaming limits your ability to succeed in your life – in regards to social development, academic achievement, and job performance. In other words instead of becoming a "Winner" you are more likely to become a "Loser."

Dunckley's research shows that, "excessive screen time appears to impair brain structure and function." She stresses that, "much of the damage occurs in the brain's frontal lobe, which undergoes massive changes from puberty until the mid-twenties. Frontal lobe development, in turn, largely determines success in every area of life--from a sense of well-being to academic or career success to relationship skills."[106]

To emphasize the associated risks, Dunckley urges parents to be vigilant, to monitor their children's screen time, and to convince other parents to do the same.

But we say, do not wait for your parents to tell you to stop prolonged video gaming. Use the self-discipline skills that you should now have started to develop, remember to control your mind with your spirit, start being more responsible for your actions and make better use of your time while you avoid physical damage to your brain. Need more evidence of the harmful effects of video gaming? Read on!

Why You Cannot Pay Attention to your Teachers or Parents, But You Can Pay Attention to Video Games

If your parents or teachers complain about your inability to pay attention, then this might also be related to too much video game playing. Are you starting to see a pattern here? Besides "frying" your brain as we have already shown, video games can also seriously stimulate your brain causing a mad release of dopamine, a brain chemical involved in focus and reward.

In Dunckley's article, *Why Can My Inattentive Child Pay Attention to Video Games?*, [107] she explained that kids only pay attention if they are presented with something interesting, and this is where the stimulation phenomenon comes in. Researchers reported, "If you have Attention Deficit Disorder (ADD) you may be drawn to video games and screens … because you can focus on them. The games provide you with sufficient stimulation for a nice dopamine surge."[108] However, this is NOT healthy.

Brain Over-Stimulation

Dunckley explains that "when you play video games, you get stimulation like rapid movement, intense colors, quick scene changes, and psychologically exciting content (violent, competitive, bizarre, surreal, fantastical, sexual, etc.)."[109]

Some of the newer video games can create even higher levels of arousal than the older ones, according to studies.[110]

Lots of screen time including video games, television, and other electronic media only make the situation worse because the constant high level of arousal caused by the electronics is not natural and prevents all young men, especially those with Attention Deficit Disorder (ADD) from developing a normal attention span, which they need to function in real life. This is even more troubling since interactive screen media are often promoted as learning tools. Dunckley emphasizes that "studies show gaming has an adverse effect on attention and impulsivity over time—especially in children who already have attention problems."[111] [112] This makes parents and teachers worry a lot, especially for kids who already have attention problems.

Brain Needs Increasing Amount of Stimulation

To make matters even worse, the more times you play video games, you may notice that you need increasing amounts of stimulation to create the same level of excitement. Dunckley says, ". . . more and more stimulation is required for focus--identical to mechanisms in drug addiction. When children report non-screen activities as 'boring,' this should be a red flag to parents and educators--the child has become accustomed to an unnatural level of stimulation."[113]

Video Gaming Is as Addictive as Drugs

Dunckley also says that video gaming elevates levels of the hormone dopamine in the brain, which becomes addictive like drugs. Eventually, more and more stimulation is required to get your brain to the same dopamine levels, which no video game or natural activity will be able to satisfy.[114] That is why some gamers feel that they need to play for 300 hours straight – as mentioned earlier. Eventually, that will not satisfy them either.

If you start to find non-gaming activities boring, you might be in danger of becoming addicted to unnatural levels of stimulation and abnormal levels of dopamine. How sad. If you do not quit, you will be robbed of enjoying the most amazing facets of your life; you will be robbed of your happiness.

If you are a young man with attention problems such as ADD, ADHD or Asperger's and already find it difficult to complete projects, and assignments, especially if you find them boring or difficult, video gaming will only make matters worse for you. You will have more trouble getting things done, more trouble focusing, more trouble controlling your impulses.

Indeed, you do not want to go through your life with a mushy brain that cannot focus. It is unrealistic to feel that your parents will take care of you for the rest of your life while you sit in your room playing video games. Right? This is not rocket science. It is common sense. Eventually, video games will not satisfy your unnatural need for constant stimulation and a dependency on high levels of dopamine. This will lead to depression, and you do not want to go down that path. If you have already dug yourself into a depression hole, consult with your parents, get medical attention, and pray to God for His help.

You need all your little gray cells to learn real life skills so that you can sustain yourself after the age of 19 or so, in college, on a mission, or in a job. Brains can repair themselves in a healthy non-tech, naturally stimulating environment – exercising or playing sports, being out in nature, learning how to cook, reading, canoeing, fishing, geocaching, orienteering, house painting, wallpapering, painting a picture, automotive mechanics, landscaping, caring for pets, designing a board game, genealogy, inventing something useful, journalism (writing an article about something that happened in your community and getting it published), gardening, first aid, learning to play a musical instrument, joining a choir, public speaking (after the age of 18 you can join the Toast Masters Club), theatre, salesmanship, or collecting. By the way, in the Boy Scouts of America, you can learn a lot of these healthy skills and much more.

SAVE YOUR BRAIN.

How Do You Know If You are Addicted to Video Games?
Check to see if you can answer "Yes" to any of the questions below. You may want to ask your parents or someone else for a second opinion because you may not be aware of your own behavior:

* Are you playing video games more than one hour per day?
* Do your parents say you have played longer than you think you have?
* Does it seem like you have only played one hour, but your mom thinks you have played three hours?

- Are you having difficulty getting along with people after playing video games?
- Do you have a violent temper sometimes and does this come after playing video games?
- Are you generally unsociable?
- Are you unable to have a relationship with a girl? (Answer only if you are 16 or older.)
- Do you lack empathy for others?
- Do you think you have depression and/or anxiety?
- Are you unable to cope with life challenges?
- Do you lack motivation?
- Have you developed vision problems since you started playing video games?
- Do you have hand or wrist pain (possible carpal tunnel syndrome) since you started playing video games?
- Are you not taking the time to go to the bathroom? Do you wear diapers instead?
- Do you get bored sometimes when you play video games?
- Do you shirk your responsibilities at home to play video games?
- Do you play video games immediately when you get home instead of doing your homework?
- Are you up late at night playing video games instead of sleeping 8-10 hours?

Again, please speak to your parents and/or counselor if you answered "Yes" to any of these questions to determine if you are addicted to video games.

So, What Is the Solution? How Do You Stop Being Addicted to Video Games?

1. Obviously, the best solution is DO NOT START playing video games for many hours at a time. Most experts would probably agree that you should limit recreational video gaming to about one hour per day.

2. Stop cold turkey. This was the best solution for Dr. Doan whom we referenced earlier. We know this is a tough option, but we offer it to you anyway. With proper motivation and determination, you can do it!

3. Slowly wean yourself off extended periods of gaming. Cut down your video-game playing time little by little. If you are playing four hours per day, try to cut it down to three. If you are playing three hours per day, try cutting it down to two. If you are playing two hours per day, try cutting it down to one hour.

4. Never play violent video games or games of low moral value. As my dad would say, "Use your own best judgment."

5. Substitute other activities for video gaming. Choose activities that are challenging physically and mentally, but choose activities that are legal and safe when using proper protection. Some have suggested sports (team and/or individual), dirt biking, downhill skiing, or other activities that require keen focus, a high level of physical activity, high energy, and skill. Proper training and preparation are the keys to safety. Learning to embrace an appropriate amount of physical and psychological risk in sports will translate into developing the ability to risk going out with friends, dating, studying, learning a new skill, or developing a business.

6. Delay gratification. Do all your homework and chores before you decide to spend any time playing video games.

7. Spend more time with your family and friends before deciding to play video games.

8. Get out in nature. Nature Deficit Disorder is real. It can set in easily if you live in a city or if you live in suburban areas and do not have access to natural environments.

9. Get plenty of sleep. This will help you reboot.

10. Eat a proper diet, including drinking plenty of water.

11. Learn to manage stress.

12. Take up art or music. Join a choir, join the school band, or paint a picture and give it to someone as a gift.

Good News: Over time, your brain can heal, but it will take some time. Even stroke victims can recover given proper treatment and therapy.

We will explain in more detail some brain-saving activities later in the book.

My Son

Writing this book prompted me to realize how excessive video gaming affected my son's life. As a single dad during a large part of his life, I watched his growth and development very carefully. From every aspect, up until the age of 10, he exhibited normal social and personal behavior. It was about age 10 that he started playing video games. At that time, I certainly did not know about the damaging effects of video gaming on the brain. Since age 5 or so, he would share his dreams with me - dreams of becoming a fireman or a racecar driver. He had goals. He told me that when he turned 16, he wanted to go explore Japan. I knew that his dreams were symbolic of someone who had strong desires to take his place in the world.

Very shortly after starting heavy video game playing he started spending a lot of time alone in his room. Our conversations slowed down and eventually stopped. He no longer spoke of future aspirations. He stopped social interactions with other members of the family. I attributed this behavior to "hormones" or "growing up" or to the fact that his mom and I had become separated. So I left him alone, thankful that he wasn't into drugs, joining a gang or getting in trouble with the law. Back then, I did not know that "babysitting by video game" was a really bad idea. I thought, "Whatever makes him happy, as long as it's not illegal or immoral, it's okay." How naive was I?

He started doing mediocre work in school, even though he had been in the *Gifted and Talented Program* for a number of years. He began to hate school and would not put his best foot forward. It wasn't so much that he didn't try - it seemed that he wouldn't and couldn't get it in gear. He lost motivation for all his subjects except art. I attempted to tutor him in math, but I would come away from these sessions frustrated because he did not seem to have the will to learn. In my estimation, he was not living up to his capacity. I knew his teachers personally and knew that they were doing their job as best they could. What I know now is that video games were sucking the life out of him and his brain.

As he grew into his mid-teens, he never seemed happy. He never smiled and always seemed agitated. He had the unusual knack of speaking (answering questions) in one- or two-word sentences. I joked about it with him, but it was really annoying to me. I asked myself if drugs could be at play, but that was not the case. So, I asked him point blank, "Why are you angry all the time." Very candidly, without thinking he said, "Dad, I don't know."

He was not a Boy Scout. I did not know about the many benefits of Boy Scouting back then. I investigated military schools for him, but I could not afford them and his mom did not agree that he should attend one of them.

I had dreams that he would become a doctor, so I asked a doctor friend of mine if my son could job shadow him for Career Day. My friend graciously accepted and allowed my son to job shadow him, but to no avail. My son was not impressed and not motivated.

He graduated high school but was not enthusiastic about attending college. He took a few courses but lost interest quickly. He never went to Japan. I encouraged him to backpack across Europe. He had no interest.

His only interests were video games, music, and art – in that order, but 90-plus percent of his interest was in video games. Music and art are excellent careers if you pursue them properly, but he had no real interest to do so.

After all, this I still did not know that he was addicted to video games. I only became aware of this addiction since I started writing this book. Thousands (maybe millions) of other parents and I did not know that our children could possibly become addicted to video games. It's nobody's fault really. It's just a societal tragedy that slowly unfolds underneath your nose until its damage is done – like

147

an insidious drug. I would not have given my son addictive drugs. Had I known that video gaming was addictive, I would have probably thought twice before buying a game for him.

When he reached twenty-one years of age, he had hand surgery for carpal tunnel syndrome. Knowing what we know now, I would say that it was most probably caused by video gaming – repetitive motion from using the game controller. Do not get me wrong, I love my son as much as anyone loves their son, and I am not blaming him for becoming addicted to video games, because he did not know about this danger either.

As I mentioned earlier, it was only when we started writing this book that we were awakened to the problem of video game addiction. Subsequently, we questioned friends and acquaintances (who are professionals), whose sons had dropped out of school. We found that their sons also played video games excessively. We shared with these parents the information we found regarding video game addiction. They were as shocked as we had been, and they immediately began to help their sons to overcome their addiction. We knew we needed to sound the alarm and provide positive solutions to help other young persons emerge from their own video gaming captivity.

To continue the story, my son, now an adult, moved to the East Coast to live in his mother's apartment while I moved to the West Coast for work.

Elaine and I got married and began the primary research for this book. Two years passed, and I could tell by the telephone conversations with my son that he showed no improvement. At some point, he had been diagnosed with depression and anxiety and was being treated. He took a Pharmacy Tech course, but did not take the licensing exam. Neither was he looking for work. The alarm bells went off immediately inside my head because his case sounded exactly like our research regarding video game addiction. We were then able to connect all the dots. We knew that excessive video gaming had caused his problem.

We got together with my son for a visit and shared our findings about video games with him. We noted that he had gained a lot of weight due to inactivity and poor food choices. After we had returned home from our visit, my wife and I began to pray for him incessantly and asked members of our church to pray for him as well. After about six months, he called us out of the blue – a changed young man. Miraculously, he told us that he had begun to avoid unhealthy foods, to jog daily, to drink sufficient water, and, as a result, had lost 50 pounds! He also told us that he was not playing games as much as before and that he was now working at a part time job that he liked because he said, "it does not require me to think." I was relieved that he was working but could not help to feel that he was burying his talents. My wife encouraged him to work on the cover design for this book.

He now speaks to me in full American English sentences. He asks questions. He listens. He laughs again like he used to do when he was around 10 or 11. He remembers to phone me on my birthday.

He tells me now that he seemed to be "in a fog" (his words) which he could not outgrow or overcome. (I know now that gaming contributed heavily to his "fog"). He sought counseling. This seems to have helped. I am so proud to say that he is now self-motivated. He helped his mother to establish a business, and he is working at a job of his own. Also, he used his God-given artistic talents to create the beautiful cover for this book for which we are so grateful. We are so thankful to Heavenly Father that our son now seems to be on his way to recovery.

I jokingly asked him when I could expect grandchildren. He laughed heartily and answered, "Maybe someday." So there is still hope.

My Stepson

My wife lovingly gave me permission to include her son Adrian's story. Adrian is Elaine's son from a previous marriage. Adrian was a sweet baby and showed all the precociousness of a well-adjusted boy. When he was eight years old, he planned to travel to China and asked for a book about China for Christmas. He received a beautiful hardcover book, bound in red and gold.

When he reached age 12, she noticed that he started being reclusive - spending lots of time in his room alone - and he was generally unsociable with family members. Although he had friends, he still seemed lonely and moody. She spoke to Adrian's vice-principal about her concerns. The vice-principal told her that her son was also spending more time alone and that it was normal to her. However, Adrian continued to seem unhappy to his mother, so she eventually took him to see a psychologist. The psychologist told her that Adrian was a philosopher like her own husband.

She would discover years later, after Adrian passed, that Adrian was being bullied at school at this time in his life. After he passed, his mother found his journal, and one of his younger sisters told her that he had been bullied throughout school. Elaine recalled that when he was nine years old he had walked home from school instead of taking the bus. At the time, he told her that boys were jumping on his back at recess. She had spoken to Adrian's teacher and asked him to supervise the children at recess more closely. Other than this incident Adrian never mentioned that he was bullied at school until one incident in high school came to light years later.

When Adrian was 12 years old he was playing video games heavily,, but again, like millions of other parents and me – she did not know that video gaming was damaging her son's brain. So Adrian was undergoing a double-whammy shot of bullying and gaming which assuredly was not healthy for him. We now know that in addition to the extreme stress of being bullied by his peers and having his brain become unwired by video gaming, he must have been having a hard time developing coping skills. Since he never mentioned being bullied to his parents when he was in elementary school (other than the once incident) and junior high school, they could not help him. In high school, he mentioned only one incident of bullying and that he "defended himself." In his journal he wrote about being bullied, defending himself physically, and being very depressed. He was depressed even though he was popular and the children at school called him "Buddy the Boxer." After Adrian's mother read his journal she discovered that he had been bullied at school repeatedly and how he truly felt. If my wife had known about the extent of the bullying, the consequences of bullying, and the consequences of excessive video gaming, she could have helped him. For Adrian, the negative effects of years of being bullied and years of excessive video gaming were cumulative.

Adrian wrote the journal entry below when he was 16 years of age. In high school, five boys had thrown lit matches at him in class, and he had challenged them, "If you want to fight, let's put on the boxing gloves!" Adrian fought the boys one at a time and won each match. The battles occurred in school. He told his mother about the incident when she asked him why his nose looked different. Not knowing any better at the time, she felt that Adrian's "standing up for himself" was healthy - that it would build his self-confidence. It was far from being healthy. We know now that children should not feel a need to defend themselves from bullies. What made matters worse for Adrian at this time in his life, was that just before these multiple boxing matches occurred, his girlfriend had ended their relationship. Adrian's mother did not know that he had a girlfriend. He had kept the relationship a secret because the girl's father was very strict and had forbidden her from having a boyfriend for cultural or religious reasons. In Adrian's journal entry, one can sense his inner turmoil due to these unhappy circumstances. He was a very tender young man, so this must have been truly painful for him.

Adrian's Journal Entry

"I know what love is now when you do not realize what you could have with her.

"Every time I fight in spite of whom I fight, I always get depressed never any rest, always with war with myself never with anybody else.

"I'm bored nothing to do. I have done everything, nothing I haven't done. The system sucks.

"I wish they would leave me alone and stop picking at my bones. I want to give up. Nothing is holding me up. I want to die, but no one will kill me. For nothing have I done. "

As the light shines through the window, I see what I have lost. To me, I have lost the only thing that brought joy and happiness to me.

Fighting did not give Adrian any satisfaction. Even though he won each boxing match. Young people should not have to defend themselves in schools. Parents do not have to defend themselves physically at work. Young people have enough to contend with - bodies that are still developing, changing hormones, a need to focus on getting good grades, and developing social skills. His mother felt that he was unhappy and asked him if there was anything wrong, but he told her, "I'm fine." His mother did not read his journal entries until after his death because she felt his journal was a private space.

Adrian had always been more of a philosopher than a fighter. He was tenderhearted but hid it hoping that if he looked tough bullies would leave him alone.

Studies have shown that, for adolescents, the relationships they have with their peers is more important to them than the relationship they have with their parents. Their relationship with peers develops their worldview. The following reference is included in Elaine's first book *Bullies and Denial Kill*, on page 41: "In her book, *The Nurture Assumption* , Judith Rich Harris argues: "Whatever our parents do to us is overshadowed, in the long run, by what our peers do to us." (*Annals of Behavior, Do Parents Matter? The New Yorker*, 1998, page 59). Adrian's relationships with his peers in school were not uplifting; therefore, he developed a negative worldview, which created a fog in his mind.

In 1998, while Adrian was studying to become a computer programmer, he failed a bench test within the condensed program at John Abbot College, in Quebec. He had been studying 12 hours per day, six days per week. He had passed UNIX and C++, but he disliked COBOL and failed two COBOL bench tests, which meant that he had to leave the program – which he felt was unfair. He appealed to the Dean of the college, to no avail. By this time, half of his class had already been eliminated from the program. The first half of the program had cost Adrian $6,500 and he had nothing to show for it - not even credits for the courses he had passed. Think twice before taking such a course. If you fail a course in most colleges and universities, you can take the course over again, and you can retain credits for the courses you pass, from which you can build a diploma or degree. Adrian felt that the college was using the course as a moneymaking scheme, and that the course was not pedagogically sound, which only reinforced his negative worldview. He committed suicide a month later, on June 28, 1998.

My stepson, Adrian, was a talented bassist in a heavy metal band while in high school and shortly after that. The band sounded quite professional and for Adrian, this was a serious undertaking. He wanted perhaps to look tough and to express feelings of dissatisfaction with the world. The other members of the band did not appear to look any tougher than he did. After Adrian's death, one of the band members posted their music to a website as a tribute to Adrian and to the band in which he had played – *Fell Winter.*

After Adrian's death and the discovery of his journal, Elaine's research into his death led her to data concerning the rise in youth violence and the correlated rise in youth suicide. In writing *Bullies and Denial Kill*, her objective was to warn parents and teachers about the deadly consequences of bullying - she wanted to save children's lives. *Bullies and Denial Kill* enables parents and teachers to understand why youth violence and youth suicide increased at an alarming rate from the 1950s to the late 1990s, and they are encouraged to be part of the solution.

Elaine also wrote *Kids Care for Kids* to help young children to understand that it is important to be kind and that it is important to develop coping skills. These two books were published in 2002. She has received letters of appreciation, for her books, from the First Lady of the United States Laura Bush and the Governor General of Canada Michaelle Jean.

After Adrian's death, his mother felt his spirit was very close by – as when a mother feels the spirit of her unborn child. Even so, she cried almost every day for three years not only because she loved and missed him but because she understood his solitude and his pain and she wished she could have helped him. Scientists have discovered that the cells of a male fetus can stay within a mother for up to 27 years (*Cell Migration from Baby to Mother.* 2007. US National Library of Medicine, National Institutes of Health). Writing *Kids Care for Kids* and *Bullies and Denial Kill* was like working with an open wound for her.

Elaine began writing *The Very Special Little Person* one of the stories in *Kids Care for Kids* five weeks after Adrian passed. She recalls poignantly that tears obstructed her view of the computer screen. The following day one of her daughters asked her to drive her to the Hudson Farmers' Market. As Elaine browsed through the market she met a woman who painted wooden hearts and had created a game called, *The Wandering Heart Game - a Long-distance Hug.* To play the game, a person places his wooden heart in a loved one's belongings, such as a briefcase or a lunch box. When the loved one finds the heart, they are reminded of the person's love and it gives them a nice warm feeling. The woman told her that she never painted two hearts alike.

Before Adrian's body was cremated in Montreal, Quebec his mother, his sisters, and his father each laid a beautiful red rose upon his chest. A week later, before they threw his ashes into the ocean they walked through the forest of Salt Spring Island, British Columbia, and picked fuchsia and white wild foxgloves. At sunset, after his father had played *The Last Post* on a trumpet, they threw Adrian's ashes into the ocean along with the foxgloves. As the sun continued to set, the foxgloves led the way to the direction in which the tide was taking his ashes.

At the farmer's market, the heart Elaine found had been painted with three foxgloves on the front. However, these foxgloves were red and gold. Red is Elaine's favorite color. She felt that someone was trying to tell her that she still had three children. She turned the heart over and there was a beautiful red and gold rose. Elaine felt that she was receiving a "long distance hug." For, the two flowers painted on the wooden heart were the same flowers she had given Adrian at his funerals. She told the artist who had painted the heart the story above, and that find the heart was a wonderful coincidence. The woman told her, "In life there are no coincidences. I don't know how, but somehow there is a connection." Elaine feels that the same positive force that gave her the heart guided her writing.

Elaine was prompted at the last minute to share the following stories with you so that you might feel the force that has guided her to co-author this book, which she says she could not have written on her own. Also, she feels that our collaboration was heaven sent because she is not a man. When Elaine and I met online I was living in Traverse City, Michigan and she was living in Victoria, British Columbia, Canada. The following stories will enable you to know how God reveals himself to us, as He teaches us "line upon line, precept upon precept."

Some of you may be contemplating suicide. Some of you may be atheists. Some of you may be agnostic. Elaine wants you to begin to know that God knows you by name, He loves you and He asked you to come to Earth for a purpose. We are all here on Earth for a purpose. God draws closer to us in our hour of need, as he did after Adrian's death for Elaine. We have only to understand his language and hear his voice.

> *What man of you, having an hundred sheep, if he lose*
> *one of them, doth not leave the ninety and nine in the*
> *wilderness, and go after that which is lost, until he find it?*

> *- Luke 15:4*

This force also saved Elaine's life. After Adrian's death, in November, she moved to the top of a heritage house. The night of the move as she lay in bed about to fall to sleep, a still, small voice telepathically prompted her to check the freezer. She had not yet bought groceries and knew that the fridge and the freezer were empty. She thought, "Why should I check the freezer?" Even though she was skeptical, she sleepily made her way to the kitchen and opened the freezer door, which gushed hot air. She immediately called the landlords who lived below. The husband came up and unplugged the refrigerator, and the following morning called an appliance serviceman. The serviceman found burnt wires. There had been an electrical fire in the freezer. The freezer happened to be close to the only exit in the upstairs unit. If Elaine had not heeded this prompting she may have perished. This enabled Elaine to feel that her life had been spared for a reason and encouraged her to continue to work and to write.

The following is a story about another gift that Elaine seems to have received through divine intervention. After Adrian's death his mother had wanted to hold an item of clothing with Adrian's scent but his grandmother had washed all of Adrian's clothes, which smelled of detergent. A few pieces of clothing were kept but after months Elaine decided to give two bags of Adrian's clothing to a second-hand shop on Gouin, Boulevard, in Pierrefonds, Quebec. Before, giving the bags of Adrian's clothing Elaine opened the bags to smell the clothing which had been stored for months, one last time, with the hope that she might smell Adrian but she only smelled detergent. So she sealed the bags and proceeded to the gray wooden collection box that had an opening about five feet from the ground, in front of the second-hand shop. As she pushed one of the bags up towards the box's opening, a leather glove fell out of a hole at the bottom of the bag. She reached into the hole and found the glove's match. Having recently lost her gloves in the month of November, she felt that they were a gift and of course kept them. When she returned to her home she placed the gloves on her bedroom dresser. Later that evening, when she went into her bedroom for something, she smelled Adrian. She looked around the room and saw the gloves. She picked up one of the gloves and smelled the inside of the glove - Adrian's scent and the scent of his aftershave was in his glove! She slept with Adrian's gloves for many months and when she woke in the middle of the night she would smell the inside of his gloves, which would soothe her until she fell back to sleep.

While Elaine was writing *Kids Care for Kids* and *Bullies and Denial Kill*, she worked in a preschool with twelve 4-year-old and 5-year-old children whom she loved. The children's sweet faces uplifted her spirits and her work grounded her as she was determined to be a positive influence in their young lives. During her second year of teaching at the preschool, a mother gave her a tape and a booklet and asked her to teach the children *The Yello Dyno Program*, which teaches children to beware of strangers. The tape contained upbeat songs to encourage children to "jump away and tell someone." However, the last song on the tape was quite different – it had a sweet melody with the following lyrics, "Mother I never told you things I wanted to say. You are my sweet inspiration…" Elaine could not help feeling that Adrian had inspired this mother to give her the tape so that she could feel Adrian's love. She quickly dismissed this notion and decided that the way the ballad made her feel was merely a coincidence.

That evening, shortly after she got home, she removed her beige colored socks and noticed that on the bottom of one of her socks there was a red, heart-shaped, fresh bloodstain. She immediately looked at her foot and, to her amazement, there was no injury on her foot – not even a pin prick. Her mind raced to find an explanation for the red, heart-shaped bloodstain but she could not find one. She had not even removed her shoes during the day. She recalled the sweet ballad that she had heard while teaching her pupils that day, and instantly felt that someone was trying to tell her that Adrian had indeed sent her a message of love and that this heart shaped blood stain was to confirm the message so that she would not have any doubts that she had received a message of love from Adrian.

Elaine keeps Adrian's journal, the wooden heart, the burnt wires, Adrian's glove, and the sock with the heart-shaped, dried bloodstain in a fireproof safe. She feels that these gifts were bestowed to enable her to feel Adrian's love and God's love so that she would turn her heart and your heart to God, and to give her the strength to continue to write during her time of mourning for her son's death.

My wife loves and misses her Adrian and thinks about him every day. His sisters miss him. His three nephews and two nieces miss him, even though they never knew him. One of his nieces is named Adrianna. His grandparents miss him. His aunts and uncles miss him. His cousins miss him. His whole family not only misses him but they also miss knowing the young woman he would have married and they miss knowing the children he would have fathered.

Adrian's death created a lot of pain. Suicide is murdering oneself. We are certain that Adrian must have regretted his decision to end his life, after he passed. Suicide is not an option. Adrian needed to tell all those who loved him how he felt. They would have helped him. He needed to be patient with himself, with other people, and with life but his brain was so damaged by years of bullying, and years of playing video games that he could not muster up the strength to focus on setting new goals, and to endure the transition period to better days.

Since my wife could feel Adrian's spirit, without a doubt, and she realized that God indeed must exist in the spiritual realm because he had blessed her so many times, the existence of God was no longer just something abstract. She felt God's presence. She was then determined to know God. She read many books including, *How to Know God* by Deepak Chopra, and *Conversations With God* by Neal Walsh. In 2003, she met two young missionaries who gave her a copy of *The Book of Mormon.* She felt the sweet spirit that emanated from the 19-year-old missionaries. They seemed to have a glow about them, they were so full of joy, and they seemed more balanced compared to Adrian and most youth she had met in schools as a teacher. She wanted her new grandsons to grow up to be like these two young missionaries.

During a period of illness she read *The Book of Mormon* and felt that it was a genuine historical account of people from one of the twelve tribes of Israel who had migrated to the America's 600 years before Jesus Christ was born, and she found that it also included an account of Jesus's visit to the people in America after He resurrected from the dead in the Middle East. In the *Bible,* there is a reference to Jesus telling the apostles that He had to leave them to visit His other flock. It made perfect sense to her that Jesus would visit people from one of the tribes of Israel in America because how else were they going to receive His teachings? There were no telephones, no televisions, no Internet in those days.

And other sheep I have, which are not of this fold:
them also I must bring, and they shall hear my voice,
and there shall be one fold and one shepherd.

-John 10:16 KJV

She investigated The Church of Jesus Christ of Latter-day Saints and found the Restored Gospel of Jesus Christ and that the church was organized as Jesus Christ intended His church to be organized. During this time she also learned that the church teaches people about the *Plan of Happiness* - our premortal existence; why we chose to come to earth, and why we are here on the earth. God knew we would all go through difficult trials in our lives and that it would feel as if we were in a fog or a "mist of darkness." It is through these times that we are to hold onto the "iron rod," which is the Word of God.

Adrian had believed in God. He wrote in his journal that he wanted to return to God. However, Adrian did not know why we are here on Earth. He had been raised a Catholic. From my experience as a former Catholic, individual Catholics were not encouraged to study the *Bible* as thoroughly as other Christian religions I have known. Also, there is plenty of historical evidence to bear this out. Therefore, Adrian's experience did not allow him to fully understand the Word of God and His plan for us. He did not know how to hold onto the "iron rod" to find his way out of the fog. He also did not know that video gaming and bullying had contributed largely to the fog that enveloped him, and that he needed to tell someone how he felt. A more complete knowledge would have empowered Adrian and saved him.

There are many young men who are trying to navigate that fog today. That is another reason why we decided to write this book – to fill young men with knowledge and light to enable them to become wise and find their way. We are motivated to impart this knowledge to young men to save their lives.

Note: In the 90s, neither children, parents, nor teachers were given any guidance from leaders in education in regards to how to manage bullying in schools. Children were not encouraged to report bullying as they are today. Back then, school administrators tended to sweep the issue of bullying under the carpet. When Elaine was studying education at the University of New Brunswick and McGill University from 1991 to 1994, bullying in schools was never discussed in her classes. She was shocked to discover that bullying was so rampant in schools when she began her student teaching, when she worked as a substitute teacher in many schools (K-12), and when she worked as a teacher in two pre-schools. Elaine, having worked with youth extensively in the 70s, observed that the general behavior of youth had changed. In the 70s, children were well-behaved in all the neighborhoods in which she worked, regardless of socio-economic status.

When Elaine was sixteen years old, she taught a group of 100 girls, ages 5-13, rhythmic calisthenics for two-hour periods, and they were as good as gold. Later the same year, she was a playground director - caring for between 20 and 80 children, on her own - without problems. When she was seventeen, she was the Assistant Coordinator of a Community Center responsible for eight playground counselors, playground activities and the children in attendance. All of the children mentioned above were well-behaved. I wonder if this would be possible today.

Today, even though the media has covered issues regarding bullying and made schools more accountable, and children are now encouraged to report bullying, it is still not unusual for young people to avoid telling their parents that they are being bullied. It is critical for you to tell people you trust your parents, your teachers, your coach, your religious leader, and your friend if you are being bullied or when someone else is being bullied. You can simply report, "I'm being bullied," or "He is being bullied," or "She is being bullied." If you are being bullied also tell them exactly how you feel, "I can't take it anymore. The bullying is sucking all my energy. I wish I was dead." This will help them to understand the severity of the bullying and how it is affecting you. You may need to educate the people in your inner circle - if so, recommend that they read *Bullies and Denial Kill*. It is available in Google Library. More tips on how to manage bullies will follow in this book.

Check the *Elevate Yourself to Manhood* website at http://www.elevateyourselftomanhood.com/videos for the availability of video about overcoming video gaming addiction.

To Get Out of the Fog Start by Increasing Your Gray Matter and Your White Matter

It should now be crystal clear to you that video gaming destroys gray matter and white matter. In your adolescence, your brain is also trying to cope with a new dose of not fully balanced hormones. You can start to heal your brain's gray matter and white matter, and begin to get out of the fog by:

1. Avoiding video games
2. Exercising regularly. "Regular exercise may lead to increased grey matter inside the hippocampus. Your hippocampus is the part of your brain that processes memories and regulates emotions."[115]
3. Learning complex skills. R. Douglas Fields writes in the U.S. National Library of Medicine, in his article, *White Matter in Learning, Cognition and Psychiatric Disorders* that, "learning complex skills, such as playing the piano, are accompanied by increased organization of white matter structure in appropriate brain tracts involved in musical performance. Importantly, the level of white matter structure increased proportionately to the number of hours each subject had practiced the instrument, indicating white matter changes in acquiring the skill rather than performance being predetermined by a limitation on white matter development."[116]

Dr. Lara Boyd, a brain researcher at the University of British Columbia, gave us these crucial, new insights about our brain's development and ability to learn throughout our lives during a TEDx Vancouver talk. She said:

*   What we know about the brain is changing at a breathtaking pace.
*   Before now, scientists thought that after childhood the brain could not change. We now know that this is not true.

- Up until know, scientists thought that a person only used parts of the brain at any given time and that it was silent when the person was not doing anything. We now know that even when a person is at rest and thinking of nothing, the brain is highly active.
- Use of new technology, like fMRI, has allowed us to learn these and many other new insights about the brain.
- Every time you learn a new fact or skill, you change your brain. We call this <u>neuroplasticity</u>.
- All of our behaviors change our brain. The key to these changes is neuroplasticity.
- Your brain is being shaped by everything that you do and everything that you don't do.
- Nothing is more effective for changing the brain than practice. The more difficult the challenge the more structural change occurs in the brain. Each person's brain changes differently.
- Study how and what you learn best. Repeat those behaviors that are healthy for YOUR brain. For one person it may be learning a musical instrument. For another person, it will be snowboarding. Yet, for another person, it might be learning a new language.
- Learning is about doing the work that your brain requires.
- Everything you do is changing your brain.
- **So, build the brain you want**.[117]

Light bulb moment: When people practice, practice, practice a complex skill the white matter in their brain increases, which enables their performance to improve. That is how people can attain genius-like performance! You can do this. Believe in yourself.

Note: Your brain does not consider mindless video gaming a complex skill, so it won't develop your brain's white matter, because you are only using a couple fingers directly in front of you, and the actions on your screen are not occurring in real life. There is no substitute for real life experience. As previously stated in the *Drop Your Game Controllers – Your Brain May Be Toast* section, when you play video games, your brain experiences loss of integrity of the white matter, and shrinkage of your gray matter.

Brain Danger #3 - Pornography

Another toxic and troublesome phenomenon has arisen in our society - pornography. Just in case no one ever told you that pornography is a bad thing, this is your official notice. If you do not know anything about pornography and have never been involved with it, then you are miles ahead of the pack. Do not go there. On the other hand, if you have, we hope that you will hear me out. Pornography addiction is a disease, and the detrimental effects of pornography on young people - both psychological, physical, and spiritual - are devastating in the short run and the long haul.

The Legislature of the State of Utah and the Governor[118] recently proposed an anti-pornography bill. They declared pornography a public health hazard leading to a broad spectrum of individual and public health impacts and societal harms. They resolved that there was a strong need for education, prevention, research, and policy change at the community and societal level in order to address the pornography epidemic that is harming the people. Here are the concerns they put forth:

* Pornography is creating a public health crisis;
* Pornography perpetuates a sexually toxic environment;
* Efforts to prevent pornography exposure and addiction, to educate individuals and families concerning its harms, and to develop recovery programs must be addressed systemically in ways that hold broader influences accountable;
* Pornography is contributing to the hypersexualization of teens, and even prepubescent children, in our society;
* Due to advances in technology and the universal availability of the Internet, young children are exposed to what used to be referred to as hardcore, but is now considered mainstream, pornography at an alarming rate;
* The average age of exposure to pornography is now 11 to 12 years of age; this early exposure is leading to low self-esteem and body image disorders, an increase in problematic sexual activity at younger ages, and an increased desire among adolescents to engage in risky sexual behavior;

- Exposure to pornography often serves as children's and youths' sex education and shapes their sexual templates; because pornography treats women as objects and commodities for the viewer's use, it teaches girls they are to be used and teaches boys to be users;
- Pornography normalizes violence and abuse of women and children;
- Pornography treats women and children as objects and often depicts rape and abuse as if they are harmless;
- Pornography equates violence towards women and children with sex and pain with pleasure, which increases the demand for sex trafficking, prostitution, child sexual abuse images, and child pornography;
- Potential detrimental effects on pornography's users can impact brain development and functioning, contribute to emotional and medical illnesses, shape deviant sexual arousal, and lead to difficulty in forming or maintaining intimate relationships, as well as problematic or harmful sexual behaviors and addiction;
- Recent research indicates that pornography is potentially biologically addictive, which means the user requires more novelty, often in the form of more shocking material, in order to be satisfied;
- This biological addiction leads to increasing themes of risky sexual behaviors, extreme degradation, violence, and child sexual abuse images and child pornography;
- Pornography use is linked to lessening desire in young men to marry, dissatisfaction in marriage, and infidelity. This link demonstrates that pornography has a detrimental effect on the family unit; and overcoming pornography's harms is beyond the capability of the afflicted individual to address alone.

In his article, *A Major Cause for the Wimpification of Men*, Joel Hilliker observes that, "Pornography has become mainstream, pervasive, socially accepted, and, thanks to the Internet, devilishly easy to get. It is also intensely addictive. The demand is monstrous. The average high school boy watches porn two hours a week."[119]

You may not realize that pornography can have a strong negative effect on you: physically, emotionally, mentally and spiritually. It affects the way you interact with women in very negative ways. If you ever expect to grow up and have a healthy relationship with a woman and get married, then you should stay away from pornography at all cost – even if your buddies are doing it.

In Hilliker's article, we learn that The Centers for Disease Control (CDC) found that regular pornography users have higher rates of depression and even more physical health problems than non-users. "The reason is that porn may start a cycle of isolation," the CDC report explained. "Porn may become a substitute for healthy face-to-face interactions, social or sexual."

To expand, recent reports from physicians show that pornography has an unexpected negative effect on a young man's physical health. Issues like erectile dysfunction, which historically only affected older men, have now started to affect young men. In the book, *Boys Adrift*, Leonard Sax, M.D., Ph.D.,[120] writes, "one in three college men now reports erectile dysfunction." That's an incredibly shocking statistic. Pornography has robbed these young men - at such a young age - of their normal biological function and has robbed them of the joy of making love to their wife.

Church leaders warn us about the negative spiritual effects of pornography, too. It hollows out your soul and makes you spiritually barren so you cannot enjoy the uplifting benefits of the Holy Spirit.

One of the traps in watching pornography is that your eyes and mind can cause you to commit sin:

> . . . *whosoever looketh on a woman to lust after her hath committed adultery with her already in his heart.*

> – Matthew 5:28 KJV

For the record, if you watch porn, it would be very difficult for you not to sin – at least in your heart and mind. This is essentially the same – as far as God is concerned – as having sexual intercourse with the woman in real life. For this reason alone, you should avoid even looking at pornographic images, reading pornographic material, or even speaking pornographically to others about it.

Also, watching porn is just another one of those modern-day time-wasters that enslave the minds of men. Along with video gaming, young men easily rack up enough wasted hours between the ages of 12 and 18 to have achieved a complete university bachelor's degree!

In their book, *The Demise of Guys: Why Boys Are Struggling and What We Can Do About It*, psychologists Philip Zimbardo and Nikita Duncan tell us that video games and online porn are rewiring the brains of men and not in a good way, claiming that this phenomenon alters the character of young men. They avoid taking risks, avoid finding jobs, avoid obtaining an education and avoid establishing healthy relationships with the female gender. "The excessive use of video games and online porn," they write, "is creating a generation of risk-averse guys who are unable (and unwilling) to navigate the complexities and risks inherent to real-life relationships, school and employment."[121] In other words, they are missing out on the most important game of their lives – the game of real life – that is much more interesting, complex, and enriching than video games.

From the spiritual perspective, men have been severely damaged by bullying, video game addiction, and online pornography.

Hilliker writes, "The frustrations so many people have over the weakness of men today all trace back to this powerful spiritual truth: MEN ARE WEAK BECAUSE OF THEIR SIN."[122]

Pornography may lead you to disobey God's commandments. That is, it may lead you to commit fornication, which to God is almost like murder, because it kills the soul.

Playing self-absorbing video games, pornography, and bullying-- these are the sins. When a man sins, he loses his spiritual protection from God and the Holy Spirit. He is then more susceptible to sin. This makes the man weak and allows the devil to do his work. Hilliker continues, "These sins are causing the collapse of manly leadership and male responsibility. They are creating weakness, insecurity, and selfishness. They are leading to the disappearance of manhood!"[123]

Also, pornography will rob you of your innocence. Pornography will rob you of the mystery, and natural curiosity pertaining to getting to know a young woman in the right order – spirit, mind, social conduct, family, marriage, and then her body. It will rob you of the joy of discovery of a real woman in real life. It may even lead you to be dissatisfied with your bride on your wedding night.

If you watch pornography as a teenager, you will get in the habit of tiring of one pornographic video and moving on to another video for the novelty of seeing a different pornographic scene for stimulation. This habit can lead to lack of sexual intimacy with your wife after marriage. A marriage with no intimacy will be difficult for you and your wife, and may lead to divorce.

A Therapist's Observation of the Behavior of Pornography Addicts

A licensed marriage and family therapist, Geoff Steurer, MS, LMFT has provided shocking insights about the effects of pornography on the life of the individual addicted to pornography and the devastating consequences for their family. Steurer observed:

"In all my years of counseling individuals and couples, I have never seen any other behavior produce a pattern of pain and misery as predictable as that which happens to an individual and his marriage when he views pornography. Let me briefly outline the pattern as I see it.

"First, long before his wife discovers his pornography use (either by his own disclosure or by her catching him), he will begin to slowly change into someone who becomes more self-centered, irritable, moody, and impatient. He will spend less focused time with his family, seek out more distractions, begin to mentally and even verbally devalue his marriage, become critical of his wife's body and character, feel more spiritually empty, and experience more internal stress. He will become more dissatisfied with his work, become easily bored with things that used to interest him, and feel restless. He will also become more resentful and blaming when things don't go his way.

"This transformation may take years, depending on how often he views pornography. If he only seeks it out every few months, he may be able to fool himself that the aforementioned challenges are situational and will pass with time. For those who view pornography more frequently, each viewing produces more disconnection from the man he could become. The repeated viewings and subsequent self-deception deepen this transformation over time. This gradual erosion eventually creates confusion and strife in the marriage. "[124]

When a Wife Discovers that Her Husband is Addicted to Pornography

For women in real life, the quality of the relationship is what is most important. Women need to feel loved. Lovemaking is the physical expression of love. The tenderness of lovemaking is most important to women. The considerate nature of her spouse is important to her out of bed and in bed. The sharing of time, thoughts, and being closer to her husband physically than she is with anyone one else is special to her. It is natural for a woman to feel love for someone with whom she is physical because her children whom she loves come forth from her physical nature.

In the article, *To the Tender Wives: What I Have Learned from My Husband's Addiction to Pornography*, when women discover that their husbands are addicted to pornography they feel betrayed and disgusted with their husband and the bond of love and trust between them becomes severed. They experience, deep sorrow and stomach pains.[125]

Steurer says, "The stress associated with discovering a husband's pornography addiction can produce sleepless nights, food issues (both overeating and undereating), traumatic flashbacks, crying spells, and feelings of hopelessness. The physical exhaustion related to these stressors can cause a once perfectly healthy woman to begin under functioning in her various roles."[126]

Many women seek to divorce a pornography addict because their husband has committed adultery, and they want to marry a righteous man who will show them genuine love. In the article, *To the Tender Wives: What I Have Learned from My Husband's Addiction to Pornography*, the author and her cousin (names withheld) represent some women who are grounded in a Christian faith, who pray that God will enable their husband to overcome the chains of pornography addiction. Through the miracle of the atonement of Jesus Christ, God's strength, and supportive wives, there are men who enable themselves to escape pornography addiction, which could have destroyed their families.[127] In Facet 4: *Elevate Your Spirit,* I will share with you how you can benefit from the atonement of Jesus Christ and God's strength to overcome addiction, and also to improve your everyday life. For we all have challenges to overcome.

If you are fortunate enough to be a virgin, be cognizant that there is an intangible special sweet union when a young man who is a "one woman man" and a young lady who is a "one man woman," are in love and marry for time and eternity. They each give each other a very special gift – the gift of their sacred virginity. After marriage, sexual intimacy is sanctioned and blessed by God because the union conforms to the laws of God and, therefore, satisfies His laws of justice. God intended that sexual intimacy would bring pleasure to married couples so that they may experience bonding and joy while replenishing the earth with their children. Children are so special – they come from Heaven. Some young married women that we know have given testimony that they have actually heard or sensed the spirit of their unborn baby asking to be born. My wife did, too. Isn't all of this wonder worth waiting for? For now, at your age, just concentrate on enjoying your youth, and become the best young man you can be.

You may have heard the term "born-again virgin." It means that someone has repented and asked God for His forgiveness through the atonement of Jesus Christ, for sins regarding sexual acts before marriage. If you have made a mistake and wish to be forgiven, you need to ask God to forgive you in Jesus's Name, and He will forgive you. Learn from your mistake and sin no more. Look for a young lady who has similar values. If you meet someone you like who does not know the gospel of Jesus Christ but is otherwise a good person – teach her to obey God's commandments.

If you want to avoid becoming weak, you must devote your energies to the "road less traveled." Avoid diversions that weaken you. Avoid addictions that suck the life out of your brain, body and soul. Avoid things that darken your conscience (the fog). Avoid things that destroy your confidence. Avoid sins that rob you of your eternal life.

Check the *Elevate Yourself to Manhood* website at http:// www.elevateyourselftomanhood.com/videos for the availability of video about overcoming pornography addiction.

Brain Danger #4 - Drug Use, Abuse or Addiction

Abusing drugs is not acceptable. Surely, you must have heard the slogan, "Just say NO to drugs" by now. Programs like the Drug Abuse Resistance Education (DARE) promote drug education and prevention across the country in most schools in America. This program was established to teach kids how to resist the temptation to use drugs.

In this section, we provide you with a comprehensive review of the dangers of drugs.

NEWS FLASH: DRUGS WILL NOT HELP YOU SOLVE PROBLEMS. DRUGS WILL ONLY AMPLIFY YOUR PROBLEMS AND GIVE YOU NEW ONES.

Look at the drug addicts in many cities who live in the streets. Perhaps they thought that doing drugs would solve their problems. The truth is that they were not able to conquer their problems because their drug habits cost hundreds of dollars each day and created new problems. They spend money on drugs that they would normally have spent on rent and food. It is a deplorable way to live. They have wasted the body God gave them. They have wasted their minds. They have wasted their time. They have forsaken their joy and happiness. Also, due to their behavior, they have also set a bad example for the children in their families, and devastated their mothers who gave them life.

Do not forget that you can get a criminal record for using illegal drugs. Did you know that if you have a criminal record you cannot get certain jobs? Take our advice and just avoid drugs.

Perhaps, if you knew the facts about drugs you would understand the risks of taking them, and you would agree with us that a reasonable person would never take illegal drugs, misuse prescription drugs, or over the counter medications. The risks to health and legal status are just too high to ignore.

Here are some common drug facts that you must know as reported on the Teen Health website and other sites as referenced:

Prescription Drugs

You should never allow prescription drugs to enter your body unless they are prescribed by a physician or pharmacist. Even then, you must use extreme caution when using these medicines. Purposeful misuse of medicines is considered drug abuse, and drug abuse can lead to addiction or other negative health consequences, including death. Be mindful – taking some prescription medications and drinking alcohol can lead to death.

Amphetamines
Amphetamines are stimulants that accelerate functions in the brain and body. They can dramatically increase heart rate, breathing, and blood pressure. They can also cause sweating, shaking, headaches, sleeplessness, and blurred vision. Prolonged use can cause hallucinations and intense paranoia. Amphetamines are seriously addictive. People who try to stop using them experience aggression, anxiety, and intense cravings for the drugs.[128]

Depressants
Depressants such as tranquilizers and barbiturates are not to be taken except under prescription. Very large doses can cause a person to stop breathing and result in death. Depressants and alcohol should never, ever be mixed as this greatly increases the risk of death. Depressants can cause psychological and physical dependency.[129]

Special Note about Anti-Depressants
If you are taking anti-depressants, please be careful to monitor for worsening depression, suicidal thinking, and behavior. The Food and Drug Administration has warned that for teens or adolescents, antidepressants can deepen depression and lead to suicide.[130]

Over the Counter Medications
The same warning goes for medicines purchased over-the-counter. Over-the-counter medicines are medicines that do not need a prescription from a doctor or pharmacist. These are medicines that can be purchased from drug stores, grocery stores, or convenience stores – things like cough medicines, or antihistamines. They should be used ONLY as directed. Never mix them with any other medicines. You can become addicted, or these medicines can create a host of health problems for you now and in the future. If you need to take more than one medicine, ask your pharmacist if there are any contraindications that could adversely affect your health.

Cold Medicines
Taking cold medicines in large quantities can cause severe injury like liver damage, heart damage, and even death if taken in high doses.[131]

Aspirin
Aspirin is a common over-the-counter medicine which may seem harmless, but that is not necessarily the case. The Mayo Clinic[132] warns that there is a serious health risk for young children and teenagers taking aspirin - it can lead to a rare but serious condition

known as Reye's (Ryes) Syndrome. According to the Mayo Clinic, Reye's Syndrome causes swelling in the liver and brain. They report that, "Signs and symptoms such as confusion, seizures and loss of consciousness require emergency treatment. Early diagnosis and treatment of Reye's syndrome can save a child's life. . . . Though aspirin is approved for use in children older than age 2, children and teenagers recovering from chickenpox or flu-like symptoms should never take aspirin. Talk to your doctor if you have concerns." Ask your pharmacist for an alternative to aspirin that is age-appropriate for young members of your family.

Illegal Drugs

Never take illegal drugs. We know there is lots of temptation and peer pressure in society to do drugs, but it is absolutely NOT in your best interest or your future family's interest for you to take drugs. Recreational use of drugs is never cool and never recommended.

Taking drugs will kill your brain cells. Taking drugs will destroy your ability to perform. Taking drugs will lead to a miserable life and depression. Taking drugs can kill you. If your friends start to do drugs, make new friends - join Boy Scouts of America, join a sports team, join a church, join a choir. Save yourself from the pit of despair. If you are curious – take control of your mind and find something else to be curious about. If you are depressed – go for a hike in nature with a friend – remember to bring a compass, plenty of water and some food.

If you are already addicted to drugs find inspiration in the stories of people who have recovered from drug addiction in the *Overcoming Addiction Challenges* section in this book, and seek help. Believe in yourself. A brand new life awaits you.

Cocaine and Crack

Cocaine is a white crystalline powder made from dried leaves of the coca plant. Crack is made from cocaine. Both are extremely dangerous. Cocaine and its derivatives affect your central nervous system. First-time users, even teens, can stop breathing or have fatal heart attacks. Using either of these drugs even one time can kill you. These drugs are highly addictive and even after one use, you can experience both physical and psychological cravings that make it extremely difficult to stop.[133]

Ecstasy
This drug is a popular club drug among teens. Many users of ecstasy experience depression, paranoia, anxiety, and confusion. There is some concern that the effects on the brain and emotions can become permanent with chronic use.[134]

Heroin
Heroin comes from the dried milk of the opium poppy, which is also used to create the class of painkillers called narcotics - medicines like codeine and morphine. Heroin is extremely addictive. Heroin can kill you. Here's how:

* Heroin can cause your body to forget to breathe while you are sleeping
* Heroin can cause your blood pressure to fall significantly, causing your heart to fail
* Heroin can cause pulmonary edema, leading to a heart attack or kidney failure

Withdrawal is intense and symptoms include insomnia, vomiting, and muscle pain. This drug puts you on a perpetual roller coaster because when you come down off a "high" you will need to take more heroin as soon as possible just to feel good again.[135] Heroin addiction is expensive.

Marijuana
Marijuana is still an illegal drug in most states. SPECIAL WARNING for teens:
Do not listen when someone says, "Oh come on, it's just marijuana" or "Oh, it's harmless" or "It's a rite of passage." Using marijuana can have serious consequences health-wise or legally.

In the words of the Partnership for a Drug-Free Canada (PDFC),[136] "The world has changed, and so have the drugs. In fact, the marijuana of today is stronger than ever before. Drug and alcohol use can lead to many negative consequences, including bad grades, broken friendships, family problems, or trouble with the law.

The PDFC website also included the following critical information regarding the negative consequences of marijuana use among adolescents:

* Marijuana use during the teen years, when brains are still developing can lead to (1) depression, (2) suicidal thoughts, and (3) schizophrenia.
* During one study, researchers found that, "Heavy users of marijuana at age 18 increased their risk of schizophrenia later in life by six times."[137]
* Studies have also found that, "marijuana use increased the risk of developing schizophrenia among people with no prior history of a disorder, and that early use of marijuana (age 15-18) increased the risk even more."[138] The risk is even greater for teens who have family members that have developed schizophrenia.

If you are experiencing dark, unhappy feelings, suicidal thoughts, or if you are having difficulty discerning what is real and imaginary, please speak to your parents and seek medical help immediately.

Methamphetamine
Methamphetamine is a very powerful stimulant. The Teen Health website shares with us that, "Users sometimes have intense delusions such as believing that there are insects crawling under their skin. Prolonged use may result in violent, aggressive behavior, psychosis, and brain damage. Methamphetamine is highly addictive."[139]

As you can see, there are numerous dangers and pitfalls awaiting you if you were to use drugs.

Check the *Elevate Yourself to Manhood* website at http://www.elevateyourselftomanhood.com/videos for the availability of the video "Your Brain on Drugs."

Brain Danger # 5 - Alcohol Use, Abuse, and Addiction

Teenagers should not drink alcohol at all. Period. There is just too much at risk for any benefit you might think you will gain. When you drink alcohol, it penetrates into all your internal organs, including the brain.

Alcohol is a depressant that alters perceptions, emotions, and senses. It can seriously affect judgment and coordination. It can also cause mental confusion, depression, short-term memory loss and slow reaction times. So you definitely do not want to be behind the wheel of a car with this stuff in your body. It can lead to your death and you could kill or harm other people.

Teens can become psychologically dependent on alcohol in order to cope with life and handle stress. Withdrawal from alcohol addiction is particularly dangerous too - even life threatening.[140]

Alcohol abuse can also lead to unwanted pregnancies and sexually transmitted diseases because it robs you of your judgment. Alcohol essentially robs you of your agency – your God-given ability to distinguish and choose between right and wrong.

Never be alone with a young woman if you have been drinking alcohol. Remember that if you rape a young woman while intoxicated, you could still be convicted of rape even if you state that you had been drinking when the rape occurred. For a young woman - any woman - being raped is a devastating experience from which many never recover. It is an act of extreme violence. No means no. A rape conviction would lead to a jail sentence and a criminal record, which would ruin your life too.

Drinking alcohol can also destroy your liver leading to cirrhosis of the liver and death.

Alcohol's Damaging Effect on the Brain

According to the National Institute on Alcohol Abuse and Alcoholism, after one or two drinks, a person could experience difficulty walking or talking with slurred speech. They might also have blurred vision, impaired memory or slowed reaction times. Heavy drinking over a long period of time will cause a person to have brain deficits that remain long after the person "gives up" drinking alcohol.[141]

Blackouts and Memory Lapses

You can also experience blackouts and memory loss after only a couple of drinks. White and colleagues[142] surveyed 772 college undergraduates about their experiences with blackouts and asked, "Have you ever awoken after a night of drinking not able to remember things that you did or places that you went?" Here is what they learned:

> Of the students who had ever consumed alcohol, 51 percent reported blacking out at some point in their lives, and 40 percent reported experiencing a blackout in the year before the survey. Of those who reported drinking in the 2 weeks before the survey, 9.4 percent said they blacked out during that time. The students reported learning later that they had participated in a wide range of potentially dangerous events they could not remember, including vandalism, unprotected sex, and driving.

Needless to say, this is dangerous behavior for your brain, the rest of your body, and other people.

Alcohol and Your Baby's Developing Brain

If you plan to get married someday and have children, you must be aware of the correlation between pregnant women drinking alcohol and Fetal Alcohol Syndrome (FAS). If your wife drinks alcohol during pregnancy, your baby's brain may be severely damaged – learning could be severely impaired, and your child's behavior could be adversely affected.[143] Also, if your pregnant wife drinks alcohol, your developing baby may develop many abnormalities including the facial features of babies with FAS (which will be a constant reminder that someone had poor judgment). According to the Mayo Clinic, here are some of the abnormalities one might be saddened to see:

* Small eyelid openings
* Short, upturned nose.
* Smooth surface between the nose and upper lip
* Small head
* Vision difficulties and hearing problems[144]

* Solution: Encourage your wife not to drink alcohol when she is pregnant. (We do not drink any alcohol.)

Brain Danger #6 - Caffeine - America's Favorite Drug

What Caffeine Does To Your Brain and Body

Caffeine is a clever drug. It tricks your body into thinking that it is adenosine, which is a "neurotransmitter" inside your body. In order to work with your nervous system, neurotransmitters connect with neural receptors. Adenosine, in order to work correctly, needs to connect with its own specific receptor. Caffeine and adenosine have a very similar chemical structure, and in fact, caffeine binds to your adenosine receptors easier than adenosine can! So it is not difficult for caffeine to trick your brain into thinking that caffeine is adenosine. Generally, you need adenosine to help you fall asleep. It dilates blood vessels to make sure you get enough oxygen while you sleep. But when you intake lots of caffeine by drinking coffee, tea, or energy drinks, adenosine cannot be absorbed by the adenosine receptors because the caffeine blocks the adenosine receptors in your brain. Because your neural circuits are now stimulated by caffeine, your body produces more adrenaline - the "fight-or-flight" hormone. This artificially keeps you awake, but this kind of stimulation is harmful to their body because it disrupts natural pathways.

After this artificial stimulation wears off, people start to feel tired or groggy, so they need to drink more coffee to start the cycle over again.

Researchers at McGill University point out that, "In general, you get some stimulating effect from every cup of coffee you drink, and any tolerance you build up is minimal. On the other hand, caffeine can create a physical dependency. The symptoms of withdrawal from caffeine begin within one or two days after you stop consuming it. They consist mainly of headaches, nausea, and sleepiness and affect about one out of every two individuals."[145]

If that's not enough, then realize that caffeine knows how to get you hooked and hooked very well. It also makes the experience a very pleasant one for you by stimulating the reward centers of the brain. McGill researchers continue, "... like most drugs, caffeine increases the production of dopamine in the brain's pleasure circuits, thus helping to maintain the dependency on this drug."[146] In other words, caffeine is addictive!

If you are a person like my wife you are not likely to become addicted to caffeine – when she drinks coffee she gets heart palpitations, and the next day and for days afterwards she feels that she has no energy. When she stopped drinking coffee as a young woman, she had an abundance of energy.

Sources of Caffeine Are Increasing

One expert agreed that caffeine intake by children was worrisome. Dr. Marielys Rodriguez Varela[147], a pediatrician at Miami Children's Hospital, said caffeine's potential effects include a rapid heartbeat, high blood pressure, and anxiety.

Varela is also concerned about obesity in those who consume coffee, soda, energy drinks that contain so much sugar. In her words, "You create a habit that will be difficult to cut off. It's not just caffeine, but all the side effects that come along with it."

Despite FDA warnings about the dangers of energy drinks like Red Bull, Monster, Rock Star, and others, sales are high which means kids are consuming them more and more. The only good news there is that sales of soda pop drinks are declining.

"Caffeine doesn't have a place in the diet of any child or adolescent," Varela said, echoing policies set forth by the American Academy of Pediatrics.

Instead of caffeinated drinks, children should drink water and moderate amounts of juice.

If they need extra energy, they can always get a boost from exercise. "Children should focus on healthy habits, not supplements that do not make us healthier," Varela said.

Effects of Caffeine on Your Brain and Nervous System

In the article "Are Energy Drinks Really That Bad", Anna Medaris Miller[148] writes, "Energy drinks are linked to heart and neurological problems, poor mental health and substance abuse among teenagers."

Studies at the University of Washington[149] outline the impact of caffeine on your nervous system:

* Increases alertness
* Reduces fine motor coordination
* Causes insomnia
* Causes headaches, nervousness, and dizziness
* Massive doses of caffeine can be lethal

My Caffeine Addiction

Before I was baptized and allowed to join my church, I needed to rid myself of unacceptable habits. Drinking alcohol, smoking, and drinking caffeine were not allowed, so I needed to cleanse myself of these things in order to be baptized. I didn't smoke - so no problem there. I routinely had wine at dinner and sometimes a beer or two, and I had no problem quitting. I quit both cold turkey. But I habitually drank 3-4 cups of coffee each day, and it was almost impossible to stop! When I tried to stop all at once, I experienced massive headaches and became quite irritable. So, I started drinking one cup per day less, and I substituted decaffeinated coffee as much as I could, which still contains traces of caffeine. I continued to reduce my total amount of caffeine intake, and my body was not happy about it; however, I was determined and highly motivated because of my faith in God and my desire to please Him. Eventually, I was drinking only decaf coffee and was able to quit altogether because, really, what's the point of drinking decaf? The taste isn't really that great and I no longer "needed" the energy boost. I found that with more exercise and a better diet, I did not need caffeine after all. So I was able to be baptized with a clear conscience. Two years on, I sometimes felt that I wanted to have a cup of coffee or a glass of wine (because my mortal body remembers the feelings), but my mind and spirit were able to overcome the temptations and restrain myself from consuming these forbidden substances. Now five years later, I have no such desires whatsoever. I also know that my body is much happier and healthier after giving up caffeine and alcohol.

What frightens me is that kids are now downing coffee, tea, and energy drinks on a regular basis.

Living in the Seattle area, Starbucks stores and other coffee shops are plentiful. Usually, they have drive-up service. Having moved here from the Midwest, I have noted on average how aggressively people drive, how much they tailgate and how impatient they are behind the wheel. I wonder how much of that is due to caffeine addiction?

Check the *Elevate Yourself to Manhood* website at http://www.elevateyourselftomanhood.com/videos for the availability of videos on two videos about how caffeine affects the body:

Video #1: The Science of Caffeine: The World's Most Popular Drug - Reactions (produced by American Chemical Society)

Video #2: Your Brain on Coffee (produced by AsapSCIENCE)

Brain Danger # 7 - Television and Too Much Screen Time

Did you know that watching too much television can impair your learning later in life? Do you sit in front of the TV for hours at a time? Is your education suffering as a result of this screen time activity? There is now evidence that if you watch TV three or four hours per day, it is highly likely that your current and future educational performance will suffer.

Daniel Wood, Staff Writer for the Christian Science Monitor, wrote in his article, *For Teens, Too Much TV Can Impair Learning Later, Study Says*, ". . . watching three or more hours of television a day leads to poor homework completion, negative attitudes toward school, bad grades, and poor performance in college."

"We found a very clear correlation between higher levels of TV watching by 14-year-olds and subsequent attention and learning problems developed during the remainder of their years," says Jeffrey Johnson, lead author of the study in the Archives of Pediatrics and Adolescent Psychiatry.

According to Wood, "The study followed 700 families for 19 years, and the same people were interviewed at ages 14, 16, 22, and 33 in upstate New York."

So, this is excellent evidence that "excessive" amounts of TV watching are also harmful to your well-being as a young man. This does not prove a direct onslaught onto your brain, but a more indirect barrier to your advancement on your quest to becoming a well-adjusted adult. It's great for you to relax sometimes and have fun watching educational, entertaining, sporting, or other events on TV (not porn, though), but limit your time. Do not allow TV to take time from other activities that might be more useful. Again, as my father told me during his lifetime, **USE YOUR OWN BEST JUDGMENT**.

Just to recap BEWARE of: (1) Bullying, (2) Internet Addiction and Gaming Addiction, (3) Pornography Addiction, (4) Drug Use, Abuse and Addiction, (5) Alcohol Use, Abuse and Addiction, (6) Caffeine, (7) Television and too much Screen Time.

This concludes the Seven Brain Dangers. Now that you know how to guard against damage to your brain let us look at how to boost it up! We will see a number of ways that will improve your well-being, your perceptions, and a whole lot more. So, hold on!

THE NINE TYPES OF INTELLIGENCES

Howard Gardner[150] is a psychologist and Professor at Harvard University's Graduate School of Education. Gardner developed the theory of multiple intelligences by studying hundreds of people over an extended period of time from many different walks of life. His methods included interviews and brain research including stroke victims, prodigies, autistic individuals, and so-called "idiot savants."

Gardner's theory is that each person's brain is comprised of multiple types of intelligence, nine to be exact. In 1983, when he first wrote about his theory in his book *Frames of Mind*, he identified seven intelligences, but in 1999 he added two more to his book *Intelligence Reframed*. Gardner contends that industrial societies overemphasized three intelligences: linguistic, mathematic logic, and spatial, but they virtually ignored other forms of human problem solving. The theory that our education system is based on, assumes that we are all born with the same type of intelligence – and only two types (see below). He disagrees.

Gardner claims that each individual has all nine intelligence types but in different amounts.

The following chart provided by Gardner[151] summarizes the nine intelligences and the suggested skills and career preferences. Which intelligences do you think most pertains to you?

Intelligence	Skills and Career Preferences
Verbal-Linguistic Intelligence Well-developed verbal skills and sensitivity to the sounds, meanings and rhythms of words.	**Skills** – Listening, speaking, writing, teaching **Careers** – Poet, journalist, writer
Mathematical-Logical Intelligence Ability to think conceptually and abstractly, and capacity to discern logical or numerical patterns	**Skills** - Problem solving (logical & math), performing experiments **Careers** - Scientists, engineers, accountants, mathematicians
Musical Intelligence Ability to produce and appreciate rhythm, pitch and timber	**Skills** - Singing, playing instruments, composing music **Careers** - Musician, disc jockey, singer, composer

Visual-Spatial Intelligence Capacity to think in images and pictures, to visualize accurately and abstractly	**Skills** - puzzle building, painting, constructing, fixing, designing objects **Careers** - Sculptor, artist, inventor, architect, mechanic, engineer, designer
Bodily-Kinesthetic Intelligence Ability to control one's body movements and to handle objects skillfully	**Skills** - Dancing, sports, hands on experiments, acting **Careers** - Athlete, PE teacher, dancer, actor, firefighter
Interpersonal Intelligence Capacity to detect and respond appropriately to the moods, motivations and desires of others	**Skills** - Seeing from other perspectives, empathy, counseling, co-operating **Careers** - Counselor, salesperson, politician, business person, minister
Intrapersonal Intelligence Capacity to be self-aware and in tune with inner feelings, values, beliefs and thinking processes	**Skills** - Recognize one's *S/W, reflective, aware of inner feelings **Careers** - Researchers, theorists, philosophers
Naturalist Intelligence Ability to recognize and categorize plants, animals and other objects in nature	**Skills** - Recognize one's connection to nature, apply science theory to life **Careers** – Scientist, naturalist, landscape architect
Existential Intelligence Sensitivity. Capacity to tackle deep questions about human existence, such as the meaning of life, why do we die, and how did we get here	**Skills** – Reflective and deep thinking, design abstract theories **Careers** – Scientist, philosopher, theologian

So as you can see, intelligence covers many different skill sets. If you think you are lousy in one area, then you might be outstanding in another one. Your job now is to identify the areas in which you can shine like the superstar that you are! Why not expand your circle of influence and delve into all nine areas? Be proactive and take control to see which areas you like best. Otherwise, you will be leaving your destiny up to chance. Do not let anyone EVER tell you that you are dumb. Discover your true worth, and your hidden talents!

MIND OVER MATTER – LEARNING NEW SKILLS AND BUILDING GOOD HABITS

Before you act, listen.
Before you react, think.
Before you spend, earn.
Before you criticize, wait.
Before you pray, forgive.
Before you quit, try.

-- ERNEST HEMINGWAY

Open up you knapsack and prepare to load up on a cache of new tools and skills to keep you on track and increase your momentum as you ascend to the summit on your quest to manhood.

MANAGING STRESS

We realize that stress can get in the way of self-improvement, especially if you are always being pounded by demands from daily life. We recognize and respect your plight and want to help you confront stress and deal with it effectively. So muster up some self-discipline and let's dive in. We are cheering for you! You are in our prayers. To start, let's try to avoid self-inflicted stress. This will put you miles ahead.

Identifying the Symptoms of Stress

When people are stressed they are more prone to fatigue, stomach pains, problems sleeping, illness, and depression. Stress can get in the way of self-improvement, especially if you are being pounded by demands from daily life. We recognize and respect your plight and want to help you confront stress and deal with it effectively. So muster up some self-discipline and let's dive in. We are cheering for you! You are in our prayers.

Your brain has an alarm system to protect you from things perceived as dangerous or stressful. Whenever you encounter a situation that your brain perceives as dangerous or stressful, your brain fires off an alert for your adrenal glands to release a burst of adrenaline. This action is called the "fight-or-flight" response. Cumulative stress can wear you down and cause mental and physical illness. Let us now explore some of the many ways teens can experience stress.

The Causes of Teen Stress

The website *Family First Aid – Help for Troubled Teens* states that "Teen stress can come from many different areas: it depends on what contexts the child moves in and what the expectations are for him or her." Please check below to see if any of these stressors pertain to you:

* **The Changes of Adolescence** - If your body develops faster or slower than most of your friends' this can cause tensions among your friends and yourself. When you are a teenager, it is important to fit in and be liked by your peers. As you grow, and your hormones cause changes in your body, this can be a source of stress causing a feeling of being out of control and a loss of self-identity.

- **Family Issues** - Tensions between parents like separation, divorce, parental infidelity, can cause teen stress. So can a parent who is not present in your life. Alcoholism, drug abuse, poverty, may all cause stress for teens. Verbal or physical abuse can generate stress that is only one part of a much larger set of problems.

  Sometimes parents live vicariously through their children – perhaps having expectations that are quite lofty – causing teen stress. You may feel that you not only have to fulfill your parents' dreams, but you have your entire family's hopes resting on your shoulders.

- **School** – If you have difficulty in school, whether or not you have a learning disability, school can cause a lot of stress. If you aspire to go to a university that requires excellent grades, you may feel extra pressure to achieve. That's good stress, yes? But this is stress nonetheless. It counts.

- **Social Issues** - The ups and down of friendship and dating can often cause stress for you. If you are hoping for acceptance from your peers or romantic love while trying to balance your own developing personality with perceptions and expectations of your peers, you might find the challenge stressful. Another issue is that you may worry not only about your problems but also about your friends' problems. If you are bullied, whether in person or via cyberbullying, this is likely to cause both stress and distress. Arguing with someone can also cause stress.

- **College Applications** - Your whole future lies open before you. Applying to colleges or universities is pivotal for every other aspect of your future life. This is significant step in your life. The long waiting period for replies causes stress for both you and your parents. So apply early to reduce stress. You may want to apply to three or four colleges or universities to give yourself a better chance of being accepted.

- **Transition** - Making the transition to high school, to learning how to drive, to holding down your first job, to getting into college and taking on increased responsibility, to moving away from home can cause major stress. This could all happen by the time you reach 18 years of age.

* **Fear** - If you live in a neighborhood where you are exposed to drug dealers, bigotry, gang activity, and so forth, this could lead to stress. Even if your area is generally safe, but you have been mugged or robbed, you may experience stress as well. Being bounced from one foster home to another can cause stress, especially when past environments in care have been less than healthy.

* **Sorrow**--The loss of a loved person or pet can result in both grief and stress.

* **Responsibility**--Having to care for others when one is still growing up oneself can cause stress. This can result from caring for younger siblings, a disabled or substance abusing parent or a failing grandparent.[152]

    Note: **Your Daycare Experience** is a factor my wife and author of *Bullies and Denial Kill*, Elaine J. Barbeau,[153] would add: Much of the stress you feel today may be related to your own pain-body of stress caused by the years you spent in daycare centers. (The book mentioned above explains this in more detail than we can cover in this book.) Briefly, many of you spent every day of the work week in daycare centers in your early years – your formative years. You may, or you may not remember your experience in daycare. It is important for you to know that your experience in daycare may have been one of "change overload" and "emotional overload," as it was, and is, for thousands of young children. David Elkind wrote about these detrimental states in great detail in his book, *The Hurried Child-Growing Up Too Fast Too Soon*154.

    The stresses you feel today may be the tip of the iceberg. The lower part of the iceberg is the pain-body of stress that you endured during your early years. Any stress that you experience today may trigger feelings of stress that you experienced in your early childhood – this compounds your feelings of stress in the present. You may have cried for hours when your parents dropped you off at the daycare center. You may have been bullied – bitten and scratched by other unhappy children. The noise level in the daycare center may have exceeded a healthy level. Your educator may have been a different person every six months. You may have developed aggressive behaviors in daycare. Ask your parents what daycare was like for you. How did the care providers treat you? How did the other children treat you? How did you behave? Understanding your past may help you to figure out why you feel so stressed in the present, and may help you to realize that most of the stress that you are feeling occurred long ago. Being aware of the severe stress that you experienced when you were a baby and a young child will help you to heal that pain. Once you have healed past wounds, you will be able to control your mind to live and feel what is happening in the present. You may be able to go through this process on your own, or with a caring psychologist. Pray to God and he will also help to lighten your burden. Getting rid of the lower part of the "stress iceberg" will enable you to have room for real tools in your knapsack as you continue on your quest to manhood.

Stress Can Lead to Chronic Fatigue Syndrome

If you become stressed out for a long period of time, you might develop Chronic Fatigue Syndrome. Monitor yourself and make sure it doesn't happen to you. There is no single test for Chronic Fatigue Syndrome (CFS) that can determine if you have it or not. Make sure that someone does not misdiagnose your condition and convince you that you are DEPRESSED when you may actually have CFS. If you get diagnosed with depression doctors may start prescribing anti-depressant medication unnecessarily. Being chronically fatigued and not able to do everything that you would like to do is difficult. It can lead to feeling sad about feeling weak. However, the sadness did not necessarily cause the chronic fatigue. It could be that too much stress caused the chronic fatigue, and the chronic fatigue is causing you to feel sad. Taking anti-depressants and going back to the stressful environment (such as bullying in school) or a stressful routine (too many activities), when you are chronically fatigued, will not help you. If you are being bullied at school, then homeschooling might be an option. Many adolescents have committed suicide while taking anti-depressants. Just be aware of these possibilities and make sure you point them out to your parents or caregivers. You may just be exhausted. Your body, adrenal glands, thyroid gland and your mind may just need time to heal, and you may need to change your environment or routine. Seek the advice of a licensed naturopath. Remember to mention stressors in your life that may have triggered chronic fatigue.

The Mayo Clinic says on its site regarding teen depression, "antidepressants carry a Food and Drug Administration (FDA) black box warning regarding a possible risk of increased suicidal behavior in some individuals under the age of 25."[155]

Symptoms of Chronic Fatigue Syndrome (CFS)

Many people who are bullied experience symptoms of Chronic Fatigue Syndrome. The principal symptoms of CFS are:

- Constant fatigue or exhaustion
- Joint and muscle pain with no apparent cause
- Occasional bursts of energy, followed by a return of pain and exhaustion
- Inability to concentrate
- Poor mental recall for words, sentence construction, etc.
- Mood swings which include anger and depression
- Difficulty in learning new information
- Imbalances in smell, taste, and appetite
- Dislike of loud noises and bright lights
- Inability to control body temperature
- Sleep disturbance - for example, sleeping by day and waking at night

- Losing balance
- Clumsiness, for instance, unable to grasp small objects, inability to separate sheets of paper

How to Mitigate Stress

Once a threat is over, your body will attempt to return to normal, but in today's world, you might find that your "Threat Alert" is going off constantly. This is why stress management is so important. You need a break from this! Stress management gives you tools that can reset your alert system.

Without stress management, high levels of stress can lead to serious physical and mental health problems. Do not wait until the stress has compounded on you to the point where you cannot cope. Start practicing a range of stress management techniques today."[156]

Keep in mind that in life there is good stress and bad stress. Planning for a wedding is an example of good stress, the death of a favorite pet is an example of bad stress. Stress in life is unavoidable at times but it can be managed.

You will feel better about your life if you manage stress by using the following stress management techniques. Managing stress is a key to having a balanced and happy life.

1. **Avoiding Self-Inflicted Stress**. To begin with, if you can avoid self-inflicted stress you will likely feel that your life is a lot less stressful – and you will be, figuratively, miles ahead. By managing self-inflicted stress, I mean avoid creating stressful situations, such as procrastinating until you have a mountain of work to do. **Action Must Come Before Motivation**. We acknowledge that sometimes, stress alone can make you feel tired, unhappy, anxious, and unmotivated. It is probably not your fault at all that you are stressed out or tired or unhappy. Life just happens. It could be your fault, but it doesn't really matter.

If you are just waiting for motivation to happen when you feel this way, you may be waiting for a long time because simply waiting is not necessarily the best strategy. Here's another news flash for you: ACTION MUST COME BEFORE MOTIVATION. Yes, you must take action first! Motivation will not just come to you. Just break the cycle – use your spirit to take control of your mind and take control of the situation. Realize your greatness within. Make a mental plan, write it down and then take action, Sir! "When mood is low, motivation follows action, rather than the other way around."[157]

2. **Get yourself organized**
   * <u>Get Rid of Clutter</u> – throw out the garbage in you room and in your drawers, give away clothes that you never wear to Goodwill, make room for your good life.
   * <u>Employ Delayed Gratification.</u> Don't let temptations get in your way. Get your work done first. If there is a job that you dislike, do a little each day even if you are not feeling well. For example, cleaning your room for 10 minutes each day is easier than having to spend one hour cleaning on Saturday morning.

3. **Practice mindfulness**. By doing this, you will be able to identify when your body is being stressed and remember how to deal with it. Remember to breathe deeply and relax every part of your body.

4. **Pray**. As I stress throughout this book, prayer also helps. Ask God to help you. God will help you find peace within yourself, which will help you manage stress. We will teach you how to pray, if you do not already know, in Facet 4: *Elevate Your Spirit.*

Ask, and it shall be given you; seek, and ye shall find; knock, and it shall be opened unto you.

– Matthew 7:7 KJV

192

Keep in mind that God may not coordinate help for you right away when you ask for help. Sometimes you may be given life challenges to help you to grow stronger - even as trees must learn to resist strong winds while they are young so that they can grow strong enough to endure adverse weather conditions after they become taller and more mature. Keep praying and have faith that help will come. In the meantime, keep taking action. If you are praying for a job, keep applying for jobs. As the saying goes, "God helps those who help themselves." If you need a student loan, but you do not bother to apply for a loan, you probably will not obtain one regardless of how much you stress about it. After you have done all that you can do, God will help you, especially if you ask in prayer, have sincere intent, and have a righteous heart. The help may come as physical help, monetary help, wise counsel, a new friendship, or some other form. These signs are some of God's ways of communicating with you. Learn God's language. We will teach you about God's language in Facet 4: *Elevate Your Spirit.*

5. **Make your bed every morning**! During a commencement speech at the University of Texas, Navy Seal, Naval Admiral William H. McRaven, Ninth Commander of the Special Operation Command, stated that when he was in training to become a Navy Seal, his bed was inspected every morning - even though they were "aspiring to be real warriors, tough, hardened Seals." He has found that, if you make your bed every morning it will encourage you to accomplish another task during the day, and then another, and another. "The little things in life matter. If you are able to do the little things right, then you will be able to do the big things right." He added, "And if you have a bad day - when you come home to a neatly made bed you will feel that tomorrow will be a better day."[158] I feel that making your bed is a small way to love yourself, and to feel proud that you have what it takes to be self-disciplined, like a Navy Seal, which helps to alleviate stress.

193

6. **Question Your Thoughts** – Your thoughts are not always right, especially if they make you feel bad.
7. **Live in the Now** – Live in the present moment – don't dwell on past painful experiences or only live for the future.
8. **Make Time for Personal Interests and Hobbies** - When I get stressed, I find that simply breaking out my bass guitar puts me in a better mood and reduces my stress levels. After a couple hours of following along on songs from iTunes, I feel happy and more relaxed. You may have another hobby, such as skateboarding, playing hacky sack, or creating origami that does the same for you.

The American Academy of Child & Adolescent Psychiatry offers the following behaviors and techniques to help manage your stress:

1. Get proper exercise and eat regular balanced meals. Eat lots of salads, including vegetables, berries, and nuts. Go for a walk each day as a start. We will cover exercise in more detail later in the book.
2. Avoid caffeine which can increase feelings of anxiety and agitation.
3. Avoid illegal drugs, alcohol, and tobacco.
4. Learn relaxation exercises (abdominal breathing and muscle relaxation techniques).
5. Develop assertiveness training skills. For example, state feelings in polite firm and not overly aggressive or passive ways: ("I feel angry when you yell at me" or "Please stop screaming.")
6. Rehearse and practice for situations that cause stress. One example is taking a speech class if talking in front of a class makes you anxious, or joining Toast Masters.
7. Learn practical coping skills. For example, learn how to break down large jobs into a series of smaller tasks.

8. Decrease negative self-talk. Do not let negative thoughts about yourself take over. Substitute alternative, neutral or positive thoughts instead. "My life will never get better" can be transformed into "I may feel hopeless now, but my life will probably get better if I work at it and get some help."

9. Learn to feel good about doing a competent or "good enough" job rather than demanding perfection from yourself and others.

10. Take a break from stressful situations. Activities like listening to music, talking to a friend, drawing, writing, or spending time with a pet, can reduce stress. Helping someone else can also relieve stress.

11. Build a network of friends who help you cope in a positive way. [159]

How to Enjoy Life Even Though It Tends to Be Stressful – Developing a Joie de Vivre

Serenity Prayer
God grant me the serenity to accept the things I cannot change, the courage to change the things I can, and the wisdom to know the difference.

– REINHOLD NIEBUHR

The French expression, *Joie de vivre*, is defined as having an exuberant enjoyment of life. You can develop a joie de vivre and enjoy life even through stressful times if you follow this sage advice:

* Develop a sense of humor. My wife has owned a beautiful, massive German wall unit for many years. This monster is ten feet wide and seven feet tall. It has thirteen doors including a huge, decorative glass door in its center. After we moved into our new house, we had almost finished re-assembling her wall unit

including the glass door, except for the back panel, which we were screwing onto the back of the wall unit when the whole thing began to wobble. It tilted forward, and then came crashing down – seemingly in slow motion – hitting a chandelier, landing partially onto a leather sofa, and broke apart. Immediately, my wife and I began to laugh in disbelief, because the scene was so absurd. Upon close inspection, we noticed that the glass door was unbroken and the chandelier was intact, miraculously. Most of the damage to the wall unit occurred inside the wall unit. It was a shame that it was damaged but the damage could have been a lot worse. The wall unit was still functional with the help of a few metal braces in the interior, and the magic of a wood stain marker. Mostly, we were very grateful that no one was hurt.

* Love someone. Preferably love many people – your parents, siblings, extended family, friends, your wife, and your children. Remember love is an action word. Show them that you love them. Most importantly, be kind and generous with your time.
* Exude a balanced spirit of good sportsmanship and competitiveness in sport, business, and other areas of life. Not everyone can be the best all the time. Be honest and realistic with yourself, and very joyful when you become the best you can be.
* Realize that during one lifetime one cannot be and do all things. In retrospect, I would have loved to have become a singing star and a surgeon. I was quite passionate about becoming a computer scientist because when I studied at university computers were the "new frontier." I was pleased with my career path because it afforded me a good life and sustained my family. There just isn't enough time to do everything. That is why it is important to choose wisely, when you are young, where you will give your life energy and your time. That way you will not have any regrets.
* Follow your passion.
* Recite the *Serenity Prayer* and integrate it into your life.

* Be joyful about living in a democratic country and having the freedoms that we enjoy.

Man's capacity for justice makes democracy possible, but man's inclination to injustice makes democracy necessary.

- REINHOLD NIEBUHR

BEWARE OF MENTAL BLIND SPOTS

We all have mental blind spots, and the following fun exercise will test to see if you have a particular one that most people have.

This is a Perception/IQ Test presented by the English Language Smart Words website.[160]

How many "F"s are there in the sentence below? Do not rush. <u>Count the Fs one time only.</u>

FINISHED FILES ARE THE RESULT OF YEARS OF SCIENTIFIC STUDY COMBINED WITH THE EXPERIENCE OF YEARS.

So how many did you count? Most people count only three "Fs." The results of this test say a lot about your perception, but it does not address your IQ. Some say that if you counted six 'Fs' the first time that is genius, five is rather rare, four is rather frequent, and three is normal. Less than three, and you need glasses, or you need to change the ones you're wearing.

The Smart Words website explains that for some obscure reasons, "we (or our brain) do not count the 'f' in 'of', maybe because the phonetic is similar to 'ov', or because during (quick) reading the brain focus on 'lexical' words, and not so much on 'grammatical' words. The point of this exercise is more than having fun. It is also to show how the brain can play tricks on you by giving you "blind spots."

If you liked the last exercise, you should love the next one.

Divergent Thinking
Take your time and count the number of balls in this picture.

Divergent Thinking
(Courtesy of La Fleur Publishing)

Did you count 5 balls?

If you did, you are correct.

But now, look away from the picture and think.

Is there anything particularly unusual about the image?

Now look at the picture again and see the hands. Did you notice how many fingers the man has? Take a closer look and count them if you have not already done that. Did you notice how many fingers the man had the first time you looked at the picture – or when we asked you to count the number of balls? Initially, we got your mind focused on counting the balls because that was your primary task. We purposely tried to distract your attention away from the number of fingers he had. We didn't ask you to look for anything unusual in the picture and report it, so perhaps your mind filtered out everything else.

The reason why we gave you this exercise is to give you a baseline view of the way most people observe and think. To elevate your mind, you will need to develop the skill of divergent thinking in which you will always be on your guard for information and data points to enhance your creativity and help you get control of your world.

Your future success in school and in the professional world will depend not only on what you know but how you can apply what you know to different situations and in creative ways. In addition, it will be critical for you to see all facets and possibilities in your environment as they truly are – for then you will be able to analyze various factors, to choose a variety of possibilities, to solve problems creatively – as in identifying good – better – best solutions.

Judy Willis MD, M.Ed., in her article *Build Your Child's Convergence*, tells us that, "The job market is fiercely competitive these days and employers are looking to get the most bang for their buck when they hire employees. They want employees who cannot only do their jobs well but employees that can "think outside the box." Colleges and universities, especially the elite ones, look to admit the brightest and most talented students as well. They want students who have the capacity to learn and excel at new skills. One new area of human development is "divergent thinking, which is the ability for a person to see beyond the target of their attention and scan the environment for unexpected or opportunistic things."[161]

Willis warns us that, "Success in the 21st century requires not just thinking outside the box, but also perceiving beyond the contents of the box. She indicates that the skills that will become more important in the future are:

* Using judgment
* Logical reasoning
* Prioritizing tasks
* Risk Assessment
* Critical analysis
* Cognitive flexibility in solving new types of problems

This is the essence of divergent thinking, and it will require you to be self-motivated and action-oriented. You must start early in your life and in your career to develop these skills. Learn how to use information in creative ways. Learn how to communicate effectively new ideas and findings to your colleagues and superiors in a way that stimulates their imagination. It will be much harder to learn these skills if you are addicted to video games, the Internet, or pornography – activities that have been shown to kill your self-motivation and consume large blocks of time.

You need to begin to develop:

* Your brainpower muscles
* Your ability to pay attention to detail
* Your analytical skills
* Your creative skills, and
* Your responsibility muscles in order to have a successful quest to manhood.

The BSA is a great organization in which to learn how to think divergently. The following is a practical example of divergent thinking:

Divergent Example

"I live four miles from work. My car gets 30 MPG. I want to use less fuel in my commute for financial and conservation reasons. Money is no object. What options do I have to reduce my fuel consumption?

"The problem is the same, but the questions change slightly. The Convergent example asks for a vehicle, whereas the Divergent example doesn't rule out options like moving closer to work, telecommuting, walking, carpooling, taking public transportation, etc.

"Both examples will produce valuable results. The convergent example may be driven by another issue – perhaps my current car was totaled and I only have a weekend to solve the problem. The divergent example may take more time to investigate – but you may discover an option that is completely different than what the user has asked you to do – like start your own company from home or invent a car that runs off of air. Or, if your brain works like Mike's did when I asked for an illustration, you may expose your inner Inspector Gadget. "[162]

Another fine example of divergent thinking is the resourcefulness of the scientists who managed to bring the Apollo 13 astronauts back to Earth after their spaceship underwent a devastating malfunction while en route to the moon. You can watch the movie *Apollo 13* to get a sense of their ordeal and their genius in using divergent thinking to solve the problem.

Our Education System May Be Failing You

If you did not notice the extra fingers, in the last exercise, it's not your fault. This could be a problem with our educational experiences over past decades. So how did our educational system promote this type of "blindness?" Perhaps it is the way that the system has encouraged single answers instead of more thoughtful, complete answers. This kind of rote learning is a remnant of the Industrial Age training, which served to train people mainly for factory jobs. Perhaps this has limited our brains ability to "stick to the facts" and ignore anything else.

This also goes back to mindfulness as we introduced it earlier - being more present or being more aware. The ability to broaden and deepen our minds will be a critical skill as we continue through the 21st century.

You Must Learn to Tolerate Ambiguity, Uncertainty, and the Risk of Making Mistakes

You will need to live with ambiguity and uncertainty and be willing to take risks when analyzing problems and coming up with solutions.

The challenge for society is to provide a learning environment where you can learn to build cognitive flexibility - where everything is not cut-and-dried or black-and-white. Put another way, in order to develop divergent thinking, you will need to observe and read for yourself while looking for details; read or listen to the observations of enlightened persons; think for yourself, weighing many different factors; analyze and come to your own wise conclusions.

As a computer programmer most of my life, I spent a lot of time writing programs which were very structured and which handled very strict logic. Then leading industry thinkers asked, "Why can we not make computers think more like the human mind?" The field of heuristics was born. Computers were then expected to think "divergently." No doubt, this type of programming has now led to the proliferation of intelligent robots and artificial intelligence.

Think about IBM's computer, Watson, which "... thinks and acts a lot like humans do. As a cognitive computing system, Watson is a natural extension of what humans can do at their best."[163]

Learning from Mistakes

Babies learn to walk by falling down. Top athletes missed a lot of baskets, footballs, baseballs, and hockey pucks before they practiced, practiced, practiced and excelled. Do not be afraid of making mistakes. That is an excellent way to learn. I do not mean purposely going out and making mistakes. I mean making "honest mistakes" where you tried to do the right thing and made an error in the process. If we are smart, we will strive to learn from our mistakes.

Thomas Edison said when he tried to invent the light bulb, "I have not failed. I've just found 10,000 ways that won't work."

Bono, lead singer of the rock group U2, noted, "My heroes are the ones who survived doing it wrong, who made mistakes, but recovered from them."

Wayne Gretzky, the great hockey player, said, "You miss 100% of the shots you do not take."

Michael Jordan, one of the greatest basketball players who ever live said, "I've missed more than 9,000 shots in my career. I've lost almost 300 games. Twenty-six times, I've been trusted to take the game-winning shot and missed. I've failed over and over and over again in my life. And that is why I succeed."

Hopefully, your parents and teachers will balance their high expectations of you with giving you opportunities to make mistakes. As you make mistakes, you may discover gaps in your understanding of life, or you may feel inadequate in some of your abilities. Take these opportunities to improve yourself. Your brain will thank you because this process will increase your neuroplasticity. Your creativity, problem-solving skills, and confidence will soar as you leverage these learning and improvement opportunities.

CREATIVE PLAY

People just need to have plain old fun sometimes instead of being stuck in a routine with your every move planned out and choreographed. What would life be like if you never had any fun? Creative play is something you can incorporate into your life to break up the monotony or to add spark to mundane tasks. Having fun helps you be more creative, and creativity is one of those dynamic behavior traits that will become very valuable to you in the future, as shown in the earlier section on Divergent Thinking. We have mentioned that schools and employers will expect students and employees to be able to think more creatively and be able to apply their education and skill in innovative ways.

In a report by the Family Institute, IBM did a survey of 1,500 corporate CEOs and identified creativity as the number one "leadership competency" of the future. They also reported that since 1990, the creativity of American youth has been declining. For children between kindergarten and sixth grade, the decline is the most pronounced.[164]

The Connection between Play and Creativity

The Family Institute reports, "...child development experts believe there's a strong link between creative problem-solving in adult life and the "practice" youngsters receive during childhood play."[165] When you and your friends have free time to play or have fun, do so. You could create a new sport by combining two or more standard sports, like Frisbee Golf was invented. Use footballs, basketballs, golf balls, Frisbees, badminton nets, baseball gloves, bats and mitts, and use a little imagination. Name your new sport, design the field of play and resolve problems as they arise around your new sport. Encourage others to participate. Establish rules for the game. Discuss good sportsmanship. Have fun.

In past generations, kids were allowed and expected to play mostly outside the house. As a kid, I almost never lounged around inside the house, because first of all, my mom insisted that I play outside. Plus, all the action was outside anyway. It was boring staying inside the house. I could hop on my bike and ride up to the country store, or I could take a walk through the woods in search of adventure. My brothers and cousins and I would invent toys or games to keep us occupied and happy. I had almost complete liberty to do as I pleased as long as I did not get into trouble, got my chores done, and made it home in time for supper. Kids who lived in town had lots of freedom too. They could walk to community parks, or visit friends without parents worrying that the kids would encounter danger. However, nowadays urban life is much too dangerous for kids to wander or play outside alone. Perhaps this has led to an excuse to stay indoors and play video games and such. In either case, kids have less time for creative play outside the home.

There is a steady flow of research that affirms that unstructured play provides an essential foundation for a life of happiness and success.[166]

Do you suffer from Play Deficit Disorder? Do you ever get out in nature for unstructured play? A good solution may be to join the Boy Scouts. This will give you tons of opportunity to get out there and have fun doing enjoyable activities while improving your mind, body and spirit!

EMPATHY

Do you think you have empathy? Empathy is defined as the ability to understand and share the feelings of others. If you have empathy for other people, you should be able to see life from their perspective, or feel what they feel, or "walk a mile in their shoes." We have already talked about excessive video gaming - or any violent video games - and how they can rob you of empathy. You must learn to have empathy for people by interacting with them, for example, listening to them or having face-to-face conversations. To get along in civil society and in individual relationships, you must develop a sense of empathy. When you find your perfect future spouse she will probably expect you to have a relatively well-developed sense of empathy.

Even animals have empathy. Here are some examples:

* Elephants have funerals! When elephants experience the death of a loved one, they will bury the body with branches and leaves, and they will guard the body for one week. Like humans, they will keep returning to the gravesite of a loved one for years.

* Dolphins have rescued swimmers from Hammerhead sharks. They have been known to surround pregnant women swimming with them, ignoring other women swimming along with them. They are also very kind to the other dolphins in their pod.[167]

* Dogs have empathy: In his article in Psychology Today titled, *Canine Empathy: Your Dog Really Does Care If You Are Unhappy*, Stanley Coren Ph.D., wrote "People often report that it seems as if their dogs are reading their emotional state and responding in much the same way that a human would, providing sympathy and comfort, or joining in their joy." He went on to tell the story about an acquaintance named Deborah that told him she had just gotten off of the phone after learning that her sister's husband had died and was sitting on the sofa wiping tears from her eyes and trying to deal with her sadness. She said, "At that moment Angus [her Golden retriever]

came over to me and laid his head on my knee and began to whimper. A moment later he quietly walked away, and then returned with one of his favorite toys and quietly put it in my lap, and gently licked my hand. I knew he was trying to comfort me. I believe that he was feeling my pain and hoping that the toy that made him happy might also help me to feel better."[168]

If animals have such empathy, how much more important is it for humans to have empathy as well?

Developing a True Conscience

Developing an authentic conscience is a consequence of empathy. One aspect of having a conscience is the desire to avoid carrying out actions that will adversely affect yourself and others. We become concerned about others more than we are worried about ourselves, especially when others are in need, as the dolphins example above illustrates. We know we have a conscience when we feel remorseful after we have hurt someone else. Now you may think that you feel this way because your parents taught you to have a conscience when you were younger, but this is only part of the picture or part of the reason you care for others.

Monkey See Monkey Do and the Phenomenon of Mirror Cells

Before we talk further about empathy, let's learn about mirror cells.

Surprising discoveries about human neurons have been made in recent years. An Italian scientist, Giacomo Rizzolatti, and his team learned in the 1980s about mirror neurons, which help us humans employ empathy.

A graduate student on Rizzolatti's team went out for a break. When he came back into the room, he was eating an ice cream cone. There was a monkey strapped into an apparatus being used for clinical experiments (let's hope the monkey was not being harmed). The researchers were monitoring the monkey's brain activity on a machine. Much to their surprise, each time the graduate student licked the ice cream cone, the monkey's brain caused the electronic monitoring device to react, even though the monkey was motionless. They discovered that the monkey's mirror neurons were mimicking what the monkey saw through his eyes.[169]

This is how mirror neurons were discovered. It turns out that mirror neurons are not only the very basis for imitation; they are the "foundation for social interaction," as stated by Dr. Rizzolatti. In an article in the *New York Times* he said, "Mirror neurons allow us to grasp the minds of others not through conceptual reasoning but through direct simulation. By feeling - not by thinking."

Mirror Neurons Help to Create Empathy

According to Izzy Kalman[170], a Nationally Certified School Psychologist, we learned empathy through Mother Nature. Neuroscientists now claim that we have a conscience because we have mirror neurons.

Mirror neurons help babies to anticipate actions of other people by one year of age. For example, an infant will notice a father carrying slices of banana and will be able to follow the banana slices with his eyes, and look at his high chair, in anticipation that the banana slices will be placed on his high chair table.[171]

Do you smile when someone else smiles at you? Do you cringe when someone else yells out in pain? Do you laugh when others laugh? Ever wonder why people say that laughter is contagious?

So how does this relate to empathy and conscience? You cannot have empathy without mirror neurons, and you cannot have a conscience without empathy.

Mirror neurons are a small circuit of cells in the premotor cortex and inferior parietal cortex of the brain. Mirror neurons appear to be the only brain cells scientist currently know about that seem to be specialized enough to code the actions of other people and also our actions - brain cells specialized for social interactions.

In the article, *The Mirror Neuron Revolution: Explaining What Makes Humans Social* an interview for *Scientific American*, Iacoboni answers the following questions:

"LEHRER: If we're wired to automatically internalize the movements and mental states of others, then what does this suggest about violent movies, television programs, video games, etcetera? Should we be more careful about what we watch?

"IACOBONI: I believe we should be more careful about what we watch. This is a tricky argument, of course, because it forces us to reconsider our long-cherished ideas about free will and may potentially have repercussions on free speech. There is convincing behavioral evidence linking media violence with imitative violence. Mirror neurons provide a plausible neurobiological mechanism that explains why being exposed to media violence leads to imitative violence. What should we do about it? Although it is obviously hard to have a clear and definitive answer, it is important to openly discuss this issue and hopefully reach some kind of "societal agreement" on how to limit media violence without limiting (too much) free speech. "[172]

If mirror neurons can absorb/encode negative and violent codes of behavior they can also absorb/encode positive codes of behavior when a person watches uplifting movies; and documentaries, about heroes, interesting work, and interesting places to see. Positive codes of behavior are even more likely if the person also surrounds himself with people who behave well and are empathetic.

If you feel that you have a lack of empathy - you can enable yourself to become more empathic by being mindful of the company you keep, and the media you watch.

The Neurons that Shaped Civilization
The brain is made up of neurons. There are about 100 billion neurons in the human brain. Each neuron makes about 1,000 to 10,000 connections with other neurons in the brain. One can calculate the number of combinations and permutations in the brain and show that the number exceeds the number of elementary particles in the universe.

Motor command neurons have been known for over 50 years. Vilayanur Ramachandran, a neuroscientist, states that mirror neurons perform a virtual reality simulation of another person's actions. He claims that civilization and culture have grown by leaps and bounds via mirror neurons through imitation and emulation, for example,

1. Tool use
2. Fire
3. Shelter
4. Language
5. Theory of Mind

All these things happened very quickly because a human was able to observe another human and emulate these actions mentally. Whenever one member of society accidently discovered something it could be quickly disseminated to other members of the group horizontally to peers or vertically to generations. Ramachandran asserts that this is how culture developed.

During a TED talk on YouTube, Ramachandran gave the following example:

If you were to touch your own hand, your neurons fire and send a signal to your body saying that you have just been touched. If you watch someone else being touched, your mirror neurons fire and, via empathy, tell you that another person is being touched. You do not actually feel that touch yourself. Why do you not get confused when you watch someone else being touched? You empathize with that person, but you cannot actually feel the sensation of their touch. Your neurons send you a signal saying, "do not worry, you're not being touched." There is a feedback signal, which vetoes the signal of the mirror neuron so that you do not consciously experience the touch on the other person's body.

But if you have your arm severed or anesthetized, then watch another person being touched, you literally feel it on your arm. (This is called a phantom arm.) In other words, you dissolve the barrier between yourself and other human beings. This is not in some abstract or metaphorical sense. **All that separates you from other people is your skin. Remove your skin and you experience that person's touch in your mind. Ramachandran claims that there is no real independent self - aloof from other human beings inspecting the world and examining other people. From our basic understanding of neuroscience, you are in fact connected by neurons to other people.**

In another example, Ramachandran says, astonishingly, if you have pain in your phantom hand, and you squeeze or massage someone else's hand, you feel the pain relief in your phantom hand, almost as if your neurons were receiving relief from watching the other person's hand being massaged.

For the longest time, we considered science and humanities as being separate and distinct. It is Ramachandran's theory that the meta neuron system is the interface bridging the gap between science and humanities. This neuron system allows us to think about issues such as consciousness, representation of self, and what separates you from other human beings. This neuron system enables you to empathize with other humans. This neuron system has also enabled the emergence of culture and civilization, which is unique to people. [173]

Empathetic Teenagers Are More Likely to Succeed

In his article, *Are Empathetic Teenagers More Likely to Be Intentionally Successful*, Licensed Professional Counselor Ugo Uche asserted that teenagers who know how to be empathetic tend to succeed in school out of a strong desire to please themselves, their parents or elder relatives. Teenagers who lack empathy or struggle with it, tend to be more self-absorbed and less caring towards others, and ironically, themselves.[174] Therefore, they do not realize that they will benefit from doing well in school.

Uche stated that "Teenagers who are more empathetic do a much better job in embracing failure, because there is little ego involved in their tasks, and setbacks - while disappointing - are rarely seen as failures, but rather as a learning experience about an approach that does not work for the task at hand."[175]

We will talk a little more about this in the section on Optimism. Your thoughts and behavior affect people close to you, and that has a ripple effect, which will not only affect people close to you but will also affect the people close to the people who know you, now and in the future. You can look upon empathy as the will to nurture yourself and others.

Narcissistic People Lack Empathy

Beware of narcissistic people because they lack empathy. They are unable or unwilling to identify with or recognize the feelings of others. At their worst, they manipulate and use people to get what they want. Some of them will pretend to care for others but in reality, they care for their possessions more than they care for people. Narcissists do not consider the pain that they inflict on others.

Dr. Les Carter, in his book, *Enough of You, Let's Talk About Me* says about narcissists, "They simply do not care about thoughts and feelings that conflict with their own. Do not expect them to listen, validate, understand, or support you." [176]

So How Can You Develop Empathy and Expand Your Empathetic Potential?

Here are some ways you can create and nourish empathy as presented by Roman Krznaric in his article, *Six Habits of Highly Empathetic People*:

Habit 1: Become curious about strangers. Try talking to the person sitting next to you on the bus. Learn to find other people more interesting than yourself. Do not examine them. Instead, be genuinely interested in them. Without trusting too much, keep yourself safe – remain in a public place.

Habit 2: Do not make assumptions about people. Do not prejudge or label people before you come to know them.

Habit 3: Walk a mile in another person's shoes. Become that person. Try one of their hobbies. See the world through their eyes. Try this with your siblings or friends and they can try your hobbies.

Habit 4: Listen intently and keep an open mind towards others. Learn the skill of "active listening." Practice it incessantly. You may learn something. You may be pleasantly surprised that the person you are listening to is more interesting than you thought, more experienced than you thought, or kinder than you thought.

Habit 5: Support social change and inspire national or global action. Find a worthy cause and find other like-minded people to help. Empathy does not need to be strictly at an individual level. It can definitely be national or global.

Habit 6: Develop an ambitious imagination. Essentially, this means using empathy as an "instrument" to understand people who have different points of view and even those who may be enemies. Understanding people who are against your views, against your beliefs gives you an ability to think like them and, therefore, develop strategies to convince them to collaborate with you or to work out problems with you. [177] This is an important skill to have within your family, society, and in international affairs.

To Recap:

* Be aware of your dealings with narcissistic people.
* Please, please, please avoid excessive video gaming – especially violent ones, and violent movies.
* Make friends and interact with others. Practice empathy.
* Build empathy by using the six habits to develop empathy and expand your empathetic potential

Test Your Empathy Quotient

Empathy Quotient tests attempt to measure and rate how much empathy you have. These test are administered by highly trained psychologists. I feel that it would be worth your while to take one or two of these tests to see how much empathy you have. Evaluate the results of the test and look for recommendations on how to build more empathy.

LEARNED OPTIMISM

As the perennial question goes, do you see the glass as half empty or half full? Asked another way, do you have a positive outlook on life or do you usually see the negative side of things? It stands to reason that having a positive outlook on life is an important trait to have. We hope you have a natural tendency to see your life in a positive light. There is so much to be thankful for in this life. Even when things are going wrong, you can find and embrace the positive side of things. You may not always have a positive disposition, but this is another skill that you can learn.

You need optimism to help inoculate yourself against depression, which is rampant in our society. Yes, even young adults get depression for various reasons: nature deficit (not enough time in nature), play deficit (not enough unstructured time having plain old fun), stress, excessive screen time, and the list goes on. These things can weigh you down. No worries, you can learn how to gain a positive worldview if you are motivated.

By the way, the correct answer to the question above is "half full." I won't accept any other answer. Sorry.

When I was a boy, my dad would sometimes give me tasks that I found very difficult. After trying a few times, exasperated, I would usually give up and tell him that the job was "too hard." "I can't do it," would be my cry. Of course my dad would give me the old routine, "There ain't no such word as can't." What he was REALLY saying is stop giving up so quickly. "Think divergently." "Be creative." "Think outside the box." "Forget about the box and re-think the contents of the box." In other words, he wanted me to go back and keep trying until I had positively tried all avenues. He was encouraging me and imparting a positive outlook on the problem. Again, I am truly indebted to my dad for these values that I still embrace today.

As a naval officer, I learned early on never to present a problem to my superior officers without also having potential solutions and logical recommendations. Also, I learned that having a positive, can-do attitude and believing in myself gave me the tenacity to stick with a problem until I had a solution.

Dr. Martin Seligman, also known as the father of the new science of positive psychology, spent over twenty years studying individuals to understand how to help people increase their positivity. His contention is that anyone can learn it, thereby improving his or her quality of life. In his book, *Learned Optimism: How to Change Your Mind and Your Life*, Seligman offers many simple techniques on how to break the "I-give-up" habit.

Seligman made the following observations about people:

Optimists react to adverse life events from a presumption of power:

1. When bad events happen in life, optimists believe that they're just temporary setbacks. Things will get better.
2. Optimists believe that unfortunate events are just isolated incidents, and chances are they will not happen again.
3. Optimists believe they can overcome bad events using their own efforts, skills, and talents.

Pessimists, however, react to unfortunate life events from a position of helplessness:

1. When bad events happen in their life, pessimists believe the events will linger for a long time.
2. When bad events happen, pessimists believe that events will undermine everything that they do. They give up quickly.
3. Pessimists blame bad events on themselves.[178]

AVOIDING LEARNED HELPLESSNESS

Through his research Seligman found that when some people experience challenges over and over again, they "give up" and become helpless. He calls this "Learned Helplessness." He discovered this by studying dogs in a lab. When the "test" dogs were exposed to a series of small electric shocks they could not control, they would eventually become helpless. In other words, they <u>learned helplessness</u>.

Expanding his work to include humans, he found that about two-thirds of both animals and humans behaved the same way. When faced with a negative situation that they could not control, they would give up and become helpless. More alarming than that, Seligman found that if the animals or humans were placed in an entirely different environment with a different annoyance that they could not control, then they would immediately relinquish or cease to fight.

Curiously though, he found that one-third of all test subjects who were exposed to uncontrollable shocks NEVER became helpless. They were fighters and would simply shake off the annoyance. They never quit![179]

What would you do in such a situation? Would you quit right away or would you fight? Or would you be resilient, shake it off?

Whenever professional ball players make a mistake or have setbacks, their coaches tell them to "shake it off," or "forget about it." They get back out there and put their best foot forward. That is the better approach.

Seligman believes that learned helplessness is a big cause of depression in our population. By recognizing what learned helpless is, though, you can guard against it happening to you.

Having optimism or learning how to generate it at will can serve you well as you progress to university, to the professional world, and throughout your personal life.

SELF-RELIANCE

"There is a time in every man's education when
he arrives at the conviction that envy is ignorance;
that imitation is suicide; that he must take himself
for better, for worse, as his portion; that though
the wide universe is full of good, no kernel of
nourishing corn can come to him but through his toil
bestowed on that plot of ground which is given to
him to till. The power which resides in him is new

*in nature, and none but he knows what that is which
he can do, nor does he know until he has tried."*

— RALPH WALDO EMERSON, SELF RELIANCE

Manly men learn how to become self-reliant so they can take care of themselves and their families. This is what they do. My dad and my stepdad exemplified this trait as we have mentioned before. In their time, society expected that every man would be self-reliant. There was, most definitely, a stigma attached to a man who did not see the need to become self-reliant.

In today's world, men are still expected to at least make an effort at being self-reliant. Young men can join the Boy Scouts to learn skills that will help them become self-reliant. If you join the scouts, you will gain confidence in knowing that you can face many challenges that may come your way. Using Learned Optimism, you will become more resilient when life comes at you hard and fast. Also, if you subscribe to the Boy Scouts motto "Be Prepared" you will be able to anticipate needs for your family and yourself and be in a better position to prevail.

Some spiritual leaders have recognized the absolute importance of self-reliance and go out of their way to help prepare adolescents to become self-reliant. In the book, *Providing in the Lord's Way: Summary of a Leader's Guide to Welfare*, The Church of Jesus Christ of Latter-day Saints teaches us that "[Self-reliance] is an essential element of our worldly and spiritual well-being."[180]

A mere desire to become self-reliant is not enough. We must make a conscious, active effort to provide for our own needs and those of our families.[181]

Bishop H. David Burton reminds us that when we have done all we can to be self-reliant, "we can turn to the Lord in confidence to ask for what we might yet lack."[182]

Being self-reliant allows us to bless others. Elder Robert D. Hales says, "Only when we are self-reliant can we truly emulate the Savior in serving and blessing others."[183]

Self-reliance is needed throughout several particular aspects of your life as explained by The Church of Jesus Christ of Latter-day Saints[184]:

1. **Education** – Study hard throughout your educational career with determination to excel. Learn to find scholarship or grant opportunities, if your parents cannot pay for your education. Work part-time or full-time if you need to do so.
2. **Health** – Start now protecting your health by avoiding illegal, unhealthy, and dangerous substances inside your body. Preserve your health so that you may grow old gracefully, having provided for and raised your family. Maintain your health for those times when you will be called upon to take care of your wife, children, and other family members. Learn proper nutrition and learn to keep in good physical shape.
3. **Employment** – Get a good education and keep abreast of the latest trends in business. Be entrepreneurial. Start your own family business and manage it well to provide the most safety for yourself and your family. Some family businesses have sustained families for generations such as Kellogg's and Heinz.
4. **Family Home Protection and Food Storage** – When you establish your own family, store up sufficient emergency food and water to last for at least a year. Install good locks, and buy a fire extinguisher, and keep it close at hand in the kitchen.
5. **Family Finances** – When you have your own family, save sufficient cash to keep you and your family solvent throughout any crisis – at least enough cash to cover three months of expenses. Work with a professional financial advisor to establish this program. Avoid debt as much as possible. Pay tithes faithfully, as the Lord will bless you and see you through all crises.
6. **Spiritual Strength** – We all experience trials in this life. Our spirituality will help us weather these storms. Get into the habit of regular prayer and come to know God. You will discover that whenever trials beset you, you will find internal peace and solace. All you need to begin your spiritual life is faith. When

you have at least the faith of a mustard seed, God will help your seed to grow and in so doing, He will demonstrate to you that He indeed exists – through personal miracles, tender mercies, and revelations.

MOTIVATION

Your life lies before you like a path of driven snow, be careful how you tread it cause every step will show.

LOWRI WILLIAMS

Motivation (also self-motivation) is the force that drives you into action - giving you the energy and desire to achieve a goal. Do you have goals? Are you motivated to achieve them? Sometimes, it may seem hard to be motivated to get out of bed, get ready for school, do homework, do chores, plan for the future, work, and keep your place clean, especially if you are not inspired to do these things. Pat yourself on the back if you are self-activated and do not need to be told to do things expected of you. On the other hand, we have an epidemic of unmotivated or under-motivated young men, who cannot seem to get themselves in gear to keep up with the basics as listed above. Lack of motivation could be caused by environmental factors, but some of the reasons are their own fault. Some young men seem to copy the behavior of others who are rebellious or just lazy. Unmotivated young men need to take responsibility for motivating themselves. Their spirit needs to take control of their mind in order to change their mindset from "unmotivated" to "motivated." We will show you how to boost your motivation shortly.

Reasons Some Young Men Lack Motivation
When it comes to school work, Dr. Leonard Sax, MD, Ph.D., author of *Boys Adrift* suggested that some young men think it's cool and

masculine to not mentally engage in school. He wrote, "Even more disturbing is the fact that so many of these boys seem to regard their laid-back, couldn't-care-less attitude as being somehow quintessentially male."[185]

"You need to care about what grade you get. It's important," one mother told her son.

"Girls care about getting good grades. Geeks care about grades. Normal guys do not care about grades," her fourteen-year-old son informed her in a matter-of-fact tone, the same tone he might use to show her how to program the DVR.

So they purposely do not get good grades so they can fit in? So they can look cool? Does this sound like a good idea to you?

We do not buy the argument that young men just want to look cool by not getting good grades. Who really wants to fail? You do not have to roll over and allow outside circumstances to rule you.

In his book, Dr. Sax pointed out different environmental reasons why boys may not be motivated - most of which are out of their control and which we have already discussed. However, he did emphasize that video gaming was one factor under their direct control. This is review, guys. We have already spoken about how video games fry your brains, so how could you possibly be motivated for schoolwork if you can only focus on video games?

Here are some other factors that may be interfering with your ability to develop self-motivation that perhaps *Boys Adrift* did NOT mention:

1. Were you bullied in school and not able to concentrate? Were you the bully and too busy thinking about the next target to bully, and just not paying attention in school? Consequently, developing huge potholes in your education.
2. Did you just waste your time and fall behind in your schoolwork - consequently developing huge potholes in your education?
3. Were there so many discipline problems in the classroom that concentrating on the teachers' lessons was next to impossible?

4. Are you afraid of success?
5. Are you, perhaps, just lazy?

Do any of the above descriptions describe you? If so, here's how you can fix these problems that may be sapping your motivation:

1. Use one of the scenarios above to describe to your parents what happened to you. Explain why you gave up on paying attention in class, studying, and doing your schoolwork. Ask your parents for their help in filling the potholes in your education. They can tutor you, or they can hire a tutor, or tutoring may be available at your public library.
2. If you are being bullied in school and the school cannot or will not stop it, ask your parents to teach you at home. You will need help from parents and tutors to catch up - to fill the potholes in your education then you can continue on a home-schooling basis (consult our website for information about homeschooling associations). However, when you have finished your studies at home, do something healthy. Socialize. Create something. Participate in scouting. Go to a gym or swimming pool. Plant a garden. Build a doghouse. Join a local theater group. Participate in church activities. Your parents are your allies. While you are being homeschooled, **STAY AWAY FROM VIDEO GAMES - THEY WILL ROB YOU OF YOUR FREE WILL, ROB YOU OF YOUR FREEDOM, ROB YOU OF A REAL LIFE, ROB YOU OF YOUR MIND.** Take control of your life.
3. If there are too many discipline problems in your school and teachers spend most of their time disciplining instead of teaching, follow the advice we offer in (2) above.
4. If you are a bully, know that being in a "fight or flight" mode all day is as damaging to your developing mind and body as it is damaging to the people you target. My wife knew someone, who bullied in school, who became mentally ill as an adult and was frequently hospitalized for

mental illness - this person was convinced that bullying led to mental illness. Bullying probably gives you a feeling of power over other people – it is addictive, but it is also self-destructive. Know that many people despise you for bullying and all of those negative thoughts towards you will eventually lead to your destruction. So exercise control over your brain and habits - stop bullying. There is never any excuse for abuse. Stubbing your toe, your dog's death, your parents' divorce, a death in your family, losing a game, not liking the color of someone else's shoelaces, are part of life, and they are not excuses for bullying. Bullying demeans another person to give you an ego boost. If you need an ego boost, have the courage to become a better person. Be of service to someone, learn skills and go on adventures in scouting, and study. Become your best self. Ask your parents to tutor you or to hire a tutor to help you to fill in the potholes in your education. Take control of your life. Do something healthy. Socialize and create. Your parents are your allies.

A Case of Natural Motivation

I had an exchange student from Sierra Leone, Africa, who stayed with my family for about a year. At 17, this young man had an incredible life story of living in abject poverty all his life. He told stories of having to hide in the jungle for weeks during the civil war in his country to keep from being slaughtered. He had dreams of becoming a Civil Engineer and supporting his family. There was absolutely nothing that was going to stand in his way. It is quite remarkable how he was able to keep up his grades in Sierra Leone schools and obtain a scholarship to come to America to study during his final year of high school. His most admirable traits were his bright shining attitude towards life, the respect he had for me, my family members and others, and his determination. His motivation was that he wanted to help his family and make a brighter future for himself. He had seen the ugly underbelly of life and wanted more. He made all A's in his senior year while staying with me, in Michigan. I lost contact with him, but through acquaintances, I learned that he eventually graduated from college and became a Civil Engineer as he dreamed. He married and is now living in Virginia. If he could stay motivated with his life circumstances, then you can too.

Our favorite documentary of all time, *On the Way to School*, directed by Pascal Plisson, [186] is about several of the bravest and most motivated children in the world. As of this writing, it is available on Netflix. **Check the *Elevate Yourself to Manhood* website at http://www.elevateyourselftomanhood.com/videos for the availability of the *On the Way to School* trailer.**

How to Boost Motivation

Mike Bundrant, in his Internet article, *Seven Causes, Seven Cures for Lack of Motivation* recommends the following ways to break yourself out of the habit of lacking motivation. I have summarized five of them here:

1. If you are the type of guy who tries to talk to himself into motivation like, "Get up off your butt! If you do not get moving, you're going to pay! You're so lazy! You must do this now" - Mr. Bundrant says that you will fail because you're being mean to yourself. Instead, he recommends that you speak nicely to yourself. Remember we said earlier that you should develop self-compassion. Well, this is one place where it might come in handy. Bundrant suggests that you speak to yourself as you would a good friend. Invite yourself to do things you have a strong desire to do AFTER you do the things you really OUGHT to do. Be pleasant with yourself. Establish a relationship with yourself based on self-respect instead of self-punishment.

2. If you are overwhelmed and just freezing up, then you have to learn how to break up large tasks into small ones. This is

one of the things I had to do while growing up on the farm. When I had to cultivate acres of crops by hand using only a hoe, I would just focus on one plant at a time, and celebrate as I completed each row of plants. It became a mental game. I would just keep a countdown of the rows as I finished them and let my mind be free, without stress, as I worked. It also made the time go faster. My motivation became the overwhelming feeling of accomplishment after each row and after the entire job was done. When I started working at my dad's factory at age 16, that same motivation trick served me well. I kept my first part-time job at the factory throughout junior high and high school. After high school, I was rewarded with a prestigious full-time job at the factory working in the laboratory as I worked my way through the first two years of college. I had "learned how to work well" in the eyes of the employer. The reward for the motivation was a steady, above-average stream of income for a teenager. Throughout high school and junior college, I always sported nice clothes, a nice car, and enough spending money to entertain myself, while giving half of my income to my family.

3. If you exhibit a lack of motivation, you might also be suffering from helplessness. We talked about this earlier in the book. Unfortunately, your body can <u>learn</u> helplessness after being beat down for some period. As mentioned before, this has been shown in clinical labs repeatedly. You have to check yourself to see if you have had a pattern of helplessness throughout your life, and you simply let life beat up on you. You must take charge to stop this behavioral pattern and seek counseling. First, ask your parents to help you. If they cannot help you, or will not help you, speak to your church leaders, school guidance counselors, scout leaders, or coaches.

4. If you are trying to please other people all the time and getting nowhere, then this will also cause you to run the risk of developing a lack of motivation. This is where self-motivation

turns into motivation according to the expectation of others -
not yourself. You have to do things to please yourself as well.
You have to identify what it is that YOU want out of life and
try to pursue that. When you know who you are, as we taught
you in the beginning chapter of this book, you will become
better able to help yourself and others. It is critical for your
own happiness to be aware of what you want in life, to have a
vision and to develop a plan for how to achieve your dreams
and goals for your life. This will boost your motivation and
confidence.

5. When you focus on unpleasant tasks first, then you will boost
your motivation. Do not think about it, just dive into it. When
you are faced with unpleasant tasks like doing the dishes, instead of focusing on the work of washing the dishes, visually
imagine the dishes being done and the area being clean first!
Ditto for doing homework. Dive in and do your most hated
subjects first. The delayed gratification will be that much
sweeter. Review the section on delayed gratification if you
need to do so.

6. Sometimes I tend to procrastinate. Then the resulting "catastrophe motivation" really drives me hard to get the job
done quickly at the last minute. This is not recommended,
of course, because it's like playing "chicken" with your life.
I'm sure you can probably perform well under pressure, but
being proactive is a much better policy. The cure for this
type of demotivation is developing self-respect and culti-
vating personal responsibility. When you begin to respect
yourself (and others) enough to act when you need to act,
then you give up the childish feeling that the world is controlling you. This helps you realize that you are in charge
of your life, and you no longer need to wait for the outside
world to pressure you to take action. You can take pride in
doing what needs to be done before circumstances pressure you to do it. [187]

Remember, lack of motivation is one of the evil pitfalls that seeks to destroy you along your quest for manhood, and later in life. I know a young man who had a wife and two little sons who loved his family, but his lack of motivation led to marital strife. His wife divorced him. Their breakup has been devastating not only to them, but to all who knew and loved them. Women expect their husbands to be responsible and motivated. Please do not let this happen to you when you get married.

Check yourself to see if you lack motivation. Practice Learned Optimism and TAKE ACTION on those things which you need to do but can't seem to get started. Learn how to instill self-motivation for those necessary tasks. Just take one step at a time. If you exercise your motivation muscles – they will become stronger with time.

Emotional Intelligence

Another crucial skill you will need to develop in order to be successful in work and social situations is emotional intelligence. To see where you stand in this area, please answer the following questions:

- Do you have the ability to identify your emotions?
- Do you sometimes not know how you feel?
- Do you feel awkward when dealing with people sometimes?
- Do you ever lose control of your emotions?
- Do you know how to decode the emotions of others?

Emotional intelligence (EQ) is the ability to know your own emotions, control your own emotions, and know how to recognize correctly the feelings of others. If you lack this knowledge, then you lack emotional maturity. If you find that you are somewhat defiant of your parents and teachers, or if you have difficulty getting along with others, you might lack emotional maturity or have a low EQ.

There was a time in our recent history when a person's intelligence quotient (IQ) was the most accepted way to determine an individual's intelligence. A person's IQ is based on the person's genes, but an individual's EQ is based on their life experience. Your future educators or employers are much more prone to evaluate you on EQ rather than IQ. Dr. Jeffrey Bernstein, Ph.D., in an article titled, *Liking the Child You Love*, said recently "Emotional intelligence fuels children's school and social success."[188]

Why You Need to Develop Emotional Maturity
Emotional maturity will help you get along with your parents, siblings, teachers, friends, co-workers, wife and children. It will also enable you to manage your feelings better. You will be able to improve your concentration and your memory, which will help you do better academically. This will give you a more balanced outlook on life.

What Does Emotional Maturity Look Like?
You will know you are emotionally mature when you have the following abilities of an emotionally intelligent person as mentioned by Bernstein:

You are more self-aware than before
Remember back at Facet 1: *Awaken Your Quest Begins* when we asked you to "Awaken and gain awareness of your world?" Now we are asking you to go deeper and begin to ponder your emotions, recognizing feelings as they occur, and discriminate between them.

You know how to manage your moods
You can handle your feelings so that they are relevant to the current situation, allowing you react appropriately. For example, it is normal to cry and grieve if a pet dies. It is not normal to cry and grieve because you have work to do and can't play video games. It is normal to feel and show anger if you are being bullied. It is not normal to feel anger if someone accidentally steps on your toes and you throw

them a punch – that is not only emotional immaturity it is an assault. However, there are mean-spirited and devious people who will hurt someone and pretend that it was an accident. Use your instincts to know the difference between bullying and a true accident. If the person who stepped on your toes is the kind of person who would not hurt a fly, accept their apology. If the person who stepped on your toes has a history of violence and hurts you deliberately, report them immediately to an authority in school or in the workplace, otherwise the violence might escalate. Distance yourself from evil people so they will not have the opportunity to do the same thing over again.

You are self-motivated
You can collect your feelings and direct yourself towards a goal, overcoming self-doubt, inertia, and impulsiveness.

You are more empathetic
You can recognize the feelings in others as you tune into their verbal communications and body language. You listen to other people in order to understand what they are saying and feeling. You notice little things like someone's red eyes, which might indicate that they have been crying, or might indicate that they are feeling ill, and you care enough to ask them how they are feeling, and offer to help.

You know how to manage relationships with others
You know how to be civil and diplomatic while solving conflicts and negotiating with others.[189]

Helpguide.org gives us some insight about how to elevate your Emotional Intelligence Quotient (EQ):

Essential Skills to Raise Your EQ

1. Learn how to reduce stress quickly while in a variety of situations. Counting to ten before reacting helps if it is not an emergency.

2. Learn how to recognize your emotions and keep them from overwhelming you. Take the time to identify why you are feeling uncomfortable. For example:

   * "I am angry." I should let the person know that I did not appreciate what he said, even if he is having a bad day.
   * "I am hurt." That football tackle was really hard, and I hurt my leg badly. I better tell the coach.
   * "I am embarrassed about my low grade." I will study more, and not at the last minute next time.
   * "I am sad that my girlfriend broke up with me." If this happens to you or another negative event happens in your life think realistic and positive thoughts. Such as – "I feel as if I had the wind knocked out of me. What can I learn from this experience? Were her reasons for ending our relationship justified?" If she ended the relationship for no good reason such as, she left because you wanted to abide by God's law and chose to wait to have sexual intimacy until after marriage then you may want to think – "This is emotionally painful, but if she did not appreciate me for who I am, she is not the right girl for me. We had different values. They say that time heals. I know that someone special will love me, someday. I just need to catch my breath. Tonight, I'll take a hot shower, maybe cry a little, and just chill out at home maybe watching a movie. Tomorrow, I'll go to the game with my friends. After all there are millions of girls in this world – there is definitely one for me. In the meantime, I will work on being the best I can be. I will focus on myself for a while."[190]

      Note: If your girlfriend broke off with you because you were physically or mentally abusive – she did herself a favor, and she did you a favor. You needed a reality check. You are emotionally immature. No self-respecting woman will love an abusive man. You will need to change. You will need to control your anger. You need to negotiate rather than impose or order a young woman to do what you want her to do. A woman has the right to say, "No." A woman has the right to see her friends and family. A woman has the right to have interests of her own. Negotiating might look like this: You could say, "Honey, I was hoping to go to a baseball game with you this Saturday. Couldn't you visit with your family next weekend?"

Your girlfriend might reply, "Mom has organized a wedding shower for my sister. I want to be there for this special day in her life. You can go to the game with one of your friends."

An appropriate response from you would be, "Oh, I didn't know that it was a special occasion. I can understand that you want to be there for her. I hope you will all have a great time."

In this scenario you would have demonstrated emotional maturity and empathy; there is no power struggle and no stressful drama.

3. Learn how to connect emotionally with others through body language. Look people in the eye and smile.
4. Learn how to use humor in challenging situations. For example, you can say, "When the going gets tough, the tough get going!"
5. Learn how to resolve conflicts with confidence. For instance, you can tell someone with whom you are arguing, "Let's talk about this civilly."

It may take you considerable time to develop the critical skill of Emotional Intelligence, but it is well worth it. You can find EQ tests online to check on your progress.

Keep up the good work!

DEVELOPING MENTAL TOUGHNESS LIKE A NAVY SEAL

We want you to develop confidence and mental toughness like a Navy Seal. Seals got their name from "Sea, Air, and Land." They are some of the toughest and most well-trained Special Forces in the world. No doubt they owe their success to excellent training and discipline. During some phases of training, the SEALs are only allowed a few hours sleep per week along with rigorous physical challenges. (Caution: While young men's bodies are developing they need sleep.) The goal of the training is to weed out those who are not physically, emotionally, and mentally tough. According to the article, *How to Be Mentally Tough Like a Navy Seal,* the following elements are essential: [191]

Goal Setting

* Keeping your eye on the particular goal you want to attain.
* Planning will put a damper on fear.
* Employing extremely short-term micro goals (minute by minute) coupled with (mid-term goals), and longer-term goals are what allow SEALS to be so successful at their jobs, and in life.

Mental Rehearsal or Visualization

Projecting outside yourself and mentally "seeing" yourself performing the task. Fast forward through the scenario several times to detect any flaws in your plan, preparing yourself for the event. This way, you will be much less stressed when the real event starts.

Positive Self-Talk

To suppress fear, talk to yourself to calm your brain using positive, confident words. Tell yourself that failure is not an option.

Arousal Control

In order to get yourself into a calm mental state and slow down the production of body chemicals that make your heart pound and your palms sweat, take slow, deep breaths. Exhale longer in order to free up more space in your lungs for fresh oxygen, which is good for your brain.[192] Breathe in deeply, hold for 5 seconds, then exhale again. Repeat a few times. You can do this anytime – in school at your desk, in an elevator, or when exercising. This exercise will help to calm you when you are upset, or nervous about something.

Recommended reading:

* *The Way of the Seal – Think Like an Elite Warrior to Lead and Succeed,* by Mark Divine
* *Navy Seal Training Guide: Mental Toughness,* by Lars Draeger

ANTICIPATING CHALLENGES AND PLANNING HOW TO REACT TO THOSE CHALLENGES

Being mentally prepared to face life's challenges is half the battle. Please find below a few examples:

1. You Encounter an Emergency Medical Situation: Are you prepared to help? If not, take a First Aid course from the American Red Cross or from Saint John's Ambulance Course.

2. Your Girlfriend Breaks Up with You: Young women have the right to choose someone with whom they feel compatible and vice versa. This is nothing new. Relationships have started and ended for centuries. There are billions of people on this earth. There is someone special for you. When one door closes another door opens. Ask yourself, "What can I learn from this experience?" Go into your "man cave" for a few days. Spending time in nature helps. Then move on. Enjoy life and if you are not enjoying life – fake it until you make it. Become the best you can be. You will meet someone else who will love you. You will love again.

3. A Family Member Dies: A family member may die - maybe both your parents. Hopefully, not soon but it will happen someday. It is hard to fathom the loss of a close family

member. Talk about this possibility with your parents, so that you can prepare by thinking about how you would react to their death, and where and how you would live. Those who have experienced the loss of a pet may be better prepared for the loss of a family member. Perhaps that is why God made animals, which would become domestic pets, to live shorter lives than humans – so that we could experience losing someone we love, in order to prepare us for the loss of a greater love.

4. You Are Approached by a Con Artist: A con artist could rob you of your dignity, virginity, self-respect, generosity, love, and money. Stay sober, stick to your values, practice saying "No," and choose your friends wisely. Remember, that trust ought to be earned. Do not trust people too quickly – get to know them well over a considerable length of time. If you make a mistake due to no fault of your own, forgive others for your own peace of mind, learn from your mistake, and become a stronger person.

5. You Are Asked to Commit a Crime or to be Complicit in a Crime: A person asks you to commit a crime in exchange for money. You are short of money and more vulnerable than you would be otherwise. Say "No." Be willing to move for employment. Be willing to do a dirty job. I know a surgeon who dug ditches to put himself through medical school. If you are going to be tough – be tough in a good way. Fight for your best life. Do not take a risk. Most gangs can never be escaped – you will lose your freedom. Millions of people who committed crimes thought that they were smart enough not to get caught. Millions of them have been incarcerated at any given time worldwide. The following statistic may bring realistic clarity. "Half of the world's prison population of about nine million is held in the US, China or Russia. Prison rates in the US are the world's highest, at 724 people per 100,000. In Russia the rate is 581."[193] You don't want to ruin your life by going to prison. In prison, men are no longer free to enjoy their life on

Earth. If they are released they are left with a criminal record, which makes it extremely difficult to find interesting employment. Most employers ask for a criminal record check.

WRITING A PERSONAL MISSION STATEMENT FOR YOUR LIFE
Another facet of goal-setting is creating a personal mission statement for your life. Stephen Covey, in his book, *7 Habits of Highly Effective People 194* provides this insight about personal mission statements:

> It focuses on what you want to be and do. It is your plan for success. It reaffirms who you are, puts your goals in focus, and moves your ideas into the real world. Your mission statement makes you the leader of your own life. You create your own destiny and secure the future you envision.

Your personal mission statement does not need to be long and complicated. It can be short and sweet, like the personal mission statements of two famous CEOs published on the Fast Company website[195]:

> "To be a teacher. And to be known for inspiring my students to be more than they thought they could be."

> — OPRAH WINFREY, FOUNDER OF OWN,
> *THE OPRAH WINFREY NETWORK*

> "To have fun in [my] journey through life and learn from [my] mistakes."

> — SIR RICHARD BRANSON, FOUNDER OF VIRGIN GROUP

You get the picture. You are unique and your goals may be different from anyone else's. Make it your own.

The authors of *Elevate Yourself to Manhood* also have a personal mission statement: "To teach. To strengthen young men, their families, their communities, and our country."

GOAL-SETTING: DEVELOPING A VISION FOR YOUR EDUCATION AND CAREER PLAN

A Mind is a Terrible Thing to Waste

(UNITED NEGRO COLLEGE FUND)

*If you stop learning, you will forget
what you already know.*

– PROVERBS *19:27 KJV*

It is important that you start early to establish educational goals and a career path, beginning with developing a plan or vision. How do you see yourself when you grow up? What are your passions? What are your talents? What does your gut tell you? What are your dreams and goals? What do you want to study? What kind of a job would you like? Where would you like to live? What kind of a girl would you like to marry? In order to achieve the end goal of a career, a home, a wife and a family, you will need an education. Planning for your future begins now by taking small steps, by planning for your education and career.

Once you figure that out, then you will need to write it down on paper to remind and to inspire yourself. Make your vision as clear as possible. You may want to place your goals on a poster board. You can add to the poster board inspiring images of a person doing the kind of job you see yourself achieving, by cutting out these images, and pasting them on the board. You can cut out the kind of car and house you would like to own – you can describe the love of your life. Doing this type of visualization can become your first step toward achieving your educational and career goals.

The University of California at Berkeley recommends the following process as adapted from Randall S. Hansen of Quintessential Careers, to create an inspirational career vision statement:

1. **Set aside some time for career planning**. Try to envision your career. Do not rush it. It may take several false starts before you get it right. Wait for things to become clear. This will allow you to plan for an ideal future.
2. **Review your career goals.** Visualize what kind of job you want. Try to picture what you want to do with your life.
3. **Suspend logic and pragmatic thinking.** When developing your career vision, assume anything to be possible to accomplish. So turn off any negative thinking that will block you from thinking big. Do not assume the future is limited to what is happening today.
4. **Brainstorm.** Think deeply about the questions and answer each as best you can:
    *   What would you like people to read in your obituary about you and your career accomplishments and how you impacted the people with whom you worked?
    *   If absolutely no obstacles stood in the way of your achieving it, what would you most like to attain in your career?
    *   Who are the people you most admire? What is it about them or their careers that attract you to them? Is there something about what they have or do that you want for your career vision?
    *   Imagine yourself in the future at a point in which you have achieved great career success. What is it that you have accomplished? What does your life look like?

- Do you feel as though you have a gift or calling? How can you share this gift or best answer the call in a way that will fulfill you?
- What's the one activity you most love? Is it part of your career? If not, how can you make it part of your job?
- Where would you like to be in your career in 20 years?

5. **Put it all together.** Write down your career vision using one sentence or a short paragraph. Write your vision in the present tense, as if it has already come true. This is the right frame of mind to instill confidence about your future rather than keeping your vision in the distant future.

6. **Keep your vision visible.** Now post your career vision all over the place and read it out loud often. Another trick is to imagine yourself successfully living your career vision. This will help you both consciously and subconsciously to develop goals and action steps that will lead you to success.

7. **Review your career vision statement regularly.** Your vision can - and most likely will - change as you move closer to it. As part of an annual career planning process, you should review your career vision statement and make any adjustments that you feel are necessary.[196]

Setting Career Development Goals

Draw out a timeline – in years – showing each milestone along your career.

The University of California at Berkeley also suggest the following tips in setting effective goals:

- Express your goals positively, rather than framing them in terms of what you don't want.
- Be precise in setting dates, times, and amounts so that you know when you have achieved your goals.

- Set priorities so that you know which of your goals to focus your attention toward and helps you avoid feeling overwhelmed by having too many goals.
- Write your goals down so that you can visually be reminded of them and so that you can craft them to be precise and clear.
- Break down your goals into small, achievable tasks so that you get frequent opportunities to accomplish them and feel motivated to take on other goals.
- Set realistic goals that you can achieve and that are in your own control.[197]

Sit down with your parents and discuss your vision and goals and ask for their feedback.

Remember to Dream Big and Aim High

Your potential is only as big as your dreams. Dream big, aim high, push yourself, and never give up! Dreams alone will not enable you to make your dreams come true. Practicing for hours and challenging yourself to attain a higher level of expertise and practicing some more will help you. Studying to gain greater knowledge in your chosen field will help you. Making an effort to meet and collaborate with people who have similar interests will help you. Never stop learning. When we die and cross over to the spiritual realm we may bring the knowledge we have gained on Earth and our earthly family with us. So you can never, ever learn too much.

WHAT WILL YOU DO TO ELEVATE YOURSELF TODAY?

Congratulations for making it through Facet 2 – *Elevate Your Mind*.
To solidify your learnings, do these things:

- Learn how to lighten up on yourself. Don't be so self-critical. Practice self-gratitude!

- Cultivate your gratitude powers and show gratitude to others in all things. Be willing to do your Gratitude Exercises each day.
- Understand how to use mindfulness to calm yourself and look internally for peace when the world becomes a bit too chaotic for you.
- Have a sense of your primary personality "color" which gives you a sense of your typical personality traits and behavioral style.
- Know how to identify your strengths, weaknesses, passions and talents. Know why it is so important to hone your abilities and to build new ones throughout your life.
- Recognize the grave dangers of Self-Doubt.
- Know how to build Self-Confidence.
- Recognize and be able to avoid the Seven Brain Dangers.
- Identify and discuss the Nine Intelligences.
- Assess the state of the health of your brain.
- Deal with stress including Chronic Fatigue Syndrome in case you're also burned out from stress.
- Think outside the box and, if necessary, re-imagine the box altogether using the practice of Divergent Thinking.
- Set aside time for play and have fun!
- Develop empathy for yourself and others.
- Be optimistic about life. Exercise the skill of Learned Optimism, if you fall short in this area.
- Develop self-reliance.
- Cure lack of motivation. Learn to KICK START yourself (respectfully, of course) like an old Harley-Davidson motorcycle when you get lazy.
- Develop mental toughness like a Navy Seal.
- Be self-reliant.
- Delay gratification.
- Practice and demonstrate emotional maturity.
- Create a written vision for your educational and professional career.

Quest Checkpoint: Your Mind

In order to satisfy the requirements for the Mind Certificate, you will need to demonstrate proficiency in the subject areas covered within this chapter by reading and completing the requirements below. After you have completed all the certificate requirements below - using the honor system – fill in the certificate with your name. **You can also download a printed copy from the *Elevate Yourself to Manhood* website at http://www.elevateyourselftomanhood.com/certificates**.

Certificate Requirements

- ☐ **Gratitude** - In your Daily Journal, each day, write down something for which you are grateful.
- ☐ **Mindfulness** - Perform the Chocolate Mindfulness exercise once per week to help ground yourself and fine-tune your senses.
- ☐ **Strengths** - Make a list of your strengths in your Daily Journal. How can you leverage them in your everyday life?
- ☐ **Weaknesses** - Make a list of what you think are your weaknesses. How can each one of them be improved? How did Michael Jordan turn weakness into strength? How can you turn your weaknesses into strengths?
- ☐ **Passions** - Write down in your journal things for which you are truly passionate! Share them with friends and family. Figure out how to make use of these passions in your everyday life, and long-term goals.
- ☐ **Talents** - Write down in your journal a list of talents you might have. Figure out how effectively you use your skills in your life. Does this list match your Passions list? Do you think you have any HIDDEN talents? Browse the Boy Scout website and view the different merit badges to see if you might have talent in some of those areas.
- ☐ **Laziness** - All of us feel lazy sometimes. Determine not to allow laziness to get in the way of accomplishing things that

need attention. Identify those times when you missed opportunity because you were lazy. Commit to avoiding laziness.

- ☐ **Self-Confidence** - Do the Self-Confidence Building exercise in this chapter weekly for 3-4 weeks. Record the results in your journal.
- ☐ **Goal-Setting** - Practice setting goals for yourself and achieving them. Start with a simple task that you can perform quickly, then increase difficulty and pick a harder goal.
- ☐ **Self-Doubt** - Identify two examples of when you failed to achieve something because you doubted yourself. What could you have done differently to ensure that you would have been successful?
- ☐ **Protecting Your Brain from the Outside** - List at least 7 ways you can protect your brain from outside physical threats.
- ☐ **Bullying** - What could you do to raise the awareness of the dangers to the brain caused by bullying? What would you do if you saw someone being bullied? Make a plan for how you would assist a bullying target both during the event and afterward. What would you do if you were bullied? Discuss this with your parents and teachers.
- ☐ **Video Gaming and Gaming Addiction** - Are you addicted to video games? In your journal, record the amount of time each day you spend video gaming. If more than one hour per day, then commit to trying to reduce the time to under one hour. If you are addicted to video gaming and you are trying to reduce the number of hours you play video games but it is not working for you, ask your parents to help you to quit "cold turkey."
- ☐ **Pornography** - Are you watching porn online or in print? Commit to stop this harmful practice. Commit to being a virgin on your wedding night. Commit to true love and desiring a naturally loving and tender relationship with a young woman. Write this commitment in your journal.
- ☐ **Drug Use** - Commit to not using illicit drugs. Period. Seek help if you need it. Write this commitment in your journal.

- ☐ **Alcohol** - Commit to not drinking alcohol. Alcohol is damaging physically, psychologically, and spiritually. Write your pledge to not drink alcohol in your journal.
- ☐ **Caffeine** - Commit to avoiding harmful drinks, especially energy drinks, sodas, and coffee. Write this commitment in your journal.
- ☐ **Television and Screen Time** - Commit to limiting the time you spend watching television, surfing the Internet, and texting (screen time) to no more than 1 hour per day. Write this commitment in your journal.
- ☐ **Intelligence** - Become familiar with the nine different kinds of intelligence. Do you recognize all of them within yourself? Which ones do you feel you possess most? Remember that we all have all nine of the intelligences inside ourselves – in varying degrees. As an experiment, see if you can become stronger in one of the intelligences in which you feel weakest. Become passionate about your highest intelligences.
- ☐ **Stress Management** - Identify the sources of stress in your life and talk to your parents and teachers about them. Use the stress management procedures provided in this chapter to help relieve your stress.
- ☐ **Divergent Thinking** - Prepare yourself for the future by learning the critical skills of becoming self-motivated, observant, analytical, action-oriented, and thinking for yourself. Do not be afraid to "go out on a limb" sometime and make mistakes – and learn from them. What lessons can you learn from Thomas Edison, Michael Jordan and Wayne Gretzky about making mistakes?
- ☐ **Creative Play** - Spend time outside in nature (no electronics allowed) and play either alone or with friends. Does your creativity seem to come easier? Record your experience(s) in your journal.
- ☐ **Empathy** - Learn the difference between sympathy and empathy. Find an occasion to empathize with someone. Record your experience(s) in your journal.

☐ **Optimism** - Is your glass half empty or half full? What is your default state of mind? Are you an optimist or a pessimist? Re-read the section on Optimism and practice changing to a more positive mindset. Record the situation and result in your journal.

☐ **Learned Helplessness** - Learn to recognize when you are falling victim to learned helplessness just like the lab dogs mentioned in the experiments. Make note in your journal of any time(s) that you felt such automatic responses to learning helplessness. Have courage. Don't just wait for someone to come rescue you. Rescue yourself or ask for help. Jump out of this rut!

☐ **Self-Reliance** - Recall the different aspects of your life that can help you to achieve self-reliance: education, health, employment, cooking (more about this in the section pertaining to the body), doing laundry, family home protection, long-term food storage. What lessons can you learn from your parents about self-reliance?

☐ **Motivation** - Learn the tricks of increasing motivation presented in this chapter. Identify the things in your life that may be de-motivating you. Practice breaking the chains caused by lack of motivation. Practice increasing motivation as shown in the chapter. Record the results in your journal – successes and failures.

☐ **Emotional Intelligence** - Follow the steps to raise your Emotional Intelligence Quotient. Record your experiences in your journal.

☐ **Mental Toughness** - Develop mental toughness by doing what Navy Seals are trained to do: Set goals, rehearse or visualize the objective, perform positive self-talk, and develop arousal control. Have fun with it. You are only competing with yourself. This exercise will also improve your self-confidence tremendously!

ELEVATE YOURSELF TO MANHOOD

QUEST CERTIFICATE – THE MIND

THIS CERTIFICATE IS AWARDED TO:

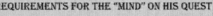

FOR DILIGENCE IN FULFILLING THE *ELEVATE YOURSELF TO MANHOOD*
REQUIREMENTS FOR THE "MIND" ON HIS QUEST

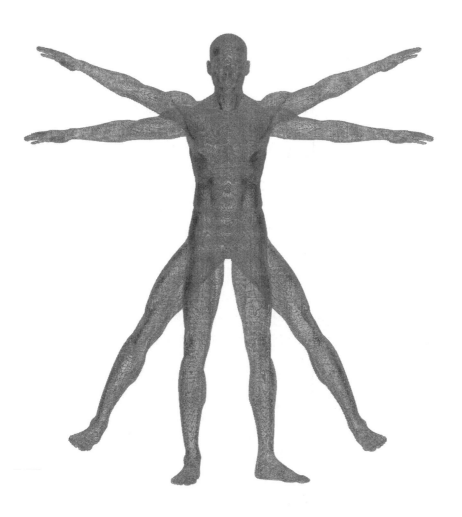

Elevate Your Body

Elevate Your Body

"What? Know ye not that your body is the temple of the Holy Ghost which is in you, which ye have of God, and ye are not your own?"

1 - Corinthians 6:19 KJV

Your body is a unique, complex organism that requires proper care and nourishment, that is, if you want to maintain good health for a very long time. With as much as we know about the human body, there are still mysteries about some of its inner-workings. In this section, we present to you the latest and best information we could find on healing and strengthening your body. **Please be sure to consult with your own personal health professionals and parents for a second opinion on the information presented here.**

But first, a little **REALITY CHECK:** Your body is not your own!

Yes, that's right. As the quote above suggests, your body does not belong to you. It is simply "on loan" to you as a loving gift from God to house your spirit (your real self) here on Earth. I honestly used to hate my body until I awoke to this realization. Now, knowing that my eager spirit was assigned to this body inside my mother's womb gives me the will to up my game in taking special care of my body. We hope that while you are on your journey through life, you possess a strong desire to protect, feed, and exercise your body to make it healthy and strong. Sometimes I wish I had learned the information we are now sharing with you when I was a teenager. I would have avoided many of the pitfalls and enjoyed the benefits of a healthy body more fully.

So first, let us begin with a mindfulness exercise to set the stage.

THE RAISIN MEDITATION

In the book *The Mindful Way Through Depression: Freeing Yourself from Chronic Unhappiness*, the authors Mark Williams, John Teasdale, Zindel Segal, and Jon Kabat-Zinn provide us with a wonderful mindfulness exercise called *Eating One Raisin: A Taste of Mindfulness.* This mindfulness exercise tests your mind and body's ability to connect with your senses. Here's how to do it:

You will need five to ten minutes alone to do this exercise. Make sure that your phone is turned off and that family or friends will not disturb you. Find a piece of paper and a pen with which to write. Your task will be to eat the fruit described in the exercise and to record your reactions afterward.

Read the instructions carefully. Only re-read them if you really need to do so. It is more important that you have the correct attitude and spirit about each of the tasks in the exercise – this is more important than following the details of each task. For each of the eight stages of the exercise, spend about twenty to thirty seconds and pause for about ten seconds in between each step.

HOLDING

Pretend that you just stepped off an alien spaceship and had just landed on earth. Take a raisin and hold it in the palm your hand. Now take it between your fingers and thumb. Place the raisin in the palm of your other hand. Can you feel its weight? (Pause 10 seconds)

SEEING

Now study the raisin carefully. You might imagine that you have never before seen a raisin. With your eyes scan it. With your mind peruse its surface with considerable scrutiny and detail. Let your eyes explore each curve, hill and valley on it. Examine the highlights where the light shines, and the darker creases. Can you see the shadow that it casts on your hand? (Pause for 10 seconds)

TOUCHING

Pick the raisin up again using your index finger and thumb. Turn it over. Can you really feel it? Is it soft? Squishy? (Pause 10 seconds)

SMELLING

Slowly bring it up beneath your nose. Does it have an aroma? Does it smell sweet? Breathe the aroma in deeply. If you do not smell anything, or if the aroma is very slight, notice that too. (Pause 10 seconds)

PLACING

Stick out your tongue. Slowly take the raisin towards your mouth. See how your hand, fingers, and arm know exactly where to put it. Gently place the raisin on your tongue. Now notice what the tongue does to "receive" the raisin. Do not chew the raisin yet. Just hold it on your tongue. Now explore the sensations of having the raisin on your tongue. If you choose to do so, continue holding the raisin on your tongue for about 30 seconds. (Pause 10 seconds)

CHEWING

You're probably ready to take a bite now, aren't you? When you're ready, consciously bite slowly into the raisin. Notice how your teeth pierce the raisin. What happens to the raisin? What happens to your mouth? Did it release any juice? What does it taste like? Feel the texture. Is it soft? Hard? Chew it slowly, but hold it in your mouth. Do not swallow yet! (Pause 10 seconds)

SWALLOWING

Become fully aware of the need or desire to swallow. How strong is this desire? Notice what the tongue does to prepare the raisin for swallowing. Can you feel the desire to swallow? Swallow now, but do not swallow it all at one time. Can you feel it move down your throat? Wait for 5 seconds then swallow again. Keep swallowing until it is all gone. Notice what your tongue does after you have swallowed. (Done)

AFTER-EFFECTS

Now, please spend time thinking about the after-effects of this experience. Is there an aftertaste? Did you automatically want to eat another raisin?[198]

Take a moment to write down anything that you noticed when you were doing the practice.

When Williams and Penman asked their clients to perform this exercise, here's what some of them said:

"The smell for me was amazing: I'd never noticed that before."

"I felt pretty stupid like I was in art school or something."

"I thought how ugly they looked . . . small and wrinkled, but the taste was very different from what I would normally have thought it tasted like. It was quite nice actually."

"I tasted this one raisin more than the twenty or so I usually stuff into my mouth without thinking." [199]

Something to Think About: So what did you think of this meditation exercise? Does this give you any perspective on how we could start paying more attention to our senses – in this case, our sense of taste, and smell? Do you think you will appreciate the textures, aromas, and flavors of food more now?

TUNING YOUR BODY FOR OPTIMAL HEALTH

The greatest wealth is health.

- VIRGIL

The human body is one incredible oxygen-consuming, blood-pumping, cell-producing, and electricity-generating machine. It is strong enough to run long distances, leap over obstacles, and carry heavy loads. However, for optimal functioning, the human body needs tuning, and it didn't come with an Owner's Manual. In this section, we will arm you with information - based on the latest research – which will help you achieve optimal health.

ROADBLOCKS TO OPTIMAL HEALTH

We will now help you navigate through the maze of health barriers that can hijack and sabotage you on your quest to becoming a healthy man. These roadblocks consist of unhealthy foods (including genetically modified foods and foods disguised to look nutritious), unhealthy drinks, and dangerous substances that you may ingest.

Other barriers include caffeine, sugary drinks (sodas and fruit juices), chemicals added to foods such as eggs in some fast food restaurants, and chemicals that leach into foods. You will need to arm yourself with this information, focus, and use your self-discipline skills in this nutrition minefield. You will need to learn how to ward off the destructive forces in this maze. You will need to build up strong defenses, and build an excellent offense to keep you alive and healthy on your quest to manhood.

When you were an infant, your parents were responsible for sustaining you and guiding you. Your parents did a good job of caring for you during the first part of your life – otherwise, you would not be alive. However, you are now capable of making choices for yourself in terms of how you take care of your body - given enough valid information, cooperation from your parents, and nutritious food from which to choose, as available. As you become more aware of the latest scientific research and what you have to choose from for maintaining your health, perhaps you may make suggestions for your family's grocery list – such as, "Let's find an alternative to processed cereals. Let's make homemade granola." (As a bonus, a recipe for delicious, homemade granola will follow.)

Nutrition

Having a proper diet that provides nutritious food and lots of water will enhance your chances for good health. In this section, we will give you a series of health tips that we feel will sum up all the best knowledge we could find to keep your body fortified. Since human biology is so complex, you would do well to adhere to guidelines here to get you started, otherwise, you may be more likely to suffer from poor health:

Health Tip #1: Drink Enough Water

How Much Water Should You Drink?

One of the most important lessons you can learn from this book is that you need to be vigilant about supplying your body with the correct amount of water and a healthful quality of water. The Daily Health Post[200] blog informs us that not drinking enough water unnecessarily causes a host of health problems. We'll jump deeper into this issue below:

As long as I can remember, I have heard that a person should drink eight 8-ounce glasses of water every day. The "eight-by-eight" rule was the one-size-fits-all answer. Even though there was no scientific research to back it up, it became the favorite response to the question, "How much water should a person drink every day?"

Your kidneys are responsible for regulation of water balance, acid balance, and excretion of waste. For the healthy person, thirst is the first compensatory response to low fluid levels. This is usually felt when the body has lost around two to three percent of its water. At the cellular level, however, damage begins to occur with as little as one percent loss of body water.

Dr. Michael Lam of the Adrenal Gland Center, tells us that adrenal glands also contribute to the hydration of the body. He says that if you become overstressed for long periods of time, your adrenal glands may not function properly.[201]

Experts now say that how much water you need to drink every day depends on a number of factors and can be different for each person. On WebMD, Dr. Trent Nessler, PT, DPT, MPT says, "It depends on your size and weight, and also on your activity level and where you live." He goes on to say, "In general, you should try to drink between half an ounce and an ounce of water for each pound you weigh every day." So if you weigh 150 pounds that would be equivalent to 75-150 ounces of water daily. To account for climate and activity level, that would be 75 ounces of water per day if you live in a cool climate, and you are somewhat sedentary. If you reside in a hot climate, and you are physically active, you would need about 150 ounces of water per day.[202]

Do Not Allow Your Body to Dehydrate

Dehydration could be making you fat and sick! Before we get to that, here is some background information about your body, its percentages of water composition, and some other useful facts.

The average human body is about 75% water!

According to Daily Health Post, the average adult loses about 10 cups of water every day simply by breathing, sweating, urinating and eliminating waste.

- The brain is about 75% water
- Blood is about 92% water

* Bones contain about 22% water
* Muscles are about 75% water

The Daily Health Post, mentioned that if you were to drinking two 8-ounce glasses of water daily before each meal (breakfast, lunch, and dinner) and at the same time reduce the portion size of your meals, you might be able to lose weight and keep it off for a year or more. [203]

Did you know that drinking cold water can speed your metabolism and burn calories? This amazing fact was mentioned in *Drinking Water May Speed Weight Loss*, a WebMD article written by Salynn Boyles, an award-winning journalist who has been writing about medical issues for more than two decades. She reported on research findings concerning water. She wrote that the effects of elevated metabolism begin about 10 minutes after consuming the water and peak at 30-40 minutes after drinking. Her piece suggested that if a person increases water consumption by 1.5 liters a day, that would burn an extra 17,400 calories over a year, which could lead to about five pounds of weight loss.[204]

Your Body Was Designed to be Powered by Water

Generally speaking, you should drink only WATER. The exception might be an occasional glass of milk. Fruit juices should be consumed in moderation. As you already know from our discussion in Brain Dangers, energy drinks are harmful to your health. In Health Tip #12, you will see that sodas ought to be avoided also. The number one source of excessive calories in the common diet is sugar-based beverages such as soda and fruit juices. Just one can of soda pop contains 35 grams of sugar (4 grams = 1 teaspoon) and 140 calories. A glass of water contains zero grams of sugar and zero calories.

Morning Tip: Have a nice cool glass of water when you first wake up. Preferably with freshly squeezed lemon juice or grated frozen organic lemon. This will improve your digestion. The addition of lemon has many health properties, which we will discuss later in this book.

Danger: You Might Be Dehydrated

In the Daily Health Post article, *Got Water? Why Dehydration Is Making You Fat and Sick*, there is a beautiful infographic, which summarizes the signs of chronic dehydration:

Fatigue – The most vital source of energy in the body is water, so when you are dehydrated the result is sluggishness and fatigue. Enzymatic activity slows down to a crawl in your body. If you are feeling sluggish, drink water instead of coffee.

High Blood Pressure - When your body is fully hydrated, your blood is about 92% water. If you become dehydrated, your blood becomes thicker. This causes an elevation in blood pressure due to higher resistance to blood flow.

Skin Disorders - When you become dehydrated, the elimination of toxins through your skin becomes impaired. This makes you more vulnerable to skin disorders like dermatitis and psoriasis, and acne. It also accelerates premature wrinkling and discoloration of the skin.

Asthma and Allergies - When you become dehydrated, your body gets creative in ways to preserve liquid. One way it accomplishes this is by restricting airways. So as your body loses more and more water, it also increases the rate of generating histamine, causing allergic reactions.

High Cholesterol - When the body is dehydrated, it will produce more cholesterol to prevent water loss from the cells.

Digestive Disorders - Digestive disorders like ulcers, gastritis, and acid reflux can be caused by a shortage of water and a shortage of alkaline minerals in the body like calcium and magnesium.

Bladder or Kidney Problems - When you are dehydrated, your body accumulates toxins and acid waste. This leads to an environment where bacteria can thrive. Possible results are infections in the bladder and kidneys, also inflammation and pain.

Constipation - Whenever your body is dehydrated, your body starts to draw water from the colon as well as other regions of the body in order to provide fluids for other critical body functions. If you do not have enough water in your body, you can become constipated because body waste moves more slowly through the colon or not at all. [205]

What Color Is Your Urine?

You can also tell quite a bit about your health by the color or your urine. The color of your urine can tell you whether or not you are drinking enough water. Your urine can come in a variety of colors, depending upon the state of your body. Take a look at this list of urine colors and what the color means with regards to your health, as noted by Dr. Oz[206]:

No Color or Transparent: You are drinking enough water. In fact, you may want to cut back a bit.

Pale Straw Color: You are normal, healthy and well hydrated.

Transparent Yellow: Normal

Dark Yellow: Normal, but you may want to drink more water soon.

Amber or Honey color: You are not getting enough water. Drink water now!

Syrup or Brown Ale color: Liver disease or severe dehydration. Drink water now and see your physician if the condition persists.

Pink to Reddish color: You may have blood in your urine, or it could be nothing serious. Contact your doctor anyway.

Orange color: You may not be drinking enough water, or you could have a liver or bile duct condition. Alternatively, it could be food dye. Contact your doctor.

Blue or Green color: Could be a rare genetic disease or certain bacterial infection, but most likely food dye. It could also be medication. See your doctor if the condition continues.

Foaming or Fizzing: Harmless effect, but could indicate excess protein in your diet or a kidney problem. See your doctor if it persists.

So, you should always maintain the color of your urine within the scale of the first four colors in this list. Remember, always hydrate with water, but do not overdo it.

What Kind of Water is Best to Drink?

Tap Water
Get to know the public water supply in the area in which you live. Public tap water should be safe, but you may need to obtain a water analysis from the public water utility in your area to be sure, or a third party because some towns and cities have committed errors in checking and reporting the water quality. Just make sure that the water you drink is safe to drink.

Public water utilities would like to maintain water pH that is near neutral. Acidic water would cause their pipes to rust. You can test the pH level of your water with pH test strips, which are available in health shops, drugs stores and some retail outlets. Dr. Mercola recommends that the water you drink should have a pH level between 6.5 and 8.[207]

Bottled Water
There are many different commercial bottled waters. There are some differences in pH among the different brands of water, but some are below the recommended range of 6.5 to 8 (more acidic). You can look up the pH of the brand of bottled water you drink on the web. Also another cause for concern is the leaching of Bisphenol A (BPA) chemicals from plastic into the water contained in plastic water bottles. We will discuss the harmful effects of BPA in the next health tip.

Ionized Water
Some people prefer water ionizers so that they can raise the alkalinity of their tap water. If this is your preference, just be sure to do research on the different brands and models of ionizers first. You can also purchase ionized bottled water.

Artesian

Our best recommendation on water – drink artesian well water. Artesian water comes from an artesian well beneath the ground where water is held and filtered within layers of rocks. The water pressure beneath the surface is sufficient to push the water to the surface above the level of the well where the water can be bottled. You can find the locations of artesian wells on the web.

Danger: Do Not Drink Too Much Water

ALERT! Too much water (or too much of any liquid) can harm you.

For decades, the public has been warned about the dangers of dehydration, but recently the public has begun to receive warnings about over-hydration, especially involving athletes or anyone involved in athletic activity. This condition is known as Exercise-Associated Hyponatremia (EAH).

According to a news report by United Press International (UPI), there are new guidelines issued by an international panel of experts who suggest that instead of gorging themselves with water out of fear of dehydration, athletes should simply drink when they are thirsty.[208]

The UPI report states that there have been more than a dozen documented and suspected runners' deaths due to EAH.

Another report by Loyola Medicine explains that if you drink too much liquid while exercising, it is possible to overwhelm the kidney's ability to excrete water. When that happens, the sodium in the blood becomes diluted, causing cells to absorb the excess water, potentially causing dangerous swelling in the brain.

Dr. James Winger, a sports medicine physician at Loyola University Medical Center, considers EAH more of a threat to the body than dehydration. He said, "No one has died on sports fields from dehydration, and the adverse effects of mild dehydration are questionable. But athletes, on rare occasions, have died from over-hydration."[209]

Home Water Testing

Testing your water supply is especially important when there is a pregnant woman, baby, nursing mother or young children in your household. As an expectant father, and when you have young children, you will be responsible for ensuring that your family has safe water to drink. Contaminated water can cause birth defects, learning difficulties and other health problems in children. The Environmental Protection Agency (EPA) recommends you "test for nitrate in the early months of a pregnancy, before bringing an infant home, and again during the first six months of the baby's life. It is best to test for nitrate during the spring or summer following a rainy period."[210]

Environmental Health News found in a study evidence that supports testing your water supply to ensure your health and the health of your future babies. Researchers studied 3,300 mothers from Iowa and Texas who had consumed nitrates in drinking water. Their babies were born with neural tube defects, oral clefts, limb deficiencies, or congenital heart defects. Results of the study showed that mothers who consumed nitrates had a higher risk of having babies with spina bifida, cleft palate and other defects. This was the first study of its kind. Used as fertilizers on crops, nitrates are one of the most widespread chemical contaminants in aquifers around the world, according to Environment Health News.[211]

Having your water tested is important for you and all members of your family.

Do you know who can test your water? As you can see there are plenty of reasons why you should test your water.

You can ask county health departments to help you test for bacteria or nitrates in your tap water, or you can have it tested by a state certified laboratory. To find a laboratory in your area, call the Safe Drinking Water Hotline at 800-426-4791 or visit www.epa.gov/safewater/labs.

HEALTH TIP #2: USE GLASS CONTAINERS INSTEAD OF PLASTIC
CONTAINERS FOR FOOD AND DRINK AND STAINLESS STEEL
POTS AND PANS OR IRON PANS FOR COOKING

The BPA content in some modern containers is a problem that is definitely avoidable, but it might take a little adjustment on your part. The Centers for Disease Control (CDC) advises that you should only drink water or eat food from BPA-Free products. BPA stands for bisphenol A, which is a chemical contained in hard clear plastic called polycarbonate and other things like sealants for your teeth, the linings of most cans containing food, and thermal paper used in some cash register receipts. BPA is a hormone disruptor. A CDC survey found that most people in the US aged 6 years and older have BPA in their system already."[212]

Researchers in Fertility and Sterility report adverse effects of BPA on sperm quality. They indicate that with increasing levels of urine BPA, there is a statistically significant association with (1) decreased sperm concentration, (2) decreased total sperm count, (3) decreased sperm vitality, and (4) decreased sperm motility.[213]

Consumer attorneys Baum, Hedlund, Aristei and Goldman, PC, provide a list of side effects from the leaching of BPA into our bodies. The firm stated that "More than 200 lab animal tests to date strongly suggest that BPA exposure, even at very small doses, creates risks of dangerous developmental, neural and reproductive health effects in infants and children. Exposure to BPA, even at small and short-term doses, is linked to a staggering number of health problems, including:

* Breast cancer
* Prostate disease and cancer
* Diabetes
* Obesity
* Hyperactivity
* Impaired, altered, and compromised immune system and functions
* Miscarriage

- Impaired female reproductive development
- Sperm defects
- Lowered sperm count
- Chromosome abnormalities
- Chromosome sorting errors
- Down's syndrome
- Turner Syndrome
- Klinefelter Syndrome
- Genitalia deformity
- Early onset of puberty
- Impaired learning and memory
- Increased aggression
- Reversal of normal sex differences in the brain structure
- Elimination of sex differences in behavior
- Changes in response to painful or fear-provoking stimuli."[214]

Even though the plastic manufacturers recognize the dangers of BPA and remove it from some products to appease the public, they replace BPA with similar chemicals. Drs. Oz and Roizen state in their article *Beware of the 'BPA-Free' Lie:* "As marketing slogans like 'BPA Free!' have started popping up on various products, the lyrics from The Who song *'Substitute'* keep coming to mind: 'Substitute your lies for fact, I see right through your plastic mac.'" "That's because while plastic manufacturers are removing hormone-disrupting bisphenol A (BPA) from (some) plastics, and (some) linings of food cans, and (some) register receipts, they are replacing it with BPS (bisphenol S), a hormone-disrupting cousin of BPA," say Oz and Roisen.

They further state, "The only difference between BPA and BPS seems to be that BPS is a bit less likely to seep into food and is slightly less effective at mimicking estrogen. But because BPS is a heartier compound, it's slower to degrade than BPA and more persistent once it gets into your body or the environment."[215]

Products that can contain BPA or BPS are water bottles, canned goods, sports water bottles, baby bottles, sippy cups, hard transparent beverage containers, sealants for your teeth, and cash register receipts. Be sure to wash your hands with soap and wear gloves if you handle a lot of cash register receipts.

Alternatives to Plastic Bottles, Canned Goods, and Aluminum:

1. So, what are the alternatives? Glass. Always drink water from glass instead of plastic if possible. Some may ask about metal water bottles, which have come into vogue in recent years. We are uncertain about the safety of aluminum bottles as we have concerns about ingesting aluminum. It is our understanding that Alzheimer's is caused by the accumulation of metals in the brain, so we are wary of using aluminum in general – even when cooking food. Also, depending on what you put in the aluminum bottle, there could be a chemical reaction with the aluminum to release aluminum into the liquid. Stainless steel bottles are probably a good alternative to plastic, but our preference is still glass.

2. Some food companies have begun to label their canned goods BPA-free, and if these are also BPS-free, we do not know. It is wise to prepare fresh vegetables, fresh meats, fresh fish, and fresh fruit on a regular basis and to avoid canned goods. Canned goods are fine to have on hand when in a hurry, or as part of an emergency supply of food.

3. By the way – stainless steel pots and pans and cast iron pans are better than aluminum and non-stick for cooking.

HEALTH TIP #3: AVOID HIGH FRUCTOSE CORN SYRUP

One of the most dangerous substances you can put in your body is High Fructose Corn Syrup (HFCS), which is a processed sweetener and food preservative made from cornstarch. There are two forms of it: HFCS-55, which is used in soft drinks and HFCS-42, which is used in canned fruit in syrup, ice cream, candy desserts, and baked goods. If you read food labels carefully, you will also find it in many sauces, dressings, cereals, yogurt, pickles, relish, and nutrition bars. It's basically everywhere. So what's the problem with HFCS?

Dr. Mark Hyman, M.D., in his article *5 Reasons High Fructose Corn Syrup Will Kill You* says that he has come to understand the role of HFCS in "promoting obesity, disease, and death across the globe."

Here are three of Hyman's reasons below:

1. <u>Large amounts of sugar consumption, in any form, causes obesity and disease</u>. As a nation, we consume way too much sugar, including HFCS. One "20 ounce HFCS sweetened soda, tea or sports drink contains 17 teaspoons of sugar." If you drink two of those per day (34 teaspoons per day), that's more sugar than our distant ancestors consumed in a whole year! The average person consumes about 60 pounds of high fructose corn syrup per year, so no wonder we have so much obesity and disease in this country.

2. <u>Cane sugar and HFCS are not the same biochemically, and your body processes them differently.</u> Cane sugar is naturally occurring, but HFCS is a compound extracted through a chemical, enzymatic process. Cane sugar is sucrose made up of <u>equal</u> amounts of fructose and glucose. When you eat it, your digestive juices break it down into glucose and fructose and then your body can absorb it. It's a different story for HFCS which is 55% fructose and 45% glucose (not equal amounts). These molecules, however, are not bound together, so your body does not need to expend any energy breaking it down. They are absorbed directly into your bloodstream. Fructose shoots straight towards your liver and sets off lipogenesis, the creation of fats like triglycerides and cholesterol. Lipogenesis creates liver damage that can trigger a condition which affects 70 million people known as "fatty liver." Another problem that high doses of high fructose corn syrup can create is to punch holes in the intestinal lining allowing toxic digestive bacteria to flow into your bloodstream, which can trigger inflammation which is the root of a whole host of problems like cancer, obesity, diabetes, dementia and accelerated aging. Fructose is sweeter than glucose, so the food industry can

serve you larger amounts of it and still make more money than by using cane sugar. Also, the food industry receives farm bill corn subsidies. That's why bottles of soda have gotten so much bigger in recent years, contributing to increases in the prevalence of obesity, diabetes, and other chronic diseases in children, and young adults.

3. <u>HFCS often contains mercury due to the manufacturing process.</u> The full extent of other chemical products besides mercury in HFCS is not known, nor their toxicity understood. The government does not test for these unknown substances that make up 15-20% of the average American's daily caloric intake.[216]

So, as you can see, high fructose corn syrup is not so sweet after all. Avoid foods containing HFCS at all costs. We want to save your body from the diseases mentioned above, if possible, to enable you to be strong on your quest to manhood.

Alternatives to High Fructose Corn Syrup:
If you need to have something sweet, eat a piece of dark, organic chocolate, and/or fruit. Oranges, strawberries, blueberries, or raspberries and cherries pair nicely with chocolate. Alternatively, prepare the Amazing Cookies recipe provided in this book.

HEALTH TIP #4: EAT SUGAR IN MODERATION
Sugar is one of the biggest food villains you will need to face.

Dr. Robert Lustig, an American pediatric endocrinologist and author of the book, *Fat Change: The Hidden Truth About Sugar, Obesity, and Disease,* has argued that sugar is as harmful as cocaine or tobacco. This was brought out in the article, *Robert Lustig: The Man Who Believes Sugar is Poison* written by Zoe Williams.[217] We all know - and she pointed out - that large amounts of processed sugar in the American diet has contributed significantly to the obesity epidemic. Besides, that sugar causes disease.

While you can find natural sugar in fruits and some vegetables, processed foods contain processed sugar, also known as "refined" sugar. This type of sugar is often added to processed food to improve the taste or to increase shelf life or both. Processed sugar is frequently listed as "Sugar" on food labels. However, there are over 60 names for sugar (listed at the end of this section). So, you need to learn how to read food labels and be able to recognize all the ways sugar has been added to the food you are planning to purchase.

Do not be confused or intimidated by all these different names. It is still sugar. Processed sugar can be hidden in sauces, ketchup, salad dressings, canned goods, processed cereals, bread, peanut butter, pizzas, yogurt, and so many more foods. I am flabbergasted at the number of foods that have sugar in them – some foods that you would not think should have sugar at all. To get the total number of grams of sugar contained in food, add up all the grams of sugar beside each of the different names for sugar. Beware of "low-fat" foods because food manufacturers tend to add more sugar to products with low-fat content to make the food taste better.

Too much sugar intake can lead to many other health concerns other than obesity – diseases such as diabetes. When I developed Type II Diabetes, I thought my life was over. Both my mother and father had diabetes and died from complications due to this potentially debilitating and fatal condition. My mother even lost a leg to the disease. So this was personal. That's when I got serious about my diet and serious about learning how to hold the disease at bay to give science a chance to find a cure. I consulted a dietitian and the first thing she recommended that I do was to cut down my sugar intake. However, I never recovered from diabetes. I want to emphasize here that "an ounce of prevention is worth a pound of cure," Benjamin Franklin. This means that in the long run it is better to prevent a disaster from occurring rather than to try to deal with the aftermath of a disaster. In other words, eating sweets once in a while all through your life is better than eating sweets every day and ending up with diabetes as an adolescent or later in life. Juvenile Type II diabetes is on the rise.

I unknowingly developed lots of bad nutritional habits as a teenager. In retrospect, our family ate far too many sweet cakes and pies (my mom was an excellent cook). Growing up in Texas, it was a cultural tradition to drink sweetened ice tea, and we did so with every evening meal. There was so much sugar in that tea, the sugar often would not dissolve and made the tea cloudy. Scary thought, yes? Eventually, I learned to drink tea without sugar – with just a little lemon, perhaps. Today, I know not to indulge in tea altogether.

Diabetes is a nasty disease that can also lead to kidney failure, heart disease, and blindness. You have the best chances in the world to avoid diabetes if you follow the guidelines in this book.

James A. Surrell, M.D., author of the book, *SOS (Stop Only Sugar)* states, "The current national statistics indicate that the average person in the United States consumes approximately 140 pounds of sugar each year. Yes, you really did read it right. And guess what your body does with all that sugar. SUGAR IS STORED AS BODY FAT!"

Surrell claims that the SOS Diet will help you painlessly lose 5 to 8 pounds per month (60 to 80 pounds per year, or more). So, if you have a weight problem, this is our recommended way to tackle the nutritional part of the problem. Of course, the other part of the problem is exercise – or the lack of sufficient exercise, which we will talk about further in this chapter.[218]

Throughout my adult life (up until recently), I struggled with weight. I started to gain extra weight when I began eating processed food while attending Junior College. Even while in the Navy, my weight went up and down like a yo-yo for years. The pattern continued after I got out of the military and worked in civilian life for decades. I became addicted to cookies. In the hospital cafeteria where I worked I bought a package of three cookies every day at lunchtime. I knew I had to finally stop eating so much sugar. So I made a strong conscious decision to cut sugar consumption down to a minimum. My first order of business was to stop the bad habit of buying cookies without thinking. Instead of buying three cookies at a time, I would buy only one cookie. After a week or so, I stopped purchasing them altogether. The cafeteria also offered a sumptuous array of fresh baked cake and pie slices. It was easy to overcome the temptation of buying these goodies because I had already overcome the craving for cookies. Mind you, I had these temptations while being diabetic. Sugar had had such a powerful hold on me that I had been rationalizing my actions and allowing myself to ingest this poison. I now know that while eating foods that contain lots of sugar, the sugar had been playing tricks with my hormones and increasing my cravings for the poison.

I joined a gym and enrolled in their Boot Camp program that involved an hour of vigorous exercise each morning Monday through Friday. On top of that I started a jogging program. People told me I looked great and I felt great. I no longer craved sweets and I lost weight but my weight plateaued at about 228 pounds. I am 6'3" tall. That's when, in 2009, I read the Stop Only Sugar (SOS) Diet at the request of my doctor. It really worked for me and I lost the amount of weight I wanted to lose. I stopped around 222 pounds. What I remember most about the SOS Diet was that Dr. Surrell recommended no more than 30 grams of sugar per day, and he suggested eating at least 30 grams of fiber each day (the section on Fiber follows).

Be careful when counting grams of sugar each day. Just one apple contains 19-20 grams of fructose. But since fructose is a natural sugar, it is much better for you than processed sugar. All sugars, including natural sugars that occur in fresh fruit, should be eaten in moderation.

Your brain has mechanisms to warn you when you have eaten enough. However, if you intake too much processed sugar, these processes are interrupted and you will continue to feel hungry and to eat. We are certain that a large portion of the population is not aware of this negative effect of sugar in addition to the other bad things sugar can do to our bodies.

As for fiber, a cup of lima beans contains 14 grams of fiber. A Lima Bean Soup recipe follows in the "Added Bonus" recipe section of this book.

These days, if I want a sweet treat, I will have a couple squares of dark chocolate after dinner. My wife also makes great cookies with low sugar content and freezes them – out of sight out of mind. I will have one cookie about once a week or whenever she bakes a batch for a church function, or for company.

The World Health Organization currently recommends no more than six teaspoons (or about 24 grams) of sugar per day. This is even more restrictive than the SOS Diet, but you get the picture. Just do not go overboard with sugar, especially processed sugar.

Beware of the Sugar Content of So-called "Healthy Drinks"

1. Do not drink fruit juices, even if they are organic, more than once or twice per week because they contain concentrated sugars. Keep in mind that one glass of fresh squeezed orange juice contains the equivalent juice of five oranges. This is too much fructose to consume daily.
2. As previously mentioned, drink water with a squeeze of fresh lemon or lime.

List of Names for Sugar

A team of health scientists from the University of San Francisco, *Sugar Science*, states that added sugar is hiding in 74% of packaged foods. They provided a list of names under which sugar may be hiding on food labels: Agave nectar, Barbados sugar, Barley malt, Barley malt syrup, Beet sugar, Brown sugar, Buttered syrup, Cane juice, Cane juice crystals, Cane sugar, Caramel, Carob syrup, Castor sugar, Coconut palm sugar, Coconut sugar, Confectioner's sugar, Corn sweetener, Corn syrup, Corn syrup solids, Date sugar, Dehydrated cane juice, Demerara sugar, Dextrin, Dextrose, Evaporated cane juice, Free-flowing brown sugars, Fructose, Fruit juice, Fruit juice concentrate, Glucose, Glucose solids, Golden sugar, Golden syrup, Grape sugar, HFCS (High-Fructose Corn Syrup), Honey, Icing sugar, Invert sugar, Malt syrup, Maltodextrin, Maltol, Maltose, Mannose, Maple syrup, Molasses, Muscovado, Palm sugar, Panocha, Powdered sugar, Raw sugar, Refiner's syrup, Rice syrup, Saccharose, Sorghum Syrup, Sucrose, Sugar (granulated), Sweet Sorghum, Syrup, Treacle, Turbinado sugar, and Yellow sugar.[219]

Alternatives to Lower Your Intake of Processed Sugar:

1. Avoid processed food with added sugars as much as possible. When you prepare your own food, you can control the amount of sugar (if any) you add to a recipe. Use fresh vegetables and fresh fruit instead of canned vegetables and fruit. Preparing homemade salad dressings is easy. Few people have time to bake bread regularly, but we can all read food labels. Choose to purchase bread that lists sugars low on its list of ingredients. If sugar is listed at the top of the list on the ingredients label, the bread will contain more sugar than bread that lists sugar as one of the last ingredients.

2. Many packaged hot cocoa mixes contain too much sugar. When making hot cocoa at home you can control the amount of sugar – mix 1- 1½ teaspoons organic sugar into 1 tablespoon *Hershey's Cocoa Powder – 100% Cacao – Natural Unsweetened*, in the bottom of a mug. (Avoid cocoa powder that contains salt.) With a fork, mix the cocoa powder, sugar and beat in ¼ cup of cold water. Fill the cup with hot milk (do not boil the milk) and stir again with the fork. The cocoa will be naturally frothy on top.

3. Add 2 teaspoons maple syrup or honey to plain yogurt and frozen fruit in smoothies. Recipes for great smoothies follow.

4. Spread a thinner layer of jam on your bread.

5. Buy dark chocolate that is 60% cacao or more. Have only one or two squares per day.

6. Never eat a whole box of chocolates. Pace yourself by enjoying and savoring two pieces once a week, instead of two dark chocolate squares. You will then have the pleasure of eating your chocolates for a longer period of time. It is fun to share chocolates with someone special. Then eating the chocolates becomes a special event and we eat fewer chocolates because we are sharing. In hot weather we keep our chocolates in the fridge.

7. Choose sweets without icing made with a lot of icing sugar. A dusting of powdered sugar on an almond croissant or a dark chocolate croissant contains less sugar than a cupcake that is piled high with icing.
8. Cream cheese icing's sugar content can be lowered, and the icing will taste great. You will need to purchase more cream cheese to cover the surface that is usually covered, without the decrease in sugar.
9. Never eat a whole large bag of caramel popcorn or an entire large bag of chips. Look for a brand of caramel popcorn that does not contain high fructose corn syrup. Pop some organic corn in olive oil in a pot that has a heavy bottom (so the popcorn does not burn). Place the regular popcorn in a bowl. Next place a few chips cooked in avocado oil on top (we like jalapeno chips), and a bit of caramel popcorn. This treat is very satisfying to munch on when watching a movie or game. However, you should not have this treat more than once a week.
10. Guacamole made with mashed avocados and a little lemon or lime, served with organic corn chips will satisfy your appetite. A spicy guacamole recipe is included in this book.
11. Peeled, cubed, frozen bananas can be pureed in a food processor into an ice cream-like consistency for a delicious treat.
12. You can slice an apple or pear and some cheese and have these with a few organic crackers for a treat. You can also have the cheese and crackers with grapes.
13. It is better to use a little organic sugar than artificial sweeteners. Preparing your own cookies, crisps, and pies is best because you can lower the sugar content in recipes. For example, many fruit crisp and fruit pie recipes call for 1 cup of sugar, but we use less. Fruit is already sweet. We use a quarter cup sugar for apple pies, and a half-cup of sugar for strawberry-rhubarb crisps because rhubarb is tart (for 9-inch pies). A great recipe for fruit crisps follows. Cookies are also

forgiving of a decrease in sugar, which means that they still look the same, and they are still very tasty – especially the Amazing Cookies, for which the recipe follows. Whereas, lowering the sugar content in cake batter may alter the texture of the cake. We would not advise this. Save your consumption of cakes for special occasions.

HEALTH TIP #5: EAT SUFFICIENT AMOUNTS OF FIBER

The SOS Diet mentioned earlier recommends a minimum of 30 grams of dietary fiber per day. Some of the benefits of eating fiber, according to Sharon Palmer, a Registered Dietitian, are reducing cholesterol levels, appetite control, and weight control. For you budding scientists, Palmer goes on to explain, "many whole plant foods are rich in different types of dietary fiber, such as pectin, gum, mucilage, cellulose, hemicellulose, lignin, and soluble fiber. Consuming a variety of fibers is suggested to gain the maximum benefits of a high-fiber diet."[220]

Brans, beans, peas, berries and ground flaxseeds are highest in fiber followed by vegetables, other fruits, and grains. Keep flaxseeds fresh by placing the bag of flaxseeds in the freezer. You can look up more detailed lists of foods containing fiber on the Internet.

HEALTH TIP #6: AVOID FAST FOOD

What did you have for breakfast today? It is quite likely that many teens dined at a fast food restaurant on their way to school. I sometimes had breakfast at a fast food restaurant on my way to work. I am cured of that habit after reading the information below. Do you really want to know what is inside fast food eggs you love so much? You may be surprised.

In a Huffington Post article titled, *These Disturbing Fast Food Truths Will Make You Reconsider Your Lunch*, Renee Jacques relates a story about eggs that made me stop eating eggs at fast food restaurants. "David Di Salvo, a writer at Forbes, decided to really look into the eggs in popular fast food breakfast sandwiches. What he

discovered was that their 'eggs' are a strange concoction that includes eggs and 'premium egg blend.' Some things that are in this
special blend contain glycerin, a solvent found in soap and shaving
cream, dimethylpolysiloxane, a silicone that can also be found in Silly
Putty, and calcium silicate, a sealant used on roofs and concrete."
[221] Some fast food restaurants do not just crack an egg and cook it
anymore. They have to process it - to death. There are many more
articles written about the disgusting contents of fast foods, but we
are not going into detail about them here. You get the point.

This little exposé on eggs is only one example of the horrors of
some fast food contents. Due to the need to prolong shelf life and to
cut costs while providing some semblance of flavor for the consumer,
food manufacturers get very creative in their processes. Some fast
food does not rot even when left out at room temperature for years.
This is not natural. Your body needs natural food. As a consumer and
as a young man hoping to have a healthy body when he grows into a
man, you must be wise and take heed of what you put into your body.
Do your research before you eat.

Alternatives to Fast Food:
Canned goods and dried goods such as soups that you reconstitute
with water are great for emergency supplies, but they have little nutritional value when compared to fresh foods. Eat fresh vegetables
and fruits; real eggs from free-range or vegetarian-fed chickens; oats
(oatmeal, oat bread); ground flaxseeds (grinding enables the body
to digest the nutrients from flaxseeds) on smoothies; uncured meats;
wild fish; natural sweeteners such as honey, and maple syrup; and
whole milk and plain yogurt. To be safe and to obtain the most nutrition, choose to eat the foods that God has provided for us, naturally.

Fast food you can make at home: For fast breakfasts, make smoothies, wheat-free muffins, granola, scrambled eggs and organic sourdough
toast, or some berries or grapes with cheese and organic grain bread.
We will supply you with a collection of excellent recipes later in this book.

For a fast lunch or supper open a BPA-free can of organic lentil
soup or a boxed organic soup – add pepper, and serve the soup

with: prepared organic salsa, organic bean dip, and organic tortilla chips from a grocery store. With a light supper such as this I like to complete the meal with one of my wife's "better-than-ice- cream" smoothies. Recipes for these smoothies will follow.

HEALTH TIP #7: AVOID EATING TOO MUCH WHEAT

Does acne plague you? Are you starting to put on weight, especially in the abdomen? You may be too young to exhibit the onset of dia-betes, arthritis, heart disease, accelerated aging, and autoimmune diseases, but guess what - if you are eating too much genetically-mod-ified (GMO) wheat or GMO corn-based foods, conditions are being set up in your body to develop these diseases according to Certified Nutritionist and Certified Trainer, Mike Geary. He wrote the books *The Truth about Six Pack Abs* and *The Top 101 Foods that FIGHT Aging*.

There is strong evidence today that eating wheat is causing a myriad of health problems such as those mentioned earlier. Guys like me - who have eaten wheat most of their lives - can tell you of the struggles with weight and other unhealthiness. Believe me, you do not want to go there. It's best to learn to eat correctly now while you are a young "whipper-snapper." So read this section carefully.

JUST REMEMBER TO CONSULT WITH YOUR OWN DOCTOR PRIOR TO FOLLOWING ADVICE IN THIS BOOK OR ANY BOOK REGARDING YOUR HEALTH. YOU SHOULD HAVE REGULAR CHECKUPS WITH YOUR DOCTOR ANYWAY AS A MATTER OF COURSE.

Dr. William Davis, cardiologist, health crusader, and author of the book, *Wheat Belly*, states, "The food you eat is making you sick, and the agencies that are providing you with guidelines on what to eat are giving dangerous advice with devastating health consequences."[222]

One of the biggest risks to public health today is the Food Pyramid put out by the US Government because it recommends eating a lot of foods containing grains such as bread and cereal. In the last 50 years grains such as wheat and corn have been scientifically geneti-cally modified and are no longer as compatible with human bodies as they once were in the 1950s and earlier. It is not the same food. This is because wheat has been genetically modified to increase crop yields, to affect certain baking characteristics, and other reasons, as we mentioned before.

In the anti- "Wheat Belly" lifestyle, all foods made with high-yield, semi-dwarf wheat – the worst crop ever created in a laboratory are rejected.

Dr. Davis was Dr. Oz's guest for three segments of the Dr. Oz Show concerning genetically modified wheat. Dr. Oz explained that in 1950 wheat was taller, bigger and had health benefits. In 2014, the wheat grown was about six inches shorter than the wheat grown in the 1950s. Dr. Davis explained that wheat now has a much higher glycemic index – it spikes your blood sugar worse than sugar. It has been linked to auto-immune diseases such as multiple sclerosis, lupus, and rheumatoid arthritis. The protein in this "Frankenwheat" can make holes in your intestinal tract, which allows toxins to get into your blood stream and cause disease. It can lead to acne, dandruff, skin rashes, and has been linked to anxiety and depression. It can also cause acid reflux, which is a burning in your esophagus.

Dr. Davis recommended eating beef, chicken, colored vegetables including mushrooms (not potatoes), nuts, salsa, cheese, and eggs, as much as you wish. He recommended eating two servings a day of, yogurt, or milk, or fruit, or lentils, or beans, or brown rice, or white rice.

Dr. Mercola's recommendations are similar. His diet consists primarily (80%) of vegetables and fruits. Kris Gunnar CEO and Founder of Authority Nutrition, and Atli Arnarson, Ph.D. in Human Nutrition, and Joe Leech, MS, Dietician, (part of Gunnar's team) also concur.

Alternatives to GMO Wheat:

1. Dr. Davis has given us a wheat free baking mix recipe and a recipe for preparing muffins. These recipes will follow in this book.

2. Eat organic breads, and organic cereals. Use organic flour when baking.
3. Eat wheat in moderation.
4. Prepare buckwheat pancakes. Soba noodles are prepared with buckwheat. Buckwheat is not wheat and it does not spike blood sugar as much as wheat.

HEALTH TIP #8: AVOID GENETICALLY-MODIFIED FOODS (FRANKENFOODS)

Studies have shown that when doctors take patients suffering from inflammatory bowel disease, allergies, asthma, autoimmune diseases, diabetes, and acid reflux off GMO foods their patients' health improves.

Non-GMO Label

Organic Label

One of the biggest changes in the American food supply in recent years has been the creation of genetically-modified foods. They are generally classified as genetically-modified organisms (GMO). There is a big debate in the world today about short-term and long-term health effects of these foods. In the article, *GMO Foods: Key Points in the Genetically Modified Debate*, Marjorie Olster says, "Much of the corn, soybean, sugar beets and cotton cultivated in the United States today contains plants whose DNA was manipulated in labs to resist disease and drought, ward off insects and boost the food supply. Though common in the U.S., they are largely banned in the 28-nation European Union."[223] We also know that wheat and canola are GMO. We will talk a lot more about these two foods later in the chapter.

People who support the use of genetically-modified foods (GMO) will say that this food is okay to consume. The fact is that scientists do not know the long-term effects of GMO foods on the body. The authors of this book are suspect of GMO foods and avoid them as much as we can. We see GMO foods as just one of the roadblocks to your optimal health.

According to the Non-GMO Project, in the U.S., GMOs are in as much as 80% of conventional processed food.[224] To avoid GMOs, look for the Non-GMO Project Verified label shown above.

To be sure your choices are genetically engineered free, all you need to remember is USDA Certified Organic = NO GMOs! (see label above)

Alternatives to GMO Foods

As much as possible, eat foods certified to be organic and non-GMO. Many grocery stores carry these options.

Health Tip #9: Avoid Meats and Milk Containing Hormones and Antibiotics

When animals are kept in unsanitary conditions and not allowed to roam free, they are more prone to disease. This is unethical. Animals ought to be treated with respect.

The meat industry gives many animals antibiotics to prevent illness. The overuse of antibiotics led to antibiotic-resistant bacteria called "superbugs." Therefore, when a person becomes very ill, there is now a significant risk that most antibiotics won't work. This is especially dangerous for pregnant women who cannot take the strongest antibiotics.

To increase the quantity of milk produced, cows are often given rBGH (recombinant bovine growth hormone), which is also banned in the European Union, as well as in Japan, Canada, New Zealand and Australia.[225]

Alternatives to Meat and Milk that Contain Hormones and Antibiotics:

1. Eat antibiotic-free meat: Today, some farms that raise animals are choosing not to give animals antibiotics, which is better for

the animals because the living conditions on these farms tend to be better for the animals. It is also better for human beings because when we purchase the meat of animals raised on these farms, we do not risk being exposed to antibiotic-resistant bacteria. The United States Department of Agriculture – Food and Safety and Inspection Services has established guidelines for labeling. Therefore, it is recommended that you eat beef and poultry that are labeled "no antibiotics added," and beef that is also labeled "no hormones administered." "Federal regulations prohibit the use of hormones," for poultry and pork. Alternatively, you can choose to eat organic meats. Choosing meats wisely will be especially important when your wife is expecting a child.

2. Wild fish high in omega-3s that do not live long lives such wild salmon, herring, and sardines are also excellent alternatives. Fish like tuna and mackerel should not be eaten more than once a week due to the mercury that has accumulated in their bodies. Tuna and mackerel live for many years in oceans that contain mercury. During those years, mercury builds up in their bodies. Pregnant women should avoid tuna and mackerel. Salmon only live for two years. Therefore, salmon are exposed to mercury in oceans for a shorter period, and therefore, they absorb far less mercury.

3. Drink organic milk.

Note: In the *Word of Wisdom*, a spiritual guide to food consumption and human behavior, we are taught that we should eat meat in moderation. As we have seen, a diet of mostly vegetables and fruit is best for most people. However, people whose ancestors thrived on meat may not thrive well on a vegetarian diet, such as the Inuits. We will discuss more about genomics in this chapter. When we eat meat or anything for that matter, we should pray to God and thank Him for the animals and the plants, the food we are about to eat. Thus, when we give thanks to God and bless the food, we receive permission to eat it.

HEALTH TIP #10: WASH PRODUCE BEFORE EATING IT TO AVOID
INGESTING PESTICIDE RESIDUE AND OTHER HARMFUL CHEMICALS

Over the decades, there have been significant changes in the way
our food has been grown and processed for market. Dr. Mercola[226]
relates that, historically, most food was fresh and grown locally. I
grew up on a farm and enjoyed excellent meals with fresh produce
daily.

Times have changed.

I went to a supermarket (I will not mention its name) to buy apples, and I struck up a conversation with the fellow handling the fruits
and vegetables. I told him that I had recently started having allergic
reactions when eating apples after they were washed with water. I
discovered that if I washed the peel of the apples thoroughly with a
"vegetable and fruit wash" for 20 seconds, including all the inden-
tations of the apple, rinsed and rubbed them under running water
until they were squeaky clean; and dried them completely with paper
towels prior to eating them, I no longer reacted. Otherwise, I would
wind up in the Hospital Emergency Room because my airways would
begin to constrict – unless I could quickly ingest a dose of Benadryl.
He informed me that he had taken to wearing gloves when handling
fruits and vegetables. I asked him why. He said that whenever he did
not wear gloves, he would notice a yellow coating on the palms of his
hands when he got home at night. Shockingly, he told me that this
yellow "stuff" he presumed to be pesticides sprayed on the foods he
handled. He went on to say that in Washington State where we live,
apples were the worst offenders.

Beware that cross-contamination of pesticides may occur in the
produce section of grocery stores. Due to grocery clerks handling
non-organic produce and then handling organic produce pesticides
can be transferred from non-organic to organic.

It is my personal belief that the problem lies in the aggressive
use of pesticides on foods to increase productivity and to ward
off diseases and pests. Perhaps my body has reached the breaking point of being able to resist and process these pesticides over

the years. All I know is that now I need to consume organic foods in order to minimize or eliminate the allergic reactions. Dr. OZ says, "Eating food that contains large doses of pesticides can wreak havoc on your nervous system and negatively affect your heart and lungs." He reports on his website that some produce had traces of more than 60 pesticides on them. He cited strawberries, apples, spinach, peaches, corn and kiwi as the dirtiest fruits and vegetables that put your health at risk.[227]

Also, we assume that as long as the pesticide residues remain below limit they are safe, but this stuff is toxic by its very nature. Besides, these chemicals have not been directly tested in humans, according to the WebMD article, *Safer Food for a Healthier You.*[228]

Another problem, as mentioned in the same article is that the safety profiles of the individual pesticides do not take into consideration the effect of their being combined together inside our bodies. I am no longer surprised that my body has begun to have "allergic" reactions to certain fruits and vegetables.

In the article, it is also reported that the FDA analyzed data collected by the nonprofit Environmental Working Group, and identified certain fruits and vegetables as having the highest levels of pesticides. Those foods are as follows:

* Peaches
* Apples
* Sweet bell peppers
* Celery
* Nectarines
* Strawberries
* Cherries
* Pears
* Imported grapes
* Spinach
* Lettuce
* Potatoes

It would be wise to choose organic options for this produce.

Alternatives to Foods with Pesticides:
The FDA also identified foods with the least pesticide residues as follows:

* Avocados
* Frozen sweet corn
* Pineapples
* Mangos
* Asparagus
* Frozen peas
* Bananas
* Cabbage
* Broccoli
* Papayas

Therefore, you can reduce your exposure to pesticides by buying organic produce for the high-pesticide items. For foods on the low-residue list, you can get away with eating non-organic if you must do so.

By all means, eat organic if you can. In either case, please reduce any contamination on your food by following these steps:

* Always wash your fresh produce well. For best results use a fruit and vegetable cleaner to remove waxes, chemicals, and soil.
* You may want to peel some non-organic produce to reduce the amount of pesticide residue. However, beware that peeling produce can reduce the amount of valuable nutrients available.
* After rinsing a peach, blanch the peach by placing it in boiling water for 2 minutes. When the peach has cooled, the skin will wrinkle and can be removed easily. You can then enjoy a bright, shiny, juicy, peel-less peach.

HEALTH TIP #11: AVOID HYDROGENATED OILS, GMO OILS, AND TRANS FATS

Americans consume over 28 billion pounds of oils annually.

Soybean Oil

Soybean oil accounts for about 65% of the oils consumed by Americans or about 18.2 billion pounds annually. According to Mercola's article, *11 Charts that Show Everything Wrong with our Modern Diet*, about 95 percent of soy is genetically engineered and loaded with the herbicide glyphosate, and the partial hydrogenation process used to make soybean oil produces trans fats that cause disease. Mercola surmises that soybean oil is one of the worst types of oil you can eat.[229]

Soybean Oil Problem #1: Glyphosate

Soybean oil contains glyphosate, the active ingredient in Roundup, a chemical used to control weeds in soybean crops. This chemical has been known to cause cancer according to the world's leading cancer agencies as mentioned on the Dr. Oz Show,[230] *The Importance of Warning Labels on Foods Exposed to Pesticides*. These GMO soybeans are used to produce soy oil, which can be found in numerous processed foods.

Soybean Oil Problem #2: Destruction of Good Bacteria in the Gut

On the website Mother Jones Tom Philpott informs us that glyphosate found in GMO and non-organic soybean food and soybean oil harm beneficial bacteria in the human gut, for example, Lactobacillus.[231] We need good bacteria in our guts to help us digest and absorb nutrients from our food properly to promote good health.

Soybean Oil Problem #3: Trans Fats

About half of the soybean oil produced is partially hydrogenated. Part of the problem with partially hydrogenated soybean oil, Dr. Mercola observes in his article, *Soybean Oil: One of the Most Harmful Ingredients in Processed Foods*, is that soybean oil contains trans fat caused by the partial hydrogenation process. Unnatural fats like trans fats cause dysfunction and chaos in your body at the cellular level.

He tells us that studies have linked trans fats to:

* Interfering with your body's use of beneficial omega-3 fats
* Cancer - The fats interfere with enzymes your body uses to fight cancer
* Diabetes – The fats interfere with the insulin receptors in your cell membranes
* Decreased Immune Function – The fats reduce your immune response
* Reproductive Problems – The fats interfere with enzymes needed to produce sex hormones
* Chronic health problems such as obesity, asthma, auto-immune disease, cancer, and bone degeneration
* Heart disease – The fats clog your arteries
* Increased blood levels of low-density lipoprotein (LDL), or "bad" cholesterol, while lowering levels of high-density lipoprotein (HDL), or "good" cholesterol[232]

Dr. Mercola warns us that "[Most] people do not have a clue they are eating this much soybean oil. They are actually getting most of it from processed foods, which often have soybean oil added to them because it is cheap. The best way to avoid soybean oil (and other nasty ingredients) is to avoid processed foods."[233]

Canola Oil

Canola is genetically modified rapeseed. Many people were allergic to rapeseed. When rapeseed was genetically modified and called canola, more people could tolerate it but the subtle effects, over time, were not known. Today, it is not uncommon for people to be allergic to canola oil. We have found that a lot of restaurants use canola oil routinely for cooking. We have also found that many processed foods found in supermarkets contain canola oil.

As a former restaurant owner, I can tell you that using canola oil is more economical than using olive oil or avocado oil. My wife, however, became allergic to canola oil, which prompted us to do a bit of research on it.

The *GMO Compass* site states:

"These improved rapeseed cultivars were free of erucic acid and glucosinolates. Erucic acid tasted bitter and had prevented the use of rapeseed oil in food. Glucosinolates, which were found in rapeseed meal leftover from pressing, are toxic and had prevented the use of the meal in animal feed. These new cultivars are known as "double-zero" rapeseed. In Canada, where "double-zero" rapeseed was developed, the crop was renamed "canola" (Canadian oil) to differentiate it from non-edible rapeseed."[234]

We recommend that you check the *Elevate Yourself to Manhood* website at http://www.elevateyourselftomanhood.com/videos for the availability of the video about how canola oil is made.

Kris Gunnars, in his article, *Canola Oil: Good or Bad?* points out that we should, at least, be suspicious of [non-organic] canola oil because it is exposed to high heat during processing. "It is certainly nothing like the simple processes used to make other popular fats and oils, like butter, olive oil or coconut oil," says Gunnars. Canola oil contains polyunsaturated fats that are sensitive to high heat. Because of this these oils oxidize quickly (become rancid). Gunnar further instructs us:

"A toxic solvent called hexane is used to extract the oil from the seeds. Trace amounts of hexane have sometimes been found in cooking oils. One study analyzed canola and soybean oils found on store shelves in the U.S. They found that 0.56% to 4.2% of the fatty acids in them were toxic trans fats (3).This is not listed on the label, unfortunately.

"Artificial trans fats are incredibly harmful and associated with many serious diseases, especially heart disease… the biggest killer in the world (4, 5).

"However, keep in mind that cold-pressed and organic canola oil has not gone through the same process and won't contain so many oxidized fats or trans fats. "[235]

Increased Vegetable Oil Consumption has Changed the American Body Fatty Acid Composition

Increased vegetable oil consumption has changed the American body fatty acid composition, which increases the risk of cancer.[236]

Dr. Mercola adds that the increased consumption of processed vegetable oils has upset the balance of omega-3 to omega-6 fats in the typical American diet. This ratio should be 1-to-1. Instead, Americans eat too much omega-6 and not enough omega-3 setting the stage for cardiovascular disease, cancer, depression, Alzheimer's, rheumatoid arthritis, and diabetes, just to name a few.[237]

Dr. Mercola's bottom line in regards to omega-3 and omega-6 fats:

* The American Heart Association's (AHA's) position on omega-6 fats runs counter to the vast majority of scientific research that supports the health benefits of lowering your omega-6 fat intake, and raising your omega-3 intake.
* Research shows that mega-3 fat deficiencies can lead to increased inflammation in your body, which predisposes you to chronic diseases like diabetes, allergies, and problems with mood and memory.
* The types of omega-3 and omega-6 fats you consume matters as much as the ratio. All dietary fats should come from whole foods that are organic, unprocessed, unrefined, and non-GMO; the AHA fails to address this.
* Your primary sources for both omega-3 and omega-6 fats should be organic, unrefined oils such as olive oil and avocado oil, raw milk and butter, free-range eggs, grass pastured beef, and whole seeds. Oils/fats you should avoid include corn, canola, soy, and margarine.[238]

Alternatives to Hydrogenated Oils, GMO Oils, and Trans Fats:

1. Sauté onions, garlic, mushroom and vegetables in "cold-pressed and naturally refined," avocado oil, or coconut oil because they do not oxidize in the pan at higher temperatures. Organic extra virgin, first cold pressed olive oil is good for making salad dressings. Butter is good for making sauces.

2. Extra virgin avocado oil has excellent flavor and is high in monounsaturated fatty acids that are good for you. Marie Wong, Cecilla Requejo-Jackman, and Allan Woolf report on The American Oil Chemists Society (AOCS) website that,"carotenoids in avocado fruit have long attracted attention for their potential anti-carcinogenic effect (inhibits development of cancer); these same carotenoids are subsequently extracted into the oil. The most significant carotenoid present in the oil is lutein (0.5-3.3 mg/kg oil). Lutein is beneficial for eye health by reducing the progression of age-related macular degeneration. The cold-pressed avocado oil also contains high levels of phytosterols (b-sitosterol being the principal sterol present), at 2.23-4.48 mg/g oil. Based on its fatty acid makeup and the presence of these phytochemicals, (extra virgin cold-pressed) avocado oil is considered to be a healthful oil."[239]

3. Eat fish rich in omega-3 (wild salmon is best) once or twice a week. If you feel that you are not getting a sufficient amount of omega-3, take omega-3 fish oil capsules that have been purified by molecular distillation to remove, heavy metals, PCBs, Dioxins, and Furans, which over time may lead to cancer. (consumerLab.com)

4. Flaxseeds and flaxseed oil capsules also contain a healthy amount of omega-3.

5. Cook with coconut oil, avocado oil, olive oil and butter. When cooking with all four of these oils, you will benefit from the different micronutrients contained in each oil.

Your body is capable of producing all the fatty acids it needs except for omega-3 and omega-6. So, it is critical, for good health, that you consume these fatty acids from natural sources on a 1:1 ratio in regards to the number of milligrams of mega-3 and omega-6. Here are some foods that contain excellent sources of omega-3 and omega-6 to help you balance out your fatty acid consumption. Check food labels to determine the amount of omega-3 and omega-6 in milligrams per serving.

Omega 6 Foods:

* Peanut butter
* Seeds
* Dairy - whole milk, real cheese, butter
* Eggs
* Beef
* Poultry

Omega 3 Foods:

* Flaxseeds and flaxseed oil
* Salmon
* Herring
* Oysters
* Sardines
* Caviar

HEALTH TIP #12: AVOID SODAS (REGULAR SODAS AND ESPECIALLY DIET SODAS)

If you want to be healthy, please do not drink sodas (also known as "soda pop" or "pop") because they can wreak havoc on your body. There are no known benefits to drinking soda of which we know.

What Happens One Hour after Drinking A Can of Regular Coke

The Renegade Pharmacist published information that struck a chord with the public about the adverse effects of Coke and Diet Coke.

Keep in mind that Coke and Diet Coke are representative of all regular sodas and diet sodas, so you should avoid all of them.

In The First 10 minutes: 10 teaspoons of sugar hit your system - well over your recommended daily intake - 6 teaspoons. You do not immediately vomit from the overwhelming sweetness because phosphoric acid cuts the flavor allowing you to keep it down.

20 minutes: Your blood sugar spikes, causing an insulin burst. Your liver responds to this by turning any sugar it can get its hands on into fat. (There's plenty of that at this particular moment)

40 minutes: Caffeine absorption is complete. Your pupils dilate, your blood pressure rises, as a response your liver dumps more sugar into your bloodstream. The adenosine receptors in your brain are now blocked preventing drowsiness.

45 minutes: Your body ups your dopamine production stimulating the pleasure centers of your brain. This is physically the same way heroin works, by the way.

>60 minutes: The phosphoric acid binds calcium, magnesium and zinc in your lower intestine, providing a further boost in metabolism. This is compounded by high doses of sugar also increasing the urinary excretion of calcium.

>60 Minutes: The caffeine's diuretic properties come into play. (It makes you have to urinate.) It is now assured that you'll evacuate the bonded calcium, magnesium and zinc that was headed to your bones as well as sodium, and water.

[Be aware that zinc is also needed for prostate health and mental health.]

>60 minutes: As the rage inside you dies down you will start to have a sugar crash. You may become irritable and/or sluggish. You have also now, literally, urinated away all the water that was in the Coke. But not before infusing it with valuable nutrients your body could have used for things like even having the ability to hydrate your system or build strong bones and teeth.[240]

What Happens One Hour After Drinking a Can of Diet Coke

The Renegade Pharmacist also published information about the damaging effects of diet sodas:

First 10 Minutes: It Attacks Your Teeth

The phosphoric acid attacks the enamel in your teeth while the artificial sweeteners like aspartame hit your system. Studies have proven aspartame triggers the taste receptors and then tricks your body into thinking it has just processed sugar.

20 Minutes: May Switch On Fat Storage Mode

Like regular Coke, this can trigger insulin, which sends your body into fat storage mode.

Data from a number of studies, including the Nurses' Health Study and the Health Professionals Follow-up Study, also reported greater risk of type 2 diabetes, high blood pressure, and heart disease.

Also, some data indicates those who consume artificially sweetened beverages double the risk of metabolic syndrome, which is related to diabetes and cardiovascular problems

40 Minutes: Can Cause Addiction

The potentially deadly combination of caffeine and aspartame creates a short addictive high similar to the way cocaine works. Excitotoxins are released which may exhaust your brain by over-stimulating its neuroreceptors, especially if consumed on a regular basis.

60 Minutes: May Deplete Nutrients, Make You Hungry and Thirsty For More

Unlike the small amount of satisfaction you get from regular Coke, your body may still crave sweets. This makes you likely to reach for another soda, or worse, some other junk food you consider to be safe and the cycle continues.[241]

A can of diet coke provides no nourishment and would replace a more nutritious drink you could have consumed instead of potentially depleting your body of essential minerals.

A diet soda will never quench your thirst as it dehydrates rather than hydrates your body. A lack of vital water can lead to brain fog, poor concentration, fatigue and feelings of irritability.

A Nurse's Experience with Diet Soda
Donna Cardillo, RN (nurse), MA, tells this compelling story about how important it is to listen to our body's needs, in her article "Is Your Diet Soda the Reason You're Not Feeling Well."

"Several years ago, a friend of mine was having a series of troubling symptoms including frequent headaches, dizziness, and nausea. She finally visited her physician who ran a series of medical tests. Everything came back negative, so the doctor further questioned my friend about her lifestyle including her diet and sleep habits. When my friend revealed that she regularly consumed 2-3 liters of diet soda each day, she was advised to discontinue her habit immediately. She did so, and all of her symptoms disappeared within a week, never to return. Her physician suspected she was experiencing side effects from the excessive amount of artificial sweeteners she was consuming in the soda.

"Needing to lose a few pounds, last year I joined a formal weight-loss program that required me to drink one-two liters of water daily. Because I've always had to force myself to drink water, I decided to use an artificially sweetened drink mix to make the liquid more palatable. It worked, and I happily chugged away for the next several weeks.

"Then I began to have heart palpitations. I considered whether I was experiencing excessive stress or anxiety in my life, but concluded that I was actually feeling rather calm and in control of late, so I didn't think that was the cause. I also do not consume caffeine and had been sleeping well. When the palpitations didn't stop after several weeks, I consulted my health-care provider. After an electrocardiogram (ECG) and exam showed nothing abnormal going on, the physician chalked up my symptoms to stress but suggested that if the symptoms didn't go away, further tests would be needed.

"I went home relieved that the tests were negative but remained troubled when the symptoms continued. Suddenly, one day I remembered my friend and her
symptoms from years prior due to her soda consumption.
Because the palpitations started shortly after I had become
a regular "user" of artificially sweetened drinks, I suspected
that this consumption could be triggering my symptoms. I
immediately stopped using the drink mix. Within a few
days the palpitations stopped, and I have been fine ever
since. "[242]

Drinking Diet Sodas Can Actually Make You Gain Weight
Drinking diet sodas on a regular basis makes your liver work so hard
detoxifying the chemical aspartame that it does not have the capacity to do one of its main jobs - breaking down fats. If you want to
lose weight and have a good quality of life as a healthy person do
not drink soft drinks more than once or twice a year. Drink water
instead.
**Note: If you want to gain muscle and weight, go to
Health Tip #22 for suggests on how to bulk up naturally and
healthfully.**

Long-Term Effects of Drinking Regular Sodas and Diet Sodas
You become what you eat and drink. Don't be fooled by multi-billion-
dollar ads and beverage companies that only want to get into your
pockets to get your hard earned money. A couple of sodas per year
at a BBQ or at a game will not hurt you, but the long term effects of
drinking sodas regularly will rob you of your health. This is definitely something you want to leave behind before heading out on your
quest for manhood.

Fatty Liver Disease
You only have one liver. It is important to take good care of it. It has
to last you a lifetime. You cannot survive without your liver.

In the on-line article *Soft Drinks Consumption and Nonalcoholic Fatty Liver Disease*, which is made available by the US National Library of Medicine, National Institute of Health, in the World Journal of Gastroenterology, William Nseir, Fares Nasser, and Nimer Assy state:

"The consumption of soft drinks can increase the prevalence of nonalcoholic fatty liver disease (NAFLD) independently of metabolic syndrome. During regular soft drinks consumption, fat accumulates in the liver by the primary effect of fructose which increases lipogenesis, and in the case of diet soft drinks, by the additional contribution of aspartame sweetener and caramel colorant which are rich in advanced glycation end products that potentially increase insulin resistance and inflammation. This review emphasizes some hard facts about soft drinks, reviews fructose metabolism, and explains how fructose contributes to the development of obesity, diabetes, metabolic syndrome, and NAFLD. "[243]

Researcher Nimer Assy reported that the aspartame in diet sodas may increase insulin resistance (causing diabetes) and trigger fatty liver disease.

Alert: The next section is a warning about the link between drinking sodas and birth defects. In order to better your chances of having healthy babies it would be wise for you and the young woman you marry to avoid drinking regular sodas and diet sodas.

Permanent Genetic Damage Due to an Accumulation of Formaldehyde The artificial sweetener aspartame, which is used in diet soda, has been reported to have harmful effects on the liver and on overall health. The website *HolisticMed.com* cites an animal study conducted at the Universitat de Barcelona, Spain. This study, conducted by Trocho et al. and published in the journal *Life Sciences* found that even small doses of aspartame caused the chemical formaldehyde (embalming fluid) to accumulate in the liver and bind to protein molecules. The site notes that formaldehyde may cause permanent genetic damage with long-term exposure.

The *Healthy Holistic Living* website informs us that when we consume aspartame, the methanol contained in the substance gets distributed throughout the body including the brain, muscle, fat and nervous tissues, then it becomes metabolized to form formaldehyde, which enters cells and binds to proteins and genetic material (DNA).[244] According to Dr. Mercola formaldehyde is a neurotoxin and known carcinogen which causes retinal damage, interferes with DNA replication and causes birth defects.[245]

Other Diseases Caused by Aspartame Consumption
According to the Healthy Holistic Living website, if it turns out that your wife is pregnant and she happens to have the genetic disorder known as Phenylketonuria (PKU) and she consumes aspartame, she will be twice as likely to give birth to a child with brain damage. You see, women who have this genetic disorder cannot metabolize phenylalanine. There are no symptoms to tell if she has the condition. She must be tested for it. Some doctors even recommend diet products to their pregnant patients to help them keep their weight down.[246] Scary. If your wife is pregnant, she should not consume artificial sweeteners.

If your wife does not carry the PKU gene, then she must not get complacent and consume aspartame. "I can have aspartame and it doesn't affect me at all," states Dr. Blaylock, describing the comments of many of his patients. But according to Dr. Blaylock, "over many years, one will start to see obvious disease in those persons". He says that those diseases, "can range from lupus and fibromyalgia to multiple sclerosis and Huntington's disease.[247]

Ingesting Preservatives in Sodas Can Lead to DNA Damage, Cirrhosis of the Liver, and Damage to Other Organs
Jennifer Byrne, a writer for Livestrong.com, talks about how preservatives added to soft drinks can damage DNA:

". . . the preservative sodium benzoate, also known as E211, may cause serious cell damage to the liver and other organs. This additive, which is used in many soft drinks to prevent mold, was reported to cause damage to the mitochondria of DNA, and eventually lead to cirrhosis of the liver and various other conditions. Although Coca-Cola reportedly phased sodium benzoate out of Diet Coke, it is still used in other diet drinks."[248]

You must exhibit self-discipline to avoid all the short-term and long-term effects of drinking unnatural substances in order to protect yourself and your future babies.

Alternatives to Sodas

* Drinking organic kombucha, which is naturally carbonated is an excellent alternative. Kombucha does not contain tea because the kombucha mushroom eats the tea and the sugar used to prepare kombucha. The result is a beverage that has a lot of health benefits. It is alkaline and a heavy metal detox. We like the original flavor, which is a bit sour, and ginger-flavored kombucha. However, there are berry-flavored and citrus-flavored varieties, as well. We choose to buy kombucha with a little residue (from the mushroom – it is called the "mother") on the bottom and strain the cold kombucha with a sieve as we are pouring it into a cold glass. We find it very refreshing. It is especially refreshing as a beverage to accompany any meal at which you are accustomed to drinking sodas. Check the "best before date" when purchasing kombucha. Kombucha is now available in many grocery stores.
* It is recommended that we drink at least two 8-ounce glasses of water before breakfast, two 8-ounce glasses of water before lunch, and two 8-ounce glasses of water before dinner. Flavoring water with freshly-squeezed lemon or lime has many health benefits.

The Amazing Health Benefits of Lemons

While writing this book I was diagnosed with (intermediate stage) prostate cancer after a biopsy to remove 12 tiny pieces of flesh from my prostate gland and tests revealed cancer. There was a two-month waiting period before the surgery to remove my prostate gland. We did not want cancer to spread during the waiting period. In the meantime, we found some very valuable information, which we hoped would mitigate my condition.

This information concerned the cancer-fighting properties of lemons, which I will share with you. The on-line article, *Who In Their Right Mind Freezes Lemons*, Hesh Goldstein, MN, talks about the incredible benefits of lemons. Some of this article's key points are:

- *"Lemon is effective in killing cancer cells because it is allegedly 10,000 (times) stronger than chemotherapy."*
- Lemon *"has a remarkable effect on cysts and tumors."*
- *"After more than 20 laboratory tests since 1970, the extracts revealed that it destroys the malignant cells in 12 cancers, including colon, breast, prostate, lung and pancreas and that the compounds of the lemon tree were 10,000 times more effective than the product Adriamycin, which is a drug commonly used chemotherapeutically in the world to slow the growth of cancer cells."*
- *"This type of therapy with lemon extract only destroys malignant cancer cells and does not affect healthy cells."*
- *"Lemon is pleasant and does not deliver the horrific effects of chemotherapy."*
- *"It has an anti-microbial effect against bacterial infections and fungi; it is effective against internal parasites and worms; it regulates blood pressure, which is too high; it acts as an anti-depressant; it combats stress and nervous disorders."*[249]

To get the best out of the lemons, buy organic lemons. Wash the lemons, and freeze them in plastic wrap and a plastic bag. The whole frozen lemon can be grated on an as-needed basis. The grated lemon can then be sprinkled in water, (especially in the morning), onto plain 2% or whole yogurt (with a drizzle of maple syrup), on salads, in sauces, on ice cream, or in smoothies.

15 Reasons You Should Be Drinking Lemon Water Every Morning
In her article, *15 Reasons You Should Be Drinking Lemon Water Every Morning*, Amy Goodrich provides the following insights about lemons:

1. Lemons improve digestion
2. Lemons boost your immune system
3. Lemons hydrate your body
4. Lemons boost energy (much healthier than energy drinks)
5. Lemons promote health and rejuvenate your skin
6. Lemons reduce inflammation
7. Lemons aid in weight loss
8. Lemons, although acidic, help to alkalize your body
9. Lemons have cleansing properties
10. Lemons have antibacterial and anti-viral properties
11. Lemons reduce mucus and phlegm
12. Lemons freshen the breath
13. Lemons boost brain power
14. Lemons have anti-cancer properties
15. Lemons will help get you off caffeine if you are addicted[250]

When we eat in restaurants, we frequently ask for either hot or cold water with a slice of lemon. Usually, it does not cost us anything.

HEALTH TIP #13: AVOID FARMED FISH
In the Huffington Post article, *Is Atlantic Salmon (Farmed Salmon) Linked to Obesity and Diabetes*, Dr. Walter Crinnion, Naturopathic Physician, writes that several studies have revealed that farmed salmon has exceptionally high levels of polychlorinated biphenyls (PCBs) and chlorinated pesticides.

He identified PCBs and the chlorinated pesticides as the substances that are most clearly linked to obesity in humans, metabolic syndrome, and diabetes.

Why are these compounds so dangerous? That is because they "persist" or remain in the body for a long time and continue to accumulate.

According to the article, studies from Japan and the U.S. have shown that if you have higher levels of PCBs in your body, you are eight times more likely to develop blood sugar problems or Type 2 diabetes in your future than someone who has lower levels of PCBs.[251]

Alternative to Farmed Fish

Primarily eat fish that are wild caught and do not live long lives such as wild-caught salmon, wild-caught herring, wild-caught sardines, wild-caught scallops, and wild-caught shrimp. I knew a man who ate a can of kippers (herring) a few times a week. He lived to be 96 years old and remained alert up until he died.

Tuna, mackerel, and halibut live long lives and, therefore, have many years to accumulate PCBs in their flesh from the oceans even if they are wild-caught. So, eat these fish in moderation. Pregnant women and nursing mothers ought not to eat these fish.

HEALTH TIP #14: AVOID LOW-FAT FOODS AND NO-FAT FOODS

We hear it all the time on television – "Eat a low-fat diet!" This is another case where the public has been led astray. Low-fat foods frequently contain too much sugar, which in the long run will be hazardous to your health.

Dr. Mercola tells us that, "Fats help your body absorb essential vitamins, including vitamins A, D, and E, and fats, which are especially important for infants and toddlers for proper growth development. The anti-fat message mostly put the blame on saturated fat and cholesterol that as decades of research has shown are harmless, while giving sugar and refined carbs (very unhealthy) a free pass."

Note: Avoid margarine that contains trans fats, potassium sorbate, and other additives.

Alternatives to Low Fat or No Fat Foods

Eat, preferably, organic or non-GMO foods that contain healthy fats – wild salmon, herring, sardines, beef, chicken, avocados, organic coconut oil, organic olive oil, organic avocado oil, cheese (real cheese – not "cheese food"), and butter, organic flaxseed oil capsules, krill oil and wild salmon oil capsules that are PCB-free, whole organic milk, and whole organic yogurt. Organic flaxseed oil capsules that contain omegas-3-6-9 are good for heart health and prostate health if used as directed on packaging.

HEALTH TIP #15: AVOID MICROWAVED POPCORN

You may be surprised that eating microwaved popcorn can be so bad for you.

According to *Natural Health News & Discoveries*, conventional microwave popcorn bags are lined with a chemical called perfluorooctanoic acid (PFOA) which is a toxin also found in Teflon (used to line non-stick pans).[252]

Dr. Oz explained that the smell (of microwaved popcorn) after you open the bag is a "chemical called diacetyl, a synthetic butter flavoring added to the product."

He explained that diacetyl is so toxic that people who work in factories where it is used became ill and developed a problem called "popcorn lung" from inhaling the gasses containing diacetyl. Dr. Oz also stated, "people who eat microwaved popcorn regularly, can develop lung problems."[253]

The other problem is that the popcorn itself is probably genetically-modified, and we have already discussed the problems with GMOs.

Alternative to Microwave Popcorn

Place organic popcorn or non-GMO popcorn in a stainless steel pot with a thick flat bottom. Add avocado oil or olive oil. Stir the corn and oil together. Flatten the kernels of corn to the bottom of the pan evenly and cover. Heat on medium high heat until the kernels start to pop wildly. Reduce the heat to medium-low until the popping sound is intermittent. Remove from the heat. Remove cover immediately. Salt immediately and eat.

HEALTH TIP #16: AVOID MSG – NOW LINKED TO WEIGHT GAIN AND BRAIN DAMAGE

Monosodium Glutamate (MSG) is a food additive widely used in the food industry to make food taste better. It is present in processed foods such as salad dressings, canned goods, chips, fast food, and such. It is used in many restaurants. MSG has been linked to many health problems.

In *Monosodium Glutamate (MSG): This Common Food Additive Now Linked to Weight Gain*, Dr. Mercola cites a study that followed the MSG intake of more than 10,000 Chinese adults. He says, "researchers found that those who ate the most MSG (about 5 grams a day) were about 30 percent more likely to become overweight than those who ate the least (less than a half-gram a day)." Historically, MSG has been mostly associated with Chinese food, but the substance is now used in a large variety of foods.

After analyzing the data, researchers found that the hormone leptin was involved in weight gain. They also found a direct correlation between MSG consumption and the hormone leptin. Leptin is the substance that primarily controls fat storage in the body. If you gain excess weight, your body produces extra leptin. Leptin is supposed to warn your brain that your body is storing too much fat and that the body should stop storing excess fat and start burning it off. Researchers suspect, however, that MSG causes leptin resistance in the body, so your body cannot properly "hear" leptin's signals.[254]

Dr. Russell Blaylock, a retired board-certified neurosurgeon and author of *Excitotoxins: The Taste that Kills*, explains in the same article that MSG is an excitotoxin, which "overexcites your cells to the point of damage or death, causing brain damage to varying degrees."

According to Blaylock, MSG's harmful side effects include:

1) Can kill brain cells
2) May cause sudden heart attacks among young athletes
3) Can lead to obesity
4) Leads to insulin resistance
5) Eye damage
6) Fatigue
7) Disorientation
8) Depression
9) Can cause learning difficulties
10) Can worsen learning difficulties
11) Can lead to Alzheimer's disease
12) Parkinson's disease
13) Lou Gehrig's disease, and
14) MSG Symptom Complex - People most at risk of developing this condition are people with asthma and people who have eaten a lot of MSG.[255]

How to Identify MSG on Food Labels

Dr. Mercola's website includes charts to help us identify which foods may contain MSG. Nowadays it is exceedingly difficult to determine if food contains MSG, even though the FDA requires that food manufacturers list the ingredient "monosodium glutamate" on food labels. This is because they do not have to label ingredients that contain free glutamic acid, even though it is the main component of MSG.

The easiest way to avoid MSG is simply to avoid processed foods, fast foods, and restaurant food, its main hideouts. However, in the event you need to check a label, here is an MSG "cheat sheet" that can help you identify it:

These ingredients contain MSG:

Autolyzed Yeast Glutamate	Calcium Caseinate	Yeast Food
	Glutamic Acid	Hydrolyzed Protein

Monopotassium Glutamate

Autolyzed Yeast Glutamate

Monosodium Glutamate

Calcium Caseinate

Glutamic Acid

Sodium Caseinate

Yeast Food

Hydrolyzed Protein

These ingredients can OFTEN contain MSG or create MSG during processing:

Flavors and Flavorings

Natural Chicken Flavoring Stock

Anything Enzyme Modified

Maltodextrin

Citric Acid

Natural Pork Flavoring Seasonings

Soy Protein

Malt Flavoring

Pectin

Powdered Milk

Protease

Anything Ultra-Pasteurized

Natural Flavors and Flavorings

Soy Protein Isolate

Malt Extract

Soy Sauce

Broth

Carrageenan

Corn Starch

Gelatin

Natural Beef Flavoring

Bouillon

Barley Malt

Enzymes

Anything Protein Fortified

Alternatives to MSG

Prepare food at home. We find that preparing large batches of soups, stews - ragouts, ratatouille, chili, paneer, congee, cassoulet, and curries and freezing these in smaller containers saves time. The benefit of eating soups and stews is that the nutrients all remain in the pot. Taking a container out of the freezer the night before and heating the main course of a meal is easy. A salad or cut vegetables with a healthful dip, or sourdough bread, or brown rice can round out the meal. You can prepare your own salad dressings - it is easy (recipes follow).

Sauté onions a long time (about 15 minutes) on medium-low heat until they are golden before adding minced garlic and water to the pot in which your soup or stew will cook. Packaged organic vegetable broths and organic chicken broths from reputable grocery stores can be used as a base for soups and stews. To enhance the flavor of soups and stews use a tablespoon or two of lemon juice, Worcestershire sauce or soy sauce. Homemade curries and homemade creole spices are very flavorful. I like parsley, sage, rosemary and thyme. We always put a couple bay leaves in a soup pot (remember to remove them before pureeing the soup). Buy grain fed, hormone free, chicken bones and beef bones from a reputable butcher to add to your soup pot - the goodness from bone marrow is healthful. Add a lot of one vegetable such as asparagus or mushroom, or choose to add a variety of vegetables in soups. Soups can be made using, lentils, or beans. Organic tomato paste and organic tomato sauce can also be used to add flavor to soups and stews, and chilies (this is good for your prostate). Fresh ginger is very fragrant and adds much flavor to Asian soups and stir-fries. Coconut milk has a delightful, delicate, and delicious flavor in curries, to which lime juice can also be added to the dish after it has been served. Cilantro, a herb known as coriander in some countries, adds flavor to guacamole, chili, and Southwestern salads - lime juice can also be added to these dishes, which will cut down on the need to add too much salt, and, of course, no MSG. We frequently add freshly ground pepper, cayenne pepper, and white pepper to dishes - sometimes all three. Adding sliced green onions to salads adds a lot of flavor. Experiment with different kinds of vinegar when making salad dressings. My favorites are cherry balsamic vinegar, white balsamic vinegar, balsamic vinegar, and apple cider vinegar with the "mother."

Elaine is working on writing a cookbook; however, she has included some of her secret recipes in this book. You can find recipe books in libraries, and there are recipes on-line, but keep in mind that not all recipes in books or on-line are good. So if something you have prepared does not taste as you feel it should - do not blame yourself. Just try another recipe. Or change the recipe you have to suit your taste.

Marry a young woman who knows how to cook. Cooking together makes cooking more fun, and less of a chore, if you are both working outside of the home. You can each share some of your favorite recipes. If you are the sole "breadwinner" while she is at home raising your children, she will be able to cook nutritious meals for herself and her family. You will all have a much better quality of life, and you will remain healthier. Remember to help her with the dishes.

HEALTH TIP #17: MINIMIZE THE USE OF SALT

"Too much salt can also kill you. Boys between the ages of 12 and 19 are especially at high risk with an average daily sodium intake of over 4,000 mg/day. The proportion of obese children and adolescents with pre-hypertension and hypertension combined is nearly 30%. Up to 74% of hypertensive children are not diagnosed with the condition because physicians have to assess age, sex and height in addition to the blood pressure measurement and they often do not take the time to do the calculations. Several studies have shown that children with high blood pressure show signs of enlargement of the left ventricle in the heart, blockage in the arteries, and diastolic dysfunction, all warning signs of heart disease."[257]

Solution: The solution is found in the recommendations posted on the Health Hub from Cleveland Clinic in the article *How Salt, Potassium Affect Your Teen's Blood Pressure.*

Current guidelines recommend limiting salt intake to 2,300 milligrams per day for healthy people. The guidelines limit salt intake to

1,500 milligrams daily for some people, notably, African-Americans, and those with high blood pressure, diabetes or chronic disease. About half of the entire U.S. population and the majority of adults would qualify for the 1,500 milligrams recommended.[258]

* 1 teaspoon salt = 2,300 mg sodium (American Heart Association)

- There is salt in bread, cheese, crackers, cookies, chips, and other processed foods. Remember to read the labels on packages to determine the number of milligrams of sodium per serving.
- Ask your doctor to calculate your age, sex, height, and blood pressure measurement.

HEALTH TIP #18: MIND YOUR POTASSIUM CONSUMPTION
Natural potassium is an important element in a healthy diet. It can easily be found in tomatoes, bananas, and avocados to name just a few foods in which it occurs naturally. However, potassium sorbate is added as a preservative to many processed foods - some fruity yogurts, some cheeses, some sauces, and other foods. It is best to check labels on processed food and to monitor the quantity of potassium you are ingesting from natural foods and processed foods. My wife became very sensitive to foods containing potassium. Whenever she ate a meal with a medium to high potassium content - such as avocados or tomato sauce or margarine (she stopped using margarine) - a rash broke out on her face. She eventually discovered that flaxseed oil depletes potassium, so she started to counteract medium to high potassium consumption by taking one or two capsules of organic flaxseed oil. It took a short while for her body to rid itself of what she suspected was an accumulation of potassium. Now if she is going to eat a meal high in potassium, she takes an organic flaxseed oil capsule, and her face remains clear.

The Mayo Clinic makes the following recommendation:

"...it is thought that 1,600 to 2,000 mg potassium per day for adults is adequate.[259] (Ask your doctor, pharmacist, or naturopath which amount is right for you.)

Remember that the total amount of potassium that you get every day includes what you get from food and what you may take as a supplement (vitamin). Read the labels of processed foods.

Your total intake of potassium should not be greater than the recommended amounts unless ordered by your doctor. In some cases, too much potassium (hyperkalemia) may cause muscle weakness, confusion, irregular heartbeat, or difficulty breathing.

The Mayo Clinic warns that a low potassium condition in the body (hypokalemia) can lead to death. Your body needs potassium, as it is an important electrolyte that enables nerve cells and muscles cells such as heart muscles to function. Common causes of excessive potassium loss are: prescription water or fluid pills (diuretics), vomiting or diarrhea or both.[260] Be sure to consult your doctor if you suspect that you are suffering from low potassium.

Therefore, do not take too many flaxseed oil capsules, as that can lead to a low potassium condition. Caring for our bodies is very scientific. It requires research, thought, perseverance, and guidance from doctors and naturopaths.

HEALTH TIP #19: EAT SOURDOUGH BREAD MORE FREQUENTLY THAN OTHER TYPES OF BREADS

Organic sourdough bread is much healthier for you than other breads. We have included here nine reasons sourdough bread is healthful from *Cookus Interruptus - Top 10 Reasons to Eat Sourdough Bread - March 16, 2013*:

1. Sourdough should not spike blood sugar as readily as other "breads."
2. Sourdough bread contains the bacteria Lactobacillus in a higher proportion of yeast than do other breads, which means more mineral availability and easier digestion.

3. The combination of bacteria and yeast combo work together to "predigest" the starches in the grains. Predigestion by sourdough means less work for your digestive system.

4. Sourdough preparation is longer. It involves soaking and rinsing. This extended preparation process results in the protein gluten being broken down into amino acids. This means easier digestion, even for those who are gluten-sensitive.

5. Acetic acid–which inhibits the growth of mold, is produced in the making of sourdough. So, sourdough naturally preserves itself. This is pretty neat considering the toxic preservatives thrown into the food supply today.

6. The fermentation process increases the content of beneficial bacteria in the bread and in your gut. A healthy gut means a happy body.

7. Additionally, these bacteria control yeast population in the gut, so yeast overgrowth and infection is less likely to occur.

8. The integrity of sourdough is so complex that it contains a host of goodness in terms of nutrients. In sourdough, you can find vitamins B1-B6, B12, folate, thiamin, niacin, riboflavin, vitamin E, selenium, iron, manganese, calcium, magnesium, phosphorus, zinc, and potassium–in addition to uniquely balanced proteins and fatty acids. This is in contrast to most commercially produced breads, which maintain only a fraction of their original nutrient content after all the processing they undergo.

9. Another good reason to eat sourdough bread is the FLAVOR. It is tangy and distinctive.[261]

Sourdough bread can be found on major supermarket shelves. Just make sure that natural ingredients are being used. Otherwise, you may want to make it at home. In either case, this is a wise choice when desiring bread.

HEALTH TIP #20: EAT COMPLETE PROTEINS BY
CONSUMING LEGUMES AND GRAINS TOGETHER

Eating complete proteins is of paramount importance for your health. Proteins build bones, muscles, blood, skin, hair, and nails. Your body uses protein to repair itself. When you eat vegetable proteins such as beans, you may have the idea that they are complete proteins, but they are not.

Meat and eggs contain complete proteins but they are animal proteins, which we have urged you to minimize to avoid switching on cancer cells. But did you know that eating peanut butter along with whole wheat bread will create a complete protein? Beans and rice; beans and cornbread; and hummus (made with chickpeas) and pita bread will also create complete proteins in your body.

As reported by Nick English, author of the article *12 Complete Proteins Vegetarians Need to Know About*, there are 20 essential amino acids that can form a protein - nine of which your body cannot produce on its own, which must be supplied by the foods that you eat.

Legumes such as beans, lentils, and chickpeas are low in methionine and high in lysine. Rice, wheat and corn are low in lysine and high in methionine. When you eat legumes with rice, corn or wheat, you are eating foods that combine to make complete proteins that are "on par with that of meat."

Other Grains that Contain Protein:

* Quinoa – like couscous but more nutritious
* Buckwheat – pancakes or soba noodles
* Soy – provides a complete protein - firm tofu, Tempeh, and Natto
* Hempseeds
* Chia
* Ezekiel Bread – made from sprouted grains[262]

If you are interested in becoming a vegetarian, do a lot of research and very carefully plan your meals. Use organic legumes and organic grains whenever possible. Speak to a naturopathic physician for guidelines regarding a vegetarian diet and taking vitamin B-12 supplements to prevent anemia.

HEALTH TIP #21: FEED YOUR GUT'S GOOD BACTERIA TO HELP WITH WEIGHT LOSS

Be smart about what you eat for snacks. Avoid eating too much sugar because you could actually be starving your gut flora. Laura Biel reports in her article, *How Your Gut Bacteria Can Help You Drop Pounds*, the negative effect of sugar on your gut's good bacteria, and the positive effects of eating key foods on your gut's good bacteria – to help you lose unwanted weight. Justin Sonnenburg, Ph.D., is cited saying, "Bacteria need complex carbohydrates, like legumes and whole grains, in order to thrive. So when you get too many calories from sweets, you're leaving your microbes (good bacteria) hungry. They either die or adapt by feeding on the mucus inside your intestine, which, experts hypothesize, could contribute to low-level inflammation, a condition that has been linked to obesity."[263] Also, we need to eat probiotic or fermented foods like yogurt, sauerkraut, miso, kefir, and kombucha that help to replenish good bacteria.

HEALTH TIP #22: BULK UP YOUR MUSCLES NATURALLY WITH FOOD AND EXERCISE

You will feel more confident and look more confident if you look and feel healthy. You may have noticed that most young women tend to want to date young men who look healthy. This is instinctual because nature has programmed women (whether they will admit it or not) to choose a healthy husband in order to have healthy babies, and also so that their husbands can help to protect them while they are busy caring for their babies.

Dr. Richard Taflinger, Clinical Associate Professor at Washington State University, explains how women choose a mate in more detail:

"The human female, on the other hand, runs into a real problem: the human mind. Remember that females must apply more criteria to select a male than males apply to a female. It is not the nearest possibility, but the best possibility that she desires. (Ehrlichman & Eichenstein, 1992) A woman's mind allows her, and indeed forces her to examine possible criteria to a much greater extent than any other animal. She can also project the consequences of choices into the future. What constitutes an alpha male, the best male with which to mate and produce the best possible offspring, depends on far more factors than any other animal on earth. The criteria for her to desire sexually a man can include strength or health or fighting ability, like the lion or the wolf. However, they can also include intelligence, money, power, prestige, position, status, attitudes, political or religious convictions, any number and combination of factors. It's whatever she believes a man should be that will result in 1) the best possible genes for her offspring, and 2) the offspring's best chance for survival and ability to pass on its genes. It is the human mind that allows her to consider the possibilities, the criteria, the future outcome of her actions. She does not go into heat and mate with the closest best bet. She makes plans, examines her choices, makes conscious decisions. Only the human female can make conscious, planned decisions about her sex life.

"Women's ability to think consciously about their sexual lives does not mean she doesn't have instinctive desires as strong as a man's. What it does mean is she will often subordinate that desire: she may desire a physically attractive man, but she will not actually have sex with him until he has satisfied more than physical criteria."[264]

When I was 14, I felt like my body was too scrawny to get girls, though I lived and worked physically on a farm. The folk hero muscle man at that time was Charles Atlas. He was the Arnold Schwarzenegger of my day. I wanted muscles like his, so I decided to work on building my physique, and bought the "Dynamic Tension" handheld device, which was the centerpiece of his system to buff up my upper body. Well, I did not become any Charles Atlas, but I built considerable weight and size, thereby increasing my self-confidence. Oh, did I tell you that I started dating at 16, so I think it worked!

If you feel that you are too scrawny, know that you can bulk up muscles every day by following these simple steps.

Eating protein at the right times during the day, in the right quantity, and the right quality is key to building muscle. Your body uses some of the proteins you eat to build muscle, and other proteins are broken down to be used to create hormones, enzymes, neurotransmitters, and much more. Vegetarian athletes such as vegan ironman Brendan Brazier build and maintain their athletic muscles with a vegetarian or a vegan diet. It may be easier and better for you to use both plant sources and meat, fish and dairy sources for your protein intake – depending on your tastes, nutritional requirements, and genetic make-up (information about genomics will follow).

Matt Frazier, author of the website *No Meat Athlete*, has done some research in regards to the amount of protein athletes need each day and stated in *Protein for Vegetarians a Simple Guide to Getting What You Need*: "Several sources I looked at cited a study which concluded that endurance athletes benefit most from 1.2 to 1.4 daily grams per kilogram of bodyweight, while strength athletes do best with 1.4 to 1.8 grams per kilogram. In pounds, that's 0.54 to 0.63 grams per pound for endurance athletes, 0.63 to 0.81 grams per pound for strength athletes."[265]

Calculate the amount of protein your body needs, to know how much protein you need to eat to develop more muscles. On-line sources with lists of food and the corresponding protein content are available. The sample menu and exercise schedule below will give you an idea of how you can plan your fitness program to build muscles:

Sample Menu and Exercise Schedule

1. Eat a good breakfast - eggs, granola with milk or yogurt, or smoothies made with yogurt and fruit.
2. Have a mid- morning snack – almonds and an apple, or an organic protein nut bar would be great! If you are allergic to nuts, eat a protein bar such as *Move Mountains Avalanche 100% Nut Free Bars*, which contain 10 – 12 grams of protein.
3. For lunch, have a bowl of chili, Lima Bean soup (recipe to follow), Hungry Boy (recipe to follow), or a peanut butter and honey sandwich. Remember to pair legumes (beans and lentils) with grains (bread or rice) in order to make complete proteins. Ask the cafeteria staff at your school to prepare legume options for school lunches.
4. Prior to exercising – eat one slice of cheese and two crackers or drink a protein shake.
5. One of the sites I read recommended eating ice cream two hours after a workout to diminish protein breakdown in your muscles. However, due to the addition of sugar and chemicals in many ice creams, I recommend having one of the "better than ice cream" smoothies included in this book.
6. Exercise your muscles every second day (as in endurance exercise- long distance running, cycling, or strength exercise – weight training), to give your muscles a chance to repair themselves. You can still take leisurely walks or hikes on alternative days.
7. At dinner, you can have a chicken breast (43 grams of protein) with, 1 cup of, broccoli (2.6 grams of protein), peas (8 grams of protein) or asparagus (3 grams of protein) and a baked potato; a chicken-broccoli stir-fry; or Salmon Panang, and rice (recipe to follow). A 7-ounce fillet of salmon contains approximately 40 grams of protein.
8. Eat a bedtime snack, which contains protein. A glass of organic milk or organic soy milk and one slice of organic bread with peanut butter, or a slice of organic bread with a side of cottage cheese and a fruit, are good options.

HEALTH TIP #23: KEEP THIS ESSENTIAL OIL IN YOUR FIRST AID KIT
Tea tree oil, also known as melaleuca, is used topically only (on the skin). It can be toxic if swallowed – keep out of the reach of young children. According to the very valuable book *Prescription for Nutritional Healing*[266], tea tree oil can be used to treat acne, athlete's foot, boils, cuts and scrapes, earache, fungal infections, hair and scalp problems, herpes outbreaks, insect and spider bites, scabies, and warts.

Be sure to consult your family doctor prior to using tea tree oil, or you can also consult a licensed naturopathic physician (ND). Some physicians are trained in both mainstream medicine and in healing with natural remedies.

My wife became familiar with *Prescription for Nutritional Healing* when she worked in the alternative healthcare industry. She noted that doctors came into the shop where she worked to purchase the book. There was also a medical student who worked part-time there who used the book. We keep a copy in our home and use it when the need arises. We recommend you and your family do the same. The book can be ordered online if you cannot find it in your local bookstore or health shop.

Take responsibility for your own health by doing research, and consulting with your parents and appropriate physicians.

HEALTH TIP #24: BEWARE OF SEXUALLY TRANSMITTED DISEASES (STDs)
The CDC reports that nearly half of the 20 million new STDs each year were among young people, between the ages of 15 to 24. They also point out that nearly 10,000 young people (aged 13-24) were diagnosed with HIV infection in 2013.[267]

Having sex with someone with Human Immunodeficiency Virus (HIV), which is an STD (even just one time) can lead to your early death. Do not play "Russian Roulette" with your life. There is no cure for HIV, and it is very contagious.

God's law to remain chaste until marriage and to remain faithful to your wife after marriage was proclaimed to protect you, your wife, and your future children because God loves you.

Before marrying someone ask her to be tested for STDs, and read the results. As well, you should give her the results from your test for STDs. Some STDs such as syphilis can be treated with antibiotics (if caught in the early stages of the disease), which you would want to do before marriage because your wife may become pregnant.

Syphilis and Your Baby

Dr. Robert Milligan, on the website, The DailyRisk.com – Your Spokane Teen Source for STD Info, states: "Syphilis can cause serious problems in pregnancy, including miscarriage or stillbirth (a baby born dead), or severe birth defects. A baby born with syphilis has a condition called congenital syphilis, which is very serious and life threatening. Symptoms usually appear within the first 3 to 7 weeks of life, but may not appear for more than 2 years. Some consequences of congenital syphilis are sores on the skin and/or in the mouth, runny nose, pneumonia, bone inflammation, low birth weight, tooth damage, deafness, facial abnormalities, and blindness. When proper medical attention is given, the syphilis can be cured with an antibiotic, but the baby may have the consequences of the infection for the rest of its life."[268]

Herpes and Your Baby

Milligan also reported, "When a baby gets a herpes infection, it's called neonatal herpes which usually affects a baby's eyes, skin, and mouth. Sometimes the infection spreads and affects the brain, lungs, liver, and adrenal glands – this is very serious and can result in death. There is medicine that can control the infection in a baby, but there is no cure. If a woman has an active outbreak at the time of delivery, a C-section may be done to protect the baby. A baby born when a mother is having her first (sometimes called a primary) outbreak has about a 50% chance of getting herpes. But a baby born to a mother having a recurrent outbreak has only about a 5% chance of getting herpes.

To reduce the risk of passing herpes to your baby, your healthcare provider may ask you to take precautions; including avoiding sexual activity during the last three months of pregnancy with any partners who also have or who may have genital herpes. Babies who are born to moms with genital herpes should be tested within 2 days after birth to make sure that the baby gets quick medical treatment if the baby has the virus."[269]

Health Tip #25: Eat a Balanced Diet and Supplement with Vitamins When Necessary

First, in order for you to have good overall health in your muscles, bones, heart, reproductive organs, eyes, skin, hair, nails, and other parts of your body, your diet should be colorful and varied, which will help to ensure that you are getting a variety of vitamins and minerals. Your diet should have a great variety of fruits, berries, vegetables, and legumes (beans, peas and peanuts), organic grains, seeds, yogurt, cheese, eggs, fish, including a little meat (poultry and red meat). However, be mindful of allergies.

Second, you may need to take a multivitamin-mineral supplement daily, especially when your stress level or activity level is high. The climate in which you live is another factor that may cause a need for you to take supplements.

Stress

Stress depletes vitamins through your urine, even if you are eating a healthful diet. Therefore, during stressful times taking a daily vitamin may help to ensure that you are getting all the nutrients you need.

Leo Galland M.D. illustrates this fact in *Magnesium: The Stress Reliever*:

"If you are like most people, when you are exposed to the stress of continuous loud noise, for example, you become irritable, easily fatigued and lose concentration. Your blood pressure may increase as the level of adrenalin, a stress hormone, increases in your blood. Under conditions of mental or physical stress, magnesium is released from your blood cells and goes into the blood plasma, from where it is excreted into the urine. Chronic stress depletes your body of magnesium. The more stressed you are, the greater the loss of magnesium. The lower your magnesium level to begin with, the more reactive to stress you become and the higher your level of adrenalin in stressful situations. Higher adrenalin causes greater loss of magnesium from cells. Administering magnesium as a nutritional supplement breaks this vicious cycle by raising blood magnesium levels and buffering the response to stress, building your resistance. Personality has a marked effect on the stress-magnesium cycle. A study done in Paris found that stress-induced depletion of magnesium was much greater for people who show the "Type A", competitive, heart-disease prone behavior pattern than for their less competitive colleagues. Dr. Bella Altura, a physiologist at the State University of New York, has proposed that depletion of magnesium among Type A individuals is the main reason why Type A individuals are at increased risk of heart attacks."[270]

Activity Level

High activity levels such as participating in many activities - sports competitions, music competitions - school, lessons, work, and a busy social life may create good stress, but it is still stress. The high demands on your body may necessitate taking a daily vitamin to supplement your diet.

The Climate in which You Live

If you live in northern climates where the sun rarely shines, or you are spending a lot of time indoors, you may need a supplement of vitamin D – sunshine enables the body to produce vitamin D on the skin. Vitamin D is essential for bone health, hormone regulation, immune response and blood pressure control.

Prescription for Nutritional Healing states:

"Vitamin D has been the ignored vitamin until recently. Studies have shown that at least 40 percent of people have less-than-optimal levels of the vitamin in their blood. As much as 70 to 80 percent of Hispanic –Americans and African-Americans may be deficient in vitamin D. Those with more coloring in the skin have a harder time absorbing vitamin D from sunlight. In addition, those who live above the 37th latitude obtain no vitamin D from sunlight between November and March. Not getting enough vitamin D in the diet or from direct sunlight has been linked to the development of several diseases including heart disease, osteoporosis, diabetes, and cancers such as breast and colon."[271]

However, too much vitamin D can be toxic. Science News reported in August 2015, on a Mayo Clinic study: Dr. Kumar notes that it is possible to ingest too much vitamin D, a condition called vitamin D toxicity or hypervitaminosis, which can result in poor appetite, nausea, vomiting and kidney complications.[272]

  * **Note:** Consult with your doctor or a pharmacist before taking a supplement of vitamin D. **Liquid forms of vitamin D must be refrigerated**.

HEALTH TIP #26: AVOID SMOKING CIGARETTES AND VAPING E-CIGARETTES

Nicotine is an extremely addictive stimulant found in tobacco. Nicotine users have an increased risk of lung disease, heart disease and stroke.[273] Especially troubling is the introduction of e-cigarettes, which are electronic cigarettes that deliver pure nicotine, along with other not-so-nice chemicals to your lungs.

  With the advent of e-cigarettes, "vape" shops are springing up everywhere. We are very concerned about this because, currently, the Food and Drug Administration (FDA) is not regulating this industry and young people are being exposed to yet another health hazard.

We promised to share with you cutting edge research. Just prior to sending the final version of the manuscript for this book to the publisher, we learned that researchers from the Lawrence National Laboratory about how vaping puts potentially harmful chemicals into smokers' bodies. The laboratory isolated six toxic compounds in e-cigarettes: propylene glycol, glycerin, nicotine, ethanol, acetol, and propylene oxide, some of which are carcinogenic (cancer-causing).

Here's the science directly from the laboratory, which explains why you should not come within a mile of e-cigarettes:

"Use of electronic cigarettes has grown exponentially over the past few years, raising concerns about harmful emissions. This study quantified potentially toxic compounds in the vapor and identified key parameters affecting emissions. Six principal constituents in three different refill "e-liquids" were propylene glycol (PG), glycerin, nicotine, ethanol, acetol, and propylene oxide. The latter, with mass concentrations of 0.4–0.6%, is a possible carcinogen and respiratory irritant. Aerosols generated with vaporizers contained up to 31 compounds, including nicotine, nicotyrine, formaldehyde, acetaldehyde, glycidol, acrolein, acetol, and diacetyl. Glycidol is a probable carcinogen not previously identified in the vapor, and acrolein is a powerful irritant. Emission rates ranged from tens to thousands of nanograms of toxicants per milligram of e-liquid vaporized, and they were significantly higher for a single-coil vs a double-coil vaporizer (by up to an order of magnitude for aldehydes). By increasing the voltage applied to a single-coil device from 3.3 to 4.8 V, the mass of e-liquid consumed doubled from 3.7 to 7.5 mg puff–1 and the total aldehyde emission rates tripled from 53 to 165 µg puff–1, with acrolein rates growing by a factor of 10. Aldehyde emissions increased by more than 60% after the device was reused several times, likely due to the buildup of polymerization byproducts that degraded upon heating. These findings suggest that thermal degradation byproducts are formed during vapor generation. Glycidol and acrolein were primarily produced by glycerin degradation. Acetol and 2-propen-1-ol were produced mostly from PG, while other compounds (e.g., formaldehyde) originated from both. Because emissions originate from reaction of the most common e-liquid constituents (solvents), harmful emissions are expected to be ubiquitous when e-cigarette vapor is present."[274]

Also, according to the American Lung Association, lung cancer is the leading cause of death from cancer for both men and women. Smoking contributes 80% and 90% of lung cancer deaths, respectively.[275]

There is no good news here. Bottom line: avoid smoking and vaping. Period. Don't experiment with smoking out of curiosity or just to fit in.

If You Are Trying to Quit, here's some advice from the National Institute of Health:

1. Make a Quit Plan

"Having a plan can make your quit day easier. A quit plan gives you ways to stay focused, confident, and motivated to quit. You can build your own quit plan or find a quit program that works for you. Check out SmokefreeTXT, QuitGuide app, or a quitline like 1-800-QUIT-NOW (1-800-784-8669) or 1-877-44U-QUIT (1-877-448-7848) to get started. If you don't know what quit method might be right for you, visit the Quit Smoking Methods Explorer to learn more. No single approach to quitting works for everyone. Be honest about your needs. If using nicotine replacement therapy is part of your plan, be sure to start using it first thing in the morning.

2. Stay Busy

"Keeping busy is a great way to stay smoke-free on your quit day. Being busy will help you keep your mind off smoking and distract you from cravings. Think about trying some of these activities:

- Get out of the house for a walk.
- Chew gum or hard candy.
- Drink lots of water.
- Relax with deep breathing.
- Go to a movie.
- Spend time with non-smoking friends and family.
- Go to dinner at your favorite smoke-free restaurant.

* Keep your hands busy with a pen or toothpick, or play a game in the QuitGuide app.

3. Avoid Smoking Triggers

"Triggers are the people, places, things, and situations that set off your urge to smoke. On your quit day, try to avoid all your triggers. Here are some tips to help you outsmart some common smoking triggers:

Throw away your cigarettes, lighters, and ash trays if you haven't already.

Avoid caffeine, which can make you feel jittery. Try drinking water instead.

Spend time with non-smokers.

Go to places where smoking isn't allowed.

Get plenty of rest and eat healthy. Being tired can trigger you to smoke.

Change your routine to avoid the things you might associate with smoking.

4. Stay Positive

"Quitting smoking is difficult. It happens one minute... one hour... one day at a time. Try not to think of quitting as forever. Pay attention to today and the time will add up. It helps to stay positive. Your quit day might not be perfect, but all that matters is that you don't smoke—not even one puff. Reward yourself for being smoke-free for 24 hours. You deserve it. And if you're not feeling ready to quit today, set a quit date that makes sense for you. It's OK if you need a few more days to prepare to quit smoking.

5. Ask for Help

"You don't need to rely on willpower alone to be smoke-free. Tell your family and friends when your quit day is. Ask them for support on quit day and in the first few days and weeks after. They can help you get through the rough spots. Let them know exactly how they can support you. Don't assume they'll know."[276]

If you need to be doing something with your hands when socializing or just relaxing, massage a "stress reliever." Actually, when I googled "stress balls" to see what was available on the market I was pleasantly surprised that stress relievers are very inexpensive when bought in bulk and come in different shapes - footballs, soccer balls, basketballs, golf balls, baseballs, hockey pucks, volleyballs, tennis balls, brain shaped balls, Earth shaped balls and even Quit balls, with a butted cigarette for the I in Quit! They can also be customized with an encouraging slogan. Stress relievers would make a great small gift to give at a party or to give to friends when they are stressed, and it might encourage them to stop smoking and vaping. In life in helps to be creative.

HEALTH TIP #27: AVOID DRINKING ALCOHOL

In the Brain Dangers section, we discussed the harm drinking alcohol can have on your brain and your babies' developing brain if your wife drinks alcohol when she is pregnant. New research also warns us that even drinking alcohol in moderation can lead to developing seven cancers.

Nicole Lyn Pesce says in her article, Bad News, Boozers: Alcohol Linked to Seven Deadly Cancers, "Talk about a buzzkill — drinking alcohol, even in moderation, likely causes at least seven kinds of cancer. New Zealand researchers published their sobering meta-analysis of alcohol and cancer studies in the journal Addiction on Thursday, and determined a causal link between drinking and developing cancer of the mouth and throat, larynx, esophagus, liver, colon, bowel and breast."[277]

Yikes!!

Don't experiment with alcohol out of curiosity or just to fit in.

HEALTH TIP #28: AVOID DRINKS CONTAINING CAFFEINE

In the Brain Dangers section, we discussed caffeine and the effects it can have on your brain. In addition, caffeine can give you heart palpitations. It can also accumulate in your body and cause you to feel poisoned and very weak. When my wife was 28 years old, doctors could not determine why she had so little energy. She started to feel better when she happened to forget to buy coffee for three weeks and did not have a cup of coffee anywhere else. The day after she got around to having a cup of coffee she felt that she had no energy. She then asked herself, "What have I done recently that I have not done over the past two weeks, during which time my energy returned?" The realization that her body was reacting adversely to coffee flooded over her. After this light bulb moment she drank decaffeinated coffee only occasionally for she found that the traces of caffeine in decaffeinated coffee would also accumulate in her body and make her feel weak. She no longer drinks any beverages that contain caffeine.

WORD OF WISDOM LEADS TO GOOD HEALTH AND LONGEVITY

It has been said that your generation is very concerned about not polluting the earth, which is great! Please add to this mission - DO NOT POLLUTE YOUR BODY!

In 1833, before science revealed the harmful effects of smoking cigarettes, drinking alcohol and consuming caffeine, Joseph Smith, the first prophet of the Church of Jesus Christ of Latter-day Saints, received revelation from God, which we now call The Word of Wisdom. This revelation warns us to avoid drinking alcohol, smoking, and drinking hot drinks (tea and coffee).

A 25-year study conducted by UCLA non-LDS professors has concluded that members of the LDS faith (also known as Mormons) live much longer than non-Mormons.

People of all denominations can benefit from this research's findings by avoiding these substances.

"Mormon men live 10 years longer than other U.S. white males. Mormon women live more than five years longer than other U.S. white females. Those are the among the results of a 25-year study into the health habits and the longevity of the Mormon lifestyle by non-Mormon UCLA professors James E. Enstrom and Lester Breslow, who summarized their research with the conclusion: 'Several healthy characteristics of the Mormon lifestyle are associated with substantially reduced death rates and increased life expectancy.' The study, conducted from 1980 to 2004, included information from question-naire responses by more than 9,800 faithful Mormon couples and concluded that practicing Mormons in California had the lowest total death rates and the longest life expectancies ever documented in a well-defined U.S. cohort. The authors concluded the findings suggest a model for substantial disease prevention in the general population. Mormons live by a health code called the 'Word of Wisdom.' They abstain from alcohol, tobacco, tea and coffee because the body is the temple of the spirit (I Cor. 3:16-17). The study revealed Mormon males had a life expectancy of 84.1 years - 9.8 years longer than that of U.S. white males. Mormon females had a life expectancy of 86.1 years - 5.6 years longer than U.S. white females."[278]

PARTICULAR HEALTH CONCERNS FOR BOYS AND MEN

By following the guidelines in the previous sections on nutrition and exercise, many health problems can be averted. In the section below, we will discuss some of the more prevalent health problems men experience so that you can take preventative measures while you are young.

CONCERN #1 – HEART DISEASE, THE #1 KILLER OF MEN

The leading cause of death for men is heart disease. We ought to add to the health tips already mentioned that relieving stress is a major factor in preventing heart disease.

Too much stress can kill you.

You can lower your stress by following these guidelines:

1. Each morning set priorities for the day. I do so before I even open my eyes. Then I feel the Holy Spirit guiding my thoughts. Remember to use your delayed gratification skills. More often than not, do what you like the least first.
2. Leave some wiggle room for interruptions. During the day, go with the flow to some extent but be ready to ask for privacy

when you need to concentrate on a task such as homework. Be disciplined but flexible.

3. Share your feelings: If you keep frustrations bottled up, even minor frustrations, you will feel stressed.

4. Eat at least one meal a day with your family or friends.

5. Build relationships. Scout meetings and activities are a great place to build healthy relationships - so are churches, choirs, school bands, and participating in sports. Talking to girls and becoming their friend and eventually dating will help to build your confidence.

6. Don't overextend yourself by participating in too many activities. You need to eat well, and you need to get plenty of sleep. Also you will acquire a greater sense of accomplishment and confidence if you can master a few skills at a time rather than doing many skills haphazardly.

7. During times of stress: Take a daily multi-vitamin/mineral supplement, which will help to replenish the vitamins and minerals excreted during stress.

8. In the evening before going to sleep find a quiet space: Turn off electronics, listen to uplifting music, or just relax on your bed and breathe deeply.

CONCERN #2 – LUNG CANCER, THE #2 KILLER OF MEN
The leading cause of death for men from cancer is lung cancer. Solution – Don't smoke!

The Mayo Clinic mentions that it is also important to avoid exposure to secondhand smoke, air pollution and exposure to chemicals (such as in the workplace).[279]

CONCERN #3 - PROSTATE CANCER, THE #3 KILLER OF MEN
Why do we need to talk about preventing prostate cancer? It is the number three killer of American men after heart disease and lung

cancer, and it is potentially debilitating. New studies have shown that prostate cancer can be avoided if boys and men eat a nutritious diet, which supplies particular nutrients throughout their lives. I wish I had known this information when I was your age. I am a prostate cancer survivor, but I am still suffering from the side effects.

The CDC admonishes that, "Except for skin cancer, prostate cancer is the most common cancer in American men. It is the second most common cause of death from cancer among Caucasian, African American, American Indian/Alaska Native, and Hispanic men, and the fourth most common cause of death from cancer among Asian/Pacific Islander men."[280] Skin cancer is easy to avoid. Use sunscreen, especially when planning to be exposed to the sun for long periods of time – at the beach, working outdoors, playing sports outdoors, and when sailing.

We hope you never get prostate cancer, but it is very common in the US. Men who opt to have their prostate removed (a prostatectomy) usually experience symptoms of incontinence and erectile dysfunction for 6 - 12 months. Some men never return to normal after the operation. A prostatectomy is a very delicate and complicated surgery, even when the prostate is removed by robotics. You can view an actual prostatectomy on YouTube if you have the stomach for it. It is our hope that by eating right throughout your life, however, you will be able to prevent this potentially deadly and debilitating disease.

I was diagnosed with prostate cancer in 2015 and decided to have my cancerous prostate physically removed because I wanted cancer out of my body as quickly as possible. There were other options, but I deemed them too risky for my taste. Because there were complications during my surgery, it took 5 hours but I had a successful outcome. All of the cancer cells were removed from my body. I was one of the lucky ones. My uncle Arzo was not so fortunate. He died of prostate cancer. He was such a great guy and he was one of my mentors growing up. He even joined our gospel music band, *The Heavenly Wonders,* which I helped form when I was young.

Knowing that I was eating lots of organic lemons before my surgery, gave me peace of mind. I also received two priesthood blessings, and my wife asked thousands of people to pray for me when she called temples and placed my name on the prayer rolls.

As an old saying goes – "an ounce of prevention is worth a pound of cure." No one knows exactly what causes prostate cancer, but we do know that prevention starts early in life with healthy nutrition. This is another important reason why we wrote this book – to help young men maintain a healthy body throughout their lives.

Note: African Americans have an increased risk of developing the most aggressive type of prostate cancer. This could be due to diet, genetics, environment or a combination of those factors. What we know is that foods with a high concentration of tomato, soy (such as tofu), and salads with many colors from a variety of vegetables, berries, fruits, nuts and seeds (with an abundance of micronutrients) can help reduce risk. When I was growing up, our family never ate salads. It took me decades to establish this as a habit and now I eat a healthy salad almost every day. I recommend butter lettuce, or romaine lettuce for the base of the salad.

Granted, while growing up on our family farm, I had a smart organic diet. However, I did have a penchant for desserts at dinner time which included cakes, pies, cobblers, and puddings. As I explained earlier, we also had lots of sugar in our glass of tea during suppertime. When I started junior college at eighteen, I became exposed to processed foods. For many years, I did not eat a proper diet consistently, nor did I know very much about nutrition. Fast foods like hotdogs, burgers, fries, chips, sodas, sweet snacks and especially cookies crept into my regular diet. I rarely ate raw vegetables or fruit.

My diet improved about 5 years before I was diagnosed with prostate cancer because I wanted to lose weight and I met my wife-to-be, but I still went to McDonald's for breakfasts, and drank bottled water (that is acidic). I was already having problems with my prostate, many years before I was diagnosed with prostate cancer. Even though my diet improved it was too late to undo the damage of a poor diet. Eating the wrong foods is like putting the wrong fuel in your car. That is why you need to be mindful about what you put into your body early in life.

It is important to have a healthy diet throughout your life so that you can have a good quality of life throughout your life. Some men are diagnosed with prostate cancer in their forties, which is young, considering that they may live to be ninety, one hundred years old, or beyond. This is a real reason for eating right.

"Let food be thy medicine."

(Hippocrates – 2000 years ago)

In the documentary, *Forks Over Knives* Dr. Colin Campbell, Ph.D., and Dr. Caldwell Esselstyn M.D. give us the benefit of research that they conducted over decades and throughout the world, in regards to preventing cancer. How to avoid prostate cancer was one of the factors studied.

Too Much Animal Protein Can Lead to Prostate Cancer

In 1958, in Japan, the people ate a traditional Japanese diet, which consisted of mostly vegetables, rice, and a little meat. One small fish or one chicken breast could feed an entire family. Meat was used for flavoring, not the main part of a meal. In 1958, the Japanese had not yet been influenced by the American diet. In 1958, the Japanese population was about half that of the population in the United States. In 1958, the number of Japanese who died from prostate cancer was 18. In 1958, the number of Americans who died of prostate cancer was 14,000!

Americans like huge steaks, fried chicken, hamburgers, and hot dogs. It has been shown that when people adopt an American diet, wherever they live, their cancer rates increase.

Forks Over Knives also discusses a study whereby rats were fed a diet of 5% casein (a protein found in milk) and, alternatively, a diet containing 20% casein. When the rats were fed a diet containing 5% casein they did not develop cancer cells. However, when the rats were given a diet containing 20% casein the cancer cells were turned on!

If 20% of your food intake is animal protein, then according to the documentary, you have a higher risk of activating cancer cells. We interpret this to mean that cancer cells could be switched on at a lower percentage of animal protein, so just beware. The Word of Wisdom encourages people to eat meat in "moderation."

When we drink skimmed milk, we are getting a higher percentage of casein per unit volume, because the fat that naturally occurs in whole milk has been removed. To me, it would seem that eating natural cheese would be less harmful than drinking low-fat milk. The French eat a considerable amount of natural (not processed) cheese, and they do not have a high ratio of heart disease, nor were the French mentioned as having high rates of cancer in *Forks Over Knives*. Europeans avoid genetically modified organisms (GMO-foods). The French eat a lot of pureed vegetable soups (even in school cafeterias). They eat cheese to end a meal with grapes and other fruits. Elaine is French Canadian. She lived in Germany close to the French border for eight years of her life.

Sea Salt and the Need to Take Edible Iodine in Order to Maintain a Healthy Prostate

Many iodized salts (table salt) contain aluminum, which can lead to an accumulation of aluminum in the brain over time. This can lead to Alzheimer's disease. Due to this risk, many families choose to use sea salt, but sea salt does not contain iodine, which is an essential nutrient for our bodies. A lack of iodine in your diet can lead to prostate cancer.

Bromine exposure: According to Dr. Mercola, when you ingest the prevailing American diet, you absorb bromine (found in baked goods, plastics, soft drinks, medications, pesticides and more). The bromine displaces iodine, causing a deficiency of iodine, leading to an increased risk of cancer of the breast, thyroid gland, ovary and prostate that we see at alarmingly high rates today.[281]

Solution: If you use sea salt that does not contain iodine, take a daily supplement of organic liquid kelp that contains edible iodine, as directed on the package. Speak to your pharmacist, a nutritionist, or a naturopathic doctor about this.

Organic Soy Milk and Organic Soy Food Such as Tofu Can Help Support a Healthy Prostate

In the article, *Does High Soy Milk Intake Reduce Prostate Cancer Incidence? The Adventist Health Study (United States)*, Jacobsen BK, Knutsen SF, Fraser GE state:

"Frequent consumption (more than once a day) of soy milk was associated with 70 percent reduction of the risk of prostate cancer (relative risk = 0.3, 95 percent confidence interval 0.1-1.0, p-value for linear trend = 0.03). The association was upheld when extensive adjustments were performed."[282]

Note: Eat only organic soy food because other soy products are genetically modified.

Organic Tomato Sauce Can Help Support a Healthy Prostate

Organic tomato sauce in pasta dishes and organic salsa contain lycopene, which is excellent for prostate health. A bit of tomato ketchup on a hot dog is not enough. Besides, most tomato ketchups contain a lot of sugar.

The problem with some canned tomatoes is that the metal can that contains them is lined with BPA. We have already discussed the harmful effects of ingesting BPA.

Alternative: Use organic tomatoes and tomato sauces that are canned in glass or tins not lined with BPA.

Zinc: A Mineral that Helps to Support the Prostate and Mental Health

Prescription for Nutritional Healing, encourages men to ensure that their intake of zinc is sufficient:

"This essential mineral is important in prostate gland function and the growth of the reproductive organs. ... Zinc is found in the following food sources: brewer's yeast, dulse, egg yolks, fish, kelp, lamb, legumes, lima beans, liver, meats, mushrooms, oysters, pecans, poultry, pumpkin seeds, sardines, seafood, soy lecithin, soybeans, sunflowers seeds, torula yeast, and whole grains. ... *Compounds called phytates that are found in grains and legumes bind with zinc so that it cannot be absorbed. If you take both zinc and iron supplements, take them at different times. If these two minerals are taken together, they interfere with each other's activity." Eating legumes and grains together creates whole proteins, which are very nutritious, but you will have to get zinc from other food source combinations."283

Michelle Kerns reports on the news site, SFGate, in the article *Zinc for Teens*: "The National Academy of Sciences recommends that teen boys between the ages of 14 and 18 should consume 11 milligrams of zinc daily. ... Zinc cannot be stored by the body, so teens need a source of zinc in their diets daily. ... **Teens who consume the recommended levels of zinc regularly may be less likely to develop neurological problems like attention deficit hyperactivity disorder, growth delays and problems with recurrent infections. They may also have a decreased risk of heart disease**, age-related macular degeneration and cancer as they grow into adulthood. ... The richest food sources of zinc for teens include shellfish, beef, pork, the dark meat in chicken or turkey and dairy products like milk, yogurt and cheese. Oysters contain the highest concentration of zinc, with 3 ounces of oysters -- approximately six cooked oysters -- providing over 70 milligrams of zinc." Kerns also reports that a teen can improve his absorption of plant-based zinc such as in pinto beans by combining the beans with beef.284 The Hardy Hungry Boy recipe in the recipe section of this book will meet this need.

Note: Remember that drinking sodas depletes the body of zinc as previously mentioned in *Health Tip #12*.

Flaxseeds Can Interfere with the Production of Prostate Cancer Cells

Men's Fitness reported in the article, *6 Reasons to Never Neglect Flaxseed* that flaxseeds may help to prevent prostate cancer. Here is an excerpt from that article:

> "Another male-exclusive benefit of flaxseeds is its ability to assist in the fight against prostate cancer. In the United States, there were 241,740 newly reported cases and 28,170 prostate cancer-related deaths in 2012. With such ominous numbers, it's no wonder researchers continue to search for ways to combat it. One study of 161 presurgery prostate cancer patients found that flaxseed appears to significantly reduce cancer cell creation rates. How? Another study indicates it's likely to disrupt the events leading to cancer cell production."[285]

Sprinkle ground flaxseeds on your smoothies. It is important to purchase ground flaxseeds or to grind them yourself. It is best to store flaxseeds in the freezer. Research would indicate that taking one capsule of organic flaxseed oil per day might help to maintain heart health as well as prostate health. Check with your pharmacist to ensure that taking flaxseed oil is right for you. You want to ensure that there are no contraindications regarding flaxseed oil and other medications you might be taking.

CONCERN #4 - INFERTILITY HAS BEEN LINKED TO THE CONSUMPTION OF FAST FOOD AND PROCESSED FOOD
Roberto A. Ferdman reported in The Washington Post article, *Researchers have Found a Striking New Side Effect from Eating*

Fast Food, the latest disturbing results about fast food and other processed food. In a study, researchers at George Washington University found that people who eat fast food have "higher rates of infertility, especially males." The research team examined the data from over 9,000 people, including their urine samples, and found that people who eat fast food have higher levels of phthalates DEHP and DiNP, which are harmful chemicals when consumed.[286]

Given these startling findings, it is no wonder that hundreds of "fertility clinics" have opened across the country to help couples to conceive.

The Reproductive Medicine Associates of New Jersey reports, "There's been a 65% increase in IVF (In Vitro Fertilization) since 2003."[287]

IVF is very expensive and not guaranteed. Infertility Resources states: "On average, IVF cost of a basic IVF cycle in the U.S ranges from about $12,000 - $15,000. Although some insurance companies cover IVF, often they don't."[288]

If you want to be a father someday, you would be wise to maintain healthy sperm by avoiding fast food and processed food. When you are ready to be a father, you will then be more likely to father babies naturally.

LEARN TO READ FOOD LABELS

As you are learning, most of the foodstuff you find in supermarkets is not fit for human consumption. So how can we possibly steer you in the right direction?

If you are to have any chance of figuring out what's in the food products you buy at the grocery store, you will need to learn how to read food labels. This is a highly-recommended skill because again, knowing what you put inside your body is very important. The next time you go grocery shopping with your parents, take the time to read labels. The U.S. Food and Drug Administration (FDA) is responsible for regulating the content of food labels. The FDA provides instructions on how to correctly read and understand food labels below:

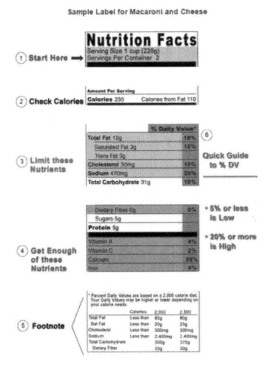

Nutrition Facts

1. **The Serving Size:** Serving sizes are standardized to make it easier to compare similar foods; they are provided in familiar units, such as cups or tablespoons or pieces, followed by the metric amount, e.g., the number of grams.

2. **Calories (and Calories from Fat)**: Calories provide a measure of how much energy you get from one serving of this food. Generally, 40 calories are low, 100 calories are moderate, and 400 calories are high. Remember that eating too many calories per day is linked to overweight and obesity.

3. **Limit These Nutrients:** (Saturated Fat, Trans Fat, Cholesterol, Sodium). Eating too much fat, trans fat, cholesterol, or sodium

(contained in salt) may increase your risk of certain chronic diseases, like heart disease, some cancers, or high blood pressure.

4. **Get Enough of These Nutrients:** (Dietary fiber, Vitamin A, Vitamin C, Calcium, Iron). Most Americans do not get enough dietary fiber. Eating enough of these nutrients can improve your health and help reduce the risk of some diseases and conditions. Eating a diet high in dietary fiber promotes healthy bowel function.

	Calories:	2,000	2,500
Total Fat	Less than	65g	80g
Sat Fat	Less than	20g	25g
Cholesterol	Less than	300mg	300mg
Sodium	Less than	2,400mg	2,400mg
Total Carbohydrate		300g	375g
Dietary Fiber		25g	30g

Percent Daily Values are based on a 2,000 calorie diet. Your Daily Values may be higher or lower depending on your calorie needs.

Percent Daily Values

5. **Note the asterisk (*)** used before the heading "%Daily Value" on the Nutrition Facts label. It refers to the Footnote in the lower part of the nutrition label, which tells you "%DVs are based on a 2,000 calorie diet." This statement must be on all food labels. But the remaining information in the full footnote may not be on the package if the size of the label is too small. When the full footnote does appear, it will always be the same. It doesn't change from product to product because it shows recommended dietary advice for all Americans--it is not about a particular food product. Look at the amounts circled in the footnote--these are the Daily Values (DV) for each nutrient listed, and they are based on public health experts' advice. DVs are recommended levels of intakes. DVs in the footnote are based on a 2,000 or 2,500 calorie diet. Note how the DVs for some nutrients change, while others (for cholesterol and sodium) remain the same for both calorie amounts.

6. **The % Daily Values (%DVs)** are based on the Daily Value recommendations for key nutrients but only for a 2,000 calorie daily diet--not 2,500 calories. You, like most people, may not know how many calories you consume in a day. But you can still use the %DV as a frame of reference whether or not you consume more or less than 2,000 calories. The %DV helps you determine if a serving of food is high or low in a nutrient. Note: A few nutrients, like trans fat, do not have a %DV because they should not be ingested – as previously discussed. Do you need to know how to calculate percentages to use the %DV? No, the label (the %DV) does the math for you. It helps you interpret the numbers (grams and milligrams) by putting them all on the same scale for the day (0-100%DV). The %DV column doesn't add up vertically to 100%. Instead each nutrient is based on 100% of the daily requirements for that nutrient (for a 2,000 calorie diet). This way you can tell high from low and know which nutrients contribute a lot, or a little, to your daily recommended allowance (upper or lower).[289]

7. **Added Sugars** – On May 2016, the U.S Food and Drug Administration issued a new food label, which includes information pertaining to added sugars. Many companies will be obliged to display the new label on their products by July 2018. Companies with less than $10,000,000 in annual food sales will have an extra year. Companies will be obliged to disclose all the amount of sugars in their products – and the percentage of added sugars.[290]

THE RISE OF NUTRIGENOMICS

The premise for the study of nutrigenomics is - scientists discovered that people of varying races, cultures, and families thrive on different diets that can vary slightly or significantly due to their genetic predisposition. That is, they are likely to thrive on the diet that their ancestor ate. It is important for us to know which foods kept our ancestors healthy and which foods made them ill because this knowledge can shed light on our personal health and what we should and should not eat.

Nutrigenomics is a multidisciplinary science
The NCMHD Center of Excellence for Nutritional Genomics defines nutrigenomics as the study of how foods affect our genes and how individual genetic differences can affect the way we respond to nutrients in the foods we eat. Our society has recently become interested in nutrigenomics because it has been recognized as having the potential for helping medical professionals learn how to prevent, mitigate and treat diseases, including certain cancers. It is envisioned that only small dietary changes would be needed, but these changes would be highly informative. We can summarize the assumptions behind this research and why scientists believe there is promise.

1. They believe that diet can be a serious risk factor for certain individuals and under certain circumstances.
2. They believe that the gene structure or gene expression can be affected by dietary chemicals.
3. They believe that a person's genetic makeup can be affected by diet and that this diet can influence the delicate balance between healthy states and diseased states.
4. They believe that diet-regulated genes can influence the onset, severity, and duration of chronic diseases.
5. They believe that personalized nutrition can be used to combat or prevent chronic disease.[291]

The NCMHD Center of Excellence explains the future expected impact of studying and putting into motion efforts to employ nutritional genomics: "The promise of nutritional genomics is personalized medicine and health based upon an understanding of our nutritional needs, nutritional and health status, and our genotype. Nutrigenomics will also have impacts on society "from medicine to agricultural and dietary practices to social and public policies" and its applications are likely to exceed that of even the human genome project. Chronic diseases (and some types of cancer) may be preventable, or at least delayed, by balanced, sensible diets. Knowledge gained from comparing diet/gene interactions in different populations may provide information needed to address the larger problem of global malnutrition and disease."[292]

PROOF OF THE THEORY OF NUTRIGENOMICS: THE INUITS' BODIES DIFFER FROM TYPICAL WESTERN BODIES

The diet of the Inuit (a people who live in the Artic) is unusually high in protein. I wonder – Did the Inuit's bodies adapt to their diet because there were very few vegetables and fruits to eat in the Artic? Or do the Inuits differ from people who have had a greater variety of food in their diet, due to the survival of those Inuits who had bodies that could cope with their high protein diet? Thereby only those who could cope with their high protein diet survived to reproduce babies who could also cope with the high protein diet. The study of nutrigenomics is intriguing.

"According to Patricia Gadsby's article, "How Can People Who Gorge on Fat and Rarely See a Vegetable Be Healthier Than We Are?" "four years ago, Loren Cordain, a professor of evolutionary nutrition at Colorado State University at Fort Collins, reviewed the macronutrient content (protein, carbohydrates, fat) in the diets of 229 hunter-gatherer groups listed in a series of journal articles collectively known as the Ethnographic Atlas. These are some of the oldest surviving human diets. In general, hunter-gatherers tend to eat more animal protein than we do in our standard Western diet, with its reliance on agriculture and carbohydrates derived from grains and starchy plants. The simplest, fastest way to make energy is to convert carbohydrates into glucose, our body's primary fuel. But if the body is out of carbs, it can burn fat, or if necessary, break down protein. The name given to the convoluted business of making glucose from protein is gluconeogenesis. It takes place in the liver, uses a dizzying slew of enzymes, and creates nitrogen waste that has to be converted into urea and disposed of through the kidneys. On a truly traditional diet, says Draper, recalling his studies in the 1970s, Arctic people had plenty of protein but little carbohydrate, so they often relied on gluconeogenesis. Not only did they have bigger livers to handle the additional work but their urine volumes were also typically larger to get rid of the extra urea. Nonetheless, there appears to be a limit on how much protein the human liver can safely cope with: Too much overwhelms the liver's waste-disposal system, leading to protein poisoning—nausea, diarrhea, wasting, and death."[293]

Ask your parents about the diet of your family members who lived long lives, and about the diet of family members who lived short lives. This may provide you with clues about which foods will strengthen you and which foods to avoid due to allergies and food sensitivities. This will also be vital information for your children.

ENERGY BALANCE AND MEASURING CALORIC INTAKE

A calorie is the unit of measure for energy. In nutrition, the calorie also stands for the amount of energy in food.

Your energy balance is the balance of calories consumed through eating and drinking compared to calories burned through physical activity. What you eat and drink is ENERGY IN. What you burn through physical activity is ENERGY OUT.

You burn a certain number of calories just by breathing air and digesting food. You also burn a certain number of calories (ENERGY OUT) through your daily routine. For example, teenagers burn calories just being students - doing things like walking to their lockers and carrying books. A list of estimated calorie requirements is shown below. This information can help you maintain a healthy calorie balance.

An important part of maintaining energy balance is the amount of ENERGY OUT (physical activity) that you do. People who are more physically active burn more calories than those who are not as physically active. The formulas for losing and gaining weight are simple:

- The same amount of ENERGY IN (calories consumed) and ENERGY OUT (calories burned) over time means your weight stays the same
- More ENERGY IN than ENERGY OUT over time and you will gain weight
- More ENERGY OUT than ENERGY IN over time and you will lose weight

Your ENERGY IN and OUT do not have to balance every day. It's having a balance over time that will help you stay at a healthy weight for the long term. You may still be growing so take that into consideration. Energy balance in children and teenagers happens when the amount of ENERGY IN and ENERGY OUT supports natural growth without promoting excess weight gain.

That is why you should take a look at the Estimated Calorie Requirement information for teenagers (below) provided by the Centers for Disease Control (CDC), to get a sense of how many calories (ENERGY IN) you need on a daily basis:

Balance Food and Activity
This calorie requirement information presents estimated amounts of calories required to maintain energy balance (and a healthy body weight) for teenagers at three different levels of physical activity. The estimates are rounded to the nearest 200 calories and were determined using an equation from the Institute of Medicine (IOM).[294]

From the 2005 Health and Human Services (HHS) - U.S. Department of Agriculture Dietary Guidelines for Americans, we find the following information for estimated calorie requirements for boys by age group and by physical activity level:

<u>Ages 9-13</u>:

* Sedentary Activity Level: 1,800 calories
* Moderate Activity Level: 1,800 – 2,200 calories
* High Activity Level: 2,000 – 2,600 calories

<u>Ages 14-18</u>:

* Sedentary Activity Level: 2,200 calories
* Moderate Activity Level: 2,400 – 2,800 calories
* High Activity Level: 2,800 – 3,200 calories

Notes:

(1) Sedentary means a lifestyle that includes only the light physical activity associated with typical day-to-day life.
(2) Moderately active means a lifestyle that includes physical activity equivalent to walking about 1.5 to 3 miles per day at 3 to 4 miles per hour, in addition to the light physical activity associated with typical day-to-day life.
(3) Active means a lifestyle that includes physical activity equivalent to walking more than 3 miles per day at 3 to 4 miles per hour, in addition to the light physical activity associated with typical day-to-day life.

The calorie ranges shown above are to accommodate the caloric needs of young men depending on their physical activity levels and age group. For children and adolescents, more calories are needed at older ages and higher activity levels. For adults, fewer calories are needed at older ages.[295]

Here is a list of foods commonly consumed by American youth, and a representative number of calories in each food (ENERGY IN your body). You can find more comprehensive lists on the web or in books:

Food	Calories
1 Beef frankfurter/wiener	184
1 Pepperoni slice	27
Ground beef, lean, ¼ pound	290
Sirloin steak, lean (grilled)	427
Bagel, plain	320
Bread, Sourdough, 1 slice	88
Won Ton Wrapper	23
Cheerios, 1 cup	5
Cheddar cheese, 1 ounce	114
Gouda, 1 ounce	101
Chocolate, 62%, 1 ounce	140
Chocolate, dark, 70%, 1 oz.	170
Chocolate milk, regular, 1 cup	210
Milk, whole, 1 cup	157
Egg, 1 large	70
Butter, 1 tablespoon	67
Ghee, 1 ounce	249
Nutella, 2 tablespoon	200
Peanut butter, smooth, 2 tablespoons	188
Apple, medium	81
Avocado, 2 or 3 slices	50
1 Banana, medium	105
Blueberries, fresh, ½ cup	41

Grapes, fresh, 1 cup	62
Kiwifruit, fresh, 1 medium	55
Lemon fresh, 1 medium	17
Mango, fresh, 1 medium	135
Orange, navel, fresh, 1 med	62
Pear, fresh, 1 medium	98
Raisins, 1 tablespoon	27
Raspberries, fresh, ½ cup	31
Strawberries, fresh, 8 berries	50
Watermelon, ½ cup diced	25
Almonds, 1 each	6
Brazil nuts, 6-8 nuts	183
Peanuts, dry roasted, 1 ounce	160
Pecan halves, ¼ cup	171
Pasta, ½ cup	200
Rice, brown, 1 cup cooked	216

ENERGY BALANCE IN REAL LIFE

Think of "energy balancing" like balancing on your skateboard or bicycle – eventually, it becomes second nature. For example, if you know you will be going to a party and may eat more high-calorie foods than normal, then you may wish to eat fewer calories for a couple of days before so that it balances out. Or, you can increase your physical activity level for a few days after the party, so that you can burn off the extra energy.

Here's another way of looking at energy balance in real life.

Eating just 150 calories more a day than you burn can lead to an extra 5 pounds over 6 months. That's a gain of 10 pounds a year. If you do not want this weight gain to happen, you can either reduce your ENERGY IN or increase your ENERGY OUT. If you want to lose weight, doing both is the best way to achieve your best weight because muscles burn fat even while you are asleep. The best way to track your ideal weight is by calculating your Body Mass Index (BMI). Remember if your BMI indicates that you are overweight, you should begin to cut down on your ENERGY IN (food intake) and increase your Energy OUT (exercise), immediately. It is much easier to lose 5 pounds or 10 pounds than it is to lose 50 pounds.

Here are some ways to burn 150 calories (ENERGY OUT), in just 30 minutes (for a 150-pound person):

- Shoot hoops
- Walk two miles
- Do yard work like gardening and raking leaves
- Go for a bike ride
- Dance with your family or friends

Portion Control Is One of the Keys to Controlling Obesity

We need to highlight another factor that turns out to be a key ingredient for good health: Portion Control.

You have heard the saying, "Everything in moderation." This expression, in regards to food, means that we should not eat too much of any food, and certain foods such as sweets should be eaten only occasionally. Too much of a good thing is not good for you. Some have said that the best exercise for regulating your weight is pushing yourself away from the table when your stomach feels 3/4 full. They have a good point too. Eat moderate amounts of food. And please do sit down to relax and mindfully enjoy your food; do not eat "on the run" all the time. This will enable better digestion and you will feel less hungry.

Do Not Over-Control What You Eat

Given all the previous health tips, some nutritionists have begun to advise that we ought to avoid over-controlling what we eat. You will need to use your head and exert your best efforts on this. If you are like me and you absolutely must have a cookie or two sometime, go ahead but eat them in moderation - meaning not every day. Eating the occasional cookie will enable your brain and body to remain balanced. More specifically, never giving into a craving for a cookie can cause your brain to send a signal to your body to go into "starvation mode" and your body will then begin to store fat to prevent starvation. In the words of Julie Barnes, a New York-based clinical psychologist, "Over-control leads to a lack of control. Just have the cookie."[296] (Notice the guideline is THE COOKIE, not COOKIES).

We encourage you to work with parents, nutritionists, and health care providers in coming up with a "balanced" diet plan specific for you, your body, your activity level, and your tastes.

Body Mass Index

The Centers for Disease Control and Prevention (CDC) defines Body Mass Index (BMI) as an easy way to screen for weight categories that can lead to health problems. You can calculate your BMI using a calculator, spreadsheet, or by hand. You will need to weigh yourself in kilograms and measure your height in meters. Your BMI is equal to your weight (kg) divided by the square of your height (m^2). The two charts below demonstrate examples showing how to track and interpret your BMI. In the first chart, the example shows a 10-year-old boy at various BMI readings. If his BMI falls within the top band (95th Percentile), he is obese. If his BMI falls between the 85th and 95th Percentiles, he is considered overweight. If his BMI falls between the 5th Percentile and 85th Percentile, he has normal weight. If his BMI falls below the 5th Percentile, then he is underweight.[297]

Calculate your own BMI. Locate your age on the chart, and plot where your BMI falls. Are you obese, overweight, normal, or underweight?

The second chart shows that two boys - one 10 years old and the other 15 years old, with the same BMI. The 10-year old is considered obese, while the 15-year-old has normal weight.

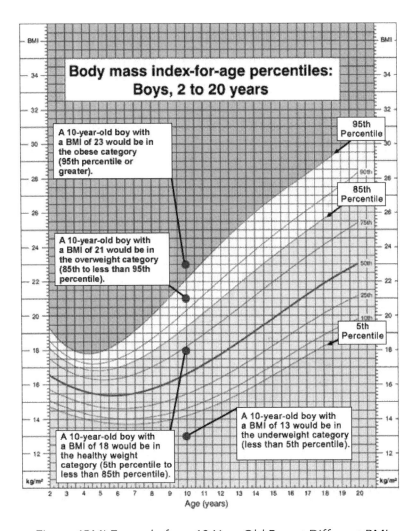

Figure 1BMI Example for a 10-Year Old Boy at Different BMI Readings to Determine Whether He is Obese, Overweight, Normal Weight, or Underweight. Image provided courtesy of The Centers for Disease Control and Prevention.

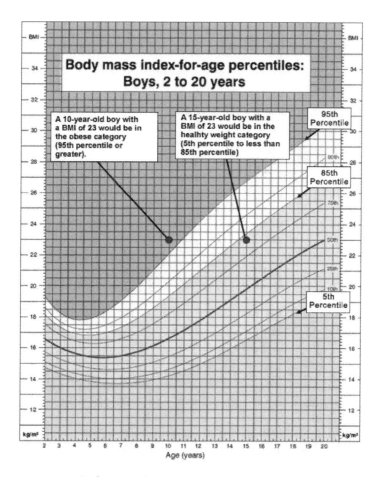

BMI Example for an Obese 10-Year Old Boy and a 15-Year Old Boy with Normal Weight - both with BMI of 23. Image provided courtesy of The Centers for Disease Control and Prevention.

LISTENING TO YOUR BODY IN REGARDS TO FOOD

Listen to your body's needs including food sensitivities and food allergies.

* If your lips begin to swell, or your throat starts to itch or you have difficulty breathing after eating certain foods, tell your parents, teacher or medical provider immediately. This may

be an allergic reaction to the food you ate. It could turn into a critical situation.

* Food sensitivities can also manifest themselves as skin rashes, sore stomachs, diarrhea, or headaches. Report any odd feelings or conditions to your parents, teachers, or medical provider.

* Adverse effects from eating food you do not know you are sensitive to or allergic to may take a long time to manifest. For example, when my wife was young she developed sore toes when she walked. She sought the advice of a doctor, and she was told that she had the onset of arthritis. She recalled the story of a Japanese surgeon who immigrated to the United States, began to eat an American diet, developed arthritis, and could no longer perform surgery. He returned to his native Japanese diet, and his arthritic condition ceased. He was able to resume performing surgery. He then introduced into his diet one at a time American foods to determine which foods aggravated his arthritis. My wife recalled that one of the foods was orange juice. She had been drinking three or four glasses of orange juice per day routinely. She felt that there might be a correlation between drinking a large amount of orange juice and her sore toes. She quit drinking orange juice and the soreness in her toes subsided. Moral of this story: listen to your body.

* Some time ago, my wife's lips would swell to twice their size sometimes after eating. She suspected a food allergy but could not figure out which food was causing the allergic reaction. Her naturopath confirmed that what she was experiencing was an anaphylactic reaction and gave her a prescription for an allergy test. She was tested for 96 foods. The results were that she was not allergic to any of these foods. However, once she knew which foods she was not allergic to, by the process of elimination, she was able to determine that she was allergic to canola oil. On the Internet, she found testimonies of other people who are allergic to this oil. Many restaurants use canola oil because it is cost effective. The moral of this story: listen to your body.

Bonus: Prepare These Easy, Healthy Recipes with Your Family

Now that you are a nutritional expert (of sorts), why not put your skills to use and treat your family and yourself to a healthy treat. Knowing how to cook nutritious meals is an important part of becoming self-sufficient.

All of these recipes should be prepared with adult supervision for younger men. Besides, preparing meals together as a family helps family members to bond. Everyone will feel the love and effort it takes to prepare a meal together. While developing cooking skills members of a family develop collaboration skills and respect for each other's work habits. Everyone will feel grateful that the task of preparing the food was not his or hers alone. This is a reflection of what family members are for in other facets of life. We are supposed to help each other. You can also prepare meals with friends.

Sharing meals with family and friends around a table is important especially when a prayer of thanksgiving is offered for the food we eat. As you shall see later in the book, prayer changes the molecular structure of water. Therefore, we feel that prayer must also change the molecular structure of food due to its water content. I believe that offering a prayer of thanksgiving improves the nutritional value of food.

Sharing food also gives us all time to focus on each other, as we unplug from our daily dose of electronic devices, work, and play. It is a special time to share what we are grateful for and any concern that we have had during the day.

Note: Safe Handling of Food

According to the CDC article, *Salmonella is a Sneaky Germ: Seven Tips for Safer Eating*, you can keep yourself, your family, and others safer by remembering to:

* **Clean.** Wash hands, cutting boards, utensils, and countertops.
* **Separate**. Keep raw meat, poultry, and seafood separate from ready-to-eat foods.

- **Cook.** Use a food thermometer to ensure that foods are cooked to a safe internal temperature: 145°F for whole meats (allowing the meat to rest for 3 minutes before carving or consuming), 160°F for ground meats, and 165°F for all poultry.
- **Chill.** Keep your refrigerator below 40°F and refrigerate food that will spoil.
- **Don't** prepare food for others if you have diarrhea or vomiting.
- **Be especially careful** preparing food for children, pregnant woman, those in poor health, and older adults.

COOKING TO LIVE WELL WITH A JOIE DE VIVRE

Eating delicious food is one of life's special pleasures. The following are my French wife's secret (until now) quick and easy recipes:

START YOUR DAY WITH ENERGY-BOOSTING BREAKFASTS

Great Granola

Ingredients

5 cups rolled oats
4 tablespoons sesame seeds
¼ teaspoon salt
2 cups nuts – walnuts, pecans, or almonds – chopped into medium size chunks (if the pieces are too small or sliced they are likely to burn) – or add coconut
1/3 cup of olive oil
1/2 cup maple syrup
1/4 cup honey
½ cup water
1/8 teaspoon cinnamon

1/4 teaspoon nutmeg, freshly grated
2 tablespoons grated frozen organic lemon zest
½ cup golden flaxseeds, ground
1 cup dried cranberries or dried cherries, and dried apricots, chopped
1/3 cup dried currants

Directions

1. Preheat oven to 300 degrees F.
2. Line a large 13in x 18in cookie sheet, with sides, with cooking parchment paper.
3. In a large bowl, stir the oats, sesame seeds, salt, and nuts.
4. Mix the oil, maple syrup, honey, water, cinnamon, nutmeg and lemon zest together. Pour this mixture over the oats and nuts. Stir until thoroughly combined.
5. Layer the granola on top of the parchment.
6. Bake for 20 minutes. Stir after 10 minutes of cooking time.
7. Remove the granola from the oven. If you are using coconut, add it at this time. Lower the oven temperature to 275 degrees F.
8. Return the granola to the oven for another 15 minutes or until the granola is very crunchy.
9. Remove the granola from the oven and add immediately the flaxseeds, the dried cranberries, currants, and apricots. Stir.
10. Cool completely. Store in an airtight container in the refrigerator.

Serve over plain yogurt with fresh berries and a drizzle of maple syrup, or honey. Alternatively, you can have the granola with organic whole milk and fresh berries.

Allergy Alert: If anyone who will partake of the granola is allergic to nuts –unsweetened shredded coconut can be substituted for nuts.

Banana Berry and Lemon Smoothie

Yogurt is a fermented food. It helps to replenish the good bacteria in your digestive system, which enables proper absorption of nutrients in the foods that you eat.

Ingredients (for 2 persons)

2 banana, sliced and frozen on Glad® cling wrap
1 1/2 cups of frozen blackberries, raspberries, and blueberries
1 cup of plain whole yogurt (nonfat yogurt tastes terrible)
2 teaspoons honey
1 tablespoon freshly grated organic frozen lemon
1/2 tablespoon ground organic flaxseeds

Directions

1. Process the first 5 ingredients in a food processor. Every ten seconds or so stir the bottom layer of smoothie to the top, process again, and repeat these two steps until all of the frozen pieces of fruit have been incorporated. It will take about ten minutes.
2. Spoon into two tall glasses.
3. Sprinkle flaxseeds on top.

*Note - The smoothies may be placed in the freezer for 5 – 10 minutes.

Mandarin Smoothie

Ingredients (for 2 persons)

5 mandarins, peeled, sectioned, and frozen on Glad® cling wrap
1 1/4 cups plain whole yogurt
2 teaspoons honey
1/8 teaspoon pure vanilla extract (optional)
½ tablespoon organic ground flaxseeds

Directions

1. Place the frozen mandarin sections, yogurt, vanilla and honey in a food processor. Process until smooth. Every ten seconds or so stir the bottom layer of smoothie to the top while pushing the fruit down to the bottom, process again, and repeat these two steps until all of the frozen pieces of fruit have been incorporated. It will take about ten minutes.
2. Spoon into two tall glasses.
3. Sprinkle organic flaxseeds on top.

Alternative: Add a frozen sliced banana or two when processing the other ingredients for a mandarin banana smoothie.

* Note: The smoothies may be placed in the freezer for 5 – 10 minutes.

Ataulfo Mango Smoothie
Ataulfo mangoes are sometimes called Champagne Mangoes. When they are ripened to a golden yellow and about to wrinkle, their texture is ultra-smooth. Ripen the mangoes at room temperature. Smoothies made with ataulfo mangoes are the smoothest smoothies.

Ingredients (for 1 – 2 persons)
2 ripened ataulfo mangoes, peeled, cubed and frozen on Glad® cling wrap
1 ¼ cup whole organic yogurt

Directions

1. Place the frozen mango cubes and yogurt in a food processor. Process until smooth. Every ten seconds or so stir the bottom layer of smoothie to the top while pushing the fruit down to the bottom, process again, and repeat these two steps until

all of the frozen pieces of fruit have been incorporated. It will take about 5-7 minutes.
2. Spoon into one or two glasses.
3. Sprinkle organic flaxseeds on top.

Note: The smoothies may be placed in the freezer for 5 minutes.

"Wheat Belly" All-Purpose Gluten-Free Baking Mix
Dr. William Davis, a cardiologist and the author of "Wheat Belly," provides the following two gluten-free recipes:

Ingredients
4 cups almond flour/meal
1 cup organic golden flaxseeds, ground
¼ cup coconut flour
2 teaspoons baking soda (We prefer to use 2 teaspoons baking powder.)

Directions
Mix all the ingredients above.

"Wheat Belly" Gluten-Free Triple Berry Quick Muffins

Ingredients (for 1 person)
1/2 cup *Wheat Belly* all-purpose baking mix
1/4 tablespoon ground cinnamon
1 tablespoon sugar
1 pinch of sea salt
1 egg
2 tablespoons milk
1 tablespoon butter, melted
1/4 cup frozen or fresh mixed berries (raspberries, blueberries, and blackberries)

Directions

1. Bake the muffin in a microwave ovenproof buttered mug or buttered ramekin.
2. In a medium bowl, combine the baking mix, cinnamon, sugar, and salt. Whisk into the dry ingredients, the egg mixture and berries. Use a rubber spatula to scrape the mixture into a large mug or a 10-ounce ramekin.
3. Microwave on high power for 2 minutes, or until a wooden pick inserted in the center comes out clean. (If using fresh berries, microwave for 1 1/2 minutes.)
4. Allow cooling for 5 minutes.[298]

Sweet Potato Asparagus Quiche
Preheat the oven to 375 degrees F.
This recipe will feed two persons. It can feed three persons if the meal also includes toast and a vegetable salad or fruit salad.

Ingredients
2 tablespoon olive oil
1 sweet potato – 8in (long) x 2in (diameter), thinly sliced (1/8in thick)
1 slice of uncured ham, chopped or 4 slices crispy uncured bacon, chopped
1in x 3in block Swiss cheese, grated
1/2 cup onion, minced
4 large eggs
1 cup whole milk
1 teaspoon prepared yellow mustard
Salt
Pepper, freshly ground
11 -12 thin asparagus spears cut five inches from the tip

Directions

1. Brush olive oil on a deep-dish pie plate.
2. Cover the pie plate with sweet potato slices. First, start by covering the bottom of the pie plate. Next, overlap the slices, slightly, on the side of the pie plate. Cover the bottom with another layer of sweet potato slices.
3. Sprinkle the cheese over the sweet potatoes on the bottom of the pie plate.
4. Cover the cheese with chopped ham or bacon.
5. Sprinkle the onion on the ham.
6. Beat the eggs.
7. Beat the mustard, salt, pepper and milk into the eggs.
8. Pour the egg mixture into the prepared pan.
9. Place the asparagus on top to resemble the spokes of a wheel. Do not peel thin asparagus. If you are using thick asparagus, peel it because the skin is thicker and will be tough. Discard the hard part at the end of the asparagus stalk but keep the middle part to add to soup.
10. Bake for 30 minutes or until the quiche is golden and a knife inserted in the center comes out clean.

French Canadian Oatmeal

Ingredients (for 1 person)
3 strips of uncured bacon, fried
2 eggs, beaten, salted and peppered
1/2 teaspoon prepared mustard
1/3 (heaping) cup Quaker's Old-fashioned oats
1 cup water
Pinch of salt
1/8 cup whole milk, or add a little water
1 tablespoon maple syrup

Directions

1. Fry the bacon.
2. Mix the water, salt and oats. Cover and bring to a gentle boil. Lower the heat to simmer until the oats are well cooked – about 10 minutes. Check after 5 minutes. Add water to achieve desired consistency.
3. Add the milk or a little more water to achieve the desired consistency. Stir. Cover and continue to simmer for about 2 minutes.
4. Meanwhile, beat the eggs with salt, pepper and prepared mustard.

Tip for scrambling eggs: Melt 1/4 tablespoon butter and ½ tablespoon olive oil in a small 6" ceramic pan on medium low heat. Pour the eggs into the prepared pan. Push the eggs across the pan every 10-20 seconds with a wooden spoon that has a flat edge on the end, until the eggs are just cooked.

5. Spoon the oatmeal into a heated bowl.
6. Drizzle maple syrup on top of the oatmeal and smooth it over the surface of the oatmeal.
7. Transfer the scrambled eggs immediately onto the oatmeal and maple syrup. Otherwise, the eggs will dry up in the pan.
8. Top the eggs with the strips of bacon and serve. Yum! My favorite.

Savory Eggcellent Wrap

Now that you know the technique for preparing scrambled eggs, from the recipe above, you can add piquant to your mornings with this spicy version of scrambled eggs:

Ingredients (for 2 persons)
2 soft organic large whole grain tortillas
2 tablespoon olive oil

6 eggs, beaten
3 green onions, sliced
2 tablespoon sun-dried tomato, cut with kitchen scissors into tiny bits
1/3 cup Swiss cheese, grated
½ tsp. prepared mustard
1/16 teaspoon salt
¼ teaspoon "Secret Spice" (recipe included)
1/8 teaspoon of freshly ground black pepper

Directions

Beat the eggs, and add the last seven ingredients – beat again. Heat the pan and olive oil on medium-low. Pour the egg mixture into the pan. Push the eggs across the pan every 10 - 20 seconds, with a wooden spoon that has a flat edge on the end, until the eggs are just cooked. Place the scrambled eggs in the center of the tortillas. To wrap: fold the bottom over the scrambled eggs, and fold the right side over then the left side over – to form a pocket filled with the savory eggs.

Congee – Asian Oatmeal

Congee is normally prepared with white rice. This delicious version uses oatmeal. Oatmeal is good for heart health and it has a low glycemic index. Prepare the congee early in the morning or the day before.

Ingredients (for 4-6 persons)

8 cups water
1 box organic chicken broth
1/4 teaspoon salt
2 cups oatmeal
1 chicken breast
3 tablespoons soy sauce
3 tablespoons dry sherry (optional – the alcohol evaporates during cooking)
½ a bunch of kale, sliced crosswise
1 pkg. mushrooms

2 tablespoons olive oil, or butter

2 tablespoons ginger root, minced

2 red peppers

Avocado oil

Hot chili sesame oil

Directions

1. Bring water and broth to a boil in a thick-bottom pot.
2. Add salt and oatmeal to the boiling water and broth.
3. Reduce heat to medium-low. Check periodically to ensure that the oatmeal does not stick. An egg flipper made of heatproof silicone or a wooden spoon with a straight edge at the bottom is ideal for scraping the bottom of pots. You want enough heat to break up the oatmeal in order to get a creamy consistency. The oatmeal should cook for about 2 hours. Add water when the congee thickens too much. The consistency desired is that of a creamy soup. If, after 2 hours the oatmeal is still not completely broken down, a handheld blender can be used to speed up the process.
4. Marinate the chicken breast for 15 minutes in a mixture of soy sauce and dry sherry. The alcohol will evaporate during cooking. (M have chosen not to consume alcohol.)
5. Add the kale to the oatmeal.
6. Slice the mushrooms and sauté in olive oil or butter (or a little of each) with a little salt. Deglaze the pan with a little water. Add the mushrooms and the mushroom au jus to the oatmeal.
7. Fry the chicken breast in 3 tablespoons of avocado oil on medium high heat. After the chicken is browned, lower the heat and simmer until still a little pink inside or just cooked. Let the chicken cool slightly until you can handle it. Julienne the chicken - (cut into 1in x ¼in slices). Set aside.
8. Add the chicken marinade to the oatmeal.
9. Deglaze the pan in which you cooked the chicken. Add this chicken au jus to the oatmeal.

10. Julienne the red pepper - (cut in long, thin slices).

11. Roast the red pepper strips in a little hot avocado oil. Avocado oil can tolerate high heat – unlike olive oil. It is OK if the strips are slightly almost burnt in spots. Add a little salt and cayenne pepper as the peppers are roasting in the pan. Set aside. Use the red pepper to decorate the top of each bowl of congee. This adds a very interesting visual and taste dimension.

12. When the oatmeal has broken up to your liking, add the chicken but do not boil after this. High heat will toughen the chicken. Taste and adjust the seasoning with a little salt if needed.

13. Serve with the roasted red pepper slivers in the center of the congee and a drizzle of chili sesame oil (this oil has a delightful aroma).

Alternative: Leftover BBQ chicken, and leftover BBQ vegetables - zucchini, red onion, sweet potato, and green pepper can be julienned and added to the congee.

SUSTAINING MEALS FOR LUNCH OR DINNER

Super-Fast and Easy Broccoli, Cauliflower, and Cheddar Cheese Soup

No chopping is needed to prepare this soup. It is very satisfying, nutritious, and comforting.

Ingredients (for 4-6 persons)

2 large pots
1 handheld blender - to puree the soup
1 large 48 oz. bag of broccoli, already cut and washed
1 medium 32 oz. bag of cauliflower, already cut and washed
4 bay leaves
1 teaspoon summer savory
1/2 teaspoon rosemary

¼ teaspoon thyme

¼ teaspoon sage

2 cups organic chicken broth (vegetarians can use vegetable broth)

1 teaspoon onion powder

1 teaspoon garlic powder

1 cup whole milk

1 cup grated cheddar cheese (you can purchase grated cheddar)

1/2 teaspoon salt

1/2 teaspoon freshly ground pepper

Directions

1. Divide all of the ingredients in half (except for the milk, cheese, salt, and pepper) and put them into the two pots. Fill the pots with water.
2. Bring the ingredients to a medium boil and cook until the vegetables are very tender. The liquid will have been reduced, and the vegetables will have cooked down somewhat.
3. Remove the bay leaves from each pot.
4. Add the milk, the cheese and the salt and pepper to <u>only one</u> pot of broccoli and cauliflower in cooking liquid.
5. With a slotted spoon add all of the vegetables from the second pot to the pot with the vegetables, milk and cheese - reserve the cooking liquid in the second pot to thin out the soup if it is too thick (the cooking liquid can also be frozen and used to make other soups - it is full of vitamins).
6. Finally, place a handheld blender (stainless steel is best) into the pot and blend the soup until creamy.
7. Taste and adjust the seasoning with salt and pepper to your liking.
8. If the soup is too thick, you can add a little of the cooking liquid from the second pot. Blend again. Viola! Easy!
9. Serve with thick slices of organic sourdough bread. Sourdough bread is more nutritious than other breads because sourdough bread has been fermented.

Asparagus Cabbage Soup

This soup is easy to prepare. It is delicious and can be served as a main course, with a slice of sourdough bread. You can end your meal with natural cheese (gouda, cheddar, or cambozola) and berries, a sliced apple, a sliced pear, grapes, or a variety of fruit. Slice the fruit just before serving to avoid browning. You may want to have another slice of sourdough bread with the cheese and fruit.

Ingredients (for 4 persons)

1 ½ pounds thin asparagus - if the spears are thick, peel the lower part with a vegetable peeler
1 medium cabbage, chopped
1 organic chicken stock box
2 onions, sliced into wedges
¼ teaspoon dried thyme
2 bay leaves
5 cups of water
Salt and freshly ground black pepper to taste.

Directions:

1. Chop off the hard white bottom end of the asparagus, and discard.
2. Cut about 2 inches off the tips of each asparagus stalk, and reserve.
3. Pour the chicken stock into a 30-cup pot, and bring it to a boil. Lower the heat and add the asparagus tips to the pot to blanch these for 2 minutes. Remove the asparagus tips, and set aside.
4. Chop the onions, and the cabbage and add these to the pot, along with the asparagus stalks (the middle part), thyme, bay leaves, and water. Cover with a tilted lid. Bring the ingredients to a medium boil, lower the heat to a gentle boil. Ensure that the vegetables remain covered with water during cooking. Continue to cook until all the vegetables are soft.

5. Remove the two bay leaves. Process the soup with a hand-held blender. If the soup is too thick add water or more chicken stock to achieve the desired consistency. Taste the soup and add salt and pepper to suit your taste and health requirements.
6. Add the asparagus tips to the pot just before serving. When these have heated through, the soup is ready to serve. If the tips remain in the hot soup for more than 5 minutes, the tips will begin to fall apart, will not taste as good, and will not look as aesthetically pleasing.

Hardy Hungry Boy

A large thick-bottomed 30-cup pot is needed. It is best to begin preparing this recipe two days before serving the Hungry Boy. The flavor of the dish will improve if it is refrigerated overnight and re-heated. Hungry Boy can be frozen in several containers to enjoy on other days - or it can feed approximately 10 hungry boys, when it is served with sourdough bread or brown rice, and cut vegetables or a salad.

This is a dish that most young men will love. I love it. Canadian Scouts used canned goods in the original recipe when they went camping. This recipe is almost as easy and much more nutritious because it is prepared from scratch.

Ingredients (for 10 persons)
6 cups organic pinto beans (the beans expand a lot)
8-ounce cube of salted pork
2 bay leaves
4 tablespoons Worcestershire sauce
2 teaspoons dry mustard, mixed with 2 tablespoons water
2 cups organic tomato sauce
4 tablespoons maple syrup, or 2 tablespoon black strap molasses
1/2 teaspoon cayenne pepper
2 teaspoons garlic powder
½ teaspoon freshly ground black pepper

2 tablespoons soy sauce

1/2 pound vegetarian-fed ground turkey, or ground chicken, or ground beef cooked in a little olive oil with a ¼ teaspoon salt and ¼ teaspoon pepper, and 1/4 teaspoon garlic powder, or to taste.

After the beans are cooked, add:

2 lbs. frozen organic green peas

Directions

1. Rinse the beans thoroughly to clean the beans, cover with water to 2 inches above the beans and soak overnight. The next day, drain the soaking water, rinse the beans and cover with water.
2. Add to the pot the cube of salt pork, bay leaves, Worcestershire sauce, organic tomato sauce, maple syrup, cayenne pepper, garlic powder, black pepper, soy sauce, and cooked ground meat.
3. Cover the beans and bring to a rolling boil on the stovetop. Lower to a medium boil. Tilt the lid to allow some of the steam to escape. Add water when the liquid boils down. Cook until the beans are very tender or to your liking – up to 4 - 5 hours. Stir occasionally to ensure that the beans are not sticking.
4. When the beans are almost tender remove the fat from the salted pork meat and return the meat to the pot.
5. When the beans are tender, add the peas.

I like Hungry Boy with black pepper and sriracha sauce on top, served with brown rice, and the maple candied walnut and blueberry salad. Recipes for these dishes follow:

Brown Rice

Brown rice has a low glycemic index. It does not spike blood sugar levels as much as white rice.

Ingredients (for 5 persons)

2 cups organic Lundberg short grain brown rice rinsed in a strainer
3 1/4 cups water
1/4 teaspoon salt

Directions

1. Combine the rice, water and salt in a thick-bottomed pot.
2. Bring to a rigorous boil for three minutes and cover. Lower the temperature to very low. Do not remove the lid.
3. Cook for about 35 minutes.
4. Fluff lightly with a fork before serving.

Maple Candied Walnut and Blueberry Salad

Ingredients (for 4-6 person)

1 head organic romaine lettuce, or 2 heads of butter lettuce
1 bunch of green onions, cut into small slices with kitchen scissors
1 English cucumber – julienned (cut lengthwise into strips)
2 red pepper, julienned
1-container blueberries

Directions for the Vegetables

1. Wash the lettuce and pat it dry with paper towels or spin it in a salad spinner.
2. Tear the lettuce into bite-size pieces.
3. Divide the lettuce into salad bowls.
4. Wash and prepare the green onions, cucumber, red pepper and blueberries.
5. Place some of each vegetable and fruit on top of the greens.

Candied Walnuts

Ingredients

1 ½ cups walnuts
1/2 tablespoon butter
¼ cup maple syrup

Directions

1. Preheat the oven to 375 degrees F.
2. Cover a baking sheet with cooking parchment paper.
3. Melt the butter in a pan, on medium heat. Add the maple syrup, stir, and then quickly add the walnuts. Stir constantly until the syrup has thickened and is coating and sticking to all the walnuts.
4. Transfer the walnuts to the baking sheet's parchment paper and bake in the oven for 8 minutes.
5. Remove from the oven and cool.

If you do not want to use all of the walnuts, they will keep very well in an airtight container in the fridge.

Salad Dressing

Ingredients

¾ cup olive oil
¼ or 1/3 cup white balsamic vinegar, depending on how much you like vinegar
1 tablespoon maple syrup
¼ teaspoon salt
¼ teaspoon freshly ground black pepper

Directions

1. Combine all of the ingredients above. Stir vigorously with a fork just before serving the salad, and spoon some of the dressing on top of each salad.
2. After drizzling the dressing onto the salad, add the maple-candied walnuts to decorate the top of each salad.

Large Pizza Dinner

To be prepared by four persons, for four hungry persons.

This is my favorite pizza. The tomato sauce in this pizza recipe is memorable. It is thick and very flavorful.

Note: The best type of pizza pan is a mesh pizza pan or a pizza pan with holes – available at Costco for businesses and online.

A great "from scratch" pizza pie takes a fair amount of time to prepare. It is fun to share the preparations with family members or friends. One person can prepare the dough. A second person can prepare the tomato sauce and purchase one 8 oz. bag of grated mozzarella cheese and a 4 oz. bag of grated Parmesan cheese. A third person can cut the vegetables. A fourth person can cook organic ground sausage, or cook uncured bacon, or bring uncured pepperoni or bring a combination of cooked uncured bacon and uncured pepperoni. Or a little uncured ham will work well, especially if the person preparing the produce brings pineapple tidbits (canned in their own juice, or fresh). Meat is optional. If you are not going to use meat – the fourth person can bring pine nuts and 1 cup or more of sundried tomatoes cut into little pieces. The next time you get together to prepare pizza, you can change who will do which task. It would be best for participants to make their portion of the pizza pie ahead of time – the morning of the pizza dinner would be best. This will save time. Then you will have time to watch a movie or to play a board game, or to play cards. Remember that socializing is important for the development of your brain.

Dough for the Pizza

2 cups organic whole-wheat flour

1 cup oat flour – (process rolled oats in a food processor to make the oat flour) - oats lower cholesterol

½ teaspoon salt

1-¼ cups of cooked organic lima beans, or organic white beans, or organic northern beans, or organic navy beans. Canned beans are ok, but drain the liquid.

½ cup warm water – to mix with the beans

½ cup of warm water (120 degrees F.)- to warm the yeast

1 teaspoon organic sugar

2 packages of dry yeast

2 tablespoons olive oil

To flavor the crust rim

2 tablespoons olive oil

¼ teaspoon garlic powder

½ teaspoon dry basil

¼ teaspoon salt

Directions

1. Combine the flours and salt and blend with a fork.
2. Puree the beans with ½ cup of water in a food processor. Beans have high fiber content.
3. Mix the ½ cup warm water and the sugar. Sprinkle the yeast over the water and stir. Let the mixture sit for 5 minutes. It is best to use a food grade thermometer to measure the temperature of the water. If the water is too hot, it will kill the yeast.
4. In a large bowl - stir the pureed beans into the yeast mixture. Add the olive oil and stir. Add the flour mixture. Stir vigorously with a fork, until all of the flour has been incorporated.

5. Sprinkle 1 tablespoon of flour on a large plate. Knead the dough on the plate – adding a tablespoon of flour whenever the dough gets sticky until it feels smooth and elastic.
6. Brush olive oil on the inside of the bowl used to mix the dough. Place the dough back into the bowl. Cover with a clean dish-towel, until the dough doubles in size – about 1 hour.
7. Clean the counter with a piece of paper towel – rinse off any soap residue. When the counter is still damp. Cover the counter with a large square of Glad® Cling Wrap. Flour the surface of the cling wrap.
8. When the dough is ready, roll the dough out with a rolling pin to just a little larger than the pizza pan about 18 ¼ inches in diameter.
9. With the help of one of your fellow pizza pals – place the meshed pizza pan over the rolled dough. Fold the cling wrap over the meshed pizza pan and working in unison reverse the dough and the pan. The pizza dough should now be on top of the pan.
10. To flavor the crust's rim roll - mix olive oil, garlic powder, dry basil, and salt.
11. Brush the seasoned oil on the inside of the circumference of the pizza dough – a ¼ inch from the very edge. Roll the pizza dough edge over this flavoring – to form a roll around the pizza that is about ½ inch wide.

Tomato Sauce for the Pizza

(The lycopene in organic tomato sauce and organic tomato paste will help to keep your prostate healthy.)

14 oz. jar organic pizza sauce (free of corn syrup)

4 oz. organic tomato paste

¼ teaspoon salt

¼ teaspoon cayenne pepper

¼ teaspoon garlic powder

1/2 teaspoon dried oregano, or marjoram

1 ½ tablespoons dried basil

Directions

1. Blend all of the ingredients above very well with a fork.
2. Spread a thick layer of sauce evenly over the dough.

Vegetables for the Pizza

3 cups of sliced mushrooms
1 large onion, very thinly sliced and quartered
1 ½ green peppers - diced
5 large garlic cloves, very thinly sliced

Directions

1. Dot the top of the tomato sauce with garlic slices.
2. Cut enough mushroom slices to cover the tomato sauce and garlic completely.
3. Sprinkle the onion slivers all over the pizza.
4. Sprinkle the green pepper all over the pizza.

Meat for the Pizza- (optional)

1/2 pound of natural ground chicken sausage or ground beef sausage or pork sausage meat (this meat is usually seasoned)
1/4 teaspoon cayenne pepper
1/4 teaspoon freshly ground black pepper
¼ teaspoon garlic powder

Directions

1. Cook the ground meat with the seasonings.
2. Sprinkle the meat onto the vegetables on the pizza.

Or:

1/4 pound uncured bacon, cooked
1/4 pound uncured pepperoni

Directions

1. Toss the bacon and pepperoni with the cayenne pepper, black pepper, and garlic powder.
2. Sprinkle the meat onto the vegetables on the pizza.

Alternative toppings: Small pieces of sundried tomatoes, black olives, and pine nuts, or ham and pineapple.

Cheese for the Pizza
8 oz. shredded mozzarella cheese
4 oz. shredded Parmesan cheese

Directions
Blend the cheeses and cover the pizza with the cheese.

Baking Instructions

1. Bake in a preheated oven at 450 degrees F. for 25 minutes. Check the pizza every ten minutes. Some ovens are hotter than others. If so, the cooking time will be less. If your oven heats at a lower temperature than indicated on the dial, it may take a few minutes longer.
2. Clear the top of the stove before removing the pizza from the oven.
3. Wear oven mitts when removing the pizza from the oven.
4. Turn the oven off.

Cut the pizza into eight equal pieces. Serve with baby carrots, celery sticks, and cucumber spears.
Alternatively, make the following salad:

Fast Salad for Pizza Dinner

Ingredients (for 4 persons)
1 head organic romaine lettuce
2 tomatoes, half a tomato per salad, cut into wedges
4 green onions, sliced
½ teaspoon dried basil, 1/8 teaspoon per salad
6 tablespoon olive oil, 1 ½ tablespoon per salad
1 lemon, juiced

Directions

1. Place washed greens in bowls.
2. Add wedges of tomatoes on top.
3. Sprinkle each salad with cut slices of green onion and a little dried basil on the top.
4. Just before serving - drizzle each salad with olive oil, and a squeeze of lemon juice.

For dessert serve – organic cherries, or organic strawberries, or orange slices, with a couple squares of dark chocolate.

If you are planning on eating pizza frequently - alternate with vegetarian pizza. Remember it is best to minimize the intake of animal protein in your diet – that includes, meat, cheese, eggs, and whole milk. Since this pizza recipe is high in animal protein, it would be best to drink water or kombucha with this meal rather than milk. Since the pizza dough is high in carbs, it would be best to avoid cake or cookies for dessert with this meal. Eating to live is a balancing act.

Best Fried Spicy Super Crispy Juicy Chicken Strips

Ingredients (for 4-6 persons)
4 large chicken breasts or 2 pounds chicken tenders
6 eggs

"Secret Spice Mix" – recipe below
4 cups panko crumbs
1 ½ cups organic flour
Avocado oil or olive oil

Directions

1. Mix all of the spices for the Secret Spice Recipe below.
2. Cut chicken breasts into strips, lengthwise, or use chicken tenders – rinse and pat dry with a paper towel. It is best to use strips of chicken because less oil is needed during the cooking process. This costs less. Therefore, a better quality of oil can be used.
3. Sprinkle the chicken strips with the Secret Spice.
4. Beat the eggs. Dip all of the chicken strips into the egg, and place on dinner plates or a large platter.
5. Mix the panko crumbs and flour and dip the seasoned chicken strips into the panko mixture. Ensure that the strips are thoroughly covered with the "breading."
6. Dip the chicken strips into the egg mixture again, sprinkle a little more of the spice mixture onto the chicken strips, and dip the chicken strips into the panko flour mixture again until well coated. Lay the breaded chicken strips down on clean plates in a single layer. Do not delay in frying the strips once they are coated, otherwise, the coating will begin to stick to the plates.

It is best to use avocado oil or olive oil for frying chicken strips.

7. Using a 12" frying pan, heat ½" avocado oil to a medium high temperature. Test with a little piece of chicken to see whether or not the oil will bubble around the chicken and cook it.

8. Add as many strips as will fit into the pan. Turn the chicken over when the side that is cooking is a medium golden color. When both sides are cooked, drain on a paper towel. Transfer the fried chicken from the paper towel and set these on a clean platter.
9. The strips may be kept in a low oven at 200 degrees F for about 10 minutes until all of the strips have been cooked, and you are ready to eat.
10. Decorate the platter of fried chicken with a little fresh parsley.

Serve the fried chicken with cooked collard greens and turnips, lima bean soup, and homemade corn bread. End this meal with thick juicy chunks of watermelon if you are having corn bread be-cause cornbread adds carbs to the meal. Therefore, it is best to have fruit. Watermelon also helps to balance hormones. Or serve the fried chicken with the "Seattle Salad." If you are serving salad instead of cornbread, you can serve "Amazing Cookies" for dessert (the recipe follows in the *Healthy Dessert* section).

Secret Spice Recipe for Fried Chicken
This recipe makes a large quantity - the extra spice can be stored in an airtight glass container.

Ingredients
1 tablespoon dried sage
2 tablespoons dried oregano
1 tablespoon thyme
3 tablespoons paprika
2 tablespoons salt
2 tablespoons black pepper, less if you do not like hot and spicy
4 tablespoons garlic powder
2 tablespoons onion powder
2 tablespoons cayenne pepper, less if you do not like hot and spicy but add another ½ tablespoon if you like very spicy chicken

1 tablespoon all natural powdered unsweetened lemon juice or organic dried lemon peel

Directions

1. Combine all of the ingredients until well blended.
2. Store in a glass container.
3. Stir the spices each time the mixture is used.

Easy Lima Bean Soup
Lima bean soup is delicious paired with cornbread, collard greens, turnips, and fried chicken. It is also very nice with cornbread and a salad for a light meal.

Ingredients (for 6-8 persons)
6 cups dried, large lima beans
1- 8 ounce cube salted pork
½ teaspoon salt (optional)
½ teaspoon freshly ground pepper
2 bay leaves

Direction

1. In a 30-cup pot, rinse the beans, soak them overnight in cold water, drain off the soaking water, rinse again and cook. The beans will swell considerably.
2. To cook - add to the prepared lima beans, salted pork, bay leaf, water to about 2 inches over the beans, salt, and freshly ground pepper.
3. Bring to a boil, lower heat to medium low. Cover with a tilted lid. Cook for 1 ½ to 2 hours. Stir occasionally to prevent sticking. Add a little water or broth from the cooked collard greens if the soup is too thick.

4. Remove the salted pork. Cut away the meat from the fat. Return the meat to the lima bean soup.
5. The soup will thicken overnight. It is best prepared the day before serving. When heated, add water to achieve the desired consistency.

Collard Greens and Turnips

Collard greens are so nutritious. For me, they are also comfort food, for they remind me of my mother's cooking. My mother passed away in 2002. She was a great cook. After eating collard greens, which are high in Vitamin K, eat meals that are low in Vitamin K for a couple days.

Ingredients (for 4-6 persons)
2 bunches of collard greens, washed
1/2 teaspoon garlic powder
1/2 teaspoon onion powder
1 bay leaf
2 tablespoons of white vinegar, or less
1/2 teaspoon salt
½ teaspoon freshly ground pepper
2 medium turnip cubed into medium pieces
1/4 pound cooked uncured bacon, chopped with kitchen scissors

Directions

1. In a large pot cover the greens with water.
2. Add to the pot garlic powder, onion powder, bay leaf, white vinegar, salt, pepper and stir.
3. Bring to a boil. Lower heat and simmer until very tender.
4. Add prepared turnip to the greens. Cook until the turnip is tender.
5. Add the chopped bacon to the greens.

Cornbread
Most packaged corn breads contain far too much sugar. This recipe is perfect.

Ingredients (for 4 persons)
3/4 cup organic, medium grind cornmeal
1 1/4 cup milk
1 egg
1/4 cup olive oil
1 cup organic flour
2 tablespoons honey
1 tablespoon baking powder
1/4 teaspoon salt - or - 1/2 teaspoon salt
½ cup grated sharp cheddar cheese

Directions

1. Preheat the oven to 400 degrees F. Butter a 9in x 9in cake pan or muffin tin.
2. Combine cornmeal and milk - let stand 10 minutes.
3. Add beaten egg and oil to cornmeal mixture.
4. Combine flour, sugar, baking powder, and salt - add these to the cornmeal and egg mixture. Pour batter into a buttered or oiled pan (olive oil) or muffin tin (makes 12 muffins).
5. Sprinkle the top of the cornbread with the grated cheese.
6. Bake for approximately 15 - 20 minutes. The cornbread will be ready to be removed from the oven when a toothpick or knife inserted comes out clean. It is best to leave the cornbread in the oven until it is a golden color on top.

Seattle Salad
Elaine created this recipe while we were living in the Seattle area – hence the name. It is a satisfying salad, which can be served for lunch

or for dinner. After the salad you can have "Amazing Cookies" for dessert because this meal is low in carbohydrates.

Ingredients (for 4 persons)
1 organic romaine lettuce head, torn into bite-size pieces
2 red pepper, julienned and cut into 1-inch strips
3 organic green onions, sliced
1 cup walnuts, broken into medium size pieces
1 cup Gouda cheese, chopped into bite-size pieces
1/3 cup Parmesan cheese, grated
4 small apples, cored and diced, just before serving

Dressing
1/3 cup olive oil mayonnaise
3 tablespoon plain whole yogurt
4 tablespoon olive oil
2 tablespoon white balsamic vinegar
¼ teaspoon freshly ground nutmeg
¼ teaspoon salt
¼ teaspoon freshly ground black pepper

Directions

1. Prepare the dressing: Whisk all of the salad dressing ingredients. Refrigerate the dressing if you are not going to use it immediately. **Anything containing mayonnaise should not be left out at room temperature for more than 30 minutes. I would rather be cautious.**
2. Place all of the prepared vegetables in a large bowl. Add the cheeses. When just about ready to serve, cut, core, dice and add the apples – otherwise, if you do so ahead of time the apples will turn brown and the salad will not be aesthetically pleasing.
3. Add the dressing, and toss the salad.
4. Divide the salad onto plates or large bowls and top with walnuts.

5. Sprinkle the top of the salad with extra freshly ground black pepper.

Avocado Croissant Sandwich
Avocado croissant sandwiches are nicely paired with broccoli slaw.

Ingredients (for 1 person)
1 large croissant, per person
½ a large avocado, per person
1 tablespoon olive oil mayonnaise, or to taste
Yellow onion, sliced paper thin
Salt and freshly ground black pepper
Crushed red pepper flakes - for those who like some heat

Directions

1. Slice the croissant in half lengthwise.
2. Toast the croissant halves under the oven's broiler for about 10 seconds. <u>Do not take your eyes off </u>of the croissant halves, for they burn easily. Remove the croissants from the oven and <u>turn off the broiler</u>.
3. Wash the avocado, and cut it in half all the way around the pit. Then cut each half in half all the way around the pit to form quarters. Jiggle a knife between the quarters to loosen the quarters of avocados from the pit. Peel each quarter.
4. Spread the bottom half of each croissant with mayonnaise. Then slice lengthwise ½ an avocado for each sandwich – placing each slice on the croissant half that is covered in mayonnaise. Sprinkle with thin slices of onion, and salt and pepper.
5. For a nice presentation - serve the avocado croissant with the top half of the croissant on the side, and broccoli slaw. Your family members and friends will then be able to see the beautiful color of the avocado slices, and then they can place the top half on top of the sandwich themselves.

Broccoli Slaw

Ingredients (for 4 persons)
1 bag broccoli prepared for broccoli slaw, with slivers of carrots (broccoli slaw is made with broccoli stems)
½ onion, thinly sliced and minced, to taste
1 cup dried cranberries
1/2 – 1 cup pecans, chopped

Toss the ingredients above.

Broccoli Slaw Dressing
3/4 cup olive oil
¼ - 1/3 cup white balsamic vinegar, or apple cider vinegar
Salt and freshly ground pepper

Beat all of the ingredients for the dressing with a fork. Pour over the vegetables and toss very well.
   Alternative: Thinly sliced cabbage can be substituted for the broccoli

Easy Thai Salmon Panang
Serve the Panang with organic brown rice.

Ingredients (for 4 persons)
2 pounds wild-caught salmon, skin removed, chopped into big chunks
3 – 4 red peppers, chopped into bite size pieces
2 tablespoons olive oil
3 onions, chopped
4 garlic cloves, minced
1 lemongrass stalk, thinly sliced
1/4 teaspoon cayenne pepper – to make the dish a Heat Level 2 (out of 5), if the red curry paste is not too hot
3 cans organic or all-natural coconut milk

¼ cup Thai red curry paste

1-2 inch cube of galangal, like a mild ginger, minced

3 kaffir lime leaves (optional if the curry paste contains kaffir lime leaves)

15-20 basil leaves, depending on the size of the leaves

1 tablespoon Thai fish sauce

1 tablespoon organic sugar

2 heaping tablespoons of Adam's <u>Smooth</u> 100% Natural Peanut Butter

10 green onions, sliced

2 limes cut into wedges

For fish stock:

1 onion

1 bay leaf

Skin from the salmon

Directions

1. Slice off the skin from the salmon and put the skin in a pot of water to make stock with an onion and a bay leaf. Use this stock to thin out the gravy if it gets too thick.
2. In a deep skillet or wok sauté in olive oil the onions, garlic, lemon grass and cayenne pepper for 1 minute and salt slightly.
3. Add the cream off the tops of three cans of coconut milk and red curry paste, continue to sauté for another 2 minutes.
4. Add remaining coconut milk, galangal, kaffir lime leaves, basil leaves, fish sauce, sugar, and peanut butter. Simmer on medium-low for 5 minutes. If the sauce thickens too much add some fish stock.
5. Then add: red pepper, and salmon.
6. Cook the salmon and red pepper for 6 minutes.
7. Pour into a deep serving dish and garnish with green onion.
8. Serve with lime wedges.

Bold Black Beans with Baked Potatoes for Busy Boys

This recipe is designed for very physically active young men. It is high in healthy calories as opposed to "junk food" calories. After a rough day, it is comforting to have an organic russet baked potato with organic sour cream or an organic yam with a pat of butter once in a while. Serve the black beans and vegetables in bowls, with baked potatoes and a simple oil and vinegar salad on the side. Add whole grain dinner rolls or squares of homemade cornbread to this meal, to ensure the synthesis of complete protein (remember nutrients in beans and grains combine to make complete proteins). However, black beans are high in calories and adding a potato and a dinner roll, or a yam and a square of cornbread makes this meal high in calories. Therefore, have fruit for dessert.

As we have learned, beans and grains will bind with zinc and prevent the absorption of zinc. Thus, for your manly health, you will need to eat a food containing zinc at another meal during the day, or take a supplement of zinc, which your pharmacist has approved. Because, as previously mentioned, your body does not store zinc.

Ingredients (for 3 persons)

3 large russet potatoes
8 ounces sour cream, or 3 tablespoons butter
1/2 cup chives, cut into bits with kitchen scissors
3 tablespoons olive oil
1 large onion, chopped
3 cups frozen organic corn, thawed
2 14-ounce cans organic spicy black beans
3 tomatoes, chopped
5-6 garlic cloves, minced
¼ or ½ teaspoon salt
¼ teaspoon freshly ground black pepper
4 tablespoons water

Ingredients for salad (for 3 persons)

9 large butter lettuce leaves, washed and pat-dried with paper towels
1/3 cup olive oil
3 tablespoon white balsamic vinegar
Salt and pepper to taste

Directions

Potatoes

1. Scrub the potato skins with a clean scrubber and water.
2. With a fork make three pricks on one side of each potato.
3. Place the potatoes (pricked side up) in a baking pan.
4. Bake the potatoes in the oven at 375 degrees F. for approximately 40 minutes – until a fork can easily pierce through the inside of the potato.

Black Beans

While the potatoes are baking, prepare the black beans (a cast iron skillet would be best):

1. Sauté the onion in 2 tablespoons of olive oil.
2. When the onion begins to stick to the pan add 2-tablespoon water to deglaze the pan by scraping up the bits on the bottom with a "straight tipped" wooden spoon and stir – the onion will become a caramel color.
3. Add the corn, remaining olive oil, salt and pepper. When the corn begins to stick to the bottom of the pan add a 2-tablespoon water and repeat the technique to deglaze the pan, and stir.
4. Add the spicy black beans including the sauce, heat through, and stir.
5. Add the tomatoes and garlic, and stir. Simmer with a tilted lid for about 20 minutes. While simmering, add a little water to achieve desired consistency.

Simple Salad

1. Beat the oil, vinegar, salt and pepper with a fork.
2. Arrange three leaves per plate one on top of the other.
3. Just before serving drizzle a little dressing over the top leaf.

Note: Just to give you an idea of the caloric content of the main ingredients in this meal - one cup of black beans contains 625 calories (ouch!), one medium russet potato 170 calories, and a dinner roll 80 calories. One medium yam contains 180 calories, and one 2-ounce piece of cornbread has 180 calories (Elaine's cornbread recipe may have fewer calories because of the lower sugar content.). Calorie counting is like learning to ride a bicycle or learning to drive a car: the information will eventually become second nature to you.

HEALTHY DESSERTS

Amazing Cookies

I love these cookies. They are delicious, and a lot healthier than packaged cookies that contain high fructose corn syrup, canola oil, and preservatives. Though I still need to eat them in moderation. I have two once in a while. They freeze very well when they are individually wrapped with Glad® Cling Wrap and placed in a Ziploc® bag.

Ingredients
1 cup butter
4 tablespoons agave syrup
6 tablespoons water
1/3 cup organic sugar
1 1/2 cups semi-sweet medium size chocolate chips
1/3 cup candied ginger, minced
1/2 cup nuts, walnuts, or pecans or macadamias, chopped (optional because some people are very allergic to nuts)

1 cup dried cranberries
3/4 cup sweetened coconut - if using unsweetened, increase the sugar by 3 tablespoons
1 cup oatmeal
2 teaspoons freshly grated organic lemon zest
2-1/4 cups organic flour
1 teaspoon baking powder (aluminum free)

Directions

1. Preheat the oven to 350 degrees F.
2. Line a cookie sheet with cooking parchment paper.
3. Place the butter, agave syrup, and water in a small pot and simmer on very low until the butter has melted. Cool to room temperature.
4. In a large bowl combine: sugar, chocolate chips, candied ginger, nuts, dried cranberries, coconut, oatmeal, and lemon zest.
5. Blend the flour and baking powder, and stir it into the oatmeal mixture.
6. Pour the butter, water, and agave syrup mixture over the ingredients in the bowl. Stir quickly and thoroughly. If the butter mixture is still barely warm, the chocolate chips will melt slightly but still remain mostly intact. This will give your cookies a light brown color and add chocolate flavor throughout the cookie. It is best to wait until the mixture is completely cooled.
7. Form a firm ball of dough with your hands. Place the ball of dough on the parchment paper and press down with the palm of your hand – until the cookie is about ¼ inch thick. Bring all the outer bits to fit snuggly into the cookie. To ensure that the cookies are done at the same time, make all the cookies the same size.
8. Cooking time should be about 15 minutes. The cooking time will vary with the type of cookie sheet, and the accuracy of the oven temperature. Some ovens run hotter than

the setting, or lower than the setting. Ceramic surfaces cook more quickly than stainless steel. Check the first batch frequently. The bottom of the cookies should be a medium-dark golden color. These cookies are best overcooked rather than undercooked. Cool for two minutes on the cookie sheet. Then remove to a cooling rack.

Note: Do a test with two cookies to determine how long you want to cook the cookies, because different ovens have different heating characteristics, as we have mentioned before.

Mini Fruit Crisps for Your Family

Encourage your family to help you to make these crisps because they are time-consuming but worth the effort. Once the crisps are prepared, they can be frozen before they are baked but they must be thoroughly thawed and at room temperature before baking.

Makes 9 round mini crisps with a bottom crust and top crust. Use round deep tins that are 5 ¾ inches in diameter. Alternatively, the recipe makes 8 rectangular tins 5-23/32 inches x 3-5/16 inches x 1-7/8 inches.

Crust

Ingredients

4 cups organic all-purpose flour
8 cups oatmeal
1 cup almond meal
3 tablespoons milled flaxseeds
3 ½ cups melted salted butter
4 tablespoons maple syrup
1 1/4 cups brown sugar
4 tablespoons butter, melted – for the top of the mini crisps
4 tablespoons maple syrup – for the top of the mini crisps

Directions

1. Blend the flour, oatmeal, almond meal, brown sugar and milled flaxseeds.
2. Mix the butter and maple syrup.
3. Then combine the oatmeal mixture (1 above) and the butter mixture (2 above), stirring rapidly, until the ingredients are blended.
4. Grease with butter all the baking tins

Fruit Filling

13 ½ cups of fruit
¾ cup organic sugar
1/3 cup organic flour

Directions

Combine 4 teaspoons organic sugar and 2 teaspoons organic flour, and pour this mixture over 1 ½ cups of fruit a little at a time and toss before filling each mini pie. Use berries, or peeled and sliced apples, or blanched, peeled and sliced peaches. Cube peaches after blanching, for a better consistency. Various fruits can be combined, such as, peaches and blueberries, or strawberries and rhubarb. Add ¼ teaspoon to ½ teaspoon of cinnamon, and add 1/8 teaspoon nutmeg to the sugar and flour mixture mentioned above to toss with apples for apple crisp.

Instructions for constructing the bottom crusts and top crusts for the crisps, and for baking the crisps:

1. Bottom crust: It is best to pat the bottom crust down with clean fingers – heat from fingers helps to keep the dough supple. Pat a <u>thin</u> layer of dough for the bottom crust all the way up the sides to the top of the pie plate. Fill the bottom crust with prepared fruit, in a slightly domed shape.
2. Top crust: Pat the dough for the top crust in a circle, 6 ¼" in diameter on a regular plate with a fork or with fingers. It should

be about 1/8 inch thick. Transfer it to the top of the fruit with an egg flipper. Mold the top crust with fingers to form a crust that does not have any holes and is sealed to the top rim of the bottom crust and sealed to the rim of the pie plate. Extra small bits of pressed dough may be needed to fill in any holes – smooth these out with your fingers.

3.   Preheat oven to 375 degrees F. about 15 minutes before placing the crisps in the oven.

4.   Before baking the crisps, brush melted butter on the top crusts. To bake, place the crisps on the middle rack. Place a cookie sheet on the bottom rack to catch any dripping; otherwise there will be a mess at the bottom of your oven.

5.   When the crisps have baked for 40 minutes – with a heat resistant silicone pastry brush, pat the top of the crusts with a coating of maple syrup and continue to bake for another 10 minutes. Bake for a total of 50 minutes, or until a medium-dark golden brown. Check periodically to avoid burning.

HEALTHY SNACKS

Spicy Guacamole

Ingredients (for 4 persons)
4 large avocados, mashed
¾ small onion, minced
1 medium tomato, chopped
1 jalapeno, seeded, minced (optional) – warning - after chopping do not touch your eyes, until your hands have been washed several times
2 handfuls cilantro/coriander, chopped
1/2 teaspoon organic lemon zest
1 small lemon, juiced
2 key lime, juiced
½ teaspoon powdered garlic

½ teaspoon paprika
½ teaspoon chili powder
1/8 teaspoon cayenne pepper
1/8 teaspoon freshly ground black pepper
1/8 teaspoon onion powder
1/8 teaspoon cumin powder
¼ teaspoon salt, or to taste
1 bag of Mexican shredded cheese

Directions

1. Chop all the vegetables except for the avocados.
2. Measure all of the spices into a small dish or glass and mix.
3. Zest the lemon.
4. Peel and mash the avocados.
5. Pour lemon and lime juice over the avocados and stir to prevent discoloration.
6. Add the chopped vegetables, lemon zest, and spices. Stir. Place the guacamole in individual serving dishes. Top with grated cheese. Serve with organic tortilla chips.

French Canadian Poutine

Many young men in Canada like to go out for poutine after playing a sport. A Montreal hockey player I know ordered poutine for his wedding guests as a late-night snack.

Thanksgiving turkey gravy is the best gravy for poutine but quick turkey gravy can be prepared at any time. Oven fried potatoes make this recipe more nutritious than poutine produced in some fast food restaurants.

Ingredients (for 4 persons)

10 - 12 large russet potatoes, peeled and sliced into thick lengths
1/3 cup olive oil
1 box organic turkey bone broth
1 pkg. organic turkey or organic chicken gravy mix

3 tablespoons cornstarch

Pinch of dried thyme or 12 tiny fresh thyme leaves

Pinch of dried sage

Pinch of summer savory

¼ teaspoon dried parsley or 1 teaspoon fresh parsley, chopped very fine

¼ teaspoon dried rosemary

½ teaspoon garlic powder

1/4 teaspoon salt

¼ teaspoon freshly ground black pepper

¼ teaspoon cayenne pepper

16 oz. cheese curds

1 bunch of green onions, chopped

Directions

1. Set oven to 400 degrees F.
2. Boil the turkey broth until it has been reduced by ¼ in a thick bottomed, medium pot. Then let it cool to room temperature.
3. Peel and cut the potatoes.
4. With your freshly washed hands grease each potato length with olive oil. Salt and pepper the potatoes. Use a very light dusting of cayenne pepper because it adds a lot of heat.
5. Bake the potatoes in the oven for approximately 45-55 minutes. Check the potatoes after about 30 minutes, and then every five minutes or so.
6. In the meantime, prepare the gravy by thickening and seasoning the broth. Whisk into the cooled broth: the gravy mix, cornstarch, parsley, sage, rosemary, thyme, garlic powder, salt and pepper. Stir constantly as the gravy is brought to a rolling boil. Then lower the heat slightly. Continue to stir the gravy with the whisk and alternately with a flat-edged wooden spoon to ensure that the gravy does not stick to the bottom of the pot. Continue to cook until the gravy has thickened - about 5 minutes. The gravy should not be too thin for it will not coat the fries, nor should it be as thick as pudding

because it will become more congealed as it cools once it is on the fries and on the plate. Taste the gravy and adjust the seasoning to your taste.

7. When the fries are crisp, place them on warmed plates. Pour some gravy over the fries, top with cheese curds, and sprinkle with green onions. Serve immediately.

Easy Homemade Root Beer

The recipe for root beer below was given to us courtesy of Bishop Eric Jacobsen who made delicious root beer for our church's BBQ. The bishop says, "The recipe for root beer is pretty easy . . ."

Mix these ingredients in a five-gallon food-grade container:

4 gallon cold, non-chlorinated water
4 pounds organic sugar – (8 cups sugar)
4 ounces root beer extract – (1/2 cup) (Cook's Root Beer Extract)
5 pounds crushed, food-grade dry ice (used for carbonation)

** Warning - Parental Supervision Necessary **

Handle dry ice with caution. Use oven mitts to handle the bag of dry ice. Use food-grade dry ice. It is available in most grocery stores, and if you ask, they may crush the dry ice for you. Do not use dry ice in individual drinks. Do not place dry ice in your mouth.

Use a food grade container. Pour water into the container, add the sugar and stir until the sugar is dissolved. Pour into the sweetened water the root beer extract and stir. Stir the dry ice into the water mixture. Keep stirring periodically, otherwise it will clump at the bottom. The dry ice will create a magical mist, which will be fun for your family and friends to watch. Let the root beer mixture bubble for an hour. Pour the root beer into glasses chilled in a freezer.

* We like Cook's Root Beer Extract. It contains natural root beer extractives. It is kosher, gluten-free, allergen-free, and non-GMO. We ordered it on-line.

** Warning ** - Do not cover the root beer as you are preparing it because the pressure created could cause an explosion.

Fermented recipes for root beer do exist in which probiotics naturally carbonate the root beer, however, these recipes require many ingredients and, if the root beer is left in bottles at room temperature for too long, the bottles will explode.

It is best to prepare root beer only a couple times a year, because as we have stated, too much sugar is not good for you. It is fun to make this root beer recipe and to share it at family reunions, or with friends at social gatherings.

POTLUCK PICNICS ARE RELAXING FOR DOUBLE DATES

Ideas for a Picnic Lunch

Picnics are a perfect outing for double dates because being in nature is both visually interesting, rejuvenating, and peaceful. Picnicking gets you away from the fast pace of life. There is time to share good food, to talk and share ideas, and to play. The cost of a potluck picnic date can be shared, to keep the cost down for each person. Another plus about having a party in the outdoors as opposed to having a party at your house is that the crumbs are left outdoors, which really cuts down on the cleanup time. Pick a fairly private spot on a public beach or at a park to have a picnic.

One person can prepare a salad. Another person can prepare sandwiches. The busiest person can bring water in glass bottles, pickles or olives, and organic strawberries. The fourth person can prepare healthful "Amazing Cookies."

Asian Jicama Orange Cranberry Salad

This salad is both refreshing and visually appealing.

Ingredients (for 4 persons)

1 large jicama (about the size of a large grapefruit), peeled, sliced and julienned

3 oranges, peeled, cut each section into three pieces

1 bunch of organic pre-washed greens

3/4 cup dried cranberries or more

1 cup walnuts, of more

1 bunch of green onions, chopped

2 red pepper, slivered

1 tablespoon black sesame seeds, dry toasted in a pan for a few minutes

Dressing

1/2 cup olive oil

1/4 cup rice vinegar

1 1/2 tsp. sesame oil - really makes a big difference

1 tbsp. agave syrup

Salt and pepper to taste

Directions

1. The morning of the picnic: In a large container, with a secure lid, assigned for the salad, mix the jicama, oranges, cranberries, walnuts, green onions, red pepper, and black sesame seeds.
2. Store the greens in a clean food safe plastic bag, and place it in the container with the other ingredients. Then the greens will not wilt.
3. Place the dressing in a clean small jar with a lid.
4. Place the container and jar in an insulated picnic tote, with a frozen packet. At the picnic, add the greens, and dressing to the other ingredients in the container just before tossing the salad.

Roast Turkey Sandwiches with Cream Cheese Lingonberry or Dijon Mustard

Give people a choice - a turkey sandwich with lingonberry jam, or with Dijon mustard, or a half of each.

Ingredients
1 turkey roll
Fresh organic sourdough bread or fresh organic whole wheat bread
1 – 8 ounce package cream cheese
Lingonberry preserves
Dijon mustard

Directions

1. Roast a turkey roll the day before. With an electric knife slice the turkey roll in very thin slices.
2. Spread a thin layer of cream cheese on each slice of bread.
3. Spread a thin layer of jam on one slice of bread for half the sandwiches. Add two turkey slices. Top with a slice of bread.
4. Spread Dijon mustard on one slice of bread for the other half of the sandwiches. Add two turkey slices. Sprinkle the turkey with salt and pepper. Top with a slice of bread.
5. Cut the sandwiches on the diagonal.
6. Wrap each sandwich individually. Bring 1 - 2 sandwiches per person depending on their appetite.
7. Place the sandwiches in an insulated picnic tote, with a frozen packet.

Water, Olives or Pickles, and Organic Strawberries

1. Bring at least 16 ounces of water for each person.
2. Bring 3-5 organic strawberries per person depending on their size.

3. Carry the chilled water, pickles or olives and strawberries in an insulated container with a frozen packet. The strawberries ought to be washed and stored in a plastic container. Serve the strawberries with the cookies.

Amazing Cookies

1. Bring 2-3 cookies (2 inches in diameter) per person.
2. Wrap the cookies individually and store them in a plastic container, in an insulated bag with a frozen packet.

Notes: When having a picnic near water always be mindful when people are in the water, especially if young children are among your party. Watch children constantly by taking shifts. Make certain that the waters are safe for wading or swimming. Remember to wear comfortable shoes, and bring a Frisbee, volley equipment; badminton equipment; or a compass if you are planning to go on a hike. In any case, the fresh air, nutritious food, and exercise in nature will be a welcomed change to your daily routines.

Bon Appétit!

EXERCISE AND FITNESS

For a healthy body, a proper diet and sufficient exercise go hand-in-hand. You have now learned some good information about managing your diet, so let's tackle exercise.

Here are some eye-popping facts about the human body:

Were you aware that by the time you reach 70 years of age, your heart will have pumped over 48 million gallons of blood through your arteries? An average heart pumps 2.4 ounces or 70 milliliters per heartbeat. An average pulse in an adult is 72 beats per minute. Therefore, an average heart pumps 1.3 gallons or 5 liters per minute. In other words, it pumps 1,900 gallons or 7,200 liters per day, almost 700,000 gallons or 2,628,000 liters per year, or 48 million gallons or 184,086,000 liters by the time someone is 70 years old.

That's not bad for a pump that weighs less than a pound!

The average adult breathes (inhales and exhales) about 7-8 liters (about one-fourth of a cubic foot) of air per minute while they are at rest. That equals to about 11,000 liters of air (388 cubic feet) each day. The air that is inhaled is about 20-percent oxygen, and the air that is exhaled is about 15-percent oxygen, so about 5-percent of the volume of air is consumed in each breath and converted to carbon dioxide. Therefore, a human being uses about 550 liters of pure oxygen (19 cubic feet) per day. That's 6,935 cubic feet per year. By the time you're 70, you will have breathed about 485,000 cubic feet of pure oxygen – that is, if your lungs remain healthy.

So if you want to be healthy when you become 70, you will need to know how to keep in shape. Let's look at some key ideas.

SCIENTIFIC 7-MINUTE WORKOUT

Recent science has shown us that we no longer need to spend hours upon hours working up a sweat to get in shape. We can do so quite a bit more efficiently and effectively using the *Scientific 7-Minute Workout*, which was developed by Brett Klika, a performance coach, and Chris Jordan, an exercise physiologist. Their work, *High-Intensity Circuit Training Using Body Weight: Maximum Results with Minimal Investment*, shows how you can get in excellent physical shape through regular aerobic and resistance training.

The steps of this very simple training regimen are:

1. Jumping Jacks Total Body
2. Wall Sit Lower Body
3. Push-up Upper Body
4. Abdominal Crunch Core
5. Step-up onto Chair Total Body
6. Squat Lower Body
7. Triceps Dip on Chair Upper Body

8. Plank Core
9. High Knees/Running in Place Total Body
10. Lunge Lower Body
11. Push-up and Rotation Upper Body
12. Side Plank Core[299]

Scientific *7-Minute Workout Drill*

Each exercise is performed for 30 seconds, with 10 seconds rest in between bouts. Total time for the entire circuit workout is approximately 7 minutes. The course can be repeated 2 to 3 times. You only need a chair, a floor, a wall, and your own body weight in order to complete the 7-minute workout, which employs both aerobic and weight training exercises. Doing this exercise routine for the first time may be challenging due to the intensity of the exercises, but as your body strengthens, the routine will become progressively easier. **If you feel discomfort while doing these exercises, reduce intensity, modify the exercise to**

alleviate the discomfort, or consult a personal trainer. Do not injure yourself.

According to Gretchen Reynolds, a reporter for the New York Times, in her article *The Scientific 7-Minute Workout*, ". . . work by scientists at McMaster University in Hamilton, Ontario, and other institutions shows, for instance, that even a few minutes of training at an intensity approaching your maximum capacity produces molecular changes within muscles comparable to those of several hours of running or bike riding."[300]

The workout is intense, yes, but just keep reminding yourself that it's only seven minutes, you're done. You'll be happy with the results in regards to your body's condition.

Check the *Elevate Yourself to Manhood* website at http:// www.elevateyourselftomanhood.com/videos for the availability of the 7-Minute Workout video.

Note: Keep in mind that your body adapts to routine. The effectiveness of any repeated exercise routine lessens over time. So, be creative. Add new exercises to your routine from time to time to challenge your body and to exercise different muscles. Also, take some time for quick-walking or running, which are important for developing cardiovascular aerobic health. Interestingly, rowing machines exercise most of the body's muscle groups, and also cardiovascular health. Strength training with weights is also important. We heartily recommend using rowing machines and weight-lifting as part of your workout regimen as well. The *Scientific 7-Minute Workout* is just a baseline.

GETTING SUFFICIENT SLEEP

The National Sleep Foundation (NSF) calls sleep "food for the brain."[301]

After all that exercise, you should be ready for a good night's sleep when bedtime comes. Getting sufficient sleep is critical for your health, and it is common knowledge these days that kids are not getting enough sleep for various reasons – environmental, stress, too much screen time, or other causes.

We now know that sleep is vital to a person's well-being.

According to the National Sleep Foundation, teens need about 9-1/4 hours sleep each night (8-1/2 is enough for some). However, a NSF study showed that on average adolescents get about 7-1/2 hours sleep on school nights - 45% of them get insufficient sleep, 31% get the borderline amount of sleep, and only about 20% actually get the optimal amount of sleep – 9 or more hours.[302]

Not getting sufficient sleep is dangerous to your health and well-being. It can even kill you.

According to Dr. Judith A. Owens, a pediatric sleep specialist at Children's National Health System in Washington, sleeplessness can increase the risk of high blood pressure, heart disease, and obesity in adolescents. She pointed out also that the lack of sleep can be fatal because it can lead to risk-taking behavior, along with depression, suicide contemplation, and car accidents.[303]

If sleep is "food for the brain," then nine hours of sleep per night ought to enable you to improve your grades in school. It is also best to do homework immediately after school whenever possible rather than late at night when you are tired.   Take the time to unwind 30 minutes before going to bed.

1. Have a glass of milk, or unsweetened soy milk, with a couple whole grain crackers and a bit of honey, or a couple whole grain crackers with a bit of peanut butter and honey.   According to Dr. Ben Kim's article *Healthy Foods that Promote Deep Sleep*, the milk, soy milk and peanut butter contain tryptophan, which will help you to sleep. The crackers contain carbohydrates that the body converts to insulin "which diverts many of your other amino acids away from your brain, leaving tryptophan with little competition to cross your blood-brain barrier to gain access to your brain," which will help you to sleep well.[304]
2. Clean your teeth. Shower.
3. Get your clothes ready for the next day.
4. Read a few pages of a good book, such as *War and Peace*.
5. Listening to calming music (not Jimi Hendricks).

Optimizing Your Sleep with Technology

Using wearable computer technology like a Fitbit can help you optimize your sleep so you can feel better and have more energy and productivity during the day. In the article, *Fitbit Says You're Using Your Alarm Clock All Wrong*, Sarah DiGiulio, a sleep reporter for *The Huffington Post*, reports that Fitbit has an app that will remind you when to sleep and vibrate to rouse you out of bed without waking up your entire household. The device can also help you get a more consistent pattern of sleep. She writes, "The new tools make personalized sleep recommendations. The app uses your previous sleep history to set optimal bedtimes and wake-up times. Users can get bedtime push notification reminders on their smartphones, and set silent alarms on their Fitbit devices based on personalized recommendations." You can track your sleep progress by accessing your personal sleep history charts. She also says that, "Science agrees that going to bed and waking up at the same time every day is one of the best things you can do for your sleep. The consistency helps set your body's internal clock, so you expect to sleep at the same time every night and you actually sleep better because your body is ready for that sleep."[305] So, take advantage of this new technological development and others as they become available to optimize your sleep. As sleep expert and adviser Els van der Helm told the *Huffington Post*, you should actually get all the sleep you need to get the benefits, but rely on your own best judgment to gauge both the quantity and quality of your sleep based on how you feel during the day.[306]

General Health Checkups

Do not forget to have regular health check-ups with your family doctor at least once a year. Using mindfulness, listen to your body. Be open and honest about what you feel or how you feel. Do not self-diagnose – that is, do not try to figure out problems alone. Share information with you parents and health professionals.

Dental Health

The same goes for dental care. Did you know that the health of your mouth, teeth and gums affects your overall health?

There are loads of bacteria in your mouth. Most of them are harmless and can be controlled by daily brushing and flossing. However, if you are not diligent in brushing and flossing, these bacteria can reach levels, which cause gum disease and tooth decay, or even periodontitis, according to the Mayo Clinic. [307]

The Mayo Clinic reports that "oral bacteria and the inflammation associated with periodontitis, a severe form of gum disease, can play a role in some disease" including endocarditis (infection of the inner lining of your heart), cardiovascular disease, diabetes, osteoporosis, Alzheimer's, and others.

Dr. Harold Katz of The California Breath Clinics confirms that bad oral hygiene is a threat to the heart and adds that it is also a threat to the brain. Referencing a study by researchers at the University of Bristol, he says, "The study showed that streptococcus, the bacteria that is responsible for gum disease and gingivitis, can open up sores in the mouth. This provides it with access to the blood, where it releases a protein that causes blood cells to clump together. These can cause dangerous blockages of blood flow to the heart and brain."[308]

To protect your oral health, you will need to do the following:

* Brush your teeth at least twice a day – preferably within 30 minutes after eating. WebMD says, "Place the toothbrush at a 45-degree angle where the teeth meet the gums. Press firmly, and gently rock the brush back and forth using small circular movements. Do not scrub."[309]
* Brush behind your teeth.
* Brush your tongue gently with a toothbrush or tongue brush (available at some drug stores).
* Floss daily, forming a "C" with the dental floss on each side of each tooth.

- Swish about 3 teaspoons of mouthwash in your mouth and hold it for 30 seconds or longer each time you brush, depending on manufacturer instructions. Tilt your head backward, gargle, and hold for 20 seconds.
- Replace your toothbrush every three to four months or sooner if bristles are frayed.
- For best results, learn to use a sulca brush daily. A sulca brush is a very small toothbrush that can fit between the gum and teeth to get rid of hidden bacteria. Trace your gum line with the brush without using toothpaste. Take 3-4 minutes for this routine in addition to brushing. Rinse with mouthwash afterward.
- If you have any minor mouth irritations, gargling with salt water and holding for 5 minutes will help.
- Schedule regular dental checkups.
- Eat a healthy diet and limit in-between-meal snacks
- Contact your dentist immediately if an oral health problem arises.

   I hope you will keep your "pearly whites" for 100 years or more.

How to Build Strong Teeth and Healthy Gums Through Your Diet

What you eat affects your teeth and gums. Dr. Don Koontz, DDS of North Creek Dental Care, wrote on his blog that there are several ways to build healthy teeth and gums via your diet:

- **Calcium** – If you are low on calcium, then your body will leach the mineral from your teeth and bones leaving you more likely to have gum disease (periodontitis)
- **Vitamin C** – Eating citrus fruits such as oranges, grapefruits, and tangerines will help repair connective tissue and help the body fight off infection

- **Fruits and Vegetables** – Crunchy fruits and vegetables such as apples, pears, celery and carrots contribute to increasing the production of bacteria-neutralizing saliva and wipe away bacteria that can cause plaque
- **Water** – Drink artesian water if it is available. Or drink water that is filtered or ionized. Preferably drink water that is slightly alkaline. Many bottled waters are acidic. Consult your dentist for more information.
- **What to Avoid** – The combination of sugar and acid (such as in sodas) come in as number one on every dentist's list of foods to avoid. This also includes gummy candies and hard candies, which can stick to your teeth.[310]

Male Sexual Health

Every man wants to have excellent sexual health, but they may not be aware of all the factors to do so. If you start taking care of your sexual health now, you will thank yourself when you are older. READ THE COMPLETE LIST BELOW:

- Learn to do **KEGEL** exercises. Kegel muscles are the same muscles you use to stop your urine flow. Squeeze the muscles, hold for a few seconds, and relax. Repeat 10 times daily.
- Eat a healthy diet.
- Exercise on a regular basis.
- Stop smoking.
- Manage stress.
- Visit your doctor every year or when you feel something is wrong.
- Do not drink alcohol.
- Do not take illegal drugs (including marijuana which may be legal in your state).
- Maintain a positive attitude.[311]

After You Have Cared for Your Body for a Lifetime, What Happens When You Die? (Food for Thought)

One day in the far-off future, after you have lived a good, long, healthy life, you will die – hopefully not before you are at least 100 years old. This is called "physical death." Everybody dies. Even though you experience physical death, the "man inside" – your spirit - will live on. Your spirit will transition to Paradise if you have been a righteous person. When Jesus returns to reign on the earth, everyone who has obeyed God's laws and has been baptized in Jesus' name will be raised from the dead or "resurrected" with a new and perfect body, and will live with Jesus.

In the next chapter, Facet 4: *Elevate Your Spirit*, you will learn more about your spirit and its very own journey. You will learn more about how awesome you truly are and what you are expected to become on this earth and beyond. This wonderful story will blow you away! Stay tuned.

What Will You Do to Elevate Yourself Today?

* Drink sufficient water for your body size, activity level and weather conditions.
* Drink artesian water, if possible.
* Avoid drinking from plastic bottles. Drink water, preferably, from glass containers. Stainless steel is an alternative.
* Avoid all of the Brain Dangers; they are harmful to your brain and your entire body.
* Eat a well-balanced diet of all the right foods specific for your body.
* Maintain a diet with a relatively low intake of animal protein.
* Learn to read food labels.
* Avoid processed foods.
* Avoid "fast foods."
* Avoid sodas.
* Avoid artificial sweeteners like those in diet sodas.

- Avoid energy drinks.
- Avoid smoking.
- Avoid alcohol.
- Avoid caffeine.
- Say "No to Drugs."
- Get plenty of exercise.
- Get 9+ hours of sleep per night.
- Get plenty of fresh air.
- Get regular health checkups.
- Get regular dental checkups.
- Eat mostly an alkaline diet - vegetables and fruits.
- Avoid beverages and foods stored in plastic containers which may contain BPA or BPS.
- Avoid canned goods lined with BPA or BPS. Look for "BPA-FREE" on the can's label.
- Drink organic kombucha. It is alkaline-forming, and it is a heavy metal detox.
- Avoid High Fructose Corn Syrup (HFCS) and refined sugar.
- Avoid GMO wheat products, and GMO corn products.
- Avoid other genetically modified foods.
- Avoid meats containing antibiotics, and hormones.
- Wash produce prior to eating to avoid ingesting pesticide residue – use a reputable fruit and veggie wash to remove wax from apples.
- Avoid hydrogenated oils, trans fats, and canola oil.
- Cook with avocado oil, olive oil and coconut oil.
- Avoid farmed salmon and other farmed fish.
- Eat wild caught fish.
- Incorporate high-intensity interval training (HIIT).
- Listen to your body.
- Grate frozen organic lemon and add it to water, on salads, on pasta, and on fish – this will also help to prevent cancer.
- Drinking organic soy milk supports prostate health.

- Eating organic vegetables and fruits supports your whole body including prostate health.
- If you use sea salt that does not contain iodine, take an organic liquid kelp supplement (edible iodine) each day to help support your general health and the health of your prostate in particular.
- Eat foods that include organic processed tomato sauce and tomato paste; the lycopene in tomato sauce supports prostate health. After the age of 40, ask your doctor to test your Prostate-Specific Antigen (PSA).
- Sometime after you reach the age of 40, speak to a naturopath about natural remedies that support prostate health, such as Saw Palmetto, African Pygeum, and Frankincense Oil.

Well, we have taken the best of what we know right now from latest scientific research and shared the knowledge with you. As the saying goes, "Knowledge is power." However, it's going to be up to you to pay attention, internalize it, and take action!

If you are a younger man, you can discuss this knowledge about nutrition with your parents. Hopefully, they will be pleased that you are interested in protecting and strengthening your body, and together you can decide on food choices for you and your family.

Quest Checkpoint: Your Body

Congratulations for reaching this checkpoint on your quest. In order to satisfy the requirements for the Body Certificate, you will need to demonstrate proficiency in the subject areas covered within this chapter by reading and completing the requirements below. After you have completed all the certificate requirements below - using the honor system – fill in the certificate with your name. **You can also download a printed copy from the *Elevate Yourself to Manhood* website at http://www.elevateyourselftomanhood. com/certificates.**

CERTIFICATE REQUIREMENTS

☐ **Mindfulness of Body** - Perform the Raisin Mindfulness exercise once per week to help ground yourself. Try this mindfulness exercise using other foods such as an apple, an orange, or a nut.

☐ **Water** - Avoid dehydration by drinking approximately eight 8-ounce glasses of water every day. You may need more as your activity level increases especially when the weather is hot, but be mindful of not drinking too much when you are very active such as playing sports – it is then best to drink only when you are thirsty.

☐ **Heed Nutritional Health Tips** - Read and study the twenty-five health tips plus the nutritional guidelines given for the particular health concerns for men. Live this healthy lifestyle. An excellent way of complying with this requirement is to start bringing into your diet each day more and more healthy foods. The right foods and water will naturally begin to crowd out the bad stuff. Keep a Food Diary of what you eat. Review this list with your parents and health advisors regularly.

☐ **Exercise and Fitness** - Be physically active each day, play team sports, swim, play golf, tennis, ping pong, badminton, go hiking, and go for walks. Do the *Scientific 7-Minute Workout* daily. Avoid playing video games for more than one hour per day, as it leads to addiction and a sedentary lifestyle.

☐ **Sleep** - Attempt to get 9 hours sleep each night. This is mandatory for your body to repair itself and prepare for the next day. Just prior to going to bed, try to do something relaxing so that your body will be ready for sleep.

☐ **Health Checkups** - Make sure to get annual health and dental checkups. In the meantime, report anything physically wrong with your body to your parents or to a health professional. Be wise by having the courage to speak up if you feel something is wrong.

ELEVATE YOURSELF TO MANHOOD

QUEST CERTIFICATE – THE BODY

THIS CERTIFICATE IS AWARDED TO:

_____

FOR DILIGENCE IN FULFILLING THE *ELEVATE YOURSELF TO MANHOOD*
REQUIREMENTS FOR THE "BODY" ON HIS QUEST

Elevate Your Spirit (The Dove Represents The Holy Spirit)

ELEVATE YOUR SPIRIT

*We claim the privilege of worshiping Almighty God
according to the dictates of our own conscience,
and allow all men the same privilege, let them
worship how, where, or what they may.*

The 11ᵗʰ LDS Article of Faith

PUT ON THE FULL ARMOR OF GOD

YOUNG MAN, BELIEVE ME, EVIL exists in this world. You see it or hear about it all the time. Each of us can be affected by evil. We must be on our guard to defend ourselves from the effects of evil and to protect our families from it at all times. This is a skill that can be learned with a bit of an effort. Do not worry; this is not a battle you have to fight on your own. You will have valiant assistance from an Almighty Source.

The battle between good and evil started even before the world was created. Satan, once an angel of God wanted to come to Earth to take away man's free will and force them to obey God. He wanted to do this to obtain all the glory for himself. Jesus had a better idea. Jesus wanted man to use his own agency to choose to do right, instead of choosing to sin (do wrong). However, there would need to be a way to erase the sin and restore man's good status with God. A way for man to repent and to be forgiven was needed.

Whenever evil is committed, the Law of Justice is invoked against the perpetrator. If left to its own devices, Justice would demand a man to pay for his sins. This punishment would be exceedingly dire - physically impossible for a man to endure. Jesus wanted a way for man to be forgiven of his sins so as not to suffer so greatly. In order to do this, Jesus would need to come to Earth to offer himself as a perfect sacrifice to satisfy the will of Justice. God accepted Jesus' proposal and Satan was angered. Satan rebelled against God and was cast out from Heaven, along with hosts of other spirits who wanted to follow him.

Satan and his followers were not allowed to have a body on earth, so they exist only as evil spirits. Their sole purpose is to cause man to sin and be miserable like them. They are miserable because they do not have a body and cannot partake of the wonders of this beautiful earth. Nor can they have the comfort of the Holy Spirit as righteous men have.

Evil is very powerful and can attack you in many blatant and subtle ways:

* Media (television, movies, Internet, video games, pornography)
* The craftiness of man (atheists, people who would deceive you and manipulate you.)
* Through laziness and apathy - "An idle mind is the devil's workshop."
* Temptation – such as sexual attraction that leads to lusting; angry feelings that lead to feelings of hatred
* Lack of morals of men and women - sexual misconduct of leaders - teachers, priests, and coaches
* Lack of knowledge - blindness to the truth
* Denial of the truth of the gospel of Jesus Christ
* Confusion about the truth

For this phase of your journey, we hearken you back to something we told you in the Awakening. There is a battle for your soul at this very moment – a battle of Good and Evil. Each day you are bombarded with images and messages from the world. For your spiritual protection, you must wear armor to save yourself from the fiery darts of the evil one (Satan).

Put on the whole armor of God that ye may be
able to stand against the wiles of the devil.

For we wrestle not against flesh and blood, but
against principalities, against powers, against
the rulers of the darkness of this world, against
spiritual wickedness in high places.
Wherefore take unto you the whole armor of
God that ye may be able to withstand in the
evil day, and having done all, to stand.
Stand therefore, having your loins girt about with truth,
and having on the breastplate of righteousness;
And your feet shod with the preparation
of the gospel of peace;
Above all, taking the shield of faith, wherewith ye shall
be able to quench all the fiery darts of the wicked.
And take the helmet of salvation, and the sword
of the Spirit, which is the word of God,
Praying always with all prayer and supplication
in the Spirit, and watching thereunto with all
perseverance and supplication for all saints."

- EPHESIANS 6:11-18 KJV

Manly men live to the glory of God.

- STEPHEN MANSFIELD, AUTHOR, MANSFIELD'S BOOK OF MANLY MEN

On your way to becoming a man, do not overlook this important maxim - that manly men live to the glory of God. You should not be afraid or ashamed to stand up and be counted as a man of God – the Creator of all things.

As we mentioned back in the Awakening, your physical body belongs to the physical plane (Earth) and your body receives life through your individual spirit.

Your spirit belongs to the spiritual world. That's the world from which it came and the place unto where it will return when you die. Although your spirit belongs to the spiritual world, it inhabits your physical body to give you life.

James Cox, in his book, *Becoming Spiritually Centered*, gives us a way to think about ourselves as having both a body and a spirit. He tells us that our being exists in three worlds: the temporal world (the Earth on which you physically live), the inner world (inside your body) and the spirit world (from hence our spirit came and will go when we die):[312]

YOUR THREE WORLDS			
The Temporal World	**YOUR (inner) World**		**The Spiritual World**
	Physical Body	**Spiritual Body**	
Your physical body lives here. This is where you: • Eat • Work • Exercise • Watch TV • Go to School • Go to Church, etc. It takes very little effort to become centered in the temporal world. All life problems are found in the temporal world.	• This combined world is your personal world – your temple. • The physical body is part of the temporal world and your inner world. • Your spirit is part of the spiritual world and gives life to your body. • Elements of these two worlds come together to form your inner world. • Your mind and your spirit control your inner world. • Using your agency, you can focus your thoughts and feelings so as to become spiritually or temporally centered.		1. Your spirit belongs to the spiritual world. 2. This is where your best friends are: • Heavenly Father • Heavenly Mother • Jesus Christ, the Savior • The Holy Spirit 3. In this world you find: • High feelings of self-worth • Peace and joy • Forgiveness of sins • Solutions to all problems • Salvation if you are righteous

Your journey on Earth is like participating in a football game or like a game of chess – a game in which you are being graded according to your performance on the field of play.

Earth is a testing ground for God's children, and the "score" depends on how well you do on your "tests." So, you see, you can never escape school! There is always more to learn. You cannot afford be lazy in these efforts. You have to "look alive" and do well because your spiritual life depends on it.

When the game of life is over (on Earth), there will be several categories of people and achievements:

Category #1: Those who recognized the game (or were taught about it), embraced it, and endured it well

Category #2: Those who died without ever recognizing there was even a game in progress (you are lucky that you are reading this, so at least you know about it)

Category #3: Those who recognized the game (or were taught about it), embraced it, however, failed to do well

Category #4: Those who knew the game (or were taught about it) and refused to abide by the rules – rejected the game and thereby became evil.

Which category would you prefer? Will your opinion change after reading this chapter – I wonder? Just keep an open mind. You have nothing to lose. This is a safe place to be. This book has been written with much love for you.

In this chapter, we will cover some of the most important topics related to boosting your spiritual nature, and your spiritual success.

ELEVATE YOUR SPIRITUAL NATURE THROUGH THE POWER OF PRAYER

One of the strongest powers on Earth is prayer. It is in prayer that we speak openly to our Father in Heaven. Prayer is a great habit to establish for yourself and your family. My wife and I have witnessed the power of prayer in our lives and in the lives of our friends and family. We confidently testify of the power of these prayers.

Prayer is more than words you speak to God. It is a dialogue, a two-way communication, between God and you. It is a time when you can humbly express your feelings to the Almighty and a time when you can be comforted, have your fears allayed, ask for strength to endure, ask for strength to conquer, ask for strength to overcome temptation, or to ask for simple blessings. You should remember that Heavenly Father loves you very much and wants nothing more than to bless you and to see you happy. Anyone can come to Heavenly Father at any time in prayer. He always has time for you. Remember to listen for His answer to your prayer. Sometimes He answers immediately. At other times, He answers through other people – someone you may know or a complete stranger.

Do not underestimate His power to know you individually despite having billions of children in this world to watch over. You are infinitely valuable to Him and He will hear prayers made to Him if you have a sincere heart and have real intent to do His Will.

Scientific Proof that the Power of Prayer Is Real

Dr. Masaru Emoto discovered a way to demonstrate, physically, the power of prayer. It is amazing to see the power of prayer revealed scientifically through water crystals in his book, *The Secret Life of Water*.

Emoto[313] has lectured around the world, and his books have become best sellers. He graduated from the Yokohama Municipal University's Department of Humanities and Sciences. Dr. Emoto discovered that when water is frozen, then allowed to defrost slightly at five degrees below zero, water crystals form and they are visible at a magnification of 200 times. The crystals appear for only two minutes under the microscope, during which time the crystals can be photographed. While working with these crystals Dr. Emoto discovered that when prayer and kind words were directed to water, the crystals that formed had beautiful symmetrical patterns. Conversely, when negative language was used towards the water, the crystals were disjointed, foggy, and even grotesque. Typically tap water did not produce crystals due to the chlorine content, but when 500 people throughout Japan prayed at the same time a prayer of love for the tap water sitting on his desk the water they prayed for formed beautiful crystals when photographed using the method above. Emoto writes, "Through this book and through these crystal photos, I hope to convey the power of prayer."[314]

When water is exposed to prayer and certain expressions such as "You are beautiful" and "I love you" – beautiful crystals result when the water is frozen. What does this really mean for us? One might conclude that the thoughts of our hearts have an impact on all life and in the creation of our world tomorrow.

As we mentioned in the chapter on the body:

* The brain is about 75% water
* Blood is about 92% water
* Bones contain about 22% water
* Muscles are about 75% water

So, imagine the impact of prayer on our bodies if someone prays for us. Imagine the effect of prayer on drinking water, which we have prayed over. Jesus taught us to pray in thanks to Heavenly Father before we partake of meals. No wonder He wanted us to do that – prayer has the power to change water and food on a molecular level! We are also supposed to give thanks and praise to Heavenly Father for His many blessings.

Emoto suggests,

"If you find yourself feeling down, overwhelmed by the daily grind, or offended by an unkind word or act, then I suggest you try something: simply look at water. Walk to the edge of a nearby pond or stream and cast your eyes on the water's gentle waves reflecting the sun. If it is raining, find a puddle and watch the raindrops make rings that appear and disappear. Or while you are washing dishes at the sink, gaze at the geometric creations made as the light from the window mingles with water cascading downward. I recommend this because you will discover that water takes you to another world where you will feel the water within being washed clean; you will be able to return to who you really are. You have just forgotten for a while that you are water. As you let the water flow gently through your mind and your body, it will heal you at your core."[315]

That's why spending time in nature is so important. Canoeing on a lake or down a river with a group of scouting buddies or your family is healing. It is healing to wake up before everyone else at the campsite and to look at the peaceful water and the occasional fish bobbing.

Walking along a beach, or staring out at the ocean, or sitting on a rock and dangling your feet in the cool waters of a lake or river or stream can also be healing.

"Returning to Bliss" When You Are Down or Unhappy

Dr. Emoto writes:

> "Think back far enough in your life and you'll probably remember a time when you felt innocent bliss. Your life had meaning, and you were so busy living that time was forgotten. But those happy feelings are not gone for good. When you are true to yourself and search for what you really want to be and do, your life will once again begin to flow.
>
> "When you do this, you will soon realize that your life has changed. You'll first feel a renewed sense of health and well-being. This is because the bliss within you will purify the water that flows through your body. If we were to take a picture of such water, the resulting crystal would most certainly astound us."[316]

Returning to bliss does not mean resume playing video games for hours. Playing video games is not real nature. Water is real – a part of real life. Your body is mostly water - real life. To find your bliss, you need to find it in real life. If you are addicted to gaming, try to travel back to a time when you did not play video games continuously. This was probably a time when you had real hopes and dreams; a time when you enjoyed playing with siblings and friends; a time when you enjoyed walking with the dog; or, a time when you were in awe of stars, clouds, flowers, and animals.

Try to pray to God on a routine basis and see how He will help you. All you need is the faith of a mustard seed. With the faith of a mustard seed and prayer, God will shower you with His love, He will send you guidance, encouragement, and blessings. Then your little mustard seed will grow to be a healthy and strong tree, enabling you to be strong and at peace.

And Jesus said unto them, Because of your unbelief:
for verily I say unto you, If ye have faith as a grain
of mustard seed, ye shall say unto this mountain,
Remove hence to yonder place; and it shall remove;
and nothing shall be impossible unto you. –

– MATTHEW 1:20 KJV

WHAT TO PRAY FOR

- **Thankfulness** – You can pray to Heavenly Father just to thank Him for His blessings in your life like your family, friends, health, strength or whatever you choose. It is always nice to start out all your prayers this way.
- **Meals** – You should always say a short prayer prior to eating meals to thank God for your food. As mentioned, science has proven that prayer actually changes the molecular structure of the water contained in food, thus, the food that we bless may nourish us on an even deeper level.
- **Peace** – You can pray for inner peace, world peace, peace of mind, peace at home, peace at school, and so much more.
- **Healing** – If you are sick or afflicted, it is wise to pray for restored health. Also, you can ask members of The Church of Jesus Christ of Latter-day Saints (LDS) how to obtain a Priesthood Blessing administered by authorized members of the Priesthood. You can also call LDS Temples to have your name placed on temple prayer rolls. As members come to the Temple, they will find your name and offer sacred prayers on your behalf.
- **Wisdom** – Pray that God will grant you wisdom in making decisions for all aspects of your life.
- **Strength** – When you are majorly stressed out, angry, afraid, or confused, and you just need strength to see your way through or to calm down, praying for strength definitely helps. You may also want to tackle a new challenge that you feel is beyond your capability. God will help you perform far

beyond your innate capacity if you pray and ask for strength to do so, but you have to put forth your best efforts.

* **Guidance** – If you need help making a decision, ask Heavenly Father in prayer – even for small, mundane things, and important life-changing decisions, such as "Which college is best for me?" In this way, over time, you will develop a relationship with Him. He does, however, want you to use your agency. Ultimately, the decision is yours to make. He also wants you to use "intestinal fortitude" because that is the way you will achieve maximum growth. However, you may inquire of God how to make wise decisions. Remember to wait for answers. Sometimes the answers will come as the still, small inner voice of the Holy Spirit a few seconds or minutes after you have inquired of God. Other times it may take hours or days to receive answers. God may send you a person to respond to your question for Him. This is called receiving answers in "God's time." I sometimes feel the Spirit immediately when a total feeling of calm comes over me. He will often speak to you in your heart or in your mind. Be patient with yourself and with God. The principle here is called "after all that we can do," ask God for help. You may have heard the expression, "God helps those who help themselves." For example, if you haven't studied for the exam, then God will not be able to help you to do well on the exam. If you have studied, God can help you to think clearly, and to remember more than you ever thought possible.

    Education is important, because the more we know, the more capacity we have. You will also be able to make wiser decisions. Apply all you know, and then ask God for assistance. He will carry you the rest of the way. Be mindful of not allowing the adversary (Satan) to influence you. Also remember that God will never ask you to harm yourself or anyone else, so do not be fooled by thoughts such as these.

* **Forgiveness (Repentance)** – One of the most important things you can pray to Heavenly Father for is forgiveness of sins. We sin when we disobey God's commandments. Everyone sins. You must repent as soon as you realize you have sinned. Do

not allow this scar to remain on your soul one second more than it already has. Your Heavenly Father will forgive you of your sins if you will only ask Him. Do not be embarrassed or too proud to repent. Asking for forgiveness requires you to come before God with a broken heart and a humble spirit, along with faith in Jesus Christ that you will be forgiven when you ask. It is surprising to me that some people refuse to repent of their sins. Two of the worst sins you can commit are adultery and fornication (sex with someone other than your lawfully-wedded wife) – sins which are second in severity only to murder! Lusting after a woman in your mind is the same as fornication, or adultery if you are married. Any sin is egregious before the Lord, and you certainly do not want to die in your sins. Have confidence that Heavenly Father will forgive your sins if you ask in the name of the Only Begotten Son, Jesus Christ.

* **Blessings for Others** – You can pray for others to be healed or blessed, such as, "Please strengthen my brother as he takes his exam tomorrow."
* **Lack of Sustenance** – When you are hungry and have no food for your family and yourself, ask God to meet your needs in prayer. God will find a way to assist you – either directly or indirectly. God often works through others to provide for His children. He may place others in your path to provide the relief you need, or to help you to find a job.
* **Protection** – Always pray for safety and protection from the evil will and actions of others which could be inflicted intentionally or unintentionally. For example, before traveling in a car, airplane, boat or any other conveyance, pray for protection. Before going to sleep at night, pray that He will see fit to allow you to awaken in the morning! The point is to pray and ask for protection whenever you think you need it.
* **Other** – Pray for whatever is in your heart - as long as it is righteous.

Since water has a delicate spiritual nature that responds to prayer, written words, and music, and since we are seventy percent water, then it would be logical to assume that we also have a delicate spiritual nature and that we are also responsive to prayer.

How to Pray

You may not have realized it, but knowing how to pray also takes a wee bit of skill to be most effective. I have already mentioned that you must have righteous intent and faith in Christ for your prayers to be heard and answered. If you are repenting and asking for forgiveness, you must have a contrite spirit and a broken heart.

Creating a prayer in your mind and heart is really simple. Not to be funny or insincere, but you can use the analogy of making a sandwich to constructing a proper prayer.

1. The top slice of bread is the opening of the prayer. You start out by addressing Heavenly Father by name, thus: "Dear Heavenly Father."
2. The bottom slice of bread is the closing of the prayer. You end it like this, "And I ask this and say this in The Name of Jesus Christ, Amen."
3. Like the contents of a sandwich, what goes in between the two slices of bread is up to you. The meat, cheese, lettuce, tomatoes, and other ingredients, can be equated to items listed in the above titled, "What to Pray For" – just to give you some idea. Your prayer, however, should not be repetitive, rehearsed or recited. Speak from your heart. Be sincere about your concerns. Your prayer may be as simple as the sample prayer below (after getting down on your knees, sitting, or standing):

*"Dear Heavenly Father, I thank Thee for all my blessings.
I ask Thee to bless this food I am about to receive. Please
bless my family, and protect us while we travel. I say
this and ask this in The Name of Jesus Christ. Amen."*

You can pray either publically at times (in church, or prior to a meeting), and you can pray privately. Either way, if you have sincere intent in your heart and belief in Jesus Christ, then God will hear your prayer. It is best to be ready to accept and respond to God's answers to your prayers no matter how He responds or when He responds. Though, you can pray for confirmation. Even though guidance from God may be challenging at times – such as attending a college you had not planned to attend, or a move to a different city, usually the reason He guided you in a different direction will be revealed.

Since prayer is a dialogue or two-way communication between you and God as we mentioned before, you must now learn how to recognize His responses to you. You can receive confirmation of your prayers by many means. Be patient though, because it may take a little time for you to learn to listen and sense responses from Heavenly Father. He may respond by sending you a visual sign, an audible sign, a dream, a messenger, or He may change your circumstances. He also uses His Holy Scriptures to send messages to us. He has responded to my prayers in very subtle ways and also in very powerful ways. Once He responded to my prayers through a song. At other times, He answered my prayer through a profound sense of peace and calmness in my heart. In 2011 after a devastating loss, He sent a messenger (a totally unknown person to me) who consoled me by telling me things that only Heavenly Father and I knew at the time. He may perform miracles for you as He has for me. I cannot deny these spiritual experiences to any man, and I reveal them to you here as a witness so as to teach you that you can receive your own responses from God. Just learn to be sensitive to His precious responses – "God's language."

AN IMPORTANT RULE ABOUT PRAYING:
Pray often - Through prayer, we can draw closer to God and get answers to our questions and find comfort. Though He may not always answer prayers right away or in the manner way we expect, we believe this scripture: "Ask, and it shall be given you; seek, and ye shall find; knock, and it shall be opened unto you." (Matthew 7:7 KJV)

SPIRITUAL PROMPTINGS

You can receive spiritual promptings. We have told you that prayer is a two-way communication between you and God. A spiritual prompting is different because it can just come to you in your mind, your heart, or just "wash" all over your body as a feeling when you least expect it. We have mentioned before that it has been described by some as "a still, quiet voice."

In the *Liahona* magazine article, *Communion with the Holy Spirit*, James E. Faust taught that spiritual promptings are personal inspiration and revelation for the small events of life as well as major events, from the Holy Spirit. He said, "If worthy, we are entitled to receive revelations for ourselves, parents for their children, and members of the Church in their callings. But the right of revelation for others does not extend beyond our own stewardship."[317]

Many people have testified of receiving promptings and not acting on them - often to their regret. That includes me. In the past, before I knew about spiritual promptings, I suffered greatly when I did not act on promptings, and was victimized by circumstances.

You must learn to listen for these cherished communications from the Holy Spirit and take necessary action. If you feel unsure, you can pray for confirmation before you act. Spiritual promptings are meant to protect us and guide us through this life. This is God's way of "leveling the playing field" for you.

Sometimes people will receive such tender mercies because the Holy Spirit wants them to feel God's grace. After a person has repented and been Baptized by emersion in water, they can receive the gift of the Holy Spirit which is a gift from God that can be bestowed upon a righteous person by a worthy priesthood holder with authority. This gift is called Confirmation. After a person is confirmed, the Holy Spirit has God's permission to reside with a person on a continual basis as long as he or she is righteous.

A young woman who had been righteous, confirmed, and was very familiar with the power of the Holy Spirit and his promptings, sinned grievously. She told me that when she began to have an intimate relationship outside of wedlock God suddenly cut her off. She

felt as if all light had been removed from her life. She said, "It was as if blinds covered all the windows." It is advisable to receive the power of the Holy Spirit with gratitude and to honor it as David did (below):
Faust adds:

> "David, the youngest son of Jesse, a mere shepherd boy, volunteered to fight the giant Goliath. David and all of the army of Israel were insulted by the humiliating taunts of this formidable giant, but David knew that inspiration had brought him to save Israel. King Saul was so impressed with the faith and determination of this young boy that he appointed him to fight Goliath. Goliath made sport of David's youth and lack of armament. David responded that he came in the name of the Lord of Hosts, the God of the armies of Israel, and that the whole assembly would learn that the Lord does not save by the sword and the spear, "for the battle is the Lord's" (1 Sam. 17:47). Then David threw a rock from his sling with such force and accuracy that the stone sank deep into the forehead of Goliath. Goliath fell to the earth a dying man, and the Philistines fled in fear."[318]

As you may have gathered from reading the chapter so far, there is more at work in the world than meets the eye. The psychiatrist Dr. Scott Peck, met many patients over his career. Of these clients, many told him about remarkable occurrences, which had saved their lives. As a scientist, Dr. Peck analyzed the statistical probability that these occurrences were just coincidences and decided that these occurrences were not merely coincidences but that there was something else working to save human lives.

Peck relates a hair-raising incident that one of his clients, a mature, respectable, and highly-skeptical scientist experienced and shared with him:

> "After our last session, it was such a beautiful day, I decided to drive home by the route around the lake. As you know, the road around the lake has a great many blind curves. I was

approaching perhaps the tenth curve of these curves when the thought suddenly occurred to me that a car could be racing around the corner far into my side of the road. Without any more thought than that, I vigorously braked my car and came to a dead stop. No sooner had I done this than a car did indeed come barreling around the curve with its wheels six feet across the yellow line and barely missed me even though I was standing still on my side of the road. Had I not stopped, it is inevitable that we would have collided at the curve. I have no idea what made me decide to stop. I could have stopped at any one of a dozen curves, but I didn't. I've traveled that road many times before, and while I've had the thought that it was dangerous, I've never stopped before."[319]

Dr. Peck could not figure out what made him stop, but we know this to be a spiritual prompting. The scientist harkened to the prompting he received. This is what saved him. The fact that he was not injured or killed can be called a "tender mercy" or a miracle from God. We often receive spiritual promptings and tender mercies, but if we are not attuned to the Spirit we may not notice them or realize we have received them. We are, however, more likely to receive promptings from the Holy Spirit when we are compliant with all of God's laws, and the heavens have not withdrawn from us.

Dr. Peck goes on to state,

"At this time I can state only a very firm but unscientific impression that the frequency of such statistically improbable occurrences that are clearly beneficial is far greater than that in which the result is detrimental.[320] Could it be that the line in the song *Amazing Grace* is true: 'Tis grace hath brought me safe thus far'?"[321]

Christians, Jews, and Muslims would all say, "Yes, it is the grace of the Creator." Although each religion may have a different name for grace and a different name for the Creator, they all believe in miracles. These religions do have some similarities. The Qur'an is another testament that Jesus Christ lived. So is *The Book of Mormon*. Did you know that Jesus Christ is mentioned 27 times in the Qur'an? The *Bible*, the Qur'an and *The Book of Mormon* all contain historical accounts of the fact that Jesus Christ lived.

The Book of Mormon gives an account of Jesus Christ visiting his flock in the Americas shortly after he rose from the dead in the Middle East. The *Bible* tells us that Israel was scattered and that the Lord will gather his flock. It is only logical that Jesus would visit his flock in the Americas to teach them the gospel of Jesus Christ. This was predicted in the Old Testament, the first section of the *Bible*, and the apostle John recorded the same proclamation, spoken though by Jesus in the New Testament, which is the second section of the *Bible*:

> *And I will gather the remnant of my flock out of all*
> *countries whither I have driven them, and will bring them*
> *again to their folds; and they shall be fruitful and increase.*
>
> *– Jeremiah 23:3 (Old Testament) KJV*

> *Hear the word of the Lord, O ye nations, and declare it*
> *in the isles afar off, and say, He that scattered Israel will*
> *gather him, and keep him, as a shepherd doth his flock.*
>
> *– Jeremiah 31:10 (Old Testament) KJV*

> *And other sheep I have, which are not of this fold:*
> *them also I must bring, and they shall hear my voice;*
> *and there shall be one fold, and one shepherd.*
>
> *– John 10:16 (New Testament) KJV*

It is important to note that in Dr. Peck's practice he met many people who relayed stories of other beneficial occurrences that were not necessarily life-saving but "life-enhancing" or "growth-producing," He also felt that these incidents happen to all of us but that many people fail to recognize the occurrence as grace or dismiss the event as a coincidence. We agree with Dr. Peck: Statistically improbable occurrences are not likely to be "just coincidences."

JESUS IS

Jesus is the "Only Begotten" son of our Heavenly Father because he was the only one conceived of our Heavenly Father and an earthly mother, Mary. Jesus is our shepherd. The biblical verses below will explain why he is called our shepherd. Jesus is also our spiritual father because through him our spirits may be reborn: by our repentance in his name we may receive forgiveness for our sins due to his atoning sacrifice, that is, the blood and life he shed for us, and the waters of baptism - as we follow Jesus' example in being baptized as he was baptized. In life our bodies are born of our mother's blood and water. Our spiritual life must be born of Jesus' blood and the waters of baptism, at which time we take on his name in spirit and covenant to abide by his commandments. When Jesus rescues us from the consequences of our sins, which would be dire spiritually without his atoning sacrifice, he becomes Our Savior. As we have seen scientifically, water has a significant spiritual nature, and therefore, so do we. The power of blood and water to cleanse us spiritually may someday be measured by science.

Then said Jesus unto them again, Verily, verily,
I say unto you, I am the door of the sheep.
All that ever came before me are thieves and
robbers: but the sheep did not hear them.
I am the door: by me if any man enter in, he shall be
saved, and shall go in and out, and find pasture.
The thief cometh not, but for to steal, and to kill,
and to destroy: I am come that they might have life,
and that they might have it more abundantly.
I am the good shepherd: the good shepherd
giveth his life for the sheep.

– JOHN 10: 7-11 KJV

The Ten Commandments (Commandments God Gave Moses)

God's most familiar standards, the Ten Commandments are as relevant today as when they were delivered to Moses. After Moses led the children of Israel out of captivity in Egypt, he went to the top of Mount Sinai and spoke with God. When Moses came back down the mountain, he had Commandments God had revealed to him engraved on stone tablets. However, when Moses saw the Israelites worshiping a golden calf he was furious. He threw the tablets inscribed with the commandments to the ground, shattering them. Moses eventually went back up Mount Sinai, and God gave him a more simplistic list of Ten Commandments because He felt that the Israelites were not ready for all of the commandments. We still follow the Ten Commandments today, thousands of years later. Later, God gave us even more commandments through Jesus.

The Ten Commandments that God gave to Moses can be found in the *Bible* (Exodus, Chapter 20 and 1 Corinthians 6:9-10 KJV), which are:

- **#1 - Thou shalt have no other gods before me. (Other "gods" can include possessions, power or prominence.)**
- **#2 - Thou shalt not make unto thee any graven image.**
- **#3 - Thou shalt not take the name of the Lord thy God in vain.**
- **#4 - Remember the Sabbath day, to keep it holy.**
- **#5 - Honor thy father and thy mother.**
- **#6 - Thou shalt not kill.**
- **#7 - Thou shalt not commit adultery.**
- **#8 - Thou shalt not steal.**
- **#9 - Thou shalt not bear false witness against thy neighbor.**
- **#10 - Thou shalt not covet.**

About Commandment #10: It is important that we learn not to be jealous or envious of one another. When our family members and friends succeed, we should rejoice with them. If they are willing to share their blessings with us, we should be grateful.

If someday you succeed, you need to remember those who have helped you along the way. It will then be your turn to "pay it forward" or to share, with your family, friends, and with those who are less fortunate.

THE TWO GREAT COMMANDMENTS GIVEN BY JESUS

Jesus said, *"I am the way, the truth, and the life."*

JOHN 14:6 KJV

Seal of the Melchizedek – A Symbol of Jesus Christ

- **#11 - First Great Commandment**: *Thou shalt love the Lord thy God with all thy heart, and with all thy soul, and with all thy mind.* (Matthew 22:37 KJV)
- **#12 - Second Great Commandment**: *Thou shalt love thy neighbor as thyself.* (Matthew 22:39 KJV)

God gave us these two Great Commandments through Jesus, and all other commandments, those that He gave Moses and the other commandments that He gave Jesus, hinge upon them. So, if we follow the commandments Jesus Christ teaches us, we will find joy in life.

Elder Richard J. Maynes in the Ensign Magazine article, **The Joy of Living a Christ-Centered Life**, shares with us a lesson about how to live a "Christ-centered life." Elder Aoba, a potter, who lives in a small mountain village in Shikoku, Japan, gave his students instruction on how to make pots of clay by using a spinning wheel. They all watched him intently and assumed that the task would be quite simple. Then he gave each of his students a chance to make a pot of their own at the wheel. One student after the other failed miserably, as they found that it was difficult to mold the clay into a pot. They mostly got lopsided pots, and for a few, the clay completely fell apart and spun away from the wheel. When asked why they failed, they answered that they had no experience, or that they had never been trained, or that they had no talent.

The potter then told them the secret: the lump of clay needed to be placed exactly in the center of the wheel. When the students tried the second time, they were all elated that they had found success![322]

In this story, the lump of clay symbolizes you and the pot symbolizes your life. It will be much easier for you to become a well-adjusted man if you lead a Christ-centered life by following his commandments.

OTHER COMMANDMENTS GIVEN BY JESUS
We can easily discern more of Jesus' Commandments from his teachings.

9 Know ye not that the unrighteous shall not inherit the kingdom of God? Be not deceived: neither fornicators, nor idolaters, nor adulterers, nor effeminate, nor abusers of themselves with mankind. 10 Nor thieves, nor covetous, nor drunkards, nor revilers, nor extortioners, shall inherit the kingdom of God.

> *11 As such were some of you: but ye are washed,*
> *but ye are sanctified, ye are justified in the name*
> *of the Lord Jesus, and by the Spirit of our God.*

> *– 1 CORINTHIANS 6: 9-11 KJV*

Verses 9 and 10 above break out into some the easily-identified commandments Jesus gave us:

* **#13 - Thou shalt not commit fornication.** (Remain chaste while dating, and only have sexual relations with your spouse.)

> *Flee fornication. Every sin that a man doeth*
> *is without the body, but he that committeth*
> *fornication sinneth against his own body.*
> *What? Know ye not that your body is the temple*
> *of the Holy Ghost, which is in you, which ye*
> *have of God, and ye are not your own?*
> *For ye are bought with a price: therefore glorify God*
> *in your body, and in your spirit, which are God's.*

> *– 1 CORINTHIANS 6:18-20 KJV*

* **#14- Thou shalt not commit adultery.** This is one of the original Ten Commandments, but Jesus added more detail. Do not lust in your heart and mind, nor with your body. You should not lust after another person for this is fornication.

> *But I say onto you. That whosoever looketh*
> *on a woman to lust after her hath committed*
> *adultery with her already in his heart.*

> *– MATTHEW 5:28 KJV*

(In other words, pornography is not acceptable. Lusting after someone in the community and masturbating is not acceptable. The LDS church addresses these issues head-on in talks given by church leaders.)

- **#15 - Thou shalt not be effeminate** - (for men, the opposite would follow for women).
- **#16 - Thou shalt not abuse yourself with mankind.** (Masochism is not acceptable.)
- **#17 - Thou shalt not be a drunkard.**
- **#18 - Thou shalt not be an extortioner.**
- **#19 - Thou shalt marry rather than burn.**

> *Nevertheless, to avoid fornication, let*
> *every man have his own wife, and let every*
> *woman have her own husband.*
> *For I would that all men were even as myself.*
> *But every man hath his proper gift of God, one*
> *after this manner, and another after that.*
> *I say therefore to the unmarried and widows, it*
> *is good for them if they abide even as I am.*
> *But if they cannot contain, let them marry:*
> *for it is better to marry than to burn.*
>
> *– 1 Corinthians 7:2, 7-9 KJV*

This is a message for the unmarried and widowed. Therefore, do not wait too long to marry. The chapter, Elevate Your Family contains advice on how to choose a young woman to marry and how to be a good husband.

- **#20 - Thou shalt not hate**

> *Whosoever hateth his brother is a murderer: and ye*
> *know that no murderer hath eternal life abiding in him.*
>
> *– 1 John 3:15 KJV*

Hatred kills the spirit of both, the one who hates and the one who is hated.

#21 - Thou shalt not turn a blind eye to those in need.

> *Hereby perceive we the love of God, because*
> *he laid down his life for us: and we ought*
> *to lay down our lives for the brethren (this*
> *also means by setting an example).*
> *But whoso hath world's good, and seeth his brother*
> *have need and shutteth up his bowels of compassion*
> *from him, how dwelt the love of God in him?*
> *My little children, let us not love in word,*
> *neither in tongue; but in deed and in truth.*
>
> *—1 JOHN 16-18 KJV*

For example: When Hurricane Katrina hit New Orleans, The Church of Jesus Christ of Latter-day Saints sent out over 30 semi-trucks with relief supplies. The church maintains warehouses of food and other supplies throughout the world ready to help those in need.

#22 - Thou shalt not be deceived by antichrists.

> *And this is love that we walk after his commandments.*
> *This is the commandment. That as ye have heard*
> *from the beginning, ye should walk in it.*
> *For many deceivers are entered into the world,*
> *who confess not that Jesus Christ is come in the*
> *flesh. This is a deceiver and an antichrist.*
> *Look to yourselves, that we lose not those things which*
> *we have wrought, but that we receive a full reward.*
> *Whosoever transgresseth and abideth not*
> *in the doctrine of Christ hath not God. He*

> *that abideth in the doctrine of Christ, he*
> *hath both the Father and the Son.*

> *– 2 JOHN 1:6-9 KJV*

#23 - Thou shalt turn thy heart to "the" children. This means care for your own children and children in general. The following scripture was mentioned in the introduction for this book. It is pivotal in motivating us to write this book.

> *Behold, I will send you Elijah the prophet before*
> *the coming of the great and dreadful day of the*
> *Lord: And he shall turn the heart of the fathers to*
> *the children, and the heart of the children to their*
> *fathers, lest I come and smite the earth with a curse.*

> *– MALACHI 4:5-6 KJV*

#24 - Thou shalt turn thy heart to thy ancestors, and do work for them which they cannot do for themselves.

> *For to this end Christ both died, and rose, and revived,*
> *that he might be the Lord both of the dead and living.*

> *– ROMANS 14:9 KJV*

> *Else what shall they do which are baptized*
> *for the dead, if the dead rise not at all? Why*
> *are they then baptized for the dead?*

> *– 1 CORINTHIANS 15:29 KJV*

*God having provided some better thing for us, that
they without us should not be made perfect.*

– Hebrews 11:40 KJV

Temple work for the dead was completed during Jesus' time. This practice is continued in LDS temples today.

- **#25 - Thou shalt develop thy talents.**
   Biblical reference: Matthew 25:14-30 KJV
- **#26 - Thou shalt repent of thy sins.**

*If we say that we have no sin, we deceive
ourselves, and the truth is not in us.
If we confess our sins, he is faithful and just to forgive us
our sins, and to cleanse us from all unrighteousness.
If we say that we have not sinned, we make
him a liar, and his word is not in us.*

– John 1:8-10 KJV

Do not delay repenting. This is a critical step towards our eternal salvation. We must repent as often as we need to repent of our sins. We need to repent with a broken heart and a contrite spirit and the intent to sin no more.

- **#27 - We are commanded to be baptized, as Jesus was by John the Baptist.**
   Biblical reference: John 3rd Chapter
   Other reference: The Inevitable Apostasy, pp 160-168
   Infants were never baptized when Jesus lived or in the early ongoing church. This practice was introduced to the church after Jesus' death, thereby corrupting the gospel.
- **#28 - Love one another as I have loved you.** (Notice that this is different from "Love your neighbor as thyself.")

A new commandment I give unto you, That ye love one another; as I have loved you, that ye also love one another.

– John 13:34 KJV

This is my commandment, That ye love one another, as I have loved you.

– John 15:12 KJV

Jesus' love for his apostles and for us was manifested through the following:

He loved us by teaching us the gospel God instructed Him to teach us. Therefore, we can show love for each other by studying the scriptures together and sharing the scriptures, the Word of God, with our families and with other people in our community.

Jesus was charitable with his time. He brought relief to the sick and those in need. So, when someone is sick, we can visit them in the hospital, or we can bring something healthful to eat to their home. We must also be vigilant in observing when people need our friendship: when they need to be accepted even though they may be of a different race, religion, or sexual orientation; when they need a pat on the back; when they need a shoulder to cry on; a helping hand with moving to another home; help with learning a difficult math concept; a meal if they are going through a tough time financially (you can buy someone breakfast or lunch or share your meal); help picking up a stack of books that they have dropped; help learning a new skill, such as swimming, or riding a bicycle;

help with preparing for an event – such as setting up chairs, or accompanying them on a musical instrument; help protecting them if you suspect they will hurt themselves or hurt someone else – you may need to speak to their parents, and a teacher, or the police, in order to protect them from themselves or to protect someone else - (RAT = Right Action Taken) – this is only a short list of ideas.

#29 - Teach the gospel of Jesus Christ in your community and throughout the world. Be a witness.

After Jesus' resurrection, He ministered on Earth for forty days, then he ascended into Heaven. The last thing Jesus told His disciples before He ascended was:

> *For John truly baptized with water, but ye shall be baptized with the Holy Ghost not many days hence. But ye shall receive power, after that the Holy Ghost is come upon you: and ye shall be witnesses unto me both in Jerusalem, and in all Judea, and in Samaria, and unto the uttermost part of the earth. (This was Jesus's last commandment before he ascended.)*
>
> *And when he had spoken these things while they beheld, he was taken up: and a cloud received him out of their sight.*
>
> *– Acts 1:5, 8, 9 KJV*

Jesus told his disciples that they would receive the power of the Holy Spirit to give them the courage they would need to give witness unto his teachings and his life, in their communities and throughout the world. When we are confirmed, we also receive the power of the Holy Ghost. However, the commandment to preach the gospel throughout the earth is for men in the priesthood. Although there are thousands of sister missionaries - for women, preaching the gospel throughout the earth is not a commandment. That is why in the early LDS church, women were not called to be missionaries unless they requested to go on a mission with their husbands. When women are confirmed they also receive power from the Holy Ghost, which includes continual guidance in their daily lives (as long as they are abiding by God's laws – the same goes for men) as they care for their families, and members of their community.

Note: Throughout scripture we are reminded to "trust in the Lord."

In thee, O Lord, do I put my trust: let
me never be put to confusion.

- Psalms 71:1

It is better to trust in the Lord than
to put confidence in man.

- Psalms 118:8

Trust ye in the Lord for ever: for in the Lord
Jehovah is everlasting strength:

- Isaiah 26:44

Ye that fear the Lord, trust in the Lord:
he is their help and their shield.

- Psalms 115:11

That thy trust may be in the Lord, I have made
known to thee this day, even to thee.

- Proverbs 22:19

OTHER RULES

1. **Study the Scriptures** – You cannot consider yourself well-read if you have not read the *Bible*. Neither can you dispute anything in the *Bible* unless you have read it for yourself. The same goes *for The Book of Mormon,* another testament of the gospel of Jesus Christ - which is an historical account of people from one of the tribes of Israel who migrated to the Americas 600 years before Jesus Christ was born, and also includes the history of 400 years of their generations after Jesus came to visit them in the Americas. The guidance that was recorded and taught to these people from their ancient Israeli prophets, and Jesus' gospel complement the teachings in the *Bible* – in that they are the same teachings. So read both of them, and then pray and ask Heavenly Father if they are true.

2. **Follow the Prophet**. We follow the prophet, because the prophet follows God. Listening to what the prophets teach will bring us peace and guide us to Heaven. Have you ever heard one person tell one side of a story, and another person telling the opposite side of the same story, and both versions sound true? With so many people and opinions competing for our attention, how do we decide what to believe? To help us know God's will — to help us figure out what is true — God calls prophets and apostles to act as His spokesmen. A prophet is a faithful, righteous man chosen by God to speak for Him here on earth. Apostles are prophets chosen by God to be special witnesses of Jesus Christ and His divinity. In order to speak for God, prophets and apostles must hold the priesthood and divine authority, which are required for such a holy responsibility.

3. **Follow The *Word of Wisdom***
Boyd K. Packer urges us to, "Honor the principle of the *Word of Wisdom* and you will receive the promised blessings. Young people, you must understand that there is something of colossal importance to justify the restrictions imposed by the *Word of Wisdom!*"[323] For example, the *Word of Wisdom*

counsels us to eat meat sparingly, but not to go overboard and not eat meat at all. In other words, do things in moderation. It advises us to do common sense things like avoiding alcohol, drugs, caffeine, and tobacco as we have already taught you. It does not promise you perfect health, but it gives you the best chance of having a body in good condition and having a mind that is alert, in order to receive those delicate spiritual promptings. Remember, your body is a temple for the Spirit of God. The *Word of Wisdom* can be found in *Doctrine and Covenants, Section 89.* Go to www.lds.org on the web.

Note: The *Word of Wisdom* was given to Joseph Smith by inspiration, from God, in the 1800's – long before science would prove that partaking of tobacco, alcohol and caffeine can be harmful. There is a lot to be said for creating a community where people who choose to live by the *Word of Wisdom* can find friendship and acceptance.

SHOCKING TRUTHS ABOUT SEXUAL PURITY

Today's society has popularized, especially to young people, the WRONG NOTIONS about sex. So some of the information in this section may come as a shock to you. Here, we want to set the record straight. We want you to know the truth about your reproductive powers, so that you can develop the correct attitude towards sex. You will need this information in order to have a healthy and happy relationship when you marry someday. If you do not read, understand and practice the information here, you will be at risk of committing extremely serious sin leading to unhappiness.

Because I grew up on a farm, I learned about sex early in my life. I could see animals mating quite frequently, so naturally I was curious about it. My parents never taught me about sex, and I did not learn about it in school because sex education was not in our regular curriculum as it is today. Despite my lack of being mentored in this area, I instinctively knew that this intimate act was specifically reserved for a husband and wife. Of course, I learned that in church.

In the Methodist church I attended in my youth I learned the Ten Commandments. One of these was "Thou shalt not commit adultery." I had a rather fuzzy notion of the interpretation of that commandment but knew that it meant I should be faithful to my wife when I married someday. Another commandment - "Thou shalt not covet" – left me clueless. I had no idea what it meant. Except, I guessed, that I should not be jealous of what other people had. Both these interpretations were very minimal and insufficient. Also, I was not that interested in finding out more for fear of looking dumb.

In my youth, sex was never portrayed on television or in other media as something people did casually – unlike today. Being the oldest child in a family of ten children, it became rather obvious to me in my youth where children came from. I knew that someday, I would grow up, get married and have children, too.

One of the most popular songs on the radio, when I was a small boy, was Frank Sinatra's *Love and Marriage* whose lyrics reinforced the idea of sex after marriage:

> *"Love and marriage*
> *Love and marriage*
> *Go together like a horse and carriage*
> *Let me tell you, brother*
> *You can't have one*
> *Without the other."*

Hint: this was long before the very explicit hip-hop music came along.

So the idea of sex AFTER marriage was ingrained in the heads of children and adults. Besides that, most people attended church on a regular basis and were taught by spiritual leaders that "Thou shalt not commit adultery". According to Rebecca Barnes, "today less than 20% of Americans regularly attend church," [324] so it is not hard to see that the gospel messages about reserving sex for marriage may not be getting out to people.

Society's view of sex has changed drastically since I began my quest for manhood. It is now the direct opposite. Never before has there been more confusion and ambiguity around sex and sex issues, but there does not need to be such confusion. The rules are quite simple.

SHOCKING FACT: You should not have sex before marriage. You should only have sex with your wife after marriage.

This means no sex with your girlfriends, no sex with friends, or "friends-with-benefits," or anyone until you are married. Then after marriage you are to only have sex with your wife. Period.

God gave husband and wives the power of procreation for the distinct purpose of creating children and raising an eternal family. Physical intimacy is a beautiful, joyful, and sacred gift that a husband and wife share, beginning on their wedding night. It is not to be used for lewd, immoral nor illegal purposes. It is for the expression of love between husband and wife. Gordon B. Hinckley, President of The Church of Jesus Christ of Latter-day Saints, in the publication *The Family: A Proclamation to the World* stated, "The sacred powers of procreation are to be employed only between man and woman, lawfully wedded as husband and wife."[325]

A Famous Football Player Chose Celibacy before Marriage

Russell Wilson, professional football player (quarterback) for the Seattle Seahawks, suggested to the lady he wanted to marry that they remain celibate until they got married. Poppie Mphuthing, News Editor for the Huffington Post, reported: "Wilson revealed during an interview with former NFL player Pastor Miles McPherson that he and famous R&B singer, Ciara, were going to wait until marriage to have sex."[326]

According to the report, Russell said to Ciara, "What would you say if we took all that extra stuff off the table? And just did it Jesus' way?" Wilson told the audience he suggested this to Ciara.

We think this is an admirable approach to courtship in a society in which celibacy has not been the norm. Russell Wilson clearly thinks for himself and is not controlled by the common immoral "group consciousness" of our society, which is largely portrayed and promoted in movies, on television, and on the Internet. In thinking for himself, he is choosing to follow the will of God. I am willing to bet that everyone in Heaven and millions of people on earth are cheering for his courage to "Choose The Right."

> *For this is the will of God, even your sanctification,*
> *that ye should abstain from fornication.*
>
> – 1 THESSALONIANS 4:3 KJV

Not Obeying God's Law of Celibacy Before Marriage Can have Fatal Consequences

Young men, choose your girlfriends wisely and mind your actions. The devil will expose you when you least expect it. Travis Alexander, a young man of the LDS faith, who had secretly committed fornication with his girlfriend, Jodi Arias, was exposed when Jodi photographed him in his shower, stabbed him 27 times, and then shot him to death. For his family, Travis' loss and the trial that followed were devastating. Arias was convicted of murder.

THE LAW OF CHASTITY

The Law of Chastity includes more than just the instructions not to have sexual relations with anyone other than your wife. It also contains instructions that before marriage you should not do anything to arouse powerful emotions. For example, no prolonged kissing, or touching in sacred parts of the bodies. Also do not lie on top of another person even when fully clothed. Neither should you arouse emotions with your body. This includes using pornography or masturbation because it causes you to lust after women with whom you are not married – even in your mind!

> *But I say unto you, that whosoever looketh*
> *on a woman to lust after her hath committed*
> *adultery with her already in his heart.*
>
> – MATTHEW 5:28 KJV

LAW OF CHASTITY NOT UNDERSTOOD

There was a young man at the University of California Santa Barbara recently who killed six people because he was lonely, sexually frustrated, and angry at women. He was angry at women because, at 22, he was still a virgin.[327] If he had known the truth about the requirements of chastity, he would have known that his virginity was a special gift and that it was preserved for a special young lady on his wedding night. If he had known the truth, it is likely that these people would not have been killed. How tragic and ironic that he thought he was abnormal because he was a virgin. If he had known the truth about chastity, he would have known that his virginity was actually virtuous.

A DISCUSSION REGARDING MASTURBATION

Many people consider masturbation to be a simple, innocent expression of sexuality. However, the church has advised us against the practice, mainly because it is a sin and we become carnal when we masturbate. In other words, we intentionally pervert our passions. The church says,

> "Masturbation is not physically necessary. There is already a way by which the male system relieves excessive spermatic fluid quite regularly through the nocturnal emission or wet dream. Monthly menstrual flow expels the female's egg and cleanses the womb. For both sexes, physical or emotional tensions can be released by vigorous activity. Thus, in a biological sense, masturbation for either gender is not necessary. In a gospel sense, it is a sin: 'Masturbation, a rather common indiscretion, is not approved of the Lord nor of His Church regardless of what may have been said by others whose norms are lower.'"[328]

Masturbation can lead to unhappiness. That notion may come as a surprise to some of you. Before marriage masturbation can lead to an unnaturally increased sexual desire and a propensity to commit fornication. It can also lead to sexually transmitted diseases, illegitimate pregnancies, and loss of dignity. So, first by reducing the amount of masturbation then abstaining from it can temporarily reduce a person's desire for sex while they are not married. So when you are dating you can feel more comfortable not being in an intimate relationship. Then you will be better able to concentrate on getting good grades, going on a religious or humanitarian mission, establishing a business, or starting a career.

After marriage, masturbation can alienate you from your wife, and lead to divorce. Pornography and masturbation deter men from being intimate with their wives.

It is normal, wholesome and sanctified by God for women to want to be intimate with their husbands. Sexual intimacy is healthy for men and for women on a physical, emotional, and spiritual level. When a husband and wife bond together physically, emotionally and spiritually the likelihood of divorce significantly decreases, which creates a safe environment for children who really want their family to remain intact. Physical intimacy produces healthy hormones such as oxytocin, which God created to enable people to bond to each other. Oxytocin is a powerful hormone. In romantic situations, for example, when you hug, kiss and become affectionate with a loved one, your body increases your oxytocin levels.

So, avoid masturbation because it is a carnal activity. Carnal behavior leads to unrighteous lust, unrighteous behavior, and misery. On the other hand, virtuous behavior will lead to confidence, serenity, and righteous behavior in all aspects of your life. If you make it a habit to behave virtuously and grow closer to God in all facets of your development, then your intimate relationship with your wife will be enriched.

HOMOSEXUALITY/SAME-GENDER ATTRACTION

God loves all his children, whether they are heterosexual or homosexual. Heterosexuals are people who are attracted to the opposite gender - men are attracted to women and vice versa. Homosexuals are people who are attracted to others of the same gender - men to men and women to women.

Before I begin to discuss the issue of same-gender attraction, I wish to express in a paragraph some "food for thought" that may guide some young men to be cautious before they label themselves "gay." Much attention is given to the lesbian, gay, bisexual, and transsexual (LGBT) community in the media. This may lead some boys, 7-8-9-10-year-olds, to believe that they are "gay" because they prefer to spend their leisure time with boys - playing with trucks, and playing sports. It is normal for young boys and even older boys to want to spend time with boys playing sports. If you felt like this when you were younger or if you still feel like this now, it does not necessarily mean that you are gay. We know boys who - when they were eight and nine years old - said that they preferred to play with boys and "Girls are yuk!" When they were 15 years old they had girl-friends, with whom they preferred to spend time. This was of their own accord. Their family did not pressure them to have an interest in girls. They developed an interest in girls naturally, likely due to hormonal changes in their bodies, even though when they were very young they could not fathom liking girls. The boys would have been loved either way – their parents were not aware of Jesus' teachings concerning same-sex intimacy.

All of us must behave kindly and with fairness towards people in the LGBT community. The media has done a fine job of supporting them. However, the media is biased; they are only focusing on giving role models of people who are practicing homosexuals. They have failed to give a voice to many people who have same-gender attrac-tion, yet still abide by God's laws. That is not objective journalism. It is not a sin to have same-gender attraction. Though it is a sin to ACT on those feelings. Thus, the media has failed to inform people who have same-gender attraction that there is an alternative. People can have same-gender attraction and at the same time obey God's laws, which can lead to a happy and rewarding life. LDS *Voices of Hope* is a website that gives people with same-gender attraction and obey God's laws a voice. Why don't CNN, CBC, BBC and other news channels interview these persons so they can tell the world about their stories of courage? (This is a rhetorical question.) If these stories were told, then many people who have same-gender attraction would not be ashamed. Having great role models would give them hope. They would not feel alone. This would cut down the suicide rate of LGBT persons. Furthermore, persons with same-gender attraction would realize the blessings that come from abiding by God's laws.

We posted the comments above on our Facebook page. Lara Buchmiller responded with the following comments:

"I love the idea of telling their stories so they can be role models for those who struggle with same-sex attraction and members [of our church] who could learn how to be a little more sensitive and supportive. I fully believe that those who live as a same-sex couple can have a fulfilled and joyful life. Just as I believe anyone who is not Christian can also have a fulfilled, joyful life. But, I agree with you wholeheartedly. The blessings we gain from following the Lord's plan and commandments are so much more than we can do on our own. The struggle with same-sex attraction is no different from any other personal struggle we may have that is opposed to God's purpose, which is our immortality and eternal life. Those that struggle with this, need support and love, not judging and condemnation as I would hope anyone would do for me with my struggles. We are not perfect, but that is why we need the Savior.

"Also, I think the media does not talk about those who struggle with same-sex attraction but chose not to follow those feelings because people would feel they are "denying" themselves or are not "being true to themselves." People do not see that they are choosing to follow a higher law. The law God has divinely decreed. Our world is becoming a world that thinks it's better to follow our desires. "Be true to ourselves." But now, more than ever, we need to be true to the Savior, forgive ourselves and others when we fall short, and turn to Christ for help and forgiveness for what we cannot do on our own."

Here are testimonies from men who are attracted to the same gender, but who <u>still abide by God's laws</u>:

Jimmy Merrel

"Jimmy works as a music therapist and enjoys helping people with cancer, emotional disabilities, neurological disabilities, AIDS, and terminal illnesses. He serves as First Counselor in a bishopric and has also served as the choir director and ward mission leader. Through his experiences with same-sex attraction, Jimmy has learned that the Lord will lighten his burdens by giving him opportunities to serve others. That sounds paradoxical, but it's a practice that has brought Jimmy much joy. Accordingly, Jimmy has served within the North Star organization as a moderator for the men's group, online groups coordinator, treasurer of the executive committee, and director of the online community. "[329]

Ethan Marston

"I am grateful for same-gender attraction. If it weren't for that, I wouldn't have clung so tightly to God as I experienced life's difficulties. I wouldn't know so much about the nature of God and the love he has for me. I wouldn't have such respect and admiration for women. I wouldn't know that love is more than a physical relationship—something that transcends the body and its desires. I wouldn't be who I am today."[330]

Brett and Shaundra Crogun

The following is a story about a very sweet young couple. It is wonderful that the young woman knew before their wedding that her future husband struggled with same-gender attraction. She loved him so much that she decided that she could cope with - perhaps less intimacy, as he also faced the same challenge to be married to her and to obey God's laws. Waiting to tell someone after marriage that one has same-gender attraction is unfair. It is best to be forthcoming long before wedding plans are made. Such is the example that this couple set.

Throughout his youth, Brett struggled quietly with something he felt no one could ever understand. After holding his feelings and frustrations entirely inside himself for years, he finally asked a dear friend to meet him. After hours of driving around together, he confided and shared with her his deepest secret - his experience with same-sex attraction. Neither of them imagined it at the time, but, to their surprise, five years later they would marry. Now, over four years into their marriage, they are certain that God is carefully directing them through life. They testify of great truths they have learned from experience, one of these truths being that when you put your faith in God, mountains can be moved. Together, Brett and Shaundra look forward to a future filled with happiness and hope.[331]

As a Christian, I must share with you what Jesus taught on the subject of being intimate with someone of the same gender. I will give God the last word.

Like all other sins, homosexual acts should be avoided and are indeed abominable in the eyes of God:

> *"Thou shalt not lie with mankind, as with womankind: it is abomination."*
>
> *– Leviticus 18:22 KJV*

> *"For this cause God gave them up unto vile affections: for even their women did change the natural use into that which is against nature: And likewise also the*

men, leaving the natural use of the woman, burned in
their lust one toward another; men with men working
that which is unseemly, and receiving in themselves
that recompense of their error which was meet."

– ROMANS 1:26-27 KJV

REPENTANCE

Repentance is one of the keys to spiritual progression. It is the process of acknowledging sins that you have committed against God's commandments. These actions could have been taken against your own body by abusing your body, against a friend, against a family member, against a classmate, against a colleague, against a neighbor or an innocent bystander. For example, bullying is a sin against God's commandments to "Love one another; as I have loved you," and, to "Love your neighbor as thyself."

You can also commit sin by omission – such as not developing your God-given talents, not repenting, not being baptized, and not sharing the gospel with others. You have the ability to determine the difference between right and wrong. Following God's commandments will help you. When you know that you have sinned, it is incumbent upon you to repent to God whom you have offended by asking for forgiveness. If you stole something, give it back. If you lie, tell the truth. The truth will set you free – otherwise, you will have to live the lie for the rest of your life. This may destroy your life or the life of another person.

If you need to repent to a human being, you should go to that person and confess the offense and ask them to forgive you and offer to make restitution, if possible. This is all part of your personal integrity and honesty. This is how you grow your character and show yourself as a decent man. You will be respected for it.

WHY YOU NEED TO REPENT

When you do something wrong, you cause the scales of justice to become unbalanced. Justice must be satisfied. The Law of Justice is a spiritual law that brings consequences for injustice, different from the laws of man. Justice also demands a penalty be paid for every sin we commit. If you ask the offended person for forgiveness, and if they forgive you, then justice would be served as far as that person is concerned, but you may have offended God as well. If you committed a serious crime, then civil authorities would also expect justice, and so would God. If you broke God's laws or commandments, then you have sinned against God and you must repent to Him and ask for forgiveness.

News Flash: *Everyone sins at some time or another. Therefore, everyone must repent to God and ask for forgiveness for their sins if they hope to progress spiritually on Earth and in the Afterlife.*

The only person who ever walked the earth without sin was Jesus Christ. He was and is the only perfect person.

Jesus came to Earth for very special reasons – to teach us the gospel, and to atone for our sins, and to overcome the sting of death by dying on the cross and resurrecting from the dead - making it possible that all could be resurrected. He knew that for humans to be able to be forgiven of their sins, which they were bound to make, He would need to atone for our sins. So, He subjected Himself to the penalty of that law required for our sins. His atonement makes His Mercy and Forgiveness available for us.

The Atonement of Jesus Christ

This great gift to mankind is called The Atonement (At-One-Ment or "at one with Jesus"). He suffered greatly for our sins in the Garden of Gethsemane. He bled from every pore in his body during his suffering (*Doctrine and Covenants* 19:18). This is one of the greatest spiritual events ever to happen on Earth, but lots of people are not aware of the Atonement. As a Methodist and as a Catholic, I was not taught that Jesus atoned for my sins in the Garden of Gethsemane and on the cross. The atonement, which He endured in the Garden of Gethsemane and on the cross, also enabled Jesus to truly understand each one of us. He knows our hearts, and He understands our pains, so he is able to succor us in our trials. Jesus suffered for us to know us.

He had the authority to use his power to stop other people from be-ing oppressed. He healed many sick people and even raised people from the dead. However, he did not have the authority to save himself. That is why when Jesus was in the Garden of Gethsemane before he began to suffer the Atonement he asked God, if He (God) would use his power to keep him from suffering excruciating pain. For, he was human like us.

> And they came to a place which was named Gethsemane:
> and he saith to his disciples, Sit ye here, while I shall pray.
> And he taketh with him Peter and James and John,
> and began to be sore amazed, and to be very heavy;
> And saith unto them, My soul is exceeding
> sorrowful unto death: tarry ye here, and watch.
> And he went forward a little, and fell on the
> ground, and prayed that, if it were possible,
> the hour might pass from him.
> And he said, Abba, Father, all things are
> possible unto thee; take away this cup from me:
> nevertheless not what I will, but what thou wilt.
> And he cometh, and findeth them sleeping,
> and saith unto Peter, Simon, sleepest thou?
> couldest not thou watch one hour?
>
> - MARK *14:32-37 KJV*

Modern revelation reveals what happened in the Garden of Gethsemane:

> Which suffering caused myself, even God, the greatest
> of all, to tremble because of pain, and to bleed at every
> pore, and to suffer both body and spirit—and would
> that I might not drink the bitter cup, and shrink.
>
> — DOCTRINE AND COVENANTS *19:18*

It is through the Atonement that man can be forgiven for sins through repentance. If you want to benefit from the great gift of Jesus' atonement, to be one with him, and to receive forgiveness and the blessings that follow when you live righteously, you need to repent. **Repenting of your sins leads to forgiveness, which erases your sins, satisfying the law of justice. This wipes your slate clean, and it feels great.**

Keep in mind that sometimes, Jesus and God know what is best for you even before you know it. Your life may take an unexpected turn - the loss of a job, an unexpected move because landlords decide to sell the house you are renting, or a girlfriend ends the relationship you had with her. Life can be very stressful during times like these, but if you are obeying God's laws, God will strengthen you. He will help you out of the conundrum. After a while you may find that there was a good reason for the change – for example: a better paying job that enabled you to accomplish all that you needed to do; time to accomplish God's work (such as writing a book for boys); or a healthier relationship with a new girlfriend. When you look back, you should give thanks thus, "Thank you Heavenly Father/God for Thy blessings". That hardship really turned out to be a blessing.

Before Jesus came to Earth, people made animal sacrifices to atone for their sins. Jesus came to Earth and became, symbolically, the sacrificial lamb for all men's sins. So in modern times, when you sin, you only need to repent to God, in Jesus' name, to be cleansed of your sins because Jesus atoned for them. Each of us should be eternally grateful to Jesus for the miracle of the Atonement.

Following Jesus by repenting, thereby benefiting from Jesus's atonement, and being baptized as Jesus was can be imagined as a vortex, an unseen path that can guide us back to our Heavenly Father and Heavenly Mother. There is much that exists in this world that we cannot see – the air we breathe, radio waves, microwaves, molecules, atoms, electrons, and protons, etc. Wouldn't it be great if someday, the power of Jesus' atonement and baptism may be observed and measured, as we can now observe the power of prayer creating change within water crystals?

I know that when I repented and was baptized making a covenant with Jesus to take upon His name, Jesus's atoning sacrifice and my baptism changed me. I became a new man inside. It is necessary to repent prior to being baptized. You must also have faith in Jesus Christ in order to partake of the Atonement already in place for you.

Satan and the world would like you to think that you do not need to repent for sins you commit. This is not true. Sin will weigh you down. Sin will rob you of your happiness.

Whenever you sin, repent immediately. Do not wait. The quicker you can remove yourself from the dark cloud of sin, and the weight of sin, the sooner you can find the peace and joy and blessings of forgiveness.

Do not deliberately break God's laws with the idea that you will just repent later. That is making a mockery of God. Instead, do the right thing always. God knows if you are faking it, so do not attempt to cover up your real intent.

How to Repent

The way you repent to God is to find a secluded place where you can meditate. Kneel down on both knees and begin to pray as we have taught you before. During your prayer, you will bring these sins to mind and ask Heavenly Father to forgive you. He already knows that you have sinned and knows that you have come to ask for forgiveness, but he expects you to say the words. Remember, words have power. When you speak the words of repentance with a broken heart and a contrite spirit, in Jesus' name, God will forgive you.

It's Never Too Late to Repent

It does not matter how long ago that you sinned. The sin is still registered on your soul as long as you have not repented. The stain is still there. The nature of the sin matters not – it still applies. The time to repent is now.

FORGIVING PEOPLE WHO HAVE OFFENDED YOU IS A GIFT YOU GIVE YOURSELF

As God forgives us, we ought to forgive people who offend us. Negative thoughts, hurt feelings, and hatred are unhealthy burdens, which cause stress and make us sick. We need to release this negativity towards people who have offended us through forgiveness. Forgiveness is a gift we give to ourselves. We may need to forgive certain people in our lives many times before the negative emotions stop creeping into our mind. In time, we can heal. When we feel that we are not able to forgive just yet, we can ask God to forgive the person who has harmed us, for our sake, and we can ask God to help us to forgive. Jesus forgave those who tortured and crucified Him. When He was dying on the cross, Jesus said: "Father, forgive them; for they know not what they do." (Luke 23:34 KJV)

As previously mentioned, one of Jesus' commandments is "Love one another, as I have loved you." Forgiving those who have offended us is another tenet of that commandment.

Prior to being immersed in baptismal waters, forgive everyone who has ever harmed you. It feels great to have such burdens lifted off your shoulders. If ever negative thoughts return, forgive again. Eventually time will heal your pain.

Note: Though you have forgiven someone, it does not necessarily follow that you should trust them – trust your instincts. Choose your friends wisely. Remember always: there is no excuse for abuse. If you are being abused tell someone, your parents, teacher, counselor, or the police, and remove yourself from that environment – then begin to forgive the person/s who has/have offended you.

FAITH

And Christ hath said: If ye will have faith in me ye shall have power to do whatsoever thing is expedient in me.

MORONI 7:33

In his article, *When Your Heart Tells You Things Your Mind Does Not Know*, President Harold B. Lee tells this story about faith:

> "I once had a visit from a young Catholic priest. I asked him why he had come, and he replied, "I came to see you."
>
> "'Why?' I asked.
>
> "'Well,' he said, 'I have been searching for certain concepts that I have not been able to find. But I think I am finding them now in the Mormon community.'
>
> "That led to a half-hour conversation. I told him, 'Father, when your heart begins to tell you things that your mind does not, then you are getting the Spirit of the Lord.'
>
> "He smiled and said, "I think that's happening to me already.'
>
> "'Then do not wait too long,' I said to him.
>
> "A few weeks later I received a telephone call from him. He said, 'Next Saturday I am going to be baptized a member of the Church because my heart has told me things my mind did not know.'"[332]

Moral of this story: The beginning of faith is when your heart tells you things your mind does not know.

BAPTISM

Having faith in Jesus Christ and repenting of your sins will prepare you for the first saving ordinance of Baptism. On this spiritual part of your quest, we hope you will come to understand the importance of baptism. Everyone who seeks eternal life must be baptized. Baptism has two parts: (1) the submersion of the person into water, which enables the death of the old self and actually rebirths the spirit, and (2) the raising up of the person out of the water, which symbolizes that the rebirth has occurred. Newborn babies come forth out of their mother's womb with blood and water, and their spirits are pure. Spiritual rebirth also occurs with blood and water – Jesus' blood that is manifest in His atoning sacrifice for the forgiveness and remission of our sins, and the waters of baptism. The ordinance of baptism is performed to spiritually cleanse a person who seeks to follow Christ and do the will of Heavenly Father (God). Combined with repentance, the act of baptism spiritually enables a person to be born again and makes them "a new creature" in Christ.

Baptism is an absolutely necessary step to be able to partake in all the ordinances established by God for his children so that they can attain eternal life. It is the first ordinance. It is the beginning of a journey on the "strait and narrow" path, which leads to eternal life. Choosing to be baptized is, therefore, a choice we must make for ourselves using our own agency.

"Jesus is "the way, the truth, and the life."

JOHN 14:6 KJV

Christ always set the example for his disciples to follow. When Jesus lived, babies were never baptized. Conscious of this responsibility, and in the presence of those whom he desired to tutor, "he took them (little children) up in his arms, put his hands upon them, and blessed them" (Matthew 19:13-15 KJV). The pattern had been set – a little child was to have hands laid upon him and be given a blessing so he might commence his journey in mortality with the benediction of God upon him."[333]

Jesus also modeled the method by which we are to receive the ordinance of baptism when he was baptized. Jesus' baptism is recorded in the following Biblical verses:

And John was clothed with camel's hair, and
with a girdle of a skin about his loins; and
he did eat locusts and wild honey;
And preached, saying, There cometh one mightier
than I after me, the latchet of whose shoes I am
not worthy to stoop down and unloose.
I indeed have baptized you with water: but he
shall baptize you with the Holy Ghost.

*And it came to pass in those days that Jesus came from
Nazareth of Galilee and was baptized of John in Jordan.
And straightway coming up out of the water,
he saw the heavens opened, and the Spirit
like a dove descending upon him:
And there came a voice from heaven, saying, Thou
art my beloved Son, in whom I am well pleased.*

– MARK *1:6-11 KJV*

The person who performs the baptism or any other ordinance must have the authority to perform the ordinance.

*The person who is called of God and has authority
from Jesus Christ to baptize, shall go down into the
water with the person who has presented himself
or herself for baptism, and shall say, calling him or
her by name: Having been commissioned of Jesus
Christ, I baptize you in the name of the Father,
and of the Son, and of the Holy Ghost. Amen.*

– DOCTRINE AND COVENANTS *20:73*

I told the story of my baptism at the beginning of this book, which is how I became a member of The Church of Jesus Christ of Latter-day Saints. The feeling I received from baptism is indescribable and permanently inscribed upon my memory. I literally became a new person in Christ. The old natural man "died" and the new man was "born" with a cleansed spirit. I can tell you that baptism works. I am a very different (and much better) person in so many ways.

When we are baptized, we take on the name of Christ and covenant to live righteously. Baptism symbolizes Jesus Christ's death, burial, and resurrection, and it also represents the end of our old lives and the beginning of our new life as one of His disciples.

THE GIFT OF THE HOLY SPIRIT

The Godhead is comprised of God (Heavenly Father), Jesus (the Only Begotten Son), and the Holy Spirit. God gave us the Holy Spirit as a spiritual companion to guide us through this life. The Holy Spirit instructs us and helps us grow as we travel along our journey on Earth. He speaks to us with a still, quiet telepathic inner voice and shows us that God knows us and that God loves us. As we have noted before, these messages from the Holy Spirit are called "promptings" to do something or not to do something. Some people refer to them also as "impressions." When we do not heed these promptings or impressions, we usually regret it. God shows that he loves us by sending us special occurrences that can only be explained as God's grace.

The more we trust in God, Jesus, and the Holy Ghost the more these "grace occurrences" will happen, if we obey God's laws. The Holy Ghost can reside with us always after we are baptized and confirmed if we obey all of God's laws.

The Holy Spirit is also called the Holy Ghost. "In the scriptures the Holy Ghost is referred to as the Comforter (see John 14:16–27 KJV; Moroni 8:26), a teacher (see John 14:26 KJV; D&C 50:14), and a revelator (see 2 Nephi 32:5). Revelations from the Father and the Son are conveyed through the Holy Ghost. He is the messenger for and the witness of the Father and the Son," says David A. Bednar.[334]

You can receive the Holy Spirit yourself through an ordinance performed at church whereby those who have authority from God can impart to you the "gift" of the Holy Spirit, through the power of the Almighty, by the laying on of hands – this is the ordinance of Confirmation. This is the only manner to receive the Holy Spirit so that it can reside with you on a continuous basis. Otherwise, the Holy Spirit can only remain with you for short periods of time. This explains why I noticed intervention of the Holy Spirit only sporadically in my life prior to being baptized and "confirmed." Now the Holy Spirit is always with me.

HOPE

When you start to live your life righteously, you will begin to have hope for a brighter future. You will start to see life in a whole different way. On its face, this is a cruel world. Things always seem to go wrong. Nothing ever seems to make you happy for very long. Sometimes you may look around you and wonder, "Is this all there is?" I know I did that on many occasions in my life. If you follow the formula given to you above, that is, to (1) repent, (2) get baptized, (3) receive the Holy Spirit, and (4) start to live a life more in alignment with what Heavenly Father desires, then you can develop a sense of hope for your earthly life – and the afterlife.

What does this mean?

- It means that you will feel that you are never alone. God will hear your prayers.
- It means that you will be confident that life's challenges can be overcome. God will help you, or He will send someone to help you. You just have to be patient because sometimes it takes God a little time to create the circumstances where you can receive the help you need. In the meantime, it is your job to "do your best – God will do the rest." For example: Once we were obliged to move suddenly to a neighboring town, two months after I underwent major surgery. I prayed to God for strength and for help. Many members of our church helped to load the moving van. However, only two men were available to help us unload the van, and one of these men had a sensitive back. Shortly before we arrived at the new house, I received a text message from someone who identified himself as "Jed" a member of our new church, and he offered to help unload the truck. Jed was not a big man yet we noticed that he was extremely strong. He did an amazing amount of work. He was even able to carry a heavy wardrobe box full of clothes and hangers up to the second floor by himself. Elaine gave each of the wonderful men who helped us load and unload the truck

a copy of one of the books she had written as a gift, but Jed had bidden us goodbye before she could give him a copy. So we brought the book to church the next Sunday, but we were unable to find him. No one seemed to know who he was. We asked the presiding Bishop if he knew Jed, he said, "No I do not. Maybe he is an angel." We asked a former Bishop if he knew Jed, he said, "I do not. Maybe he is an angel." We certainly felt that he was God sent, not only for us, but also for the member of our old church who had a sensitive back.

* Hope means that, instead of seeing life as a one-way street that ends in death and nothing else, you will see that your spiritual self has an eternal future living with Heavenly Father, your loved ones, and all the other hosts of heaven.

When that realization comes to you, you will be able to enjoy your life that much more no matter what happens.

Doubters will not experience proof of the power of prayer unless they (1) pray, and (2) study the *Bible* and *The Book of Mormon*.

SERVICE TO OTHERS (ALSO CALLED CHARITY)

Everybody can be great...because anybody can serve. You do not have to have a college degree to serve. You do not have to make your subject and verb agree to serve. You only need a heart full of grace. A soul generated by love.

- MARTIN LUTHER KING, JR.

One way to energize your spiritual journey is by giving service to others. If you are a Boy Scout, you already know this principle.

When you serve others, you become a disciple of Christ, fulfilling his will. As you help others, you will feel the love inside your heart for the ones you are helping. This is the Holy Spirit in concert with you, helping others – especially the poor and needy. It is very pleasing to God. You will find that your capacity will increase to enable you to accomplish more than you would have been able to before.

The other aspects of charity are:

* Patience
* Sharing of your time – calling your grandparents – reading a bedtime story to a sibling or cousin – playing catch or shooting hoops with a sibling or a neighbor
* Understanding
* Listening
* Careful counsel
* Feeding the hungry
* Visiting the sick
* Keeping a journal for your posterity
* Completing ordinances in a Temple for your ancestors who have passed so that they can be reunited with you
* Sharing the gospel of Jesus Christ

> *He saith unto him the third time, Simon, son of Jonas,*
> *lovest thou me? Peter was grieved because he said unto*
> *him the third time, Lovest thou me? And he said unto*
> *him, Lord, thou knowest all things; thou knowest that*
> *I love thee. Jesus saith unto him, Feed my sheep.*
>
> *– JOHN 21:17 KJV*

SPIRITUAL HAPPINESS AND THE PLAN OF HAPPINESS

In an earlier chapter, we spoke mainly about the happiness of a "temporal" or earthly nature. Many people realize that even when they find what they call success, they are still not truly happy. Earthly happiness can only take you so far.

In this section, we will talk about Spiritual Happiness, and specifically The Plan of Happiness.

Spiritual happiness comes from:

* Obeying God's Laws
* Being grateful for Jesus's atoning sacrifice
* Being of service to other people
* Discovering for yourself your mission here on earth (a Patriarchal Blessing, which is a message from God that is transmitted through a church member who has been called to be a Patriarch, is a helpful guide for the rest of your life), and
* Following the Plan of Salvation, which is also called the Great Plan of Happiness and Our Eternal Life.

Please check our website http://www.elevateyourselftomanhood.com/videos for the availability of the video, *Our Eternal Life* and read the transcript below which describes the Plan of Happiness thoroughly – it is awesome!

"We live in a world that never seems to stand still. Each day technology advances. Information moves across the globe. People die. Children are born, and life continues on. Most of us have wondered at some point in our lives, what is the point? What is the purpose of it all?

"In today's fast-moving world, it is easy to feel lost and alone. Lots of us think we are on a dead-end journey with no real destination or that there is no help to get us there. Have you ever wondered why you are here, where you were from, and where you were going? These three questions have crossed the minds of many people all over the world.

"We'd like to tell you that there is a purpose to your life. We call it God's Plan of Salvation, or the Great Plan of Happiness. This simple plan will answer many of your questions.

"Let's start with the first question: Where did we come from? We lived with God as spirits before we came to earth. We call this our premortal life. God, our Heavenly Father, is the father of our spirits. We are all brothers and sisters and part of His family.

"Next we came here to earth. So why are we here? Coming here was part of God's plan of happiness. First we came to get a physical body. When we came to this world, our spirit joined together with our body. To experience all the joy that Heavenly Father wants us to have, we need to have a physical body.

"We are also here to gain experience that we could not obtain in any other way. This would include being tested by making choices. If we continually make good choices, we can prepare to live with God again. So God's plan for us here on earth is fairly simple--to find happiness by gaining experience, getting a body, and by proving ourselves to Him.

"Eventually, we all die. Death separates our spirits from our bodies and is one of the obstacles that keeps us from living with God again. However, we will not be "dead" forever. Part of God's plan includes the resurrection when our spirit will reunite with our body. Rest assured that just like birth, death is another step in our eternal journey.

"The other obstacle that separates us from God is sin. Sin is when we do something that we know is wrong. Because of our sins, we cannot live with God again. Heavenly Father knew that we would make wrong choices and sin. He knew that we would die. So to overcome sin and death, Heavenly Father sent His Son, Jesus Christ.

"Jesus Christ was the first person to be resurrected, and through His divine power, all of us will be resurrected and live again. Jesus Christ also suffered for our sins and made it possible for us to repent and to be forgiven. Repentance is as simple as turning away from our sins and changing our hearts. If we repent and follow Jesus's example, we can become clean and live with God again.

"Knowing that God has not left us alone to wander through this life has brought great peace and joy into our hearts. We hope that you will find the same happiness that we have by considering God's plan for you." [335]

THE SPIRITUAL DESTINY OF OUR COUNTRY

The story of America gives me great comfort and makes me realize that our country is unique and specially blessed. The founding fathers of our country were all giants of spirit. *The Declaration of Independence* was founded in a spiritual context.

Ezra Taft Benson said, "The Declaration of Independence is much more than a political document. It constitutes a spiritual manifesto—revelation if you will—declaring not for this nation only, but for all nations, the source of man's rights. Nephi, a prophet in *The Book of Mormon*, foresaw over 2,300 years ago that this event would transpire. The colonies he saw would break with Great Britain and that 'the power of the Lord was with [the colonists],' that they 'were delivered by the power of God out of the hands of all other nations' (1 Nephi 13:16, 19). The Declaration of Independence was to set forth the moral justification of rebellion against a long-recognized political tradition—the divine right of kings. At issue was the fundamental question of whether men's rights were God-given or whether these rights were to be dispensed by governments to their subjects. This document proclaimed that all men have certain inalienable rights. In other words, these rights came from God."[336]

I now know that God did not want there to be a king at the head of the United States of America because when Jesus comes to reign on earth, the seat of His government will be in the United States, and He will be the Lord and King of all nations.

In their book, *The Miracle of Freedom: Seven Miracles that Saved America*, Chris Stewart and Ted Stewart bring this message home by pointing out that only 5% of the world's populations, including all the people who have ever lived, have lived in freedom. The United States is one of the rare countries in which people enjoy freedom. How fortunate are we?

Chris Stewart and Ted Stewart ask, "Did God intervene to save us? Did He intend for us to serve as an example of democracy and freedom to the rest of the world?"

They assert that "the evidence is overwhelming. At critical points in our history, when the odds were stacked against us, God has provided miracles to assure this nation's survival." Specifically, *Seven Miracles that Saved America* explores these seven events:

1. Christopher Columbus's unlikely discovery of the New World
2. The miracle at Jamestown that led to the English colonists' survival
3. The Battle of New York during the Revolutionary War, in which an inexplicable fog allowed George Washington and his army to escape the advancing British troops
4. The miraculous creation of the United States Constitution
5. The miracle involving Abraham Lincoln and Gettysburg, in which God answered the president's desperate prayer
6. The unlikely scenario that played out in the Battle of Midway during World War II paving the way for the allies to win the war
7. The miracle that saved the life of President Ronald Reagan, who went on to play a major role in defeating Communism337

We all need to pray that God will help us preserve our freedom, but God can only assist us if we follow His laws. If we are to set an example to the world, we must as a nation become morally straight which will then enable us to have moral authority and the power of God.

A good example is Joan of Arc, who led the French to victory against the British in the 15th century, by encouraging the men under her leadership to repent and to obey God's laws. God rewarded the French with incredible victories. In one battle three French soldiers died while three thousand British soldiers died.

Many of us do not realize how very fortunate we are to live in a country where people enjoy freedom. As a former military officer,

I am saddened for anyone who has lost a son or a daughter to war. War is dreadful. I am also very thankful for the sacrifice that so many soldiers around the world have made to preserve freedom. Thanks be to the soldiers and thanks be to God.

CREATION AND EVOLUTION

"I myself am convinced that the theory of evolution, especially the extent to which it has been applied, will be one of the great jokes in the history books of the future. Posterity will marvel that so flimsy and dubious an hypothesis could be accepted with the incredible credulity that it has."

MALCOLM MUGGERIDGE JOURNALIST AND PHILOSOPHER, PASCAL LECTURES, UNIVERSITY OF WATERLOO, ONTARIO, CANADA

Within the scientific debate about creation versus evolution lies the truth about God. Does God exist or does He not exist? Belief in Creation leads one to believe in God. Belief in Evolution does not necessarily preclude someone from believing that God exists, but it does lead many people to believe that what is written in the *Bible* is only symbolic. Although Jesus used symbolism in the stories/parables, He told his followers to avoid persecution, not all aspects of the *Bible* are merely symbolic. Many people would like to think that the *Bible* is only symbolic because they want to do whatever they please, which generally means not obeying God's commandments - many of these same people have never read the *Bible*. So let's keep an open mind and explore this debate because you will not have the opportunity to study both Creation and Evolution in school. Exploring new ideas along your quest, especially those ideas that have the potential to enlighten you, is certainly worthwhile. You can make up your own mind because God has given you agency.

How do you think the first humans came to be on Earth? Do you believe God created them as the *Bible* says? Or do you believe humans evolved from apes? Or rocks? If you think that we evolved from apes or rocks, then where did these apes and rocks come from in your opinion? Did an amoeba, a single-celled organism in a pond, decide to become an ape? We say, No. God created each <u>kind</u> of animal.

Do you believe God created Earth, the animals, plants and humans, the universe including the planets, moons, stars, galaxies, and constellations? Or do you think they were the result of the "big bang," which also created Earth?

How you answer these questions and what your beliefs are towards these issues will prove most important in your life. How you come to understand the origins of man will determine your worldview, your spiritual identity, and the direction of your life.

These are only some of the questions you will encounter and will need to grapple with when you think, read, or hear about the "creation versus evolution" issue. Each one of us humans will need to discover our own answers to these questions. Each of us should contemplate the origin of humans, the earth, and the universe. It's only logical that one would want to know where we came from, what we're doing here, and where we're going when we die.

<u>So What Is the Big Disagreement?</u>

Most head-to-head arguments around evolution and creationism give a person the sense that if you believe in evolution, then you cannot believe in creationism, and vice versa. Very few people see where these two camps can overlap or support each other. People who believe in evolution say that creationism is anti-science and silly. Creationists say that evolutionists are God-less because they do not believe the *Bible*'s account of Creation. Some creationists believe that evolutionists lack morals because they do not believe in God.

In this book, we do "take sides" in this argument. We believe that Creation is the truth so we provide you with supporting information from the creationists' side of the argument – information that you may have never received before. We do this because you have probably been brainwashed all your life about evolution in the school system. As part of your growth, we want to give you a PROPER CHANCE of coming to your own conclusion in the matter.

Dr. Kent Hovind Ph.D. is a former high school science teacher. He taught science for fifteen years and is a creationist. Hovind shared his experience in Russia while giving a lecture on Creation Versus Evolution at a university. In the audience, one of the professors was crying. Dr. Hovind asked his interpreter why the professor was crying. The interpreter answered saying that the professor had never heard the Creation Story before – that all his life, he had only been taught evolution.[338]

Dear reader, my heart also cries for you. I fear that you are in the same boat as this Russian professor whose heart was burst open with joy for finally hearing the truth – a truth his heart knew when he beheld the wonders of nature and studied the wonders of nature but to which his mind had been deprived for so long. Our society has similarly systematically brain-washed our youth so that they can only believe in evolution. Young minds have been brainwashed since kindergarten or even as babies, and they are ignorant of the noble truth of creation. They have never been taught the beautiful Creation Story either in school or in church?

Our public schools enthusiastically teach evolution with all its trappings and misconceptions, but not Creation! Some teachers have sued schools to be able to teach Creationism to their students, but the courts (Peloza v. Capistrano School District – 1994) would not allow it.[339] The Supreme Court has also blocked the teaching of creationism in schools (Epperson v. Arkansas - 1968). The court says that it violates the First Amendment to the U.S. Constitution because teaching creationism would violate the separation of church and state. These unfortunate interpretations of the law may have prevented you – our precious reader – from learning the truth about Creation.

It is important to note the differences among macroevolution, microevolution, and creationism. Evolutionists believe in macroevolution and microevolution, but they do not believe in creation. People who believe in creation also believe in microevolution, but they do not believe in macroevolution.

It stands to reason that, before we can decide what to believe when there is controversy, we need to learn about the subject at hand. Otherwise people can pull the wool over our eyes to keep us from seeing the truth. Thus we would remain naïve and vulnerable. Strong men are wise – they can express their beliefs with truth and conviction. In order to become educated and wise, one must keep an open mind and seek the truth.

Macroevolution means changing, through evolution, from one kind to another. For example if an ape evolved into a man, that would be macroevolution.

We do not believe that macroevolution occurred in the past. Nor do we believe that macroevolution happens in our time today. Nor do we believe that macroevolution will ever occur in the future.

Scientists who believe in macroevolution usually believe in the Big Bang theory; and believe that life developed from rocks or amoebas– for example, that birds came from dinosaurs; and, do not believe that God created anything. These scientists have led the public to believe a host of misconceptions, which are still being taught in schools.

Scientists who believe in Creation know that the Big Bang Theory is a tall tale at best, or the adversary's (satan's) way of deterring people from knowing the truth about God's creation.

Scientists who believe in Creation and microevolution agree with evolutionists – that microevolution means evolutionary changes within a kind. For example, if you breed two dogs of different breeds, they give birth to a dog which may have different characteristics from the parents, but it will still be a dog - not a frog or an apple, as evolutionists would have us believe.

And God made the beast of the earth after his kind, and
cattle after their kind, and every thing that creepeth upon
the earth after his kind: and God saw that it was good.

– Genesis *1:25 KJV*

465

Donell Cox & Elaine J. Barbeau Cox

During the thousands of years that humans have recorded history, amoebas and apes have always been basically the same. Humankind has not observed them developing into other kinds of animals. Generally, organisms and animals produce their own kind, with slight variations. Slight variations due to interbreeding within the same species, such as breeding dogs of different breeds, have generated new breeds that can reproduce but they are still dogs under the umbrella of the species *Canis familiaris.*

Evolution could not have created the variety of species we know exist today because when animals of different species mate, most offspring, called hybrids, cannot reproduce, such as the offspring of a horse and a donkey, which is called a mule. The reason that animals from different species cannot reproduce an offspring that can reproduce is because they have different chromosomal structures. Furthermore, many hybrid animals suffer from health problems and a poor quality of life. The Institute for Creation Research (ICR) gives more evidence (below) that evolution could not produce higher-order organisms:

The ICR in the article *The Natural Direction of Life Is Degeneration Not Evolution*, explains, "Mutations (producing hybrids) lead to the loss of genetic information and consequently the loss of genetic potential. This results in what is termed "genetic load" for a population of organisms. Genetic load is the amount of mutation in a kind of organism that affects its fitness for a particular environment. As genetic load increases, the fitness decreases and the organism progresses towards extinction as it is unable to compete with other organisms for resources such as food and living space."[340]

Evolutionist have for centuries falsely led generations to believe that humans evolved from apes. This has never been observed. There is no scientific evidence or fossil record to support this archaic theory. Zero. Zip. Zilch. Nada. So why is this theory being taught in schools?

Jeffrey P. Tomkins, Ph.D., in his article for the Institute for Creation Research (ICR) *New Research Debunks Human Chromosome Fusion* explains, "Humans and great apes differ in chromosome

466

numbers—humans have 46 while apes have 48."[341] This shows defini-tively that man could not have evolved from apes.

What about plants? God created many different kinds of plants including the sweet scented tiny lilies-of-the-valley and the awesome giant sequoias. There is an enormous difference between these plants. Look at a sweet little lily and then com-pare it with the giant sequoia. The Giant Sequoias and Museum website states, "the largest tree on Earth, the undisputed King of the Forest, the General Sherman tree is not only the largest liv-ing tree in the world, but the biggest living organism, by volume, on the planet. The most famous giant sequoia (Sequoiadendron Giganteum), named "General Sherman," is:

* 2,100 years old
* 2.7 million pounds
* 275 feet tall
* 100 feet wide at its trunk"[342]

This massive organism stands in testament to the Creation. It is interesting to note that trees that look similar, such as the giant se-quoias and the giant redwoods, have significant differences. The Giant Sequoias and Museum website also tells us that, "While they are mem-bers of the same family, redwoods and sequoias are actually different species, and distinct in many interesting and fascinating ways! Both also require very specific, though very distinct, climates to survive."[343]

All of this diversity did not evolve from one little amoeba in a pond. God in His infinite wisdom planted the sequoias and the red-woods where they would thrive.

What about the earth? Do you believe God created the earth? Or do you believe the earth was formed from the Big Bang?

How old do you think the earth is? Billions of years old? Millions of years old? Or thousands of years old?

Creation is the belief and the science which supports the fact that the earth, the heavens, and all things - living and non-living - were created by God.

Evolutionists claim that creationists ignore science or do not believe in science, but they are wrong. Creationists believe that God also created science and encouraged man to explore and understand the creation so that they could draw closer to Him.

In the words of the website, Creation.org, "Creationists contend that it is actually we who are standing on the side of science, against religious beliefs that would hold us back. We recognize firstly that there *must* have been a Creator (God). Just as any car must have had a designer even more so life on Earth shows evidence of incredible built-in design."[344]

Americans grew up watching Bill Nye "The Science Guy" on his immensely popular educational television shows. It turns out that Nye is a staunch evolutionist and firmly believes in all the things that evolutionists typically believe: that man evolved from apes, that the universe was created by the Big Bang, and other such theories.

The following is a summary of the "logical discussion" that Bill Nye and Dr. Hovind had to prove that the theory of macroevolution is also a religion and that it is not based on science, as students in schools and in universities are falsely led to believe. From the YouTube video titled: *Dr. Kent Hovind Obliterates Evolutionist Bill Nye!*[345]

Dr. Hovind stated evolutionists believe that the Big Bang exploded from nothing 20 billion years ago and that 4.6 billion years ago the rocks cooled down, it began to rain, which made a soup, and something found something to marry and something slowly evolved into everything we see today.

"Dr. Hovind asked the professor, 'Where did all of the matter come from?'

"The professor answered, 'We do not know.'

"Dr. Hovind asked the professor, 'Who gave the universe the laws of centrifugal force, gravity, and inertia that govern the universe?'

"The professor answered, 'I do not know.'

"Dr. Hovind asked the professor, 'Where did the energy to make this Big Bang come from?'

"The professor answered, 'I do not know for sure.'

"Dr. Hovind stated, 'The law of Conservation of Angular Momentum is such that if a spinning object breaks apart, all of the fragments will spin in the same direction.'

"The professor stated, 'Yes I am aware of the law of conservation of angular momentum.'

"Dr. Hovind said, 'Evolutionists state that the Big Bang began as a swirling dot. Why do two of our planets spin backward?'

"The professor said, 'That's interesting.'

"Dr. Hovind said, 'That's kind of hard on your Big Bang theory. Not only that but six moons are spinning backward.' He asked the professor, 'Why?'

"The professor said, 'I do not know.' The professor then asked Dr. Hovind, 'Why do you think they are going backward?'

"Dr. Hovind said, 'I was hoping you were going to ask that. If I told you that God created Heaven and the Earth as the *Bible* teaches, you're going to ask, 'And where did God come from?' Then I will say, 'I do not know.' But you said, 'I do not know. I do not know for sure.' (many times) No sir, do not tell me that what I believe is religion and that yours is science. No sir, they are both religion.'"

From the conversation above, you can begin to see some of the many questions that are unanswerable in evolution "theory" – if you can even call it a theory. We say that evolution is a "religion" because it requires belief in something that occurred when none of us were around to witness it first-hand. If we use science as the mediator, then creationism wins because science supports creation more than it supports evolution.

Why do schools allow the religion of evolution to be taught while God and Creation are forbidden? Why do textbooks contain much evolutionary literature that supports the false teachings of the man-made religion "macro" evolution?

There are still lots of people who do not know the Creation story, which is – literally - the first information the *Bible* offers. The *Bible* is also a history book. History is studied in schools, therefore, the *Bible* should be given equal time. Millions of people who have read the *Bible* know that the Creation story is true – including many scientists. For anyone to understand our origins, they must know the Creation Story. I strongly urge you to read the entire Creation Story in the Book of Genesis in the *Bible* for yourself and ponder it in your heart. Also, consider the scientific facts in this chapter supporting creation.

THE CREATION STORY

In the King James Bible, Genesis 1:1 reads, "In the beginning God created the heaven and the earth."

You should know that Creation took place about 6,000 years ago and took six days to complete. The first 31 verses of Genesis Chapter 1 provide the day-by-day events of each Creation Day:

Creation Day 1: God created the heaven and earth. The earth was initially without form and was dark. He created light and called the light "Day" and the darkness "Night."

Creation Day 2: God created the firmament and separated the waters. God named the firmament Heaven. Firmament is atmosphere or sky.

Creation Day 3: God gathered together the dry land and called it Earth. He gathered together the water and called them seas. On this day, God created the grasses, herb yielding seed, and fruit trees yielding fruit and their seeds.

Creation Day 4: God created lights in the firmament to give light to the earth. He also created the sun, moon and stars to indicate day, night, signs, seasons, days, and years.

Creation Day 5: God created sea creatures and fowls.

Creation Day 6: God created beasts, cattle, and "everything that creepeth upon the earth." God also made man and woman on this sixth and final day of creation.

Day 7: God rested from His work. This is known as the Sabbath Day. In the Ten Commandments, we are commanded to "Remember the Sabbath Day and keep it holy" which means we are not to labor on the Sabbath Day. We are to spend time doing things like worshiping God, spending time with family or friends, visiting the sick, and writing in our personal journals.

It would be best to do your homework on Friday evenings so that you can enjoy the rest of the weekend, and abide by God's law - to keep the Sabbath Day holy. Of course at times there are extenuating circumstances. Some people, such as nurses and doctors, must work on the Sabbath to support themselves and their families – though they do not work every Sunday.

The Creation Story flies in the face of evolutionists, as we will see later. Some scientists are still hard at work trying to disprove creationism and prove evolution theory, but so far no hard evidence has been given to prove evolution.

CAUTION: In this section, when we speak of "evolution," we must be mindful to remember that there are different kinds of evolution, as we have previously mentioned. Also remember, for the sake of having a debate, that in this part we use the word "evolution" the way that most people use the word evolution, including the theory that man evolved from apes, or birds evolved from dinosaurs, which is more precisely macroevolution, and other forms of evolutionary theory which we will discuss later: Cosmic Evolution, Chemical Evolution, Stellar and Planetary Evolution, and Organic Evolution. To be clear: WE DO NOT AGREE WITH ANY OF THESE THEORIES. On the other hand, to confirm once again, we support the concept that certain members of a species may change slightly between generations but basically they retain the appearances and functions associated with that particular kind of species, which is

called microevolution. Everyone agrees that microevolution is true: therefore, there is no need to discuss it in this segment.

In order to further understand the origins of man and the study of evolution, you will need to know about the Great Flood, which is also mentioned in the *Bible*. As noted previously, evolutionists dispute the account of the biblical creation, but there is little dispute that the Great Flood really happened. What evolutionists fail to acknowledge is the effect of Noah's flood on the topology of the earth and the fossil deposits. We will talk more about that later. For now, let's take a look at the story of The Great Flood as documented in the *Bible*.

The Great Flood

About 1,600 years after the Creation, the human race had multiplied greatly, but there was much wickedness in the world. The earth was corrupt and full of violence. Things became so bad that God began to regret having made man. The *Bible* says:

> *"5 And God saw that the wickedness of man was*
> *great in the earth and that every imagination of the*
> *thoughts of his heart was only evil continually.*
> *6 And it repented the Lord that he had made man*
> *on the earth, and it grieved him at his heart."*
> *7 And the Lord said, I will destroy man whom I have*
> *created from the face of the earth; both man, and*
> *beast, and the creeping thing, and the fowls of the*
> *air; for it repenteth me that I have made them.*
>
> *– Genesis 6:5-7 KJV*

You should, of course, read the biblical account of The Flood for yourself (Genesis 6:9 – 9:17 KJV). A condensed version follows:

God decided to destroy all humanity on Earth because of the rampant evil. The only people on Earth at that time who were faithful to

God were Noah and his family, so God decided to save them so that they could replenish the earth after the flood was over. Remember how the waters first covered the earth on Creation Day 2? God decided to restore the earth back to its previously watery condition and start over again. (In essence, the earth would be baptized or "born again.") So he asked Noah to build an ark and collect two of every kind of animal. He did not need to collect fish or other reptiles or mammals capable of surviving in water because there would be plenty of water on the earth.

The ark was huge. The *Bible* says the ark was 450 feet long and 45 feet high. The *Bible* uses "cubits" for its measurements. A cubit was the length of a man's arm from fingertips to elbow.

The ark had space for a large number of animals. The Bible specifies that Noah took two of "every kind" of animal on the ark. Some scientists contend that "every kind" does not necessarily mean "every species." This reduced the number of animals needed to replenish the earth to a much smaller number. Noah was given young males and young females of every **kind** of animal because they would take up less space than fully-grown animals. The animal population on the ark included mammals, birds, reptiles, and amphibians.

This is where the story gets interesting. Since you were a baby, you have been taught that dinosaurs lived "millions" of years ago. That would mean that the earth was millions of years old. That would also mean that the creation story we told you before was not true because we also told you that Creation occurred about 6,000 years ago. But we have reason to believe that dinosaurs were present during Noah's time and that some baby dinosaurs were on the ark along with the other animals![346] In recent years, scientists have been shocked to find dinosaur soft tissue from T. Rex bones dug up in Montana.[347] The article *Dinosaur Shocker* published on Smithsonian.com describes, "a tiny blob of stretchy brown matter, soft tissue from inside the leg bone, which suggests the specimen had not completely disintegrated as science would suggest. We say that this proves that this dinosaur is not 68 million-years-old as the article states, but much, much younger. Anyway, back to the story of the Great Flood.

Torrential waters flowed from beneath the earth and also from above for forty days and forty nights, filling the earth with water. The *Bible* tells us that this was a global flood. The floodwaters lasted 150 days, after which the waters started to recede. After the seventh month, Noah's Ark came to rest somewhere upon Mt. Ararat in Turkey (Genesis 8:4).

This is all documented in the *Bible*. If it all sounds too simplistic, keep in mind that God, The Omnipotent, has all power and He assisted Noah and his family in designing and constructing the ark, compelled the animals to appear at the ark in the appropriate pairs, and helped to manage the animals while onboard.

It is interesting to note that many cultures throughout the world have recorded oral histories of a Great Flood occurring. I am certain that if my grandparents had been Noah and his wife and had told me that they had experienced such a catastrophic event I would tell my children and grandchildren and they would likely tell their children and grandchildren and so on for many generations because so many people died and our ancestors were chosen by God to live. Long ago, there were fewer distractions than we have today – very few people were able to read and write and the printing press to print books had not been invented. For these people telling historical stories, and current stories orally was a crucial means for teaching and acquiring knowledge. In Jesus' time, his disciples recorded what Jesus had taught them by hand on scrolls, these scrolls were hidden until they were compiled to print Bibles.

Henry M. Morris, Ph.D. in his article *Jesus and the Flood* explains how Jesus, who had the power to heal the sick and raise the dead, gave testimony that the Bible's account of the Great Flood is true:

"For as in the days that were before the flood they were eating and drinking, marrying and giving in marriage, until the day that Noah entered into the ark, And knew not until the flood came, and took them all away; so shall also the coming of the Son of man be" (Matthew 24:38-39 KJV).

"The Lord Jesus Christ not only believed in the special, recent creation of all things by God (note Mark 10:6-8 KJV), but also in the worldwide Flood of Noah's day, including the special preservation of life on the Ark. The Flood in which He believed was obviously not a "local flood," for He compared it to the worldwide future impact of His Second Coming.

"Neither was it a 'tranquil flood,' nor a 'selective flood,' for Jesus said, 'the flood came, and destroyed them all' (Luke 17:27 KJV). It is clear that He was referring to--and that He believed--the Genesis record of the great Flood! There it says that the whole earth was 'filled with violence' (Genesis 6:13 KJV), having first been filled with people, and that the resulting world-cleansing deluge was so cataclysmic that "every living substance was destroyed which was upon the face of the ground, both man, and cattle, and the creeping things, and the fowl of the heaven; and they were destroyed from the earth" (Genesis 7:23 KJV). Indeed, "the flood came, and took lliterally `lifted'l them all away.

"This is what Jesus said, and what He believed, and therefore, those who are truly His disciples must also believe this. The destructive effects of the Flood can still be seen today, not only in the Biblical record, but also in the abundant evidences of cataclysmic destruction in the rocks and fossil graveyards all over the world. To refuse this evidence, as do many modern intellectuals, can only be because they 'willingly are ignorant,' as Peter said in referring to this testimony (II Peter 3:5 KJV)."[348]

Fewer scientists now dispute The Flood, and they are now grappling with understanding how this "catastrophic deposition" of geological material affected the earth.

Scientific evidence now proves the feasibility of the Great Flood. Deborah Netburn reported on November 21, 2015, on the Los Angeles Times website that scientists updated the calculation for underground water beneath the earth's crust. In her article, she said that Tom Gleeson, a hydrogeologist from the University of Victoria in British Columbia, Canada and his team reported that there are 6 quintillion gallons of groundwater in the upper 1.2 miles of the Earth's crust. This water, if spread out over all the continents, would amount to about 600 feet of water – or twice the height of the Statue of Liberty.[349] It is worth mentioning that the waters on which Noah sailed was not simply rain water. Vast amounts of the Great Flood waters spewed up from the depths of the earth.

*In the six hundredth year of Noah's life, in the second
month, the seventeenth day of the month, the same
day were all the fountains of the great deep broken
up, and the windows of heaven were opened.
And the rain was upon the earth
forty days and forty nights.*

GENESIS 7:11-12 KJV

This is critical information because acknowledgment of The Flood affects the way we understand fossils and sediment layers. Most critically, textbooks used in school to teach evolution do not take the Great Flood into account. These texts are frequently outdated and were written by evolutionists who refuse to believe in creation and other historical accounts recorded in the *Bible*, thereby teaching students incorrect information.[350]

WHAT CREATIONISTS BELIEVE

As we have mentioned, Creationists believe the *Bible* and the scientific evidence that supports the *Bible*. They subscribe to the Biblical account of Creation and The Flood. They believe in God and they believe in SCIENCE, which God also created. God created science so that man could learn to develop the world, control disease, grow healthy food to feed multitudes of people, and to learn to understand the universe and the nature of God.

Creationists believe that the human race, the earth, creatures, and plants are only about 6,000 years old – as opposed to 4.5 billion years old, which evolutionists want us to believe. Be aware that many evolutionists are essentially self-proclaimed atheists and do not want others to believe in God.

How they can deny the scientific evidence that the Earth and the universe are only about 6,000 years old, as accounts from the *Bible* teach us, is beyond me. It is truly exasperating. The Institute for Creation Research (ICR) has an animated video *Evidence from the Physical*

Sciences, which explains scientific proof that our universe and Earth are young. The following is a portion of the transcript from the video:

> "As the moon orbits the Earth its gravity pulls on the oceans causing tides. As tides pull on the moon they cause it to move about an inch and a half away from the Earth each year. That means that about 6,000 years ago the moon would have been about 800 feet closer to the Earth. If the Earth and moon were 4 billion years old they would be touching and that wouldn't have been good."[351]

As a college freshman taking my first courses in physics and engineering, I was immediately astounded by the symmetry and logic between physics, mathematics, music, and other sciences. Later in life, as I studied anatomy and physiology, I was dumbstruck by the graceful complexity of the human body. As the recipient of miracles in my life, I cannot deny my Creator. Once we come out of our fog, we can immediately see the hand of God in all things. We can know in our hearts and heads that God is the Designer and Creator.

Speaking of hearts – did you know that there are many heart-shaped lakes on the earth? Did God make these heart-shaped lakes to let us know that He loves us?

There is such order and beauty in the world that He created for us. Molecules are all strictly ordered. There is order between men and women – generally women are physically weaker than men – if it were not so many men would likely expect women to bear children and do all of the heavy lifting, too. God planned that men and women would share the load of creating a home and a family. Also, God created differences between men and woman to create more joy in the world, as when men and women lift their voices to sing. The harmonies created by great choirs such as the Mormon Tabernacle Choir (Consider the Lilies and Love One Another are marvelous); Metro Singers (Someday, and Walk Together Children are amazing); Morgan State University Choir; the U.S. Naval Academy Glee Club; U.S. Air Force Academy Cadet Chorale; the Harlem Gospel Choir; the

Trinity College Choir; and singers like Andrea Bocelli and Celine Dion singing The Prayer are all a testament to God's design, and creation.

As we mentioned before in the Creation Story, God created the heaven and the earth (Genesis 1:1 KJV).

We are also taught in the *Bible* that Jesus, before he came to the earth as a man, assisted God in creating Earth and the universe.

> *For by Him [Jesus] all things were created that are in*
> *heaven and that are on earth, visible and invisible,*
> *whether thrones or dominions or principalities or powers.*
> *All things were created through Him and for Him.*
>
> – COLOSSIANS *1:16 KJV*

Creating Earth was a colossal miracle that many people take for granted every day.

From latter-day revelation, we now know further details about the creation. We now know that God's action was that of an architect-first creating the earth on a conceptual and spiritual level, then having His son, Jesus, physically create or act as the builder of the earth. In a Brigham Young University speech titled *Christ the Creator*, Mark E. Petersen stated:

> ... Almighty God was the Creator, and he has revealed the truth about the origin of life and all else in creation. He himself says, "And worlds without number have I created; and I also created them for mine own purpose; and by the Son I created them, which is mine Only Begotten" (Moses 1:33). Then it was through Christ that the Creation came to be.[352]

Everything you see in nature is beautifully, colorfully, and intricately designed. Take a look at plants, animals, and especially humans. As you learn more about the human body, you will see how astonishing it is. The human eye has over 137 million electrical connections within one square inch wired directly to the brain. A person would be a fool to think that this was not part of an intelligent design.

Creationists believe that if there is intelligent design, then there must be an intelligent designer (God).

The great Albert Einstein, in his book *The World As I See It*, said, ". . . The harmony of natural law . . . reveals an intelligence of such superiority that, compared with it, all the systematic thinking and acting of human beings is an utterly insignificant reflection" (p. 267-68).

As previously mentioned, creationists support microevolution. Essentially, all of the different animals that came forth from the first kinds of animals, which survived the Great Flood on Noah's Ark, developed through microevolution – BUT THEY REMAINED THE SAME KIND OF ANIMAL. Creationists believe that the greater part of evolution "theory," macroevolution, is illogical and that it contradicts the *Bible*. Actually "evolution" does not qualify scientifically as a theory, because each year the information changes and scientists seem to go back to square one. Evolutionist – through constant discoveries in science – to their dismay, are playing "catch up" with the *Bible*. But this is a game that they cannot win.

Humans are commanded by God to learn the truth and to be able to answer those who question the validity of the scriptures and the things that Christians believe. That is why we are arming you with this knowledge. You need to know the truth about your human origins. Then you will be able to properly answer those who will inevitably challenge you about whether you believe in evolution or creation:

> *But sanctify the Lord God in your hearts: and be ready*
> *always to give an answer to every man that asketh you a*
> *reason of the hope that is in you with meekness and fear:*

> — 1 PETER 3:15 KJV

We are expected to study the scriptures to learn the truth about all things so we can attain ammunition and defenses for the war of words, which will ensue. The words of non-Christians turn to action as we see that Christianity is being assaulted on an increasing basis each year – Jesus Christ's birth is no longer celebrated in schools. Christ the Creator of our world and His creation are not discussed in school.

Creationists believe in Jesus Christ. There are many historical accounts that Jesus lived. We study other historical figures. We ought to study about Jesus and his creation and about his life.

The majority of people in the U.S. would like their children to be taught about Jesus. In 2004, Bootie Cosgrove-Mather reported in CBS News that the results of a poll taken in the U.S. indicated that 65% of all Americans favored schools teaching creationism and evolution.[353] This is honorable, it would be educational, and it would benefit our children. However, as we have seen lobbying governments for this cause has not worked because governments insist upon separating religion and state, which seems to be a double standard when considering that much of what is being taught in regards to evolution is false doctrine. Essentially, it is a false religion. Interestingly, the poll also revealed that only 13% of Americans believe that people evolved and that God did not guide the process.

Solution:

Young man, if you want to learn more about creation and other historical and spiritual truths, be proactive, go to church and read the Holy Scriptures. If you want your children to learn more about creation and other truths take them to a church that offers Sunday School lessons, and share the Holy Scriptures with them. It just takes a little planning, and a little sacrifice – such as not sleeping in on Sunday mornings. You can do it. The reward will be an enriched life for you and your family.

Proof that Jesus Christ truly existed is not only mentioned in the *Bible*; He is mentioned in other history books, such as *The Book of Mormon*, including 25 times with great respect, in the Quran. The website Islam101offers the following information on the subject:

"CHAPTER 2: JESUS IN THE QURAN
"CHRISTIANS UNAWARE
"The Christian does not know that the true spirit of charity, which the Muslim displays, always, towards Jesus and his mother Mary spring from the fountainhead of his faith- the Holy Quran. He does not know that the Muslim does not take

the holy name of Jesus, in his own language, without saying Hazrat Eesa (meaning revered Jesus) or Eesa alai-hiss-salaam i.e. (Jesus peace be upon him).

"Every time the Muslim mentions the name Jesus (pbuh) without these words of respect, he would be considered dis-respectful, uncouth or barbaric. The Christian does not know that in the Holy Quran Jesus (pbuh) is mentioned by name five times (5x) more than the number of times the prophet of Islam is mentioned in the Book of God. To be exact - twenty-five times as against five."[354]

WHAT EVOLUTIONISTS BELIEVE

The fear of the Lord is the beginning of knowledge:
but fools despise wisdom and instruction.

PROVERBS *1:7 KJV*

If you believe that life developed on its own, or the universe came about through a giant explosion, you are considered an evolutionist. As previously mentioned, evolutionists also believe that the earth, human beings, creatures, and plants evolved over millions or billions of years.

Some people take the middle ground and say that their belief in evolution does not mean they do not believe in God. They think that God created life through macroevolution. This concept contradicts the literal words of the *Bible* and current scientific evidence.

We do not believe that all that we call "life" could have evolved from low-level organisms or from inanimate objects like rocks. In the words of Mark E. Peterson in his article *Christ the Creator*, "Now note what the scripture says about the origin of life, which so many believe was but a spontaneous chemical reaction from inanimate objects . . . under no cir-cumstance did life ever spring from nonlife—not ever from any inanimate substance. Zero plus zero equals zero; no life plus no life equals no life."[355]

WHAT IS EVOLUTION ANYWAY?

If someone wants to talk to you about evolution, you need to first understand what kind of evolution they are talking about. The word "evolution" has many meanings, but only one of the meanings is actually scientific:

1. Cosmic Evolution – the theory that time, space and matter came into existence all by themselves or as the result of the Big Bang. **(This has never been observed.)**
2. Chemical Evolution - the theory that all the higher chemical elements originated from hydrogen, the simplest element. **(This has never been observed.)**
3. Stellar and Planetary Evolution – the theory that the planets and stars originated from space dust. The fact is that no one has ever seen a star form. **(This has never been observed.)** Boyle's Law will not allow dust to congeal into a solid star.
4. Organic or Naturalistic Evolution – the theory that matter created itself - that all life sprang from non-organic material like rock. Do you truly believe that your ancestors were rocks? **(This has never been observed.)**
5. Macroevolution – the theory that life developed from rocks and that one kind of animal can change into another kind of animal, e.g., reptiles changing into birds or mammals. **(Nothing like this has ever been observed.)**
6. Microevolution – variations developing within a species - such as in *Canis familiaris*, which is the scientific name for the species "dog," in that breeds of dogs develop within the species. **This is the only scientific evolution and the only kind of evolution that has actually been observed.**

Shocking Fact: As a student, you have been brainwashed into believing the "evolution theory" in ALL its forms. Here's how it is done. First, you are taught about microevolution (#6 above); then you are led to believe that all the other types of evolution are valid too!

This is not true. "Evidences" for evolution presented in the past have all been refuted, except for microevolution.

> *"Scientists who go about teaching that evolution is a fact of life are great con-men, and the story they are telling may be the greatest hoax ever. In explaining evolution, we do not have one iota of fact."*

DR. T.N. TAHMISIAN, A PHYSIOLOGIST FOR THE
ATOMIC ENERGY COMMISSION, USA

EVOLUTION LIES THAT SCHOOLS ARE TEACHING STUDENTS

When I grew up, neither evolution nor creationism was taught in school. Society took the *Bible* at its word, so there was no need to teach creationism in school. We believed the Book of Genesis when it said that "God created the heavens and the earth."

We do not object to schools teaching evolution, however, we object to students being lied to about evolution. When teaching students about the origins of the earth and about the origins of the people, animals and plants who inhabit the earth it would be wise to relate the historical account of creation as told in the *Bible*. It would also be wise to learn the differences between microevolution and macroevolution as we will study in more detail here.

EVOLUTION MISCONCEPTIONS IN TEXTBOOKS

Dr. Kent Hovind, Ph.D., - as previously mentioned - a high school science teacher for fifteen years, created a video series on Creation and Evolution.[356] He scoured through student textbooks and identified "evolution lies" being taught to students. The list below contains some of the more common misconceptions about evolution. The list is not exhaustive, but it contains evolution theories such as the Big Bang theory which I mentioned earlier:

Misconception #1: *The Grand Canyon was created by the Colorado River through erosion over millions of years.*

The Truth: The Grand Canyon was created by the biblical flood. Geologists are now reversing their theories and coming to a consensus that the Grand Canyon was created by Catastrophic Deposition. According to John D. Morris, Ph.D., the sedimentary layers in the Grand Canyon were caused by "water-related processes operating at increased rates and intensities in the past. Evidence of underwater turbidity currents is found in the Tapeats Sandstone, the Redwall Limestone, and others."[357]

Nathan Jones, in *The Christ in Prophecy Journal*, wrote that when Mount Saint Helens erupted in 1980, a canyon was created overnight that looks like Grand Canyon. It didn't need to take millions of years to form.[358]

Misconception #2 *The reason why the missing link between apes and humans still persists is that evolution happened so fast.*

Evolutionists contradict themselves. On the one hand they state that evolution was a very slow process, and when they cannot explain something or have no evidence that evolution occurred as they would have liked to believe, they simply state that it happened fast and did not leave any evidence.

The Truth: Evolutionists have not found any fossil records that show that apes evolved into men.

Misconception #3 – *Carbon dating measures the age of fossils.*

The Truth: Carbon dating, which was invented in 1940, can measure the quantity of Carbon 14 in a specimen, and the rate of decay. However, it cannot tell us when something first existed because we do not know the exact amount of C14 it had originally. Also, the specimen could have been contaminated by other sources of carbon 14.

Dr. Andrew A. Snelling, in his October 2010 article *Carbon – 14 Dating, Understanding the Basics,* in Answers Magazine, does a very thorough job of explaining the science behind carbon dating. He concludes his article with the following:

". . . And because the half-life of carbon-14 is just 5,730 years, radiocarbon dating of materials containing carbon yields dates of only thousands of years, not the dates of millions and billions of years that conflict with the framework of earth history provided by the *Bible*, God's eyewitness account of history."[359]

Another example of carbon-14 dating errors: "Lava flows in New Zealand were shown dated at 275,000 years old, when in actuality those lava flows were made in 1949."[360]

Misconception #4 – *"Natural selection," (the getting rid of weakness in a species), created new species.*

The Truth: Hovind's analogy explains why this concept is a lie. If you worked in an automobile factory and got rid of every defect in the cars produced, would you ever produce an airplane? In other words even if only the strongest plants survived they could never have produced an animal. Besides how would many plants have survived without bees to pollinate them? God created all kinds of plants, kinds of animals and humans in a short period of time because they live in ecosystems that are interdependent.

*Let no man deceive himself. If any man among
you seemeth to be wise in this world, let him
become a fool, that he may be wise.
For the wisdom of this world is foolishness with God. For
it is written, He taketh the wise in their own craftiness.*

– 1 CORINTHIANS 3: 18-19) KJV

Note: This scripture means it is better to know the truth about something and be called a fool than to believe lies and be called wise.

Misconception #5 – *Charles Darwin proved the "theory of evolution" when he studied birds on the Galapagos Islands and concluded that they all had a common ancestor.*

The Truth: Yes, the birds on the Galapagos Islands did have common ancestors – two birds – a male and a female. Darwin had discovered <u>microevolution</u> (not macroevolution). He had discovered that over time, different breeds of birds had evolved – but note: THEY WERE STILL BIRDS. Much like when breeders of dogs manage to create a new breed of dog today by breeding two dogs of different breeds. However, Darwin's theory did not prove the origin of the initial male and female bird on the Galapagos Islands – they certainly did not come forth from amoeba, or plants or from fish – for in the thousands of years of recorded history that has never been ob-served because it is scientifically impossible. It was God who created the birds, which were likely decedents of the birds kept on Noah's ark.

Misconception #6 - *That the famous "Geologic Column" shows earth's history through layers of rocks and index fossils is an accurate representation of Earth's evolution.*

The Truth: Charles Lyell, a Scottish lawyer - wrote the book *Principles of Geology* in 1830. He is responsible for creating the Geologic Column, which is totally inaccurate. Each layer of rock is given a name (such as Palaeozoic, Mesozoic, Cenozoic), and an age with a corresponding fossil index. It was thought that these layers represented millions of years. This was done before there was any way to date geological structures us-ing carbon dating techniques. The Geologic Column is the bible for evolutionists. It can only be found in one place in the world - in the textbooks! A principal factor that rips apart the Geological Column is the discovery of tall, petrified trees (de-picted in a photograph in *Bob Jones Earth Science* p. 306) that run through many layers of sediment. Had they been covered a little at a time they would have rotted before another layer of sediment covered another section of their trunk.

Another truth concerning the geologic column is that scientists currently use strata of soil and rocks to date fossils. But wait. They also use fossils to date strata of soil and rocks! This is circular reasoning and, therefore, impossible to resolve. Even the famous evolutionist Niles Eldredge says, "Paleontologists cannot operate this way. There is no way simply to look at a fossil and say how old it is unless you know the age of the rocks it comes from and this poses something of a problem: if we date the rocks by their fossils, how can we then turn around and talk about patterns of evolutionary change through time in the fossil record?"[361]

If millions of years of evolution were true, then how were mammoths preserved in "muck" in areas of barren Siberia where no mountains stood from which erosion could have occurred? The answer lies in the fact that layers of soil were created through catastrophic events, such as the Great Flood that is mentioned in the *Bible*, volcanoes erupting, and earthquakes. Layers of soil were created <u>suddenly</u> not over millions of years.

Misconception #7 - *Human embryos growing in their mothers' wombs have "gill slits."*
   The Truth: Hovind states, "Those little folds of skin are not gills. Those little wrinkles under your chin when you are growing up (in the womb), grow into bones in your ear and glands in your throat. They never have anything to do with breathing."

Misconception #8 – *Birds evolved from dinosaurs.*
   The Truth: If a dinosaur's egg hatched a bird, where did its mate come from? It takes a male and a female to produce offspring.

Misconception #9 - *The human tailbone is vestigial, and when humans evolved we lost our tails.*

The Truth: You can easily understand that it would have been "handy" for us to have a tail to hold onto things, especially when we find that we do not have enough hands. Why would we have wanted to lose our tail?

Misconception #10 – *Dinosaurs lived millions of years ago.*
The Truth: On Creationism.org we found some compelling arguments to support the existence of dinosaurs during the time our ancestors lived. There are historical accounts of dinosaurs (dragons) in many countries. Humans and dinosaurs, like man and tigers today, lived in different areas. That is why there are few records of human remains, and dinosaur remains in the same archeological dig.

The Institute of Creation Research sheds more light on research projects where both human and dinosaur tracks appear together. Dr. Morris points out that "In the last ten or fifteen years, however, many scientists and laymen alike are waking up to the fact that much solid scientific evidence exists that contradicts evolutionary notions. One of the most shattering pieces of evidence comes from the Paluxy River basin in central Texas, near the town of Glen Rose, where fossilized tracks of man and dinosaur appear together."[362]

The ten misconceptions mentioned above are just a short list that evolutionists have been peddling for over a century. There are more "evolution" concepts that have already been shown to be false. Even more will be revealed as science becomes more sophisticated.

IRREDUCIBLE COMPLEXITY
We like to use the concept of irreducible complexity as an example to show that God created us just as we are and that we did not evolve from apes, rocks, plants, or anything else. Take our eyes for example.

According to the article, *Reverse Engineering the Brain*, by John K. Stevens in Byte Magazine the retina of the eye has 137 million electrical connections within one square inch wired directly to the brain. ". . . it would take a minimum of 100 years of Cray [supercomputer] time to simulate what takes place in your eye many times every second," says Stevens.[363],

Human eyes are amazingly complex and could not have evolved from light-sensitive patches of skin as evolutionists might have you think. If you removed one or more of the components of the eyeball, I think that you would have serious issues seeing properly, no? This is just common sense.

In his book, *Darwin's Black Box: The Biochemical Challenge to Evolution*, Michael Behe defines irreducible complexity:

"By irreducibly complex I mean a single system composed of several well-matched, interacting parts that contribute to the basic function, wherein the removal of any one of the parts causes the system to effectively cease functioning. An irreducibly complex system cannot be produced directly (that is, by continuously improving the initial function, which continues to work by the same mechanism) by slight, successive modifications of a precursor system, because any precursor to an irreducibly complex system that is missing a part is by definition nonfunctional. An irreducibly complex biological system, if there is such a thing, would be a powerful challenge to Darwinian evolution."[364]

Neurosurgeon Ben Carson points out that the kidneys and eyes have components that are useless without all the other components. So, these "useless" components should have been dropped if we "evolved." He deduces, "According to the theory of evolution, it is impossible for any complex component to exist unless it just spontaneously formed overnight. That sounds crazy to me, but then again, if you believe matter can form from non-matter, then I guess you can believe that an eyeball can form overnight."[365]

Of course an eyeball spontaneously developing overnight has never been observed because it never happened. The fact is that God created a whole man and a whole woman with fully functioning eyeballs - namely Adam and Eve, who are our ancestors.

EVOLUTIONISTS DO NOT USE THE SCIENTIFIC METHOD

In order to prove that macroevolution is true, for example, that apes have evolved into a man or that they have a common ancestor, scientists or evolutionists would need to use the Scientific Method. If you have taken any science class in high school, you probably know the Scientific Method. The scientific method provides a way of asking and answering scientific questions by making observations and doing experiments. When using the scientific method we follow these steps:

1. Ask a question or come up with an idea about something.
2. Do the background research through observing the phenomenon and by collecting data.
3. Construct a hypothesis.
4. Test the hypothesis by experimentation.
5. Analyze the data from the experiment and draw a conclusion.
6. Communicate the results of the experiment to allow others to validate findings.

In the recipe above, one would ideally want to observe apes evolving into humans. Well, no one has actually ever observed apes evolving into humans, nor has any viable evidence ever been produced to show that man evolved from apes. This has not been shown to be true scientifically.

No viable evidence has been produced that shows that the earth, stars, moon, sun, planets, or galaxies were produced from a "big bang." It cannot be classified even as "theory" according to the Scientific Method because it has not been observed. It is all conjecture. So if you assume these things to be true, you are mistaken.

These things are all lies perpetrated upon the public by "macroevolutionists" who seek to discredit the *Bible*. When giving talks or writing papers, they cite facts about microevolution, which are true, and they hope that you will not notice the lies they tell concerning macroevolution. It's pretty clear what Jesus meant when He told us about the creation of men and women:

"But from the beginning of the creation
God made them male and female."

– MARK 10:6 KJV

He made man directly as a man – not as an ape to evolve into a man millions of years later.

As new discoveries are made, it seems that science is providing proof of the Creation. The Creation Museum in Petersburg, Kentucky houses numerous other examples of science helping to prove Creation. This is exciting!

We present this information to you so you can study it and use your agency - "your own best judgment," as my dad would always tell me. You need to be able to discern fact from fiction to decide which teaching, creation or evolution, has the most plausible historical account of the origins of the universe, the earth, and mankind – loving Creators, or a Big Bang.

As for me, I bet my life and my eternal life on these things, which are taught in the *Bible* and by Christians who are well-educated scientists. We firmly believe that God and His Son, Jesus, created the heaven and earth as stated in the *Bible*.

WHY IT IS IMPORTANT TO BE A CREATIONIST INSTEAD OF AN EVOLUTIONIST

I cannot overstate the necessity for you to study carefully and come to an understanding of these issues. Each year the theory of evolution changes due to new scientific discoveries. We believe that these scientific discoveries will only further the case for creationism as God pulls away another layer of the onion skin.

After studying all the information available, you must make your choice because your life actually does depend on your choices.

Here are five good reasons to be a creationist:

1. It feels good to be on the side of truth – the winning side! As the *Bible* says, "Prove all things; hold fast that which is good." 1 Thessalonians 5:21 (King James Bible)
2. Your choice will influence whether or not you seek to know God, Jesus, and the Holy Ghost.
3. Your choice will influence whether or not you abide by God's laws.
4. Your choice will influence who you choose to be your friends.
5. Your choice will influence who you will marry and how you will raise your children.

BE RESPECTFUL AND KIND WHEN DISCUSSING EVOLUTION VERSUS CREATIONISM

In our discussions with others about this topic, we need to remember to be loving, kind, and respectful to each other as we delve deeper into the subject – instead of attacking each other. Neither should we mock those with whom we disagree. As my mother taught me, "If you don't have anything nice to say, don't say anything at all." In the corporate world, I learned to make only comments – during meetings - that were additive to the ongoing conversation. To do otherwise would be frivolous, time-wasting, and unprofessional.

The ideas and beliefs you develop about evolution or creation will have a tremendous impact on your life. You will need to decide for yourself what you believe, but you will need to take a stand – on one side or the other.

You may want to educate family and friends about Creation, and teach children about Creation in Sunday School, as well.

WHAT HAPPENS TO YOUR SPIRIT WHEN YOU DIE?

It is our prayer that you will live a happy and hearty life for 100 years or more, but each of us, whether rich or poor, will eventually die, hopefully, from natural causes when our time is up on this earth. As a young man, you probably do not think of this eventuality too much, but it is certainly a topic that you should keep in mind. Young people die unexpectedly, too, from violence, disease, or accidents. Being aware of your mortality enables you to focus on making the most of each day and it enables you to start early in life to prepare your spirit for the afterlife. A very basic question you might ask is, "What happens when I die?" In short, your body becomes lifeless and begins to decay or decompose back to its natural elements. In this chapter, you will learn that your spirit will separate from your body and continue to live on - in the Spirit World.

In the Spirit World, there are two destinations:

(1) Paradise – a place of immense love and joy, and
(2) Spirit Prison – a place of immense unhappiness and misery.

No one knows the time and date of their death on this earth. At least we ought not to know, for that would likely mean planned suicide, which is against God's laws. We can decide - here and now - where we would like our spirit to go when we die, and govern ourselves accordingly while we are still living.

WHAT IS THE SPIRIT WORLD LIKE?

As we already mentioned, Paradise is a place of immense joy and happiness, while Spirit Prison is a place of immense unhappiness and misery. The destination at which your spirit arrives will be determined by your spiritual status here on Earth at the time of your death.

Essentially, if you obey God's laws, your spirit will go to Paradise. If you disobey God's laws, your spirit will go to Spirit Prison.

Just as God has a perfect plan for everything in this world from atoms to the universe, he has a perfect plan for the afterlife. Just as there are criteria to fulfill when you apply for a job, or apply to get into college, or attend a grand ball, there are also criteria to meet in order to be accepted into Paradise. People with evil intent or who have committed sins will not be admitted, unless they have repented, been baptized as Jesus was baptized, and have received the Holy Spirit by the laying on of hands. People who have chosen not to believe in God and Jesus will not be admitted. These decisions are strictly up to each person to make.

Brent L. Top, the author of *Life After Death: 6 Insights into the Spirit World*, wrote the following:

> "Clearly ancient prophets had some understanding of the spirit world. In the Old Testament, the author of Ecclesiastes wrote that after we die we "return unto God" (Ecclesiastes 12:7 KJV). Jesus, speaking to the thief on the cross, said, "Today shalt thou be with me in paradise" (Luke 23:43 KJV). Peter clearly taught that Christ went to preach the gospel in the spirit world (see 1 Peter 3:18–20; 4:6 KJV). But these ancient prophets don't give us any description of what the spirit world is like or where it is."[366]

Top says that through the revelation of latter-day prophets more truths about the spiritual realm have been revealed. I would like to point out eight lessons spoken about in this article and from teachings of church leaders:

1. **The Spirit World is Right Here on Earth**. Our loved ones who lived righteously here on Earth and have since passed away are now in Paradise. They are living close beside us in a dimension that we cannot see. They are among us. They can see us and can help to guide us. This brings to my mind the true life story told in the movie *The Cokeville Miracle*. The events in the movie occurred in real life on May 16, 1986. Our children

and grandchildren were inspired by this movie. We encourage you to watch it. **Check out the trailer for this movie on the** *Elevate Yourself to Manhood* **website http://www.elevatey-ourselftomanhood.com/videos.**

2. **Spirits are active even after the body dies**. Says Top, "Spirits continue to be interested and intimately involved in the Lord's work on both sides of the veil." The Veil is the invisible barrier that separates the living from the dead. Our ancestors help to guide us here on the earth, and they also teach the gospel to those who are in Spirit Prison. Spirits who were not righteous on Earth (they did not obey God's laws) go to Spirit Prison when their body dies.

3. **When we die, we retain our spiritual talents and quali- fications gained here on Earth.** Wilford Woodruff says, "The priesthood and offices we hold in this life go with us into the spirit world. We engage in the same types of service and ministry there that we use our priesthood for here." The Priesthood, in general, is the authority given to man to act for God. Every man ordained to any degree of the Priesthood has this authority delegated to him.

4. **Your spirit will eventually have a "Life Review" after your body is dead.** The results of your Life Review will determine your permanent (eternal) status. We all must pay for our sins committed here on Earth, that is, unless we repent of them. Sins are committed when we disobey God's laws. If we have repented of our sins, obeyed God's laws, and we have received all of God's ordinances we will be among the First Born at the First Resurrection. Then we will live with Jesus here on a per- fect earth during the Millennium for 1,000 years, during which time we will perform work for our dead ancestors who did not accept the gospel while on earth but have repented, and now wish to do so. By repenting in the name of Jesus Christ, our sins are forgiven and the stain of sin is washed away from us. We are made new again. We have the opportunity to repent of sins while we are alive. It is much better to repent while you

are alive rather than waiting until you die and find yourself in Spirit Prison. Once in Spirit Prison, you will need to wait for some undetermined amount of time before you have the opportunity to hear the gospel and repent. After that you will need to be baptized and confirmed, and receive other special ordinances by proxy by one of your living relatives on Earth prior to your Life Review at the Second Resurrection. Keep in mind that if you die before receiving these ordinances you will have the agency to accept or reject the work that your family members will be willing to do for you, so that you can be released from Spirit Prison, but you may have to wait a long time. It is explained in Top's article that "when we repent, the Atonement of Jesus Christ cleanses and purifies us; we are made new creatures. So, yes we will have a life review, but the life review will be of the new creature, or the new life that Christ has created in us." I can testify to you that when I repented, was baptized and confirmed in 2011, I felt brand new and I lost all desire to sin. There were many sins for which I needed to repent. Also, I quit drinking alcohol and coffee before my baptism in accordance with the Word of Wisdom. Weaning myself off caffeine took six months but I was determined to do so. For a while I had withdrawal headaches and other symptoms, but now I choose to no longer take these substances. That is not to say that I do not still have the occasional urge for a glass of Cabernet Sauvignon or Merlot. That is not to say that I do not desire a cup of my favorite Café Con Leche (Mexican coffee), Café Sua Da (Vietnamese coffee), or just a plain old Starbucks sometimes. Since being baptized and confirmed with the Holy Spirit, I have truly become a new person. Also, since then, I have been sealed to my wife for "time and eternity" in the Holy Temple by a Sealer who holds the authority to seal couples, which gives me the privilege to be among the First Born at the First Resurrection. As mentioned above – the First Resurrection will mark the beginning of the Millennium where Jesus will live on Earth again with us – this time for 1,000 years, in peace and harmony. During that time, our spirit will return to Earth in its resurrected state, from Paradise to reside within our new resurrected bodies. Our body will not be corruptible, as our current bodies are. We will have perfect Gloried Bodies built to last an eternity. We will feel no pain.

5. **What will the spirit world look like to us?** The Spirit World and our earthly world resemble each other to a large degree. It was revealed to the Prophet Joseph Smith, "That which is spiritual [is] in the likeness of that which is temporal; and that which is temporal in the likeness of that which is spiritual." (*Doctrine and Covenants*, Section 77). Top cites another past president of the church, Brigham Young, as saying that the spirit world will appear to us just as natural as the current world does, however, "it will be suffused with "inexpressible glory." Top jokingly says that, "earthly life might be compared to regular television as it was first invented, and the spirit world is more like high-definition television, enhanced with incredible resolution and beautiful detail."

6. **How will we travel? Communicate?** Brigham Young, in his description of the Spirit World said that we will be able to move or travel at extremely high speed. In the *Journal of Discourses*, Young said, "As quickly as the spirit is unlocked from this house of clay, it is free to travel with lightning speed to any planet, or fixed star, or to the uttermost part of the earth, or to the depths of the sea, according to the will of Him who dictates."[367] I imagine that to mean faster than light speed – more like the speed of thought. If we decide to go someplace, we can arrive there instantaneously. "These realizations," Brigham Young said in *The Teachings of the Presidents of the Church*, "furnish a fine illustration of the ability and power of the Almighty. When we pass into the spirit world we shall possess a measure of this power."[368]

7. **Enhanced Communication**. Elder Orson Pratt spoke extensively about how we will be able to communicate with angels and with each other with ease in the spirit world – without using

the spoken language of our current earthly state, but with a sort of mind-to-mind and spirit-to-spirit communication in the spirit world. In this medium, Pratt suggests that spirits are able to perceive vast amounts of information from many sources all at the same time and to have a much deeper perception than men in their mortal state. There, he informs us, communication is not dependent on vibrations, sound waves, and human ears.[369] Top reports that in his research he came across people who had near-death experiences and who spoke about telepathic communication while in the spirit world.

8. **Enhanced Learning**. Top says, "There is another aspect of this enhanced capacity of righteous spirits in the spirit world that I really look forward to — increased ability to learn and retain knowledge. President Brigham Young stated, 'I shall not cease learning while I live, nor when I arrive in the spirit-world; but shall there learn with greater facility.' Orson Pratt explained this ability by declaring: 'Instead of thinking in one channel, knowledge will rush in from all quarters; it will come in light like the light which flows from the sun, penetrating every part, informing the spirit, and giving understanding concerning ten thousand things at the same time; and the mind will be capable of receiving and retaining all.'"

How truly amazing the Spirit World must be!

Top concludes, "These are but of a few of the teachings of prophets and apostles about the spirit world. They are like snowflakes on the tip-top of the iceberg. The more I study and learn about the spirit world, the more it enriches my life. Our knowledge of what it will be like then and there helps us to know what we should be like here and now. Gospel insights about dying teach us a great deal about living."

If we are to receive the blessings of living in Paradise and during the Millennium, we must obey God's commandments while we live on physical Earth. It will definitely be worth the effort.

BEWARE OF EVIL IN THE WORLD AND CHOOSE THE RIGHT

WARNING: Evil is real in this world. But, how did evil begin? How did it enter the world? The *Bible* teaches us that evil started with a war in heaven.

Gordon B. Hinckley, one of the religious leaders in the United States who met with President George Bush shortly before the president addressed the nation after the attack on the World Trade Center on September 11, 2001, stated in a General Conference address:
"

And there was war in heaven: Michael and his angels fought against the dragon; and the dragon fought and his angels,

"And prevailed not; neither was their place found any more in heaven.

"And the great dragon was cast out, that old serpent, called the Devil, and Satan, which deceiveth the whole world: he was cast out into the earth, and his angels were cast out with him.

"And I heard a loud voice saying in heaven, Now is come salvation, and strength, and the kingdom of our God, and the power of his Christ" (Rev. 12:7–10). ...

"From the day of Cain to the present, the adversary has been the great mastermind of the terrible conflicts that have brought so much suffering.

"Treachery and terrorism began with him. And they will continue until the Son of God returns to rule and reign with peace and righteousness among the sons and daughters of God.

"Now, brothers and sisters, we must do our duty, whatever that duty might be. Peace may be denied for a season. Some of our liberties may be curtailed. We may be inconvenienced. We may even be called on to suffer in one way or another. But God our Eternal Father will watch over this nation and all of the civilized world who look to Him. He has declared, "Blessed is the nation whose God is the Lord" (Ps. 33:12). Our safety lies in repentance. Our strength comes of obedience to the commandments of God.

"Let us be prayerful. Let us pray for righteousness. Let us pray for the forces of good. Let us reach out to help men and women of goodwill, whatever their religious persuasion and wherever they live. Let us stand firm against evil, both at home and abroad. Let us live worthy of the blessings of heaven, reforming our lives where necessary and looking to Him, the Father of us all. He has said, 'Be still, and know that I am God' (Psalms 46:10 KJV)."[370]

The story below illustrates how these evil spirits work, by creeping upon us, little by little, to cause us to be unhappy, to tempt us to make wrong decisions, and for some of us who are unaware of their subtle ways – destroy our righteous spirit, and keep us from blessings that Heavenly Father has in store for us.

As the old story goes, if you put a frog into a pot of boiling water, it will leap out right away to escape the danger. But, if you put a frog in a pot that is filled with water that is cool and pleasant, and then you gradually heat the pot until the water starts boiling, the frog will not become aware of the threat until it is too late. The frog's survival instincts are geared towards detecting sudden changes.

This story illustrates how people can be led astray into evil. Before they know it, they can become addicted to alcohol, drugs, porn, or gambling. They can find themselves living a life of crime, which can ruin their lives, and the lives of others. It begins with small degrees of wrong choices, a little marijuana, a few drinks of alcohol, a couple porn movies, a poor choice of friends, and so on. That is why choosing your leisure time activities and friends are so critical. Choosing the wrong friends and the wrong leisure time activities can lead you into the "frog's pot" - or put another way - the "slippery slope into the dungeons of evil."

Philip Zimbardo the author of *The Lucifer Effect: Understanding How Good People Turn Evil* states in a TED talk: "Evil is the exercise of power to intentionally, harm psychologically, hurt physically, destroy mortally or spiritually, or commit crimes against humanity."[371]

CHOOSING THE RIGHT

When you choose to do the right thing, it has a compounding effect – in little increments you become a healthier, stronger, righteous man – positively influencing your wife and children, your community, and your nation. When millions of young men choose the right, along with you, you become a force with which to be reckoned. By obeying God's commandments, choosing your friends wisely, choosing to care for your mind, your body, and your spirit, you save yourself, your family and society from the frog's hot pot, which is the devil's grip.

There are many human beings who have demonstrated the power of the good:

* Thomas Garret, a Quaker abolitionist, saved 2500 African Americans from slavery and death through the "underground railroad," to the safe haven Canada. He did so over a 40-year period. Is so doing he risked his own life again and again. His actions showed a deep and lasting commitment to choosing what was right. The movie "Freedom," illustrates this well.
* Joan of Arc a 19-year-old ordinary farm girl liberated France from British tyranny. Her story illustrates how the power of God guided her. The movie Joan of Arc, which originally aired on BYUtv, November 26, 2015, is compelling.[372]
* Marquis de Lafayette a wealthy French aristocrat was 19 years old, when he chose to help General George Washington win the Revolutionary War against the British.
* Millions of young men who fought in the Revolutionary War, the American Civil War, World War I, and World War II, also chose the right – and every time the right won. Historically, the most righteous usually prevail.
* Irena Sendler – worked as a plumber in Nazi camps. She smuggled out and saved 2500 Jewish children.
* Nicholas Winton a 29-year-old London stockbroker who wrote *The Power of the Good* – saved 600 Jewish children from Nazi Germany.

- Oskar Schindler was a businessman who saved the lives of 1200 Jews. Schindler's List a movie directed by Steven Spielberg illustrates this story well.
- Joseph Smith, an ordinary 14-year-old farm boy chose the right even though he was persecuted for following God's guidance. Joseph founded The Church of Jesus Christ of Latter-day Saints, and restored the original gospel of Jesus Christ to the earth. He was martyred when he was 38 years old. The LDS church now has 15,000,000 members in 150 countries.
- Mother Teresa of Calcutta, a Catholic nun spent 69 years of her life loving and caring for some of the poorest people on earth. Catholic on-line reports: "Hundreds of thousands of people from all classes and all religions, from India and abroad, paid their re-spects. ...Presidents, prime ministers, queens, and special envoys were present on behalf of countries from all over the world."[373]

If you judge people, you have no time to love them.

(MOTHER TERESA)

Kind words can be short and easy to speak,
but their echoes are truly endless.

(MOTHER TERESA)

If you can't feed a hundred people, then feed just one

(MOTHER TERESA).

The lyrics to the song below illustrate how the Holy Spirit guides us when we choose the right. In order to exercise your ability to be a mentor, you may want to share the song *Choose the Right* with your younger siblings and or younger cousins.

Song: *Choose the Right*

Choose the right when a choice is placed before you. In the right the Holy Spirit guides. And its light is forever shining o'er you. When in the right your heart confides. (Chorus) Choose the right! Choose the right! Let wisdom mark the way before. In its light, choose the right! And God will bless you ever more.

Choose the right! Let no spirit of digression. Overcome you in the evil hour. There's the right and the wrong to ev'ry question; Be safe thru inspiration's pow'r.

Choose the right! There is peace in righteous doing. Choose the right! There's safety for the soul. Choose the right in all labors you're pursuing. Let God and heaven be your goal.

Text: Joseph L. Townsend, 1849-1942Music: Henry A. Tuckett, 1852-1918

TITHES AND OFFERINGS

One of the many blessings in my life is the privilege of paying tithes. When I was a young boy, I remember my Aunt Lois's unpopular mantra about paying tithes to the church and how blessings would flow from that. Nobody I knew paid tithes, except for Aunt Lois. In the *Bible*, we are taught that we should give 10% of our earnings (10 cents of every dollar) to God, for He has given us so much. This money, in turn, is used for spreading the gospel of Jesus Christ by printing the Bible and The Book of Mormon, maintaining the church's website, and building churches and temples. In the Church of Jesus Christ of Latter-day Saints members also give a "fast offering" once a month. Family members (8-year-olds and above) will skip eating two meals (breakfast and lunch) on the first Sunday of the month, and they will offer as a fast offering the money they would have spent on those two meals, in order to help members in need and for victims of disasters, such as the victims of Hurricane Katrina.

Soon after becoming a member of the LDS church I began to tithe, and I thought of my Aunt Lois's testimony. I can attest that there is great power in doing so.

The Law of Tithing requires sacrifice. If you obey the law of tithing, you will receive blessings far greater than anything you ever give up. The commandment for tithing is mentioned in the *Bible* where the prophet Malachi teaches us:

"Bring ye all the tithes into the storehouse, that there may be meat in mine house, and prove me now herewith, saith the Lord of hosts, if I will not open you the windows of heaven, and pour you out a blessing, that there shall not be room enough to receive it"

– MALACHI *3:10 KJV*

The expression "windows of heaven" refers to the many blessings that the Lord has promised you when you pay tithing – even if you have only earned a very small amount of money, and you give ten percent of that sum. As you obey this law, the Lord will bless you both spiritually and in worldly means.

In my mind, tithing and offerings are similar to giving service to others. We are asked to give of our time, talent and treasure to God.

What has God given us, you may ask? He has given us:

* Our life
* Our bodies
* The gospel
* This earth
* Our sun
* Our moon and the stars
* The food we eat
* Mountains
* Oceans

- Beautiful flowers of every color
- Beautiful animals of every color
- Beautiful people of every color
- Physically strong men
- Wise men
- Perceptive women
- Gentlewomen
- Sweet children
- An ability to love
- An ability to learn
- An ability to create music
- An ability to sing in wonderful harmonies
- An ability to dance
- A good sense of humor
- An ability to wonder
- An ability to have gratitude
- And so much more

So, God deserves 10% of our earnings. I love God and Jesus who have done so much for us.

BE ON YOUR GUARD ABOUT "NEW AGE" RELIGION

As a young man of fourteen, spreading my spiritual wings searching for "truth", I stumbled upon a book about what was then called "the occult." This is what New Age was called back then. Being young and naive, and having been raised in a Christian church (Methodist), I was fascinated by the contents of this "secret knowledge" as the title had suggested. Reading this book led me into a wide array of "mystic" philosophies, into which I delved ever so deeply. At about this same age, I was introduced to masturbation, too. Perhaps you can imagine how quickly my young, hormone-driven life plunged into two obsessions: new age thinking, and sex. Christian values I had been taught did not seem to be able to corral the intensity of my carnal and spiritual sensibilities and the direction I was headed.

At eighteen, after enrolling in college, I found myself spending a disproportionate amount of my study time in the library poring over the entire collection of New Age books, as they were by then formally called. New Age had become my religion and it had taken over my life. I began to judge people by their "sign" and tried to figure out life through the lens of New Age thinking. Eventually, I got into some of the "black arts" of the occult when, at 20, I was confronted by divine intervention - a strong prompting forced me to STOP suddenly. I was startled by the sudden shock received by this impression I received in my heart and in my mind. I know now that it was a warning from the Holy Spirit, and I am so thankful that it confronted me. I had started my journey seeking "truth" but wound up on a slippery slope down the wrong spiritual path. As an inquisitive teenager, I was like a frog swimming in cool, pleasant water, while someone gradually turned up the heat in the pot– I did not notice that the water was getting ready to boil and cook me until it was almost too late. I could not perceive that I was being diverted away from light and truth, as I became enshrouded in darkness. Nobody was there to warn me. I had no spiritual guidance at the time. It was not my intent to betray God and unknowingly pay homage to Satan. I know now that if I wanted to get to know Jesus and God, I should have spent my time in prayer and reading the Holy Scriptures. Adhering to the Word of God (the "iron rod") would have led me more surely, safely, and quickly through the darkness of my life and into the light of truth.

Do not be confused or misled by New Age religion. There are lots of misconceptions which can easily distract you or lead you down forbidden paths. I am sure there are many more, but I am only providing three big misconceptions of New Age that you should consider:

NEW AGE MISCONCEPTION #1: THE BELIEF THAT THERE IS NO EVIL IN THE WORLD.

We already talked about this topic earlier – about how the Evil One lurks around every corner and cannot wait to pounce upon innocent souls who let down their guard. Anyone who listens to the news knows about terrorists, murderers, and rapists. These are some of the obvious examples of evil in the world, but there are other more commonplace ones. Many members of society, probably someone you know, ROUTINELY break the laws of the Ten Commandments, the result of which is evil. Review the Ten Commandments to see if you agree.

NEW AGE MISCONCEPTION #2: THE BELIEF THAT BLENDING BIBLICAL SCRIPTURES WITH THE PHILOSOPHIES OF MAN WILL LEAD TO TRUTH

New Age thinking is a buffet or smorgasbord of ideas. With New Age religion, people essentially create their own brand of religion by borrowing ideas from the sacred *Bible* and sprinkling in their idea, resulting in beliefs which stray from the truths of the scriptures. This is how the world fell into apostasy after Jesus died, furthering the spread of evil in the world. Instead of wading through the complexities and confusion of New Age religion, ask for guidance from God to find truth by reading the *Bible*.

If any of you lack wisdom, let him ask of
God, that giveth to all men liberally, and
upbraideth not; and it shall be given him.

– JAMES 1:5 KJV

Ask, and it shall be given you; seek, and ye shall
find; knock, and it shall be opened unto you.

– MATTHEW 7:7 KJV

NEW AGE MISCONCEPTION #3: ALL PATHS LEAD TO GOD.

This is a blatant lie perpetuated by Satan. All paths DO NOT lead to God, as my personal experience attests. You have to be smart and look in the right places for God. Biblical scriptures clearly show us how to find Him.

Jesus said, "I am the way, the truth, and the life. No one comes to the Father except through me." So, as you can see, there is only one channel to the Father, and that is through Jesus Christ. In this book, we seek to lead you down the "strait and narrow path" as mentioned by St. Matthew:

> *13 Enter ye in at the strait gate: for wide is the gate,*
> *and broad is the way, that leadeth to destruction,*
> *and many there be which go in thereat:*
> *14 Because strait is the gate, and narrow is the way,*
> *which leadeth unto life, and few there be that find it.*
> *15 Beware of false prophets, which come to you in*
> *sheep's clothing, but inwardly they are ravening wolves.*
>
> *– MATTHEW 7:13 KJV*

IT MUST BE IMPORTANT TO FOLLOW JESUS

Most of Jesus' twelve apostles were martyred for preaching the gospel. The twelve apostles were from all walks of life before they followed Jesus. Many were fishermen. Bartholomew was of royal blood. Matthew had been a hated tax collector, and John was from a well-to-do family. While following Jesus they felt his sweet spirit, listened to his teachings, witnessed his many miracles, witnessed that he rose from the dead, and ascended into heaven. After Jesus had died Judas the apostle who betrayed Jesus hanged himself. After Jesus ascended, the eleven other apostles left Jerusalem and spread to the far corners of the earth to preach Jesus' gospel in Iran, Syria, Italy, Ethiopia, India, Turkey, and Greece. Eventually, they were persecuted and all except one was martyred – Peter asked to be crucified upside down because he felt unworthy to be crucified like Jesus; Andrew asked to be crucified on a cross shaped like an "X" for the same reason; Thomas was killed with a spear; James' body was sawed into pieces; Bartholomew's body was flayed alive with knives; Jude was killed by arrows; Philip died by hanging, and Matthew and James were also martyred.[374] [375]

They knew Jesus personally and they risked their lives and died to preach Jesus' gospel because they knew it was more important than their own life.

The Need for Spiritual Clarity

People have a natural desire to become more aware of their spiritual selves, but what is the goal? Is the goal simply to get to know yourself better? Is the goal to find Jesus? God? The writer Barbara Curtis, in her article, What is 'New Age' Religion, and Why Can't Christians Get on Board?, points out a few of the devices New Agers use to achieve higher consciousness – "meditation, breathing exercises, yoga, diet, crystals, channeling, spirit guides, and more." However, she also thinks that "New Agers are in a lot of confusion because they haven't found the Truth, but only what fits into the spiritual perspective they have constructed. As in the Garden of Eden, the lie has never changed."[376]

Through the gospel of Jesus Christ, you can find peace and truth. The peace comes from repentance, the Atonement of Jesus Christ, the knowledge of the Plan of Salvation, and knowing that you are on the right path to return to Heavenly Father.

Final Word in Spirituality

Our knowledge about our current life and our future life in the spirit world enables us to know how we ought to behave now while we are alive. We should live righteously and learn to progress spiritually as much as we can by following all God's Laws and observing covenants we make with God. We should learn how to live a Christ-centered life. We should deepen our faith and learn to walk in righteous paths always.

We are taught that the only aspects of our earthly life that we will bring with us when we cross over to the spirit world are the knowledge and talents we gain here on Earth. Thus, we ought to learn as much as we can while we are here on Earth. We are taught that we can be reunited with our families in the spirit world. By our own efforts, we should do all within our power to enable ourselves and our family members to live a righteous life, so that we may be reunited and all receive a full measure of God's glory.

Who shall inherit the kingdom of God? The *Bible* says thus:

15 And they brought unto him also infants,
that he would touch them: but when his
disciples saw it, they rebuked them.
16 But Jesus called them unto him, and said,
Suffer little children to come unto me, and forbid
them not: for of such is the kingdom of God.
17 Verily I say unto you, Whosoever shall
not receive the kingdom of God as a little
child shall in no wise enter therein.
18 And a certain ruler asked him, saying, Good
Master, what shall I do to inherit eternal life?
19 And Jesus said unto him, Why callest thou me
good? none is good, save one, that is, God.
20 Thou knowest the commandments, Do not commit
adultery, Do not kill, Do not steal, Do not bear false
witness, Honour thy father and thy mother.
21 And he said, All these have I kept from my youth up.
22 Now when Jesus heard these things, he said unto
him, Yet lackest thou one thing: sell all that thou
hast, and distribute unto the poor, and thou shalt
have treasure in heaven: and come, follow me.
23 And when he heard this, he was very
sorrowful: for he was very rich.
24 And when Jesus saw that he was very
sorrowful, he said, How hardly shall they that
have riches enter into the kingdom of God!
25 For it is easier for a camel to go through a needle's
eye, than for a rich man to enter into the kingdom of God.
26 And they that heard it said, Who then can be saved?
27 And he said, The things which are impossible
with men are possible with God.

28 Then Peter said, Lo, we have left all, and followed thee.
29 And he said unto them, Verily I say unto you, There
is no man that hath left house, or parents, or brethren,
or wife, or children, for the kingdom of God's sake,
30 Who shall not receive manifold more in this present
time, and in the world to come life everlasting.

– LUKE 18:15-30 KJV

Use your agency to determine what you will do to elevate yourself past what the world says you should be.

Always remember and never forget these things:

* You are a child of God.
* God knows you personally.
* God loves you very much.
* God made the Heavens and Earth and all things therein.
* Through Him, all good things are possible.
* Read the Holy Scriptures daily.

Learn to elevate yourself spiritually so you can begin to be the kind of man God would be proud to welcome back home into His loving arms.

WHAT WILL YOU DO TO ELEVATE YOURSELF TODAY?

Every day in your gratitude journal write down five things for which you are grateful including any occurrences of grace/miracles great and small which are unusual that were not likely to happen but did happen and for which you are grateful. So start being more mindful of the graces that occur in your life.

QUEST CHECKPOINT: YOUR SPIRIT

Congratulations for reaching this checkpoint on your quest. In order to satisfy the requirements for the Spirit Certificate, you will need to demonstrate proficiency in the subject areas covered within this chapter by reading and completing the requirements below. After you have completed all the certificate requirements below - using the honor system – fill in the certificate with your name. **You can also download a printed copy from the** *Elevate Yourself to Manhood* **website at http://www.elevateyourselftomanhood.com/certificates.**

CERTIFICATE REQUIREMENTS

☐ **Spirit** - Recall that you are more than just a physical body; you have a spirit which gives you life. Contemplate this and write your thoughts in your journal.

☐ **Spiritual Nature** - Recall the story of the highly skeptical and respectable scientist who had a profound spiritual experience while driving his car around a blind bend in the road. Record in your journal any spiritual experiences (unexplainable by science) you have had.

☐ **The Power of Prayer** - Recall the story of how prayer affects water and come to realize how prayer must affect the human body since we are mostly water! Write any thoughts you may have on this subject in your journal. **Prayer**
  - Commit to saying a short prayer before each meal
  - Commit to saying a prayer before going to bed each night
  - Commit to saying a prayer after waking up in the morning
  Extra Points: See how many other prayers you can fit into the day. You can say them in your mind, on the school bus, while you work, or when you begin to daydream.

☐ **Ten Commandments** - Recall or be able to recite the Ten Commandments of God. What are the other commandments humans were given by God through Jesus Christ? Read the *Bible* and find, if you can, additional commandments given by God and Jesus.

☐ **Law of Chastity** - Remember the Law of Chastity. Remember that Heavenly Father expects you to preserve sexual intercourse until after marriage with your Eternal Companion. Reflect in your journal how you plan to remain chaste until marriage.

- ☐ **Hanging Out and Dating** - Casual dating begins at sixteen. Double date so as to guard against temptation. Do not be exclusive with a girl until you meet the girl you would like to marry. In the meantime, enjoy the platonic company of many young ladies. Identify couples with whom you feel comfortable double-dating. Ask your parents for guidance.

- ☐ **Repentance** - Explain in your own words how you would go about repenting and obtaining forgiveness. Think of something that you may have done wrong. Kneel in prayer and ask God for forgiveness using the format provided in this chapter. Use the Spirit to compose your own prayer to Heavenly Father.

- ☐ **Faith** - Recall the story of the Catholic priest and how his heart told him things his mind did not know. This is the beginning of faith. Pray that you will be able to increase your faith in God. Record your thoughts in your journal.

- ☐ **Baptism** - Pray and think about being baptized. Each person must use their own agency to determine whether they are ready for baptism or not. Have you developed faith? Have you repented? Write your thoughts and feelings down in your journal, discuss with your parents and church leaders.

- ☐ **Hope** - Having hope means that you feel confident about your purpose in this life, and that you look forward to an even better life after death. In your journal, list ways in which you feel you have hope. Talk with others, including parents, teachers, counselors, if you do not feel hope or if you are depressed.

- ☐ **Charity/Service -**
  - Write down ten ways you could provide service to or help someone.
  - Look around for opportunities and offer to help someone in need. Do this each day, or whenever the opportunity arises.

⁕ Sign up as a volunteer on one of several Volunteer/Service websites in your community.

☐ **Tithes and Offerings** - Learn the value of sharing your wealth. Set aside ten percent of your earnings for tithing to your church or for charity. Record the blessings you receive.

☐ **Spiritual Happiness and the Plan of Happiness** - Become familiar with the Plan of Happiness and what it means for your spiritual destiny. Explain the Plan of Happiness to someone you know. Write your thoughts in your journal.

☐ **The Creation Story** - Read and understand the full Creation Story in the *Bible* (Genesis Chapter 1, verses 1-25 KJV) and review the section in this book titled: What Creationists Believe.

☐ **The Story of the Great Flood** - Read and understand the Flood Story and how the flood has affected the fossil record of the world and how it renders most of what man believes about "evolution" as false.

☐ **Misconceptions about Evolution** - Read and understand the sections "What Evolutionists Believe" and "What is Evolution Anyway?" Of the six kinds of evolution mentioned, observe that only one type of evolution is true: Microevolution. Make note that all the other types of evolution: Cosmic, Chemical, Stellar/Planetary, Organic, and Macro, are FALSE. Belief in these types of "evolution" means that you do not believe in God the Creator and runs counter to your spiritual well-being, growth, and maturity.

☐ **The Spirit World**. Contemplate where you would want your spirit to go after you die. Record your thoughts in your journal. Discuss this with your parents and spiritual leaders.

ELEVATE YOURSELF TO MANHOOD

QUEST CERTIFICATE – THE SPIRIT

THIS CERTIFICATE IS AWARDED TO:

_____

FOR DILIGENCE IN FULFILLING THE *ELEVATE YOURSELF TO MANHOOD*
REQUIREMENTS FOR THE "SPIRIT" ON HIS QUEST

Elevating Your Character

ELEVATE YOUR CHARACTER

You mold your character and future
by good thoughts and acts.

- SPENCER W. KIMBALL

THE VALUES YOU LEARN WILL help determine the type of person you become. How well you learn these good values and apply them to your life will determine the quality of your character. There are many character traits. Let us begin by discussing positive and negative character traits.

CHARACTER TRAIT CATEGORIES

Ron Kurtus is an author and student of human behavior. He asserts that your whole character is a combination of your personal traits, your social traits, and your cultural traits.

PERSONAL CHARACTER TRAITS

Personal character traits are attitudes that you have towards your own actions and achieving goals. Since all of us have faults, each person has a combination of positive traits and negative traits.

Although you are a work in progress, you should always strive to do your best and become the best person you can be. Kurtus provides us an outline, as he sees it, of positive (good) traits that we hope you develop and the corresponding negative (bad) traits:

Positive or Good Traits	Negative or Bad Traits
Courageous	Cowardly
Conscientious	Careless
Determined	Easily Discouraged
Confident	Unsure
Hard working	Lazy

Studying the information above, we can understand the claim that positive (good) character traits tend to lead to positive outcomes, while the negative (bad) personal traits usually lead to failure.[377]

It is crucial that you aspire to developing positive character traits and avoid the negative traits. So let us dig a little deeper into each character trait to obtain a better understanding.

Courage

Courage (also bravery) is the ability and willingness to do something in the face of fear and or hard work. Having confidence in yourself helps fuel your courage, but the truly courageous may proceed with a formidable task feeling totally inadequate for the job!

Melanie Greenberg, Ph.D., a Clinical Psychologist, published *The Six Attributes of Courage* in *Psychology Today* with hopes of guiding persons to become their "best and bravest self." She enumerated those attributes of courage, along with some inspiring quotes. We have also included a few of our favorite quotes.

1)   Feeling Fear Yet Choosing to Act[378]

> *I learned that courage was not the absence of fear,*
> *but the triumph over it. The brave man is not he who*
> *does not feel afraid, but he who conquers that fear.*

— NELSON MANDELA

> *We must build dikes of courage to*
> *hold back the flood of fear.*

- MARTIN LUTHER KING, JR.

Unfortunately, many of our young men today – for some reason – seem to fear things like getting a higher education. It seems too daunting for them. Yes, it does take courage to tackle the job of getting an education – whether it means becoming a teacher, a banker, a lawyer, a machinist, a plumber, a police officer, or you name it, the rewards are great and necessary.

> *Education, then, beyond all other devices of human*
> *origin, is the great equalizer of the conditions of*
> *men -- the balance-wheel of the social machinery.*

HORACE MANN

2)   Following Your Heart[379]

> *And most important, have the courage*
> *to follow your heart and intuition. They*
> *somehow already know what you truly want to*
> *become. Everything else is secondary."*

— STEVE JOBS, STANFORD COMMENCEMENT SPEECH, JUNE 2005

Using your agency, your imagination, and your passion, determine that the thing you are about to set out to do is the right thing for you at the right time. Remember that sometimes your heart tells you something that your mind does not know. That is inspiration. That is spirit. So you need to find the courage to commit to it and do it.

3)   Persevering in the face of adversity[380]

> *When we are afraid we ought not to occupy ourselves with endeavoring to prove that there is no danger, but in strengthening ourselves to go on in spite of the danger.*
>
> — MARK RUTHERFORD

> *You have within you the strength, the patience, and the passion to reach for the stars and change the world!*
>
> - HARRIET TUBMAN

> *When you become detached mentally from yourself and concentrate on helping other people with their difficulties, you will be able to cope with your own more effectively. Somehow, the act of self-giving is a personal power-releasing factor.*
>
> - NORMAN VINCENT PEALE

Never give up the fight even though the going gets tough. Look deep down inside for the courage you need to withstand the headwinds and darts being thrown at you. In a TED talk, a Social Psychologist, Amy Cuddy, stated that she had been a gifted child. She said that in her youth she was in a terrible automobile accident, which left her with a brain injury. Her doctors told her that she would never learn easily again, and suggested that she would not be able to attain a university degree. Undaunted she pursued her education, graduated with an undergraduate degree and was accepted to Harvard. At Harvard she felt overwhelmed and that she did not belong. A mentor told her, "Fake it until you make it." She faked it until she made it. After that she was able to share this precious message with other young people – and to you, through me.[381]

4) Standing Up For What Is Right[382]

> *Sometimes standing against evil is more important*
> *than defeating it. The greatest heroes stand*
> *because it is right to do so, not because they*
> *believe they will walk away with their lives.*
> *Such selfless courage is a victory in itself*

— N.D. WILSON, DANDELION FIRE

> *Our lives begin to end the day we are*
> *silent about things that matter.*

- MARTIN LUTHER KING, JR.

> *Great spirits have always encountered violent*
> *opposition from mediocre minds.*

- MARTIN LUTHER KING, JR.

When you stand for things that are right, you can rest assured of the assistance of angels who can help shore up your courage.

(5) Expanding Your Horizons; Letting Go of the Familiar[383]

Man cannot discover new oceans unless he has
the courage to lose sight of the shore.

— LORD CHESTERFIELD

"This world demands the qualities of youth;
not a time of life but a state of mind, a temper
of the will, a quality of the imagination, a
predominance of courage over timidity, of the
appetite for adventure over the life of ease."

— ROBERT F. KENNEDY

Pray to the Almighty for the expansion of your capacity – for the ability to see beyond borders and to step out into the unknown with courage. Indeed this is the only way to grow.

(6) Facing Suffering With Dignity or Faith[384]

The ideal man bears the accidents of life with dignity
and grace, making the best of circumstances.

— ARISTOTLE

There may be times when we are powerless
to prevent injustice, but there must never
be a time when we fail to protest.

- ELIE WIESEL

No one can make you feel inferior without your consent.

- ELEANOR ROOSEVELT

When you know the *Plan of Happiness* that was laid out for each of us before the Earth was established, you already know that you will encounter turbulence during your life. Like a young tree, you need to learn how to withstand strong winds early in your life so that as you grow older and taller you will not be toppled by the raging storms, which will enable you to enjoy peaceful times.

Courage-Building Exercise

Greenberg suggests that you can build courage by following a particular process. Grab a notebook and pen, then go find a quiet space where you can reflect for a while.

Now go back to the first definition of courage we mentioned above: "Feeling Afraid Yet Choosing to Act." Answer the following questions while keeping that statement in mind. Think of a situation when you felt afraid, yet chose to face your fear.

(a) What did you observe, think, and feel at the time? (e.g., "I saw the deep swimming pool and I got that dark, sinking feeling in the pit of my stomach").

(b) What did you or the people around you say, think, and do to help you face your fear? (e.g., "My friends told me not to worry that they had my back").

(c) At what point did your fear start to go down? How did you feel afterward?

(d) Now think back to an earlier situation in childhood in which you faced your fear. How did you handle it?

(e) Finally, think of a situation you are currently facing that creates fear or anxiety. What are you most afraid of?

(f) Now, is there a way to apply the same skills you used in the two earlier situations to be more courageous in this situation? Remind yourself that you have these skills and have used them successfully in the past. What mental or environmental barriers stand in the way of using these skills? How can you cope with or get rid of these obstacles?

(g) Now to burn in Greenberg's process, you must repeat this exercise over a 6-day period, each time using one of the attributes of courage above. On the seventh day, develop your own definition or attribute of courage and repeat the process.

(h) Check for the availability of the video on Courage Building on the Elevate Yourself to Manhood website at http://www. elevateyourselftomanhood.com/videos.

Conscientiousness

Conscientiousness means being thorough, careful, and vigilant in doing one's actions. If you are a student, being conscientious isn't about just getting to school and into your classroom on time. It means that you have completed all your assignments, and you are ready, willing, and able to engage with your teacher and classmates in the task of learning. Learning is your job, and you are ready, willing, and able to do your job.

Determination

Determination is steadfastness and firmness in achieving a goal. If you have envisioned what your future success looks like, and you have the determination to achieve it, then you have a much better chance of making it happen. Having optimism helps to bolster your determination.

Confidence

As previously stated in the Confidence section of Facet 2 – Elevate Your Mind confidence is trust in your own knowledge and abilities. Confidence will give you the courage to take action: to face problems and find solutions, to seek higher education, to seek a good job or to start your own business, to have a social life, to marry, to raise a family, and to be the best you can be. **Visit the *Elevate Yourself to Manhood* website at http://www.elevateyourselfto-manhood.com/videos to check the availability of the video on self-confidence.**

Hard Work

This final component of courage, hard work, is the engine that drives all the other components. It matters not how much courage you have if you do not act on it.

SOCIAL CHARACTER TRAITS

Kurtus goes on to talk about one's social traits - those attitudes you have toward other people and how you deal with them. Whenever you employ positive social character traits, you get good results (success). Having negative social traits and behaviors leads to failure in those relations. The negative traits can cause you to be distrusted or even disliked. There are also extremes of these traits, as well as those in-between:

Positive or Good Social Character Traits

* Honest
* Kind
* Reliable
* Fair
* Considerate

Negative or Bad Social Character Traits

* Dishonest
* Cruel
* Unreliable
* Biased
* Inconsiderate[385]

These behavioral traits are self-explanatory.

How would you rate yourself in these areas? How would you rate your friends? How do you feel about friends who have all or most of the positive social traits? How do you feel about friends or acquaintances who have some of the negative character traits? Which of these two characters would you want to be?

Remember to choose your friends wisely. Friends with negative traits can lead to trouble.

What Do You Stand For?

A man should stand for something. As you mature and obtain more life experience, you may find yourself thinking about current social or political issues. An awareness of current issues will give you confidence because you will be able to understand what's going on in the world, the country, the state, or in your local area. You will understand what people are expressing when they speak or write their opinion on a particular topic. We do not expect you to have strong political opinions at this stage of your life, though some of you undoubtedly do have well-defined opinions regarding many political topics. As a citizen, you will eventually want to develop your own worldview of issues. Here are a few examples of things you can do or think about in this regard:

- Watch or read the news on television or cable channels (domestic and international) or on the Internet
- Read magazines (good ones , not trashy ones)
- Watch political debates and figure out what candidates you like best
- Figure out who you would vote for and why. For example, are you Pro Life or Pro Choice? Which candidate will do the most for your generation? Which candidate is most honest? Which candidate seems to be the most logical and realistic? Which candidate will command respect from leaders of other countries and protect our country?
- You may want to keep your thoughts private, share them with your family, or you can get involved in political campaigns when there is a candidate you would like to support.

- Which sports do you like best? Which teams do you like best? Follow your favorite sport. Knowledge about sports will enable you to have conversations when in social situations.
- Are you committed to eating a healthy diet? What are your favorite foods? Which restaurants do you prefer? Talking about food can lead to pleasant conversation.
- Would you be an advocate for the homeless?
- Do you feel that we should say "Merry Christmas" or "Happy Holidays?"
- What type of music do you like? If you like many "genres" of music it is OK to say, "I have eclectic taste in music." Talking about music is also a pleasant subject for conversation.
- Which famous artists do you like best?
- What are your favorite books?
- As you mature your opinions may remain the same or your opinions and tastes may change. However, at any given time you will know who you are and the issues you support or are against. Developing opinions, passions, and goals will help you develop your character and boost your self-confidence.

CULTURAL CHARACTER TRAITS

Finally, Kurtus tells us that cultural character traits reflect how well you adhere to or follow the laws and rules of society.

"Most people are members of community, culture and religions. Those groups have rules and laws that they expect members to follow. A person who follows or obeys the rules is judged as having good cultural character. He or she may be considered an outstanding, law-abiding citizen, a good member of the group or a devout, religious person," says Kurtus. "Those who do not follow the rules are considered law-breakers, trouble-makers or sinners. Their character is said to be immoral, unethical, or corrupt. Most laws and rules are stated in the negative sense, telling what you cannot do."[386]

SPECIAL CHARACTER TRAITS

INTEGRITY

Integrity has seven related attributes: honesty, decency, chastity, holiness, self-respect, keeping promises, and personal worth.

"Integrity means thinking and doing what is right at all times, no matter what the consequences. When you have integrity, you are willing to live by your standards and beliefs even when no one is watching. Choose to live so that your thoughts and behavior are always in harmony with the gospel." (LDS.org – *Youth Standards*)

> *Do what is right; then if men speak against you calling you evil names, they will become ashamed of themselves for falsely accusing you when you have only done what is good. Remember, if God wants you to suffer, it is better to suffer for doing good than for doing wrong!*

1 PETER 3:16 THE LIVING BIBLE

Keep promises that you make. It will increase trustworthiness.

Demonstrate moral courage - doing what you think is right even when there is no great pressure to do otherwise.

Honesty

If you behave honestly, in thought, word, and deed, you will build a good reputation for yourself. People will trust you. You will be more likely to have good friends, to get a good job, and to have a healthy, happy, and active social life.

"Be honest with yourself, others, and God at all times. Being honest means choosing not to lie, steal, cheat, or deceive in any way. When you are honest, you build the strength of character that will allow you to be of great service to God and others. You will be blessed with peace of mind and self-respect.

Being honest will enhance your future opportunities and your ability to be guided by the Holy Ghost. Be honest at school; choose not to cheat in any way. Be honest in your job, giving a full amount of work for your pay. Do not rationalize that being dishonest is acceptable, even though others may think it does not matter." (LDS.org – Youth Standards)

Decency

Acting decently towards others – Do not abuse others, especially vulnerable people. Treat other people as you would like to be treated; even when they cannot see or hear what you are doing, such as, when you are preparing food for them or when you are talking about them.

Chastity

Chastity is sexual purity. Chaste people are morally clean in their thoughts, words, and actions. Chastity means not having any sexual relations before marriage. It also means complete fidelity to your wife during marriage.

Regrettably, in light of events in the news, I warn you to beware of predatory adults who will try to take advantage of your youthful naiveté, and virginity. Teachers, coaches, scout leaders, priests, ministers, and parents of friends (male or female) should never ask to be alone with you. Protect your body.

Every person has the God-given right to choose a spouse and to give to his or her spouse the gift of love, virginity, and intimacy on their wedding day. Robbing a young person of this sacred gift, which he or she would have given to their spouse, is a crime. If they are under age it is a crime against the laws of the land and against God's laws. If they are of legal age to consent but are not married to the person with whom they are being intimate, it is still a crime against God's laws. Robbing them of their innocence and robbing them of the delight of discovery with a loving spouse is sacrilegious.

Pedophilia is an act of physical and psychological violence - an assault on the children's bodies and minds. Be on your guard for adults that make you feel uncomfortable in this area. Trust your instincts. Children cannot recover the sacred gift of virginity stolen from them. Neither can they recover their innocence and peace of mind.

Do not be led astray by "favors" offered in exchange for giving up your virginity and self-respect. Obtaining a chance to play on a sports team, or acceptance for a lead part in a movie or play or financial gain is not worth your virginity, nor your self-respect – you will regret it.

Do not be led astray by peer pressure, or curiosity – you will regret it. Your virginity is sacred, so protect it at all costs until you are married.

I realize that some of you who are reading this book may be even more vulnerable because you are just slightly over the age of consent, which differs from state to state. However, the spiritual and emotional scars will be the same for you if you are coerced into having sex before marriage so be careful, be sober so that you can remain mindful of protecting your body. You will also protect your body from sexually transmitted diseases, and the responsibility of unwanted pregnancy.

If you are sexually abused, tell someone. You have a responsibility to yourself so that it does not happen again. You also have a responsibility to help protect other young people from perpetrators. If you are abused, please know that it is not your fault; God knows that and other adults will know that. Seek counseling.

The documentary film, *The Hunting Ground*, which received excellent reviews at the Cannes Film Festival, and aired on CNN November 22, 2015, shed much-needed light on the fact that students on campuses across the United States have been sexually assaulted by other students, at a much more alarming rate than people ever imagined. Young women and young men, as well, need to be careful not to become victims of these crimes. The problem has gotten so bad that the federal government now has the right to cut off Title IX funding to colleges and universities that do not prosecute perpetrators of sexual assault. Post-secondary institutions will now be more likely to expel and prosecute perpetrators of sexual crimes.

Hopefully, someday you will meet a young woman who has been mindful of protecting the gift of her virginity so that she can give you her special gift on your wedding night. Hopefully, you will have done the same for her, and hopefully someday, you will have beautiful healthy babies together.

True Men Protect Virtue

> *True manhood does not seek to compromise a woman's*
> *purity, true manhood stands up to heroically protect it.*
>
> - *GENERATION LIFE*

"Generation Life is a movement of young people committed to building a culture of life by spreading the pro-life and chastity messages."[387]

Self-Respect

Shakespeare, speaking through Polonius, reminds us:

> *This above all: to thine own self be true,*
> *And it must follow, as the night the day,*
> *Thou canst not then be false to any man.*

Much of our self-respect is built by our own hard work, and by trying to be as independent as possible. Self-respect also includes: caring for our health, personal hygiene, and chastity; protecting our self from bullies; avoiding dishonest people, taking the time to enjoy life through healthy activities, and peaceful moments of contemplation.

Personal Worth

In the words of James E. Faust, from his talk, The Dignity of Self, "May we all have a feeling of personal worth and dignity born of the knowledge that each of us is a child of God, and be strengthened by looking upwards in the pursuit of holiness. As we look up may we be worthy to receive the inspiration that comes constantly from God, which inspiration is sacred, real, and often very private."[388]

RESPONSIBILITY

Learning to be responsible is another highly desirable character trait for a young man to develop. With the right opportunity, you can start taking on responsibilities quite early in life. You should sit down and discuss this topic with your parents.

Before taking on responsibility, you must demonstrate an appropriate level of maturity.

Show maturity by doing things around the house without being told, for example, doing your homework, doing chores, taking care of pets, taking care of younger siblings, and other responsible tasks. Observe curfews, observe laws and be a good citizen. Choose your friends and associates well. Do not give your parents gray hairs. In other words, show your mature self. Be a good teammate and do your share.

So by showing maturity, you are already demonstrating that you are a responsible person.

Now when it comes time for you to ask your dad to borrow the car, you will be in good stead - providing that you have shown enough maturity to take Drivers' Education, pass the tests, and obtained your Drivers' License.

Self-Sacrifice

The desire and ability to self-sacrifice for yourself, your family, people in your community, your country, and the planet will reap you rich rewards. Sacrifice, once discussed in Catholic Schools and Protestant Schools, is still mentioned in churches but with fewer people attending church, some young men may not be familiar with the term self-sacrifice. I feel a need to discuss this character trait because it can enhance your happiness, the happiness of others and the welfare of the planet.

Merriam-Webster Dictionary defines sacrifice as the act of giving up something that you want to keep, especially in order to get or do something else or to help someone.

Some of the greatest examples of self-sacrifice are:

1. Your mother, who carried you and gave birth to you. She sacrificed her young body, and endured pain and suffering to give you life. She sacrificed sleep when you were a baby to nurture you and sacrificed sleep when you were ill to bring you back to health, for years.
2. Jesus Christ who atoned for our sins in the Garden of Gethsemane and died for our sins so that through him our sins would be forgiven, if we repent.
3. Soldiers who have fought and died to preserve our freedom.

Self-Sacrifice for Your Own Welfare

On a very simplistic level just to get you started to think about sacrifice and what it feels like, imagine that you feel like eating a pound of chocolates but you don't because you do not want to gain weight. The sacrifice of not over indulging will help you to maintain a healthy weight.

Another motive for not eating a pound of chocolate might be to share it with your girlfriend whenever she comes over to watch a movie – thereby impressing her with your self-control and willingness to share, which will strengthen your relationship. Sacrificing some of your chocolates to give to your girlfriend will enable you to savor these chocolates more.

Another scenario of self-sacrifice might be – you are married, but your earnings don't cover all of your family's expenses. Therefore, your wife needs to work. When she gets home during her workweek, there are still groceries to purchase, laundry to be done, meals to be prepared, dishes to be done, and children who need help with their homework and who need to be chauffeured to their activities. She is exhausted from work outside and inside the house and needs time to unwind in a warm bath, to relax with a good book, or to sleep. If you are willing to sacrifice most of your personal time at happy hour, playing golf, or other activities outside the home during the child-rearing years to help with household chores and child-rearing, and if you are willing to understand that your wife may need some free time, you will help to create a happy family. "Happy wife, happy family, happy life."

Self-Sacrifice for Your Family
An example of sacrificing for your family's welfare would be: Your wife gives birth and wants to care for her own baby. She does not want to place your baby in a daycare center, and therefore does not plan to return to work. You also want what is best for your baby. You were hoping to buy a new car but on one salary you can barely make ends meet. In order to ensure that your family will have sufficient funds to purchase healthful food you decide to sacrifice getting a new car. You may not get your new car soon but you will find great joy in seeing your baby grow to be healthy and strong. Hopefully, with experience and seniority or a better job you will be able to get that new car.

Self-Sacrifice for Your Country
When countries are invaded by people who would rob its citizens of their freedom men enlist to go to war to protect their families and their country. They sacrifice years of their lives and too often they sacrifice their life. It is unfathomable that these atrocities happen, but if men who know the value of freedom do not defend their country evildoers will try to control life on earth with hard-to-believe disregard for human rights. When Pearl Harbor, Hawai'i was attacked on December 7, 1941 during World War II and when the World Trade Center attacked in New York City on September 11, 2001, men and women joined the armed forces to protect the United States. I had worked for Cantor Fitzgerald on the 105th floor of the World Trade Center. A year before the awful events of 9/11, I was recruited away to another company. In the aftermath, I lost many vibrant, intelligent, sweet colleagues that day. I think about them every day. I am grateful for my life and my freedom to work where I want to work, to choose who I want to marry, and to practice my religion. I am grateful for the young men and women who have fought to preserve my freedom, the United States of America, and other countries that value freedom. I served in the Navy for 10 years during which time I was involved in the Iranian hostage rescue attempt. I would have been willing to do anything that I was called to do for my country.

Elevate Yourself To Manhood

Self-Sacrifice for Your Planet

Preserving our planet for our own enjoyment and for the enjoyment of future generations is everyone's responsibility. On-line there are lists of many easy things you can do to save planet Earth every day – it just takes a little planning, perhaps changing old habits, and a little sacrifice, which would first entail taking the time to actually read about what you can do to save your planet.

Self-Sacrifice in the Service of Others

Self-Sacrifice in the service of others is also called volunteer work, which can enrich your life. Often those who give of their time to help others will testify that they received much more in return. They develop friendships, learn new skills, meet people who are inspiring in spite of their situation or circumstances in life, and they recall a feeling of peaceful contentment. There are thousands of volunteer organizations. JustServe.org is one option. You can volunteer in senior residences, summer camps, within your church, in hospitals, with special needs children and adults, and within animal shelters. Treasure in Heaven - The John Tanner Story is a remarkable story about self-sacrifice in the service of others. **Please check the *Elevate Yourself to Manhood* website at http://www.elevateyourselftomanhood. com/videos for the availability of the video *The John Tanner Story*.**

BOY SCOUT CHARACTER TRAITS

Boy Scouts use purposeful hands-on experiential learning to build character. Through the Scout Law, the Boy Scouts of America mentor young men by using as a guide a set of character traits similar to those mentioned above; however, they go into more depth. Each scout is bound by the Boy Scout Law by which they attempt to acquire these honorable traits:

- Trustworthiness
- Loyalty

- Helpfulness
- Friendliness
- Courtesy
- Kindness
- Obedience
- Cheerfulness
- Thriftiness
- Bravery
- Cleanliness
- Reverence

Although the scouts do not earn a merit badge for each of these character traits. Badges are earned for other skills like hiking, citizenship, and camping. They acquire the traits as a result of interacting with each other, through real-life experience, and through mentoring. We strongly recommend scouting as a way to broaden your world and attain the desirable traits needed for optimal growth into manhood.

How to Be a Gentleman

*Being a gentleman is timeless; these are ideals
that will never be obliterated by technology,
the latest social ideology, or protests from
men who are content to do less.*

- JOHN BRIDGES, *HOW TO BE A GENTLEMAN*

There is a big difference between being a man and being a gentleman. A gentleman is a more refined version of the common man. Gentlemen often garner more respect because they have qualities that command more respect than men without such qualities. If you were a Cub Scout or a Boy Scout, you would probably pick up a lot of the character traits that would qualify you as a gentleman. Any man or boy can learn to be a gentleman. The basic behaviors can be learned any time in any walk of life. These traits are mostly a matter of good taste, honor, courage, bravery, common courtesy and civility.

You should always strive to be - not only a "good" man but a "gentlemanly" man.

There are literally hundreds of unofficial "rules" - covering a wide variety of situations - that suggest how to be a gentleman. We present some of the more common behaviors, gleaned from a number of sources as well as our own favorites in this book for your consideration. When you behave like a gentleman, speak like a gentleman, dress like a gentleman, and eat like a gentleman, you will feel like a gentleman!

General Manners of a Gentleman

* Always hold ladies in high regard and with utmost respect.
* Never belittle or objectify women.
* Have good posture. Do not slouch.
* Have a firm handshake with men, but shake a woman's hand more gently. Shake people's hand up and down only.
* Be chivalrous; for example, offer your coat to a young lady who might be cold and without cover.
* Offer to carry or move heavy objects for a woman of any age.
* Avoid any offensive actions in public like spitting on the pavement.
* Treat others with respect.
* Always be courteous.
* Remember to say "Please" when asking someone for assistance.
* Remember to say "Thank You" when anyone does even the slightest of kind gestures towards you.
* Always try to make others feel comfortable.
* Be polite and care for your lady.
* Be faithful to your lady.

- Stand up for your lady and be prepared to defend her.
- Never ask a lady her age – unless you expect she is too young to date (under 16) – (do not be fooled by makeup).
- Never ask your lady about former boyfriends.
- Admit when you're wrong.
- Always carry a clean handkerchief or tissue to offer to a lady when needed.
- Never blame others for your mistakes.
- Laugh at other people's jokes even if you do not think they are funny.
- Do not ask your lady to buy things for you.
- Surprise your lady with flowers every once in a while. Simple cut field flowers will do most times. At appropriate times, offer a formal bouquet.
- Do not forget special occasions like birthdays and anniversaries.
- Go out of your way to make your lady happy.
- Never physically man-handle a lady, even if she man-handles you.
- Be of good cheer and co-operative.
- Smile often.
- Never let your lady walk home alone.
- When you are walking down a street with a woman, walk on the side closer to the traffic.
- Do not hold grudges. Always forgive.
- Your lady is more important than video games - treat her that way.
- Never be late for a date.
- When riding in a bus always offer your seat to an older person, to people who are handicapped, or to any women. This makes it less likely that they will be injured while in a moving conveyance.
- Wash your hands before preparing food.
- Wash your hands before eating meals.
- When at a buffet – return to the buffet table with a clean plate, in order to avoid the transfer of germs to the buffet.

- When having dinner as a guest at someone's house help to clear the table and offer to help with the dishes.

A Gentleman Walks Through a Door

- A gentleman always opens a door for a lady. Do not ask. Just do it. If the lady declines you, then relent with a smile and say "sorry." The vast majority of women (and other gentlemen) will appreciate the gesture and say "thank you."
- A gentleman always glances behind himself when he walks through a door.
- He never slams a door in another person's face. It does not matter whether the other person is a man or a woman.
- If a gentleman is approaching a door ahead of another person who is burdened down with packages, or if the door is a heavy one, he offers his assistance, without comment, and without waiting for a "thank you."
- Be extra careful with revolving doors. Do not share a revolving door slot with anyone. Enter and exit gracefully, making sure others are able to get through the revolving door safely.

Communicating to Gain Respect

- Say "please" whenever you ask for anything (as previously mentioned).
- Say "thank you" whenever someone does anything for you (as previously mentioned).
- When you are introduced to someone shake his or her hand immediately and say, "How do you do?" which is a greeting, not a question. Saying "Pleased to meet you," is middle class.
- Do not use profane or vulgar language – you will lose credibility.
- Never talk down to anyone – doing so makes you seem egotistical.

- Speak about positive subjects. For example, do not complain about the weather.
- Wait for your turn to speak. Do not cut other people off.
- Do not make racist, bigoted, sexist, homophobic comments. Not even when you are joking.
- Use good grammar. Avoid slang or colloquial ("common") language.
- Be truthful.
- Be a good listener. Learn "active" listening.
- Say nice things - make sincere compliments.
- Avoid bringing up controversial or uncomfortable topics such as politics, sex, or anything gross.
- Text or call your girlfriend or wife often - with discretion.
- Reply to texts, emails, social media messages, and voicemails promptly.
- Never talk behind someone's back – if you do, you will lose people's trust.
- Compliment your lady often.
- Never insult your lady - even if you are joking around.
- Do not brag.
- Do not reveal too much information about others – do not gossip – maintain integrity.

A GENTLEMAN AND HIS CELL PHONE

A gentleman does his best to use his cell phone in the most unobtrusive manner possible. He knows that, while many may consider a cell phone a necessity, there is no reason he should be obnoxious when using one. A gentleman knows that constant use of his cell phone when he is with other people can only make it clear that he values the person on the other end of the telephone conversation far more highly than the persons who are in his company. Such behavior is, at its best, ill-mannered and irritating. A gentleman's phone calls — whether they concern business or private matters — are still his personal affair. He does not force others to listen to his conversation. If a gentleman finds that he truly must initiate or receive a phone call while he is in a public place, he moves to the place where he is least likely to become a nuisance to others. Even in a business meeting, or when he is conducting business at mealtime, a gentleman still says, "Excuse me" before answering a call - even if it is related to the business at hand.

WHEN A GENTLEMAN DOES NOT TALK ON HIS CELL PHONE

- When he is behind the wheel of a vehicle of any type.
- In the midst of a church service or during a theater performance, a movie, or a concert.
- At a table in a restaurant of any kind - be it fast food or first class.
- In the waiting room, or in the examining room, at a doctor's office.
- When standing in line at the grocery store, the post office, a deli, or another place where customers may find themselves trapped as unwilling witnesses to his conversation.
- In an elevator, unless he is alone, or in the company of only friends or coworkers.
- In the workout room at his gym.
- While traveling in the "quiet car" of a train.
- In the cabin of an airplane.
- The only exceptions to the above are an emergency call or a call from a young child – pull over to the side of the road if you are in a car.
- In any place where signage, or a public announcement, notifies him that the use of cell phones is not permitted.

BODY LANGUAGE AND NON-VERBAL COMMUNICATIONS BASICS
Body language is the science of how people communicate with their physical body - the expressions on their face, their eyes, their hands,

their feet, and their posture. You should study body language in order to present yourself in the best light and to develop a better understanding of people in social situations. Not many young men have been taught to learn non-verbal cues or body language. Mostly, we think, that instead of trying to figure it out, young men today just give up and decide to go shoot baskets, play computer games, text, email, or skateboard.

It has been said that non-verbal communications (body language) are more important that verbal communications (what you say). Do not despair. We have a few essentials for you to consider. There are many books on body language that you can check out to give you more detailed information, but keep in mind that there is no "one size fits all" for body language. We are all different, but there are a few key points of guidance we can offer you:

1. Have good posture. Stand tall, gut sucked in with your shoulders back.
2. Maintain good eye contact, but do not stare. Smile but do not over-do it. Be genuine.
3. Make purposeful hand and arm gestures. Do not swing your arms or move them around unnecessarily.
4. Speak slowly, deliberately, and clearly. Allow space in between sentences. Enunciate your words instead of slurring or swallowing your words. Be articulate – coherent, expressive and easy to understand.
5. Keep your tone of voice moderate or lower, not squeaky if you can help it.
6. When you walk into a room, enter with confidence in an orderly fashion, engaging others with eye contact.
7. Have a firm, strong handshake. Not limp. Not too tight.
8. Dress well.
9. Be aware of cultural differences. Learn about people with whom you will be engaging.
10. Avoid strange facial expressions. As we mentioned earlier, smile, but be genuine. Do not "fake smile".

11. Keep a comfortable conversation distance from people (depending on culture and relationship). Respect their personal space.
12. Beware of hand gestures, as they also vary by culture.
13. Beware of touching. Cultures differ in this regard as well. For example, do not try to shake the hand of a Muslim woman. They are not permitted to shake hands with men.

As you grow older and obtain more life experience, pay close attention to body language. Read books and study people, learn good habits within your culture and become aware of other cultures' body language rules.

Dress, Appearance, and Hygiene

At home or out in the world, you should always be mindful of your hygiene, the way you dress, and your general appearance. How you present your body to the world should mean a lot to you. It also means a lot to others with whom you come into contact. Did you also know that the way you dress affects the way you act? The way you dress also affects the way people treat you. Psychological forces behind the way you dress will influence your behavior in the short-term and in the long-term.

In general, dress according to the way you want people to see you and treat you. More importantly, dress to reflect what you want to become.

Here are some rules of hygiene, dress and appearance:

* Always keep your body clean and well groomed.
    * Make sure your nails are clean and trimmed.
    * Keep your hair clean and neat.
    * Shower or bathe each day - multiple times if necessary. Be sure to wear fresh clothes afterward.
    * Do not be afraid to use body wash, shampoo, conditioner, aftershave, and cologne (but not too much cologne).
    * Keep facial hair neat.

- Wear deodorant. Beware of antiperspirants that contain aluminum. Aluminum is a metal. It can get absorbed into your body and brain, which can cause severe health problems.
- Take special care of your teeth. (See section on Dental Care)
- Dress modestly. Always choose to be more on the classy side than the trashy side of fashion.
- Never lower your dressing standards for the sake of others.
- Do not disfigure your body with tattoos and body piercings. Tattoos and body piercings can eliminate you from obtaining certain positions of employment.
- Dress as appropriate for the occasion. When attending an event, always inquire about the dress code and dress accordingly.
- Do not wear your pants hanging halfway off your derriere - exposing your underwear. Although dressing like this appears "cool" to a minority of people, it has nefarious roots and sends the wrong message, especially if you are escorting a young lady. Respect yourself and the young lady. Your pants should be worn with a belt around your waist, not around your buttocks. Also exposing your underwear is obscene. Such dressing habits are not condoned by polite society.
- When dating, always dress nicely for the occasion to show respect for the young lady. If she is worth dating, then she deserves a handsome, well-dressed, respectful young man as her escort. Your clothes should be clean and pressed.
- When attending church, always show respect for the Lord by dressing appropriately - a suit, dress shirt, and tie. Always wear nicely kept, polished shoes as well. You do not need to pay a fortune for a good suit. Discount retailers offer reasonable prices. At times, you can even buy a good suit at a second-hand shop.
- Learn how to tie a tie, for example, the *Four-in-Hand Knot*, the *Windsor Knot*, and a bow tie.
- If you must rent your event clothes (a prom or ball for example), always choose smart, conservative clothes.

- Always wear clean shoes. Polish your shoes well, and don't forget the soles. When you meet a lady, she often checks out your shoes first! We're not sure why, but she has her reasons.
- Always make sure your clothes fit properly. Pants not too long nor too short. Shirt or coat not too large nor too small.
- Minimize loud colors and wild patterns. I have some embarrassing personal stories to tell about this one.
- Make sure your clothes do not have holes or wrinkles. Some styles allow wrinkles or even rips, but a gentleman does not consider them appropriate for public wear.

By staying well-groomed and by dressing well, you will feel more self-assured and confident. More importantly, you will automatically command more respect from others. Besides, you can never know when you will meet "Miss Right."

DINING / TABLE MANNERS

- Put your cell phone on vibrate or turn it off.
- Offer to take your date's coat. Gently ease the coat off her shoulders and hand it to the coat check clerk, carry it or hand it to your date.
- When ready to sit down at the table, pull out your date's chair to facilitate ease of sitting.
- Do not check text messages or send text messages while seated at the table. Pay attention to other people at your table. Same rules apply when dining at home. If you must use the phone, excuse yourself first.
- A gentleman says grace before eating his meal.
- If the food set before him is intended to be eaten piping hot (or icy cold), and if a gentleman is the first person to be served at his table, he waits for one other person to be served before he begins to eat.

- If a gentleman and his fellow diners are all served at the same time, and if there is a lady at the table, he waits until she lifts her fork before he takes his first bite.
- If a gentleman's meal is slow to arrive from the kitchen, and if others at the table have been served, he urges them, "Please, go ahead without me." And he means it.
- A gentleman places the napkin on his lap prior to commencing to eat.
- A gentleman does not put his elbows on the table at any time.
- A gentleman breaks his bread, and he butters a small portion of the bread at a time - not the entire serving of bread.
- A gentleman does not stack his plates at the end of the meal.
- A gentleman does not cut up all his food at once.
- A gentleman never places a piece of dirty flatware back on the table – it sits on his plate. If it falls on the floor, leave it there and ask the server for a replacement.

     When a gentleman needs to take a break while eating, he places his knife and fork on the lower right side of your plate with the handles SEPARATED at an angle. This sends a message to the waiter that you are not done – you're just taking a break. When you leave the table during a meal, fold your napkin neatly and place it discreetly on the table next to your plate. Do not place it in your chair because that is just gross.

- When a gentleman has finished eating, he places his knife and his fork on his plate side by side, as if they were the hands of a clock set at the 10-20 position. The tines of the fork and the sharp end of the knife point to the 10 o'clock position and the handles, placed together, point to 20 minutes past the hour.
- A gentleman never salts his food before tasting it. Otherwise, he might ruin his meal because it could be well-salted already. Also, he would never insult the cook that way.
- Ditto for using ketchup.

* When a gentleman has an unpleasant time in a restaurant, he does not badger the wait staff. He lodges his complaint with the management. Unless he is a glutton for punishment, he does not patronize that restaurant again.
* Pay for your date's meal.
* Always tip appropriately. My personal rule is 20%, but the amount you tip should be at your discretion. The amount of tip should reflect the quality of the service you receive. Generally, when people receive good service, they leave a 15-20% tip. If you pick up food at the counter or food bar, you should not feel obligated to tip.
* A gentleman never comes to the table only in underclothes.
* Do not pick your nose at the table or anywhere else in public. Retreat to the restroom to do the deed. Be sure to wash your hands.
* If you need to pick your teeth, retreat to the restroom for that as well.

TABLE SETTINGS AND MANNERS FOR A YOUNG GENTLEMAN

A huge part of being a gentleman is demonstrating proper table manners. If you learn all the table manner rules in this book, you will be in good stead. You may find yourself in the White House someday. Why not aim high?

When you start to date that special young lady, you will probably want to impress her with your knowledge of the finer points of courtesy and grace. One of the first things you should know about when it comes to dining is the proper way to use utensils at a properly set table. This stuff is fairly straightforward, but could prove to be crucial to you. Besides, this information will enhance your confidence in any dining situation. So let's jump into table settings and manners.

In general, silverware that is used by the left hand is placed on the left of the plate, and the silverware used by the right hand is on the right side of the plate. Forks are on the left, knives and spoons are on the right. A seafood cocktail fork is an exception. It is placed on the right since it is used in the right hand unless an individual is left-handed. The sharper side of the knife is turned toward the plate. The formal table setting diagram provided shows a more sophisticated table setting for a more elegant formal dinner. There is no need to utilize the formal table setting diagram if you do not have enough flatware to accommodate it. Use it as a guideline.

The water glass is placed on the right at the tip of the dinner knife. Goblets may be substituted at luncheon or dinner. If wine is to be served, the glasses are to the right of the water glass. They are arranged in a diagonal line toward the spoons. The first wine to be served is placed nearer the right hand of the guest. As a reminder, we do not endorse drinking wine or any other alcoholic beverages for physical and spiritual reasons we have addressed already. There could be legal reasons, too, if you are under age.

The use of bread plates is up to you. They provide space for bread, pickles and olive pits. If you are having a casual type party with cocktail ribs or chicken wings or something with a toothpick, include this kind of plate for the waste. It is better to have bread plates than to have the dinner plates assume the role of a garbage can.

When setting a table, the napkin can be placed in either of two positions. At a luncheon or dinner party when the first course is to be served after the guests are seated, it may be folded into a rectangle and placed across the plate. It is also OK to put the neatly folded napkin to the left of the forks. The open corner may be toward or away from the plate though all napkins on the table should be folded and turned in the same direction. Do not waste your time trying to learn fancy napkin folds. The food is more important. A napkin folded into a rectangle fits into the design of table arrangement better than any other shape. My wife and I actually prefer napkin rings.

If a salad is to be on the table, it is placed to the left of the forks. Small, individual salt and pepper shakers are placed at the top of the plate. Salt and pepper shakers at each place are not required for a good service, but they allow guests to continue the conversation rather than to try to find a break in which to say, "Please pass the salt."

At a large dinner party place cards simplify seating. Place cards may be used for a small party if it is a festive occasion or if place cards are desired to carry out the theme of the party.

Please consult the *Elevate Yourself to Manhood* **website at http://www.elevateyourselftomanhood.com/videos for the availability of the video on dining etiquette.**

Formal Place Setting

WHAT WILL YOU DO TO ELEVATE YOURSELF TODAY? QUEST CHECKPOINT: YOUR CHARACTER

Congratulations for reaching this checkpoint on your quest. In order to satisfy the requirements for the Character Certificate, you will need to demonstrate proficiency in the subject areas covered within this chapter by reading and completing the requirements below. After you have completed all the certificate requirements below - using the honor system – fill in the certificate with your name. **You can also download a printed copy from the** *Elevate Yourself to Manhood* **website at http://www.elevateyourselftomanhood. com/certificates.**

CERTIFICATE REQUIREMENTS

- [ ] **Positive or Good Personal Character Traits** – What are some of the positive or good personal character traits mentioned in this section? Do you possess these traits? Write down some ideas in your journal about how you might develop these desirable traits.

- [ ] **Negative or Bad Personal Character Traits** - What are some of the negative or bad personal character traits mentioned in this section? Do you possess any of these traits? Write down some ideas pertaining to how you may go about ridding yourself of these undesirable traits.

- [ ] **Positive or Good Social Character Traits** - What were some of the positive or good social character traits mentioned in this section? Do you possess these traits? Write down your thoughts on how you might go about acquiring or fine-tuning these desirable traits.

- [ ] **Negative or Bad Social Character Traits** - What were some of the negative or bad social character traits mentioned in this section? Do you possess any of these traits? Write down your thoughts on how you might go about ridding yourself of these undesirable traits.

- [ ] **Positive of Good Cultural Character Traits** - What were some of the positive or good cultural character traits mentioned in this section? Do you possess these traits? Write down your thoughts on how you might go about acquiring or fine-tuning these desirable traits.

- [ ] **Negative or Bad Cultural Character Traits** - What were some of the negative or bad cultural character traits mentioned in this section? Do you possess any of these traits? Write down your thoughts on how you might go about ridding yourself of these undesirable traits. Do you adhere to the laws of the land? Do you adhere to the laws of your culture as long as they do not conflict with the laws of the land?

☐ **Integrity** - What is the definition of the special trait: integrity? Explain how it relates to the positive character attributes of honesty, decency, chastity, holiness, self-respect, and personal worth. Write down your thoughts in your journal.

☐ **Responsibility** - What are your thoughts about responsibility? How does it relate to maturity? Do you act responsibly? What have you done lately to demonstrate responsibility to your parents, teachers, yourself and others? Write down your thoughts in your journal.

☐ **Boy Scouts** - How do the Boy Scouts of America help to develop the character of young men? What are some of the noble traits mentioned in the Boy Scout Pledge?

☐ **Being a Gentleman** - Why is it important to want to be a gentleman instead of just being a man? Study the traits of a gentleman. Which traits do you already possess? Which traits do you think you need to work on? Each week, pledge to work on one or two gentlemanly traits. Practice these traits out in public.

☐ **Dress, Appearance, and Hygiene** - Why is it important to pay attention to how you dress and appear to others? Do you have the appropriate nice clothes to wear in public when you go on dates? When you seek employment? When you go to church? Why is it important to always have good personal hygiene?

☐ **Dining/Table Manners** - Why is it important to develop good dining etiquette and table manners? Prior to going out on a date or with a friend, go out to a friendly restaurant alone and practice good table manners.

☐ **Escorting / Dating a Young Lady** - Do you know how to properly escort or date a young lady? Write a list of DOs and DON'Ts and practice in real life.

☐ **Language/Speech** - Why is proper language or communication important? Review the excellent pointers in this section on language/speech and practice incessantly!

- [ ] **Body Language** - Review the section on body language and practice daily. Mastering basic body language techniques as mentioned here will improve the image of how people see you, improve your self-respect, and increase your self-confidence.
- [ ] **Character connection to Mind, Body, and Spirit** - Can you see how your mind, body, and spiritual development tie directly into your character development? In your journal, write down your thoughts on this topic.

ELEVATE YOURSELF TO MANHOOD

QUEST CERTIFICATE – CHARACTER

THIS CERTIFICATE IS AWARDED TO:

_____

FOR DILIGENCE IN FULFILLING THE *ELEVATE YOURSELF TO MANHOOD*
REQUIREMENTS FOR "CHARACTER" ON HIS QUEST

Elevate Your Family

ELEVATE YOUR FAMILY

WHETHER YOU ARE FROM A nuclear family, single parent family, or foster care family the following chapter will allow you to get a sense of factors that enable fully intact families to develop and to grow to be more loving and supportive of each other throughout their life together. Many of you will also discover the reason God created families.

YOUNG MEN IN SINGLE PARENT FAMILIES AND FOSTER CARE FAMILIES

Life isn't easy and never has been easy for most people who live on earth. At times, the lives of the rich and famous look easy but they frequently have their hardships as well. For example, two members of the Kennedy family were assassinated – President John F. Kennedy and Senator Robert Kennedy.

As I am writing this section my grandsons who are eighteen and seventeen years old are grieving the loss of their father who died suddenly of natural causes. This is about as tough as it gets in life. One of my grandsons told me, "It's been tough but I am remaining positive." Their father would have wanted them to remain positive throughout life to overcome all of their life's vicissitudes. They are fortunate to have a good mother who loves them. Their mother became a single parent when they were much younger. Even so, they were very close to their father, and had recently lived with him for a year and sailed to Mexico with him. Their father loved them and was a significant influence in their lives.

Young men from single parent families can succeed very well in life and grow to be wonderful husbands and fathers - such as President Barak Obama and Prime Minister Justin Trudeau.

Many young men who live in foster care are safer in care than they would have been with their biological parents. Some young men entered foster care because they were orphaned or because their parent became too ill to care for them. Many young men who have been in foster care have lived with more than one foster family. They have led tragic and very difficult childhoods. If you are in foster care hopefully you are now living with a kind family, you have a roof over your head and an opportunity to go to school.

Hopefully, the mentorship in this book will enable you to deal with the effects of your childhood, and help to enable you to have a loving, healthy family of your own someday. Many people who were foster children have become very successful and many have become famous, such as Dave Pelzer the author of the book *A Child Called It* and other best-selling books. Pelzer was severally abused by his mother. His wife Marsha Pelzer states: For over 8 years Dave's mother tortured and dehumanized her son.

If you met Dave for the first time or watched him from a distance, you'd never recognize the lows of his past or the heights of his success. "I never expected any of this," Dave says. "I love my life. My biggest blessings are not my work as an author and communicator, but are my wife, Marsha, and my son, Stephen. Accolades and status in one's career are nice and open doors to make more of a difference in this world, but the heart of what I do is for my family. To make things better for my son today than when I was growing up. To me, life is an adventure, and with every day there's another opportunity to go out there and do something!"[389]

THE IMPORTANCE OF FAMILIES

WE ARE ALL PART OF God's family. We are all His children. Human families are central to the makeup of our society and God's Eternal Plan.

God created the earth because He loves us, and He wanted us to have the opportunity to experience life in our physical bodies in this world living with our families. "The creation of the earth provided a place where families can live" states Julie Beck, Relief Society General President of The Church of Jesus Christ of Latter-day Saints. She continues, "God created a man and a woman who were the two essential halves of a family. It was part of Heavenly Father's plan that Adam and Eve be sealed and form an eternal family."[390]

It is within the family that a person begins to learn how love feels and how to love. After all, to "love one another" is one of God's commandments as we have seen before. Ideally, in your boyhood family you are learning how to love from feeling the love your parents show you each day. From their love, you learn to love yourself - how to take care of your mind, body and spirit. You also learn to love your parents and your siblings. This loving environment helps you to have a love for members of your extended family: your grandparents, aunts, uncles, cousins, and ancestors. You should then be able to show love to friends, to neighbors, to people in your community, to your wife and children, to fellow countrymen, to other people of the world, and to God. This is part of God's plan for us on Earth.

God established the ordinance of marriage (called the sacrament of marriage in some churches) to give couples the lawful right or license to have children because He wants us to: (1) experience that special love parents have for their children, to know how it feels to love someone so completely, (2) to create a safe environment for children, and (3) to provide children with both male and female role models.

FAMILIES ARE ORDAINED OF GOD

The family being ordained of God makes the family central to His plan for the eternal destiny of His children. That makes it possible for families to be united eternally, and to return to His presence.[391]

ONE BIG HUMAN FAMILY

In God's eyes, we are all His children, and we are all brothers and sisters. If you think about it, you will begin to see that all people are related to each other somewhere down the line. Logically, we would need to be if we accept Adam and Eve as the original parents. The point is that families are what tie all of us together into one big human family!

GROWTH WITHIN YOUR FAMILY

It is through love that we progress as humans – in mind, body and spirit. Your parents' love for you prompted them to protect you from harm, to keep you clean, to feed you, to have fun with you, and to teach you. If your parents had not loved you, perhaps you would not even be alive today. Not loving you would have been extreme laziness and neglectful on their part. Loving you and caring for you, however, taught your parents many valuable lessons, which they would not otherwise have learned. As you learn to care for yourself, you will learn many valuable lessons, and someday when you have a wife and children to care for, you will also learn new and precious lessons, which you will share with them. Active love transcends the atrophy (withering away) of the human mind, body and spirit. Active love enables human growth.

As a human being who has grown through love, and who has grown to be a strong, righteous human being, you can enable yourself and your family to have a better life on Earth and to be reunited with your family after death to live with God for eternity in peace and harmony. Living with God will be blissful. There will be no sorrow. There will be no pain. There will be love. This is God's plan.

MARRIED UNTIL DEATH DO US PART OR FOR TIME AND ALL ETERNITY? WHICH WOULD YOU PREFER? UNTIL DEATH DO US PART

"Until death do us part" is the famous vow in the traditional Christian marriage rite. That means that when either the man or the woman dies, the marriage contract is no longer valid. Isn't that really sad for two people who love each other and have been together for many years? Just to think that you will no longer be a part of the other person's life can be quite heartbreaking. Not only is the other person gone, but your loved one is no longer married to you.

MARRIED FOR TIME AND ETERNITY

In my marriage/sealing to spouse - my wife and I were married "for time and all eternity" which means that we will always be married even after death. That is so comforting to me because I cannot imagine not being married to my wife. She is a vital part of me - of who I am. In our church, The Church of Jesus Christ of Latter-day Saints, we were "sealed" in marriage to each other. This is a stronger, more enduring marriage bond than just being married until one of us dies. We believe that we lived with God as spirit children before we were born and that we will return to live with God after we die. Being "sealed" while we are here on earth during a sealing ceremony in a Holy Temple assures us that we will always be together, even after death. This bonding is a vital part of God's plan for our spiritual lives and our spiritual happiness.

FAMILIES CAN BE TOGETHER FOREVER

In the Holy Temples of The Church of Jesus Christ of Latter-day Saints children are sealed to their parents so that they can be reunited together again after they die to live within their family for eternity. When children are born to parents who are sealed in an LDS temple, the children are born into the covenant and therefore they are essentially sealed to their parents as soon as they are born. When couples are sealed after their children are born, the children may be sealed to them.

This is the only scenario that makes sense to us. We humans are part earthly and part spirit. Our bodies die (the earthly part) but our spirits live on. Being sealed to our family members is an earthly ordinance, which means that the sealings can only take place on Earth in the Temple. When Jesus comes to Earth again, all those who have died, and obeyed his commandments in their earthly existence, will be resurrected, given a new body, and will be reunited with their family. God has created order on a molecular level and also on a spiritual level – such is the nature of God.

Also, your parents can be sealed to their parents, and they can be sealed to all their children, and your grandparents can be sealed to their parents and so forth. Thus, you may all be reunited. Only people who obey God's commandments will have this privilege. Children from single parent families can be sealed to their parents if one parent is deceased and sealed to the other parent. Or when the parent who has raised them remarries the children can be sealed to their parent and stepparent.

LIVING WITHIN YOUR CURRENT FAMILY

An excellent and very well respected university math professor once told me, "My twelve-year-old thinks that I am stupid." My reply of encouragement was, "That will change with time." This child apparently did not know that all of her father's students thought that he was one of their best professors. Children have lived in the world for a very short period of time – their perspective is limited. What a child may consider annoying in childhood, he may consider a blessing later on in life as he gains a greater understanding of responsibility, health, safety, education, social norms, and spiritual resilience.

LEARNING SELF-RELIANCE AND RESPONSIBILITY WITHIN THE FAMILY

Some of the most significant lessons in your life can be learned as you grow up within your own family. You learn to be obedient to your parents, share in family responsibilities, perform chores, learn to get along with others, and learn to be self-reliant.

In days past, the main goal of most of the young teenaged men I knew was to grow up and become independent. That usually meant getting a girl and a car of their own and eventually getting married. That was a tall order and meant that you needed to have money as well. I was allowed to work on a payroll when I turned 16. That's when I bought my first car and started to consider myself independent. However, as early as age 10, I had done odd jobs to make money in the summertime or after school. In addition to my chores at home when I was very young, I sold newspapers, picked berries, worked in graveyards, worked in fields, and sawed wood for money – until I was old enough to find a regular part-time or full-time job while in school.

As I mentioned in the dedication of this book, my dad was forced to quit school and help his family on the farm. This was his contribution to helping to support his mother, father and siblings.

A lot of the money I made working as a teenager went to helping to support our large family as well. This was a valuable lesson in selflessness that I learned from my father at an early age.

You can start developing your work skills and earning money in middle school and high school by "scrambling for work." Offer your services for pay to family members, and neighbors. You can cut lawns, plant bulbs and flowers, shovel snow, wash windows, create websites, clean blinds, fix window screens, wash cars, help care for a large litter of puppies, and walk dogs.

This will enable you to meet new people and build a network, learn to follow directions, learn responsibility, earn money, and be self-reliant – all leading to your ultimate maturity.

REMEMBER GOD'S 5ᵀᴴ COMMANDMENT?
Honor thy father and thy mother.

WHAT KIDS WANT PARENTS TO KNOW
Earlier we mentioned the professor who said his twelve-year-old daughter thought he was stupid. Well, you may have feelings like that towards your parents sometimes. Rachel Vail, author of the article *Top 15 Things Your Middle School Kid Wishes You Knew* captured *the* feelings of young men and young women in the section below.

Under each of the statements, we have made suggestions regarding how you can discuss these concerns with your parents.

1. **Respect me. I'm my own person, not just your kid. Sometimes I might have opinions that differ from yours. Sometimes I just want to be your baby. Respect me either way.**[392]

   We agree and recognize that your parents should respect you and love you unconditionally. Children are people, too. They have their own thoughts, dreams, and aspirations. If you are lucky enough to be born into a family with righteous parents and wholesome values, you will be rightly guided. Listen to your parents because they have years of experience dealing with life. Share with them your opinions - most parents will find discussions with their developing children fascinating and they will be open to learning something new, but they may not always agree with you especially if your "opinion" compromises your health and safety. While you are living in your parents' home, it is important to obey your parents. Obey your parents because they love you; it is the fifth commandment from God "Honor thy father and thy mother;" and it is a part of your job as a member of your family to help to keep peace in your household. Always be open to asking your parents to explain things, which you may not understand. Parents have the responsibility to raise you up properly so allow them to do so. Keep the channels of communication open with your parents to avoid misunderstandings.

2. **I still want to have fun with you, and feel like home is safe and happy. Smile at me.**[393]

   To relieve stress, it is a good idea to purposefully take time out just to have fun - to enjoy each other's company and to build those bonds that are so important to maintain healthy relationships. Ask your parents to set aside one day a week for "Family Home Evenings." Family home evenings are a special time set aside for your entire family to participate in activities together each week without fail so that everyone in the family can look forward to this special time. There are over 100 ideas for family home evenings at the end of this section.

Family members should be particularly mindful that building family relations is foundational to the stability of the family and the stability of society. Spending leisure time together having fun enables a family to bond. However, unstructured play with siblings and friends is also enormously important.

3. **I need to make some of my own choices, and maybe some of my own mistakes. Do not do my work for me or get me out of every jam. You do not need to be better than me at everything. Do not condescend; you do not need to impart your elderly wisdom on me if I have a problem. Please wait for me to ask for your help. If I do not ask for it, I might want to work it out for myself. Let me rant without offering advice. Sometimes that's all I really need, just to talk my way through something and for you to just listen to me.**[394]

   By all means, within reason, make your own choices as long as they are within bounds of God's Laws, societal laws, and parents' rules. It is expected that people will explore their world and learn. People make mistakes, but that is not a license to be reckless. During the course of your everyday life, you may make honest mistakes. Everyone does. That is okay. That is often how we grow. Allow yourself to make a reasonable number of errors, but ask questions before you indulge too much or too quickly into things you do not know about. Be responsible when exploring your world.

4. **Sometimes I'm going to be moody and annoyed and frustrated. You need to just let that happen (though you shouldn't let me be rude to you; that's weird and embarrassing). It might just be a mood, or something might be going on that I'm not ready to talk about yet. If you hang around doing stuff near me and do not interrupt or try to solve it as soon as I start, I might feel comfortable talking to you about things.**[395]

   We have all been teenagers before, so we know what you mean and how you may feel sometimes. Again, it is better to talk to your parents, or friends, or counselors about how you feel so that anger and pressure do not continually build up inside. Keep in mind that your parents love and respect you as a person and want you to grow up healthy and well-adjusted. Remember that they have already shown you so much love and attention. Your mother carried you for nine months and insured that her diet was healthful for you when you were just a little fetus. Your parents took care of you when you were teething and sick. They kept you clean and well fed so that you would be healthy. Now it is time for you to become responsible for part of the care that you need. For a parent it is a little like watching a baby bird take its solo flight, only the solo flight lasts for years. Your parents are happy for you when you are able to resolve things on your own, but they want to be there for you if you need their help. They want to be able to catch you if you begin to fall, which is unlike the ability of a mother bird although the mother bird would probably like to catch her baby bird when he begins to fall. I have seen dead baby birds on the ground. So be thankful that you have human parents who are capable of being able to help you. Keep in mind that your actions (or inactions) may also be stressing out your parents. It is probably best not to challenge their authority and respect them first. You may need to teach them how to talk calmly and gently to you so as to avoid uncomfortable feelings and awkward situations.

5. **Trust that I'll do my work. If I do not, you can help me manage my time, but wait until I'm not taking care of responsibilities to think I can't. Do not just assume I can't handle responsibility because of my age. Believe in me.**[396]

   Being open and honest about things can build trust. With the lure of video games, cell phones, iPads, porn, and other distractions, parents can no longer make an assumption that kids are faithfully behind closed doors doing their homework. If you are supposed to be doing work, give your parents a report periodically that shows that you are doing your job. Parents are busy and do not really have time to micro-manage teenagers. It is expected that you will show signs of maturity and responsibility and recognize the situation in which both you and your parents find yourselves and work with it, which means learn to be flexible and realistic. If your parents have trusted you to do school work on your own and have been shocked to see your grades plummet to Cs and Ds you can expect that they will want to see exactly what you have accomplished every evening, going forward. It is a good idea to keep your parents up-to-date at the best of times even if you are doing well in school. If you were working at a job, you would not want the foreman or supervisor breathing down your neck all the time to see how you were doing. You would want to be proactive, as any good team member would do, and make sure that others are kept up-to-date on the status of your work as it relates to the project. "The project" in regards to homework is; submitting assignments on time, preparing well for exams, and doing the best you can. "The project," in regards to chores is – just get them out of the way. When planning to do homework and chores remember to use your delayed gratification skills. It is up to you to make sure that your parents do not stress out about it. Employ your self-discipline skills, also. You can double your efforts to impress your parents by demonstrating responsibility and maturity.

6. **It feels really good when you ask me to teach you about what I'm learning or what I'm good at. You do not have to be awesome at computer programming to let me teach you some cool stuff, for instance. I have to be a beginner constantly. Show me it's OK to stay relaxed and present when you are struggling to learn something.**[397]

This is a good thing. By learning new skills and teaching them to others, it solidifies your knowledge. Teaching others feels good because it is human nature to want to help each other. Giving service to others is one of the highest achievements we can attain as humans. When I was a teenager, I enjoyed building metal detectors from mail order electronic kits. My dad and my uncles thought it was pretty cool and considered me the expert in my family when it came to electronics. It also made me feel good and radically boosted my confidence. Pretty soon, I started to branch out into other areas of science. I read *Popular Science* and *Popular Mechanics* magazines religiously and kept up-to-date on the latest gadgets. I loved "teaching" my uncles new things as they also shared their knowledge with me. I went on to become an engineer. Whatever your passion, use it to help, entertain, and inspire your family and extended family. They are also a safe audience in case you make mistakes. Practice your skills with your family, learn from your mistakes, perfect it, and then share with the world!

7. **I do not like the drama either, and it surprises me as much as it does you. You think it's rough having this alien lunatic in your house? Try having it in your body, and you can't even get away.**[398]

I once asked my 12-year old son why he was angry all the time. He told me bluntly, "Dad, I do not know." It's tough being a teenager. You can probably be assured that the "alien lunatic" in your body is some weird cocktail of hormones your body is generating just because you are going through puberty. By recognizing this fact, you are a long way down the road with mastering it. You must always stay in control. Use your spirit to control your mind. Talk to your parents and counselors about it. Avoid drugs and alcohol, which only make matters worse. See a medical professional regularly to make sure that things are on the up-and-up physically, but stay diligent and hang in there. You are at a critical juncture in your developmental cycle, and you must keep that in mind. You will need to develop the strength to counteract violent urges. Maybe try physical exercise or sports to dissipate some of your energy in a positive way. Remain mindful that this is just a phase you necessarily must transition through. Be patient with yourself.

However, going through the transition phase from "alien lunatic" to a healthy young man will never give you an excuse to abuse other persons. Remember the Golden Rule, "Do unto others as you would have them do onto you." The Golden Rule is truly one of Jesus' Great Commandments, which I mentioned earlier in Facet 4: *Elevate Your Spirit*. It is expressed in other ways throughout the *Bible* so it must be critical.

Therefore all things whatsoever ye would that
men should do to you, do ye even so to them:
for this is the law and the prophets.

- MATTHEW 7:12 KJV

And as ye would that men should do to
you, do ye also to them likewise.

- LUKE 6:31 KJV

8. **If you do not like my friends, it feels like you do not trust my judgment or like I am stupid about choosing friends. Or both. Ask me what I like about them, or what we have fun doing together, or just to tell you about a new friend. Stay open-minded. Still, if you think my friends are being bad to me, I need you on my side that much more.**[399]

Talk to them about the situation, by all means. Maybe they will change their minds after a while. Be open. Invite your friends over so your parents can get to know your friends better. If after meeting your friends your parents still feel the same way, then I would side with your parents. Look at the other side of the coin.

This is an area where you should definitely rely on your parent's advice. First of all, your parents have more experience than you do. Their negative opinion about your friends is not an indictment of your judgment. Your parents are only interested in protecting you short-term and long-term. Second, they are your parents, and their wishes should be respected. If you are on a quest to grow up into a well-adjusted adult male, you owe it to yourself to side with your parents and be supportive of them, especially when they have your own best interest in mind. Give your parents the respect they deserve and you will be better off in the long run. Remember the commandment, "Honor thy father and thy mother." That means listening to them with deference, as you would like you children to do for you.

9. **Sometimes I am completely overwhelmed and need to zone out for a while. I am not becoming a slug and will not stay in my room staring at a screen for the rest of my life. Maybe just for the rest of the afternoon.**[400]

Zoning out for a while is definitely okay. It can be therapeutic. It can just give your mind a break. It can help you be creative. Just tell your parents what you need to do and they will most likely understand. If you are like most teenagers, you are probably sleep-deprived, and your brain could be temporarily overwhelmed. Again, open communications are key. You might be amazed how many problems can be resolved with proper communications. However, as you now know, playing video games all afternoon is not a recommended choice for downtime – escaping by reading a novel in your room, or sleeping, or talking to a friend on the telephone, or going for a hike, or visiting with a friend are better alternatives.

10. **I will fight you every step of the way if you make me do stuff I do not want to do (get some exercise, do my homework, write a thank-you note, practice piano, apologize to my sister, take a shower, wear deodorant... so many things), but you should probably make me do them anyway. I know I will feel better if I sweat and shower each day, and develop my study skills, and show up tomorrow prepared, and, and, and. I know! But please do not overwhelm me. I might not be able to do what I should right away. I might need reminders, later, which will annoy me completely. Remind me anyway.**[401]

You are spot on with this one. At least, you recognize yourself in this situation. It is the parent's role to guide you in the path you are to go and to make sure you stick to it. Your brain is distracted enough, and parents try to maintain that delicate balance between allowing you the freedom to demonstrate maturity on your own and playing cop to make sure you do not fail. Giving you gentle reminders is a small price to pay for the insurance that you are managing your time properly and have a good chance of being successful in school and in your life. If you are overwhelmed, please let your parents know so they can help you or find help for you. However, remember to use your "delayed gratification" skills. If you procrastinate and you get behind in your schoolwork and chores, then you will feel overburdened. Be wise. At your age, you should not need to be prodded at every turn. If you do, you likely have a problem. Are you playing video games instead of doing what you ought to do? You may want to discuss the issue respectfully with your parents.

11. **Explain why I'm being criticized or punished. It feels scary if I do not understand anything beyond that you are mad at me. And sometimes what I need more than a scolding is a hug or a cuddle. Especially when I am more porcupine than a puppy.**[402]

    This is another reason why you must communicate well with your parents. Let them know that you need a hug when things are not going well for you. Better yet, walk up to them and hug them yourself. They will get the message. Parenting is a two-way street. Parents should be sensitive to you and your needs and adjust their parenting methods accordingly. Parents cannot read minds so do try to be transparent and reveal your vulnerabilities to them. Because they love you, they will understand you better and perhaps forgive you quicker for any screw-ups. Be honest, though, because parents can usually spot an invalid excuse due to laziness, or an outright lie – this will only make them more upset.

12. **I need to have private jokes with my friends and not explain them to you. It's how we bond. You do not need to be involved in every aspect of my life to still be loved and needed by me.**[403]

    We agree with you here. Each generation has its own fads and lingo. Parents do not always "get" what kids are talking about, and that's okay. Maybe when you're hanging out with your parents, you can get them caught up on the latest trends and urban slang (as long as it's clean). It might make for a fun conversation. It might bring you closer to your parents because they need to feel that you love them too, and sharing new trends in language is a good way to share your love with them. If a parent senses that private jokes might be destructive, then they may feel the need to intervene. There are certain timeless universal truths in regards to what is an appropriate joke. Sexist, racist, bigoted, homophobic jokes should never be tolerated because they instill hatred – essentially they are hate propaganda, at best they are in extremely poor taste. If you keep the company of people who encourage such joke telling you will lose credibility, especially, if you are caught saying such a joke on a recording that could be played 20 years from now when you are trying to get a good job, or run for political office.

When Mitt Romney, a Republican, ran for the presidency of the United States in 2012 against Barack Obama the Democrats capitalized on what Romney called "Tomfoolery," – a joke. When Romney was a young man, he and some of his friends jumped on a youth who had long hair and cut his hair. Romney and his friends thought it was a joke at the time but this incident came back to haunt Romney because thousands of Americans thought that Romney and his friends behaved like bullies. Romney lost the election and Barack Obama won. What you think and do today will affect your tomorrow.

Parents often have to rely on extra-sensory perception or gut instinct in order to protect their children. Do not be insulted if they are only exercising caution on your behalf. A parent will always be your parent, even after you are an adult. They will eventually need to let their little bird fly from the nest. Even though they might have less influence on your life when that happens, they will still feel a sense of responsibility borne out of a lifetime of love for you. Just be sensitive to their innate need to protect you regardless of your age. You will likely be the same with your children. Remember that mothers can carry cells from the babies they carried in their wombs for up to 27 years. No wonder your mother still feels connected to you. She is!

13. **If my social life gets to be too much, I may need you to force a little vacation from it on me. But most of the time what I need is to work through how to navigate life online and with peers. Now is my chance to learn how to deal with this, with your help. Just shutting it down keeps me from learning how**

to build my life online with scaffolding provided by you. Stay calm and cool, let me explain what's going on, and talk things through with me. Ask more, tell less.[404]

As you grow older and as you demonstrate sufficient maturity, your parents may feel that you can have more autonomy. With the number of predators in our society, we believe that kids should always be mindful of the dangers of the Internet as well as all the good that can be derived from it. I can't stress this enough: communication with your parents is paramount. Do not be too secretive because this will only breed suspicion. Also, it will be harder to bail you out of a sticky situation. Yes, learning how to navigate the complexity of life online and offline is daunting, but you are not in this game all by yourself. Your parents are an integral part of your life. When you meet your future spouse, she will be even more integral in your life. So you are better off learning how to deal with that now. You will be a stronger person if you learn to leverage these family relationships in dealing with your life. It is your family's responsibility to help to protect you. We agree that it would behoove parents to learn to handle situations diplomatically to avoid hard feelings, so gently let them know if you feel that they are overbearing. However, listen to them and respect their authority and position too. **Reminder:** Spending time with friends from school, sports teams, band, choir, scouting, church groups, cousins (basically people that you know) face-to-face is healthier for you than spending time on-line. Scheduling a meeting with a stranger that you have met on-line without discussing it with your parents is not a good idea. Because some men who want to harm young men pretended to be girls on-line. Be wise and stay safe.

14. **Especially if I've been feeling stressed, maybe you could just hang out with me. Go to the park or get an ice cream or have a catch, whatever; it feels good to just do something together without discussing or solving or teaching anything.**[405]

Yeah, that sounds great. Take a look at the *101 Things You Could Do for Fun with Your Family* at the end of this chapter. Having good, clean fun with your family is a tremendous way to build rapport and express love for each other.

15. **I like it when you think I'm funny. Or interesting. Or awesome. I actually do care what you think about me. Please find something specific you actually like about me because sometimes I can't find anything in myself to like at all. I might roll my eyes, but your words and judgments do matter to me, and I will remember them, the good and the bad. I will keep them with me like treasures even when I lose my keys and wallet and ID. Which I probably will. More than once. Sorry.**[406]

Be honest. Tell them how you feel. When you roll your eyes you are giving your parents a negative message. Your parents don't want to alienate you by being obnoxious. If you roll your eyes when they give you a compliment they may not give you another compliment out of fear of alienating you. If they tend to complement you about things that don't matter to you - tell them that you would rather feel that they appreciate something else that you are capable of doing. Communication is key.

For parents, there is no lovelier dream than successfully raising their children to adulthood and seeing them become fruitful and happy. This is not an easy road for either the parents or the children. The path is fraught with danger, pain, laughter, joy, misery and more often than not, success. A family is truly made in heaven. Parents are indeed blessed if they have children. Children are indeed blessed if they are born to or adopted by loving parents. This is our constant prayer, but often that is not the case.

APPRECIATE AND RESPECT ALL YOUR FAMILY
MEMBERS AND THEY WILL HAVE YOUR BACK

Be thankful for your family. Be thankful for your parents. Be thankful for your siblings if you have them. Be thankful for your forbears because without them neither you nor your parents would be here.

Always feed and nourish your relationship with your family because your knowledge, talent and your family are the only things you will take with you to the spirit world. Families are truly FOREVER. Hopefully, you will be sealed to your parents, your spouse and your children in a Temple so that on that Great and Terrible Day you will all be together under the protective arm of Jesus Christ.

BE KIND TO YOUR PARENTS

1. Be respectful to your parents and hopefully they will be respectful to you. Do not roll your eyes as this is definitely a sign of disrespect. Never raise your voice to your parents. Never have a "tone" of voice with them that signals disrespect.
2. Call them to let them know how you are doing throughout your life. Make as much of an effort to speak to your parents as you do to speak to your friends because your parents love you more than your friends do and they have been pivotal in your life, and they are bound to remain pivotal. Friends tend to come and go in this transient society.
3. Show your parents that you appreciate them. Give them a card. Help them with a chore. Bring your mother a rose. If you have younger siblings, give your parents a break from parental responsibility by offering to babysit to give your parents a date night.

BE KIND TO YOUR SISTER

Share your feelings with your sister and listen to her feelings. Sometimes two heads are better than one at sorting out feelings and life's problems. Since you both come from the same generation, family and culture you are likely to understand each other very well. Write a poem or a letter to your sister, which she will treasure for a lifetime. The following poem is an example:

Poem for a Sister

Thanks
Remember the time, I got into trouble,
You helped me up, out of the rubble.
I never had to go far for advice,
Talking with you, has always been nice.

Looked at others, tried to compare,
Quickly realized, you were more fair.
I just had to politely ask,
And you would help me with any task.

We always had each other's back,
Especially when, our days were black.
To a great sister, just want to say thanks,
Hope you enjoyed, my jokes and my pranks.
(by anitapoems.com)

Be Kind to Your Brother

How lucky you are to have a brother. If you don't have a biological brother, ask your favorite cousin or your best friend to be your brother. Make a pact to keep in touch no matter where life takes you. You can build commonality and build wonderful memories with your brother – through scouting, sports, church activities, and family outings. Write a poem or letter for your brother, which he will treasure for a lifetime. The following poem is an example:

Poem for a Brother

My Brother and Friend

I'm so happy;

you're my brother and friend.
A few verses of love,
I'd just like to send.

I always enjoy,
spending time with you.
In so many ways,
together we grew.

We share a close bond
and a very strong link.
We openly express,
whatever we think.

Just want to thank you,
for all you have done.
You've always been,
hilarious and fun.

You're one of those people,
that is genuinely nice,
You're always willing,
to offer advice.

My life has been blessed,
with a brother like you.
With you by my side,
life's easier to chew!
(by anitapoems.com)

YOUTH LIVING IN FOSTER FAMILIES

If you are living with a foster family, the insights above still apply, mostly, even if you were not living with your foster family when you were little. Changing families is tough. Keeping lines of communication open with your foster family and your social worker is still a key factor in having a successful experience in foster care. Report any abuse promptly to your social worker – keep a record of events, times, and dates, to give to your social worker if need be.

While you are in foster care establishing a pivotal stable environment of caring people in your life, outside of your home, is critical to your well-being in the present and the future. Becoming a member of Boy Scouts of America will help to provide you with a measure of stability if you ever have to move to a different foster family. If you have to move to a different area, you may have to change scout troop as well but you will find caring mentors in any scout troop and can still build upon the scouting skills and badges that you have already earned. These skills will help you to find a job when you leave foster care so that you do not become homeless. Scouts will provide you with a network of people who know you and can recommend you for jobs and can help you to find housing because scouts are raised to help each other and other people. Essentially, scouts can become your family, as well. Someday, you can become a scout leader and help boys like yourself to become the best they can be. Joining a church will give you spiritual sustenance and a sense of belonging to God's family.

Your Life Priorities and a Road Map

As you travel along your quest for manhood, it might be helpful to have a roadmap. Now that you have considered your mind, body, spirit, character, and you have begun to understand the importance of family, you might wonder how it all fits together.

I suggest you consider your life priorities (roadmap) in this order:

* Developing a knowledge of God
* Keeping your mind, body and spirit healthy
* Developing a gentlemanly, kind, and dependable character

- Loving your 1st family (mother, father, siblings, grandparents, and ancestors)
- Loving your 2nd family (wife, and children)
- Being an active member of society (community, nation, world)

Since we already covered in this book your mind, body and the spiritual parts of your journey, and we are covering the family in this chapter, logically society will be covered in the next chapter.

So let's continue by exploring the next phase or what follows in your progression – dating, marriage and having children.

PREPARATION FOR MARRIAGE

Virtue loveth virtue; light cleaveth unto light.

- DOCTRINE AND COVENANTS 88:40

HANGING OUT AND DATING

Before you build a family, you will probably spend some time hanging out with girls and dating girls to eventually find a wife. So, let's get a handle on hanging out and dating.

What is "hanging out"? In some parts of the country hanging out with girls means spending time with a group of friends both male and female. Many teens use the term "hanging out" when spending time with girls individually or in groups. Activities can include, for example, school dances, church functions, school sporting events, and everyday things like working on a school project, or watching a movie at a friend's house or preparing a large pizza, or baking cook-ies. In other parts of the country the term "casual dating" with girls means, spending one on one time with a girl, accompanied by an-other couple on a double dating basis, but also spending time with other girls at different times, which we recommend after attaining the age of sixteen. Examples of activities for casual dating include: going out for lunch, hiking, attending parties, visiting museums, visiting a botanical garden, and touring a zoo. These types of activities will enable you to casually get to know the young women better. This will allow you to discern the best qualities in young ladies you would like to have in your eternal partner.

What is "serious dating"? Today in some parts of the country to "date" someone means that a young man and a young woman are seeing each other exclusively. However, for the purpose of this book when a young man and young woman decide to exclusively accompany each other to social events, they are seriously dating (not dating anyone else) – double dating with another couple is still recommended. Activities for serious dating could include going to church together, going to the beach, singing in a choir, acting in a play, going out to dinner, attending spectator sports, hiking, visiting with friends, planting a garden, learning how to dance, attending weddings and funerals, attending graduation ceremonies, and everyday things as well such as shopping, and watching a movie at home.

The booklet *For the Strength of Youth* informs us that a date is simply a planned activity for you and a female companion to get to know each other, practice social skills, and develop a friendship.

Do not start (serious) dating right away. Go out with different young ladies – not the same person all the time (casual dating). Do not get too serious too quickly. You do not want to limit your opportunity to get to know more young ladies. It will also help avoid immorality.[407]

We recommend that you wait until you are at least sixteen (preferably seventeen) before seriously dating a young woman exclusively. The young lady should be a minimum of sixteen years of age as well. When you first start dating, be sure to invite at least one other couple to go along.

When choosing someone to date, be sure to select a young lady who has high moral standards that mirror yours. While on a date, it is the responsibility of both the young man and the young woman to protect each other's honor and virtue – as remaining chaste before marriage and avoiding fornication is one of God's Laws.

Choose your dating activities and locations wisely. Activities should be safe, spiritually uplifting (as in having fun and being happy and as in feeling the spirit of God), and inexpensive. You just want to be able to have a good time and get to know each other better. Only go to places where you will be able to maintain good order, decorum, and moral standards.

The *For the Strength of Youth* booklet suggests, "Young men generally take the initiative in asking for and planning dates. Always be kind and respectful when you ask for a date or when you accept or decline one. While on a date, be courteous as you listen to others and express your own feelings."[408] Practice your gentleman skills.

"If young people court (date) one another without being sexually involved they can more objectively determine whether they should proceed further or whether they should part and seek other more compatible companions," states *Mature Intimacy: Courtship and Marriage, A Parent's Guide*, The Church of Jesus Christ of Latter-day Saints.

The Lord condemns every sexual relationship outside of marriage. Sexual sins are more serious than any other sins except murder and denying the Holy Ghost (see Alma 39:3-5). If you are not married, you should not have sex. If you are married, you should have sex only with your legal spouse. Of course, this is your choice. However, we caution you to use your moral agency to do the right thing, otherwise, there will be spiritual consequences – as we have discussed in Facet 4: *Elevate Your Spirit*.

It is important to know this because if you adhere to this law, you will be blessed. Also, if you adhere to this law while dating you will be creating a foundation of respect, which will strengthen your relationship and enable you to overcome the tumultuous times during your life together after you are married.

Kisses

When dating seriously, sweet kisses to say hello and good night are lovely. If you both choose not to kiss that is fine as well. There is no hurry. Some people prefer to wait until their wedding day to kiss for the first time.

However, it may be important for you to know whether or not the young woman you are dating is as affectionate as you are, and whether or not you like each other's kisses. How to kiss someone can be learned at any time. For some people, it comes naturally, but others need to be taught or still for some people it is a matter of preference – some people prefer soft kisses, other people prefer passionate kisses. Soft kisses are likely to be more appropriate when dating seriously. Passionate kisses may be best after marriage because they may lead to the temptation of further sexual contact.

When dating seriously, some time after the first kiss, it is important to discuss these preferences. You do not want to lose the girl you are contemplating to marry because she finds your kisses too harsh or too soft. This may sound silly, but it happens. Keep in mind that some young ladies may need to be kissed softly even after marriage until trust in your tenderness is established.

Note: The first kiss is like a present you give to each other. It is best not to talk about the present until it is opened.

How to Choose a Spouse

Some day you may want to make one of the most important decisions of your life – you will ask a young woman to marry you. Finding the right marriage partner takes maturity and "people smarts." You must be a good judge of character. First, before you plan to propose to a young lady, you must start by preparing yourself to BE the right spouse.

Prepare Yourself to be the Right Spouse

You might want to start by asking yourself a series of questions to determine if you are someone a young woman would want to marry. First look at your habits: how you talk, how clean you look and how you dress. There are also other factors to consider such as:

- Do you have a weight that is heavier than most people would appreciate? If so, after reading Facet 3: *Elevate Your Body*, you should be able to quickly take charge of developing a healthy body.

- Are you eccentric? Most people have little eccentricities, so you need to take a look at yours. Take the time to analyze them. An anonymous author wrote on yahoo a list of their own eccentricities, which included: (1) Quickly leafing through paperback books so they create a draft (wind), just before he read them, (2) Ranting (sometimes angrily, sometimes humorously) about every little thing no matter how insignificant. Assuming that the author is a man the former eccentricity would not be a problem for a young lady, the latter eccentricity would be a problem, and (3) Making sure all pen lids' clips point towards the writing down the pen. This eccentricity may be an indication that someone has an obsessive-compulsive disorder. That coupled with "ranting about every little thing," would be cause for concern for any young woman. She should run away from a man with such a temperament. If you have similar eccentricities seek psychological help prior to beginning a serious relationship with a young woman.

- Are you too selfish? If anyone has told you that you are selfish, they may be right. If so, practice thinking about how you would feel if you were treated in the same manner. Realize that if you would not like being treated that way, or would be sad due to an unfortunate event, another person is likely to feel the same. For example, if you and a girlfriend are meeting to do homework together, don't eat an apple in front of her without offering her an apple or offering to share your apple before you bite into it.

- Do you have annoying habits such as smacking when you are eating or chewing with your mouth open? Chewing as quietly as possible is courteous. Also, please keep your mouth closed while chewing, and don't talk with food in your mouth.

* Do you have a warm and cold personality? Is your behavior friendly one day and unfriendly the next? Having a balanced attitude towards people will enable people to trust that they will feel liked or loved by you on a constant basis.

* Are you dull or are you over-the-top exuberant? If you are dull make an effort to read or listen to the news, to enable yourself to communicate about current events. If you are shy, rehearse a comment or two in private before attending a social situation. If you have been told that you are too exuberant – be your exuberant self with someone who is like you and remember to actively listen while making an effort to understand what other people are expressing.

* What personality traits do you like in other people? Emulate those traits if they are pleasing and righteous.

* Are you hanging out in the right places to meet the right girl for you? It isn't easy to meet people these days because few communities organize community socials and community dances like in the old days. Therefore, you will have to take charge of your destiny. Don't expect that the young woman of your dreams will simply fall into your lap. Go find her. Join a church. Join a special interest club at your school, college or university. Join a choir. Participate in a play. Take a cooking class. Join a canoeing club. Play tennis. Play golf. Be open to personal introductions from relatives, and friends.

WHEN IS THE RIGHT TIME FOR MARRIAGE?

The right time for getting married is when you are ready to be the right spouse for someone else who is the right spouse for you.

What does this mean? Many of us see the faults in other people, but we do not see our own faults. Therefore, before you begin to search for a young woman with the qualities that you want in a spouse, you must first identify your own weaknesses. Then start to correct them before you begin to date and while you are dating – prior to marriage. Your strengths will contribute to the success of your marriage.

You are in part a product of your upbringing to a certain extent. Your background does not necessarily dictate your future, but in general, good family relationships help us have healthy marriages. The converse is also true to a certain extent. Poor family environments can lead to weak or troubled marriages. But you are in charge, so you can learn to overcome any shortcomings you may have had in your background and decide to do the things necessary to create a good marriage. Start by choosing the right young woman at the right time.

This issue of timing is a delicate balancing act. You shouldn't wait too long, but neither should you jump into marriage too quickly:

- <u>Do not put off marriage for too long.</u> Gordon B. Hinckley offered this counsel about timing: "I hope you will not put off marriage too long. I do not speak so much to the young women as to the young men whose prerogative and responsibility it is to take the lead in this matter. Do not go on endlessly in a frivolous dating game. Look for a choice companion, one you can love, honor, and respect, and make a decision."[409]
- <u>Do not jump into marriage too quickly.</u> Take the time to find the girl of your choice. Take the time necessary to communicate about your hopes and dreams; strengths and weaknesses; likes and dislikes; attitudes towards finances; attitudes towards each other's family; religious beliefs and values; and the lifestyle you foresee for your family.

I can offer you an example of the latter:

When I got married at 22 years of age, I had just joined the Navy. After our wedding day (in Texas), I was shocked to discover that my bride did not want to move to Florida with me where I was posted. She wanted to finish her college courses. Three torturous months passed before she joined me, and as we drove to my new station in Maryland, she cried all the way because she missed her family. This was very upsetting to me, to say the least. I was morti-fied. It took several months before she calmed down and started to feel at home.

In retrospect, we had not communicated sufficiently. Perhaps it would have been best for me to marry a young woman who was ac-customed to a military lifestyle or a Foreign Service lifestyle - some-one who was accustomed to change.

One thing is sure; we hardly knew each other. We had met on a college campus where there were very few women. I had almost no experience dating women. I just knew I wanted to be married.

My parents had a good marriage, and that was what I wanted for myself. They would eventually be married for over 50 years.

My bride and I had dated only twice before I was deployed to Europe and, over manual correspondence; somehow, we had decided to get married when I came home from deployment. We had not had sufficient time to get to know each other properly. Hopefully, some of you will learn from my mistake. After this mar-riage failed - I finally learned to date many women without becom-ing too serious at first, to find someone with whom I would be compatible on all levels — intellectually, emotionally, spiritually, and physically. I learned to determine when a relationship was not healthy, and ended a poor relationship as soon as I knew it was a poor relationship — so as not to waste my time — time I could spend finding the right woman. I was able to recognize quickly when a woman was not the right one for me and kept searching until I found the love of my life.

The Ensign Magazine article, *Choosing and Being the Right Spouse*, recommends that "Sincere, positive communication prac-ticed in dating and courtship increases the likelihood of greater com-mitment, better conflict resolution, and more love between partners in marriage. Good communication begins with a righteous heart."[410]

Out of the abundance of the heart the mouth speaketh.

- Matt. *12:34*

On the other hand, communication from a selfish heart is generally just manipulation. Elder Marvin J. Ashton said: "If we would know true love and understanding one for another, we must realize that communication is more than a sharing of words. It is the wise sharing of emotions, feelings, and concerns. It is the sharing of oneself totally."[411]

SHOW RESPECT FOR YOURSELF TOO

Of course, you will want to marry a woman to whom you can show respect. That goes without saying. But at the same time, you must respect yourself as well. The self-respect that prepares one well for marriage is not, as Harold B. Lee has said, "an abnormally developed self-esteem that becomes haughtiness, conceit, or arrogance, but a righteous self-respect that might be defined as 'belief in one's own worth, worth to God, and worth to mankind (which includes his wife and family).'"[412]

Lee also mentions one young wife's comments about her husband which illustrates how a poor sense of self-worth can harm a marriage. The wife said, "I love him, and I hope he will change. He has poor self-esteem. In any discussion of problems in our relationship, he puts up defenses and throws everything back on me or says he is worthless."[413]

In *Psychology Today*, published on May 1, 2012, Stephen J. Betchen wrote, in his article *Knowing When Someone's Not Right for You*, a compelling personal story about trusting and respecting your own instincts:

"When I was in my late teens, I was fortunate enough to be approached at a summer party by an extraordinarily beautiful girl. This young lady was as close to a so-called supermodel as someone other than a rock star could get—and my male friends wholeheartedly agreed. Tall, slim, and with perfectly symmetrical features, there was only one way a person could be this beautiful—you'd have to be born that way.

"Now this wasn't the kind of thing that usually happened to me, but rather than being wrought with insecurity I distinctly remember feeling eerily calm; as if the experience wasn't real enough to fret over. The truth is, I was waiting to wake up—and I soon did.

"While I'll never forget that night, it was on our first formal date—the following week—that my icon injected reality directly into my veins - at least five times within the first couple of hours she asked me how tall I was. And while I answered straight-up, she continued to ask until I realized that I was in the middle of something Shakespeare might have appreciated. In speaking to the crowd following Caesar's assassination Mark Antony referred several times to Brutus as "an honorable man." It was Antony's way of telling the crowd that he was particularly displeased that Brutus was involved in the assassination.

"My teenage dreamboat conveyed time and again that she was displeased with the disparity in our height: I swear she was only about one inch taller than I was. Can you imagine, one inch from being a teen ubermensch; one inch from being elevated beyond an average boy's high school station? I do not mean to sound like an ingrate, but at the time I would've rather had severe acne—at least I wouldn't have suffered false hope.

"Part of me wanted to believe that this girl really liked me. For a brief moment, I fantasized that by repeatedly asking the same question she was hoping to get a different answer...and a different reality. But shy of orthotics, or a pair of high-heeled shoes from the Disco era, as we say in Jersey: 'Forget about it.' So I did the only logical thing: I told her that it was okay with me if she wanted a taller guy; that I would quietly steal away into the night so that she could pursue a better fit. Gallant, don't you think? A little like King Arthur allowing Guinevere to go to her true love, Lancelot. Surprisingly however, she denied that height was a problem. 'You're crazy,' she said, 'I'd be shallow to base a relationship on height.'

"I wanted to buy her story so-o-o-o bad. I thought the rest of my life was riding on it—or at least the rest of high school—and she told it with such passion and sincerity. But I was sure I was right. So I pulled myself out of her arms and left, never to have seen her again. I assume she's married to a basketball player by now...and that's fine."[414]

STUDY FEMALE BODY LANGUAGE

Girls can at times be confusing. It is sometimes difficult to read their body language. A young woman named Lizzie posted these tips on YouTube, telling guys what signs girls give out when they are not interested. I feel that they are quite helpful in navigating the "Whom do I ask out on a date?" stage of dating. In order to find a girl who likes you, you need to know the signs a girl gives when she does not like you.

SIGNS A GIRL GIVES WHEN SHE DOES NOT LIKE YOU

The YouTube video that Lizzie Ereezay published gives these valuable insights that might prove to be useful to know as you interact with young ladies:

1. She is clearly uncomfortable with physical contact. She moves away when you touch her arm.
2. She does not laugh at your jokes.
3. She backs away when you talk to her.
4. She does not want to hug you in an affection way. She just pats one of your shoulders instead of hugging you underneath your arms.
5. She is too busy to spend time with you.
6. She is vague about making plans. There is no enthusiasm for the plans you wish to make.
7. If she likes you, she will touch her hair gently with long strokes. If not, she is likely to touch her hair with short jerky movements.

8. If she likes someone else, chances are she does not like you – although this could change.
9. Her conversations are only about what she is doing and not about what she is feeling.
10. She does not go out of her way to talk to you.
11. She does not care that much about your life. She does not ask you questions about your life because she does not want to get to know you better.[415]

While it is recommended to wait until the age of sixteen to date, and to double date with friends for a few years while you get to know many different girls before you decide which type of girl you prefer. It is a good idea for 12-year-olds to begin to talk to girls in school and to practice reading their body language, which gives clues about how they are feeling. Practice makes perfect!

Occasionally, a boy and a girl meet at sixteen and love each other so much they never date anyone else – they marry and stay married for 60, 65, even 72 years, until death takes one of them. Frequently, for these couples the one left behind dies just a few weeks after or only a year or so after their spouse dies because they miss their spouse and lose the will to live.

WHO IS THE RIGHT GIRL FOR YOU?
A girl you respect and love with all your heart.

HOW TO KNOW WHETHER OR NOT A GIRL IS THE RIGHT GIRL FOR YOU
If both you and the girl feel a very special connection on all levels, she is likely the right girl for you. Thirty signs that you have a genuinely good relationship:

1. You both have a spiritual commitment to God's laws.
2. You respect each other.
3. You respect yourselves.

4. You both feel at ease with each other.
5. You enjoy spending time with each other.
6. You share goals for the future.
7. You have common interests, for example, in regards to friends, music, and food.
8. You are intellectually similar. It is wonderful to have a companion with whom you can communicate on topics that interest both of you.
9. You work well together – doing schoolwork, or volunteering, or gardening.
10. You have similar beliefs on important topics such as family life and how to manage money.
11. The girl wants the same number of children as you do.
12. She shows you that she cares for you with her actions, and you show her that you care for her with your actions such as taking care of each other when you are not feeling well.
13. She shows that she cares for other people. She is kind to her parents, kind to her siblings, kind to her friends, and kind towards children. She is also kind towards your family.
14. She dresses appropriately.
15. Her language is appropriate.
16. She has good manners.
17. She has good hygiene and personal grooming.
18. You trust each other.
19. You love each other for who you are (you are not trying to change each other).
20. You can have a disagreement and resolve conflicts civilly.
21. You both respect each other's need to have private interests, for example, volunteering with scouting, reading, painting a picture.
22. You like each other's friends and family.
23. You both encourage each other to be the best you can be and boost each other's confidence when you are down.
24. You both feel comfortable in social situations together.
25. You enjoy holding hands.
26. You like each other's kisses (16 years or older only).

27. You both believe that you have found the right person with whom to share your life.
28. The girl's very presence inspires you to be the best you can be.
29. You are both inspired to be loving and loyal to each other.
30. The girl is healthy and is likely to carry healthy babies unless you are willing to make the sacrifice of potentially not having children.

It is important for young people to not use harmful substances, especially if they are planning to have children. As we have seen, if the young man and young woman avoid foods with harmful chemicals, and they avoid drugs, they are more likely to have children without birth defects. Substances such as sodas, caffeine, alcohol, tobacco, cocaine, marijuana, aspartame (see Health Tips) and some prescription medications are not conducive to good health – especially for a young mother who is expecting a baby. We have been warned by the prophets to avoid polluting "the fountains of life" which could harm a child inside the womb.

A healthy mother is an advantage to a developing fetus. Fundamental hygiene is important, including regular bathing and clean, fresh clothing. Diet is crucial. The mother should eat healthy foods and drink plenty of water long before pregnancy and during pregnancy, so that the baby will receive enough nourishment through the umbilical connection between the placenta and the uterus. Get a doctor's advice about prenatal vitamins. Your wife should exercise during pregnancy to maintain proper blood circulation and healthy respiration. Exercise during pregnancy will also minimize unnecessary weight gain to facilitate postnatal recovery.

When you find a relationship such as the one covered by the 30 markers above, you will know that it is a relationship worth nurturing and developing. Develop yourself until you have the necessary fortitude of character to be worthy of such a relationship. Also, become financially stable enough to marry her.

ESTABLISHING FINANCIAL STABILITY BEFORE MARRIAGE

Financial stability does not mean being rich. It is possible to marry your sweetheart while you are both in college if you both have - part time jobs, apply for student grants, and live frugally. The wedding and reception can be organized on a frugal basis as well, as you shall see later on in the book.

Alicia Rades makes a fascinating argument for getting married while attending college. Rades discovered from her personal experience that a couple can save many thousands of dollars by qualifying for grants after marriage and living off campus as a married couple (working part time) - which she shares in *Why It Makes (Financial) Sense to Marry Before Graduation*. They were married in early 2012 and filed their *Free Application for Federal Student Aid* (FAFSA) after the wedding for their 2012-2013 school year. As of 2014, when Rades article was published, she was happily married and as a couple, she and her husband had saved around $28,000. Some of their savings helped to pay for the cost of their wedding. However, Rades does not recommend marrying someone down the hall just to save money. Rades and her boyfriend had planned to be married since high school.[416]

THE BLESSINGS OBTAINED IN CONSUMMATING A HAPPY MARRIAGE

There are profound blessings to be obtained in consummating a happy marriage. There are physical, spiritual and eternal joys awaiting those who enter into marriage with proper intentions. In his presentation, *The Plan of Happiness*, Boyd K. Packer states:

> "Ideally, mating begins with romance. Though customs may vary, it flourishes with all the storybook feelings of excitement and anticipation, even sometimes rejection. There are moonlight and roses, love letters, love songs, poetry, the holding of hands, and other expressions of affection between a young man and a young woman. The world disappears around the couple, and they experience feelings of joy.

"And if you suppose that the full-blown rapture of young romantic love is the sum total of the possibilities which spring from the fountains of life, you have not yet lived to see the devotion and the comfort of longtime married love. Married couples are tried by temptation, misunderstandings, financial problems, family crises, and illness, and all the while love grows stronger. Mature love has a bliss not even imagined by newlyweds.

"True love requires reserving until after marriage the sharing of that affection which unlocks those sacred powers in that fountain of life. It means avoiding situations where physical desire might take control. Pure love presupposes that only after a pledge of eternal fidelity, a legal and lawful ceremony, and ideally after the sealing ordinance in the temple are those procreative powers released in God's eye for the full expression of love. It is to be shared solely and only with that one who is your companion forever.

"When entered into worthily, this process combines the most exquisite and exalted physical, emotional, and spiritual feelings associated with the word *love*. *That* part of life has no equal, no counterpart, in all human experience."[417]

During your married life, you will encounter challenges. To meet these challenges, you will need to be steadfast, courageous, creative, inventive, flexible, communicative, optimistic, determined and dependable. Scouting will help you develop fortitude of character through the development of life skills. Learning to do things that are tough – like hiking a 50-mile trek – will prepare you for times when life gets tough, and as the saying goes "When the going gets tough, the tough get going."

As on a 50-mile scouting trek and in life when the going gets tough it is good to have friends to give you a helping hand. You will find that kind of friendship in scouting, and you will find that type of friendship as a member of a church. As a scout and as a member of a church, you will not be alone in your youth or in your married life.

It is important for a man to be able to support his wife because after childbirth your wife may be too weak to go back to work even if she wants to go back to work. Some babies do not sleep well at night, and young mothers suffer from sleep deprivation until the baby is several months old. Some babies need to feed every two hours. Some babies suffer from painful colic (stomach cramps). After that, teething begins, and again the baby does not sleep through the night. Add to this colds and flu, measles, and chicken pox and you can see that at times a mother will need to nap when her little children nap during the day. Also, many women find it tough to leave their babies with someone else when they become mothers. They would rather care for their babies and prepare nutritious meals for their family. Studies have shown that young children's intellectual development, social development, emotional development, and behavioral development are all greater when cared for at home, than when they are cared for in daycare.

The Myth of Quality Daycare written by Mr. Violato and Ms. Snow of The National Foundation for Family Research and Education (NFFRE), appeared in the Canadian National Post on May 2, 2000. It is an indication that someone cares enough about babies and little children to seek and speak the truth. The NFFRE gave our children who cannot speak for themselves, a voice, by speaking out against a socially accepted norm that is detrimental to the healthy development of children - daycare. The aforementioned article by Violato and Snow states the following:

> "Indeed, the meta-analysis shows that daycare seems to have a small, negative effect on the intellectual, social, and emotional functioning of children who experience it for more than 25 hours per week. And there appear to be even larger negative consequences for daycare children when it comes to behavioral outcomes and their attachments to their mothers.
>
> "These results are disquieting in and of themselves. Even more disturbing was the discovery that the quality of the daycare seems to have no mediating effect on these outcomes.

"In analyzing the data on more than 32,000 children brought together through the meta-analysis, the researchers looked at such variables as the sponsor of care (for-profit nursery schools versus government-run care centers versus "the nice woman down the street"), education of the caregivers, caregiver-to-child ratios and program quality.

"Irrespective of the nature or quality of the program studied, the children in daycare fared, on average, less well on all significant developmental indicators – intellectual, emotional and social – than their stay-at-home counterparts."[418]

In other words: Young men should prepare to support their future families.

JUGGLING WORK AND PARENTING

As you can see the best environment for raising children is their parents' home. Some women and occasionally a man want to work at home to care for their small children even if they have attained a post-secondary education. In so doing they may sacrifice momentum for their degrees will become obsolete in a couple of years. They will sacrifice job seniority, monies they would have earned, and a higher rate of social security when they retire – that is if they decide to enter the workforce when the children start school.

Some women and men know that they would find working at home full time too difficult – they would feel cut-off from mainstream society. They would feel too vulnerable due to the divorce rate. They have already sacrificed and worked hard to attain their post-secondary education and to develop their skills and talents. They are eager to pursue their passion in the workplace – as actors, doctors, musicians, dancers, athletes, lawyers, engineers, accountants, hairdressers, photographers, midwives, and so forth.

Our position is:

1. When a woman or a man decide to make the sacrifice to stay home out of wanting the joy of raising their little children, for they are so precious and those early years go by so quickly – may God bless them with fruitful careers afterwards.

2. When a man and a woman have little children, and they both want to work, may they each find a part time job "job sharing," to enable each parent to pursue their careers by keeping their foot in the door of the workforce on a part-time basis, which will keep their experience in their chosen fields current. More job sharing opportunities need to be created in the workplace. Also, couples can share a business. They can work different shifts – this is hard – one of my stepdaughters and her husband did this to keep their babies out of daycare. Nonetheless, it worked. May God bless these couples, as well.

3. Planning your career goals with your future children in mind is essential for your children's well-being.

BENEFITS OF GETTING MARRIED SOONER RATHER THAN LATER

There are three very significant reasons to marry sooner rather than later in life.

1. The availability of good single women is greater when you are young. During your high school and college years you will have the greatest opportunity to meet women with whom you have something in common – at school, at social events, in church, at political rallies, and through friends and relatives. Once you begin to work in an office with a small staff and work over time to launch your career, your choices will be limited. Choose wisely and treat her well for the same reason. You do not want to have a divorce ten years after marriage to find that the women you want to date are not interested in marrying an older man because they want to have healthy babies of their own.

2. To have a few years as a couple to enjoy time together without the responsibility of children. When you marry at a young age there is no need to begin to have children immediately.

3. To reduce the odds of having children with birth defects - It is through marriage that you attain the highest level of love and human relationship especially when you have children. Because the optimum child-bearing age for young women is around 18-28, you might consider starting to think about marriage sometime after your first year of college. Just plan to marry sooner rather than waiting until later in life because when couples conceive after the woman has attained the age of thirty, birth defects become more likely - actually the odds of conceiving a baby with birth defects increases with each passing year. The same is true if a man is older, even if he marries a much younger woman because semen counts deteriorate with each passing year, which affects fertility, and genetic disorders are more likely to occur. Chris Gayomali reported for The Week in his article *At What Age Does a Man's Sperm Quality Deteriorate?* that, "The decline in sperm quality may start as early as age 35, according to *New Scientist*. Researchers at Reproductive Technology Laboratories in Los Angeles reached their conclusion after examining roughly 5,000 men between the ages of 16 and 72. Sperm, like any other cell, spend their lives constantly regenerating. And with every cell division comes an increased risk of genetic mutation, which is why some studies have linked older fathers (40 and up) to children with diseases like autism and schizophrenia."[419]

4. To have a long and healthy relationship with your wife and children. To have the energy to play with your children when you are relatively young. To raise them before the age of deterioration when people begin to die more frequently. My step grandsons lost their father of natural causes when they were seventeen and eighteen years old. That was tough.

MAKING THE DECISION TO MARRY HER

In Choosing and Being the Right Spouse by Thomas B. Holman we also find:

Before you propose, you can ask for confirmation from God.

First, you must be worthy of receiving the inspiration from God. Being worthy includes not lusting after other women on porn sites, or in magazines or books; paying tithing to your church; obeying all of God's commandments, and observing all your covenants.

Secondly, you need to understand the balance between agency (free will) and inspiration. As Elder McConkie taught us,

"We make our own choices, and then we present the matter to the Lord and get his approving, ratifying seal." The experience of one young man illustrates this: "There are two things in my life that I've always felt would be important: a career and marriage. Yet at the time I didn't feel like I was getting a response (from God). I prayed, 'Heavenly Father, this is so important, I need to know whether or not it's right.' Then toward the end of our courtship, I went to the temple. I was so frustrated because I wasn't getting an answer either way. After praying and waiting for an answer, I got more frustrated and gave up. That was when an impression came to me: 'You already know the answer.' Then I realized that God had answered my prayers. The decision to marry Becky always made sense and felt right. I can see now that God had been telling me in my heart and in my mind that it was a good decision. And later, at the time of the ceremony, I had another confirmation that what I was doing was right."[420]

Thirdly, you may want to ask several times for confirmation from God. In His infinite love, mercy, and patience, our Heavenly Father is generous with His counsel and response to His children.

Fourth, we can learn to discern the differences between inspiration, infatuation, and desperation.

Inspiration, as we have already seen, comes when one is living worthily, exercises agency righteously, and studies the situation out carefully. It can be confirmed by multiple spiritual enlightenments and peaceful feelings.

Recognize that infatuation may give you a false sense of love. Infatuation is immature love. It has the hallmarks of jealousy, possessiveness, clinginess, and overdependence.

Also, be aware of desperation where you might want to get married just to get out of certain personal or cultural situations. Recognize this as immature love that needs to be re-examined.

Fifth, seek spiritual confirmation, where both of you pray for an answer from Heavenly Father that you are worthy and are entering into a healthy relationship. Elder Dallin H. Oaks has discussed this issue: "If a revelation is outside the limits of stewardship, you know it is not from the Lord, and you are not bound by it. I have heard of cases where a young man told a young woman she should marry him because he had received a revelation that she was to be his eternal companion. If this is a real revelation, it will be confirmed directly to the woman if she seeks to know. In the meantime, she is under no obligation to heed it. She should seek her own guidance and make up her own mind. The man can receive revelation to guide his own actions, but he cannot properly receive revelation to direct hers. She is outside his stewardship."[421]

How to Propose to the Right Girl

I doubt if you will learn how to propose to a girl at school or in scouting, or in church. A good marriage proposal is imperative because many girls dream about the moment their special beau will propose marriage to them. Understandably, you will want to meet her expectations with regards to your wedding proposal to her. This will enable you to embark on your life's journey and adventure together starting on the right foot.

The information below is only meant to be food for thought - to help you to prepare for this special moment in your life. You may want to return to these reference years from now.

<u>Plan to give her the right engagement ring before you propose</u>
Plan to give your sweetie the ring of her dreams, within your budget of course. Someday when you are talking about dreams, in general, bring up the subject of rings. Or if you have friends that have recently become engaged you can ask your sweetie what she thought about the ring. Was it just the right size? Or was it too chunky? What did she think about the stone? What is her favorite stone? If your girlfriend has unusual taste, and you do not want to ruin the proposal by giving her a ring she would not want to wear, have a look at rings on-line together. Or when you are taking a walk, stop at a jewelry shop to have a look at rings, and other things "just for something to do." If you hope to give her an heirloom ring, which once belonged to a relative, you will have to ensure that she likes the ring beforehand. For if she does not like the ring, the thought of rejecting it would put her in a very awkward situation. She may be reluctant to offend you or your family. Some girls would be honored to be symbolically invited into your family with a special heirloom ring. When Prince William proposed to Kate Middleton, he gave her Diana, Princess of Wales' engagement ring. Princess Diana was Williams' late mother. Other girls prefer to have a new ring that has never been worn by anyone else.

<u>Pick the right time</u>
Make sure that you are both ready for the responsibilities that come with marriage. Your girlfriend will need to feel secure when she thinks about spending the rest of her life with you before you propose. Below please find some ideas that will help her feel secure about having a lifelong relationship with you.

    1) Demonstrate that you truly love her. You can show her that you love her by actually listening to her when she speaks to you, by helping her when she needs help (such as carrying groceries), by being a gentleman (review the section "How to Be a Gentleman"), by taking an interest in her family and friends, and by surprising her with little

thoughtful gifts such as a rose, a small box of chocolates to share, a well-planned date.

2) Your girlfriend will need to feel secure that you will be able to support her if she were to have a baby. Therefore, talk to her about your education, and career goals. Demonstrate that you are responsible on the job by being punctual, alert, proactive, and industrious. Be a dependable person.

3) She will need to feel confident that you are a righteous man - demonstrate honesty, and caring for people by being of service to her and to others. Show your willingness to grow spiritually, and a desire to share in the responsibilities of raising a spiritually centered family, by going to church with her.

A surprise proposal is romantic

Wait for some time after talking about rings to propose. You should have already purchased the ring prior to the proposal. Be sure to take care of the ring because it is precious and probably pricey. Pick a time in both your lives that is relatively stress-free, such as, after exams or after any other major events that she is helping to plan. Then the proposal will feel like a celebration. However, life, in general, can be busy. Do not worry about not having the time to plan a wedding. If you want to marry her do not wait too long - propose and you will figure out the details for the wedding later.

Plan to propose in a romantic location

Here are a few ideas:

1) If she is a "foodie" take her to a restaurant where the food is fabulous but not necessarily expensive. The restaurant should be at least very clean and it should have at least a cozy atmosphere. Reserve a table in a secluded part of the restaurant.

2) You may want to choose to propose to her where you first met or where you first expressed your love for each other.

3) If she loves the outdoors, you may want to propose to her in a breathtaking outdoor setting.

4) If in her family other people have proposed with their family gathered around you may want to organize a party, which will include your family and her family, and propose to her in front of both families. That is if you are confident that she is likely to say, "Yes." That is if such a circumstance would be pleasing to you also.

How to make a memorable marriage proposal
Write down what you plan to tell her, and practice. Keep the proposal short and sweet so that she can remember exactly what you said. Begin by telling her why you love her, that you are lucky to have met her and that you want to spend the rest of your life with her. Then ask, "Will you marry me?"

PLANNING FOR THE WEDDING DAY

> *Have ye not read, that he which made them at the beginning made them male and female, and said, for this cause shall a man leave father and mother, and shall cleave to his wife: and they twain shall be one flesh? Wherefore they are no more twain, but one flesh. What therefore God hath joined together, let not man put asunder.*
>
> MATTHEW 19:4–6 KJV

Planning for the wedding ahead of time will save you and your fiancée stress and embarrassment. For example, ensure that you book a venue for the wedding night months in advance. I know a young man who did not book a venue for his wedding night. After the reception the groom told his young bride that they would find a hotel room but all of the hotel rooms were booked for miles around due to a car-racing event. They finally found a motel room at 4:00 am. The bride could not hide her disappointment. She had planned all of the other aspects of the wedding and felt that he had been inconsiderate. The groom was embarrassed and became aloof. This was not a good way to start a marriage. Indeed, their marriage was unhappy and ended in divorce. To avoid such a misadventure plan ahead of time. Bookstores sell wedding planners to help you and your fiancée to prepare all the important details.

Note: Do not do things that will jeopardize what is supposed to be the most important day of your life. Such as, do not wear cufflinks that a former girlfriend gave you on your wedding day, as Prince Charles did when he married Lady Diana. This will break your bride's heart.

WEDDING CEREMONY

Discuss with your fiancée your hopes and dreams for the wedding ceremony. Will the wedding be held in a temple, in a church, in a synagogue, in a mosque, or on a beach? If you plan to say your own vows, write them weeks before the ceremony and practice what you plan to say to each other either individually or together. Most members of The Church of Jesus Christ of Latter-day Saints marry in an LDS temple, which is free. LDS churches are also free of cost for weddings for all members but photography is not permitted in the temple nor in the church during the wedding ceremony. Photos are taken afterward. My daughter married in a Catholic church, which was not in her parish. The rental cost for the Catholic Church was $400 and the cost for the priest's time was $200 even though she is Catholic. She was told about the cost for the priest's time about a week before the wedding. She was shocked and dismayed.

Elaine and I were married in a gazebo in a park next to a beautiful lake, in July 2012, presided over by Bishop Seamons – unforgettable. Although we had a small wedding, the space was quite large and we could have had a much larger wedding there. Being a public space, we only paid $25.00/hour plus the cost of furniture rentals, and so forth. So, don't let cost be a barrier for getting married to your sweetie! It must be noted that this ceremony was a typical "civil" ceremony. Later, in January 2013, we had a second wedding ceremony called a "sealing" in the Seattle, Washington, LDS Temple – it was a most joyful, spiritually uplifting and deeply religious occasion with eternal consequences. This ceremony was necessary in order to be married "for time and all eternity" as we have described previously. This ceremony is available to anyone who is a member of the church.

WEDDING RECEPTION

For the wedding reception, focus on the highest quality within your budget. Wedding receptions need not be elaborate and expensive. There are many magazines with lovely ideas for weddings to suit all budgets. It is important not to go deeply into debt. If you are having a smaller wedding, you can find private rooms in some restaurants that can accommodate 12 to 30 people for a wedding reception – and you pay only for the cost of food and beverages – at no cost for the room. Hotel restaurants such as the Fairmont Olympic and more casual restaurants such as the Claim Jumper have such spaces. You just need to inquire. Some restaurants also offer fixed menus for as little as $15 to $40 per person. At times, guests can choose from a fixed menu their preferred entrée, their preferred dessert, and their preferred beverage all for a fixed price. It is easy to budget for a wedding with a fixed menu and fixed price. Be mindful to ask about food allergies before planning for food or wedding favors.

You can also hold a wedding reception in a church cultural hall – in some churches for free if you are a member. Recently, we attended a lovely wedding in a church hall. The round tables were set with white linen and fresh flowers. The buffet had a wide assortment of food to please people of all ages. There were approximately 150 guests.

During the wedding reception, it is most important that you remember to focus on your bride, your eternal partner. It is her day so make it extra special for her. Tell her that she looks beautiful. Smile at her. Dance with her. Be kind, gentle and sweet with her. Love her. As I always like to say, a man's wife is his centerpiece.

Donell Cox & Elaine J. Barbeau Cox

*Husbands, love your wives, even as Christ also
loved the church, and gave himself for it.*

Ephesians 5:25 KJV

Wedding Night

As parents and as church goers, we often forget that we need to teach our children about sexual expression after they are married. This point was brought home by a member of our church who is a surgeon by profession and who teaches the gospel lessons at our church. He said that we need to teach our children that after marriage God ordains sexual expression, that it is holy, that it is an expression of love, and that it is joyful.

We found some inspirational quotes on this subject from other church leaders whom we believe are guided by God. Since marriage is pivotal in God's plan for his children, we feel that it is best to let God speak through His leaders here on earth:

In our church we utilize the book written by church leaders, A Parent's Guide, in which we learn more about mature intimacy, courtship, and marriage:

"The courtesy and friendship the couple has shown during courtship are vital on their wedding night. The first night requires nearly perfect courtesy, consideration, and, in many cases, a gentle sense of good humor. They must be the very best of friends on this first occasion when they are able to begin to know one another completely. They may be ill at ease, even awkward, and would do well to smile at their awkwardness. Each must remember that the other person is vulnerable to embarrassment. And, they must realize that the greatest passions of marriage lie ahead, to increase over the years through experience and growth. A truth not generally known to newly married couples is that in virtuous marriages passions increase over the years between the couple.

604

Couples can find great joy through fidelity, childbirth, rearing and teaching their children, providing a home, and striving to live gospel truths."[422]

On intimacy, David O. McKay counseled:

"Let us instruct young people who come to us, first, young men throughout the Church, to know that a woman should be queen of her own body. The marriage covenant does not give the man the right to enslave her, or to abuse her, or to use her merely for the gratification of his passion. Your marriage ceremony does not give you that right.

"Second, let them remember that gentleness and consideration after the ceremony are just as appropriate necessary and beautiful as gentleness and consideration before the wedding.

"Third, let us realize that manhood is not undermined by the practicing of continence, notwithstanding what some psychiatrists claim. Chastity is the crown of beautiful womanhood, and self-control is the source of true manhood if you will know it, not indulgence. Sexual indulgence whets the passion and creates morbid desire.

"Let us teach our young men to enter into matrimony with the idea that each will be just as courteous, and considerate of a wife after the ceremony as during courtship."[423]

We learn more about the honeymoon night from the guidance given in *A Parent's Guide*:

"The honeymoon ought to be a time when the partners learn about one another's minds, emotions, bodies, and spirits. It is not a time for sexual excess. It is not a fling of worldly diversions that is scheduled between the temple (or where ever the wedding took place) ceremony and a return to serious living. The honeymoon and early weeks of marriage are a time for private discovery on all levels: physical, social, emotional, and spiritual.

"In sexual matters, as in all other aspects of marriage, there are virtues to be observed: 'If it is unnatural, you just do not do it. That is all. There are some people who have said that behind the bedroom doors anything goes. That is not true, and the Lord would not condone it.' (Spencer W. Kimball, The Teachings of Spencer W. Kimball, p. 312).

"Both husbands and wives have physical, emotional, psychological, and spiritual needs associated with this sacred act. They will be able to complement each other in the marriage relationship if they give tender, considerate attention to these needs of their partner. Each should seek to fulfill the other's needs rather than to use this highly significant relationship merely to satisfy his or her own passion.

"Couples will discover differences in the needs or desires each partner has for such a relationship, but when each strives to satisfy the needs of the other, these differences need not present a serious problem. Remember, this intimate relationship between husband and wife was established to bring joy to them. An effort to reach this righteous objective will enable married couples to use their complementary natures to bring joy to this union.

"The intimate relationship between husband and wife realizes its greatest value when it is based on loving kindness and tenderness between the marriage partners. This fact, supported by valid research data, helps newly married couples recognize that the so-called sex drive is mostly myth. Sexual intimacy is not an involuntary, strictly biological necessity for survival like breathing and eating. Sexual intimacy between a husband and wife can be delayed or even suspended for long periods of time with no negative effect (for example, when the health of one or the other requires it). Husbands and wives are not compelled to mate because their genes or hormones order them to do so. Sexual powers are voluntary and controllable; the heart and mind do rule. While sex drive is a myth, husbands and wives do have physical and emotional needs that are fulfilled through sexual union. If they perceive and appreciate their masculine and feminine natures as important, complementing, but not controlling, parts of their lives, becoming as one flesh can be one of life's richest and most rewarding experiences."[424]

Future Family Life

How to have a Long and Happy Marriage

If you want to have a long happy marriage, you need all the help you can get. You start by looking inward at yourself and making yourself suitable for marriage. Then you go about finding the right person to marry and marry her at the right time of your life and her life. After you are married, you will then need tools and skills to keep the marriage alive. But do not fret. Others have been happily married for a lifetime. If one couple can do it, so can you! As it is wise to study any subject, it is wise to study what leads to a successful marriage. This is not taught in school. So where else are you going to learn this? You have to learn from the experience of elders who have had successful marriages.

Here are two inspirational stories from people who have been married for 50 years or more from the book *Married for Life* by Bill Morelan.

Always Treat Your Wife Like a Lady

> HUSBANDS ...BE CONSIDERATE AS YOU LIVE WITH
> YOUR WIVES AND TREAT THEM WITH RESPECT.
>
> – *1 Peter 3:7 KJV*

Sol and Edna Weiss
Married: June 16, 1946

New York City, New York

Sol and Edna met at a party when he was fourteen, and she was thirteen. "We still hold hands," Sol says. "And I still put up with his sense of humor Edna laughs."

Showing a woman honor and respect involves so much more than chivalrous gestures such as holding a door, rising politely at the dinner table, or laying one's coat over a puddle of rainwater. A husband's treatment of his wife like a lady begins with his attitude toward her. Does he truly value his spouse or does he take her for granted? Does he view her as a gift from heaven above or as a burden, "the old ball and chain"? The *Bible* describes a wife of noble character as "her husband's crown" (Proverbs 12:4 KJV), "worth far more than rubies" (Proverbs 31:10 KJV). A godly wife is a treasure to be cherished, deserving her husband's highest compliments and praise.

Honoring his wife begins with his thoughts and feelings toward her, but it doesn't end there. Picture a valiant young knight striving to win his lady's affections and revealing his heart to her through his words and deeds! He gives her his full attention when she is speaking. He considers her point of view. He respects her opinions and empathizes with her feelings. In addition, he regards the issues that concern her as important. And he celebrates her triumphs and commends her for her virtues.

God is calling wives to be true ladies, kindhearted and worthy of respect; He is calling husbands to be sincere gentlemen, and to give their wives the honor they have earned.

You Only Get Out of Marriage What You Put Into It

"Whoever sows generously will also reap generously,"

– 2 CORINTHIANS 9:6 KJV

"Eldon and Ginny Phillips

"Married: October 30, 1946

"Belle Center, Ohio

"Eldon and Ginny went to high school together: His first move: he stole her shoes during a play rehearsal! "It took him eight years to convince me to marry him," laughs Ginny.

"A young entrepreneur starts with an idea for a unique, new product. He carefully lays plans for a start-up business, calculating revenues and expenses. He meets with consultants, accountants, and attorneys. He works hard to sell the concept to banks and investors to raise capital. In time, he leases space, purchases equipment, and hires employees. Finally, he is ready to begin. He works hard, pouring himself into the business, determined to make it succeed. And it thrives. But does he now merely sit back, relax, and enjoy the fruit of his labor? No! He works harder than ever while conjuring up ideas for improving efficiency, bettering customer relations, bolstering profits.

"If a marriage is to last a lifetime, it requires the same level of devotion and energy. Both partners must give 100 percent. Each must be available to the other when needed, fully present, ready to listen, to talk, and to act. Both spouses must pour their heart and soul into this enterprise, making whatever sacrifice necessary to ensure success.

"Yet what an investment! The payoff is a rich, healthy, loving relationship that lasts. And everyone involved reaps countless rewards. Sound good? Devote time and energy to your marriage."

BECOMING A FATHER

Imagine the Kind of Father You Want to Be

Before coming to Earth, we were all spirit children of God. If God is a father, being a father must truly be a privilege. Today, some of God's spirit children are still waiting to be born so that they may also obtain a physical body and an earthly experience. You can prepare to be a good parent for your children all through your life by preparing to be the best person you can be. Imagine holding your first newborn baby. What name would you choose for a baby boy? What name would you choose for a baby girl? What kind of family do you want?

Dr. Peck, the leading psychiatrist who wrote *The Road Less Traveled* (sounds like a quest to me) wrote these words of wisdom to help you to begin to imagine what type of parent you would want to be so that you can start to prepare for your role as a parent. He wrote:

"If a child sees his parents day in and day out behaving with self-discipline, restraints, dignity and a capacity to order their own lives, then the child will come to feel in the deepest fibers of his being that this is the way to live. If a child sees his parents day in and day out living without self-restraint or self-discipline, then he will come in the deepest fibers of being to believe that that is the way to live.

"Yet even more than role modeling is love. For even in chaotic and disordered homes genuine love is occasionally present, and from such homes may come self-disciplined children. And not infrequently parents who are professional people - doctors, lawyers, club women and philanthropists - who lead lives of strict orderliness and decorum but yet lack love, send children into the world who are as undisciplined, destructive and disorganized as any child from impoverished and chaotic homes."[425]

I am thankful to my parents who served as role models and mentors who managed to raise my eight siblings and myself into responsible citizens who would raise their own families. How did my parents do this? They did it by displaying discipline and love even in the midst of the chaos of having a large family in a small house.

How Love Works to Grow Children Perfectly

When you start to have children, I am sure you will want to raise them well, too. As with my parents, it will take self-discipline and love eternal. We are certain you have this capability within you. Peck has more on the subject:

> "Ultimately love is everything. The parents who devote time to their children even when it is not demanded by glaring misdeeds, [they] will perceive in them subtle needs for discipline, to which they will respond with gentle urging or reprimand or structure or praise, administered with thoughtfulness and care. They will observe how their children eat cake, how they study, when they tell subtle falsehoods when they run away from problems rather than face them. They will take the time to make these minor corrections and adjustments, listening to their children, responding to them, tightening a little here, loosening a little there, giving them little lectures, little stories, little hugs and kisses, little admonishments, little pats on the back.
>
> "So it is that the quality of discipline afforded by loving parents is superior to the discipline of unloving parents. But this is just the beginning. In taking the time to observe and to think about their children's needs, loving parents will frequently agonize over the decisions to be made, and will, in a very real sense, suffer along with their children. The children are not blind to this. They perceive it when their parents are willing to suffer with them, and although they may not respond with immediate gratitude, they will learn also to suffer. "If my parents are willing to suffer with me,' they will tell themselves, 'then suffering must not be so bad, and I should be willing to suffer with myself.
>
> "This is the beginning of self-discipline."[426]

Always remember that love is an action verb as much as it is a feeling.

ENABLE YOUR CHILDREN TO DEVELOP A HABIT OF PRAYER
Have you had the opportunity to watch the movie, *The Cokeville Miracle*, which is based on a true story? The town of Cokeville, Wyoming made national headlines when 100 elementary school children and their teachers were herded into a small room by a mad man and a woman who had a bomb. The bomb went off in the center of the room and, by experts' estimation, the room should have been leveled with many people dead. However, only two people died that day: the man and the woman who had brought the bomb into the room. Each person who left that room alive has a story to tell about prayer and divine intervention. This story is about the prayer of children and how powerful these prayers can be.

Our Heavenly Father knows us and loves us and wants us to communicate with Him through prayer. The Lord Jesus Christ commanded, "Ye must always pray unto the Father in my name" (3 Nephi 18:19).

A good habit for yourself and for your future children is to always remember to pray. You have already been shown the power of prayer when we talked about the "secret life of water" and other examples.

When I was a child, on the wall above my bed, my parents hung a poster with a prayer written on it:

Now I lay me down to sleep,
I pray the Lord my soul to keep,
If I should die before I wake,
I pray the Lord my soul to take. Amen.

It is a favorite prayer for children and has been around for many years. My parents taught me to recite this prayer each night, kneeling on the floor next to my bed, before I went to sleep. It was a simple thing to do, and I did it dutifully just because my parents asked me to do so. Even today, I remember this prayer often, and it brings a strong sense of comfort to me. It reminds me of simpler times when I was under the protection of my parents, and I didn't have a care in the world. I'm sure Heavenly Father liked it when I prayed this prayer, even though I probably didn't know what it meant back then and may have been a little scared that I might not wake up! Fast-forward to today, actually,

I still think about that possibility and each night before I go to bed I kneel down and ask Heavenly Father to watch over me while I sleep and allow me to wake up the next day refreshed and ready to face my duties.

I have learned that "canned" or prewritten prayers like the one above are not as meaningful as they could or should be. A prayer should spontaneously flow from the heart of a person in thanks to God or about current concerns. For your child, you can help them remember the things they may want to mention in prayer to get them started. Spontaneous prayers are much more meaningful to Heavenly Father, the person to Whom prayers are directed. This is especially true for children since they are so innocent and close to the spirit.

FAMILY HOME EVENINGS

Life can get so busy that family members spend little time together. Children have activities in the evenings. Parents have meetings in the evenings. However, in the LDS church members are counseled to reserve Monday evenings for "Family Home Evenings." This is when families organize their schedule so that all the members of their family are available to spend time together on Monday evenings. Different members of the family can take turns planning for the family home evening. The Family Home Evening usually begins with a prayer and a scripture to share. After the scripture reading and discussion of the scripture, the family can sing a hymn or do any other wholesome activities the family has prepared. There are many activities that families can do together after sharing a scripture (see the list of example activities below). Make it fun, but most importantly, enjoy the time together as a family. It is a time of caring, growth, and bonding. Family Home Evenings usually end with a prayer. Let this be a time that your leadership and stewardship skills shine brightest. Build special memories with your family of sharing quality time together – sharing thoughts about the day and dreams and goals – learning and laughing. Remember that families are forever and that Family Home Evenings are necessary tools, which will enable you and your wife to keep your family together.

115 Things You Could Do for Fun with Your Family

Most of these great ideas came from *101 Family Home Evening Activities* by Rachel Bruner. There are really 115 ideas, but as the author says, "Who is counting?"

1. Visit the zoo.
2. Find out about your area's community center and/or park activities.
3. Wash the dog. (A neighbor's dog if you do not have one!)
4. Have a family slumber party.
5. Build a fort. (Use large appliance boxes outside, or pillows and sheets inside.)
6. Get out the family photo album.
7. Research your family history.
8. Visit the Genealogical Library.
9. Play stickball.
10. Play hopscotch.
11. Play games.
12. Clean the house together. (Have a pick-up party.)
13. Make up a play. Take it to a nursing home.
14. Fly kites.
15. Go on a family trip/historical excursion.
16. Did it snow? Go sledding and make a snowman.
17. Make a collage out of pictures from old magazines.
18. Set up a lemonade stand on a warm day.
19. Shoot hoops together. Play H.O.R.S.E.
20. Draw pictures of members of your family.
21. Make a family calendar.
22. Tell stories around a campfire. (Or at the barbecue?)
23. Organize a game of capture the flag.
24. Make miniature boats and float them in some water.
25. Write letters to grandparents or a missionary.
26. Play freeze-tag.
27. Tell scary stories (With lights out.)
28. Play broom ball.

29. Go for a hike.
30. Go for a bike ride together.
31. Go get ice cream and walk around the Temple grounds.
32. Learn to play the guitar together.
33. Listen to classical music, lights off, lying on the floor, and take turns saying what it sounds like.
34. Attend community concerts or listen to a local band.
35. Organize a community clean-up.
36. Visit the library.
37. Go ice skating or roller skating/blading.
38. Paint a picture, a mural, or a room.
39. Learn how to use a compass.
40. Organize 72-hour emergency kits.
41. Plant a tree or some flowers.
42. Learn the metric system.
43. Learn sign language.
44. Learn Morse code.
45. Go swimming.
46. Go bird watching.
47. Walk the dog. (A neighbor's dog if you do not have one!)
48. Visit the countryside.
49. Visit the City. (Maybe on a bus?)
50. Pick berries/fruit together.
51. Bake cookies or bread.
52. Make homemade jam.
53. Take treats to neighbors or friends.
54. Plant a garden.
55. Join a family choir.
56. Start a family journal.
57. Go to a museum.
58. Take a nature hike trail.
59. Play cards. (Try Nephi's Boat or Scripture Cards.)
60. Start a family exercise group.
61. Sing in the car.
62. Visit a local bookstore.

63. Make crafts together. Give them away.
64. Make Christmas ornaments together.
65. Write a story together.
66. Put a sleeping bag out in the back yard and watch the night sky through binoculars.
67. Go fishing.
68. Play touch football.
69. Have a culture night. Make a meal and learn about another culture.
70. Take photographs.
71. Invite friends over. Cook ethnic food.
72. Do yard work together.
73. Play Frisbee or Ultimate Frisbee.
74. Make your own family cards for the holidays or birthdays.
75. Play chess, bridge, or checkers.
76. Go camping.
77. Go for a long walk.
78. Play charades.
79. Do a rain dance.
80. Go around the table after dinner and have everyone say what they love best about each other.
81. Go dancing, have a family dance, or take a dance class together.
82. Climb a tree.
83. Watch the sunset. Watch the sunrise. Figure out when the sun will rise and set in your location.
84. Have a big party and celebrate a TV free week.
85. Have a picnic. (If it's raining, have a picnic in the family room on a blanket.)
86. Invite a family over for a barbecue.
87. Memorize the Articles of Faith.
88. Memorize a family hymn.
89. Learn how to fold the American Flag (or your country's flag). Have a patriotic night. Have a flag ceremony.

90. Visit an elderly person or someone shut in.
91. Have a first-aid night. Invite other families to come. Call the fire department for a class.
92. Learn what to do if you are lost.
93. Have a budgeting class. Save for a family trip.
94. Learn how to build a fire and cook hot dogs.
95. Have an etiquette night. Practice your skills over a formal dinner.
96. Talk about drugs. Do role-playing.
97. Have a friend come and discuss good nutrition and health practices. (Kids do not listen to their mom.)
98. Learn home repairs for an activity. Make sure the girls learn too.
99. Prepare a family group sheet/four generation pedigree chart. Interview an older family member.
100. Start a family collection. (Coins, rocks, stories, dress-up, clothes, treasures.)
101. Have a family testimony meeting.
102. Have a bubble blowing contest. (Bubbles or bubble gum.)
103. Blow bubbles outside. Try different instruments.
104. Have a baking contest.
105. Adopt a grandma or grandpa from your church.
106. Have a family fireside.
107. Watch an old movie (maybe a western) together.
108. Make a family goal chart.
109. Have a service car wash.
110. Learn to play golf together.
111. Go miniature golfing.
112. Make a family cookbook.
113. Have a family treasure hunt.
114. Have a family dance. Everyone can bring partners.
115. Solve a puzzle together (crossword, word search, or jigsaw).[427]

PREPARING YOUR FAMILY FOR EMERGENCIES

Savings, Emergency Food Storage, and other Supplies

When I lost my job, developed cancer and had surgery, our savings, and food supply lasted for almost one year. After that, the LDS church helped us until I was able to work again. It was a humbling experience. However, I was glad that we were well prepared. The deep freezer was well stocked. We had plenty of canned goods and dry goods such as large bags of rice and large bags of beans.

The prophets have also advised members of the church to prepare for other emergencies such as earthquakes, tornadoes, ice storms, and forest fires. It is important to have plenty of water stored, about a gallon of water per day, per person for drinking, cooking, and bathing.

We are also advised to pack a backpack or two (depending on the size of our family), in case we have to leave our homes suddenly, with the following: a flashlight, toilet paper (a roll fits perfectly into yogurt containers to keep it dry), waterproof matches, candles, enough water for 72 hours (the quantity would have to be rationed), tiny packets containing emergency blankets, a little folding stove and fuel, a small pot, cups, nuts, coconut, fruit leathers, powdered soups, little packets containing rain ponchos, a change of underwear for every member of the family, a Swiss Army knife, soap, toothbrush and toothpaste. Statically, it usually takes about 72 hours for emergency responders to arrive during a catastrophe. Remember to bundle up the children and pets to keep them safe. Also, pray for God's protection.

Life Insurance

Life is unpredictable. Three thousand people who expected to live long lives died in the 9/11 attacks. On any given day we could be victims of an event that could end our lives. When a man is responsible for supporting his family, he must have permanent life insurance to replace his income and to cover his family's immediate and future expenses if he dies. Life insurance benefits will ensure that your wife and children will be able to survive in the event of your demise. (This is a sad thought but it happens.) Getting insurance to cover your family's needs is a very loving, responsible action. Life insurance ensures that your wife will be able to pay for the mortgage or rent, education for your children, and daily living expenses. Otherwise, your loved ones could become "homeless."

Homelessness is on the rise in the United States. In the Newsweek article, *Child Homelessness in U.S. Reaches Historic High, Report Says*, Stav Ziv writes that "One out of every 30 children in the U.S. experienced homelessness last year. That makes nearly 2.5 million children who, in 2013, lived in shelters, on the streets, in cars, on campgrounds or doubled up with other families in tight quarters, often moving from one temporary solution to another."[428]

Locking into a permanent life insurance policy in your teens or twenties when you are young and healthy will be relatively very inexpensive and it will guarantee your insurability. Also, getting a permanent life insurance policy early in life will protect your future family. Life insurance that is included in company benefits is unreliable because it does not last beyond the term of employment – as soon as you lose your job you lose your benefits, which include your life insurance. Therefore, you should also have your own personal policy, which would follow you whether you are employed or not. Furthermore, if you wait until later in life to get a permanent life insurance policy, it may be too expensive due to your age, or you may be denied or rated due to an illness or due to your occupation such as being a pilot.

The life insurance benefit for your loved ones can be augmented with a rider, which is added to the policy that you decide to purchase. A "rider" is an optional benefit that can be added to an insurance policy. Here is one of New York Life's offering:

"Policy Purchase Option (PPO) Rider guarantees the right to purchase another life insurance policy with a face amount up to $150,000 periodically, without providing evidence of insurability.

This guarantee, which can be exercised on scheduled 'Option Dates,' is available until you reach age 46 regardless of your health or occupation."According to the New York Life website, this rider can be purchased at issue (when you apply for the life insurance policy) with New York Life's Whole Life, Custom Whole Life, and Level Premium Convertible Term 5, Level Premium Convertible Term 10-20, and Yearly Convertible Term policies. The new policies you purchase by exercising the PPO Rider may be any one of the permanent insurance products offered by New York Life (with the exception of Survivorship policies or policies that offer increasing amounts of insurance).[429]

***Note**: Term life insurance policies are not permanent life insurance. The premiums for term insurance will increase considerably with your age. Term insurance can be purchased if dollars are scarce. Term insurance can be added as a rider to permanent life insurance or as a separate policy to cover a mortgage or to increase your total insurance coverage when your children are young.

It is important to purchase a permanent life insurance policy when you are young (1) to guarantee that you have insurance to protect your future family, (2) to have the option of adding on life insurance in order to increase the benefit as your family grows, and (3) to accumulate cash value. The cash value will help pay for the insurance premiums if you are ever without employment. Speak to an insurance agent from a leading insurance firm.

Tip: The transfer of wealth through life insurance is one of the ways the rich get richer. Fathers leave their children wealth through insurance, which their children can invest in businesses, which they bequeath to their children, and so on. The family's assets grow through life insurance and investments for successive generations.

QUEST CHECKPOINT: YOUR FAMILY
Congratulations for reaching this checkpoint on your quest. In order to satisfy the requirements for the Family Certificate, you will need to

demonstrate proficiency in the subject areas covered within this chapter by reading and completing the requirements below. After you have completed all the certificate requirements below - using the honor system – fill in the certificate with your name. **You can also download a printed copy from the *Elevate Yourself to Manhood* website at http://www.elevateyourselftomanhood.com/certificates.**

CERTIFICATE REQUIREMENTS

☐ **The Importance of Families**
  * Why are families so important?
  * Why did God ordain families?
  * How can you obtain growth of your mind, body, and spirit within a family?
  * How can families be together forever?
  * How are all God's children considered one big family?

☐ **Hanging Out, Casual Dating, Serious Dating, and Preparation for Marriage**
  * How old should you be before you start dating and being romantic with young ladies? Search through this section to find the answer if you do not know.
  * What character traits should you look for in a young woman that you might want to marry someday?
  * How do you know if a young lady is right for you?

☐ **Marriage**
  * Why is marriage important?
  * Who ordained marriage? (Hint: He was the Creator of this world.)
  * Marriage was ordained between a man and a woman. This is logical since only a man and a woman can have biological children. Please record your thoughts in your journal.
  * Explain how two people can be married "for time and all eternity" instead of only "until death do us part." Why is this so critically important for a man and woman?

☐ **Children**
- Why is it so important for married couples to have children? Do you plan to get married and have children some day? Write your thoughts about this in your journal.

☐ **Commandments**
- What is the Fifth Commandment? What does it mean to you? Do you carry out the Fifth Commandment?

☐ **Fatherhood**
- What kind of father do you plan to be? Do you think this book will help you develop into a good father?

☐ **Finances**
- Ask your parents and financial advisor about obtaining a life insurance policy that will guarantee your insurability and enable you to increase the benefit later on when you have a family.

ELEVATE YOURSELF TO MANHOOD

QUEST CERTIFICATE – FAMILY

THIS CERTIFICATE IS AWARDED TO:

_____

FOR DILIGENCE IN FULFILLING THE *ELEVATE YOURSELF TO MANHOOD*
REQUIREMENTS FOR "FAMILY" ON HIS QUEST

*E*levate Your Place in Society

Elevate Your Place in Society

Showing Yourself to Be a Man

THERE'S NO HUGE RUSH FOR you, as a teenager, to start acting as an adult male would act. At this point, we are only interested in making sure you are aware of the path you should strive to take to becoming a man. By all means, live your life as a teenager, but do so safely and with a bit of purpose. After all, you have your whole life in front of you, and a bit of preparation won't hurt.

As you have now learned how to awaken; how to strengthen your mind; how to help your body grow strong; how to develop excellent character traits; how to feed your inner spirit; how to interact and communicate with family members; how to plan for your own family it's now time to think about effectively interacting within society and creating a man's mindset.

So, when do you become a man? Society has confusing rules in that regard. You can vote when you're 18. You can join the military when you are 17. At age 18, you are considered a legal adult so you can apply for a loan to purchase a house. The legal age for purchasing and drinking alcohol is 21 in most states.

Do these things make you a man? Does any chronological age make you a man? That would be debatable.

I say, you are a man whenever you start acting responsibly like one – when you have awakened from your teenaged life slumber and have come to the realization that, "Hey, there's a wonderful world out there. There is so much opportunity to learn and grow. What do I need to do to grab my share of opportunities and do my part?"

The movie based on a true story, *The Pursuit of Happyness,* starring Will Smith, is an excellent example of a young man, a single father, taking the proverbial "bull by the horns" and carving a place for himself in the modern world with only his courage and intellect.

As a teenager, your brain still has a lot more physical growing to do. The National Institute of Mental Health article, *The Teen Brain: Still Under Construction* says this about the teenage brain: "In key ways, the brain doesn't look like that of an adult until the early 20s." [430] But do not be too self-conscious about that. Just keep in mind that you probably have a tendency to take some risks that you probably should not take – especially when you are around your friends, which could cost you your life.

When you are around your friends, consciously use your mind and good judgment to think and act responsibly with integrity and courage – like a mature man should. Fake it until you make it, if you need to do so. For example, never get into a car when the driver has been consuming alcohol or who is under the influence of drugs. Have the courage to say, "No thank you," and try to convince the person not to drive. In any given situation there are always "good," "better," and "best," responses. In this case, it would be best to establish friendships with young men who neither drink alcohol nor take drugs – in order to preserve your own life.

DAILY POSITIVE AFFIRMATIONS TO KEEP YOU ON TRACK
Prior to going out into the world each day, practice these fortifying, positive affirmations. Say them consciously or, preferably, out loud if your situation permits:

* I am patient.
* I am disciplined.
* I can delay gratification.
* I am determined to be my best at home, at school, at work, at play and in my interactions with others.
* I use Step-Wise Refinement to tackle large, complicated projects.

- I use my God-given talents.
- I am developing new skills and talents.
- I can control my mind.
- I know that God loves me and knows me personally.
- I have a realistic view of the world, which I continually update to make self-improvements.
- I understand that I have the agency to choose between right and wrong.
- I choose the right course of action, in my thoughts and in my deeds.
- I am ready to personally manage my life responsibly with guidance from my parents, mentors, and the Holy Spirit.
- I am self-compassionate.
- I am grateful for the privilege to live in my great country.
- I am willing to do whatever I can to improve my town, city, and country.
- I am happy to the core of my being and understand that sometimes people have problems that they must overcome.
- I have an optimistic point of view.
- I am able to view hard times as learning experiences, and look forward to better times. I can see the "silver lining."
- I will stand up for victims.
- I am confident in my abilities.
- When I have done all that I can do I pray that the *Armor of God* will protect me from evil and that God will fight the battles, which I cannot fight.
- I respect life and try my best not to harm others or myself.

FINE-TUNING YOUR PEOPLE SKILLS

Creating and maintaining friendships is vital for your social development. It also "buffers against stress and protects against medical problems such as depression and anxiety," according to Karen L. Schiltz, Ph.D., clinical psychologist.[431]

Try to make friends in real life not just online. Face-to-face inter-actions with people are critical for developing people skills, which you will need throughout your life.

If you feel socially awkward or find that you have difficulty in this area, talk it over with you parents. Perhaps you and your parents can act out different social scenarios to give you practice in a safe place to enable you to feel comfortable with communicating using spoken words.

Here are some rules, offered by Schiltz, to help you get along with people:

- Learn how to initiate conversations easily
- Do not interrupt others when they are talking
- Join in the fun rather than sitting on the sidelines observing
- Do not be physical or verbally aggressive with peers
- Learn to understand visual signals such as facial expressions or gestures.
- Realize that not everyone feels the way you do. Each person has his or her own set of emotions.
- Do not be too bossy or domineering (telling others what to do)
- Learn what you should not talk about in certain situations. For example, do not tell a sad story when everyone else is having fun. It is a "downer."
- Stop yourself from getting frustrated when you do not under-stand the intent or goal of a conversation. Stay calm and try to figure it out. Or look it up on the Internet. Or just ask.
- Do not talk about yourself too much. Ask questions about others. (People like those who truly listen to them).
- Keep calm when you have a conflict with others.
- Try to maintain relationships that are reciprocal. Value your-self and consider dropping those relationships that are not reciprocal.
- Do not exaggerate to others the number of friends you have. (In life, if you have one true friend, you are very lucky.)

- Do not behave inappropriately in order to make friends like siding with bullies or buying friendships or taking drugs.
- Learn to make eye contact with people.
- Do not exhibit unusual quirks that are out of the ordinary.
- Be friendly to others who might be developmentally challenged.
- Do not always take things literally. Learn little nuances in the language of a conversation.
- Do not spend all your time with others playing video games or watching television (do other stuff together as well). For example, shoot baskets, go to a batting cage, work out in a gym, go fishing, go for a hike, or work on your golf swing.
- Do not criticize or judge others.
- Recognize physical or social boundaries. Do not crowd other's personal space too much; however, stand back while maintaining a confident posture. Do not touch someone who does not want to be touched.
- Do not freak out when you are stressed. Have self-control.
- Do not have an overly serious facial expression all the time.
- Do not laugh at inappropriate times, for example, when someone else is suffering. Offer help instead.
- Self-correct errors in your behavior or conversations.
- Learn to say "I'm sorry" or "excuse me" when you are in error
- Discern the difference between intentional and accidental actions such as when someone happens to bump into you in the hallway at school. Do not be offended when someone accidentally bumps into you – forgive them.
- Always be aware of the volume and tone of your voice.

At its best, these values and actions will help you make and maintain friendships with your peers. These actions, along with your moral values, and the character attributes you have learned about should make others comfortable around you and help you bond with them.

At its worst, be aware that violation of any of these things might cause others to try to bully you. According to Schiltz, bullies themselves may have a high level of social competence. They may have high social status and have lots of friends or followers. Bullies might "perceive themselves in a positive light, with an inflated sense of self," says Schiltz. Bring issues of bullying up to your parents, teachers and others in authority if that happens. Do not let them get the best of you, nor should you take the law into your own hands and become violent. It's not worth the amount of trouble you will get yourself into or the hurt you will cause others. Remember your own self-worth and take a stand against bullying but handle it properly. Violent retaliation would put an indelible stain on your own soul and tarnish your fine character. Jail time for assault will lead to a criminal record and will keep you from finding employment in many fields including banking, retail, healthcare, legal, financial, or teaching.

Are you a bully? Do you bully others face-to-face or indirectly by lying about the target or by cyberbullying? Examine your own behavior to determine if you are a bully.

Schiltz points out that a person might be a bully if they show any of these signs:

* They have a tendency to show verbal or physical aggression
* They are unable to control their own anger
* They need to "win" all the time
* They have a strong sense of entitlement
* They refuse to accept responsibility for the conflicts they create themselves
* They always blame others for the "unsafe" environment

Is this you? Is this anyone you know?

Bullying is ugly, and it has dire consequences for all involved. Avoid bullies if you can. Do not be a bully. Report bullying to authorities.

OPEN DOORS THROUGH SCOUTING

To truly elevate yourself socially, become a Boy Scout! What a wonderful way to make friends, spend time with mentors, and round out your social life, character and life experience. The Boy Scouts have more than 100 Merit Badges you can achieve, which reflect the development of your life skills.

You should join the Scouts with the specific goal of ultimately becoming an Eagle Scout – the highest level of scouting achievement, which you may add to your resume throughout your life. You'll be in the fine company of 40+ astronauts, President Ford, Michael Bloomberg, Robert Gates (former Secretary of Defense), Bill Gate's father, and many other men of illustrious achievement.

An Eagle Scout designation on your resume will impress college and university admissions personnel and potential employers. It represents a sociable individual who has courage and a steadfast attitude. A gentleman we know recounted that he regretted not earning the last few badges to attain his Eagle Scout, because the criteria to earn one of the badges was to correspond with someone by letter as a "pen pal," which he thought was not cool. After college, at his first job interview he was asked if he was an Eagle Scout. Being an Eagle Scout may open doors for you socially, in education, and in the workplace.

EDUCATION

Broaden your horizons and give yourself more choices after high school by obtaining higher education. You might think, "Hey, there are many folks who didn't finish high school or college and became millionaires or billionaires." And I say that's great for them! I will also point out that the famous people we know who did that had a vision, a fire in their belly and luck. If that's you, then go for it. For the rest of us, we need to hedge our bets and get more education as a foundation for launching a business, seeking employment, going into politics, teaching or getting into medicine. Keep in mind that every company you apply to work for will want to know your education status and their jobs all have minimum educational requirements. The more competitive companies will want to hire employees with the highest academic achievement. Not only do they want employees with the highest academic achievement, but they will want to know how well the prospective employees have demonstrated the use of those academic achievements (recall the section on Divergent Thinking). You may also add on your resume volunteer experience, sports that you have played, special interests such as playing a musical instrument, and reading.

Besides all of the above – we have learned from scriptures that when we pass into the afterlife, we will take our knowledge and talents with us. That is why we have been given the commandment to continue to learn and develop our talents (Matthew 25 KJV). These talents we will use during Jesus' reign on Earth to build a new earth. In the parable of the "pounds" Jesus also warns us to increase our wealth (Luke, 19:11-26 KJV).   As we increase our wealth through education, so ought Jesus' church to increase in membership as people pay tithing (10% of after tax income) to sustain and grow his church. Why would Jesus want his church to increase? The answer is simple: To save more of his brothers and sisters so that they may return to God our Father in heaven.

COLLEGE AND UNIVERSITY

Education enables you to glow on the inside,
so you can shine on the outside.

ELAINE J. BARBEAU COX

Hopefully, you are making excellent grades in high school and have taken a few Advanced Placement (AP) courses to get some college credits before you graduate from high school, which will give you a head-start in college. This could shorten the number of courses and semesters you would need to graduate from university.

In high school, you should prepare carefully for college entrance exams like the ACT or the SAT. Do your best on these tests because colleges and universities will use these scores as one of the factors in deciding to admit you to their school or not. Other factors may include any volunteer work or leadership experience you have gained. You can gain this experience through scouting, coaching, working with youth as a camp counselor, or working with the elderly. Having a part-time job, or a summer job will also be a factor that colleges and universities will consider in assessing the level of maturity you have attained. Essay writing skills are an important factor in college entrance decisions, as well. The best way to become a good writer is to read, read, read every day. Read the news online, read cereal boxes, read novels, read magazines or whatever. Oh, and practice writing a lot too!

Be mindful of not over-extending yourself – creating a plan and balance in your life is key. You need time to do your homework, time to socialize with family and friends, time to earn money at a part-time job, time to read and time to sleep.

Exercise maturity and discipline during your high school years. Visualize your academic path through high school, college and even into graduate school for a Masters' degree or Ph.D. Education is a gift that you give yourself, which will help you to sustain yourself and your family later in life. No one can take away your academic achievements.

How to Go to College or University
Without a High School Diploma

As a former teacher who witnessed bullying in schools, my wife is not surprised that according to the U.S. Census Bureau 31.4 million Americans do not have a high school diploma or the equivalency - a General Education Development (GED) certificate. If you are a high school dropout you might be interested to know the information below. On the website *Classes and Careers*, the article *How To Go To College Without a High School Diploma* tells us that there are four ways to attend a college or university without a high school diploma:

1. **Enroll in a community college.** Enroll in a community college. Many colleges have Ability to Benefit programs for people who dropped out of high school and do not have a

high school diploma nor a GED. After contacting the admission office to inquire about the date of placement tests, passing these tests, and proving that your well-being would be enhanced by a college education and if you have a family that your family's well-being would be greatly improved, you will be admitted to the college within the Ability to Benefit Program. You may also apply for financial assistance.

2. **Get a GED**. "The best way to get your GED is to get your hands on some test study materials. You can either buy your own, or join a study group. Study materials are available online, as well as at your state Department of Education and Centers for Workforce Education. **A note of caution:** You cannot take the GED test online. Any website claiming to offer a GED test (as opposed to a practice test) and a high-school diploma for a fee is a scam. Don't fall for it."

3. **Apply for non-traditional student status**. Some colleges recognize that although someone may not have a high school diploma or a GED, they may be self-taught and they may have learned a great deal from real life, work experiences, or volunteer work experiences, and may have developed organizational skills, people skills, determination, dedication, and savoir-faire. Such applicants may be admitted to these colleges as "non-traditional" students.

4. **Double-dip and multitask**. You can ask the college registrar where you want to attend if you can take high school courses at a high school and college courses at their college during the same semester. This is called a "concurrent enrollment program." Bonus: Many high schools will double the high school credits that you complete when you are taking college courses."[432]

Persons Who have Learning Difficulties Can also Attain a College or University Education

Today, there are many colleges that offer assistance to students who have learning difficulties – tutoring, time management and organization, reading and writing strategies, housing assistance, and so forth. Francesca Fulcinit gives students with learning difficulties who wish to attend a college or university, great guidance in her extensive article for PrepScholar, *The 18 Best Colleges for Students with Learning Disabilities.* She provides such information such as: when applying to these colleges and universities remember to apply to their learning disability program. Two colleges that do not charge fees for their learning disability services are: Augsburg College and Fairleigh Dickinson University. Augsburg has the *Center of Learning and Accessible Student Services* (CLASS), and Fairleigh Dickinson University has their *Regional Center for Learning Disabilities.*[433] Other colleges such as Beacon College in Leesburg, Florida and Landmark College in Putney, Vermont, cater only to students who "learn differently."

Graduate School

After obtaining a four-year bachelor's degree, you may decide to continue your studies for a Masters' degree (an additional two years), or after attaining a Master's, a Doctorate – Ph.D. (an additional four to five years).

If you look at the bibliography of this book and read the names of the authors of source material for this book, a lot of them are doctors, clinicians, therapists or researchers who have attained advanced educational degrees. We rely heavily on these "thought" leaders to help us solve societal problems.

Specialty Training

This is the realm of special advanced schools such as medical school, law school, dental school, and pharmacy school. The following

* Medical doctors and surgeons are there to help keep us all alive when disease or injuries happen to our loved ones or us. There are various branches in medical school, for

example, general; ophthalmology (correcting eye injuries and diseases); podiatry (correcting injuries to feet); orthopedics (correcting injuries to bones and muscles); neurology (treating disorders of the nerves and nervous system in the brain and in the spine); urology (treating urinary and reproductive issues); otolaryngology (treating ear, nose, and throat problems); and plastic surgery.

* Since we are a country of laws, lawyers play a vital role in society as well. There are various branches in law school: Admiralty Law; Bankruptcy Law; Business Law; Civil Law; Criminal Law: Entertainment Law; Family Law; Health Law; Immigration Law; Intellectual Property Law; International Law; Labor Law; Military Law; Personal Injury Law; Real Estate Law; and Tax Law.
* Veterinarians treat sick farm animals, exotic animals, and our pets (each of these is a specialty).
* Pharmacists calculate and dispense medicines. They are very knowledgeable about dangerous drug interactions.
* Dentists care and treat teeth and gum conditions, dental implants, TMJ (temporomandibular joint) disorders, and restorative surgical procedures.
* Naturopathic doctors treat many conditions including, allergies, hormonal imbalances, and fertility problems. They are licensed to use prescription drugs but prefer to use natural remedies that have no negative side effects.

TRADE SCHOOLS

Trades learned in trade schools are also an honorable way to earn money for a family. Depending on your passions, you might want to pick up a high-paying skill such as plumbing, electrical work, or machining. Given one of these skills, you could either work for an established company or start your own business. I have read reports for Master Plumbers and home builders that indicate they cannot seem to find enough young men who wish to become apprentices in their trades. The companies complained that they often had to search in other countries to find workers with enough interest and drive to take up these crafts and undergo on-the-job training for a couple of years to sufficiently learn the skill. This is a sad statement for our American youth. On-the-job training is a great opportunity to get paid to learn versus accumulating student debt.

*Note:** When choosing a program of study after high school, choose a field that is projected to have many job openings at the time you graduate. Consult recruiters, industry leaders, guidance counselors, and those working in the profession.

GOING ON A LONG-DISTANCE MISSION OR VOLUNTEERING ABROAD?

Before you begin your college or university program, or after your first year or two of study, you may want to go on a long distance mission through your church or volunteer abroad through one of the organizations mentioned in the review *2016 Best Volunteer Abroad Programs, Organizations, and Projects*, on the Forever Volunteer website, posted February 29, 2016 by Sarah Vandenberg.[434]

Three of the more affordable volunteer programs that piqued my interest in this review are: Love Volunteers $175 USD per week; Volunteer Solutions $200 USD per week; and Agape Volunteers "project fee starts at USD $510 and already includes the registration fee and travel insurance."

You may begin to save for your mission while you are in high school. You can fundraise to volunteer abroad. On the Volunteer Forever site, you may find *Volunteer Abroad Fundraising Tips* from Ruth, by Steven Weddle, July 14, 2013.

The movie, *The Best Two Years* will give you an idea of what a missionary experience abroad might entail. The more serious drama *The Saratov Approach* issues a warning about being cautious when serving a mission abroad. I recommend watching these two movies before going on a mission or volunteering abroad. Also, avoid war zones. You are needed to make a difference in the world.

Boy Scouts and Eagle Scouts will be well prepared to take part in an adventure of a lifetime - a mission or volunteer abroad project. If I were a young man I would personally want to wait until completing my mission or volunteering abroad before getting married because during that two year period my perspective might change, but that decision is up to you.

My wife met with missionaries in 2005 and I met with missionaries in 2011. We are both converts. Becoming a member of our church was the best and most important decision of our lives. We are so grateful to the missionaries who dedicated their time to meet with us and would like to extend here our sincere "Thanks."

We have noticed that young men who go through the scouting program and serve missions or volunteer abroad tend to have more resilience during their lives and they tend to be more successful, generally speaking, than those who do not go through these experiences early in life. These experiences are beneficial for young persons from all walks of life. Prince Williams and Kate Middleton both volunteered abroad after high school.

GoAbroad.com reports: You see, both William and Kate spent a gap year that included experiences abroad — as did William's brother, Prince Harry.[435]

FINDING EMPLOYMENT

After finishing college or university, you will probably want to find work. That means (1) starting your own business, (2) working as an employee for an established company, (3) joining the military, or (4) going into public or foreign service. Let's explore these options further.

ENTREPRENEURSHIP

Want to be your own boss? Becoming an entrepreneur may, at first, be very challenging, but it can also be very rewarding. Do you recognize any of these names and companies, which were established in recent times (just to name a few)?

Steve Jobs (Apple)
Jerry Yang (Yahoo)
Michael Dell (Dell)
Bill Gates (Microsoft)
Mark Zuckerberg (Facebook)
Larry Page (Google)
Jeff Bezos (Amazon)
Jack Ma (Alibaba)
Jack Dorsey (Twitter)

If starting your own business interests you, search the Internet for information about these entrepreneurs and their partners and read their stories. See if their experiences resonate with your own personal passions and talents.

Keep in mind that doctors, lawyers, certified public accountants (CPA), financial advisors, plumbers, electricians, retail store owners, and farmers, can also have their own businesses.

A recent article in Inc Magazine written by Minda Zetlin states that 63% of 20-Somethings want to start a business, so it is likely that you might be drawn to private enterprise ownership.[436]

According to Forbes Magazine, there are over 22 million self-employed people working in small businesses in the United States.[437]

The United States Small Business Associate (SBA) suggests that if you are considering going into business for yourself, you should consider it if you have the following characteristics and behaviors:

- **Comfortable with taking risks:** Are you comfortable taking risks? Are you ok with making tough decisions?
- **Independence:** You will need to make a lot of decisions on your own and bear the consequences. Can you bear the prospect of someone saying "no" to you sometimes?
- **Persuasive:** Can you make the case for your ideas to other people? Do you enjoy speaking to others to help them see things your way?

- **Able to negotiate:** Do you have the ability to negotiate successfully?
- **Creative:** Are you able to come up with new ideas? Do you enjoy solving problems? Do you have the ability to easily detect new opportunities?
- **Supported by others:** Do you have a support network of parents, friends, acquaintances who can assist you?[438]

One day you may consider opening your own business, but do not feel rushed into doing so. Do your homework first. Study your desired field well. Discuss plans with parents, mentors and friends to get confirmation. Pray about it! When you own your own business you can deduct from your taxes a portion of your household bills (see a tax advisor about this).

The best time to start your own business is before you have children, because starting a business frequently demands 12-15 hours of work per day for 6 or 7 days a week. You do not want to miss the precious early years with your children. When they will bond with you.

WORKING AS AN EMPLOYEE FOR A COMPANY

There are over 100 million people working full-time in the US. Most people who work are working for someone else. So before you finish your education you will need to: (1) identify the job opportunity you would like to pursue, and (2) interview for that job.

Some young people, while they are still in college, start out as interns with little or no pay to test-drive jobs and companies to see if they are a good fit for them and the company. If you have already finished your education and want to start your career, then perhaps you can obtain an "entry level" job or an apprentice position.

It's probably premature now, but you may be interested to know how people currently look for work. By the time you're ready for the job market, things may be different, but let's pretend that you were looking for a job today.

1. There are plenty of Internet sites that list jobs. The biggest ones are **Monster.com**, **CareerBuilder.com**, **Indeed.com**. On these sites, you set up a profile and upload your resume, then use their search engines to find jobs for you. These job sites have a bot (robotic agent) that can be programmed to send the job notices directly to your email account for easy access.

2. Similar to Facebook, people currently working or people looking for employment can maintain their profiles on websites like **LinkedIn.com** where they can be found by job recruiters or where they can read other searchers' stories about job-hunting, job opportunities, and so forth.

After connecting with a recruiter from a prospective company, you can set up a date and time for an interview. In today's world recruiters may want to connect with you by phone or video first for screening. They will see if you qualify for the job in terms of:

- Education
- Experience
- Required skills
- Certifications
- Other requirements that the company may specify

If you get past this step, then they may schedule a date and time for another interview with the manager who is in charge of hiring someone for the position you are seeking. The manager will further review your qualifications and personal attributes to see if you might be a good candidate for the job.

If you get past the manager's virtual interview then, you may be asked to come into the company for a face-to-face interview. At this point, the company will have already narrowed their search to one or two candidates including yourself! Using your interview skills, demonstrating your outstanding character, poise, knowledge, and self-confidence, you have an excellent chance of getting the job. Congratulations!

To give you an idea of how companies screen job candidates, here is a sample Job Description for a Staff Accountant right out of college:

Job Responsibilities:

- Work with team developing annual budgets and financial forecasts
- Assist in preparation, system entry and report review
- Research and analyze monthly financial results
- Create and maintain spreadsheets, databases, and financial reports used to communicate monthly results.
- Prepare and review presentations for executive reviews and meetings.
- Create analysis and reporting to measure the financial impact of business decisions and monitor performance.

Job Qualifications

- <u>Education</u>: Bachelor's degree in Accounting, Finance or Business related field, MBA or progress towards
- <u>Grades in College</u>: 3.0 GPA or greater preferred
- <u>Experience</u>: Financial Planning & Analysis, Accounting or previous related internship/work experience preferred
- <u>Skills:</u> Strong proficiency with Excel, Word and PowerPoint

So you see, you must get good grades and know how to actually apply what you have learned in college. Work with your professors and mentors to ensure that you are gaining all the skills you need in school to prepare you for the job world. High school is not too early to start.

I suggest that while in high school you write your first resume. If you have any paid work experience or volunteer work, put that on your resume. Put down any leadership positions you have held in school or coaching as well. Colleges will use this information as a screening tool for admissions. Here is a sample resume:

YOUR NAME
555 XYZ Street, StarStocker, Ca 99999
Home: (111) 555-1212 Cell: (111) 555-0011
yourname@emailaddress.com

OBJECTIVE
Interested in a paid summer camp work experience for up to 40 hours per week.

EDUCATION
Prepadan Central High School, Prepadan WA
High School Diploma anticipated in May 2018
Sophomore, GPA 3.84
Electives: Art, Music
Activities: Soccer, Tennis

VOLUNTEER & COMMUNITY SERVICE

- Volunteer Camp Counselor
- ABC Home for Aged, Bothell, Washington - Ongoing
- Library Volunteer. Run errands or do assignments for library staff.
- Bothell Recreation Department, City of Bothell, WA, Summer 2007

SPECIAL SKILLS & INTERESTS

- Able to follow written and verbal instructions
- Good with computer software
- Can do internet research using Internet browser
- Love to work with computers
- Can create attractive drawings using graphic software
- Trombone player in the jazz and concert bands

FUTURE GOALS

- Planning to study Sociology or Engineering as a major in college
- Join the National Honor Society in Junior year

Keep your eye on your goals and use discipline to elevate yourself to the heights necessary for getting a good-paying job.

JOINING THE MILITARY

Joining the military is an honorable way to make a living if you have a strong passion for serving while defending your country. If you join right out of high school, you will become an enlisted man and acquire a particular job skill similar to a trade school in civilian life. Only a high school education is required of enlisted people. After finishing boot camp, you would receive orders to a military school where you would learn about the profession that best fits the military's needs and, hopefully, your desires.

If you want to become a military officer, you will need to obtain a Bachelor's Degree or higher from any accredited college or university. After college, you would go to officer training school's boot camp to attain the basics of military life.

A hybrid approach to that is to join the Reserve Officers' Training Corp (ROTC) Program at some colleges or universities. In this program, you are set apart from the civilian students in college in that you study military topics and wear a uniform while attending classes.

If you are thinking about attending one of the military academies to become an officer, then you will need to obtain a letter of recommendation from your congressperson or senator. There are five U.S. service academies:

- The United States Military Academy (USMA) in West Point, NY
- The United States Naval Academy (USNA) in Annapolis, MD
- The United States Coast Guard Academy (USCGA) in New London, CT
- The United States Merchant Marine Academy (USMMA) in Kings Point, NY
- The United States Air Force Academy (USAFA) in Colorado Springs, CO

When Dealing with Others, Be Kind and Assertive

*The only thing necessary for the triumph of
evil is for good men to do nothing.*

Edmund Burke

It is important to be kind to others. The *Bible* says to "love" everybody - that's an order from God, but this may take many years of spiritual development to actually understand what that means and how to practice it, so do not despair. Be kind, but also, be assertive. Learn to find that delicate balance in order to be the most effective with people. Being kind does not mean being a doormat. Being a doormat does not benefit anyone - either you or other people. As a leader, protector and provider for your family, you will need to learn assertiveness and how to use it judiciously. In my personal experience over many years, people would often mistake my kindness for weakness. Do not let that happen to you. Be kind, but also, be firm and assertive. Say what you mean and mean what you say. Yes, some people will try to take advantage of you (walk all over you) like a "doormat" if you do not learn to say "No" sometimes. It's important to learn when and how to say "no." Use your head and your agency. If you ask the Holy Spirit for guidance and strength, you cannot go wrong. Do what you know is right.

Dr. Peck adds important information in regards to when it is appropriate to hold one's tongue:

"The selective withholding of one's opinions must also be practiced from time to time in the world of business or politics if one is to be welcomed into the councils of power. If people were always to speak their minds on issues both great and small, they would be considered insubordinate by the average supervisor, and a threat to an organization by management. They would gain reputations for abrasiveness and would be deemed too untrustworthy ever to be appointed as spokesmen for an organization. The road that a great executive must travel between the preservation and loss of his or her identity and integrity is extraordinarily narrow, and very, very, few really make the trip successfully. It is an enormous challenge."[439]

Assertive people take action to protect innocents because they know right from wrong and have the courage to do so. Do not be deluded by the world. Do not allow yourself to be fooled by the world's popular beliefs and opinions. See clearly be assertive in doing the right thing. Take lessons from Martin Luther King, Jr., Edmund Burke, President FW De Klerk and Nelson Mandela. How many years did de Klerk withhold his true opinion about ending apartheid in South Africa, which enabled him to become president of South Africa? How many times did Nelson Mandela withhold his opinion about de Klerk's inability to stop the violence in South Africa just as negotiations were taking place to end apartheid? Sometimes opinions must be withheld for the greater good, and at other times, they need to be voiced clearly and emphatically for the greater good.

Nobelprize.org shows that The Nobel Peace Prize 1993 was awarded jointly to Nelson Mandela and Frederik Willem de Klerk "for their work for the peaceful termination of the apartheid regime, and for laying the foundations for a new democratic South Africa."[440]

In 1994, Nelson Mandela became the first president of the post-apartheid era in South Africa. That was monumental.

FW de Klerk and Nelson Mandela both traveled the narrow road, as Dr. Peck says above, "between the preservation and loss of (their) identity and integrity" to the successful completion of the extraordinarily difficult task of ending apartheid.

CIVILITY

Cecile Blais Barbeau, my mother-in-law, taught her children, "Turn your tongue twice before you speak," which means that before you say anything, think of the consequences of the words you are about to speak. If you know the consequences and you feel that it will add joy, justice, solve a problem, or be useful to someone as in educating someone about something, or what you are about to say will be useful to yourself such as in asking someone to go out with you somewhere, then go ahead and speak. If you feel that what you are about to say is unjust, or a lie, or will hurt a kind person's feelings then hold your tongue. Remember, that once something is spoken or written it cannot be taken back; and what you have said may change your relationship with the recipient forever - even if what you said was said as a "joke." Saying something hurtful and disguising it as a joke is "passive aggressive behavior" it is psychologically abusive. Be mindful.

Sometimes, even when you have a kind heart, your choice of words and the way you express words can be hurtful to others. When you hurt someone unintentionally, always ask for forgiveness and explain what you meant to say. Remember that - at least - your Heavenly Father knows your intentions, and also YOU know your intentions. With patience, humility, and honesty you should be able to correct any misunderstandings. It has been my experience that eventually good always overcomes evil, and that bad experiences can also be overcome if there were good intentions. Test this theory out for yourself.

Why Join a Church?

A member of our church mentioned in a talk that while having lunch in a restaurant, one of his colleagues asked him, "What do you get by being a member of a church?" The church member answered, "That's an easy question to answer, Hope, Commitment, and Community. Hope for an eternal life with Jesus, God and my family. Commitment to God, my family and my church members gives my life meaning and direction. Community gives me a sense of belonging, and security in that I do not feel alone."

His colleague surmised, "You are lucky."

Members of the church become partners with you as you proceed through life. I have heard many women thank the members of their church for helping to raise their children as teachers in Sunday School, and in the Young Men meetings and in the Young Women meetings.

When I was diagnosed with cancer and experienced a pulmonary embolism (PE) and deep vein thrombosis (DVT), I received priesthood healing blessings, and support in numerous other ways. I believe that it was a miracle - through the grace and power of God – that saved me.

When I first developed PE/DVT, Elaine sent emails to priesthood holders and asked them to pray for me. At the time we did not know why I was ill. She also called temples around the country and placed my name on their prayer rolls. I went to the local Urgent Care and was misdiagnosed with dehydration and low electrolytes and I was told to go home and drink Gatorade. Three days later my condition worsened and I allowed Elaine to call 911, which she had wanted to do three days earlier. Before the ambulance arrived she sent another email to four bishops asking them to pray for me. In the hospital's Emergency Room, we felt a deep sense of peace, and I began to recover on blood thinners. I was blessed to have survived. About 25% of people with a DVT and PE die within the first 30-60 minutes.

Bishops and counselor in the church are receptive to private, confidential conversations. With these spiritually-inspired individuals, you can share things which you would never share with anyone in your extended family or at work because you would not want to worry your family, and you would not want your colleagues to know your private business.

On the other hand, I have often marveled at how openly members of the church share their innermost feelings about hardships, shortcomings, and lessons learned and the manner in which other members offer their support and appreciation. You need never feel alone as a member of a church. Church members become an extension of your family.

Personal Finance and Investments

Managing personal finances is a core skill that you will need to get a handle on – sooner rather than later. Some high schools are starting to make financial management a requirement for graduation, and you would be doing yourself a big favor to study the subject if you have not already done so. It's never too early to start learning how to manage your money.

A friend of mine started teaching his kids money management principles when they were very young. He gave them three quart jars labeled: SPENDING, SAVING, and CHARITY and assisted them in figuring out how much needed to go into each jar whenever they received money. For example, if one of his children received a dollar, ten cents would go into CHARITY, ten cents would go into SAVING and eighty cents would go into SPENDING.

This is an excellent way of teaching very young children how to manage money and it could be extended and modified to meet your personal needs.

Checking Accounts

You should get yourself a checking account when you are in high school so you can get practical experience managing your own money. By the time you are in college, you should have experience handling money and credit cards.

Within your checking account you can have expense money at your disposal in four categories for buying "something you need," such as food and paying the rent, "something you want," such as new sports running shoes, and ice cream or gelato, "personal gifting" for buying a friend or family member a small gift, and for "charity." Be sure to spend this money according to your overall budget, which you should keep in a log or in a spreadsheet. Be thrifty and do not waste money. Be sure to pay all bills on time.

Saving Money

Learning to save money is a valuable skill to acquire. As a child, you may have heard your parents talking about "saving for a rainy day." You might have even had a little piggy bank. If you did, you probably remember the good feeling you had as you dropped the coins down the slot. You probably felt even better when you were able to use some of that money to buy an ice cream or a toy.

Do you save money now? If not, you may want to get back into the habit of saving. This is good practice for when you become a man and have a family. You will be responsible for setting aside and maintaining savings for your family's needs, for emergencies and for your retirement. Open a savings account at a bank and make it a habit of depositing a part of your money in your account. In essence, saving is paying yourself.

Categories of Savings

Within your savings account you can allocate money in several categories, including "emergencies" such as a job loss, "long term goals" such as education, a mission, and "short-term goals" such as saving for something special that you want such as new bicycle, or a canoe, or a new car. In regards to saving for a period of job loss, the financial industry recommends saving enough to cover at least three months' rent, food, gas, utilities, technology, telephones, and for costs associated with finding employment such as purchasing new shoes and clothing.

Saving for Retirement

There are various ways that you can save to prepare for your retirement. Again, it's never too early to start saving - especially for retirement.

Retirement might seem a very long way off, but the wise young man knows to start saving for this eventuality as soon as practical.

What are your dreams and goals? Do you want to live comfortably in retirement – without financial worries? If so, saving each month in an annuity with flexible premiums will enable you to invest and grow your earnings throughout your years of employment, and will enable you to receive a monthly income from that annuity when you retire for the rest of your life. Annuities work for you as a tax shelter also. Annuities are essentially a private pension plan. There are different types of annuities and insurance companies have differing policies. With some insurance companies, you may begin to invest in an annuity when you are eighteen. It is important for you to do your own research. When you find the type of annuity you feel would be best for you speak to a trusted financial advisor. Remember it is easy to get into an annuity but it is not easy to get out of an annuity without paying financial penalties – so you want to make certain that the annuity is right for you.

Another benefit of having your investments in an annuity is that you can designate a revocable beneficiary of the annuity in case you pass before you retire – which would be sad but it happens. At first, you may want to choose your parents to be beneficiary, but after you marry you ought to change the designated beneficiary to your wife's name and you may want to name your children also– to enable your wife and your children to receive your investment if you die. Having said that, we do hope you will have a long and healthy life.

Be sure to work with a trusted financial planner to assist you make these decisions and get them into place.

When you start work, your company may provide you with a 401K savings and investment plan. If so, please take advantage of this vehicle and make the best of it, again, by consulting with a trusted financial advisor.

Other ways of saving money include Individual Retirement Accounts (IRAs), Roth IRAs, and Certificates of Deposits (CDs). These are beyond the scope of this book, but after you have full-time employment, be sure to consult that financial advisor we mentioned several times earlier.

One word of caution: Be sure to keep enough money on hand to handle your current expenses easily, along with emergencies. Don't make the mistake of locking up too much of your money so that it is not accessible when you need it or that you have to pay a high penalty to access it. Plan wisely.

CREDIT CARDS AND DEBIT CARDS
One day you will need to decide when you need a credit card. Perhaps the first credit card you will use will be your parent's credit card. They may offer you a credit card on their account for you to use to make specific purchases. Or they may allow you to carry one of their cards when you start driving – in case of emergencies like running out of gas or having a flat tire or other reasons.

Eventually you ought to get a credit card of your own – one in which you are responsible for the charges, in order to establish your credit rating. It would be beneficial for you to use your checking account to pay off the card each month so that you learn that debt from the credit card is only "borrowed" money that must be paid back each month.

If you are using a debit card, be sure that you have sufficient funds in your checking account prior to making purchases. This will save you potential embarrassment from being declined at a cash register.

If you have given your debit card to a company to bill you online and there are insufficient funds in your checking account, there could be a "Non-sufficient Funds" fee of about $40.

Learn to manage cash balances in your checking account, savings account, and credit card accounts in order to gain proficiency in managing money. This will help you learn responsibility and increase your self-reliance and confidence.

CREDIT REPORT AND CREDIT SCORES
When you start using credit, it will become important to understand your credit report and credit scores. If your high school offers

personal financial management classes, it is advisable to take these courses to prepare yourself for financial responsibility. Here are a few things, which you should know:

1. There are three major credit-reporting companies: Experian, Equifax, and Trans Union. Each one maintains a database with credit history records for individuals.

2. You can obtain a credit report from these companies directly, or you can obtain credit reports through certain websites like www.freecreditreport.com and others. Each person is now allowed one free credit report per year from each of the credit bureaus or through the other companies. It is a good idea to check your credit report periodically for errors, omissions, and for the accuracy of information. In order to do that, you must learn how to properly read and understand your credit report.

3. You should be mindful of your credit score, which is shown in your credit report. Your credit score determines the quality of your credit and will become important when you are preparing to rent an apartment, or when buying a house or a car. Some jobs will require you to have decent credit. Landlords will check your credit score to determine whether they want to rent to you. Mortgage companies will check your credit score to determine whether or not to approve your mortgage so that you can buy a house. Car dealerships will also check your credit score before allowing you to purchase a car. All of these entities check people's credit scores because they want to ensure that you will make the rent payment or mortgage payment on time each month, and the car payment on time each month.

4. Your credit score will help determine the interest rate of your mortgage when you purchase a house. A higher credit score will yield a lower interest rate on your mortgage than a lower one, which will save you money - money which you can then save or invest. So don't over spend. Be sure to pay off those credit cards promptly. Live within your means.

Investing

If you are interested in investing, discuss ideas with your parents and with a certified financial securities advisor. Always study on your own to be able to make wise decisions - even if you have a financial security advisor assisting you. Listen to or read financial news, study historical markets, and read about how other men and women have made their fortunes. Keep track of your results and learn from your mistakes.

What Will You Do To Elevate Yourself Today? Quest Checkpoint: Your Place in Society

Congratulations for reaching this checkpoint on your quest. In order to satisfy the requirements for the Society Certificate, you will need to demonstrate proficiency in the subject areas covered within this chapter by reading and completing the requirements below. After you have completed all the certificate requirements below - using the honor system – fill in the certificate with your name. **You can also download a printed copy from the *Elevate Yourself to Manhood* website at http://www.elevateyourselftomanhood. com/certificates.**

Certificate Requirements

- ☐ **Manhood -** What does it mean to you to "be a man?" Record the answer in your journal.
- ☐ **Manhood -** Name a few men you admire and note what contributions they have made to society. Record the answer in your journal.
- ☐ **Fine Tuning Social Skills**
  - ⚬ Practice a new social skill or two each day. "Fake it until you become it." Practice, practice, practice, in your mind and socially.
  - ⚬ Having progressed through the book studying about Mind, Body, Spirit, Character, Family, and Society do you

now have a good sense of how to deal comfortably with family, peers, friends, neighbors, and colleagues? How has this book helped you in this regard? Discuss this with your friends, parents, teachers, and others.

☐ **Scouting** - Can you see how becoming a Boy Scout or Eagle Scout can help you elevate yourself? Make a plan to join Boy Scouts of America, become a Scout Leader, or support the Boy Scouts.

☐ **Positive Affirmations** Identify positive affirmations that reso-nate with you and use them to create positive self-talk to help you in your relationships with others in society. During quiet time, repeat these affirmations each day until they become a part of you.

☐ **Education, Training, and Continual Learning** - Can you see the value of continuous learning even after you finish high school? Outline your plans to attend a college, university or trade school.

☐ **Skill/Profession** – Ask your career guidance counselor at school to give you an aptitude test to determine what kinds of jobs you may enjoy. However, remember that this is only a guideline. If you are passionately interested in something else pursue that. Also, ask your career guidance counselor for an extensive list of jobs. Go to job boards on the Internet to see what kinds of jobs major companies are offering.

☐ **Mission** - Do you plan to go on a mission to help others?

  • You can go on a mission through The Church of Jesus Christ of Latter-day Saints

  • You can work through secular volunteer organizations like JustServe.Org, AmeriCorp Vista, Red Cross, Doctors Without Borders, Love Volunteers, Volunteer Solutions, Agape Volunteers.

☐ **Employment or Business Ownership** - What are your plans for becoming self-reliant? Will you start your own business or seek to work for someone else? Record your plans in your journal.

☐ **Resume** – Use the sample resume template to create an actual resume for yourself on your computer.

☐ **Marriage/Family** – Families are the building blocks for our society. What are your plans for starting a family? Discuss your tentative plans with parents or mentors.

☐ **Kindness and Assertiveness** - Learn to find that delicate balance between being kind to others yet being assertive when you need to be so.

☐ **Civility** - In society, one must know how to "be civil" by keeping a kind tongue and behaving like a gentleman. This is a personal challenge that you must learn at home, in school and at work. Think of ways you can be civil even when someone is yelling angrily at you.

☐ **Personal Finance and Investments** -
   * Open a checking account at a reputable bank.
   * Open a savings account at a reputable bank.
   * Deposit your earned money into these accounts and manage your bills or payments by writing checks or using bank cards.
   * Obtain a credit card. Pay the balance monthly.
   * Establish a budget. How many categories are there in your basic savings account? How many categories are there in your basic checking account?
   * Learn how to manage your credit and monitor your credit score.
   * Learn about investments, which may be appropriate for your age and status. Seek the counsel of a financial advisor.
   * Buy a life insurance policy when you are young, which guarantees your future insurability and that you can increase the benefit to your beneficiaries in order to protect your future family and accumulate cash value.

ELEVATE YOURSELF TO MANHOOD

QUEST CERTIFICATE – SOCIETY

THIS CERTIFICATE IS AWARDED TO:

_____

FOR DILIGENCE IN FULFILLING THE *ELEVATE YOURSELF TO MANHOOD* REQUIREMENTS FOR "SOCIETY" ON HIS QUEST

Create Your Legacy

FACET 8

CREATE YOUR LEGACY

WHAT WILL YOU DO TO create a beautiful legacy for your children and grandchildren? There are three facets to creating a legacy - financial, historical, and spiritual.

CREATING A FINANCIAL LEGACY

For many people leaving a financial legacy means leaving an inheritance to their children. Often people do so because they want to help to raise up future generations with enough money to maintain the family business and to provide funding for education for their children and grandchildren. Frequently, there is an underlying desire to pay forward the financial lift that was offered to them by their parents and grandparents, and, therefore, they want to do the same for their children by leaving them a financial legacy. Some people who never received an inheritance and struggled through life want to strengthen their families by leaving them a financial legacy so that they will be able to weather whatever happens to them in life – in health or sickness. Financial legacies also help to care for special needs children who have physical and mental challenges.

GETTING STARTED

Steven Covey, author of the famous book, *The 7 Habits of Highly Effective People*, suggests that you "begin with the end in mind."[441] It is best to start planning for the future while you are young. When considering leaving a financial legacy for your family, it is best to speak to a financial security advisor who is also a qualified life insurance agent who can help you develop a plan that will make your dreams and goals come true. However, here are a few basic principles for leaving a legacy for your children:

1. Life insurance on your life will help to cover taxes on the proceeds from the sale of your house in the event of your death if you are leaving your children a house.

2. If you are leaving your house to one of your children, they will need to pay taxes on gaining a house – life insurance can cover these taxes. Plus life insurance can provide an inheritance for your other children.

3. Laws regarding the transfer of wealth may differ from country to country, and state to state. As previously mentioned, it is best to speak to a financial security advisor to establish a plan for your legacy. Brad Wiewel,[442] reporting for ABC News in the United States, in his article *Inheritance 101: How to leave your home to your kids* says, remember to "include the 'right words' in the deed to your home. Those words can either be Transfer on Death or Joint Tenant with Right of Survivorship. (Tenants by the Entireties is another option between spouses in some states). Either option lets you give your home to your loved one(s) at your death without the delays associated with probate or the cost of setting up a trust."

4. It is important to plan and save for your retirement. Otherwise, you may not be able to leave your children your house or your business.

5. Getting a good paying job should enable you to save for your retirement and to leave a legacy for your children.

6. Investing wisely so that you do not lose your hard earned money should also enable you to leave a financial legacy. My wife became a financial security advisor about a month before the devastating 2008 financial market crash. That

crash exposed many crooked financial advisors. Earl Jones, a Canadian financial security advisor, stole a million dollars from his own brother. He also stole the savings of friends, widows, and seniors. In the United States, Bernard Madoff stole 20 billion dollars from his clients and was sentenced to 150 years in prison for running the biggest fraudulent financial investment scheme in U.S. history. BOTTOM LINE: BE CAREFUL WHERE YOU PARK YOUR HARD-EARNED MONEY.

How to Spot a Financial Scammer

Protecting your nest egg for yourself and your family requires vigilance. Be wise. Ken Fisher, author of *How to Smell a Rat*, provides guidance on recognizing the warning signs of a financial scam that may threaten your financial assets:

1. Your advisor also has access to your money. Your assets are commingled into pools of assets. Your money account is not in your name.

2. The plan for your investments was too complicated for your advisor to explain so that you could understand where and how your money was being invested: you should understand the pros, cons, options, company's history as assessed by a third party, and the history of the investment as assessed by a third party.

3. Returns on your investments are continuously growing. There is no downturn at all when the markets experience a downturn. (This is not normal.)

4. Your advisor makes you feel that you are part of an exclusive club, with unique strategies, and that you should be grateful that they let you in. They deter you from asking questions with authoritative comments, "You take care of your health and I will take care of your finances." You have the right to ask questions to protect your money. If your advisor does not answer your questions seek financial advice elsewhere.

5. A trusted friend or family member referred you to the advisor. You did not take the time to check the advisors credential and the credentials of the company.[443]
6. Do research before you invest. It is your money. It is your responsibility.

CREATING A HISTORICAL LEGACY

1. If you want your children to grow up to be righteous, healthy, happy and courageous, you will need to set an example they will want to emulate. Live your life as if the eyes of your children and grandchildren were looking at you. If you would not want them to see your behavior, you should not be behaving in such a manner that would negatively influence them.
2. Remember how much power words have on water. There is a saying, which describes the power of our actions, "Actions speak louder than words." Actions have a ripple effect in our personal lives and in the lives of our children and grandchildren. If the actions we take are positive the ripples will be positive – if the actions we take are negative the ripples will be negative.
3. Keep a journal from which to write your memoirs. The stories of your life will delight and inspire your children and grandchildren. Take great joy in your youth. You are physically strong. You have stamina. Use some of that strength and stamina to speak to your children and grandchildren in your journal.

"Language allows us to reach out to people,
to touch them with our innermost fears, hopes,
disappointments, victories. To reach out to
people, we'll never meet. It's the greatest
legacy you could ever leave your children or
your loved ones: The history of how you felt."

~ SIMON VAN BOOY

4. During photo shoots remember to think of your children and grandchildren. How would you want them to see you? Be the kind of person they will want to know. When you smile for photographs, imagine that you are smiling at your children and grandchildren because they will be looking at that photograph someday – smiling right back at you. They will be happy that you were happy. They will be glad that you had a good childhood and a good life. They will be pleased that you were courageous and achieved your goals. It will help them to feel that they can also be happy and that they can also achieve their goals.

5. Ancestral photographs enable generations to feel connected. In looking at ancestral photos, people may see that their physical traits resemble those of their forbears. These photos enable us to get a sense of our ancestors' personalities – they become more than just a name – we then feel spiritually closer to them. These precious photos can be uploaded to websites like *Family Search* or *Ancestry* so that the photographs can be made available to future generations. In our home, my wife and I have displayed our ancestral photographs dating back to the 1800s, on a couple of walls in our hallway. These photographs are so precious to us, all the more so because our ancestors looked distinguished. We look forward to continuing our own genealogical work – searching for new names and documenting them in the system. We hope you will do the same.

My father-in-law, Arthur Barbeau, uploaded family home movies onto DVDs. He wrote his career memoirs. His childhood friend Fernando DiLabio gave my wife a photograph of the boyhood friends he and Arthur played with in the 1930s (The Balsam Street Pals), and a high school photograph. Please find four photographs of Arthur below. Fernando DiLabio became an aeronautical engineer. As of this writing, he is 86 years old and still runs 6 miles per day. He and his wife (whom he met when he was in high school) have given of their time to share Arthur's childhood stories, which Arthur planned to write himself the day he died.

As you see the friendships Arthur built have influenced the life of his daughter and this book, in ways that he could not have imagined when he was a boy. This is an example of the ripple effect that your life will have upon your posterity. In this case, the ripples were positive. His ability to care for his family of seven children and his joie de vivre were a testament to his strength of character, which has inspired his entire family.

Your life lies ahead of you like a field of untouched snow.
Be careful the way you walk in it for every step will show
(and will influence many lives as well as your own).

– UNKNOWN

This is Elaine Barbeau Cox writing. We are fortunate to have one good photograph of Ray Cox (Donell's father) when he was young, which we included in his dedication at the beginning of this book. Ray accomplished a great deal in his life. His greatest accomplishments were providing for and inspiring his family of nine children. Therefore, I feel that we ought to share photographs of Donell when he was becoming a man, for they reflect the positive influence that Ray Cox had on his son Donell and his entire family.

Lifting a race up from slavery, lifting a culture up from historical tensions was championed by men like Ray Cox and my father, Arthur Barbeau. They sought to be the best they could be to lift themselves up, to lift their families up and in so doing lifted their communities. This is an ongoing challenge for all men.

We can never take for granted the freedoms and privileges that we now possess. Each generation has a responsibility to do their part in maintaining our rights to equal opportunity to pursue happiness, to have a fulfilling life, and to enjoy the freedom we possess and benefit from today. To achieve this, men of every culture and race must continue to strive to set a good example for their families and members of their community.

What do men like Ray Cox, Arthur Barbeau, Donell Cox, Fernando DiLabio, Gordon Nishimoto, Shane Leavitt, Scott Ashworth and so many men whom I admire have in common? When they were young, they spent time in nature doing essentially what boy scouts do. They began working towards specific non-curricular goals, at chores, and odd jobs early in life. They are able to do hard things well. They study to get a formal education or they become self-educated. They abide by God's commandments and repent when they sin. They obey the laws of the land. They provide for and are of service to their families. They are of service to members in their community and to their country. They never give up – and when the going gets tough, they keep meeting all of life's challenges, by overcoming or changing course. They have a zest for life. They have a vision for themselves and their family. They respect themselves, and other people. This is their legacy for which I will be eternally grateful. I pray that you will follow their example.

Balsam Street Pals

ARTHUR BARBEAU - MEDALLIST -46 -47 – 48

Arthur Barbeau's Perfect Flyaway off the High Bar

JUNIOR CANADIAN GYMNASTIC TEAM 1947 – MAYOR PRESENTING THE
CITY OF OTTAWA CREST FOR CANADIAN CHAMPIONS

Mr. Greer (coach), Gerry Cotter, Ray Gauthier, Art Barbeau, Mr. Wallen
Plus The Mayor - (Note- Art is made up for MC' ing HS Variety Show)

Arthur Barbeau and other Team Members Win
the Canadian Gymnastics Championship

1ˢᵗ TROMBONE SOLO – OTTAWA MUSIC FESTIVAL - 16 YR OLD

16-Year-Old Arthur Barbeau Wins Trombone Competition

Donell Cox & Elaine J. Barbeau Cox

Donell Cox High School Graduation

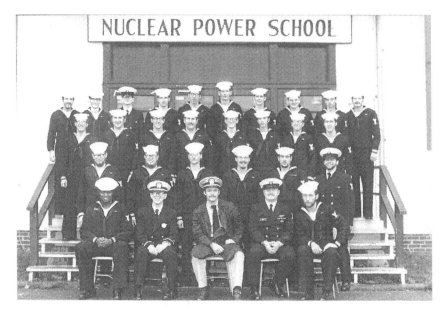

*Donell Cox (First Row, Left Corner), US Navy Nuclear
Power School, Bainbridge, Maryland*

*Lieutenant Donell Cox, Admiral's Aide, Commander Naval Sea
Systems Command (COMNAVSEASYSCOM), Washington, D.C.*

CREATING A SPIRITUAL LEGACY

I am convinced that the greatest legacy we can leave our
children are happy memories: those precious moments so
much like pebbles on the beach that are plucked from the
white sand and placed in tiny boxes that lay undisturbed
on tall shelves until one day they spill out and time repeats
itself, with joy and sweet sadness, in *the child now an adult.*

~ OG MANDINO

In his article, *Our Legacy*, Stephen B. Oveson[444], a member of the Quorum of the Seventy, quoted Gordon B. Hinckley speaking to students at Ricks College, "To you I say with all of the energy of which I am capable, do not become a weak link in the chain of your generations. You come to the world with a marvelous inheritance. You come of great men and women. Never let them down. Never do anything which would weaken the chain of which you are a fundamental part" (Scroll, 14 Sept. 1999, 20).

Oveson added: "To me that means that we must do all in our power to ensure that we instill within our loved ones the great legacy of an abiding testimony of the gospel of Jesus Christ."

In a presentation titled, *Our Legacy*, Stephan B. Oveson discusses many more aspects of building a meaningful legacy:

1. Be an example of one who puts the Savior and His Gospel first in his life.
2. Teach your family how to pray.
3. Build a life of honesty and integrity.
4. Be responsible and dependable.
5. Provide well for your family.
6. Repent of your mistakes and learn from them.
7. Set aside a special day each week to spend with your family.
8. Do interesting activities together. Have fun.
9. Be a good neighbor and a loyal friend.
10. Have control over your temper.

11. Forgive people who have hurt you.
12. Be of service to others.
13. Leave a legacy of knowledge, wisdom, and love to your family.

Record in your journals when God has answered your prayers, tender mercies that He has bestowed, and miracles, which you have been fortunate to receive. These will be a source of spiritual legacy for your children and grandchildren.

QUEST CHECKPOINT: YOUR LEGACY

Congratulations on reaching the end of your quest. In order to satisfy the requirements for the Legacy Certificate, you will need to demonstrate proficiency in the subject areas covered within this chapter by reading and completing the requirements below. After you have completed all the certificate requirements below - using the honor system – fill in the certificate with your name. **You can also download a printed copy from the *Elevate Yourself to Manhood* website at http://www.elevateyourselftomanhood.com/certificates.**

CERTIFICATE REQUIREMENTS

- ☐ **Financial Legacy**
  - **Life Insurance** - Ask your parents about getting a life insurance policy that will guarantee your insurability, and to which you can add a rider that will allow you to increase the benefit when you have a family. Before you marry, your parents can be the beneficiaries of your insurance policy, which will be fair especially if they are paying for the policy. Once you start working, you can take over the payments. Remember to designate the beneficiary as "revocable." When you get married you can change the beneficiary to your wife's name by calling your life insurance company and requesting a change of beneficiary form – fill it out with your

wife's name, mail it back. Two weeks later call the company to double-check that the beneficiary of your policy is your wife. Then, God forbid (but it does happen), if she is pregnant and you are in an automobile accident and die she will have at least some money to help her to cope financially.

- ☐ **Historical Legacy**
  - **What life lessons will you pass on to your children?** Record these lessons in your journal. This will provide rich content for your memoirs that your heirs will enjoy forever. Be judicious as you write down your thoughts, actions, observations, and dreams.
  - **Purchase a fireproof safe for your journals.** Find a safe place to store and protect your journals – perhaps a fireproof safe where you keep all your other valuable documents like your passport and your marriage license.
  - **Photos**. Smile whenever someone takes your photo. The pictures you take today will create precious memories. Consider keeping printed copies of photos in a safe place as well as electronic/online photos.

- ☐ **Spiritual Legacy**
  - Start recording in your journal instances when God has answered your prayers, tender mercies that He has bestowed, and miracles, which you have been fortunate to receive. These will be a source of spiritual legacy for your children and grandchildren.
  - Learn the Holy Scriptures well so that you may guide your children.
  - Attend a church that offers Gospel Lessons.
  - Be mindful of acting in congruence to your values, beliefs, the laws of the land and God's laws.
  - Behave in such a manner that your children and grandchildren will be glad to call you their father and grandfather.

ELEVATE YOURSELF TO MANHOOD

QUEST CERTIFICATE – LEGACY

THIS CERTIFICATE IS AWARDED TO:

_____

FOR DILIGENCE IN FULFILLING THE *ELEVATE YOURSELF TO MANHOOD*
REQUIREMENTS FOR "LEGACY" ON HIS QUEST

In Closing

Repeat the "Happy" Test

Now that you have almost completed this book, we are interested to know if your life perspective has changed. Go back to the Happy Test and take it again to see if your score has improved. Please send an email to info@elevateyourselftomanhood.com to let us know.

A Message to America that I Hope You Will Share When It Is Your Turn to Mentor Young Men

In order for our young men to grow into healthy, happy, and morally strong men, we as a society need to help them. It truly does "take a village" to raise a child. Without quality role models and without proper guidance when they need it, we can't expect our boys to grow up into men that will be able to sustain families and become leaders. There are many pitfalls and distractions threatening to lure them off their chosen paths. To help our young men survive the teenage years and become successful men, society needs to do its part too. Society includes you. We need wise and gracious people like you to help mentor young men to adulthood. I pray that you will heed this honorable calling for the sake of young men everywhere and our marvelous Earth.

MY TESTIMONY

And with that I bear my personal testimony that God and Jesus live. I testify that Jesus atoned for our sins in the Garden of Gethsemane, and if we repent with a broken heart and a contrite spirit, we shall be forgiven. I testify that if you put your faith in God and Jesus, they will be your help throughout your life – in your weakness, in your sadness, and in your joy - in ways unimaginable. I pray that when your spirit shall have departed this life, your children will keep their hearts turned to God and Jesus and that they will keep your remembrance and legacy alive. I say this in the name of Jesus Christ. Amen

I leave you this simple hymn that describes the relationship one can develop with God and Jesus:

I Feel My Savior's Love

I feel my Savior's love
In all the world around me.
His Spirit warms my soul
Through ev'rything I see.

I feel my Savior's love;
Its gentleness enfolds me,
And when I kneel to pray,
My heart is filled with peace.

I feel my Savior's love
And know that he will bless me.
I offer him my heart; My shepherd, he will be.

I'll share my Savior's love
By serving others freely.
In serving, I am blessed.
In giving I receive.

Chorus
He knows I will follow him,

Give all my life to him.
I feel my Savior's love,
The love he freely gives me.

Music by K. Newell Dayley
Text by Ralph Rodgers Jr.
K. Newell Dayley
Laurie Huffman

A FINAL THOUGHT

When I was a young man, an older woman gave me a wooden plaque with a poem inscribed upon it. There were little footprints made of brass surrounded by white beach sand glued to the plaque beneath a poem. I graciously accepted the plaque, but throughout my life I always pondered its meaning and why she singled me out to receive this gift. Having gained significantly more life experience, I have now come to know and appreciate its meaning more clearly:

Footprints in the Sand

One night I dreamed I was walking
along the beach with the Lord.
Many scenes from my life flashed across the sky.
In each scene, I noticed footprints in the sand.
Sometimes there were two sets of footprints,
other times there was one set of footprints.

This bothered me because I noticed
that during the low periods of my life,
when I was suffering from anguish,
sorrow or defeat,
I could see only one set of footprints

So I said to the Lord,
"You promised me, Lord,
that if I followed you, you would walk with me always.
But I have noticed that during the
most trying periods of my life
there has only been one set of footprints in the sand.
Why, when I needed you most, have
you not been there for me?"

The Lord replied.
"The times when you have
seen only one set of footprints, my child,
is when I carried you."

(MARY STEVENSON, 1936)

Congratulations! You have completed the book, and now you have the roadmap, the tools, and the mindset to complete your quest. **Be brave, have fun, and may God be with you.**

NOW GO OUT THERE AND ENJOY YOUR LIFE

Now that you have a broader perspective of life, and a deeper appreciation for your youthful vigor, spend that energy constructively to build a strong foundation for the rest of your life while having fun. Here are some suggestions:

1. Join the Boy Scouts of America
2. Take a road trip with friends
3. Camp out under the stars with fellow scouts
4. Participate in an Outward Bound excursion
5. Participate in a NOLS excursion
6. Learn a foreign language
7. Travel to a foreign country with your parents
8. Take a walk in the rain

9. Go to an outdoor band concert
10. See a Shakespearean play
11. Learn to play your favorite musical instrument
12. Learn to cook something that you like and share with your family
13. Go to a professional ball game
14. Host a movie marathon (G-Rated)
15. Vote as soon as you are 18
16. Become a White House Intern
17. Become a Congressional Page
18. Study abroad
19. Make a comical YouTube video
20. Become an astronaut
21. Sing a solo in public
22. Run a marathon
23. Act on stage in a play
24. Start a small (legal) business
25. Read the *Bible*
26. Go to Disney World or Disneyland or both
27. Swim with dolphins
28. Get your body into tip-top shape
29. Do a public speech
30. Go on a safari
31. Go on a 50-mile trek
32. Fish and eat your catch
33. Brew your own root beer
34. Go to an Olympics
35. Take a bath in a hot spring
36. Trek to Machu Pichu
37. Dance the Macarena
38. Go to a drive-in movie theater
39. See the Northern Lights
40. Learn to juggle
41. Ride a horse
42. Make a pizza

43. Watch a meteor shower
44. Write a letter to the President
45. Volunteer at a nursing home
46. Write a short story
47. Write a song
48. Do Geo-Caching with friends
49. Plant a tree
50. Grow a garden
51. Swim a mile in a pool
52. Earn an advanced college degree
53. Love deeply. Love your parents, love your wife, love your children, love your grandparents, love other members of your family, and love your neighbors. Put your love into action.
54. Now, put down the cell phone, video game controller and television remote and elevate yourself to manhood!

BIBLIOGRAPHY

n.d. Accessed March 30, 2016. http://www.catholic.org/clife/teresa/.

n.d. http://www.achooallergy.com/learning/famous-asthma-sufferer-teddy-roosevelt/.

n.d. *101 Family Home Evening Activities.* Accessed October 12, 2015. http://lds.about.com/od/familynight/a/101-Family-Home-Evening-Activities.htm.

n.d. *11 Facts About Teens and STDs.* Accessed April 5, 2016. https://www.dosomething.org/facts/11-facts-about-teens-and-stds.

2014. *11 Ways Dehydration Could Be Making You Fat and Sick.* July 24. Accessed October 18, 2015. http://dailyhealthpost.com/11-ways-dehydration-could-be-making-you-fat-and-sick/.

2014. *16 Cancer Causing Foods You Probably Eat Every Day.* March 9. Accessed December 5, 2014. http://naturalon.com/10-of-the-most-cancer-causing-foods/1/.

AACAP Staff. 2005. *American Academy of Child & Adolescent Psychiatry - Helping Teenagers With Stress.* May. Accessed October 12, 2014. http://www.aacap.org/AACAP/Families_and_Youth/Facts_for_Families/Facts_for_Families_Pages/Helping_Teenagers_With_Stress_66.aspx.

n.d. *Added Sugar Vs Natural Sugar.* Accessed November 1, 2015. http://thatsugarfilm.com/blog/2015/03/16/added-sugar-vs-natural-sugar/.

Administration, U.S. Food and Drug. 2014. *How to Understand and Use the Nutrition Facts Label.* June 18. Accessed October 23,

2014. http://www.fda.gov/Food/IngredientsPackagingLabeling/ LabelingNutrition/ucm274593.htm#seeimage4.

2004. "Alcohol Alert." *U.S. Department of Health & Human Services, National Institute of Health, National Institute on Alcohol Abuse and Alcoholism.* October. Accessed October 2014, 2014. http:// pubs.niaaa.nih.gov/publications/aa63/aa63.htm.

n.d. *American Heart Association.* Accessed September 12, 2015. www.heart.org/advocacy.

American Lung Association. n.d. *Lung Cancer Fact Sheet.* Accessed March 15, 2016. http://www.lung.org/lung-health-and-diseases/ lung-disease-lookup/lung-cancer/learn-about-lung-cancer/ lung-cancer-fact-sheet.html?referrer=https://www.google.com/.

2014. *American Psychological Association - Marriage and Divorce.* October 4. Accessed October 4, 2014. http://www.apa.org/topics/divorce/.

Andrea Watcher, Marriage and Family Therapist. 2014. "Which Wolf Are You Feeding?" *The Blog.* October 8. Accessed October 8, 2014. http://www.huffingtonpost.com/andrea-wachter/law-of- attraction_b_4292517.html.

Andreasson, S. et al. 1987. "Heavy Users of Marijuana at Age 18 Increase their Risk of Schizophrenia by Six Times Later In Life." *Lancet:Cannabis and Schizophrenia: A longitudinal study of Swedish Conscripts* 1483-1486.

Anita Poems Staff. n.d. *AnitaPoems - Let's Bring Joy to their Hearts.* Accessed August 15, 2015. http://www.anitapoems.com/poems- for-brothers.html.

Answers in Genesis Staff. 2000. *Were Dinosaurs on Noah's Ark.* April 3. Accessed August 15, 2015. https://answersingenesis.org/ dinosaurs/were-dinosaurs-on-noahs-ark/.

Antes, Emily. 2010. *Inside the Bullied Brain - The Alarming Neuroscience of Taunting.* November 28. Accessed October 8, 2014. http://www.boston.com/bostonglobe/ideas/articles/2010/11/28/inside_the_bullied_brain/?page=full.

Arseneault L., et al. 2004. "Casual Association between Cannabis and Psychosis: Examination of the Evidence." *British Journal of Psychiatry 184* 110-117.

Ashton, Marvin J. 1976. *Family Communications.* May. Accessed October 11, 2015. https://www.lds.org/general-conference/1976/04/family-communications?lang=eng.

n.d. *ASPARTAME AND PREGNANCY WHAT ARE THE RISKS?* Accessed November 22, 2015. http://www.healthy-holistic-living.com/aspartame-and-pregnancy.html.

Balch, Phyllis A. 2004. *Prescription for Nutritional Healing.* New York: Penguin.

Balch, Phyllis A., CNC. 2010. *Prescription for Nutritional Healing, Fifth Edition: A Practical A-to-Z Reference to Drug-Free Remedies Using Vitamins, Minerals, Herbs & Food Supplements.* New York: Avery.

Barbeau, Elaine J. 2002. *Bullies and Denial Kill - Let us Teach Our Children Not to be Abusive While We Teach Them to Survive.* West Mount, Quebec: Price Patterson LTD.

Barker, Eric. 2014. *4 P's for Happiness.* October 8. Accessed October 8, 2014. http://www.bakadesuyo.com/2014/01/the-way-to-happiness/.

Barnes, Rebecca, and Lindy Lowry. 2012. *100 Percent Americans Will Attend Church This Week.* December 10. Accessed August 15, 2015. http://www.8to15.com/home/2012/12/10/100-percent-of-americans-will-attend-church-this-week.html.

2014. *Baum, Hedlund, Aristei & Goldman, PC.* Accessed October 30, 2014. http://www.baumhedlundlaw.com/bpa/bpa_side_effects. php#sthash.LMFFukz0.EosOX4gs.dpuf.

BBC. n.d. *World Prison Populations.* Accessed August 1, 2016. http:// news.bbc.co.uk/2/shared/spl/hi/uk/06/prisons/html/nn2page1.stm.

Beck, Julie. 2009. *Teaching the Doctrine of the Family.* August 4. Accessed November 15, 2014. https://www.lds.org/liahona/2011/ 03/teaching-the-doctrine-of-the-family?lang=eng.

Bednar, David, A. 2010. *Receive the Holy Ghost.* October. Accessed October 14, 2015. https://www.lds.org/general-conference/2010/ 10/receive-the-holy-ghost?lang=eng.

Behe, Michael. n.d. *Darwin's Black Box: The Biochemical Challenge to Evolution.*

BeliefNet. n.d. *10 Celebrities Who Overcame Their Addictions.* Accessed April 20, 2016. http://www.beliefnet.com/Entertainment/ Celebrities/Galleries/10-Celebrities-Who-Overcame-Their-Addictions.aspx?p=1#OF1fxaKQtbzOMWuv.99.

Benson, Ezra T. 1976. *Our Priceless Heritage.* October. Accessed October 14, 2015. https://www.lds.org/general-conference/1976/10/our-priceless-heritage?lang=eng.

Berkeley, University of California at. 2014. *Goal-Setting: Developing a Vision & Goals for Your Career Plan.* October 12. Accessed October 12, 2014. http://hrweb.berkeley.edu/learning/career-development/goal-setting/career-plan-vision.

Bernhoft, Robin Dr, and Jeff Smith. 2912. *GMO Foods: Are They Dangerous to Your Health?* October 17. Accessed November 22,

2014. http://www.doctoroz.com/episode/gmo-foods-are-they-dangerous-your-health.

Bernstein, Jeffrey PhD. 2014. *Emotional intelligence fuel's children's school and social success.* March 23. Accessed October 13, 2014. http://www.psychologytoday.com/blog/liking-the-child-you-love/201403/crucial-skill-will-help-your-child-succeed.

Betchen, Stephen J, DSW. 2012. *Knowing When Someone's Not Right for You.* May 1. Accessed July 18, 2016. https://www.psychologytoday.com/blog/magnetic-partners/201205/knowing-when-someones-not-right-you.

BibleInfo.Com. n.d. *Who were the 12 disciples?* Accessed May 12, 2016. http://www.bibleinfo.com/en/questions/who-were-twelve-disciples#andrew.

Biel, Laura. n.d. *How Your Gut Bacteria Can Help You Drop Pounds.* Accessed January 11, 2016. http://www.fitnessmagazine.com/weight-loss/tips/advice/gut-bacteria/.

Bilton, Nick. 2014. *Steve Jobs Was a Low-Tech Parent.* September 10. Accessed February 16, 2016. http://www.nytimes.com/2014/09/11/fashion/steve-jobs-apple-was-a-low-tech-parent.html?_r=1.

n.d. "Book of Mormon." *Doctrine and Covenants 42.*

Boy Scouts of America. 2016. *Boy Scouts of America.* Accessed February 16, 2016. http://www.scouting.org/About/FactSheets/presidents.aspx.

Boyd, Lara, Ph.D. n.d. *After watching this, your brain will not be the same.* Accessed June 25, 2016. https://www.youtube.com/watch?v=LNHBMFCzznE.

Boyles, Salynn. 2004. *Drinking Water May Speed Weight Loss.* January 5. Accessed October 18, 2015. http://www.webmd.com/diet/20040105/drinking-water-may-speed-weight-loss.

Brody, Jane E. 2014. *Hard Lesson in Sleep for Teenagers.* October 14. Accessed October 23, 2014. http://well.blogs.nytimes.com/2014/10/20/sleep-for-teenagers/?_php=true&_type=blogs&_r=0.

Brown, J., and K. Dutton. 1995. "The Thrill of Victory, the Complexity of Defeat: Self-Esteem and People's Emotional Reaction to Success and Failure." *Journal of Personality and Social Psychology* (Journal of Personality and Social Psychology) 68:712.

2014. *Building Self-Confidence.* October 15. Accessed October 15, 2014. http://www.mindtools.com/selfconf.html.

Bundrant, Mike. 2013. November 3. Accessed October 12, 2014. www.naturalnews.com/042764_self_motivation_discipline_inspiration.html.

Burton, David H. 2009. "The Blessing of Work." *Liahona*, December: 37.

Byrne, Jennifer. 2015. *Diet Soda's Effects on Liver Functions.* October 8. Accessed November 21, 2015. http://www.livestrong.com/article/224712-diet-sodas-effects-on-liver-functions.

Callister, Tad R. 2006. *The Inevitable Apostasy and the Promised Restoration.* Salt Lake City, Utah: Deseret Book Company.

Cannon, Mark W, and Danielle Stockton. 2010. *UCLA study proves Mormons live longer.* April 13. Accessed July 31, 2016. http://www.deseretnews.com/article/705377709/UCLA-study-proves-Mormons-live-longer.html?pg=all.

Cardillo, Donna, RN, MA. 2011. *Is Your Diet Soda the Reason You're Not Feeling Well?* September 9. Accessed August 12, 2015. http://www.doctoroz.com/blog/donna-cardillo-rn-ma/diet-soda-reason-youre-not-feeling-well.

Carmichael, Joe MSEd. 2009. *Permanent Adolescence - Why Boys Don't Grow Up.* Far Hills, NJ: New Horizons Press.

Carmichiel, Joe MSEd. 2009. *Permanent Adolescence: Why Boys Don't Grow Up.* Far Hills, NJ: New Horizons Press.

Carson, Ben MD. 2014. *One Nation.* New York City: The Penguin Group.

Carter, Les. 2008. *Enough About You, Let's Talk About Me: How to Recognize and Manager the Narcissists in Your Life.* San Francisco: Jossey-Bass.

2014. *CBS Denver.* October 8. Accessed October 8, 2014. http://denver.cbslocal.com/2013/11/17/windsor-boy-saves-brothers-life-in-choking-incident/.

CDC. n.d. *About Child & Teen BMI.* Accessed November 23, 2015. http://www.cdc.gov/healthyweight/assessing/bmi/childrens_bmi/about_childrens_bmi.html.

Charron, Phil. 2011. *Divergent Thinking vs Convergent Thinking.* October 26. Accessed April 27, 2016. https://www.thinkbrownstone.com/2011/10/divergent-thinking-vs-convergent-thinking/.

Ciarrochi, Joseph. 2012. *Get Out of Your Mind and Into Your Life: A Guide to Living an Extraordinary Life.* Oakland, CA: New Harbinger Publications.

Classes and Careers. n.d. *How To Go To College Without a High School Diploma.* Accessed May 20, 2016. http://blog.classesandcareers.com/advisor/how-to-go-to-college-without-a-high-school-diploma/.

Cleveland Clinic. 2015. *Cleveland Clinic Health Essentials.* April 27. Accessed August 13, 2015. http://health.clevelandclinic.org/2015/04/how-salt-potassium-affect-your-teens-blood-pressure/.

Clinic, Mayo. n.d. *Healthy Lifestyle - Stress Management.* Accessed September 26, 2014. www.mayoclinic.org/healthy-living/stress-management/basics/relaxation-techniques/hlv-20049495.

Clinton, Bill. 2004. *My Life.* Knopf Publishing Group.

Cohen, Sharon. 2014. "Inner-city school applauds first college graduates." *San Jose Mercury News - Breaking News.* June 8. Accessed October 13, 2014. http://www.mercurynews.com/breaking-news/ci_25926922/inner-city-school-applauds-first-college-graduates.

Comedy, That's. 2014. *That's Comedy.* October 12. Accessed October 12, 2012. http://www.thatscomedy.com/religious/religious007.htm.

Cookus Interruptus. 2013. *Top 10 Reasons to Eat Sourdough Bread.* March 16. Accessed August 16, 14. Cookus Interruptus - Top 10 Reasons to Eat Sourdough Bread .

Coren, Stanley PhD. 2012. *Psychology Today.* June 7. Accessed August 9, 2015. https://www.psychologytoday.com/blog/canine-corner/201206/canine-empathy-your-dog-really-does-care-if-you-are-unhappy .

Cosgrove-Mather, Bootie. 2004. *Poll: Creationism Trumps Evolution.* November 22. Accessed December 30, 2015. http://www.cbsnews.com/news/poll-creationism-trumps-evolution/.

Covey, Sean. 2006. *The 6 Most Important Decisions You'll Ever Make - A Guide for Teens.* New York, NY: Simon & Schuster.

—. 2013. *The 7 Habits of Highly Effective Teens.* New York, NY: Simon & Schuster.

—. 2013. *The 7 Habits of Highly Effective Teens, Personal Workbook.* New York, NY: Simon & Schuster.

Covey, Stephen R. n.d. *Stephen Covey.* Accessed January 10, 2016. https://www.stephencovey.com/7habits/7habits-habit2.php.

—. 1989. *The 7 Habits of Highly Effective People.* New York: Free Press.

Cox, James. 2012. *Becoming Spiritually Centered.* Nampa, Idaho: National Marketing, Inc.

Creationism Staff. n.d. *Dinosaurs.* Accessed August 15, 2015. http://www.creationism.org/topbar/dinosaurs.htm.

Creationism.org Staff. n.d. *Creationism.* Accessed August 15, 2015. http://www.creationism.org/topbar/creationism.htm.

Crinnion, Walter, Dr. 2012. *Is Atlantic Salmon (Farmed Salmon) Linked to Obesity and Diabetes?* April 24. Accessed August 12, 2015. http://www.huffingtonpost.com/dr-walter-crinnion/salmon-diabetes_b_1332820.html.

Cuddy, Amy. 2002. *Amy Cuddy: Your Body Language Shapes Who You Are.* June. Accessed May 19, 2016. https://www.ted.com/talks/amy_cuddy_your_body_language_shapes_who_you_are?language=en#t-14469.

Curtis, Barbara. 2008. *What is 'New Age' Religion, and Why Can't Christians Get on Board?* April 18. Accessed March 30, 2016.

http://www.crosswalk.com/faith/spiritual-life/what-is-new-age-religion-and-why-cant-christians-get-on-board-11573681.html.

Curtis, Ken, Ph.D. n.d. *Whatever Happened to the Twelve Apostles?* Accessed May 12, 2016. http://www.christianity.com/church/church-history/timeline/1-300/whatever-happened-to-the-twelve-apostles-11629558.html.

Davis, William Dr. 2015. *Wheat and Grains Make You Sick.* June 13. Accessed August 15, 2015. http://www.wheatbellyblog.com/2015/06/wheat-and-grains-make-you-sick/.

Dawursk, Glen, Jr. 2007. *Pupil Services: True Colors Testing.* April 7. Accessed November 28, 2015. http://www.yuthguy.com/classroom/super/pupilservicestruecolors.htm.

Deiner, E., and F. Fujita. 1995. "Resources, Personal Strivings, and Subjective Being: Linking Goals and Affect Through the Self." *The Journal of Personality and Social Psychology* 68:926.

De-Kun Li, M.D., Ph.D., ZhiJun Zhou, M.D., Ph.D., Maohua Miao, Ph.D., Yonghua He, Ph.D., JinTao Wang, Ph.D., Jeannette Ferber, M.P.H., Lisa J. Herrinton, Ph.D., ErSheng Gao, M.D., M.P.H., Wei Yuan, M.D., Ph.D. 2011. "Urine bisphenol-A (BPA) level in relation to semen quality." *Fertility and Sterility* 95 (2): 625-630.e4. Accessed August 10, 2015. doi:10.1016/j.fertnstert.2010.09.026.

Demedeiros, James. n.d. *6 Reasons to Never Neglect Flax Seed.* Accessed May 4, 2016. http://www.mensfitness.com/nutrition/what-to-eat/6-reasons-to-never-neglect-flax-seed?page=.

Diener, E., R.A. Emmons, R.j. Larsen, and S. and Griffin. 1985. "The Satisfaction with Life Scale." *Journal of Personality Assessment* 49 71-75.

DiGiulio, Sarah. 2016. *Fitbit Says You're Using Your Alarm Clock All Wrong.* June 21. Accessed June 22, 2016. http://www.huffingtonpost.com/entry/fitbit-alarm-clock-app_us_5769ae2ee4b065534f481c00.

n.d. *Dinner Party Menu Ideas.* Accessed October 10, 2015. http://www.dinner-party-menu-ideas.com/table-setting-diagram.html.

Disease Control Staff, Center. 2013. *National Biomonitoring Program.* July 23. Accessed August 10, 2015. http://www.cdc.gov/biomonitoring/BisphenolA_FactSheet.html.

2014. *Divorce - Love to Know.* October 4. Accessed October 4, 2014. http://divorce.lovetoknow.com/Main_Page.

2013. *Do Animals Feel Empathy?* April 11. Accessed October 12, 2014. http://blog.nus.edu.sg/lsm1303student2013/2013/04/11/do-animals-feel-empathy/.

Doan, Andrew P., MD, PhD. 2012. *Hooked on Games.* Corallville: F.E.P. International, Inc.

Doheny, Kathleen. 2011. *Strokes in Children and Young Adults on the Rise.* September 1. Accessed November 21, 2015. http://www.webmd.com/stroke/news/20110901/strokes-in-chldren-and-young-adults-on-the-rise.

Dr. Phil Staff. n.d. *A Call to Action against Bullying.* Accessed August 15, 2015. Bullying can be physical, emotional.

Dunckley, Victoria. 2014. *Gray Matters: Too Much Screen Time Damages the Brain.* February 27. Accessed October 10, 2014. http://www.psychologytoday.com/blog/mental-wealth/201402/gray-matters-too-much-screen-time-damages-the-brain.

Dunckley, Victoria L. M.D. 2014. *Why Can My Inattentive Child Pay Attention to Video Games?!* February 1. Accessed October 11, 2014. http://www.psychologytoday.com/blog/ mental-wealth/201402/why-can-my-inattentive-child-pay-attention-video-games.

Durnell, Linda. 2014. June 25. Accessed October 14, 2014. http:// www.huffingtonpost.com/linda-durnell/train-your-brain-using-th_b_5527152.html.

2014. "Eagle Scout Award." *Boy Scouts of America.* October 8. Accessed October 8, 2014. http://www.scouting.org/filestore/ boyscouts/pdf/542-900.pdf.

2014. *Effects of Caffeine on the Nervous System.* October 11. Accessed October 11, 2014. http://faculty.washington.edu/ chudler/caff.html.

Eldredge, Niles, and Gould Stephen Jay. 1985. *Evolution and the Theory of Punctuated Equilibria.* New York: Simon and Schuster.

Elkind, David. 1988. *The Hurried Child.* Reading, Massachusetts: Addison-Wesley.

Emoto, Masaru. 2005. *The Secret Life of Water.* New York, NY: Atria.

English Language Smart Words. n.d. *Count the Number of Fs.* Accessed October 3, 2015. http://www.smart-words.org/humor-jokes/language-humor/count-number-f-sentence.html.

English, Nick. 2014. *12 Complete Proteins Vegetarians Need to Know About.* April 29. Accessed January 9, 2015. http://greatist.com/ health/complete-vegetarian-proteins.

Environmental Health News. 2013. *Nitrates in mom's drinking water linked to birth defects in kids.* June 27. Accessed April 30, 2016. http://www.environmentalhealthnews.org/ehs/newscience/2013/06/nitrate-in-moms-drinking-water.

Ereezay, Lizzie. 2014. *13 Signs a Girl Doesn't Like You.* January 16. Accessed August 15, 2015. https://www.youtube.com/watch?v=p4b8aaMCgx8.

Family First Aid Staff. 2014. *Family First Aid for Troubled Teens.* October 12. Accessed October 12, 2014. http://www.familyfirstaid.org/parenting/emotional/teen-stress/.

Farberov, Snejana. 2014. *Daily Mail.* December 26. Accessed August 9, 2015. http://www.dailymail.co.uk/news/article-2887841/Best-Christmas-present-Heartwarming-moment-app-developer-reveals-parents-paid-mortgage.html.

Faust, James E. 2002. *Communion with the Holy Spirit.* March. Accessed May 11, 2016. https://www.lds.org/liahona/2002/03/communion-with-the-holy-spirit?lang=eng.

—. n.d. *The Dignity of Self.* Accessed March 23, 2016. https://www.lds.org/general-conference/1981/04/the-dignity-of-self?lang=eng.

Feller, Stephen. 2015. *Athletes's Best Bet is to only drink when thirsty.* June 29. Accessed August 10, 2015. http://www.upi.com/Health_News/2015/06/29/Athletes-best-bet-is-to-only-drink-when-thirsty/5351435610372/?spt=su&or=btn_fb.

Ferdman, Roberto A. 2016. *Researchers have Found a Striking New Side Effect from Eating Fast Food.* April 15. Accessed June 25, 2016. https://www.washingtonpost.com/news/wonk/wp/2016/04/15/

researchers-have-found-an-alarming-new-side-effect-from-eating-fast-food/?tid=hybrid_experimentrandom_2_na.

Fields, Helen. 2006. May. Accessed May 25, 2015. http://www.smithsonianmag.com/science-nature/dinosaur-shocker-115306469/?no-ist.

Fields, R. Douglas. 2008. *White Matter in Learning, Cognition,, and Psychiatric Disorders.* June 5. Accessed April 24, 2016. http://www.ncbi.nlm.nih.gov/pmc/articles/PMC2486416.

Fisher, Ken, and Lara Hoffmans. 2009. *How to Smell a Rat.* Hoboken: John Wiley & Sons, Inc.

n.d. *Fleur-de-lis Designs.* Accessed September 20, 2015. http://www.fleurdelis.com/meanings.htm.

Fontane, P. 1996. "Exercise, Fitness, and Feeling Well." *American Behavior Scientist* 39:288.

Fottrell, Quentin. 2015. *Soda and junk foods are not making you fat.* November 6. Accessed November 8, 2015. http://www.marketwatch.com/story/soda-and-junk-foods-are-not-making-you-fat-2015-11-06?dist=lcountdown.

Frazier, Matt. n.d. *No Meat Athlete.* Accessed May 4, 2016. http://www.nomeatathlete.com/where-vegetarians-get-protein/#sthash.8bSVYPQs.dpuf.

Fredrickson, Barbara L. PhD. 2009. *Positivity.* New York, NY: MJF Books.

Fulciniti, Francesca. 2015. *The 18 Best Colleges for Students with Learning Disabilities.* September 12. Accessed March 2016, 2016. http://blog.prepscholar.com/the-18-best-colleges-for-students-with-learning-disabilities.

Gadsby, Patricia. 2004. *How can people who gorge on fat and rarely see a vegetable be healthier than we are?* October 2004. Accessed October 31, 2014. http://discovermagazine.com/2004/oct/inuit-paradox.

—. 2012. *How Can People Who Gorge on Fat and Rarely See a Vegetable Be Healthier Than We Are?* January 8. Accessed August 13, 2015. http://annchilders.blogspot.com/2012/01/how-can-people-who-gorge-on-fat-and.html.

Galland, Leo, MD, FACN. n.d. *Magnesium: The Stress Reliever.* Accessed April 8, 2016. http://www.healthy.net/Health/Essay/Magnesium_The_Stress_Reliever/74.

Gardner, Howard. 2014. *Multiple Intelligence.* October 12. Accessed October 12, 2014. http://web.cortland.edu/andersmd/learning/mi%20theory.htm.

Gayomali, Chris. 2013. *At what age does a man's sperm quality deteriorate?* July 26. Accessed May 20, 2016. http://theweek.com/articles/461711/what-age-does-mans-sperm-quality-deteriorate.

General Electric. n.d. *50 Fact of Grey Matter.* Accessed April 24, 2016. https://medium.com/@generalelectric/50-grey-matters-you-might-not-know-about-your-brain-9a6063dd2e99#.ds4knzig4.

Generation Life. n.d. Accessed August 1, 2016. http://www.generationlife.org/about-us.

Gentile, Douglas A., et al. 2012. "Video Game Playing, Attention Problems, and Impulsiveness: Evidence of Bidirectional Causality." *Psychology of Popular Media Culture 1, no. 1* 62–70.

Germer, Christopher K., PhD. 2009. *The Mindful Path to Self-Compassion - Freeing Yourself from Destructive Thoughts and Emotions.* New York: The Guildford Press.

Ghose, Tia. 2012. *Live Science.* November 15. Accessed August 9, 2015. http://www.livescience.com/24800-animals-emotions-morality.html.

n.d. *Giant Sequoias and Museum.* Accessed October 14, 2015. http://www.visitsequoia.com/giant-sequoia-trees.aspx.

GMO, Compass. 2015. *GMO Compass.* August 11. Accessed August 11, 2015. http://www.gmo-compass.org/eng/grocery_shopping/crops/21.genetically_modified_rapeseed.html.

GoAbroad. n.d. Accessed March 29, 2016. http://www.goabroad.com/blog/2011/04/28/prince-william-kate-middleton-inspire-students/.

Goldstein, Hesh. 2015. *Who in Their Right Mind Freezes a Lemon?* February 24. Accessed August 12, 2015. http://www.realfarmacy.com/freezes-lemon/.

Golgowski, Nina. 2014. *Washington teen shot by cousin in deadly high school shooting forgives shooter, tweets 'rest in peace'.* October 27. Accessed October 27, 2014. http://www.nydailynews.com/news/national/wash-teen-shot-deadly-high-school-shooting-forgives-shooter-article-1.1989489.

Goodrich, Amy. 2014. *15 Reasons You Should Be Drinking Lemon Water Every Morning.* July 3. Accessed August 12, 2015. http://blogs.naturalnews.com/15-reasons-drinking-lemon-water-every-morning/.

Government, US. 2014. *Statistical Abstract of the United States 1958 vol., 79th annual edition, Table 179.* October 4. Accessed October 4, 2014. www.archives.gov/research/military/vietnam-war/casualties-statistics.html.

Grant, Adam. 2013. *A Better Way to Discover Your Strengths.* July 2. Accessed October 8, 2014. http://www.huffingtonpost.com/adam-grant/discover-your-strengths_b_3532528.html.

Green, C. Shawn and Daphne Bavelier. 2003. "Action Video Game Modifies Visual Selective Attention." *Nature 423, no. 6939* 534–537.

Greenberg, Melanie, Ph.D. 2012. *The Six Attributes of Courage.* August 23. Accessed February 16, 2016. https://www. psychologytoday.com/blog/the-mindful-self-express/201208/ the-six-attributes-courage.

Gunnars, Kris. 2014. *Authority Nation.* Accessed November 3, 2014. http://authoritynutrition.com/11-graphs-that-show-what-is-wrong-with-modern-diet/.

Gunnars, Kris, BSC. 2015. *Canola Oil: Good or Bad?* August 13. Accessed August 13, 2015. http://authoritynutrition.com/canola-oil-good-or-bad/.

Hales, Robert D. 2009. "A Gospel Vision of Welfare: Faith in Action." *Basic Principles of Welfare and Self-Reliance,* 2.

Harris, Bradley D. 2011. *Trails to Testimony - Bringing Young Men to Christ Through Scouting.* Charleston, SC: Unknown Publisher.

Hayes, Steven C PhD and Spencer Smith. 2005. *Get Out of Your Mind and Into Your Life: The New Acceptance and Commitment Therapy.*

Health and Human Services, U.S. Department of. 2010. "Questions and Answers on Antidepressant Use in Children, Adolescents, and Adults." *U.S. Food and Drug Administration - Protecting Your Health.* July 19. Accessed October 13, 2014. http://www.fda.gov/ Drugs/DrugSafety/InformationbyDrugClass/ucm096305.htm.

Health and Human Services, US Dept of. 2014. *Be More Than and Bystander.* October 14. Accessed October 14, 2014. http://www. stopbullying.gov/respond/be-more-than-a-bystander/index.html.

Health Central. n.d. *10 Tips for Men's Sexual Health.* Accessed May 11, 2016. http://www.healthcentral.com/sexual-health/cf/ slideshows/10-tips-for-men-s-sexual-health?972842&ap=825.

Health, Teen. 2014. *Drugs: What You Should Know.* October 10. Accessed October 10, 2014. http://kidshealth.org/teen/drug_ alcohol/drugs/know_about_drugs.html#.

Healthwise Staff. n.d. *Proper Angle for Brushing Your Teeth.* Accessed November 29, 2015. http://www.webmd.com/oral-health/ proper-angle-for-brushing-your-teeth.

Helpguide.org. 2014. *Emotional Intelligence (EQ).* October 13. Accessed October 13, 2014. http://www.helpguide.org/articles/ emotional-health/emotional-intelligence-eq.htm.

Hilliker, Joel. 2013. *A Major Cause for the Wimpification of Men.* January 18. Accessed October 10, 2014. http://www.thetrumpet. com/article/10285.21921.0.0/society/a-major-cause-for-the-wimpification-of-men.

Hinckley, Gordon B. 1991. "Articles of Belief - Bonneville International Corporation Management Seminar."

—. 1995. "The Family: A Proclamation to the World." *The Church of Jesus Christ of Latter-Day Saints.* September 23. Accessed October 18, 2014. https://www.lds.org/topics/ family-proclamation.

—. 2001. *The Times in Which We Live.* October. Accessed March 30, 2016. https://www.lds.org/general-conference/2001/10/ the-times-in-which-we-live?lang=eng.

Holland, Jeffrey R. n.d. "For Times of Trouble." LDS.org.

Holman, Thomas B. 2002. *Choosing and Being the Right Spouse.* September. Accessed November 23, 2014. https://www.lds.org/ensign/2002/09/choosing-and-being-the-right-spouse?lang=eng #footnote10-22909_000_015.

Hong, Soon-Beom, Jae-Won Kim, Eun-Jung Choi, Ho-Hyun Kim, Jeong-Eun Suh, Chang-Dai Kim, Paul Klauser, et al. 2013. "Reduced Orbitofrontal Cortical Thickness in Male Adolescents with Internet Addiction." *Behavioral and Brain Functions 9, no. 1* doi:10.1186/1744-9081-9-11.

Hovind, Kent, Ph.D. 2012. *Evolution Lies in Textbooks.* January 21. Accessed May 22, 2015. https://www.youtube.com/watch?v=3Q0qC4_uTVU.

2014. *How Drugs Affect Neurotransmitters.* 12 October. Accessed October 12, 2012. http://thebrain.mcgill.ca/flash/i/i_03/i_03_m/i_03_m_par/i_03_m_par_cafeine.html.

How Stuff Works. n.d. *How Marijuana Works.* Accessed October 3, 2015. http://science.howstuffworks.com/marijuana5.htm.

Hyman, Mark MD. 2014. "5 Reasons High Fructose Corn Syrup Will Kill You." *Dr. Mark Hyman.* October 18. Accessed October 23, 2014. http://drhyman.com/blog/2011/05/13/5-reasons-high-fructose-corn-syrup-will-kill-you/#close.

Hymowitz, Kay S. 2011. *Manning Up.* New York: Basic Books.

IBM Staff. 2014. *What is Watson.* October 12. Accessed October 12, 2014. http://www.ibm.com/smarterplanet/us/en/ibmwatson/.

Infertility Resources. n.d. *IVF Costs - In Vitro Fertilization Costs.* Accessed June 25, 2016. http://www.ihr.com/infertility/ivf/ivf-in-vitro-fertilization-cost.html.

Institute for Creation Research. n.d. Accessed May 22, 2016. http://www.icr.org/mutation.

Iocoboni, Marco. 2008. *Scientific American.* July 1. Accessed August 9, 2015. http://www.scientificamerican.com/article/the-mirror-neuron-revolut.

Islam101. n.d. *Christ in Islam.* Accessed March 23, 2016. http://www.islam101.com/history/people/prophets/jesus/christ_in_islam2.htm.

Jacobsen, BK, SF Knussen, and GE Fraser. 1998. "PubMed: Does high soy milk intake reduce prostate cancer incidence? The Adventist Health Study (United States)." *Cancer Causes Control* 553-557. http://www.ncbi.nlm.nih.gov/pubmed/?term=Does+high+soy+milk+intake+reduce+prostate+cancer+incidence%3F.

Jacques, Renee. 2013. *These Disturbing Fast Food Truths Will Make You Reconsider Your Lunch.* November 20. Accessed October 4, 2015. http://www.huffingtonpost.com/2013/11/20/fast-food-truths_n_4296243.html.

2014. *James Earl Jones and His Unmistakable Voice.* December 5. Accessed January 2, 2016. https://www.youtube.com/watch?v=I2LkdNls4bw.

2015. *Joan of Arc.* November 26. Accessed March 30, 2016. http://www.byutv.org/watch/98102eb7-69d9-45e5-9322-2e9d7284c3a6/joan-of-arc-joan-of-arc.

Johnson, Jeffrey. n.d. *Archives of Pediatrics and Adolescent Psychiatry.*

Jones, Nathan. 2013. *The Christ in Prophecy Journal.* June 21. Accessed March 23, 2016. http://www.lamblion.us/2013/06/creation-training-carbon-destroys.html.

Kalman, Izzy. 2010. *Resilience to Bullying.* January 23. Accessed October 28, 2014. http://www.psychologytoday.com/blog/psychological-solution-bullying/201001/mirror-neurons-conscience-development-and-the-fallacy-ac.

Kalyanaraman, James D. Ivory and Sriram. 2007. "The Effects of Technological Advancement and Violent Content in Video Games on Players? Feelings of Presence, Involvement, Physiological Arousal, and Aggression." *Journal of Communication 57, no. 3* 1460-2466.

Katz, Harold Dr. 2010. *Oral Bacteria May Cause Serious Problems Throughout the Body.* September 13. Accessed January 11, 2016. http://www.therabreath.com/articles/oral-care-industry-news/oral-bacteria-may-cause-serious-problems-throughout-the-body-1596/.

Kerns, Michelle. n.d. *Zinc for Teens.* Accessed April 8, 2016. http://healthyeating.sfgate.com/zinc-teens-4589.html.

Kim, Ben, Dr. 2011. *Healthy Foods that Promote Deep Sleep.* June 20. Accessed March 26, 2016. http://drbenkim.com/best-foods-sleep.html.

Kimmel, Michael. 2008. *Guyland - The Perilous World Where Boys Become Men.* New York, NY: Harper.

Kiyosaki, Robert. 2012. *Rich Dad Poor Dad - What the Rich Teach Their Kids About Money - What the Poor and Middle Class Do Not.* Scottsdale, AZ: Plata Publishing, LLC.

Klika, Brett, and Chris Jordan. 2013. "HIGH-INTENSITY CIRCUIT TRAINING USING BODY WEIGHT: Maximum Results With Minimal Investment." *ACSM's Health & Fitness Journal* 8-13. http://journals.lww.com/acsm-healthfitness/Fulltext/2013/05000/HIGH_INTENSITY_CIRCUIT_TRAINING_USING_BODY_WEIGHT_.5.aspx.

Koepp, J J. et al. 1998. "Evidence for Striatal Dopamine Release during a Video Game." *Nature 393, No. 6682* 266-268.

Koontz, Don DDS. 2013. *How to Build Strong Teeth and Healthy Gums with your Diet.* October 7. Accessed November 3, 2014. http://donkoontzdds.com/healthy-living/how-to-build-strong-teeth-and-healthy-gums-with-your-diet/?gclid=CMLN9ubq3sEC FQVffgodl3IAOA.

Krznaric, Roman. 2012. *Six Habits of Highly Empathic People.* November 27. Accessed October 12, 2014. http://greatergood.berkeley.edu/article/item/six_habits_of_highly_empathic_people1?utm_source=GGSC+Newsletter+-+August+2014&utm_campaign=GG+Newsletter++-+August+2014&utm_medium=email.

—. 2012. *Six Habits of Highly Empathic People.* November 27. Accessed October 29, 2014. http://greatergood.berkeley.edu/article/item/six_habits_of_highly_empathic_people1.

Kurtus, Ron. 2013. *Three Character Trait Classifications.* January 29. Accessed November 7, 2014. http://www.school-for-champions.com/character/three_classifications.htm#.VF1-A_nF9h5.

Lam, Michael MD,MPH, Justin Dr Lam, and Dorine RDN,MS,MPH Lam. n.d. *Adrenal Fatigue Center.* Accessed March 24, 2016. https://www.drlam.com/blog/fluid-balance-and-adrenal-fatigue-syndrome-part-1/6408/.

Latter-Day Saints, The Church of Jesus Christ of. 2014. *Catching the Vision of Self-Reliance.* October 12. Accessed October 12, 2014. https://www.lds.org/topics/welfare/the-church-welfare-plan/catching-the-vision-of-self-reliance?lang=eng#notes.

—. 2014. *Catching the Vision of Self-Reliance.* October 12. Accessed October 12, 2014. https://www.lds.org/topics/welfare/the-church-welfare-plan/catching-the-vision-of-self-reliance?lang=eng#notes.

—. 2001. *For the Strength of Youth.* Salt Lake City: The Church of Jesus Christ of Latter Day Saints.

—. 2009. *Providing in the Lord's Way: Summary of A Leader's Guide to Welfare.* Salt Lake City: The Church of Jesus Christ of Latter-Day Saints.

2014. *LDS.org.* October 9. Accessed October 9, 2014. www.lds.org.

Lee, Harold B. 2002. *When Your Heart Tells You Things Your Mind Does Not Know.* June. Accessed November 23, 2014. https://www.lds.org/new-era/2002/06/when-your-heart-tells-you-things-your-mind-does-not-know?lang=eng.

Lepper, H. 1996. *In Pursuit of Happiness and Satisfaction in Later Life.* Ph.D. Dissertation, Riverside: University of California.

Lin, Fuchun, Yan Zhou, Yasong Du, Lindi Qin, Zhimin Zhao, Jianrong Xu, and Hao Lei. 2012. "Abnormal White Matter Integrity in Adolescents with Internet Addiction Disorder: A Tract-Based Spatial Statistics Study." *PloS One 7, no. 1* 10:137.

Lipworth, Elaine. 2012. *Samuel L Jackson: 'I drank and I used drugs. I fancied myself as Oliver Reed'.* April 26. Accessed April 20, 2016. http://www.telegraph.co.uk/culture/film/starsandstories/9214431/Samuel-L-Jackson-I-drank-and-I-used-drugs.-I-fancied-myself-as-Oliver-Reed.html.

Lisle, Jason Dr. 2009. *The Ultimate Proof of Creation - Resolving the Origins Debate.* Green Forest, AR: Master Books.

Louv, Richard. 2008. *Last Child in the Woods - Saving Our Children from Nature-Deficit Disorder.* New York, NY: Algonquin Books of Chapel Hill, a division of Workman Publishing.

Luciani, Joseph J, PhD. 2007. *Self-Coaching - The Powerful Program to Beat Anxiety & Depression.* Hoboken, NJ: John Wiley & Sons.

Lyubomirsky, S. and L. Ross. 1997. "Hedonistic Consequences of Social Comparison." *Journal of Personality and Social Psychology* (Journal of Personality and Social Psychology) 73:1141.

Lyubomirsky, S. 1994. *The Hedonistic Consequences of Social Comparison: Implications for Enduring Happiness and Transient Mood.* Ph.D. Dissertation, Palo Alto, California: Stanford University.

Mann, Denise. 2011. *Study Identifies Risks for Video Game Addiction.* January 18. Accessed October 9, 2014. http://www.webmd.com/parenting/news/20110118/study-identifies-risks-for-video-game-addiction.

Mansfield, Stephen. 2013. *Mansfield's Book of Manly Men - An Utterly Invigorating Guide to Being Your Most Masculine Self.* Nashville, TN: Nelson Books.

Marilyn Price-Mitchell, PhD. 2014. *Mindful Warriors: Meditation for Teenagers.* October 8. Accessed October 8, 2014. http://www.rootsofaction.com/meditation-children-teens-mindful-warriors/.

Mas, Susana. 2014. *Justin Trudeau memoir: 7 surprising revelations from Common Ground.* October 20. Accessed November 14, 2015. http://www.cbc.ca/m/touch/news/story/1.2805502 .

Matsummara, Molleen, and Louise Mead. 2007. *Ten Major Court Cases about Evolution and Creationism.* July 31. Accessed May 25, 2015. http://ncse.com/taking-action/ten-major-court-cases-evolution-creationism.

Maynes, Richard J. 2015. *The Joy of Living a Christ-Centered Life.* November 1. Accessed March 20, 2016. https://www.lds.org/ensign/2015/11/saturday-morning-session/the-joy-of-living-a-christ-centered-life?lang=eng.

Mayo Clinic. 2015. August 14. Accessed April 5, 2016. https://www.sciencedaily.com/releases/2015/08/150814091322.htm.

—. n.d. *Fetal alcohol syndrome.* Accessed April 27, 2016. http://www.mayoclinic.org/diseases-conditions/fetal-alcohol-syndrome/basics/symptoms/con-20021015.

—. n.d. *Mayo Clinic - Diseases and Conditions.* Accessed November 17, 2015. http://www.mayoclinic.org/diseases-conditions/reyes-syndrome/basics/definition/con-20020083.

—. n.d. *Men's health: Prevent the top threats.* Accessed April 8, 2016. http://www.mayoclinic.org/healthy-lifestyle/mens-health/in-depth/mens-health/art-20047764.

Mayo Clinic Staff. n.d. *Diseases and Conditions - Teen Depression.* Accessed August 15, 2015. http://www.mayoclinic.org/diseases-conditions/teen-depression/in-depth/antidepressants/art-20047502.

—. 2014. *Health Lifestyle - Stress Management.* October 12. Accessed October 12, 2014. http://www.mayoclinic.org/healthy-living/stress-management/basics/stress-basics/hlv-20049495.

—. n.d. *Symptoms - Low potassium (hypokalemia).* Accessed November 23, 2015. http://www.mayoclinic.org/symptoms/low-potassium/basics/definition/sym-20050632.

n.d. *Mayo Clinic: Potassium Supplement (Oral Route, Parenteral Route).* Accessed November 22, 2015. http://www.mayoclinic. org/drugs-supplements/potassium-supplement-oral-route-parenteral-route/description/drg-20070753.

McGraw, Jay. 2000. *Life Strategies for Teens.* New York, NY: Simon & Schuster.

McRaven, William Admiral. 2014. *Admiral McRaven's Life Lesson #1: Make Your Bed.* June 18. Accessed August 9, 2014. https://www. youtube.com/watch?v=jflUvxQLkgs.

Medalla, Shosh Shlam and Hilla. 2014. *China's Web Junkies.* January 19. Accessed October 8, 2014. http://www.nytimes.com/2014/01/20/ opinion/chinas-web-junkies.html?_r=0.

Medicine, Loyola. 2015. *Drinking too much water can be fatal for athletes.* June 15. Accessed August 10, 2015. http:// www.loyolamedicine.org/news/drinking-too-much-water-can-be-fatal-athletes-09022014.

Mental Floss. n.d. Accessed April 22, 2016. http://mentalfloss.com/ article/25552/quick-10-10-people-perfect-pitch.

Mercola, Dr. 2014. *11 Charts that Show Everything Wrong With Our Modern Diet.* February 24. Accessed October 18, 2015. http:// articles.mercola.com/sites/articles/archive/2014/02/24/modern-diet.aspx.

—. 2013. *Iodine Supplements May Be Too Much of a Good Thing.* June 29. Accessed August 13, 2015. http://articles.mercola.com/ sites/articles/archive/2013/06/29/iodine-deficiency-risk.aspx .

—. 2011. *Monosodium Glutamate (MSG): This Common Food Additive Now Linked to Weight Gain.* June 16. Accessed August 13, 2015.

http://articles.mercola.com/sites/articles/archive/2011/06/16/this-common-food-additive-now-linked-to-weight-gain.aspx.

Mercola, Joseph M Dr. 2014. *11 Charts That Show Everything Wrong with Our Modern Diet.* February 24. Accessed November 1, 2014. http://articles.mercola.com/sites/articles/archive/2014/02/24/modern-diet.aspx.

Mercola, Joseph M Dr. 2012. *Guidelines to Help Your Teen Safely and Effectively Improve His or Her Physique.* December 7. Accessed November 3, 2014. http://fitness.mercola.com/sites/fitness/archive/2012/12/07/teens-whey-protein.aspx.

Mercola, Joseph M.D. 2010. *Alkaline Water: If You Fall for This "Water Fad" You Could Do Some Major Damage.* September 11. Accessed March 24, 2016. http://articles.mercola.com/sites/articles/archive/2010/09/11/alkaline-water-interview.aspx.

Mercola, Joseph, Dr. 2012. *Major Trouble Ahead If You Don't Fix Omega-3 Fat Deficiency.* January 12. Accessed June 22, 2016. http://articles.mercola.com/sites/articles/archive/2012/01/12/aha-position-on-omega-6-fats.aspx.

Mercola, Joseph, M, M.D. 2014. *How Artificial Sweeteners Confuse Your Body into Storing Fat and Inducing Diabetes.* December 23. Accessed November 21, 2015. http://articles.mercola.com/sites/articles/archive/2014/12/23/artificial-sweeteners-confuse-body.aspx.

Mercola, Joseph, M.D. 2014. *11 Charts That Show Everything Wrong with Our Modern Diet.* February 24. Accessed March 24, 2016. http://articles.mercola.com/sites/articles/archive/2014/02/24/modern-diet.aspx.

—. 2011. *Aspartame: By Far the Most Dangerous Substance Added to Most Foods Today.* November 6. Accessed November 22, 2015.

http://articles.mercola.com/sites/articles/archive/2011/11/06/
aspartame-most-dangerous-substance-added-to-food.aspx .

—. 2013. *Soybean Oil: One of the Most Harmful Ingredients in Processed Foods.* January 27. Accessed March 24, 2016. http://
articles.mercola.com/sites/articles/archive/2013/01/27/soybean-oil.aspx.

Miller, Anna Medaris. 2015. *Are Energy Drinks Really That Bad?* January 16. Accessed August 12, 2015. http://health.usnews.
com/health-news/health-wellness/articles/2015/01/16/
are-energy-drinks-really-that-bad.

Miller, Steve. 2014. *CBS Chicago.* October 8. Accessed October 8, 2014. http://chicago.cbslocal.com/2014/02/23/chicago-boy-scout-to-receive-special-award-for-shielding-girlfriend-from-bullets/.

Milligan, Robert, M.D. n.d. *Pregnancy & STDs.* Accessed April 5, 2016. http://www.thedailyrisk.com/pregnancy/pregnancy-and-stds.

Mind Tools Group. 2014. *Building Self-Confidence - Preparing Yourself for Success.* October 15. Accessed October 15, 2014. http://www.mindtools.com/selfconf.html.

Monson, Thomas. 1987. "Guiding Principles of Personal and Family Welfare." *Tambuli*, February.

Morelan, Bill. 2004. *Married for Life.* Hallmark.

Morris, Betsy. 2002. *Overcoming Dyslexia.* May 13. Accessed March 28, 2016. http://archive.fortune.com/magazines/fortune/fortune_archive/2002/05/13/322876/index.htm.

Morris, Henry M., Ph.D. n.d. *Jesus And The Flood.* Accessed May 12, 2016. http://www.icr.org/article/18379.

Morris, John D., Ph.D. 2015. *Grand Canyon: Is It Really 'Exhibit A' For Evolution And The Old Earth?* May 22. Accessed May 22, 2015. http://www.icr.org/article/grand-canyon-it-really-exhibit-a-for-evolution-old/.

—. n.d. *The Paluxy River Tracks.* Accessed February 16, 2016. http://www.icr.org/article/paluxy-river-tracks/.

Mphuthing, Poppie. 2016. *Ciara and Russell Wilson's Engagement Proves Waiting to 'Put Out' Isn't a Crazy Idea.* March 14. Accessed March 26, 2016. http://www.huffingtonpost.com/entry/ciara-russell-wilson-engaged_us_56e70726e4b065e2e3d6cace.

Murray C., and M.J. Peacock. 1996. *A Model-Free Approach to the Study of Subjective Well-Being.* Report, Thousand Oaks, California: Sage: Mental Health in Black America.

National Institute of Health. n.d. *Balance Food and Activity.* Accessed August 15, 2015. Estimated Calorie Requirements .

National Institute of Mental Health. n.d. *The Teen Brain: Still Under Construction.* Accessed May 20, 2016. http://www.nimh.nih.gov/health/publications/the-teen-brain-still-under-construction/index.shtml.

2014. *National Sleep Foundation.* Accessed October 21, 2014. http://sleepfoundation.org/sleep-topics/teens-and-sleep.

2006. "National Sleep Foundation." *Sleep in America Poll 2006.* Accessed October 23, 2014. http://sleepfoundation.org/sites/default/files/2006_summary_of_findings.pdf.

Nazar, Jason. 2013. *16 Surprising Statistics About Small Businesses.* September 9. Accessed November 13, 2014. http://www.forbes.com/sites/jasonnazar/2013/09/09/16-surprising-statistics-about-small-businesses/.

Neff, Kristin PhD. 2014. *A Healthier Way to Relate to Yourself.* October 16. Accessed October 16, 2014. http://www.self-compassion.org/.

—. 2014. *Definition of Self-Compassion.* October 16. Accessed October 15, 2014. http://www.self-compassion.org/what-is-self-compassion/definition-of-self-compassion.html.

—. 2014. *Self-Compassion - Test Your Self Compassion.* October 8. Accessed October 8, 2014. http://www.self-compassion.org/test-your-self-compassion-level.html.

Neimiec, Ryan M. PsyD. 2014. *Things to Do to Create Personal Happiness.* October 8. Accessed October 8, 2014. http://www.psychologytoday.com/blog/what-matters-most/201212/7-new-exercises-boost-happiness.

New York Life. n.d. *Policy Purchase Option (PPO) Rider: Multiple benefits for policyholders.* Accessed March 28, 2016. http://www.newyorklife.com/learn-and-plan/policy-purchase-option-rider-multiple-benefits-policyholders.

Niles, Eldredge. 1985. *Time Frames: Rethinking of Darwinian Evolution and the Theory of Punctuated Equilibria.* New York, New York: Simon and Schuster.

Nobelprize.org. n.d. Accessed May 20, 2016. http://www.nobelprize.org/nobel_prizes/peace/laureates/1993/.

North Creek Dental Care Blog. 2013. *How to Build Strong Teeth and Healthy Gums with your Diet.* October 7. Accessed August 15, 2015. http://donkoontzdds.com/healthy-living/how-to-build-strong-teeth-and-healthy-gums-with-your-diet/.

Nseir, William, Fares Nassar, and Nimer Assy. 2010. "Soft drinks consumption and nonalcoholic fatty liver disease." *World Journal of Gastroenterology* 2579-2588. Accessed August 12, 2015. http://www.ncbi.nlm.nih.gov/pmc/articles/PMC2880768/.

Nutburn, Deborah. 2015. *There are 6 quintillion gallons of water hiding in the Earth's crust.* November 21. Accessed December 30, 2015. http://www.latimes.com/science/sciencenow/la-sci-sn-modern-groundwater-20151116-story.html.

Nutritional Genomics Staff. n.d. *The NCMHD Center of Excellence for Nutritional Genomics.* Accessed August 2014, 2015. http://nutrigenomics.ucdavis.edu/?page=information.

Olson, Adam C. 2004. *Where Is My Iron Rod?* January. Accessed November 1, 2015. https://www.lds.org/new-era/2004/01/where-is-my-iron-rod?lang=eng.

Olster, Marjorie. 203. *GMO Foods: Key Points in the Genetically Modified Debate.* August 2. Accessed October 4, 2015. http://www.huffingtonpost.com/2013/08/02/gmo-foods_n_3693246.html.

2014. *Outward Bound.* October 8. Accessed October 8, 2014. http://www.nols.edu/about/.

Oveson, Stephen B. 1999. *Our Legacy.* October. Accessed October 12, 2015. https://www.lds.org/general-conference/1999/10/our-legacy?lang=eng.

Oz, Mehmet, M.D. 2015. *Dr. Oz Reveals Monsanto's Statement on Glyphosate.* April 7. Accessed November 21, 2015. http://www.doctoroz.com/episode/how-outsmart-identity-thieves-after-your-money-and-medical-data?video_id=4158826902001.

Oz, Mehmet, M.D., and Dr. Mike Roizen. 2014. *Beware of 'BPA-Free' Lie.* AccessedOctober30,2014.http://www.NewsmaxHealth.com/Dr-Oz/bpa-bps-dr-oz-plastic/2014/01/16/id/547409/#ixzz3Hetztm1P.

Packer, Boyd K. 2015. *The Plan of Happiness.* April. Accessed August 14, 2015. https://www.lds.org/general-conference/2015/04/the-plan-of-happiness?lang=eng.

Packer, Boyd K. n.d. *How to Live the Word of Wisdom.* Accessed March 22, 2016. https://www.lds.org/youth/article/how-to-live-the-word-of-wisdom?lang=eng.

—. 2015. *The Plan of Happiness.* May. Accessed January 2, 2016. https://www.lds.org/ensign/2015/05/saturday-morning-session/the-plan-of-happiness?lang=eng.

Palmer, Sharon RD. 2008. "The Top Fiber-Rich Foods List." *Today's Dietitian* 10 (7): 28.

Partnership for a Drug-Free Canada (PDFC). n.d. *Marijuana.* Accessed October 3, 2015. http://www.canadadrugfree.org/drug-info/marijuana/.

PBI, The Palm Beach Institute. 2014. *This is What Alcohol is Really Doing to Your Body.* October 10. Accessed October 10, 2014. http://www.pbinstitute.com/alcohol-really-body/?utm_source=Content_Marketing&utm_medium=SEO&utm_campaign=BlogFeed.

Peck, Scott M., MD. 2011. *The Road Less Traveled - A New Psychology of Love, Traditional Values, and Spiritual Growth.* New York, NY: Touchstone.

—. 1978. *The Road Less Travelled.* New York: Touchstone.

—. 1978. *The Road Less Travelled.* New York: Touchstone.

Pegalis, L. 1994. *Frequency and Duration of Positive Affect: The Dispositionality of Happiness.* Ph.D. Dissertation, Athens: University of Georgia.

Pelzer, Dave. n.d. *The Self-Made Man Behind the Marvel.* Accessed May 19, 2016. https://www.bookbrowse.com/author_interviews/full/index.cfm/author_number/145/dave-pelzer.

Pesce, Nicole Lyn. 2016. *Bad news, boozers: Alcohol linked to seven deadly cancers* . July 22. Accessed July 31, 2016. http://www.nydailynews.com/life-style/health/bad-news-boozers-alcohol-linked-deadly-cancers-article-1.2721651.

Petersen, Mark. 1977. *Christ the Creator.* December 13. Accessed August 15, 2015. https://speeches.byu.edu/talks/petersen-mark-e_christ-creator/.

Peterson, Mark, E. 1977. *Christ the Creator.* December 13. Accessed January 1, 2016. https://speeches.byu.edu/talks/mark-e-petersen_christ-creator/.

Pharmacist, Renegade. 2015. *Diet Coke Exposed: What Happens One Hour After Drinking Diet Coke, Coke Zero Or Any Other Similar Diet Soda.* August 2. Accessed August 12, 2015. http://therenegadepharmacist.com/diet-coke-exposed-happens-one-hour-drinking-diet-coke-coke-zero-similar-diet-soda/.

—. 2015. *What Happens One Hour After Drinking A Can Of Coke.* May 3. Accessed August 12, 2015. http://therenegadepharmacist.com/what-happens-one-hour-after-drinking-a-can-of-coke/.

Philpott, Tom. 2014. *Monsanto GM Soy Is Scarier Than You Think.* April 23. Accessed November 21, 2015. http://www.motherjones.com/tom-philpott/2014/04/superweeds-arent-only-trouble-gmo-soy.

Pilcher, J., and E. Ott. 1998. "The Relationship Between Sleep and Measures of Helth and Well-Being in College Students: A Repeated Measures Approach." *Behavioral Medicine* 23:170.

Pillemar, Karl, PhD. 2011. *30 Lessons for Living - Tried and True Advice from the Wisest Americans.* New York, NY: Penguin Group.

2014. *On the Way to School.* Directed by Pascal Plisson. https://www. youtube.com/watch?v=elsQ0B43Q9Y.

Pratt, Orson. n.d. *Discourse On language or the medium of communication in the future state and on the increased powers of locomotion (October 22, 1854).* Accessed January 2, 2016. http://jared.pratt-family.org/orson_histories/orson-discourses-1854-oct.html.

Price-Mitchell, Marilyn. n.d. *Mindful Warriors: Medication for Teenagers.* Accessed October 4, 2014. http://www.rootsofaction. com/meditation-children-teens-mindful-warriors/.

Public Broadcasting Service. n.d. *The Roosevelts: An Intimate History.* Accessed April 20, 2016. http://www.pbs.org/kenburns/ the-roosevelts.

Rades, Alicia. 2014. *Why It Makes (Financial) Sense to Get Married Before Graduation.* June 2. Accessed May 20, 2016. http://www. careermeh.com/makes-financial-sense-get-married-graduation/.

Ramachandran, Vilayanur. 2009. "TED Talk: The Neurons that Shaped Civilization." *Born to Copy? Media Violence and Mirror Neurons.* Accessed October 29, 2014. http://drdavewalsh.com/posts/61.

Rath, Tom. 2007. *Strengths Finder.* New York, NY: Gallup Press.

Reding, Joy. 2014. *Men Stuck in Adolescence: Why It's Everyone's Problem.* August 2. http://www.yourtango.com/201173900men-stuck-adolescence-why-its-everyones-problem.

Reinberg, Steven. 2014. *Sources of Caffeine for Kids Increasing - Effects of excessive caffeine intake on youngsters aren't yet known, experts warn.* February 10. Accessed October 11, 2014. http://www.webmd.com/parenting/news/20140210/energy-drinks-coffee-increasing-sources-of-caffeine-for-kids-cdc-says.

Reproductive Medicine Associates of New Jersey. 2015. *Infertility in America 2015 Survey and Report.* Accessed June 25, 2016. http://www.rmanj.com/wp-content/uploads/2015/04/RMANJ_Infertility-In-America-SurveyReport-_04152015.pdf.

Reuters. 2007. *Bill Gates Keeps Close Eye on Kids' Computer Time.* February 20. Accessed February 16, 2016. http://www.reuters.com/article/us-microsoft-gates-daughter-idUSN2022438420070221.

Reynolds, Gretchen. 2013. *The Scientific 7-Minute Workout.* May 9. Accessed November 3, 2014. http://well.blogs.nytimes.com/2013/05/09/the-scientific-7-minute-workout/?_php=true&_type=blogs&_r=0.

Rowe, Seth. 2014. *Star Tribune.* October 8. Accessed October 8, 2014. http://www.startribune.com/local/south/236249111.html.

Ryan, M.J. 2005. *The Happiness Makeover - How to Teach Yourself to Be Happy and Enjoy Every Day.* New York, NY: MJF Books.

n.d. *S.C.R. 9 Concurrent Resolution on the Public Health Crisis.* Accessed April 24, 2016. http://le.utah.gov/~2016/bills/static/SCR009.html.

Saints, The Church of Jesus Christ of Latter-Day. 2004. *True to the Faith.* Salt Lake City: The Church of Jesus Christ of Latter-Day Saints.

Sansom, Will. 2011. *Related studies point to the illusion of the artificial.* June 27. Accessed August 12, 2015. http://uthscsa.edu/hscnews/singleformat2.asp?newID=3861.

Sarfati, Jonathan, PhD. 2013. *Refuting Evolution 2.* Powder Springs, GA: Creation Book Publishers.

Sax, Leonard, MD. 2007. *Boys Adrift - The Five Factors Driving the Growing Epidemic of Unmotivated Boys and Underachieving Young Men.* New York, NY.

Scharper, Julie. 2014. *10 centenarians share secrets to long life.* November 2. Accessed November 12, 2014. http://seattletimes.com/html/living/2024905209_1000plusyearsofliving10centenarianssharesecretstoalonglifexml.html.

Schiltz, Karen PhD. 2012. *Beyond the Label: A guide to unlocking a child's educational potential.* November 1. Accessed November 11, 2014. http://www.psychologytoday.com/blog/beyond-the-label/201211/power-bullies-and-victims.

Scope, E. 1999. *A Meta-Analysis of Research on Creativity.* Ph.D. Dissertation, New York, NY: Fordham University.

Seligman, Martin E.P. Ph.d. 2006. *Learned Optimism - How to Change Your Mind and Your Life.* New York, NY: Vintage Books a division of Random House.

Sequoia and Kings Canyon National Parks. n.d. *Giant Sequoias and Museum.* Accessed August 14, 2015. http://www.visitsequoia.com/giant-sequoia-trees.aspx.

Shattuck, Kelly. 2014. *7 Startling Facts: An Up Close Look at Church Attendance in America.* Accessed October 19, 2014. http://www. churchleaders.com/pastors/pastor-articles/139575-7-startling-facts-an-up-close-look-at-church-attendance-in-america.html.

Shayne, Vic, Dr. 2007. *What Happens To Your Body Within An Hour Of Drinking A Coke.* October 24. Accessed August 12, 2014. What Happens To Your Body Within An Hour Of Drinking A Coke.

Shlam, Shosh, and Hilla Medalia. 2014. *China's Web Junkies.* January 20. Accessed October 2, 2015. http://www.nytimes.com/video/opinion/100000002657962/chinas-web-junkies.html.

Skae, Teya. 2008. *How a Stressful State Leads to Chronic Fatigue.* September 20. Accessed October 14, 2014. http://www.natural-news.com/024268_stress_body_fatigue.html#ixzz3GAxSieeX.

Sleiman, Mohamad Sleiman, and Jennifer M. et al Logue. 2016. "Emissions from Electronic Cigarettes: Key Parameters Affecting the Release of Harmful Chemicals." *Environmental Science and Technology.* July 27. Accessed July 31, 2016. http://pubs.acs.org/doi/abs/10.1021/acs.est.6b01741.

Smith, Ian K., MD. 2010. *Happy - Simple Steps for Getting the Life You Want.* New York, NY: St. Martin's Griffin.

Smokefree.Gov. n.d. *Quit Day: 5 Steps.* Accessed July 31, 2016. https://smokefree.gov/steps-on-quit-day.

Snelling, Andrew Dr. 2010. *Carbon-14 Dating.* October 1. Accessed August 15, 2015. https://answersingenesis.org/geology/carbon-14/carbon-14-dating/.

Solomon, J. 1996. "Humor and Again Well." *American Behavior Scientist* 39:249.

Staff, American Experience. 2014. *American Experience Website.* Accessed November 20, 2014. http://www.pbs.org/wgbh/americanexperience/features/biography/clinton-bill/.

Staff, Dr. Oz. 2014. *The Urine Color Palette.* October 14. Accessed August 11, 2015. http://www.doctoroz.com/article/urine-color-palette.

Staff, Examined Existence. 2014. *How to Be Mentally Tough Like a Navy Seal.* October 14. Accessed October 14, 2014. http://examinedexistence.com/how-to-be-mentally-tough-like-a-navy-seal/.

Staff, Fox News. 2014. *Dr. Oz Reveals the Hidden Dangers of Microwave Popcorn.* April 28. Accessed December 5, 2014. http://insider.foxnews.com/2014/04/28/dr-oz-reveals-hidden-dangers-microwave-popcorn.

Staff, LDS. 2014. *Why is family important?* Accessed November 15, 2014. https://www.lds.org/youth/learn/yw/marriage-and-family/family?lang=eng.

Staff, LDS.org. 1985. *A Parent's Guide - Chapter 6: Mature Intimacy: Courtship and Marriage.* Accessed November 23, 2014. https://www.lds.org/manual/a-parents-guide/chapter-6-mature-intimacy-courtship-and-marriage?lang=eng.

Staff, Mayo. 2014. *Bullying: Help your child handle a bully: Childhood bullying can have lifelong consequences. Listen to your child's concerns. Then help your child stop bullying in its tracks.* October 14. Accessed October 14, 2014. http://www.mayoclinic.org/healthy-living/childrens-health/in-depth/bullying/art-20044918.

Staff, Mayo Clinic. 2014. *Oral health: A window to your overall health.* Accessed November 3, 2014. http://www.mayoclinic.org/healthy-living/adult-health/in-depth/dental/art-20047475?pg=1.

Staff, Non-GMO Project. 2014. *Non-GMO Facts.* Accessed November 22 2014, 2014. http://www.nongmoproject.org/wp-content/uploads/2013/08/NonGMO_Pocket_TriFold_US.pdf.

Staff, SBA. 2014. *Is Entrepreneurship For You?* Accessed November 13, 2014. http://www.sba.gov/content/entrepreneurship-you.

Staff, Teen Stress - Family First Aid. 2014. *Teen Stress - Family First Aid.* October 12. Accessed October 12, 2014. www.familyfirstaid.org/parenting/emotional/teen-stress/,.

Staff, The Family Institute. 2010. *Play Deficit Disorder.* July 10. Accessed October 12, 2014. http://www.family-institute.org/about-us/tip-of-the-month/family-tip-of-the-month/335-play-deficit-disorder-april-2011.

Staff, WebMD. 2015. *WebMD.* August 10. Accessed August 10, 2015. http://www.webmd.com/diet/water-for-weight-loss-diet?page=2.

Stern, Marlow. 2014. *'Web Junkie' Is a Harrowing Documentary on China's Internet Addiction Rehab Clinics.* January 20. Accessed October 3, 2015. http://www.thedailybeast.com/articles/2014/01/20/web-junkie-is-a-harrowing-documentary-on-china-s-internet-addiction-rehab-clinics.html.

Steurer, Geoff MS, LMFT. n.d. *The Effect of Pornography on the Spouse of an Addict.* Accessed April 26, 2016. http://salifeline.org/article/effects-of-pornography-on-a-spouse/help-for-spouses.

Stevens, John K. 1985. "Reverse Engineering the Brain." *Byte Magazine.* April. 287.

Stewart, Chris, and Ted Stewart. 2012. *Seven Miracles that Saved America.* Salt Lake City: The Shipley Group, Inc. and Brian T. Stewart.

—. 2011. *The Miracle of Freedom: 7 Tipping Points that Saved the World.* Salt Lake City: Shadow Mountain.

—. 2011. *The Miracle of Freedom: The 7 Tipping Points that Saved The World.* Salt Lake City: The Shipley Group, Inc and Brian T. Stewart.

Sugar Science. n.d. *Sugar Science.* Accessed March 24, 2016. http://www.sugarscience.org/hidden-in-plain-sight/#.VvRJkeIrKhc.

Sumpio, BE, JT Riley, and A. Dardik. 2002. "Cells in focus: endothelial cell." *International Journal of Biochemistry and Cell Biology* 1508-1512. http://www.ncbi.nlm.nih.gov/pubmed/12379270.

Surrell, James, A., M.D. n.d. *SOS (Stop Only Sugar) Diet.* Accessed November 1, 2015. http://www.sosdietbook.com/.

Swing, Edward L, et al. 2010. "Television and Video Game Exposure and the Development of Attention Problems." *Pediatrics 126, no. 2* 214–221.

Taflinger, Richard, Ph.D. n.d. *Taking ADvantage: Social Basis of Human Behavior: Sex.* Accessed May 4, 2016. http://public.wsu.edu/~taflinge/socsex.html.

Tavernise, Sabrina. 2016. *F.D.A. Finishes Food Labels for How We Eat Now.* May 20. Accessed May 20, 2016. http://www.nytimes.com/2016/05/21/health/fda-nutrition-labels.html?_r=0.

The Centers for Disease Control. 2015. *Cancer Prevention and Control.* August 13. Accessed August 13, 2015. http://www.cdc.gov/cancer/dcpc/resources/features/ProstateCancer/index.htm.

—. 2015. *Prostate Cancer.* August 13. Accessed August 13, 2015. http://www.cdc.gov/cancer/prostate/basic_info/index.htm.

—. n.d. *Sexual Risk Behaviors: HIV, STD, & Teen Pregnancy Prevention.* Accessed April 5, 2016. http://www.cdc.gov/healthyyouth/ sexualbehaviors/index.htm.

The Church of Jesus Christ of Latter-day Saints. n.d. *Chapter 5: Teaching Adolescents: from Twelve to Eighteen Years.* Accessed November 29, 2015. https://www.lds.org/manual/a-parents-guide/chapter-5-teaching-adolescents-from-twelve-to-eighteen-years?lang=eng.

—. n.d. *Our Eternal Life.* Accessed December 30, 2015. https://www.lds. org/topics/plan-of-salvation/our-eternal-life/video?lang=eng.

The Church of Jesus Christ of Latter-Day Saints. n.d. *Prayer.* Accessed August 14, 2015. https://www.lds.org/topics/prayer?lang=eng.

The Church of Jesus Christ of Latter-day Saints. 2013. *To the Tender Wives: What I Have Learned from My Husband's Addiction to Pornography.* July. Accessed April 26, 2016. https://www.lds.org/ ensign/2013/07/to-the-tender-wives-what-i-have-learned-from-my-husbands-addiction-to-pornography?lang=eng.

The Church of Jesus Christ of Latter-Day Saints. 2015. *Voice(s) of Hope - Brett and Shaundra Cragun.* Accessed August 14, 2015. http://ldsvoicesofhope.org/voice.php?v=78#.VbwahHhhP0d.

—. 2014. *Voice(s) of Hope - Ethan Marston and Allison Tenney.* Accessed August 15, 2015. http://ldsvoicesofhope.org/voice. php?v=77#.Vc6cBPlVhBc.

—. 2015. *Voice(s) of Hope - Jimmy Merrell.* Accessed August 14, 2015. http://ldsvoicesofhope.org/voice.php?v=77#.Vc6cBPlVhBc.

The Dr. Oz Show. 2014. *25 Acid-Promoting Foods.* January 10. Accessed August 13, 2015. Dr. Oz http://www.doctoroz.com/ article/25-acid-promoting-foods.

—. 2014. *25 Alkaline-Promoting Foods.* January 10. Accessed August 13, 2015. Dr. Oz http://www.doctoroz.com/article/25-alkaline-promoting-foods.

—. 2014. *Dr. William Davis Makes His Gluten-Free All-Purpose Baking Mix.* January 28. Accessed November 29, 2015. http://www.doctoroz.com/recipe/wheat-belly-triple-berry-quick-muffin.

—. 2010. *Produce and Pesticides: What You Need to Know.* September 23. Accessed October 4, 2015. http://www.doctoroz.com/article/produce-and-pesticides-what-you-need-know.

The Free Dictionary By Farlex. 2015. *Medical Dictionary - The Free Dictionary by Farlex.* August 13. Accessed August 13, 2015. http://medical-dictionary.thefreedictionary.com/PH+balance.

The Giant Sequoias and Museum. n.d. *The Giant Sequoias and Museum.* Accessed December 30, 2015. http://www.visitsequoia.com/giant-sequoia-trees.aspx.

The Institute for Creation Research. n.d. *Evidence from the Physical Sciences.* Accessed May 12, 2016. http://www.icr.org/physical-science.

The Seattle Public Library. n.d. Accessed April 17, 2016. http://www.spl.org/audiences/literacy-esl-and-citizenship/esl-calendar#/?i=4.

The Stuttering Foundation. n.d. *Stuttering and the King's Speech.* Accessed April 18, 2016. http://www.stutteringhelp.org/stuttering-and-kings-speech.

Tolle, Eckhart. 1997. *The Power of Now.* Vancouver: Namaste Publishing.

—. 1999. *The Power of Now; A Guide to Spiritual Enlightenment.* Vancouver: Namaste.

Tomkins, Jeffrey, Ph.D. n.d. *New Research Debunks Human Chromosome Fusion.* Accessed May 22, 2016. http://www.icr.org/article/new-research-debunks-human-chromosome/.

Top, Brent L. 2014. *Life After Death: 6 Insights into the Spirit World.* November 2014. Accessed January 1, 2016. http://www.ldsliving.com/Life-After-Death-6-Insights-into-the-Spirit-World/s/77329.

Totheroh, Gailon. n.d. *Evolution Outdated.* Accessed August 15, 2015. http://www.cbn.com/spirituallife/churchandministry/evangelism/evolution_outdated.aspx.

Trudeau, Justin. 2015. *Je t'aime, Papa: Justin Trudeau's eulogy to his father.* October 23. Accessed November 14, 2015. http://www.theglobeandmail.com/news/politics/jetaimepapa-justin-trudeaus-2000-eulogy/article26923529/ .

Tuma, Rabiya. 2006. *The Dana Foundation.* July 1. Accessed August 9, 2015. http://www.dana.org/Publications/Brainwork/Details.aspx?id=43665.

U.S. Environmental Protection Agency. n.d. "Home Water Testing." *U.S. Environmental Protection Agency.* Accessed April 30, 2016. https://www.epa.gov/sites/production/files/2015-11/documents/2005_09_14_faq_fs_homewatertesting.pdf.

Uche, Ugo MS, LPC. 2010. *Promoting Empathy With Your Teen.* May 3. Accessed October 28, 2014. http://www.psychologytoday.com/blog/promoting-empathy-your-teen/201005/are-empathetic-teenagers-more-likely-be-intentionally-succes.

US Department of Health & Human Services. n.d. *Balance Food and Activity.* Accessed August 14, 2015. https://www.nhlbi.nih.gov/health/educational/wecan/healthy-weight-basics/balance.htm.

Vail, Rachel. 2014. *Top 15 Things Your Middle School Kid Wishes You Knew.* September 9. Accessed August 25, 2015. http://www.huffingtonpost.com/rachel-vail/top-15-things-your-middle-school-kid-wishes-you-knew_b_5844308.html.

Vandenberg, Sara. 2016. *2016 Best Volunteer Abroad Programs, Organizations, & Projects - See more at: https://www.volunteerforever.com/article_post/2016-best-volunteer-abroad-programs-organizations-projects#sthash.pZ8bRO30.dpuf.* February 29. Accessed March 29, 2016. https://www.volunteerforever.com/article_post/2016-best-volunteer-abroad-programs-organizations-projects.

Vinocur, Leigh, MD FACEP. 2011. *The Dr. Oz Show.* November 14. Accessed August 10, 2015. http://www.doctoroz.com/blog/leigh-vinocur-md-facep/how-much-water-do-you-really-need.

Violato, Claudio. 2000. "The Myth of Quality Daycare." *National Post.* May 2. 18.

Vozza, Stephanie. n.d. *PERSONAL MISSION STATEMENTS OF 5 FAMOUS CEOS (AND WHY YOU SHOULD WRITE ONE TOO).* Accessed January 10, 2016. http://www.fastcompany.com/3026791/dialed/personal-mission-statements-of-5-famous-ceos-and-why-you-should-write-one-too.

Walsh, Dave Dr. 2011. *Born to Copy? Media Violence and Mirror Neurons.* June 2. Accessed October 29, 2014. http://drdavewalsh.com/posts/61.

Watson, Julie. 2014. *The Huffington Post: Crime.* May 24. Accessed October 19, 2014. http://www.huffingtonpost.com/2014/05/24/santa-barbara-shooting_n_5384839.html.

WebMD Staff. 2015. *Safer Food For a Healthier You - Produce and Pesticide Residue.* Accessed October 4, 2015. http://www.webmd.com/diet/safer-food-healthier-you?page=3.

WebMD. n.d. *Water and Your Diet: Staying Slim and Regular With H2O.* Accessed June 19, 2016. http://www.webmd.com/diet/water-for-weight-loss-diet?page=2.

White, A.M., D.W. Jamieson–Drake, and H.S. and Swartzwelder. 2002. "Prevalence and correlates of alcohol–induced blackouts among college students: Results of an e–mail survey. ." *Journal of American College Health* 51:117–131.

2014. *Why Dehydration is Making You Fat and Sick.* July 24. Accessed October 24, 2014. http://dailyhealthpost.com/11-ways-dehydration-could-be-making-you-fat-and-sick/.

Wiewel, Brad. 2015. *Inheritance 101: How to Leave Your Home to Your Kids.* August 1. Accessed January 10, 2016. http://abcnews.go.com/Business/inheritance-101-leave-home-kids/story?id=32788920.

Williams, A., D. Haber, G. Weaver, and J. Freeman. 1998. "Altruistic Activity." *Activities, Adaptation, and Aging* 22:31.

Williams, J.M.G., J.D. Teasdale, and Z. V & Kabat-Zinn Segal. 2007. *The Mindful Way Through Depression - Freeing Yourself from Chronic Unhappiness.* New York, NY: The Guilford Press.

Williams, Mark, and Mark Penman. 2011. *Mindfulness an Eight-Week Plan for Finding Peace in a Frantic World.* New York, NY: Rodale.

Williams, Zoe. 2014. *Robert Lustig: the man who believes sugar is poison.* August 24. Accessed November 1, 2015. http://www.theguardian.com/lifeandstyle/2014/aug/24/robert-lustig-sugar-poison.

Willis, Judy MD, MEd. 2014. *Build Your Child's Divergence - So they can perceive beyond the box.* October 12. Accessed October 4, 2014. http://www.psychologytoday.com/blog/radical-teaching/201404/build-your-child-s-divergence.

Winch, Guy, PhD. 2014. *The Squeaky Wheel.* May 1. Accessed October 28, 2014. http://www.psychologytoday.com/blog/the-squeaky-wheel/201405/how-mastering-all-5-senses-can-get-you-what-you-want.

Wong, Marie. 2010. *What is unrefined, extra virgin cold-pressed avocado oil?* April. Accessed August 15, 2015. http://www.aocs.org/Membership/FreeCover.cfm?ItemNumber=1099.

Wood, Daniel B. 2007. *For teens, too much TV can impair learning later, study says.* May 10. Accessed October 12, 2014. http://www.csmonitor.com/2007/0510/p03s02-ussc.html.

Woodruff, Mandi. 2014. *A 27-year-old millionaire reveals how he built his wealth.* November 7. Accessed November 14, 2014. http://finance.yahoo.com/news/27-year-old-millionaire-anton-ivanov-financessful-184823184.html.

Yang, Stephanie. 2014. *5 Years Ago Bernie Madoff Was Sentenced to 150 Years In Prison – Here's How His Scheme Worked.* July 1. Accessed January 10, 2016. http://www.businessinsider.com/how-bernie-madoffs-ponzi-scheme-worked-2014-7.

Young, Brigham. n.d. *Chapter 38: The Spirit World - Teachings of Presidents of the Church: Brigham Young (1997) pp 279-84.* Accessed January 1, 2015. https://www.lds.org/manual/teachings-brigham-young/chapter-38?lang=eng.

—. 1868. *Funeral of the Late President Daniel Spencer.* December 10. Accessed January 1, 2015. http://jod.mrm.org/13/75.

Young, Caroline. 2013. *7 Most Common Genetically Modified Foods.* December 3. Accessed November 22, 2014. http://www.huffingtonpost.com/builtlean/diet-and-nutrition_b_4323937.html.

2014. *YouTube: Dr. Kent Hovind Obliterates Evolutionist Bill Nye.* December 3. Accessed August 14, 2015. https://www.youtube.com/watch?v=IHFqFP-Li_o.

Zennie, Michael. 2014. *Daily Mail.* October 8. Accessed October 8, 2014. http://www.dailymail.co.uk/news/article-2478172/Teen-dies-saving-lives-car-crashes-way-home-final-project-Eagle-Scout.html#ixzz3CYJwHOKc.

Zetlin, Minda. 2014. *Survey: 63% of 20-Somethings Want to Start a Business.* Accessed November 13, 2014. http://www.inc.com/minda-zetlin/63-percent-of-20-somethings-want-to-own-a-business.html.

Zhou, Yan, Fu-Chun Lin, Ya-Song Du, Ling-di Qin, Zhi-Min Zhao, Jian-Rong Xu, and Hao Lei. 2011. "Gray Matter Abnormalities in Internet Addiction: A Voxel-Based Morphometry Study." *European Journal of Radiology 79, no. 1* 92–95.

Zimbardo, Philip G., and Nikita Duncan. 2012. *The Demise of Guys.* Seattle: Amazon.

Zimbardo, Philip. 2014. *PHILIP ZIMBARDO: The Lucifer Effect Understanding How Good People Turn Evil.* November 14. Accessed March 30, 2016. https://www.youtube.com/watch?v=Jc_e9M8M-RU.

Ziv, Stav. 2014. *CHILD HOMELESSNESS IN U.S. REACHES HISTORIC HIGH, REPORT SAYS.* November 17. Accessed March 28, 2016. http://www.newsweek.com/child-homelessness-us-reaches-historic-high-report-says-285052.

END NOTES

1. (Fleur-de-lis Designs n.d.)

2. (Fleur-de-lis Designs n.d.)

3. (Fleur-de-lis Designs n.d.)

4. (Fleur-de-lis Designs n.d.)

5. (Fleur-de-lis Designs n.d.)

6. (US Government 2014)

7. (Stewart and Stewart, The Miracle of Freedom: 7 Tipping Points that Saved the World 2011)

8. (American Psychological Association - Marriage and Divorce 2014)

9. (Divorce - Love to Know 2014)

10. (Mas 2014)

11. (Trudeau 2015)

12. (Peck, The Road Less Traveled - A New Psychology of Love, Traditional Values, and Spiritual Growth 2011), p. 134

13. (Peck, The Road Less Traveled - A New Psychology of Love, Traditional Values, and Spiritual Growth 2011), p. 137

14. (Hymowitz 2011)

15. (Carmichiel 2009)

16. (Tolle, The Power of Now; A Guide to Spiritual Enlightenment 1999)

17. (Doctrine and Covenants Section 42)

18. (Boy Scouts of America 2016)

19. (Boy Scouts of America 2016)

20. (Boy Scouts of America 2016)

21. (Boy Scouts of America 2016)

22. (Louv 2008) p. 72

23. (Louv 2008) p. 74

24. (Louv 2008) p. 121

25. (Louv 2008) p. 300

26. (Boy Scouts of America 2016)

27. (S. Miller 2014)

28. 28 (Rowe 2014)

29. (Zennie 2014)

30. (CBS Denver 2014)

31. (Outward Bound 2014)

32. (Olson 2004)

33. (Golgowski 2014)

34. (Book of Mormon n.d.) D&C 128:21

35. (Book of Mormon n.d.) D&C 93:11-17

36. (Peck, The Road Less Traveled - A New Psychology of Love, Traditional Values, and Spiritual Growth 2011), p. 27

37. (Peck, The Road Less Traveled - A New Psychology of Love, Traditional Values, and Spiritual Growth 2011), p. 27

38. (Peck, The Road Less Traveled - A New Psychology of Love, Traditional Values, and Spiritual Growth 2011)

39. (Peck 2011, p. 19)

40. (Price-Mitchell n.d.)

41. (Marilyn Price-Mitchell 2014)

42. (Ciarrochi 2012)

43. (Williams and Penman 2011)

44. (Williams and Penman 2011)

45. (Neff, Definition of Self-Compassion 2014)

46. (Neff, A Healthier Way to Relate to Yourself 2014)

47. (Neff, Self-Compassion - Test Your Self Compassion 2014)

48. (Smith 2010)

49. (Diener, et al. 1985)

50. (Neimiec 2014)

51. (Barker 2014)

52. (S. Lyubomirsky 1994)

53. (Lyubomirsky and Ross 1997)

54. (Brown and Dutton 1995)

55. (Murray and Peacock 1996)

56. (Diener and Fujita 1995)

57. Williams, et al. 1998)

58. (Pegalis 1994)

59. (Lepper 1996)

60. (Solomon 1996)

61. (Pilcher and Ott 1998)

62. (Fontane 1996)

63. (Scope 1999)

64. (Emoto 2005, p. 25)

65. (Farberov 2014)

66. (Andrea Watcher 2014)

67. (Williams and Penman 2011)

68. (Dawursk 2007)

69. (Grant 2013)

70. (B. Morris 2002)

71. (The Seattle Public Library n.d.)

72. (James Earl Jones and His Unmistakable Voice 2014)

73. (The Stuttering Foundation n.d.)

74. (Public Broadcasting Service n.d.)

75. (Lipworth 2012)

76. (BeliefNet n.d.)

77. (BeliefNet n.d.)

78. (BeliefNet n.d.)

79. (Peck 2011, p. 275)

80. Peck 2011, p. 271)

81. (Hinckley, Articles of Belief - Bonneville International Corporation Management Seminar 1991)

82. (Holland n.d.)

83. (Mind Tools Group 2014)

84. (Mind Tools Group 2014)

85. (Mind Tools Group 2014)

86. (Mental Floss n.d.)(Staff, Mayo 2014)

87. (Staff, Mayo 2014)

88. (Staff, Mayo 2014)

89. (Dr. Phil Staff n.d.)

90. (Antes 2010)

91. (Antes 2010)

92. (Skae 2008)

93. (Barbeau 20029(U. D. Health and Human Services 2014)

94. (U. D. Health and Human Services 2014)

95. (U. D. Health and Human Services 2014)

96. (McGraw 2000)

97. (U. D. Health and Human Services 2014)

98. (Shlam and Medalia 2014)

99. (Reuters 2007)

100. (Bilton 2014)

101. (Doan 2012)

102. (Mann 2011)

103. (Gentile 2012)

104. (Mann 2011)

105. (V. Dunckley 2014)

106. (V. Dunckley 2014)

107. (V. L. Dunckley 2014)

108. (Koepp 1998)

109. (V. Dunckley 2014)

110. (Ivory and Kalyanaraman 2007)

111. (Gentile 2012)

112. (Swing 2010)

113. V. Dunckley 2014)

114. (V. L. Dunckley 2014)

115. (General Electric n.d.)

116. R. D. Fields 2008)

117. (Boyd n.d.)

118. (S.C.R. 9 Concurrent Resolution on the Public Health Crisis n.d.)

119. (Hilliker 2013)

120. (Sax 2007)

121. (P. G. Zimbardo 2012)

122. (Hilliker 2013)

123. (Hilliker 2013)

124. (Steurer n.d.)

125. The Church of Jesus Christ of Latter-day Saints 2013)

126. (Steurer n.d.)

127. (The Church of Jesus Christ of Latter-day Saints 2013)

128. (Health 2014)

129. (Health 2014)

130. (U. D. Health and Human Services 2010)

131. (Health 2014)

132. (Mayo Clinic n.d.)

133. (Health 2014)

134. (Health 2014)

135. (Health 2014)

136. (Partnership for a Drug-Free Canada (PDFC) n.d.)

137. (Andreasson 1987)

138. (Arseneault L. 2004)

139. (Health 2014)

140. (Health 2014)

141. (Alcohol Alert 2004)

142. (White, Jamieson–Drake and and Swartzwelder 2002)

143. (Alcohol Alert 2004)

144. (Mayo Clinic n.d.)

145. (Effects of Caffeine on the Nervous System 2014)

146. (How Drugs Affect Neurotransmitters 2014)

147. (Reinberg 2014)

148. (A. M. Miller 2015)

149. (Effects of Caffeine on the Nervous System 2014)

150. (Gardner 2014)

151. (Gardner 2014)

152. (Family First Aid Staff 2014)

153. (Barbeau 2002)

154. (Elkind 1988)

155. (Mayo Clinic Staff n.d.)

156. (Mayo Clinic Staff 2014)

157. (Williams and Penman 2011)

158. (McRaven 2014)

159. (AACAP Staff 2005)

160. (English Language Smart Words n.d.)

161. (Willis 2014)

162. (Charron 2011)

163. (IBM Staff 2014)

164. (Staff, The Family Institute 2010)

165. (Staff, The Family Institute 2010)

166. (Staff, The Family Institute 2010)

167. (Ghose 2012)

168. (Coren 2012)

169. (Walsh 2011)

170. (Kalman 2010)

171. (Tuma 2006)

172. (Iocoboni 2008)

173. (Ramachandran 2009)

174. (Uche 2010)

175. (Uche 2010)

176. (Carter 2008)

177. (Krznaric, Six Habits of Highly Empathic People 2012)

178. (Seligman 2006)

179. (Seligman 2006)

180. (Latter-Day Saints, Providing in the Lord's Way: Summary of A Leader's Guide to Welfare 2009)

181. (Monson 1987)

182. (Burton 2009)

183. (Hales 2009)

184. (Latter-Day Saints, Catching the Vision of Self-Reliance 2014)

185. (Sax 2007)

186. (Plisson 2014)

187. (Bundrant 2013)

188. (Bernstein 2014)

189. (Bernstein 2014)

190. (Helpguide.org 2014)

191. (Staff, Examined Existence 2014)

192. (Durnell 2014)

193. (BBC n.d.)

194. (S. R. Covey, Stephen Covey n.d.)

195. (Vozza n.d.)

196. (Berkeley, University of California at 2014)

197. (Berkeley, University of California at 2014)

198. (Williams, Teasdale and Segal 2007)

199. (Williams and Penman 2011)

200. (11 Ways Dehydration Could Be Making You Fat and Sick 2014)

201. (Lam, Lam and Lam n.d.)

202. (WebMD n.d.)

203. (Why Dehydration is Making You Fat and Sick 2014)

204. (Boyles 2004)

205. (Why Dehydration is Making You Fat and Sick 2014)

206. (D. O. Staff 2014)

207. (J. M. Mercola 2010)

208. (Feller 2015)

209. (Medicine 2015)

210. (U.S. Environmental Protection Agency n.d.)

211. (Environmental Health News 2013)

212. (Disease Control Staff 2013)

213. (De-Kun Li 2011)

214. (Baum, Hedlund, Aristei & Goldman, PC 2014)

215. (Oz and Roizen, Beware of 'BPA-Free' Lie 2014)

216. (Hyman 2014)

217. (Z. Williams 2014)

218. (Surrell n.d.)

219. (Sugar Science n.d.)

220. (Palmer 2008)

221. (Jacques 2013)

222. (Davis 2015)

223. (Bernhoft and Smith 2912)

224. (Staff, Non-GMO Project 2014)

225. (C. Young 2013)

226. (J. M. Mercola 2014)

227. (The Dr. Oz Show 2010)

228. (WebMD Staff 2015)

229. (D. Mercola, 11 Charts that Show Everything Wrong With Our Modern Diet 2014)

230. (Oz, Dr. Oz Reveals Monsanto's Statement on Glyphosate 2015)

231. (Philpott 2014)

232. (J. M. Mercola, Soybean Oil: One of the Most Harmful Ingredients in Processed Foods 2013)

233. (J. M. Mercola, 11 Charts That Show Everything Wrong with Our Modern Diet 2014)

234. (GMO 2015)

235. (K. B. Gunnars 2015)

236. (K. Gunnars 2014)

237. (J. M. Mercola 2014)

238. (J. D. Mercola 2012)

239. (Wong 2010)

240. (Pharmacist, What Happens One Hour After Drinking A Can Of Coke 2015)

241. (Pharmacist, Diet Coke Exposed: What Happens One Hour After Drinking Diet Coke, Coke Zero Or Any Other Similar Diet Soda 2015)

242. (Cardillo 2011)

243. (Nseir, Nassar and Assy 2010)

244. (ASPARTAME AND PREGNANCY WHAT ARE THE RISKS? n.d.)

245. (J. M. Mercola, Aspartame: By Far the Most Dangerous Substance Added to Most Foods Today 2011)

246. (ASPARTAME AND PREGNANCY WHAT ARE THE RISKS? n.d.)

247. (ASPARTAME AND PREGNANCY WHAT ARE THE RISKS? n.d.)

248. (Byrne 2015)

249. (Goldstein 2015)

250. (Goodrich 2014)

251. (Crinnion 2012)

252. (16 Cancer Causing Foods You Probably Eat Every Day 2014)

253. (F. N. Staff 2014)

254. (D. Mercola, Monosodium Glutamate (MSG): This Common Food Additive Now Linked to Weight Gain 2011)

255. (D. Mercola, Monosodium Glutamate (MSG): This Common Food Additive Now Linked to Weight Gain 2011)

256. (D. Mercola, Monosodium Glutamate (MSG): This Common Food Additive Now Linked to Weight Gain 2011)

257. (American Heart Association n.d.)

258. (Cleveland Clinic 2015)

259. (Mayo Clinic: Potassium Supplement (Oral Route, Parenteral Route) n.d.)

260. (Mayo Clinic Staff n.d.)

261. (Cookus Interruptus 2013)

262. (English 2014)

263. (Biel n.d.)

264. (Taflinger n.d.)

265. (Frazier n.d.)

266. (P. A. Balch 2004)

267. (The Centers for Disease Control n.d.)

268. (Milligan n.d.)

269. (Milligan n.d.)

270. (Galland n.d.)

271. (P. A. Balch 2010)

272. (Mayo Clinic 2015)

273. (Health 2014)

274. (Sleiman and Logue 2016)

275. (American Lung Association n.d.)

276. (Smokefree.Gov n.d.)

277. (Pesce 2016)

278. (Cannon and Stockton 2010)

279. (Mayo Clinic n.d.)

280. (The Centers for Disease Control 2015)

281. (D. Mercola, Iodine Supplements May Be Too Much of a Good Thing 2013)

282. (Jacobsen, Knussen and Fraser 1998)

283. (P. A. Balch 2010)

284. (Kerns n.d.)

285. (Demedeiros n.d.)

286. (Ferdman 2016)

287. (Reproductive Medicine Associates of New Jersey 2015)

288. (Infertility Resources n.d.)

289. (Administration 2014)

290. (Tavernise 2016)

291. (Nutritional Genomics Staff n.d.)

292. (Nutritional Genomics Staff n.d.)

293. (Gadsby, How can people who gorge on fat and rarely see a vegetable be healthier than we are? 2004)

294. (National Institute of Health n.d.)

295. (US Department of Health & Human Services n.d.)

296. (Fottrell 2015)

297. (CDC n.d.)

298. (The Dr. Oz Show 2014)

299. (Klika and Jordan 2013)

300. (Reynolds 2013)

301. (National Sleep Foundation 2014)

302. (National Sleep Foundation 2006)

303. (Brody 2014)

304. (Kim 2011)

305. (DiGiulio 2016)

306. (DiGiulio 2016)

307. (Staff, Mayo Clinic 2014)

308. (Katz 2010)

309. (Healthwise Staff n.d.)

310. (North Creek Dental Care Blog 2013)

311. (Health Central n.d.)

312. (Cox 2012)

313. (Emoto 2005) p. 30

314. (Emoto 2005) p. 23

315. (Emoto 2005) p. 39

316. (Emoto 2005) p. 16

317. (Faust, Communion with the Holy Spirit 2002)

318. (Faust, Communion with the Holy Spirit 2002)

319. (Peck, The Road Less Traveled - A New Psychology of Love, Traditional Values, and Spiritual Growth 2011)

320. (Peck, The Road Less Travelled 1978, 256)

321. (Peck, The Road Less Travelled 1978, 241)

322. (Maynes 2015)

323. (B. K. Packer, How to Live the Word of Wisdom n.d.)

324. (Barnes and Lowry 2012)

325. (Hinckley, The Family: A Proclamation to the World 1995)

326. (Mphuthing 2016)

327. (Watson 2014)

328. (The Church of Jesus Christ of Latter-day Saints n.d.)

329. (The Church of Jesus Christ of Latter-Day Saints 2015)

330. (The Church of Jesus Christ of Latter-Day Saints 2014)

331. (The Church of Jesus Christ of Latter-Day Saints 2015)

332. (Lee 2002)

333. (Callister 2006)

334. (Bednar 2010)

335. (The Church of Jesus Christ of Latter-day Saints n.d.)

336. (Benson 1976)

337. (Stewart and Stewart, Seven Miracles that Saved America 2012)

338. (Hovind 2012)

339. (Matsummara and Mead 2007)

340. (Institute for Creation Research n.d.)

341. (Tomkins n.d.)

342. (The Giant Sequoias and Museum n.d.)

343. (The Giant Sequoias and Museum n.d.)

344. (Creationism.org Staff n.d.)

345. (YouTube: Dr. Kent Hovind Obliterates Evolutionist Bill Nye 2014)

346. (Answers in Genesis Staff 2000)

347. (H. Fields 2006)

348. (H. M. Morris n.d.)

349. (Nutburn 2015)

350. (Totheroh n.d.)

351. (The Institute for Creation Research n.d.)

352. (Petersen 1977)

353. (Cosgrove-Mather 2004)

354. (Islam101 n.d.)

355. (Petersen 1977)

356. (Hovind 2012)

357. (J. D. Morris, Grand Canyon: Is It Really 'Exhibit A' For Evolution And The Old Earth? 2015)

358. (Jones 2013)

359. (Snelling 2010)

360. (Jones 2013)

361. (Eldredge and Jay 1985)

362. (J. D. Morris, The Paluxy River Tracks n.d.)

363. (Stevens 1985)

364. (Behe n.d.)

365. (Carson 2014)

366. (Top 2014)

367. (B. Young, Funeral of the Late President Daniel Spencer 1868)

368. (B. Young, Chapter 38: The Spirit World - Teachings of Presidents of the Church: Brigham Young (1997) pp 279-84 n.d.)

369. (Pratt n.d.)

370. (Hinckley, The Times in Which We Live 2001)

371. (P. Zimbardo 2014)

372. (Joan of Arc 2015)

373. (16Ma)

374. (BibleInfo.Com n.d.)

375. (K. P. Curtis n.d.)

376. (B. Curtis 2008)

377. (Kurtus 2013)

378. (Greenberg 2012)

379. (Greenberg 2012)

380. (Greenberg 2012)

381. (Cuddy 2002)

382. (Greenberg 2012)

383. (Greenberg 2012)

384. (Greenberg 2012)

385. (Kurtus 2013)

386. (Kurtus 2013)

387. (Generation Life n.d.)

388. (Faust, The Dignity of Self n.d.)

389. (Pelzer n.d.)

390. (Beck 2009)

391. (Staff, LDS 2014)

392. (Vail 2014)

393. (Vail 2014)

394. (Vail 2014)

395. (Vail 2014)

396. (Vail 2014)

397. (Vail 2014)

398. (Vail 2014)

399. (Vail 2014)

400. (Vail 2014)

401. (Vail 2014)

402. (Vail 2014)

403. (Vail 2014)

404. (Vail 2014)

405. (Vail 2014)

406. (Vail 2014)

407. (Latter-Day Saints, For the Strength of Youth 2001)

408. (Latter-Day Saints, For the Strength of Youth 2001)

409. (Holman 2002)

410. (Holman 2002)

411. (Ashton 1976)

412. (Holman 2002)

413. (Holman 2002)

414. (Betchen 2012)

415. (Ereezay 2014)

416. (Rades 2014)

417. (B. K. Packer, The Plan of Happiness 2015)

418. (Violato 2000)

419. (Gayomali 2013)

420. (Holman 2002)

421. (Holman 2002)

422. (Staff, LDS.org 1985)

423. (Staff, LDS.org 1985)

424. (Staff, LDS.org 1985)

425. (Peck, The Road Less Travelled 1978) p. 21-22

426. (Peck, The Road Less Travelled 1978) p. 23

427. (101 Family Home Evening Activities n.d.)

428. (Ziv 2014)

429. (New York Life n.d.)

430. (National Institute of Mental Health n.d.)

431. (Schiltz 2012)

432. (Classes and Careers n.d.)

433. (Fulciniti 2015)

434. (Vandenberg 2016)

435. (GoAbroad n.d.)

436. (Zetlin 2014)

437. (Nazar 2013)

438. (Staff, SBA 2014)

439. (Peck, The Road Less Travelled 1978) p. 62

440. (Nobelprize.org n.d.)

441. (S. R. Covey, The 7 Habits of Highly Effective People 1989)

442. (Wiewel 2015)

443. (Fisher and Hoffmans 2009)

444. (Oveson 1999)

Made in the USA
San Bernardino, CA
14 March 2017